Communications
in Computer and Information Science   1782

Rationale

The CCIS series is devoted to the publication of proceedings of computer science conferences. Its aim is to efficiently disseminate original research results in informatics in printed and electronic form. While the focus is on publication of peer-reviewed full papers presenting mature work, inclusion of reviewed short papers reporting on work in progress is welcome, too. Besides globally relevant meetings with internationally representative program committees guaranteeing a strict peer-reviewing and paper selection process, conferences run by societies or of high regional or national relevance are also considered for publication.

Topics

The topical scope of CCIS spans the entire spectrum of informatics ranging from foundational topics in the theory of computing to information and communications science and technology and a broad variety of interdisciplinary application fields.

Information for Volume Editors and Authors

Publication in CCIS is free of charge. No royalties are paid, however, we offer registered conference participants temporary free access to the online version of the conference proceedings on SpringerLink (http://link.springer.com) by means of an http referrer from the conference website and/or a number of complimentary printed copies, as specified in the official acceptance email of the event.

CCIS proceedings can be published in time for distribution at conferences or as post-proceedings, and delivered in the form of printed books and/or electronically as USBs and/or e-content licenses for accessing proceedings at SpringerLink. Furthermore, CCIS proceedings are included in the CCIS electronic book series hosted in the SpringerLink digital library at http://link.springer.com/bookseries/7899. Conferences publishing in CCIS are allowed to use Online Conference Service (OCS) for managing the whole proceedings lifecycle (from submission and reviewing to preparing for publication) free of charge.

Publication process

The language of publication is exclusively English. Authors publishing in CCIS have to sign the Springer CCIS copyright transfer form, however, they are free to use their material published in CCIS for substantially changed, more elaborate subsequent publications elsewhere. For the preparation of the camera-ready papers/files, authors have to strictly adhere to the Springer CCIS Authors' Instructions and are strongly encouraged to use the CCIS LaTeX style files or templates.

Abstracting/Indexing

CCIS is abstracted/indexed in DBLP, Google Scholar, EI-Compendex, Mathematical Reviews, SCImago, Scopus. CCIS volumes are also submitted for the inclusion in ISI Proceedings.

How to start

To start the evaluation of your proposal for inclusion in the CCIS series, please send an e-mail to ccis@springer.com.

Deepak Garg · V. A. Narayana · P. N. Suganthan ·
Jaume Anguera · Vijaya Kumar Koppula ·
Suneet Kumar Gupta
Editors

Advanced Computing

12th International Conference, IACC 2022
Hyderabad, India, December 16–17, 2022
Revised Selected Papers, Part II

Springer

Editors
Deepak Garg
SR University
Warangal, India

V. A. Narayana
CMR College of Engineering & Technology
Hyderabad, India

P. N. Suganthan
Nanyang Technological University
Singapore, Singapore

Jaume Anguera
Ramon Llull University
Barcelona, Spain

Vijaya Kumar Koppula
CMR College of Engineering & Technology
Hyderabad, India

Suneet Kumar Gupta
Bennett University
Greater Noida, India

ISSN 1865-0929   ISSN 1865-0937 (electronic)
Communications in Computer and Information Science
ISBN 978-3-031-35643-8   ISBN 978-3-031-35644-5 (eBook)
https://doi.org/10.1007/978-3-031-35644-5

This Springer imprint is published by the registered company Springer Nature Switzerland AG
The registered company address is: Gewerbestrasse 11, 6330 Cham, Switzerland

Preface

The objective of the 12th International Advanced Computing Conference (IACC 2022) was to bring together researchers, developers, and practitioners from academia and industry working in the domain of advanced computing. The conference consisted of tracks in Advances in Machine Learning and Deep Learning, Advances in Applications of Artificial Intelligence in Interdisciplinary Areas, Reinforcement Learning, and Advances in Data Science. The conference took place on 16th and 17th December 2022 at CMR College of Engineering and Technology, Hyderabad. All editions of the series are successfully indexed in ISI, Scopus, DBLP, Compendex, SJR, and Google Scholar. The current version of the conference proceedings is published in the prestigious CCIS series of Springer.

The conference has the track record of acceptance rates of less than 20% in the last 11 years. More than 12 IEEE/ACM Fellows hold key positions of the conference committee, giving it a quality edge. In the last 11 years the conference's citation score has been consistently increasing. This has been possible due to adherence to quality parameters of review and acceptance rate without any exception, which allows us to make some of the best research available through this platform.

The conference organizers have followed the standard process for assessing papers based on the methodology & empirical study in the article, the novelty of the work, its significance, and the contribution made by the authors.

Keeping the quality benchmarks of the conference, in the 12th IACC also the acceptance rates were within our limits of 20%: 415 research papers were submitted and after single-blind review 97 papers were accepted. Out of these 97, 81 papers were registered for presentation at the conference. 6 out of 81 were selected in the short papers category and the rest in the full-length category. The final recommendation of papers was made by the general/program co-chair of IACC-2022 after receiving the review comments from the reviewers.

In the coming years, we would like to further enhance the visibility of the conference in terms of the number and quality of the papers. We are also consistently trying to reach out to under-represented regions of the world for quality papers.

Our sincere thanks to the Springer staff for their continuous support and help in taking the conference and series to the next level.

December 2022

Deepak Garg
Conference General Co-chair,
12th IACC 2022

Organization

Honorary Co-chairs

Sundaraja Sitharama Iyengar   Florida International University, USA
Sartaj Sahni   University of Florida, USA
Jagannathan Sarangpani   Missouri University of Science and Technology, USA

General Co-chairs

Deepak Garg   SR University, India
Suneet K. Gupta   Bennett University, India
Vijaya Kumar Koppula   CMR College of Engineering & Technology, India
V. A. Narayana   CMR College of Engineering & Technology, India

Proceeding Editors

P. N. Suganthan   Nanyang Technological University, Singapore
Jaume Anguera   Universitat Ramon Llull, Spain

Program Co-chairs

Kit Wong   University College London, UK
George Ghinea   Brunel University London, UK
Carol Smidts   Ohio State University, USA
Ram D. Sriram   National Institute of Standards & Technology, USA

Sanjay Madria   University of Missouri, USA
Oge Marques   Florida Atlantic University, USA
Vijay Kumar   University of Missouri-Kansas City, USA
Ajay Gupta   Western Michigan University, USA

Special Issue Co-chairs

Akansha Singh	Bennett University, India
Dilbag Singh	Gwangju Institute of Science and Technology, South Korea

Technical Program Committee/International Advisory Committee

Shivani Goel	Bennett University, India
Sumeet Dua	Louisiana Tech University, USA
Roger Zimmermann	National University of Singapore, Singapore
Seeram Ramakrishna	National University of Singapore, Singapore
B. V. R. Chowdari	NUS and Nanyang Technological University, Singapore
Hari Mohan Pandey	Edge Hill University, UK
Selwyn Piramuthu	University of Florida, USA
Bharat Bhargava	Purdue University, USA
Omer F. Rana	Cardiff University, UK
Javed I. Khan	Kent State University, USA
Harpreet Singh	Wayne State University, USA
Rajeev Agrawal	North Carolina A&T State University, USA
P. Prabhakaran	St. Joseph University, Tanzania
Yuliya Averyanova	National Aviation University (NAU), Ukraine
Mohammed M. Banet	Jordan University of Technology, Jordan
Dawid Zydek	Idaho State University, USA
Wensheng Zhang	Iowa State University, USA
Bal Virdee	London Metropolitan University, UK
Qun Wu	Harbin Institute of Technology, China
Anh V. Dinh	University of Saskatchewan, Canada
Lakshman Tamil	University of Texas, USA
P. D. D. Dominic	Universiti Teknologi Petronas, Malaysia
Muhammad Sabbir Rahman	North South University, Bangladesh
Zablon Akoko Mbero	University of Botswana, Botswana
V. L. Narasimhan	University of Botswana, Botswana
Kin-Lu Wong	National Sun Yat-sen University, Taiwan
Pawan Lingras	Saint Mary's University, USA
P. G. S. Velmurugan	Thiagaraja College of Engineering, India
N. B. Balamurugan	Thiagaraja College of Engineering, India
Mahesh Bundele	Poornima University, India
N. Venkateswaran	Sri Sivasubramaniya Nadar College of Engineering, India

S. Sundaresh	IEEE Madras Section, India
Premanand V. Chandramani	SSN College of Engineering, India
Mini Vasudevan	Ericsson India Pvt. Ltd., India
P. Swarnalatha	VIT, India
P. Venkatesh	Thiagaraja College of Engineering, India
B. Venkatalakshmi	Velammal Engineering College, India
M. Marsalin Beno	St. Xavier's Catholic College of Engineering, India
M. Arun	VIT, India
K. Porkumaran	Dr. N.G.P. Institute of Technology, India
D. Ezhilarasi	NIT Tiruchirappalli, India
Ramya Vijay	SASTRA University, India
S. Rajaram	Thiagaraja College of Engineering, India
B. Yogameena	Thiagaraja College of Engineering, India
S. Joseph Gladwin	SSN College of Engineering, India
D. Nirmal	Karunya University, India
N. Mohankumar	SKP Institute of Technology, India
A. Jawahar	SSN College of Engineering, India
K. Dhayalini	K. Ramakrishnan College of Engineering, India
Diganta Sengupta	Meghnad Saha Institute of Technology, India
Supriya Chakraborty	Amity University, India
Mamta Arora	Manav Rachna University, India
Om Prakash Jena	Ravenshaw University, India
Sandeep Singh Sengar	University of Copenhagen, Denmark
Murali Chemuturi	Chemuturi Consultants, India
Madhu Vadlamani	Cognizant, India
A. N. K. Prasannanjaneyulu	Institute of Insurance and Risk Management, India
O. Obulesu	G Narayanamma Institute of Technology & Science, India
Rajendra R. Patil	GSSSIETW, India
Ajay Kumar	Chitkara University Institute of Engineering & Technology, India
D. P. Kothari	THDC Institute of Hydropower Engineering and Technology, India
T. S. N. Murthy	JNTUK Vizianagaram, India
Nitesh Tarbani	Sipna College of Engineering & Technology, India
Jesna Mohan	Mar Baselios College of Engineering and Technology, India
Manoj K. Patel	CSIR, India
Pravati Swain	NIT Goa, India
Manoj Kumar	University of Petroleum and Energy Studies, India

E. S. Gopi	National Institute of Technology Tiruchirappalli, India
Mithun B. Patil	NKOCET, India
Priya Saha	LPU, India
Sahaj Saxena	Thapar Institute of Engineering and Technology, India
Dinesh G. Harkut	Prof Ram Meghe College of Engineering & Management, India
Pushpendra Singh	National Institute of Technology Hamirpur, India
Nirmala J. Saunshimath	Nitte Meenakshi Institute of Technology, India
Mayank Pandey	MNNIT, India
Sudeep D. Thepade	Pimpri Chinchwad College of Engineering, India
Pimal Khanpara	Nirma University, India
Rohit Lalwani	MIT University of Meghalaya, India
Loshma Gunisetti	Sri Vasavi Engineering College, India
Vishweshwar Kallimani	University of Nottingham, UK
Amit Kumar Mishra	DIT University, India
Pawan Whig	Vivekananda Institute of Professional Studies, India
Dhatri Pandya	Sarvajanik College of Engineering and Technology, India
Asha S. Manek	RV Institute of Technology and Management, India
Lingala Thirupathi	Methodist College of Engineering & Technology, India
P. Mahanti	University of New Brunswick, Canada
Shaikh Muhammad Allayear	Daffodil International University, Bangladesh
Basanta Joshi	Tribhuvan University, Nepal
S. R. N. Reddy	IGDTUW, India
Mehran Alidoost Nia	University of Tehran, Iran
Ambili P. S.	Saintgits Group of Institutions, India
M. A. Jabbar	Vardhaman College of Engineering, India
Lokendra Kumar Tiwari	Ewing Christian College, India
Abhay Saxena	Dev Sanskriti Vishwavidyalaya, India
Kanika Bansal	Chitkara University, India
Pooja M. R.	Vidyavardhaka College of Engineering, India
Pranav Dass	Bharati Vidyapeeth's College of Engineering, India
Avani R. Vasant	Babaria Institute of Technology, India
Bhanu Prasad	Florida A&M University, USA
Barenya Bikash Hazarika	NIT Arunachal Pradesh, India
Ipseeta Nanda	Gopal Narayan Singh University, India
Satyendra Singh	Bhartiya Skill Development University, India

Sudip Mandal	Jalpaiguri Govt. Engineering College, India
Naveen Kumar	IIIT Vadodara, India
Parag Rughani	National Forensic Sciences University, India
K. Shirin Bhanu	Sri Vasavi Engineering College, India
R. Malmathanraj	NITT, India
Latika Singh	Sushant University, India
Gizachew Hailegebriel Mako	Ethio telecom, Ethiopia
Tessy Mathew	Mar Baselios College of Engineering and Technology, India
Grzegorz Chodak	Wroclaw University of Science and Technology, Poland
Neetu Verma	DCRUST, India
Sharda A. Chhabria	G.H. Raisoni Institute of Engineering & Technology, India
Neetesh Saxena	Cardiff University, UK
R. Venkatesan	Ministry of Earth Sciences, India
V. Jayaprakasan	IEEE Madras Section, India
D. Venkata Vara Prasad	SSN College of Engineering, India
Jayakumari J.	Mar Baselios College of Engineering and Technology, India
P. A. Manoharan	IEEE Madras Section, India
S. Salivahanan	IEEE Madras Section, India
P. Santhi Thilagam	National Institute of Technology Karnataka, India
Umapada Pal	Indian Statistical Institute, India
S. Suresh	NIT Trichy, India
V. Mariappan	NIT Trichy, India
T. Sentilkumar	Anna University, India
S. Chandramohan	College of Engineering, India
D. Devaraj	Kalasalingam Academy of Research & Education, India
J. William	Agnel Institute of Technology & Design, India
R. Kalidoss	SSN College of Engineering, India
R. K. Mugelan	Vellore Institute of Technology, India
V. Vinod Kumar	Government College of Engineering, India
R. Saravanan	VIT, India
S. Sheik Aalam	iSENSE Intelligence Solutions, India
E. Srinivasan	Pondicherry Engineering College, India
B. Surendiran	National Institute of Technology Puducherry, India
Varun P. Gopi	National Institute of Technology Tiruchirappal India
V. Vijaya Chamundeeswari	Velammal Engineering College, India
T. Prabhakar	GMRIT, India

V. Kamakoti	IIT Madras, India
N. Janakiraman	KLN College of Engineering, India
V. Anandakrishanan	NIT Trichy, India
R. B. Patel	MMEC, India
Adesh Kumar Sharma	NDRI, India
Gunamani Jena	JNTU, India
Maninder Singh	Thapar University, India
Manoj Manuja	NIT Trichy, India
Ajay K. Sharma	Chitkara University, India
Manjit Patterh	Punjabi University, India
L. M. Bhardwaj	Amity University, India
Parvinder Singh	DCRUST, India
M. Syamala	Punjab University, India
Lalit Awasthi	NIT Jalandhar, India
Ajay Bansal	NIT Jalandhar, India
Ravi Aggarwal	Adobe Systems, USA
Sigurd Meldal	San José State University, USA
M. Balakrishnan	IIT Madras, India
Malay Pakhira	KGEC, India
Savita Gupta	PU Chandigarh, India
Manas Ranjan Patra	Berhampur University, India
Sukhwinder Singh	PU Chandigarh, India
Dharmendra Kumar	GJUST, India
Chandan Singh	Punjabi University, India
Rajinder Nath	Kurukshetra University, India
Manjaiah D.H	Mangalore University, India
Himanshu Aggarwal	Punjabi University, India
R. S. Kaler	Thapar University, India
Pabitra Pal Choudhury	Indian Statistical Institute, India
S. K. Pal	DRDO, India
G. S. Lehal	Punjabi University, India
Rajkumar Kannan	Bishop Heber College, India
Yogesh Chaba	GJUST, India
Amardeep Singh	Punjabi University, India
Sh. Sriram Birudavolu	Oracle India Limited, India
Ajay Rana	Amity University, India
Kanwal Jeet Singh	Punjabi University, India
C. K. Bhensdadia	DD University, India
Savina Bansal	GZSCET, India
Mohammad Asger	BGSB, India
Rajesh Bhatia	PEC, India
Stephen John Turner	VISTEC, India

Ramakanth Kumar P.	RVCE, India
S. N. Omkar	IISC Bangalore, India
Balaji Rajendran	CDAC, India
Annapoorna P. Patil	MSRIT, India
K. N. Chandrashekhar	SJCIT, India
Mohammed Misbahuddin	CDAC, India
Saroj Meher	ISI, India
Jharna Majumdar	NMIT, India
N. K. Cauvery	RVCE, India
G. K. Patra	CSIR, India
Anandi Jayadharmarajan	Oxford College of Engg., India
K. R. Suneetha	BIT Mesra, India
M. L. Shailaja	AIT, India
K. R. Murali Mohan	GOI, India
Ramesh Paturi	Microsoft, India
S. Viswanadha Raju	JNTU, India
C. Krishna Mohan	IIT Chennai, India
R. T. Goswamy	Techno International New Town, India
B. Surekha	K S Institute of Technology, India
P. Trinatha Rao	GITAM University, India
G. Varaprasad	BMS College of Engineering, India
M. Usha Rani	SPMVV, India
P. V. Lakshmi	SPMVV, India
K. A. Selvaradjou	PEC, India
Ch. Satyananda Reddy	Andhra University, India
Jeegar A. Trivedi	Sardar Patel University, India
S. V. Rao	IIT Guwahati, India
Suresh Varma	Aadikavi Nannaya University, India
T. Ranga Babu	RVR & JC College of Engineering, India
D. Venkat Rao	Narasaraopet Inst. of Technology, India
N. Sudhakar Reddy	S V Engineering College, India
Dhiraj Sunehra	Jawaharlal Nehru Technological University, India
Madhavi Gudavalli	Jawaharlal Nehru Technological University Kakinada, India
B. Hemanth Kumar	RVR & JC College of Engineering, India
A. Sri Nagesh	RVR & JC College of Engg., India
Bipin Bihari Jaya Singh	CVR College of Engg, India
M. Ramesh	JNTU, India
P. Rajarajeswari	GITAM University, India
R. Kiran Kumar	Krishna University, India
D. Ramesh	JNTU, India
B. Kranthi Kiran	JNTU, India

K. Usha Rani	SPM University, India
A. Nagesh	MGIT, India
P. Sammulal	JNTU, India
G. Narasimha	JNTU, India
B. V. Ram Naresh Yadav	JNTU, India
B. N. Bhandari	JNTUH, India
O. B. V. Ramanaiah	JNTUH College of Engineering, India
Anil Kumar Vuppala	IIIT Hyderabad, India
Duggirala Srinivasa Rao	JNTU, India
Makkena Madhavi Latha	JNTUH, India
Anitha Sheela Kancharla	JNTUH, India
B. Padmaja Rani	JNTUH, India
S. Mangai	Velalar College of Engg. & Tech., India
P. Chandra Sekhar	Osmania University, India
Chakraborty Mrityunjoy	IIT Kharagpur, India
Manish Shrivastava	IIIT Hyderabad, India
Uttam Kumar Roy	Jadavpur University, India
Kalpana Naidu	IIIT Kota, India
A. Swarnalatha	St. Joseph's College of Engg., India
Aaditya Maheshwari	Techno India NJR Institute of Tech., India
Ajit Panda	National Institute of Science and Technology (NIST), India
R. Anuradha	Sri Ramakrishna Engg. College, India
B. G. Prasad	BMS College of Engg., India
Seung-Hwa Chung	Trinity College Dublin, Ireland
D. Murali	VIT, India
Deepak Padmanabhan	Queen's University Belfast, UK
Firoz Alam	RMIT University, Australia
Frederic Andres	NII, Japan
Srinath Doss	Botho University, Botswana
Munish Kumar	Maharaja Ranjit Singh Punjab Tech. University, India
Norwati Mustapha	UPM, India
Hamidah Ibrahim	UPM, India
Denis Reilly	Liverpool John Moores University, UK
Ioannis Kypraios	De Montfort University, UK
Yongkang Xing	De Montfort University, UK
P. Shivakumara	UM, Malaysia
Ravinder Kumar	TIET Patiala, India
Ankur Gupta	Bennett University, India
Rahul Kr. Verma	IIIT Lucknow, India
Mohit Sajwan	Bennett University, India

Vijaypal Singh Rathor	Thapar University Patiala, India
Deepak Singh	NIT Raipur, India
Simranjit Singh	Bennett University, India
Suchi Kumari	Bennett University, India
Kuldeep Chaurasia	Bennett University, India
Indrajeet Gupta	Bennett University, India
Shakti Sharma	Bennett University, India
Hiren Thakkar	PDPU, India
Mayank Swankar	IIT(BHU), India
Tapas Badal	Bennett University, India
Vipul Kr. Mishra	Bennett University, India
Tanveer Ahmed	Bennett University, India
Madhushi Verma	Bennett University, India
Gaurav Singal	NSUT, India
Anurag Goswami	Bennett University, India
Durgesh Kumar Mishra	Sri Aurobindo Institute of Technology, India
S. Padma	Madanapalle Institute of Technology & Science, India
M. A. Jabbar	Vardhman College of Engineering, India
Deepak Prashar	Lovely Professional University, India
Nidhi Khare	NMIMS, India
Sandeep Kumar	IIT Delhi, India
Dattatraya V. Kodavade	D.K.T.E Society's Textile & Engineering Institute, India
A. Obulesu	Anurag University, India
K. Suvarna Vani	V.R. Siddhartha Engineering College, India
G. Singaravel	K.S.R. College of Engineering, India
Ajay Shiv Sharma	Melbourne Institute of Technology, Australia
Abhishek Shukla	R.D. Engineering College Technical Campus Ghaziabad, India
V. K. Jain	Mody University, India
Deepak Poola	IBM India Private Limited, India
Bhadri Raju M. S. V. S.	S.R.K.R. Engineering College, India
Yamuna Prasad	IIT Jammu, India
Vishnu Vardhan B.	JNTUH College of Engineering Manthani, India
Virendrakumar Bhavsar	University of New Brunswick, Canada
Siva S. Skandha	CMR College of Engineering, India
Vaibhav Anu	Montclair State University, USA
V. Gomathi	National Engineering College, India
Sudipta Roy	Assam University, India
Srabanti Maji	DIT University, India
Shylaja S.S.	PESU, India

Shweta Agrawal	SIRT, India
Shreenivas Londhe	Vishwakarma Institute of Information Technology, India
Shirin Bhanu Koduri	Vasavi Engineering College, India
Shailendra Aswale	SRIEIT, India
Shachi Natu	TSE College Mumbai, India
Santosh Saraf	Graphic Era University, India
Samayveer Singh	Ambedkar National Institute of Technology, India
Sabu M. Thampi	IIITM Kerala, India
Roshani Raut	Vishwakarma Institute of Information Technology, India
Radhika K.R.	BMSCE, India
R. Priya Vaijayanthi	Institute of Technology, India
M. Naresh Babu	NIT Silchar, India
Krishnan Rangarajan	Dayananda Sagar College of Engineering, India
Prashant Singh Rana	Thapar Institute of Engg. & Tech., India
Parteek Bhatia	Thapar Institute of Engineering & Technology, India
Venkata Padmavati Metta	BIT, India
Laxmi Lydia	VIIT, India
Nikunj Tahilramani	Dolcera IT Services Pvt. Ltd., India
Navanath Saharia	IIIT, India
Nagesh Vadaparthi	MVGR College of Engineering, India
Manne Suneetha	VR Siddhartha Engineering College, India
Sumalatha Lingamgunta	JNTU Kakinada, India
Kalaiarasi Sonai Muthu Anbananthen	Multimedia University, Malaysia
K. Subramanian	IIT Kanpur, India
Singaraju Jyothi	Sri Padmavati Mahila Visvavidyalayam, India
Vinit Jakhetiya	IIT Jammu, India
Yashwantsinh Jadeja	Marwadi University, India
Harsh Dev	PSIT, India
Yashodhara V. Haribhakta	Government College of Engineering, India
Gopal Sakarkar	GHRCE, India
R. Gnanadass	Pondicherry Engineering College, India
K. Giri Babu	VVIT, India
Geeta Sikka	B R Ambedkar National Institute of Technology, India
Gaurav Varshney	IIT Jammu, India
G. L. Prajapati	Devi Ahilya University, India
G. Kishor Kumar	RGMCET, India
Md. Saidur Rahman	Bangladesh University of Engineering and Technology, Bangladesh

Wali Khan Mashwani	Kohat University of Science & Technology, Pakistan
Krishna Kiran Vamsi Dasu	Sri Sathya Sai Institute, India
Sisira Kumar Kapat	Utkal Gaurav Madhusudan Institute of Technology, India
Kuldeep Sharma	Chitkara University, India
Zankhana H. Shah	BVM Engineering College, India
Rekha Ramesh	Shah and Anchor Kutchhi Engineering College, India
Gopalkrishna Joshi	KLE Technological University, India
Ganga Holi	AMC Engineering College., India
K. Kotecha	Symbiosis International, India
Radhakrishna Bhat	MAHE, India
Kuldeep Singh	Carnegie Mellon University, USA
Binod Kumar	JSPM's Rajarshi Shahu College of Engineering, India
Raju Kumar	Chandigarh University, India
Nitin S. Goje	Webster University in Tashkent, Uzbekistan
Pushpa Mala S.	Dayananda Sagar University, India
Ashish Sharma	GLA University, India
Ashwath Rao B.	Manipal Institute of Technology, India
Deepak Motwani	Amity University, India
V. Sowmya	Amrita School of Engineering, India
Jayashri Nair	VNR VJIET, India
Rajesh C. Sanghvi	G.H. Patel College of Engineering & Technology, India
Ashwin Dobariya	Marwadi University, India
Tapas Kumar Patra	*Odisha* University of Technology and Research, India
J. Naren	Rathinam College of Arts and Science, India
Rekha. K. S.	National Institute of Engineering, India
Mohammed Murtuza Qureshi	Digital Employment Exchange, India
Vasantha Kalyani David	Avinashilingam Institute for Home Science and Higher Education for Women, India
K. Sakthidasan	Hindustan Institute of Technology and Science, India
Shreyas Rao	Sahyadri College of Engineering and Management, India
Hiranmayi Ranganathan	Lawrence Livermore National Laboratory, USA
Sanjaya Kumar Panda	National Institute of Technology Warangal, India
Puspanjali Mohapatra	IIIT Bhubaneswar, India
Manimala Mahato	Shah & Anchor Kutchhi Engineering College, India

B. Senthil Kumar	Kumaraguru College of Technology Coimbatore, India
Jyoti Prakash Singh	National Institute of Technology Patna, India
Abhinav Tomar	Netaji Subhas University of Technology, India
M. G. Sumithra	Dr. N.G.P. Institute of Technology, India

Contents – Part II

Innovations in AI

System Security and Communication using AI

Use of AI in Human Psychology

Use of AI in Music and Video Industries

Contents – Part I

Application of AI for Disease Classification and Trend Analysis

Design of Agricultural Applications using AI

Disease Classification using CNN

About the Editors

Dr. Deepak Garg Vice Chancellor, SR University Director leadingindia.ai, He has been Dean, Computer Science and Engineering, Bennett University and Director, NVIDIA-Bennett Center of Research on Artificial Intelligence.

Dr. Garg is leading the largest Development, Skilling and Research initiative in AI in India with more than 1000 institutional collaborators. He is a chief consultant for algorithmguru.in. He has done his Ph.D. in efficient algorithm design in 2006. He served as chair of IEEE Computer Society, India IEEE Education Society (2013–15). He has handled funding of around INR 700 million including RAENG, UK on MOOCs, Machine Learning and AI. He has 110+ publications with 1400+ citations and Google h-index of 18. In his 24 years of experience, he has delivered 300+ invited talks and conducted 100+Workshops and 15+ Conferences across the country. He has Supervised 14 Ph.D. and 35 Students. He is a blogger in Times of India named as breaking shackles. For details please visit http://www.gdeepak.com.

Ponnuthurai Nagaratnam Suganthan (Fellow, IEEE) received the B.A. and M.A. degrees from the University of Cambridge, U.K., and the Ph.D. degree in computer science from Nanyang Technological University, Singapore. He is currently a professor with Qatar University.

Dr. Suganthan was the recipient of the IEEE Transactions on Evolutionary Computation Outstanding Paper Award in 2012 and the Highly Cited Researcher Award by the Thomson Reuters in computer science in 2015. He is currently an Associate Editor for the IEEE Transactions on Evolutionary Computation, the IEEE Transactions on SMC Systems, Information Sciences, and Pattern Recognition and the Founding Co-Editor-in-Chief for Swarm and Evolutionary Computation Journal.

Dr. Jaume Anguera IEEE Fellow, founder and CTO at the technology company Ignion (Barcelona, Spain). Associate Professor at Ramon LLull University and a member of the Smart Society research group. He is an inventor of more than 150 granted patents, most of them licensed to telecommunication companies. Among his most outstanding contributions is that of the inventor of Antenna Booster Technology, a technology that fostered the creation of Ignion. The wireless industry has adopted many of these products worldwide to allow wireless connectivity to IoT devices through a miniature component called an antenna booster that is ten times smaller than conventional antennas. Author of more than 270 widely cited scientific papers and international conferences (h-index 52). Author of 7 books. He has participated in more than 22 competitive research projects financed by the Spanish Ministry, CDTI, CIDEM (Generalitat de Catalunya), and the European Commission for an amount exceeding $13M as a principal researcher in most of them. He has taught over 40 antenna courses worldwide (USA, China, Korea, India, UK, France, Poland, Czech Republic, Tunisia, Perú, Brazil, Canada, Spain). With over 23 years of R&D experience, he has developed part of his professional experience with Fractus in South Korea in designing miniature antennas for large Korean companies such as Samsung and LG. Since 2017 he has been with Ignion in the role of CTO. He leads the company R&D activity to create new products, envisage new technologies, technical evangelism, and provide technology strategy to scale the company business. He has received several national and international awards (ex. 2004 Best Ph. D Thesis -two prizes, one given by Telefónica Mobile, 2004 IEEE New Faces of Engineering, 2014 Finalist European Patent Award). He has directed the master/doctorate thesis to more than 160 students, many of them have received awards for their thesis (COIT, COITT, Ministry of Education). His biography appears in Who'sWho in the World and Who'sWho in Science and Engineering. He is an associate editor of the IEEE Open Journal on Antennas and Propagation, Electronics Letters, and a reviewer in several IEEE and other scientific journals. He is an IEEE Antennas and Propagation Distinguished Lecturer and vice-chair of the working group "Software and Modeling" at EurAAP. More info at http://users.salleurl.edu/~jaume.anguera/.

Major Dr. V. A. Narayana is Professor in the Department of Computer Science & Engineering and Principal at CMR College of Engineering & Technology. He received his bachelor's degree in Mechanical engineering from University College of Engineering, Osmania University in 1994, Masters Degree in Computer Science and Engineering from University College of Engineering, Osmania University in 2004. He received his Ph.D. in Computer Science and Engineering from JNTU Hyderabad in 2014. He has over 28 years of experience out of which 11 years of service in the Indian Army and 17+ years of research and teaching experience. He has contributed more than 26 research papers in various Scopus Indexed and IEEE Journals. His areas of interest include Data Mining, Web Mining and Database Management Systems etc., He has provided guidance for more than 22 M.Tech student projects. He is currently guiding 3 Ph.D scholars in eminent institutes such as IIT Bombay, JNTUH, and Bennett University. He has delivered many invited talks and Guest Lectures at National and International levels and has authored four books. With the keen interest to promote and develop research, he has organized many International and National Conferences and various Workshops, Seminars etc., He has received many awards and honors for his service which include "SARVOTHAM ACHARYA PURASKAR", "Organizational Excellence in Technical Education", "Best Educationist", "DEWANG MEHTA", "Best faculty", "Best HOD" etc., He has been part of teaching, research, training and consultancy at CMRCET since 2006. With his rich academic and research experience, he has been instrumental in executing more than 25 Sponsored Research and consultancy projects funded by various funding agencies like DST, and AICTE and other renowned agencies.

Dr. Vijaya Kumar Koppula Professor & Dean (Academics), Department of CSE has completed his B.Tech with Computer Science and Systems Engineering from Andhra University, M.Tech with Computer Science & Technology from Andhra University and Ph.D with Computer Science from University of Hyderabad.

He has more than 23 years of teaching experience. He is resource person for Infosys campus program, worked as a visiting scientist for page segmentation project in CVPR Unit, ISI Kolkata. He received an award for Teaching Excellence from Indo-American Education Summit 2016. He is a paper setter for various universities, reviewer for various international conferences and guided more than 100 B.Tech and M. Tech projects. He has published papers in various International/National journals and IEEE International/National conferences. He published papers in top IEEE International conferences like ICDAR 2011 and ICPR 2012. His papers are indexed in Scopus, DBLP and IEEE xplore. PhD supervisor in eminent institutes such as JNTUH, GRIT, and Bennett University. One of the research scholar completed PhD degree under his supervision.

Suneet Kumar Gupta is Associate Professor in the Department of Computer Science Engineering at Bennett University, Gr. Noida. His current research interests are Wireless Sensor Network, Internet of Things, Natural Language Processing and Brain-Computer Interaction. Presently Dr. Gupta has completed a Wireless Sensor Network based project funded by Department of Science and Technology, Uttar Pradesh.

Dr. Gupta is also part of a project funded by the Royal Academy of Science London entitled with Leadingindia.ai. He has more than 80 research articles, authored 2 books and 3 book chapters in his account.

Innovations in AI

GCOMSP: Design of a GWO Based Model for Continuous Optimization of Multidomain Stock Prediction Performance

Rachna Sable[1]([✉]) [iD], Shivani Goel[2] [iD], and Pradeep Chatterjee[3] [iD]

[1] Bennett University, Greater Noida 201310, UP, India
rachna.sable@gmail.com
[2] School of Computer Science Engineering and Technology, Bennett University, Greater Noida 201310, UP, India
[3] Head Digital Transformation and Customer Experience, GDC, Tata Motors, Pune, MS, India

Abstract. The goal of stock market prediction using various techniques of machine learning and deep learning is to create more accurate models. Stock price prediction from multidomain datasets requires design of data collection, preprocessing, aggregation, pre-filtering, feature representation and variance-based selection, prediction model design, and post processing processes. Existing models that perform these tasks are highly context-sensitive and cannot be scaled for multiple stock markets. Most of these models do not incorporate continuous learning mechanisms, which limits their scalability. To overcome these issues, this work proposes, design of a novel Grey Wolf Optimization (GWO) based model for continuous optimization of multidomain stock prediction performance. It aggregates datasets from multiple sources like stock prices, global news, local news, social media information, and commodity prices. The model is developed using Convolutional Neural Networks (CNNs), which assisted in providing high accuracy for multiple stock types. The CNN based model's performance is continuously tuned via use of a GWO based optimization layer which assists in incremental learning to optimize stock prediction efficiency for multiple use cases. The proposed GWO model uses a fitness function that incorporates prediction accuracy, computational delay, and precision values in order to identify optimal CNN configuration for better performance. Performance of the model was tested on Indian, American and Chinese stock markets and compared with various state-of-the-art models. Based on this comparison, it is observed that the proposed model has improved prediction accuracy by 7.6% and precision by 8.5%, while reducing computational delay by 5.9% across multiple evaluations.

Keywords: Stock market · Prediction · CNN · GWO · Accuracy · Precision

1 Introduction

Researchers from several professions have spent a great deal of time studying the prediction of stock movement. Prices are influenced by a variety of variables, such as firm performance, historical trends, and other variables. Traditional research concentrated

© Springer Nature Switzerland AG 2023
D. Garg et al. (Eds.): IACC 2022, CCIS 1782, pp. 3–16, 2023.
https://doi.org/10.1007/978-3-031-35644-5_1

on a stock's time series and technical analysis, i.e., forecasting stock movements using patterns from previous price signals. Price signals alone, however, are unable to account for market surprises and the effects of rapid, unexpected events. Stock price prediction from multidomain datasets is a highly specialized area of signal processing that combines real-time data crawling, pre-filtering for removal of outliers, sentiment analysis, feature representation and variance-based selection, prediction of stock and its processing operations. To design an efficient stock price prediction model, it is recommended that data collection, feature identification and prediction models must be optimized. It is observed that these tasks can currently be performed by existing models, but they are very context-sensitive and cannot be scaled for other stock markets. Additionally, the lack of continuous learning processes in the majority of these models restricts their potential to scale. The Grey Wolf Optimization (GWO) supports incremental learning of the model to enhance stock prediction efficiency.

The major contribution of the paper is design and implementation of a unique GWO based model for continuous optimization of multidomain stock prediction performance which has addressed the problems of development of a multidomain stock prediction system that collects data from various sources, including stock prices, national, international, local, social media, and commodity prices. Convolutional Neural Networks (CNNs) are used in the model's development to help it provide excellent accuracy for a variety of stock kinds. The suggested model employs a fitness function that takes prediction accuracy, computational latency, and precision values into account. The model can be used for a broad range of real-time use cases and scaled to various stock markets.

Rest of the paper is organized as follows: Sect. 2 covers the related work in the field of stock market prediction. Methodology used is presented in Sect. 3. Section 4 discusses all results and compares these models in terms of their real-time performance levels, which assist in validating its usability. Finally, this paper offers some insightful conclusions regarding the suggested paradigm and suggests ways to further enhance its functionality.

2   Related Work

Stock market is highly volatile and non-linear in nature. Researchers have found it extremely difficult to make accurate predictions. The relative ranking or order of stocks is considered important so that the price or performance of a single stock in order to make sensible investment selections was the idea proposed in [1]. It was suggested that stock-related information can improve the stock ranking prediction. A graph-based approach along with machine learning models to improve prediction performance was employed [2] which focused on various feature selection algorithms along with Random Forest classifier to improve performance. A wide variety of stock value prediction models are proposed by researchers, and each of them vary in terms of their internal operating characteristics. DQN along with CNN was used in [3] to test the model on chart images as input for making global market predictions. The results showed that artificial intelligence-based stock price forecasting models can be used in relatively small markets, even when there was insufficient data for training. Deep Clue's efficiency in assisting with stock market investment and analysis tasks was the work in [4]. For instance, work in [5, 6] proposed use of metaheuristic search and efficient word embedding with deep learning-based model for high efficiency stock value prediction operations. These models showcased high prediction accuracy, but cannot be scaled to multiple stock types. To overcome this issue, work in [7] proposed use of candlestick charting with Ensemble Machine Learning (CC EML), which assisted in improving prediction performance under multiple use cases.

Similar models were discussed in [8–10], which proposed use of augmented textual features, Hybrid Red Deer-Grey Algorithm (HRDA), and Hybrid Time-Series Predictive Neural Network (HTPNN) which assisted in augmenting input feature sets in order to improve quality of prediction for different stock types. These models were extended via the work in [11–13], which proposed use of Recurrent Neural Networks (RNNs), Auto Regressive Integrated Moving Average (ARIMA), Long short-term memory (LSTM), and No Free Lunch Model, which assisted in improving prediction accuracy via estimation of high-density technical markers, and then analyzing them for different input types. These models showcased high accuracy and can be extended for multiple stock markets with better prediction efficiency levels. The work in [14] outlined a clustering technique that combined k-means clustering and morphological similarity distance (MSD) for mining related stocks. Hierarchical Temporal Memory (HTM), was utilized to identify trends in comparable stocks and produce forecasts finally designated as C-HTM. It was shown that C-HTM had higher forecast accuracy as compared to HTM, which had not learned similar stock patterns. An intelligent PLR (IPLR) model was developed by integrating Genetic algorithm with the Piecewise Linear Representation to iteratively raise the threshold value [15]. As a result, the model's profitability was increased even more. Many influences of events issue, which was not taken into consideration by the current methodologies was discussed in [16]. To address this issue, a two-component multi-element hierarchical attention capsule network was proposed. It was shown that the model's ability to quantify the many influences on occurrences increased forecast accuracy. Multimodal Event-Driven LSTM was proposed in [17], to address unique challenges in processing multimodal data. An intelligent agent-based market prediction system iJADE Stock Advisor using Hybrid Radial Basis Function Recurrent Network (HRBFN) showed better results [18].

Ouyang et al. highlighted use of many techniques for pattern identification in stocks like Temporal Pattern Attention and Long-Short-Term Memory (TPA-LSTM), Toeplitz Inverse Covariance-Based Clustering (TICC) and Multivariate LSTM-FCNs [19]. According to empirical findings, the portfolio based on the suggested three-stage architecture performed better than the portfolio based on the stock market. A model with various sources and instances that could efficiently incorporate events, feelings, and quantitative data into a thorough framework named multi source multiple instances was proposed in [20]. The model simultaneously determined the significance of the information and forecasted how the stock market would move. To lessen volatility's concentration property, a hybrid model based on GARCH-type models and a cutting-edge non-linear filtering technique was proposed in [21]. It was observed that the suggested hybrid model (VU-GARCH-LSTM) achieved a performance boost of 21.03% when compared to the mean performances of the current hybrid models. A novel approach to make simpler, noisy filled financial temporal series via sequence reconstruction by leveraging motifs using a convolutional neural network to detect the spatial structure of time series after that was proposed in [22]. The proposed method using feature learning outperformed conventional signal processing with accuracy improvements of 4% to 7%. The long-term temporal features and the short-term spatial features from market data were extracted using trend predictive model (TPM)'s application of the PLR approach and CNN in first phase [23]. It was based on an encoder-decoder framework. To pick and combine pertinent dual features and forecast the direction of the stock price, an encoder-decoder framework based on the dual attention method was applied in second phase.

The experimental results demonstrated that, in terms of prediction accuracy, the proposed TPM surpasses the current state-of-the-art approaches, including CNN, SVR, LSTM, and TPM NC. A thorough examination for the selection of the fewest possible relevant Technical Indicators using CSFTNB was conducted in [24] with the goal of enhancing accuracy, decreasing misclassification costs, and raising investment return. Zhang et al. proposed a stock index movement prediction method [25]. It was based on signal decomposition and the newly defined instantaneous frequency. It proved to be more effective than BP neural network. But most of these models are highly context-sensitive, and cannot be scaled for multiple stock markets. Moreover, most of these models do not incorporate continuous learning mechanisms, which limits their scalability when applied to real-time market scenarios. The next section outlines ways to resolve these problems by designing a novel Grey Wolf Optimization (GWO) based Model for Continuous Optimization of Multidomain Stock Prediction performance. The model is evaluated for different stock markets and compared with a wide variety of state-of-the-art methods under different use cases, which assists in validating its performance for real-time stock types.

3   Methodology

To address the aforementioned issues, design of a novel Grey Wolf Optimization (GWO)-based Model for continuous optimization of multidomain stock prediction performance is depicted in Fig. 1.

In order to discuss about GWO and its internal working operations, this section initially briefs about stock value prediction models. The News and Social Media datasets are crawled for updates about current stock (or its primary owner entities).

These searches include:

- Mention: Stock name in News Feeds and Tweets
- Mention: Stock's company name (Stock of Google will be directly related to its parent company ABC ltd.) in News Feeds and Tweets
- Mention: Company's board of directors in News Feeds and Tweets

Equation 1 given below evaluates the final sentiment of the stock based on the above extracted data using a Word2Vec-based sentiment analysis model.

$$S_{out} = w(N) * S(N) + w(CN) * S(CN) + \sum_{i=1}^{ND} w(BD_i) * S(BD_i) \qquad (1)$$

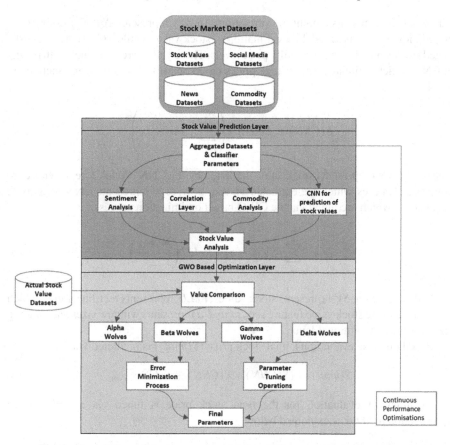

Fig. 1. Overall flow of the proposed model for continuous optimization process.

where, $w(N)$ represents weight of stock's name, $S(N)$ represents sentiment of the stock's name, $w(CN)$ represents weight of stock's company name, $S(CN)$ represents sentiment of the stock's company name, $w(BD)$ represents weight of Board of Director's name, $S(N)$ represents sentiment of the Board of Director's name, while ND represents number of relevant directors (or other socially active members) in the company.

Similarly, a correlation value is estimated, which assists in evaluating link between company's stock value and commodity prices via Eq. 2,

$$C(S, C) = \frac{n(\sum S, C) - (\sum S)(\sum C)}{\sqrt{\left[n\sum S^2 - (\sum S)^2\right]\left[n\sum C^2 - (\sum C)^2\right]}} \tag{2}$$

where, S and C represents stock values and corresponding commodity values, while $\boldsymbol{n}$ represents number of samples used for analysis. Based on this correlation, stock value is estimated via Eq. 3,

$$S(C) = C(S, C) * w(C) * ARIMA(S) \tag{3}$$

where, $w(C)$ represents weight of correlation, *ARIMA* represents Autoregressive integrated moving average model for estimation of stock value, while $S(C)$ represents estimated stock value due to commodity price levels. These values are combined with results of CNN, which estimates output stock prices based on Soft Max activation function via Eq. 4,

$$S(CNN) = SoftMax\left(\sum_{i=1}^{N_f} f_i * w_i + b_i\right)$$ (4)

where, $S(CNN)$ represents stock value predicted by the CNN Model, f_i represents convolutional features which are extracted via Eq. 5, w_i & b_i represents CNN weights & bias values, which are tuned via the GWO based optimization process.

$$f_i = \sum_{a=-\frac{m}{2}}^{\frac{m}{2}} SV(i-a) * ReLU\left(\frac{m+a}{2}\right)$$ (5)

In this equation, *SV* represents stock values, *ReLU* represents rectilinear unit, which is used to activate stock value feature sets, *m and a* represents window sizes and padding sizes for the convolutional layers.

Based on these evaluations, final stock price ($S(final)$) is predicted via Eq. 6,

$$S(final) = (S(CNN) * w(CNN) + S(C)) * S_{out}$$ (6)

Accuracy of evaluation for the final stock price is tuned via a GWO based optimization method as explained below.

GWO Optimization process
Step 1: Setup the initial parameters for GWO
Total wolves used for optimization (N_w)
Total iterations for which these wolves will be used (N_i)
Learning rate of the wolves (L_w)
Current values of individual weights:
$w(N)$, $w(CN)$, $w(BD)$, $w(C)$, $w(CNN)$, $b(CNN)$
Predicted and actual value of stock S(P), S(A)
Step 2: Mark all the wolves as 'Delta' wolves, which will assist in modifying their configurations
Step 3: Scan through each wolf for N_i iterations, via the following process
Skip the wolf if it is not marked as 'Delta Wolf'
For all other wolves, generate their internal configurations via the following process
Stochastically select N_p parameters via Eq. 7 $N_p = STOCH(L_w * N, N)$ (7) Where, N represents number of weights that can be tuned, while STOCH represents a stochastic process for generation of numbers between given value sets

(continued)

(continued)

Modify these values via Eq. 8 $w_i = w_i \pm L_w$ (8) Where, w_i represents i_{th} weight, and $i \in (1, N_p)$
Based on the new weights, wolf fitness can be evaluated via Eq. 9 $f_w = \frac{A+P+R}{3}$ (9) Where, A, P and R represents accuracy, precision & recall of stock prediction, which is evaluated via Eq. 10, 11, and 12 respectively $A = \frac{N_c}{N_t}$ (10) $P = \frac{N_{cc}}{N_t} \ldots (11)$ $R = \frac{N_{ci}}{N_t} \ldots (12)$ Where, $N_c, N_{cc}, N_{ci}, \& N_t$ represents number of correctly predicted entries, number of correctly predicted entries with correct stock sentiments, number of correctly predicted entries with incorrect stock sentiments, and total number of stock values used for the prediction process
Step 4: Repeat this task for each wolf, and then estimate iteration threshold via Eq. 13 as follows $f_{th} = \sum_{i=1}^{Nw} f_{wi} * \frac{L_w}{N_w}$ (13)
Step 5: At the end of each iteration, modify wolf status via the following process
Mark wolf as 'Alpha' if $f_w > 2*f_{th}$
Else, mark wolf as 'Beta', if $f_w > f_{th}$
Else, mark wolf as 'Gamma', if $f_w > L_w * f_{th}$
Otherwise, mark wolf as 'Delta' wolf, and repeat the process
Based on this evaluation, identify wolf with highest fitness levels, and use its identified weights for tuning stock prediction operations. Due to selection of wolf with highest fitness, this model is capable of improving accuracy of the stock prediction process. To validate its performance, the model is evaluated in terms of precision, recall, accuracy, delay values, and compared with other methods in the next section.

4 Result Analysis and Experimentation

A wide variety of tests were conducted to evaluate the model's performance. These include news analysis, stock market analysis, and stock movement prediction based on social sentiment. Market values are estimated using indicator-based analysis, which combines local and global stock sentiment with indicators to get the final stock value. Stock and commodity prices were gathered using the Yahoo! Stock API, social feeds were retrieved using the Twitter API, international news was retrieved using the BBC, and local news was retrieved using the NDTV API for these experiments. Using these datasets, performance metrics such as precision, recall, accuracy and area under the curve (AUC) of intra-day value estimation were calculated. Reliance Jio, Tata Motors, Zomato, Google, Apple, and Asian Paints all had their parameter means calculated, after that these values were evaluated over a period of 60 days. The average values of the parameters for each day were recorded. These stock prices were forecasted for 60 days with daily monitoring. With regard to the models described in HTP NN [10], MEH CAN [16], and CNN w/o GWO, which make use of equivalent inputs as the proposed model for the final stock price estimate, these readings help evaluate the performance of the proposed model under different scenarios. Based on this strategy, average accuracy for stock prediction with reference to number of days is shown in Table 1.

Table 1. Comparative Accuracy of stock prediction models.

Days	Acc. HTP NN [10]	Acc. MEH CAN [16]	Acc. CNN w/o GWO	Acc. GCOM SP
5	56.7	73.5	77.2	83.5
14	57.4	75.5	78.63	84.65
20	57.93	76.98	79.73	85.88
28	58.45	78.45	80.85	87.08
35	58.98	79.93	81.98	88.28
42	59.33	80.28	82.4	88.73
49	59.68	80.35	82.7	89.03
54	59.85	80.35	82.83	89.18
56	60.03	80	82.78	89.13
58	60.42	80.96	83.55	89.96
60	60.73	81.89	84.23	90.7

Based on the evaluation in Table 1 and Fig. 2, the proposed model showcases 25.5% improvement in accuracy when compared with HTP NN [10], 8.5% improvement when compared with MEH CAN [16], and 5.9% improvement when compared with CNN w/o GWO process, which makes it highly useful for high accuracy stock prediction applications. This is possible due to continuous optimizations via the GWO Model, which assists in improving its stock value prediction performance under real-time use cases.

Similarly, performance of precision of stock value prediction is shown in Table 2.

Based on the evaluation in Table 2 and Fig. 3, the proposed model showcases 29.5% improvement in precision when compared with HTP NN [10], 12.5% improvement when compared with MEH CAN [16], and 13.9% improvement when compared with CNN w/o GWO process, which makes it highly useful for high precision stock prediction applications. This is possible due to continuous optimizations via the GWO Model, which assists in improving its stock value prediction performance under real-time use cases.

Similarly, performance of recall of stock value prediction is shown in Table 3.

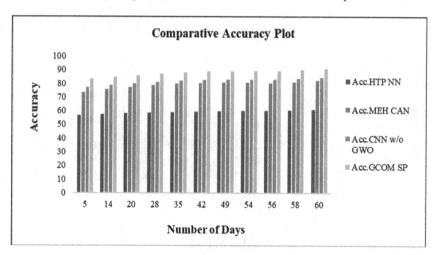

Fig. 2. Comparative Accuracy of stock prediction models.

Table 2. Comparative Precision of stock prediction models

Days	Prec. HTP NN [10]	Prec. MEH CAN [16]	Prec. CNN w/o GWO	Prec. GCOM SP
5	47	58.25	59.5	71
14	47.75	60.5	61.25	73
20	48.75	62.75	63	75
28	49.75	65	64.75	77
35	50.5	65.75	65.25	77.75
42	51.25	66	65.75	78.5
49	51.5	66	65.75	78.75
54	51.75	65.5	65.75	78.75
56	52.4	66.94	67.02	80.16
58	52.98	68.4	68.02	81.37
60	53.71	69.89	69.26	82.86

Based on the evaluation in Table 3 and Fig. 4, it can be observed that the proposed model showcases 14.2% improvement in recall when compared with HTP NN [10], 5.9% improvement when compared with MEH CAN [16], and 6.1% improvement when compared with CNN w/o GWO process, which makes it highly useful for high recall stock prediction applications. This is possible due to continuous optimizations via the GWO Model, which assists in improving its stock value prediction performance under real-time use cases.

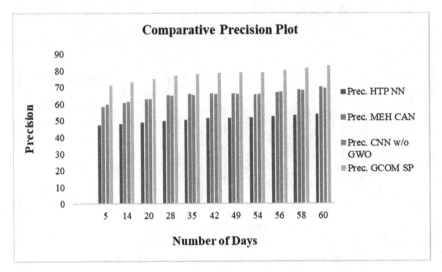

Fig. 3. Comparative Precision of stock prediction models

Table 3. Comparative Recall of stock prediction models

Days	Rec. HTP NN [10]	Rec. MEH CAN [16]	Rec. CNN w/o GWO	Rec. GCOM SP
5	41.25	46.75	47.5	53.5
14	41.75	48	48.5	54.5
20	42.25	49.25	49.5	55.5
28	42.75	50.25	50.25	56.5
35	43	50.75	50.5	56.75
42	43.25	50.75	50.75	57
49	43.5	50.75	50.75	57
54	43.75	50.5	50.75	56.75
56	44.18	51.16	51.36	57.4
58	44.44	51.97	51.84	57.91
60	44.79	52.66	52.44	58.55

Similarly, performance of delay needed for stock value prediction can be observed from Table 4 as follows,

Based on the evaluation in Table 4 and Fig. 5, the proposed model showcases higher delay when compared with existing models, thus requiring higher computational capabilities for efficient performance. This is due to highly iterative GWO Model, which assists in improving accuracy performance via continuous optimization process. Thus, the model is useful for high accuracy, better precision, and good recall applications, but

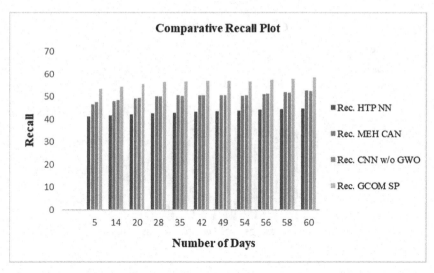

Fig. 4. Comparative Recall of stock prediction models

Table 4. Comparative Delay of stock prediction models

Days	D (ms)	D (ms)	D (ms)	D (ms)
	HTP NN [10]	MEH CAN [16]	CNN w/o GWO	GCOM SP
5	23	26.75	27	33.5
14	23.5	28	27.88	34.75
20	24	29.25	28.88	36
28	24.5	30.63	29.88	37.25
35	24.88	30.88	30.38	37.75
42	25.25	31	30.63	38
49	25.5	31	30.75	38.13
54	25.75	30.63	30.63	38.13
56	26.2	31.51	31.23	39
58	26.49	32.29	31.85	39.8
60	26.88	33.11	32.47	40.64

has higher complexity, which increases its deployment requirements under real-time use cases.

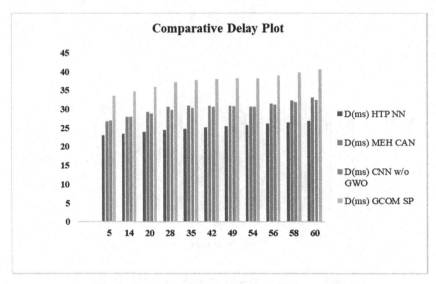

Comparative Delay of stock prediction models

5   Conclusion and Future Work

The proposed GCOMSP Model uses a combination of different deep learning methods which are optimized via the GWO process. To perform this optimization, weights for each of the prediction models are modified via an intelligent stochastic process. The model is continuously learning and can provide stock values with better accuracy. The proposed model is capable of achieving 25.5%, 8.5% and 5.9% improvement in accuracy, 29.5%, 12.5% and 13.9% improvement in precision, 14.2%, 5.9% and 6.1% improvement in recall when compared with HTP NN [10], MEH CAN [16] and CNN w/o GWO process respectively. The proposed model showcased higher delay when compared with existing models, thus requiring higher computational capabilities for efficient performance. This is due to highly iterative GWO Model, which assisted in improving accuracy performance via continuous optimization process. In future, performance of the model can be improved via integration of Q-Learning, Generative Adversarial Networks (GANs), Recurrent NNs, etc.

References

1. Saha, S., Gao, J., Gerlach, R.: Stock ranking prediction using list-wise approach and node embedding technique. IEEE Access **9**, 88981–88996 (2021)
2. Yuan, X., Yuan, J., Jiang, T., Ain, Q.U.: Integrated long-term stock selection models based on feature selection and machine learning algorithms for china stock market. IEEE Access **8**, 22672–22685 (2020). https://doi.org/10.1109/ACCESS.2020.2969293
3. Lee, J., Kim, R., Koh, Y., Kang, J.: Global stock market prediction based on stock chart images using deep Q-network. IEEE Access **7**, 167260–167277 (2019). https://doi.org/10.1109/ACCESS.2019.2953542

4. Shi, L., Teng, Z., Wang, Le., Zhang, Y., Binder, A.: DeepClue: visual interpretation of text-based deep stock prediction. IEEE Trans. Knowl. Data Eng. **31**(6), 1094–1108 (2019). https://doi.org/10.1109/TKDE.2018.2854193

5. Alsulmi, M.: Reducing manual effort to label stock market data by applying a metaheuristic search: a case study from the Saudi stock market. IEEE Access **9**, 110493–110504 (2021). https://doi.org/10.1109/ACCESS.2021.3101952

6. Kilimci, Z.H., Duvar, R.: An efficient word embedding and deep learning based model to forecast the direction of stock exchange market using Twitter and financial news sites: a case of Istanbul stock exchange (BIST 100). IEEE Access **8**, 188186–188198 (2020). https://doi.org/10.1109/ACCESS.2020.3029860

7. Lin, Y., Liu, S., Yang, H., Wu, H.: Stock trend prediction using candlestick charting and ensemble machine learning techniques with a novelty feature engineering scheme. IEEE Access **9**, 101433–101446 (2021). https://doi.org/10.1109/ACCESS.2021.3096825

8. Bouktif, S., Fiaz, A., Awad, M.: Augmented textual features-based stock market prediction. IEEE Access **8**, 40269–40282 (2020)

9. Alotaibi, S.S.: Ensemble technique with optimal feature selection for Saudi stock market prediction: a novel hybrid red deer-grey algorithm. IEEE Access **9**, 64929–64944 (2021). https://doi.org/10.1109/ACCESS.2021.3073507

10. Wang, Y., Liu, H., Guo, Q., Xie, S., Zhang, X.: Stock volatility prediction by hybrid neural network. IEEE Access **7**, 154524–154534 (2019)

11. Nabipour, M., Nayyeri, P., Jabani, H., Shahab, S., Mosavi, A.: Predicting stock market trends using machine learning and deep learning algorithms via continuous and binary data; a comparative analysis. IEEE Access **8**, 150199–150212 (2020). https://doi.org/10.1109/ACCESS.2020.3015966

12. Idrees, S.M., Afshar Alam, M., Agarwal, P.: A prediction approach for stock market volatility based on time series data. IEEE Access **7**, 17287–17298 (2019). https://doi.org/10.1109/ACCESS.2019.2895252

13. Bousono-Calzon, C., Bustarviejo-Munoz, J., Aceituno-Aceituno, P., Escudero-Garzas, J.J.: On the economic significance of stock market prediction and the no free lunch theorem. IEEE Access **7**, 75177–75188 (2019). https://doi.org/10.1109/ACCESS.2019.2921092

14. Wang, X., Yang, K., Liu, T.: Stock price prediction based on morphological similarity clustering and hierarchical temporal memory. IEEE Access **9**, 67241–67248 (2021). https://doi.org/10.1109/ACCESS.2021.3077004

15. Chang, P.-C., Fan, C.-Y., Liu, C.-H.: Integrating a piecewise linear representation method and a neural network model for stock trading points prediction. IEEE Trans. Syst. Man Cybern. Part C (Appl. Rev.) **39**(1), 80–92 (2009). https://doi.org/10.1109/TSMCC.2008.2007255

16. Liu, J., Lin, H., Yang, L., Xu, B., Wen, D.: Multi-element hierarchical attention capsule network for stock prediction. IEEE Access **8**, 143114–143123 (2020)

17. Li, Q., Tan, J., Wang, J., Chen, H.: A multimodal event-driven LSTM model for stock prediction using online news. IEEE Trans. Knowl. Data Eng. **33**(10), 3323–3337 (2021). https://doi.org/10.1109/TKDE.2020.2968894

18. Lee, R.S.T.: iJADE stock advisor: an intelligent agent based stock prediction system using hybrid RBF recurrent network. IEEE Trans. Syst. Man Cybern. - Part A: Syst. Hum. **34**(3), 421–428 (2004). https://doi.org/10.1109/TSMCA.2004.824871

19. Ouyang, H., Wei, X., Wu, Q.: Discovery and prediction of stock index pattern via three-stage architecture of TICC, TPA-LSTM and multivariate LSTM-FCNs. IEEE Access **8**, 123683–123700 (2020). https://doi.org/10.1109/ACCESS.2020.3005994

20. Zhang, X., Qu, S., Huang, J., Fang, B., Yu, P.: Stock market prediction via multi-source multiple instance learning. IEEE Access **6**, 50720–50728 (2018)

21. Koo, E., Kim, G.: A hybrid prediction model integrating GARCH models with a distribution manipulation strategy based on LSTM networks for stock market volatility. IEEE Access **10**, 34743–34754 (2022). https://doi.org/10.1109/ACCESS.2022.3163723
22. Wen, M., Li, P., Zhang, L., Chen, Y.: Stock market trend prediction using high-order information of time series. IEEE Access **7**, 28299–28308 (2019). https://doi.org/10.1109/ACCESS.2019.2901842
23. Chen, Y., Lin, W., Wang, J.Z.: A dual-attention-based stock price trend prediction model with dual features. IEEE Access **7**, 148047–148058 (2019). https://doi.org/10.1109/ACCESS.2019.2946223
24. Alsubaie, Y., Hindi, K.E., Alsalman, H.: Cost-sensitive prediction of stock price direction: selection of technical indicators. IEEE Access **7**, 146876–146892 (2019)
25. Zhang, L., Liu, Na., Yu, P.: A novel instantaneous frequency algorithm and its application in stock index movement prediction. IEEE J. Sel. Top. Signal Process. **6**(4), 311–318 (2012). https://doi.org/10.1109/JSTSP.2012.2199079

Self Supervised Learning for Classifying the Rotated Images

Sidharth Roy[2,3], Aboli Marathe[2,4], Rahee Walambe[1,2(✉)],
and Ketan Kotecha[1,2]

[1] Symbiosis Institute of Technology (SIT), Symbiosis International (Deemed University), Pune 412 115, Maharashtra, India
`rahee.walambe@sitpune.edu.in`
[2] Symbiosis Centre for Applied Artificial Intelligence (SCAAI), Symbiosis International (Deemed University), Pune 412 115, Maharashtra, India
[3] Mahindra United World College India (MUWCI), Paud 412 108, Maharashtra, India
[4] Machine Learning Department, Carnegie Mellon University, Pittsburgh, PA 15213, USA

Abstract. As the applications of image classification models have grown, there has emerged a need to develop classifier models which are invariant to the orientation of the image. Traditionally, image augmentation is applied during training of classification models to encourage the quality of rotation invariance. In our work, we propose an alternate method of classifying rotated images in which the 2d rotation transformation applied to an image is identified and reverted before being passed to an image classifier, thus increasing classification accuracy. The rotation correction is achieved by feeding the input images through a Rotnet, a deep convolutional model which has been trained to identify the orientation of images, and rotating the images back to the original orientation. We find that our method achieves an increase in image classification accuracy over the baseline model on the CIFAR10 dataset. Specifically, when images are rotated and passed to an image classifier with an accuracy of 94% on the CIFAR10 classification task, the accuracy drops to 59.1%. However when the randomly rotated input images were corrected for rotation using our method before being fed to the classifier, the accuracy increases to 75.8%.

Keywords: Unsupervised Representation Learning · Image Classification · ConvNet · Rotnet

1 Introduction

There has been a widespread adoption of deep learning algorithms for computer vision tasks. These algorithms have achieved state of the art performances on image classification [10,18], image segmentation [13], and object detection [3,9] tasks. In the case of image classification, the image data fed to the classifier

D. Garg et al. (Eds.): IACC 2022, CCIS 1782, pp. 17–24, 2023.
https://doi.org/10.1007/978-3-031-35644-5_2

is not always guaranteed to contain correctly oriented images, thus the ability to classify images accurately when they are rotated becomes important. This is especially useful in applications such as remote sensing, microscopy imaging, medical imaging, and other image classification tasks where the rotation of the images should not affect the interpretation of the content [15].

In this work, a method for correction of the image rotations using a ConvNet based Rotation Net (Rotnet) [8] is proposed. The Rotnet is trained to recognize the 2d rotation transformation applied to images, which allows for reorienting the images correctly before passing them through a classifier.

The key contributions of this paper are summarized as follows:

- Demonstrated that there is a drastic drop in accuracy when randomly rotated images are fed to an image classifier which has been trained on images without any rotation.
- Proposed a method for classifying images which may have 2d rotations applied to them using a Rotnet, and demonstrated that our method yields higher accuracy performance in comparison to the baseline model for image classification of rotated images.
- As the proposed method separates the Rotnet model completely from the downstream classifier model, this allows for a modular framework in which rotation correction can be easily incorporated into other downstream tasks by correcting images for rotation before passing them to a specialized model.

The rest of this paper is organized as follows: the second section contains the literature review which discusses published works in the field of self supervised learning, the third section details the methods and materials used in training the Rotnet and image classifier models, the fourth section provides an overview of the framework used, the fifth section discusses the results obtained, and the conclusion is presented in the sixth section.

2   Literature Review

Successes in computer vision using supervised learning draw on the availability of large scale datasets with manually annotated data. However, manual data labeling is a time consuming, expensive, and laborious task [1]. Self supervised learning (SSL) is a recent learning paradigm in which supervisory signals are generated from a dataset of unlabeled data and are used to learn representations without the need for manual annotation [2]. After this initial training phase, the learned representations of the model can be fine-tuned to a downstream task [11]. Broadly, SSL algorithms can be categorized into auxiliary pretext tasks and contrastive learning [19]. Our discussion will be mainly centered around pretext tasks.

While contrastive learning allows for representation learning through the use of positive and negative image pairs, auxiliary pretext tasks are used to learn representations by automatically generating pseudo labels from the image data, which may be a property of the data or a part of the data itself. Popular pretext tasks include prediction of the 2d rotation transformation applied to an image [8], prediction of the position of an image patch relative to another [5], identification of the permutation applied to shuffle patches of an image [16], colorization of grayscale images [22], and more.

In the rotation prediction pretext task, Gidaris et al. [8] rotated image inputs by a randomly chosen angle of 0, 90, 180 or 270°. A ConvNet was trained to predict the 2d rotation transformation applied to the input image. In order to succeed at the task, the model learned to recognize the salient features of the image and their orientation. The learned representations were later fine-tuned and used in downstream tasks such as image classification, object detection, and segmentation. A ConvNet trained in this manner is referred to as a Rotnet.

Due to the simplicity of the Rotation task, it has been utilized as a pretraining step in image classification and image generation tasks as well as other downstream tasks with limited labeled data [4,14,21]. Yamaguchi et al. [20] propose an enhanced image rotation prediction task to allow for learning of representations which capture image shape as well as texture. Feng et al. [7] propose a method for decoupling representations from image rotations, thus allowing for rotation invariant image instance classification.

In contrast to the Decoupling method and other works, our proposed method separates the Rotnet model completely from the downstream classifier model. This allows for a modular setup in which the Rotnet model can be plugged into the pipeline of other downstream tasks such as image segmentation or object detection to allow for rotation correction of images before being passed to a specialized model.

3   Methods and Materials

3.1   Datasets

We use a Resnet-50 [10] followed by a fully connected dense layer with 4096 parameters and a four way softmax classification layer for the Rotnet model. The model has a total of 32M parameters. For training, we use images from the PASCAL VOC 2007 dataset [6]. The PASCAL Visual Object Classes (VOC) contains 20 object categories for object classification and object detection tasks. A total of 9000 images from the dataset were used for training (labels were discarded as we make use of the self supervised learning paradigm which does not require labels). The dataset was chosen as it contains few images with ambiguous orientations. A few samples are shown in Fig. 1. Four distinct rotations were generated for each image and no preprocessing was applied aside from the rotation transformations. Four rotations were used following the original Rotnet paper [8], in which the authors demonstrated that a Rotnet trained on four discrete rotation transformations resulted in better performance on the image recognition downstream task than when trained on two or eight discrete rotation transformation. However, as we do not finetune the model on a specific downstream task, increasing the number of discrete rotation transformations may result in improved image classification performance for rotated images. The model was trained using SGD with batch size 256 and momentum 0.9. As each batch contains four rotated versions of each image, the model in fact sees 64 distinct images per batch. A learning rate of 0.01 was used and reduced by a factor of 5 after epochs 20 and 40. We train using the Tensorflow backend on the Google Colab platform with a GPU for a total of 50 epochs.

Fig. 1. Sample images from the PASCAL VOC 2007 Dataset.

3.2   RotNet

The Rotnet was proposed by Gidaris et al. [8], in which image features are learnt by training the ConvNets to detect the orientation of the image. The ConvNet is trained to learn a feature extractor $F(\cdot)$ to recognize the transformation α applied to X^{α}, where X^{α} is the input image X rotated by $\alpha \in A$. Such a ConvNet is referred to as the Rotnet. The set $A = \{0, 1, 2, 3\}$ corresponds to the set of the four applied rotations $\{0°, 90°, 180°, 270°\}$. The model receives as input a rotated image $X^{\overline{\alpha}}$, where $\overline{\alpha} \in A$ is the unknown rotation transformation applied to X, and outputs a probability distribution over the four rotation transformation classes of A:

$$F(X^{\overline{\alpha}}|\theta) = \{F^j(X^{\overline{\alpha}}|\theta)\}_{j=0}^{4}$$

where the feature extractor $F(\cdot)$ is parameterized by θ, and $F^j(X^{\overline{\alpha}}|\theta)$ is the predicted probability that the input image has been transformed by the rotation A_j.

Given a set of N images, the model must learn to solve the objective:

$$\min \frac{1}{N} \sum_{i=1}^{N} loss(X_i, \theta)$$

where

$$loss(X_i, \theta) = -\log(F^{\overline{\alpha}}(X_i^{\overline{\alpha}}|\theta))$$

and $\overline{\alpha}$ is the unknown rotation transformation applied to X.

In order to succeed at the optimization task, the ConvNet based model is forced to learn the orientation of salient features in the image [8]. The generic pipeline for the Rotnet model is as shown in Fig. 2.

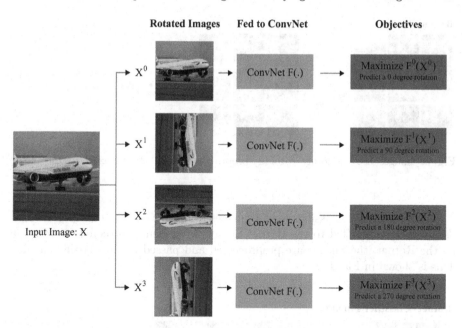

Fig. 2. A rotation transformation of 0, 90, 180, or 270°C is applied to the input image. A ConvNet is trained to learn a feature extractor $F(\cdot)$ to identify the rotation transformation applied to the image. For each of the four classes, the ConvNet outputs a probability $F^j(X^{\overline{\alpha}})$: the probability that the input image $X^{\overline{\alpha}}$ on which the rotation transformation $\overline{\alpha}$ is applied has been rotated by transformation j.

3.3 Image Classifier Model

For the image classifier, we use a Resnet-50 pretrained on ImageNet [17] followed by two fully connected layers with relu activation and a ten way softmax classification layer, resulting in a model with 26M parameters. The model was fine-tuned to the CIFAR10 dataset [12], yielding a testing accuracy of 94% (note, however, that this is not the SOTA for this dataset). The CIFAR-10 dataset contains 50000 training images and 10000 test images of size 32×32 in colour. The images are divided across 10 classes. During training, the images were preprocessed such that each color channel is zero-centered with respect to the dataset and were upsampled by a factor of 7 to obtain image sizes of 224×224. The model was trained on Google Colab with a GPU.

4 System Design

This section outlines the pipeline used for the baseline model and the proposed Rotnet+Classifier model. For the baseline model, images from the CIFAR10 dataset are randomly rotated, preprocessed, and fed to the classifier model, as shown in Fig. 3.

Baseline Pipeline

Fig. 3. Images are randomly rotated, preprocessed, and then passed to the image classifier.

For the Rotnet+Classifier model, images from the CIFAR10 dataset are randomly rotated and fed to the Rotnet model. After being corrected for rotation by the Rotnet, the images are preprocessed and passed to the classifier model. This is shown in Fig. 4.

Rotnet+Classifier Pipeline

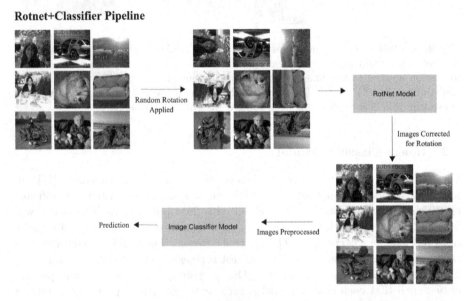

Fig. 4. Images are randomly rotated and passed to the Rotnet. The Rotnet identifies the applied rotation and the images are reverted back to the original orientation. These rotation corrected images are preprocessed and then passed to the image classifier.

5   Results and Analysis

During testing, the image classifier performed with 94.0% accuracy (note that this is not the SOTA for the dataset, however it serves as a proof of concept) on non-rotated images from the CIFAR10 dataset. However, when the images were rotated, the accuracy dropped to 59.1%. When the randomly rotated input images were corrected for rotation before being fed to the classifier in the Rotnet+Classifier model, the accuracy increased to 75.8%. These results are tabulated in Table 1.

Table 1. Classification accuracy for the Resnet-50 based image classifier when no rotation is applied, when a random 2d rotation is applied, and when the randomly rotated images are passed to the proposed Rotnet+Classifier model.

Model	Input Transformation	Accuracy
Resnet-50 Image Classifier	No random rotation applied	94.0%
Resnet-50 Image Classifier	Images randomly rotated	59.1%
Rotnet+Classifier	Images randomly rotated	75.8%

6   Conclusion

Thus we demonstrate that the classification accuracy of an image classifier model trained on correctly oriented image data drops drastically when fed images which are randomly rotated. Our method of using a Rotnet to correct for image rotation effectively improves accuracy in the classification task for the CIFAR10 dataset. Specifically, we found that when images are rotated and passed to an image classifier with an accuracy of 94% on the CIFAR10 classification task, the accuracy drops to 59.1%. When the randomly rotated input images were corrected for rotation using our method before being fed to the classifier, the accuracy increases to 75.8%. As the Rotnet model which identifies the rotation transformation applied to the image is separated from the downstream classifier model, this allows for a modular framework in which rotation correction can be easily incorporated into other downstream tasks by correcting images for rotation before passing them to a specialized model.

References

1. Albelwi, S.: Survey on self-supervised learning: auxiliary pretext tasks and contrastive learning methods in imaging. Entropy **24**(4) (2022). https://doi.org/10.3390/e24040551. https://www.mdpi.com/1099-4300/24/4/551
2. Chen, L., Bentley, P., Mori, K., Misawa, K., Fujiwara, M., Rueckert, D.: Self-supervised learning for medical image analysis using image context restoration. Med. Image Anal. **58**, 101539 (2019). https://doi.org/10.1016/j.media.2019.101539
3. Chen, L.C., Papandreou, G., Kokkinos, I., Murphy, K., Yuille, A.L.: DeepLab: semantic image segmentation with deep convolutional nets, atrous convolution, and fully connected CRFs. IEEE Trans. Pattern Anal. Mach. Intell. **40**(4), 834–848 (2018). https://doi.org/10.1109/TPAMI.2017.2699184
4. Chen, T., Zhai, X., Ritter, M., Lucic, M., Houlsby, N.: Self-supervised generative adversarial networks. CoRR abs/1811.11212 (2018). http://arxiv.org/abs/1811.11212

5. Doersch, C., Gupta, A., Efros, A.A.: Unsupervised visual representation learning by context prediction. CoRR abs/1505.05192 (2015). http://arxiv.org/abs/1505.05192

6. Everingham, M., Van Gool, L., Williams, C., Winn, J., Zisserman, A.: The pascal visual object classes (VOC) challenge. Int. J. Comput. Vis. **88**, 303–338 (2010). https://doi.org/10.1007/s11263-009-0275-4

7. Feng, Z., Xu, C., Tao, D.: Self-supervised representation learning by rotation feature decoupling. In: Proceedings of the IEEE/CVF Conference on Computer Vision and Pattern Recognition (CVPR) (2019)

8. Gidaris, S., Singh, P., Komodakis, N.: Unsupervised representation learning by predicting image rotations. CoRR abs/1803.07728 (2018). http://arxiv.org/abs/1803.07728

9. He, K., Gkioxari, G., Dollár, P., Girshick, R.B.: Mask R-CNN. CoRR abs/1703.06870 (2017). http://arxiv.org/abs/1703.06870

10. He, K., Zhang, X., Ren, S., Sun, J.: Deep residual learning for image recognition. In: 2016 IEEE Conference on Computer Vision and Pattern Recognition (CVPR), pp. 770–778 (2016). https://doi.org/10.1109/CVPR.2016.90

11. Holmberg, O., et al.: Self-supervised retinal thickness prediction enables deep learning from unlabelled data to boost classification of diabetic retinopathy. Nat. Mach. Intell. **2**, 719–726 (2020). https://doi.org/10.1038/s42256-020-00247-1

12. Krizhevsky, A.: Learning multiple layers of features from tiny images. University of Toronto (2012)

13. Liu, W., et al.: SSD: single shot multibox detector. In: Leibe, B., Matas, J., Sebe, N., Welling, M. (eds.) ECCV 2016. LNCS, vol. 9905, pp. 21–37. Springer, Cham (2016). https://doi.org/10.1007/978-3-319-46448-0_2

14. Lucic, M., Tschannen, M., Ritter, M., Zhai, X., Bachem, O., Gelly, S.: High-fidelity image generation with fewer labels. CoRR abs/1903.02271 (2019). http://arxiv.org/abs/1903.02271

15. Marcos, D., Volpi, M., Tuia, D.: Learning rotation invariant convolutional filters for texture classification. CoRR abs/1604.06720 (2016). http://arxiv.org/abs/1604.06720

16. Noroozi, M., Favaro, P.: Unsupervised learning of visual representations by solving jigsaw puzzles. CoRR abs/1603.09246 (2016). http://arxiv.org/abs/1603.09246

17. Russakovsky, O., et al.: ImageNet large scale visual recognition challenge (2014). https://doi.org/10.48550/ARXIV.1409.0575

18. Simonyan, K., Zisserman, A.: Very deep convolutional networks for large-scale image recognition (2014). https://doi.org/10.48550/ARXIV.1409.1556

19. Tao, L., Wang, X., Yamasaki, T.: Self-supervised video representation using pretext-contrastive learning. CoRR abs/2010.15464 (2020). https://arxiv.org/abs/2010.15464

20. Yamaguchi, S., Kanai, S., Shioda, T., Takeda, S.: Image enhanced rotation prediction for self-supervised learning (2019). https://doi.org/10.48550/ARXIV.1912.11603

21. Zhai, X., Oliver, A., Kolesnikov, A., Beyer, L.: S^4l: self-supervised semi-supervised learning. CoRR abs/1905.03670 (2019). http://arxiv.org/abs/1905.03670

22. Zhang, R., Isola, P., Efros, A.A.: Colorful image colorization. In: Leibe, B., Matas, J., Sebe, N., Welling, M. (eds.) ECCV 2016. LNCS, vol. 9907, pp. 649–666. Springer, Cham (2016). https://doi.org/10.1007/978-3-319-46487-9_40

Unsupervised Learning Method for Better Imputation of Missing Values

B. Mathura Bai[1]([✉]), N. Mangathayaru[1], and B. Padmaja Rani[2]

[1] Department of IT, VNR VJIET, Hyderabad, TS, India
{mathurabai_b,mangathayaru_n}@vnrvjiet.in
[2] Department of CSE, JNTUH, Hyderabad, TS, India
padmaja_jntuh@jntuh.ac.in

Abstract. The main objective of any clustering method is to improve the clusters quality. Such an improvement can be achieved using graph partitioning algorithm which partitions the graph into maximum components with minimum cut which represents the optimality of spectrum partitioning. The commonly used graph portioning algorithm is spectral algorithm called known popularly as spectral clustering. Such a unsupervised method can be used during imputation for identifying the optimal clusters. Optimal clusters reduce the search space during imputation and thus achieve dimensionality reduction. The proposed method uses MKNN-MBI imputation method in which the non-missing dataset used for imputing the missing values is reduced. The reduction is achieved by using spectral partitioning method for which the non-missing dataset is represented as a graph. The spectrum of a Laplacian graph is obtained using spectral clustering from which the optimal l eigen values are identified as optimal cluster centers for imputation. The imputation is done using this reduced optimal non-missing dataset. The imputed dataset is evaluated by comparing the accuracies of classifiers like SVM, C4.5, NB and kNN. Proposed method has improved the accuracies of the imputation on optimal reduced datasets.

Keywords: Data Imputation · Clustering · Spectral Partitioning

1 Introduction

In today's world medical data quality is utmost important and concern for accurate decision making. Medical data and quality of data [1] plays a prominent role in machine learning and data mining tasks. In [26], the authors have identified challenges in data mining. The quality of the medical data can be improved by replacing the missing values. Missing data is one of the challenges identified by [2]. The missing values can be replaced by different imputation methods like data driven, machine learning based and hybrid method. One such imputation method is defined by the author in [10, 12] and extended to [14]. The search space is huge which consumes more time for scanning and for identifying the most similar instance for imputation. There is a need for reducing the search space for improving the imputation process.

© Springer Nature Switzerland AG 2023
D. Garg et al. (Eds.): IACC 2022, CCIS 1782, pp. 25–34, 2023.
https://doi.org/10.1007/978-3-031-35644-5_3

The reduced search space can be achieved by clustering. One such popular clustering algorithm is spectral clustering. Spectral clustering is popular because of its simplicity and no assumptions on the cluster structure. More advantages are specified in [3]. In spectral clustering, the graph can be partitioned using eigenvectors of the graph adjacency matrix [4] and partitions the points into clusters with high similarity within cluster and low between clusters similarity. Spectral clustering can be used for huge datasets in the graph but should be sparse. Author in [5] suggested using second smallest eigenvalue which represents the bi-partitioning of the graph Laplacian. Spectral graph partitioning method therefore uses Fiedler vector [5] which is the second eigenvector-a separator of a Laplacian graph. Spectral clustering is also used for learning from a similarity matrix specified in terms of sparsity as indicated by the author in [6] and is robust to irrelevant attributes. Graph Laplacians can be used to partition the graphs. They are used for unsupervised and semi-supervised learning. Such a learning in spectral clustering is used for identifying the optimal instances of non-missing dataset whose laplacian function value is small indicates the data points are more similar in nature where graph is tightly connected.

The proposed method is divided into Sect. 2 discussing the detailed survey of the existing literature done by the researchers on spectral clustering. Section 3 describes the proposed method MKNNMBI imputation with DR (Dimensionality Reduction). In Sect. 4 experiments are conducted on iris and pima missing datasets and the results are collected. Section 5 performs a detailed study on the experimentation. Section 6 briefs the conclusions.

2 Literature Survey

The learning accuracy of any classifier can be improved by Dimensionality Reduction (DR). Dimensionality Reduction (DR) techniques which are popular in machine learning are feature selection and feature extraction methods. In [21] one such DR method is defined by the authors. In their method, feature goodness is defined as how much the feature is correlated to class labels. If the value is high then the feature is treated as highly correlated to that class label. In the same manner the degree of similarity is defined in [10, 12]. This can be extended to be considered as a similarity measure as in [20] and can also be used in spectral clustering. Authors in [22] detailed explained the challenges of feature selection methods. To reduce the computational time while maintaining accuracy is considered as a major challenge in DR. Another challenge identified in [22] is scalability and stability of DR method. These challenges along with consideration of data distribution either vertically or horizontally need to be considered when designing any DR method. One such suitable method is spectral partitioning algorithm. Authors in [23] discussed seven different heuristic techniques for selecting good subsets from a set. One of the techniques as mentioned by the authors in [23] called as elimination of data points which are very similar to other as they posses very little discriminatory information. This method is implemented as PCA, LDA methods. Even spectral graph partitioning algorithm also uses the same pattern recognition concept as specified in [23].

Authors in [24] proposed linear complexity algorithms for instance selection purpose reducing the complexity from polynomial or log linear to linear and also reduce the execution time, resource consumption. Equal literature is also done in instance selection or prototype selection just like feature selection in DR. Authors of [25] has done an exhaustive literature survey on Prototype Selection (PS) techniques. The authors based on their detailed literature survey suggested guidelines while applying PS methods. Author of [27] defines concept drift problem i.e., as time elapses the concept and data distribution also remain unstable. To maintain stability different approaches to handle concept drift are mentioned by author in [27] and one such method is instance selection. Author in [28] proposed class conditional nearest neighbour (cnn) for instance selection. The degree distribution in between class graph is used for instance selection. In instance-based learning the neighbor identification is done only at run time and so it is called as a lazy learning method. The runtime in the classification can be reduced by prototype selection. Authors in [29] proposed a Prototype Selection by Clustering (PSC) method. Authors in [30] proposed Maximum Variance Cluster (MVC) algorithm for partitional clustering. The advantage of MVC is that there is no need to determine number of clusters in advance as in K-Means and GMM.

Spectral clustering when used for text documents in [7] identified that the clustering quality is dependent on the similarity degree. The conductance or the eigenvalue gap reflects the good measure for clustering quality. Conductance is always the robust version of connectivity and lies between 0 and 1. The conductance value if it is closer to 0 means that we have a better cluster. The subset of vertices in a graph whose conductance value is small indicates a partition or cluster. Cheeger's inequality theorem specifies the same as in [5]. Authors in [8] specifies conductance as a generalization metric to quantify the clustering quality in which the vertices are given equal importance irrespective of count of the similar neighbors for it and each vertex is associated with a weight to reflect the importance. For clustering similar points, conductance seems to be a best measure. The proposed method aim is to find k-partitioning of the graph with the maximum conductance. In [8] the authors analyzed clustering algorithm quality in terms of conductance which can be defined as the time taken to find top k eigen vectors which can be a polynomial. The speed of algorithm should be linear and depend on the number of nonzero entries i.e., sparsity.

Spectral partitioning algorithm is a linear method which finds graph sparse cuts with cheeger inequalities as a quality measure for partitioning. Authors in [9] proposed a bi-criteria method for conductance with approximation equal to cheeger's inequality. In [11] the authors discussed the issues of spectral clustering algorithms which cluster the data points using eigenvectors of graph. Authors define spectral methods as alternative methods for clustering which are popularly used in image segmentation, VLSI design and Computer Vision. Spectral partitioning methods in which the second eigenvector defines a semi-optimal cut and guarantees for an approximation optimal cut in the Laplacian graph. Authors in [11] presented a clustering algorithm which takes data points as input and use affinity matrix A for graph representation of data points, obtain eigenvectors for normalized A and cluster them using K-means algorithm. Authors in [13] proposed an approach for image segmentation by proposing a novel criterion global measure called as normalized cut in graph partitioning. The advantage of this is that it measures both the intra group similarity and as well inter group dissimilarity. Normalized cut graph partitioning and other eigenvector-based graph partitioning techniques when compared the author found that the normalized cut balances between finding clumps and finding splits. The authors in [13] showed that by using eigenvalue system, they have proposed a normalized cut and applied this method for image segmentation.

3   Proposed Method

3.1   MKNNMBI Imputation with Dimensionality Reduction (DR)

Lee et al. 2014 [15] in their work showed that the no. of components which are connected in graph G can be represented using the eigenvalue whose value is zero i.e., $\lambda_l = 0$ iff G has at least l number of connected components. Authors in Alon et al. 1984, 1985 [16, 17] stated that the Cheeger's or isoperimetric inequality for graphs show that the second lowest eigen value of laplacian matrix of G is related to structure of G. The higher eigen values and the Cheeger's inequality can be used for optimization problems.

In proposed method randomly projected instances of non-missing datasets are used by MKNNMBI for imputation [14]. These randomly projected instances are identified by the proposed method by applying l-partitioning spectral algorithm. The l partitions of graph G are the optimal instances for imputation in the proposed method and these instances are the optimal representations of the graph G represented for the non-missing dataset. This proposed method not only reduces the non-missing dataset size but also improves the quality of spectral clustering. The procedure to find minimum cut in G is the objective of the proposed method. The spectrum of graph G is derived using spectral algorithm which includes eigen values and eigen vectors of G.

3.2   Algorithm

The proposed method extends the Cheeger's inequality by using higher eigen values [18] of the Laplacian graph. The proposed method is a combination of MKNNMBI method of [14] and MBI method of [12]. In this method, the MKNNMBI imputation method is done by considering the reduced non-missing dataset during imputation. The proposed method defines the procedure of how to obtain the reduced non-missing dataset before applying MKNNMBI imputation. The proposed method architectural diagram is shown in Fig. 1. The main procedure of the proposed method is it executes the MKNNMBI Imputation method where first the incomplete dataset is divided into non-missing and missing datasets as per the framework of imputation. The non-missing dataset is given as input to the proposed method. The proposed method applies Spectral Clustering and selects the l optimal instances or prototype based on the smallest eigen values of Spectral clustering. The identified l optimal instances define the reduced non-missing dataset which is used in place of actual or original non-missing dataset for MKNNMBI Imputation.

The detailed explanation of proposed method is shown as an algorithm in Fig. 2.

4   Experimentation

The experimentation is carried on two datasets by name iris and pima which contain the missing values. The imputation of these missing values is done by the proposed method by combining MKNNMBI imputation done on the reduced non-missing dataset. The

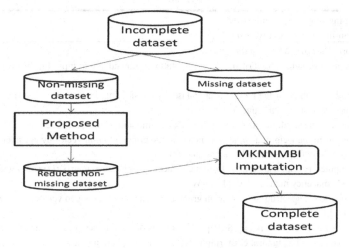

Fig. 1. Architectural Diagram of Proposed Method

non-missing dataset of iris dataset is n = 101 and the reduced non-missing datasets as derived by the proposed method were l = 3,25,50,75,100 (l < n) and the imputation on these reduced non-missing datasets is computed and checked for accuracies by using SVM, C4.5, kNN, NB as stated in Table 1. The k value column denotes the k value of MKNNMBI imputation method.

The accuracies were improved with the reduced non-missing iris dataset as seen in Table 1. The pima dataset non-missing dataset has size n = 378 and the reduced non-missing dataset considered by the proposed method is l = 150 (l < n). The kNN classifier applied for the imputed dataset computed by MKNNMBI imputation using both actual non-missing dataset (n) and reduced non-missing dataset (l). The accuracies is improved from 72.65 to 73.7 and the non-missing dataset size if reduced from 378 to 150 for imputation as shown in Table 2. This dimensionality reduction has improved the accuracy of imputation method.

5   Results and Discussion

The accuracies on iris dataset can be seen in Fig. 3. The iris dataset with actual non-missing dataset size n = 101 and with this dataset after MKNNMBI imputation the accuracies achieved for SVM is 95.33, for C4.5 is 94.66, for kNN is 96.66 and for NB is 94. The MKNNMBI imputation on reduced non-missing dataset has improved these accuracies.

The accuracies of imputation on reduced non-missing dataset size l = 3 are for SVM is 94.66, for C4.5 is 96 (improved from 94.66 with the actual non-missing dataset size n = 101), for kNN is 95.33 and improved a little for NB from 94(n = 101) to 94.66(l = 3). The accuracies of imputation on reduced non-missing dataset size l = 25 are for SVM is 94, for C4.5 is 94.66, for kNN is 96, for NB is 92.66. It is observed that the reduced non-missing dataset size with l = 2 is better for C4.5 and NB classifiers whereas for l = 25 reduced size there is no improvement in accuracy. The accuracies of imputation

Input: Non-missing dataset with size n
Output: Non-missing dataset with size l (l <=n)

Step 1: Start (Start of the Proposed Method)

Step 2: The non-missing dataset of size n for imputation is considered as input for the proposed method

Step 3: Build a graph G for the non-missing dataset by considering the instances as vertices and similarity among instances as edge weights

Step 4: Consider the similarity as stated in MKNNMBI method of Bai et.al, 2022 [14, 20].

Step 5: Transform the weighted adjacency matrix of the graph into unit vector by considering the threshold as λ=0.99 (representing higher similarity)

Step 6: Compute the Laplacian matrix from the adjacency and degree matrix (D) computed from the weighted adjacency matrix (W) as L=D-W

Step 7: Compute the spectrum of Laplacian graph or eigen values and eigen vectors for Laplacian matrix form of G.

Step 8: As stated by the authors in [18, 19] find l subsets of the Laplacian graph such that the maximum expansion i.e., natural clustering is achieved by minimizing the sparse cuts among the graph G. Thus, spectral clustering obtains the optimal subsets or optimal non-missing instances by improvising the spectral clusters quality. This can be represented by the top l eigen values of the graph G.

Step 9: The non-missing dataset of KNNMBI whose number of instances was n is now reduced to l optimal non-missing instances where l can be much less than n (l <=n)

Step 10: The non-missing dataset with reduced size from n to l is now used for imputation by MKNNMBI Method as specified in [14].

Step 11: The MKNNMBI imputation method fills the missing values with estimated values and forms a complete dataset for classification

Step 12: The complete dataset is then applied with various classifiers like SVM, C4.5, kNN and Naïve Bayes (NB) to compute the accuracies

Step 13: The classifier accuracies are calculated and compared for different search spaces both actual and reduced non-missing dataset sizes and with different l values of MKNNMBI method

Step 14: Stop

(End)

Fig. 2. Proposed Method algorithmic steps

on reduced non-missing dataset size l = 50 also has no improvements in accuracies i.e., for SVM is 94.66, for C4.5 is 94.66, for kNN is 95.33 and for NB is 93.33.

The accuracies of imputation on reduced non-missing dataset size l = 75 and l = 100 has improved the accuracies as shown in Fig. 3. The accuracy with reduced dataset size l = 75 for SVM is 95.96 (more than 95.33 with n = 101 non-missing dataset size), for C4.5 is 95.16 (more than 94.66 with n = 101), for kNN is 97.58 (much higher than 96.66 with n = 101), for NB is 95.16 (higher than 94 with n = 101). Similarly for reduced non-missing dataset size l = 100 also the accuracies computed are for SVM is 95.33 (same as 95.33 with n = 101), for C4.5 is 94.63 (same as 94.66 with n = 101), for kNN is 96.66 (same as 96.66 with n = 101), for NB is 94.66 (little improvement than 94 with n = 101). From the results the same or higher accuracies can be achieved by the proposed method with reduced non-missing dataset size from n = 101 to n = 75,100.

Table 1. MKNNMBI Imputation on iris dataset with different search space sizes and various classifier accuracies

MKNNMBI Imputation		Classifier Accuracies			
Search Space(No. of Instances)	k value	SVM	C4.5	kNN	NB
101	3	95.33	94.66	96.66(k = 5)	94
3	1	94.66	96	95.33(k = 3)	94.66
25	1	94	94.66	96(k = 1)	92.66
50	1	94.66	94.66	95.33(k = 5)	93.33
75	3	95.96	95.16	97.58(k = 11)	95.16
100	1	95.33	94.63	96.66(k = 11)	94.66

Table 2. MKNNMBI Imputation on pima dataset with and without Dimensionality Reduction (DR) and kNN Classifier accuracies

MKNNMBI Imputation (k = 3)	Classifier Accuracies
Search Space (No. of Instances)	kNN
378	72.65(k = 7)
150	73.70(k = 11)

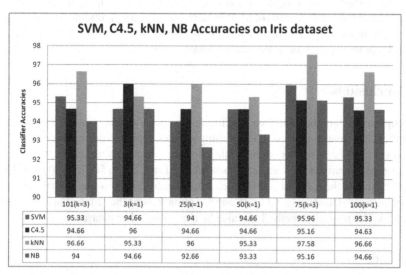

Fig. 3. Different classifier accuracies on iris dataset using MKNNMBI Imputation with different search spaces

Thus achieving the dimensionality reduction from n = 101 to l = 75 using proposed method.

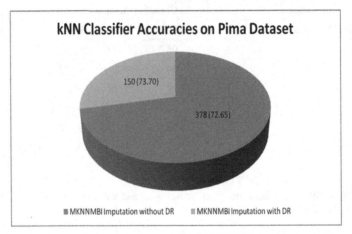

Fig. 4. kNN classifier results on iris dataset for MKNNMBI imputation with and without Dimensionality Reduction (DR)

The proposed method has achieved an accuracy of 72.65 for kNN classifier with the non-missing dataset size as n = 378 and a high accuracy of 73.70 for kNN classifier with the reduced non-missing dataset size as l = 150 as shown in Fig. 4. Thus the method proposed can improve the results of MKNNMBI imputation by reducing the non-missing dataset size drastically. The dimensionality reduction with improved quality clusters formed by proposed method is the main contribution.

6 Conclusions

The proposed method has improved the imputation accuracy on reduced dataset during imputation. The search space is reduced using proposed method during imputation. This method can also be tested on other missing datasets unlike iris and pima. This method can be tested on various reduced search spaces like l = 2, 3, 25, 50, 75, 100, 125, 150… etc. and conclude the reduced size for each dataset accordingly as like for iris dataset the optimal reduced dataset size is l = 75 and for pima dataset the reduced optimal dataset is l = 150. The proposed method can also be applied to other datasets.

References

1. Cios, K.J., Moore, G.W.: Uniqueness of medical data mining. Artif. Intell. Med. **26**(1–2), 1–24 (2002)
2. Bai, B.M., Mangathayaru, N., Rani, B.P.: Exploring research issues in mining medical datasets. In: Proceedings of the International Conference on Engineering & MIS 2015, pp. 1–8 (2015)

3. Von Luxburg, U.: A tutorial on spectral clustering. Stat. Comput. **17**(4), 395–416 (2007)
4. Donath, W.E., Hoffman, A.J.: Lower bounds for the partitioning of graphs. IBM J. Res. Develop. **17**, 420–425 (1973)
5. Fiedler, M.: Algebraic connectivity of graphs. Czechoslovak Math. J. **23**, 298–305 (1973)
6. Bach, F., Jordan, M.: Learning spectral clustering. In: Thrun, S., Saul, L., Scholkopf, B. (eds.) Advances in Neural Information Processing Systems (NIPS), vol. 16, pp. 305–312. MIT Press, Cambridge (2004)
7. Cheng, D., Kannan, R., Vempala, S., Wang, G.: On a recursive spectral algorithm for clustering from pairwise similarities (2003)
8. Kannan, R., Vempala, S., Vetta, A.: On clusterings: good, bad and spectral. J. ACM (JACM) **51**(3), 497–515 (2004)
9. Gharan, S.O., Trevisan, L.: Approximating the expansion profile and almost optimal local graph clustering. arXiv preprint arXiv:1204.2021 (2012)
10. Bai, B.M., Mangathayaru, N., Rani, B.P.: An approach to find missing values in medical datasets. In: Proceedings of the International Conference on Engineering & MIS 2015, pp. 1–7 (2015)
11. Ng, A., Jordan, M., Weiss, Y.: On spectral clustering: analysis and an algorithm. In: Advances in Neural Information Processing Systems, vol. 14 (2001)
12. Bai, B.M., Mangathayaru, N., Rani, B.P., Aljawarneh, S.: Mathura (MBI)-a novel imputation measure for imputation of missing values in medical datasets. Recent Adv. Comput. Sci. Commun. (Formerly: Recent Patents on Computer Science) **14**(5), 1358–1369 (2021)
13. Shi, J., Malik, J.: Normalized cuts and image segmentation. IEEE Trans. Pattern Anal. Mach. Intell. **22**(8), 888–905 (2000)
14. Bai, B.M., Mangathayaru, N.: Modified K-nearest neighbour using proposed similarity fuzzy measure for missing data imputation on medical datasets (MKNNMBI). Int. J. Fuzzy Syst. Appl. (IJFSA) **11**(3), 1–15 (2022)
15. Lee, J.R., Gharan, S.O., Trevisan, L.: Multiway spectral partitioning and higher-order cheeger inequalities. J. ACM (JACM) **61**(6), 1–30 (2014)
16. Alon, N.: Eigenvalues and expanders. Combinatorica **6**, 83–96 (1984). Theory of computing (Singer Island, Fla., 1984). MR0875835
17. Alon, N., Milman, V.D.: λ1, isoperimetric inequalities for graphs, and superconcentrators. J. Comb. Theory Series B **38**(1), 73–88 (1985)
18. Louis, A., Raghavendra, P., Tetali, P., Vempala, S.: Algorithmic extensions of cheeger's inequality to higher eigenvalues and partitions. In: Goldberg, L.A., Jansen, K., Ravi, R., Rolim, J.D.P. (eds.) APPROX/RANDOM 2011. LNCS, vol. 6845, pp. 315–326. Springer, Heidelberg (2011). https://doi.org/10.1007/978-3-642-22935-0_27
19. Louis, A., Raghavendra, P., Tetali, P., Vempala, S.: Many sparse cuts via higher eigenvalues. In: Proceedings of the Forty-Fourth Annual ACM Symposium on Theory of Computing, pp. 1131–1140 (2012)
20. Mathura Bai, B., Mangathayaru, N., Padmaja Rani, B.: A similarity measure to find Nearest Neighbours for heart disease to improve prediction accuracy. Int. J. Adv. Res. Comput. Commun. Eng. **11**(7), 36–41 (2022)
21. Yu, L., Liu, H.: Feature selection for high-dimensional data: a fast correlation-based filter solution. In: Proceedings of the 20th International Conference on Machine Learning (ICML 2003), pp. 856–863 (2003)
22. Bolón-Canedo, V., Sánchez-Maroño, N., Alonso-Betanzos, A.: Feature Selection for High-Dimensional Data. Springer, Cham (2015)
23. Mucciardi, A.N., Gose, E.E.: A comparison of seven techniques for choosing subsets of pattern recognition properties. IEEE Trans. Comput. **100**(9), 1023–1031 (1971)
24. Arnaiz-Gonzalez, A., Diez-Pastor, J.F., Rodriguez, J.J., Garcia-Osorio, C.: Instance selection of linear complexity for big data. Knowl.-Based Syst. **107**, 83–95 (2016)

25. Garcia, S., Derrac, J., Cano, J., Herrera, F.: Prototype selection for nearest neighbor classification: taxonomy and empirical study. IEEE Trans. Pattern Anal. Mach. Intell. **34**(3), 417–435 (2012)
26. Yang, Q., Wu, X.: 10 challenging problems in data mining research. Int. J. Inf. Technol. Decis. Mak. **5**(04), 597–604 (2006)
27. Tsymbal, A.: The problem of concept drift: definitions and related work. Comput. Sci. Dept Trinity Coll. Dublin **106**(2), 58 (2004)
28. Marchiori, E.: Class conditional nearest neighbor for large margin instance selection. IEEE Trans. Pattern Anal. Mach. Intell. **32**(2), 364–370 (2009)
29. Olvera-Lopez, J.A., Carrasco-Ochoa, J.A., MartinezTrinidad, J.: A new fast prototype selection method based on clustering. Pattern Anal. Appl. **13**(2), 131–141 (2010)
30. Veenman, C.J., Reinders, M.J.T., Backer, E.: A maximum variance cluster algorithm. IEEE Trans. Pattern Anal. Mach. Intell. **24**(9), 1273–1280 (2002)

DR-A-LSTM: A Recurrent Neural Network with a Dimension Reduction Autoencoder a Deep Learning Approach for Landslide Movements Prediction

Praveen Kumar[1](✉) ⓘ, Priyanka[1] ⓘ, K. V. Uday[2] ⓘ, and Varun Dutt[1] ⓘ

[1] ACS Lab, Indian Institute of Technology Mandi, Mandi 175075, Himachal Pradesh, India
bluecodeindia@gmail.com, varun@iitmandi.ac.in
[2] Geotechnical Engineering Lab, Indian Institute of Technology Mandi, Mandi 175075, Himachal Pradesh, India
uday@iitmandi.ac.in

Abstract. Landslides are a challenging problem in India and the world. Different weather conditions and soil properties could trigger landslides. The Machine learning (ML) models could predict landslides' movements. The ML model may overfit the high-dimensional feature of weather and soil data. Dimension reduction techniques could reduce the dimension of the features. The autoencoder model was developed to reduce the data dimension in this experiment. The four months, April to August 2022, time series data of the landslide monitoring station (LMS) from the five landslides in Himachal Pradesh, India, were considered to train the ML models. The dimension reduction autoencoder long-short-term memory (DR-A-LSTM), an autoencoder and LSTM model ensemble, was developed. Furthermore, the ensemble of principal component analysis (PCA) and LSTM (PCA-LSTM) model was developed to reduce the dimension by PCA. The DR-A-LSTM model was compared with the simple LSTM and PCA-LSTM models to predict landslide movements. The data was split in the 80:20 ratio to train and test the ML models. The simple LSTM model produced 82.3% accuracy in the training data and 71.8% in the testing data. The simple LSTM model showed overfitting in the training data. The PCA-LSTM model produced 76.5% accuracy in training and 88.2% in testing. Next, the DR-A-LSTM model produced 97.8% accuracy in training and 100% in testing. The findings of this experiment suggest that the DR-A-LSTM model performed better than the simple LSTM model and PCA-LSTM. As a result, the DR-A-LSTM model could be developed for real-time landslide movement predictions.

Keywords: Landslide · Autoencoder · Simple LSTM · PCA-LSTM · DR-A-LSTM

1 Introduction

Landslides are a challenging problem in India and the world [1]. Different factors could affect the landslides, such as weather parameters and soil properties [2]. The movements in the landslides could be predicted by inputting these features into the machine learning

© Springer Nature Switzerland AG 2023
D. Garg et al. (Eds.): IACC 2022, CCIS 1782, pp. 35–49, 2023.
https://doi.org/10.1007/978-3-031-35644-5_4

(ML) models [3, 4]. The landslide monitoring system (LMS) could be installed on the landslide surface to record the weather and soil parameters [5]. The LMSs could record the weather parameters temperature, humidity, rainfall, atmospheric pressure, and sunlight) and the landslide parameters (soil movement and soil moisture). However, the dimension of these features is high and could overfit or infer the performance of the ML models [6]. Dimension reduction techniques could reduce the dimension of the feature space [7].

Several researchers developed linear discriminative analysis (LDA), principal component analysis (PCA), and autoencoder techniques to reduce the dimension of data [7–10]. For example, Wang et al. (2016) developed the autoencoder model to reduce the dimension of the handwritten digit of the MNIST and faces from the Olivetti face datasets [7]. The PCA transforms the data in linear space, whereas the autoencoder transforms the data in nonlinear space and finds more information. The autoencoder could be developed to reduce the dimension to find more information in compressed data.

Several researchers developed the autoencoder model for the prediction of landslide displacement [11–13]. For example, Nam & Wand (2020) developed the autoencoder model for landslide susceptibility area assessment and prediction of rainfall-induced landslides in Japan [11]. Either researcher developed the autoencoder model for the landslide susceptibility or the slope risk factors but not on the time series data of the weather and soil parameters recorded from the landslide surface by LMS.

Several researchers developed recurrent neural network (RNN) models for landslide movement prediction from the time series data [14–17]. For example, Jiang et al. (2020) developed the support vector regression (SVR), long short-term memory (LSTM), and hybrid of LSTM with SVR model for landslide displacement prediction [14]. The LSTM models were primarily used in the literature for time series data prediction for landslide movements. The ensemble of an autoencoder and LSTM model could be developed for landslide movement prediction in time series data.

From the ML literature survey, first, it was observed that the PCA, LDA, and autoencoder models could be used for dimension reduction of the high dimensional feature space. Second, the autoencoder models were developed for the landslide susceptibility assessment and the landslide classification by risk factors. But autoencoder was not developed for the landslide classification by time series data of weather and soil properties. Third, the LSTM and SVR models were mostly developed for the landslide displacement prediction on the time series data. Therefore, this paper aims to fill the literature gap by developing an autoencoder and a PCA for dimension reduction and the LSTM model to predict the landslide movement by the time series data. For this research, four-month time series data from the five landslide locations of Himachal Pradesh, India, is considered for this study.

First, the background literature is detailed on various dimension reduction techniques and ML models for predicting soil movements. Then, the data and construction of ML models for soil movement predictions are detailed. Furthermore, in the result section, the model's performance is evaluated by comparing its predictions on a test dataset. We close this study by discussing the relevance of dimension reduction via ML models for landslide movement predictions.

2 Background

Several researchers developed the LDA, PCA, and autoencoder techniques to reduce the dimension of high dimensional input data [7–10]. For example, Wang et al. (2016) developed the autoencoder model to reduce the dimension of the handwritten digit of the MNIST and faces from the Olivetti face datasets [7]. The researcher compared the autoencoder with PCA and LDA dimension reduction techniques in this experiment. The result shows that the autoencoder outperformed and learned different meaningful encoding than the PCA and LDA techniques. Furthermore, Lazzara et al. (2022) developed a long-short-term memory (LSTM) and autoencoder-based model for dimension reduction to predict the aircraft's dynamic landing response over time [8]. In this development, the PCA and the Convolutional-Autoencoder models were compared with LSTM-Autoencoder. The result shows that the LSTM-Autoencoder model outperformed the other dimension reduction models. Next, Wang et al. (2022) developed the PCA and autoencoder model to reduce the dimension of the dataset for the intrusion detection system (IDS) [9]. Results revealed that the dimension reduction by the autoencoder model increased the IDS performance more than the PCA. Furthermore, Boquet et al. (2020) developed the variational autoencoder (VAE) to reduce the dimension of the road traffic data [10]. By reducing the dimension of the dataset, the author found that the model learns the more meaningful characteristics of the data. Results suggest that the VAE could be developed for road traffic prediction.

Several researchers developed the autoencoder model for the prediction of landslide displacement [11–13]. For example, Nam & Wand (2020) developed the autoencoder model for landslide susceptibility area assessment and prediction of rainfall-induced landslides in Japan [11]. In this experiment, a sparse autoencoder (SpAE), a stacked autoencoder (StAE), a random forest (RF), a support vector machine (SVM), and a combined model of RF with SpAE and StAE were developed to compare the performance. The result shows that the hybrid RF with the autoencoder model was better than the other individual models. Furthermore, Huang et al. (2020) developed the fully connected sparse autoencoder (FC-SAE) for landslide susceptibility prediction in Guizhou Province, China [12]. In this experiment, the dataset contained 27 environmental features as the input of FC-SAE. Next, the performance of the FC-SAE was compared with the SVM and back propagation neural network (BPNN). Results revealed that the FC-SAE model outperformed the SVM and BPNN models. Next, Tan et al. (20221) developed the stacked autoencoder (SAE), artificial neural network (ANN), and radial basis function models for landslide prediction [13]. In this experiment, the models were trained on 14 slope risk factors of the landslide, such as slope hydrology, geology, and topology. The result shows that the SAE model has better accuracy than ANN and RBF models.

Several researchers developed the RNN models for landslide movement prediction from the time series data [14–17]. For example, Jiang et al. (2020) developed the SVR, LSTM, and hybrid of LSTM with the SVR model for landslide displacement prediction [14]. These models were trained on the precipitation, reservoir water level, and previous displacement recorded from China's three gorgeous reservoir areas. The result shows that the hybrid model performed better than the SVR and LSTM models for the prediction of displacement of landslides. Furthermore, Lin et al. (2022) developed the LSTM and LSTM fully connected (LSTM-FC) models for predicting the displacement trend of the landslide [15]. The extra fully connected layer was added to the LSTM's hidden layer in the construction of LSTM-FC. These models were trained on the rainfall and reservoir water level features of China's Baishuihe and Bazimen landslides. Results revealed that the LSTM-FC model outperformed the LSTM model for predicting landslide displacement trends. This survey observed that the LSTM and SVR models were mainly used for the landslide displacement prediction on the time series data. Furthermore, several researchers developed the LSTM models to predict the displacement in the landslide [16, 17]. The soil movement time series data from the real-world landslide were considered in the experiment. The experiment's findings suggest that the LSTM model could be developed for landslide movement prediction.

Several researchers in the literature used pre-trained models in natural language processing and computer vision-related problems [18]. However, these pre-trained models work best for sentence prediction and image-related tasks. The pre-trained models were never used for landslide prediction via time series data. Therefore, there is a need for the development of the model from scratch.

The ML literature survey observed that the PCA, LDA, and autoencoder models were developed to reduce the dimension of data. The state-of-art autoencoder model was mainly developed for landslide hazard zonation mapping. The autoencoder was also considered for landslide classification by geological and hydrological attributes. However, an autoencoder was not developed for landslide classification by time series weather and soil properties data recorded from LMS. Therefore, the main contribution of this paper is to develop an autoencoder and a PCA to reduce the dimension of the time series data for the landslide movement classification.

3 Methodology

3.1 Data

Several LMSs installed on the landslides in the state of Himachal Pradesh in India. Figure 1 shows the LMS installed on several real-world landslide locations in Himachal Pradesh. Figure 1a shows the real-world landslide, and the LMS shown in Fig. 1b installed on the top of the landslide in Fig. 1a is marked with red. Figure 1c shows the LMS installed at another landslide, and some visible cracks are shown in a red eclipse. The LMS measures the weather parameters of the location, such as temperature (Temp) in degrees Celsius, humidity (Hum) in percent, rainfall (Rain) in inches per hour, atmospheric pressure (Press) in millibars, and sunlight (Light) in lux. Apart from this, it measures the soil g-force in three-direction (gFx, gFy, and gFz) by an accelerometer sensor and angular rotation in degrees per second (Wx, Wy, and Wz) by a gyroscope sensor. The LMS's capacitive soil moisture sensor measures the soil's volumetric moisture content (Mos) in percent. Whenever a change in g-force is more significant than a predefined threshold (0.02), the system records it as a landslide movement (Mov). The LMS sends these thirteen attributes to the cloud every ten minutes. During the four months of the monsoon season from April to August 2022, the LMSs from the five locations recorded the landslide movements. We had the four-month time series data with thirteen attributes from the five landslide locations for this research. The total number of data points was eighty-five thousand in the LMS dataset. We defined the prediction problem as a binary class classification, where the landslide movement attribute's value zero means no-movement, and one implies movement. The sample data points recorded from the LMS are shown in Table 1. As seen in Table 1, the change in g-force in the serial number (SN) 4 to 5 breached the threshold, and LMS recorded it as a movement.

Fig. 1. The LMSs installed on several real-world landslide locations.

Table 1. Sample data points of the landslide recorded from the LMS.

SN	Temp	Hum	Rain	Press	Light	gFx	gFy	gFz	Wx	Wy	Wz	Mos	Mov
1	22	62	0	819	46	−0.97	0.20	−0.25	−6.52	−2.07	−6.52	60	0
2	22	62	0	819	13	−0.97	0.19	−0.24	−7.62	−2.93	−7.62	60	0
3	20	66	0	819	13	−0.97	0.19	−0.25	−7.87	−3.41	−7.87	60	0
4	20	68	0	819	12	−0.96	0.19	−0.25	−8.17	−3.23	−8.17	60	0
5	19	69	0	819	10	−0.94	0.25	−0.27	−5.92	−1.70	−0.13	60	1

3.2 Machine Learning Models

PCA. The principal component analysis is a prevalent technique for reducing data dimension [19]. The PCA is an orthogonal linear transformation that projects the input data to the principal components. The principal components are the data directions explaining the greatest variance. The first principal component has the maximum variance, and so on. The dimension could be removed by considering only some principal components and ignoring the rest of them.

Autoencoder. Autoencoder is a particular artificial neural network with the same input and output [20]. The autoencoder's hidden layer size is smaller than the input and output layer size. The middle-hidden layer of network is known as the bottleneck or latent vector (z). The input layer to the bottleneck network is known as an encoder function $g_\emptyset(.)$ parametrized by $\emptyset$. The bottleneck to the output layer is known as a decoder function $f_\theta(.)$ parametrized by θ. The encoder compresses the input data (x) in the bottleneck and learns the encoded features in the input data. The encoded features are known as latent space. In the latent space, similar features are close together, whereas the distinct features are farther away. The decoder takes the bottleneck input and regenerates the input ($\hat{x}$), similar to the original input. The bottleneck size is smaller than the input, which means the autoencoder reduces the dimension of the input data. In training, the autoencoder model learned the data representation in the latent space and ignored the insignificant data. The autoencoder with the nonlinear activation function transforms the data in the nonlinear space. As a result, the autoencoder can learn nonlinear manifolds [21]. The architecture diagram of the autoencoder model is shown in Fig. 2. As shown in Fig. 2, x is the input to the encoder and $\hat{x}$ is the regenerated input by the decoder. The symbol z is a latent vector. The key equations of the autoencoder model are as follows:

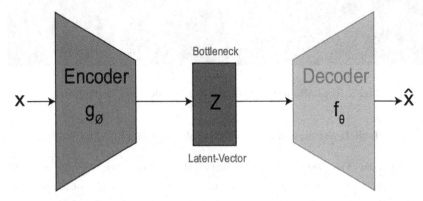

Fig. 2. Illustration of the autoencoder architecture.

$$z = g_\emptyset(x) \tag{1}$$

$$\hat{x} = f_\theta(z) \tag{2}$$

The mean squared error (MSE) loss function is used in the autoencoder, which minimizes the difference in original input x and regenerated input $\hat{x}$. The loss function is defined as follows:

$$MSE(\emptyset, \theta) = \frac{1}{n} \sum_{i=1}^{n} (x_i - f_\theta(g_\emptyset(x_i)))^2 \tag{3}$$

where x_i is the input. The $g_\emptyset$ and f_θ are the encoder and decoder nonlinear transformation functions. The variable n represents the total number of inputs.

RNN Model. The RNN model is a special type of artificial neural network which can predict the next time stamp with feedback from the previously predicted output [22]. The RNN contains a memory cell of the previously predicted output and feedforwards it to the next time stamp. The memory cell has a recurrent connection. The RNN model suffers from a vanishing gradient problem, where RNN cannot handle the long-term dependency on the data from the past [23].

The LSTM is a variant of the RNN, which avoids the vanishing gradient problem by selective reading, writing, and forgetting the information [24]. The LSTM has three gates that perform the selective read, write, and forget operation on the memory cell and the current input. An LSTM cell contains a memory cell (c_t) that stores the long-term dependency in the input data sequence. The model's memory is limited, and it needs to keep only the necessary information in the memory cell. The output gate (o_{t-1}) selectively writes the data from its past memory cell state (c_{t-1}) to the new vector (h_{t-1}). The logistic activation function (σ) decides what fraction of information pass to the next state, where 0 means not passed, and 1 means passed. The tanh activation function makes sure that the values are between -1 and 1. The new vector (h_{t-1}) is passed to the next state. The weighted sum of current input (x_t) and h_{t-1} construct and new temporary cell state ($\tilde{c}_t$). The input gate (i_t) selectively reads from the $\tilde{c}_t$. The forget gate (f_t) selectively forgets some information from the previous cell state (c_{t-1}). Figure 3 shows the interaction of input, output, and forget gates with the memory cell state. The operator $\odot$ represents the element-wise product between two vectors. The equation for selectively read, write, and forget are shown as follows:

$$o_{t-1} = \sigma(U^o x_{t-1} + W^o h_{t-2} + b^o) \tag{4}$$

$$h_{t-1} = tanh(c_{t-1}) \odot o_{t-1} \tag{5}$$

$$\tilde{c}_t = tanh(Ux_t + Wh_{t-1} + b) \tag{6}$$

$$i_t = \sigma(U^i x_t + W^i h_{t-1} + b^i) \tag{7}$$

$$f_t = \sigma(U^f x_t + W^f h_{t-1} + b^f) \tag{8}$$

$$c_t = (f_t \odot c_{t-1}) + (i_t \odot \tilde{c}_t) \tag{9}$$

where U and W are the weight matrix and b is a bias. The LSTM model learns the weight matrix and bias from the training data. The prediction of the movement or no-movement is the binary class classification. The binary cross entropy (BCE) loss function is used for classification. The BCE function is defined as follows:

$$BCE = -\frac{1}{N} \sum_{i=1}^{N} y_i \cdot \log(p(\hat{y}_i)) + (1 - y_i) \cdot \log(1 - p(\hat{y}_i)) \tag{10}$$

where N is a total number of packets. The y_i is the true label and $p(\hat{y}_i)$ is the probability of the packets belonging to the movement class.

Proposed Dimension Reduction Autoencoder LSTM (DR-A-LSTMS) Model. The dimension of the time series data is high (12 features) to classify the movement and no-movement classes in this experiment. The unimportant features could overfit the ML models. Thus, the dimension of the input features needs to reduce.

The proposed model first reduces the input features' dimension by the autoencoder's trained encoder (see Fig. 4). The encoder takes the input features (x) and yields the

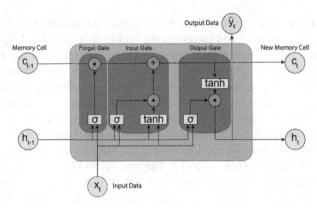

Fig. 3. A simple LSTM cell interacting with input, output, and forget gate.

encoded component as output (z), and the data packets are constructed from the encoded components. The construction of the data packets is explained in the next section. Next, these data packets are the inputs for the LSTM model. The LSTM model finds the recurrent relationship in the input data packet and passes it to the dense layer. Next, the SoftMax function predicts the movement or no-movement class for the next timestamp. In real-time, the DR-A-LSTM model gets data from LMS, encodes the inputs by the encoder, and then indicates whether a movement on no-movement in the landslide for the next timestamp.

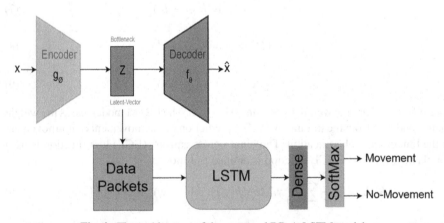

Fig. 4. The architecture of the proposed DR-A-LSTM model.

The Construction of Data Packets. The construction of the data packets is shown in Fig. 5. As shown in Fig. 5, the encoded dimension from the encoder is five, the lag value is three, and every row has a corresponding label for movement (1) and no-movement (1). For example, in Fig. 5, the movement label is one in the nth timestamp, then $n - 1$ to n-lag encoded feature values (x') are selected for the prediction of the movement in the next timestamp. The lag value was varied to construct the different lengths of data packets. Same as the data packets could be constructed for the no-movement class.

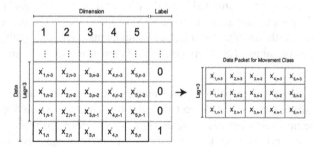

Fig. 5. The construction of the data packet for the movement class.

PCA-LSTM. This model first reduces the input features' dimension by the PCA. The PCA takes the input features (x) and yields the desired number of principal components as output (z). The data packets are constructed from the principal components. Next, these data packets are the inputs for the LSTM model same as DR-A-LSTM.

3.3 Model Construction

Autoencoder. The input and output layers dimension of the autoencoder model was 12. Next, the number of hidden layers was one or two. Furthermore, the bottleneck size varied from 3 to 10. The activation function changed to the linear, rectified linear unit (ReLU), logistic, and tanh function. The Adam optimizer and MSE loss function were selected for the autoencoder. The early stopping technique was used to avoid overfitting the models. The early stopping stops the training of the model when the test error increases. Table 2 depicts the various parameter ranges of the model.

Simple LSTM. The input dimension of the model was in 3D (batch size, lag, and 12 features). The batch size was 32 or 64, and the lag value varied between 1 and 100. The memory size varied from 50 to 500. Next, the dense layer size ranged from 10 to 100. Furthermore, the activation function changed to the ReLU, logistic, and tanh. The final layer was the SoftMax layer with the SoftMax activation function and two outputs. The BCE loss function with Adam optimizer was selected for the model. The early stopping technique was used to train the models. For regularization of the model, the dropout technique with twenty percent probability was applied to the LSTM's outputs. Table 3 depicts the various parameter ranges of the model.

DR-A-LSTM. After training the autoencoder, the data packets were constructed from the encoder output and passed to the LSTM model. The input dimension of the LSTM of the DR-A-LSTM model was in 3D (batch size, lag, and the number of reduced features).

The rest of the parameters varied the same as the simple LSTM model. Table 3 depicts the various parameter ranges of the model.

PCA-LSTM. The number of desired principal components varied between 3 to 10, and the data packets were constructed from the principal components and passed to the LSTM model. The input dimension of the LSTM of the PCA-LSTM model was in 3D (batch size, lag, and the number of principal components). The rest of the parameters varied the same as the simple LSTM model. Table 3 depicts the various parameter ranges of the model.

Data Packets. Several data packets were created for movement and no-movement classes. Eighty-five data packets belonged to the movement class, and more packets belonged to the no-movement class. Next, eighty-five random packets were selected from the no-movement class to make class balance. The random eighty percent of packets were selected from each class for the training, and the rest were for the testing.

Table 2. The different parameters varied in Autoencoder.

Parameter	Range of Parameter
Input size	12
Hidden layers	1 or 2
Bottleneck size	3 to 10
Loss function	MSE
Activation function	ReLU, tanh, logistic
Optimizer	Adam
Epochs	500 with early stopping

Table 3. The different parameters varied in the simple LSTM and DR-A-LSTM.

Parameter	Range of Parameter		
	Simple LSTM	PCA-LSTM	DR-A-LSTM
Lag	1 to 100	1 to 100	1 to 100
Reduced features	12	3 to 10	3 to 10
Memory size	50 to 500	50 to 500	50 to 500
Dense layer size	10 to 100	10 to 100	10 to 100
Batch size	32, 64	32, 64	32, 64

(continued)

Table 3. (*continued*)

Parameter	Range of Parameter		
	Simple LSTM	PCA-LSTM	DR-A-LSTM
Loss function	BCE	BCE	BCE
Activation function	ReLU, tanh, logistic	ReLU, tanh, logistic	ReLU, tanh, logistic
Optimizer	Adam	Adam	Adam
Epochs	500 with early stopping	500 with early stopping	500 with early stopping

4 Results

The ML models' parameters were optimized in training. The best parameters value for the autoencoder model was selected, which yielded the best classification accuracy of the DR-A-LSTM. The MSE loss for the best autoencoder model was 0.02 in 14 epochs. The optimized parameters for the autoencoder model are shown in Table 4. As can see in Table 4, the autoencoder model produced the lowest error with a ReLU activation function. Next, Table 5 shows the calibrated parameters for the simple LSTM, PCA-LSTM, and DR-A-LSTM models. For example, all the models have shown the highest accuracy with memory size 100 with tanh activation and dense layer size 10 with ReLU activation. The simple LSTM and DR-A-LSTM models showed the highest accuracy with a lag value of 10, whereas the PCA-LSTM model showed the highest accuracy with a lag value of 12. Furthermore, PCA-LSTM was best with six reduced dimensions, and the DR-A-LSTM model was best with the five dimensions.

Furthermore, Table 6 shows the performance of the simple LSTM, PCA-LSTM, and DR-A-LSTM models during the training and testing. As can see in Table 6, the simple LSTM model produced 82.3% accuracy in the training data and 71.8% in the testing data. The simple LSTM model showed overfitting in the training data. Similarly, the PCA-LSTM model showed 76.5% training and 88.2% testing accuracy. Next, the DR-A-LSTM model produced 97.8% accuracy in the training and 100% in the testing.

Figure 6 shows the confusing matrix of the best-performed DR-A-LSTM model in the training and testing. As shown in Fig. 6, the DR-A-LSTM model predicted the three-movement points as no-movement points in the training, but in the testing, it classified all the data correctly.

Table 4. The best value of the parameters for the autoencoder calibrated from the training data.

Parameter	Range of Parameter
Input size	12
Hidden layers	2

(*continued*)

Table 4. (*continued*)

Parameter	Range of Parameter
Bottleneck size	5
Loss function	MSE
Activation function	ReLU
Optimizer	Adam
Epochs	14

Table 5. The calibrated parameters for ML models from the training data

Parameter	Range of Parameter		
	Simple LSTM	PCA-LSTM	DR-A-LSTM
Lag	10	12	10
Reduced features	12	6	5
Memory size	100	100	100
Dense layer size	10	10	10
Batch size	32	32	32
Loss function	BCE	BCE	BCE
Activation function	tanh in LSTM, ReLU in Dense layer	tanh in LSTM, ReLU in Dense layer	tanh in LSTM, ReLU in Dense layer
Optimizer	Adam	Adam	Adam
Epochs	15	130	288

Table 6. The results of the ML models from training and test dataset.

Model	Training Accuracy (in %)	Test Accuracy (in %)
Simple LSTM	82.3	71.8
PCA-LSTM	76.5	88.2
DR-A-LSTM	97.8	100

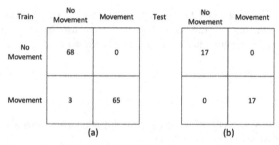

Fig. 6. The confusion matrix of the DR-A-LSTM. (a) From the train data. (b) From the test data.

5 Discussion and Conclusion

The movements in the landslides could be predicted by the ML models. The prediction of the movement in the landslide timely could save the lives and thread related to the landslides. The LMSs could be installed on the landslide to record the pattern of movements. The recorded data could be high dimensional and may be overfitting the ML models. The PCA and autoencoder models have been developed in this experiment to reduce the data dimension. For training the PCA and autoencoder models, 4-month time series data of LMSs from the five landslides were utilized. The time series data was split in the 80:20 ratio, where 80 percent was used for training and 20 percent for testing. Next, a simple LSTM, PCA-LSTM with PCA, and a DR-A-LSTM model with an autoencoder were developed to classify the movement and no-movement in the next timestamp. All the high-dimensional features were provided to the simple LSTM model. In contrast, the PCA-LSTM and DR-A-LSTM models received reduced data from the PCA and bottleneck layer of the autoencoder, respectively.

This experiment's findings revealed that the simple LSTM model produced 82.3% accuracy in the training data and 71.8% in the testing data. The simple LSTM model showed overfitting in the training data. Furthermore, the autoencoder model was trained and showed 0.02 MSE loss in the reconstruction of the input data. Next, the PCA-LSTM model produced 76.5% accuracy in the training and 88.2% in the testing. Furthermore, the DR-A-LSTM model produced 97.8% accuracy in the training and 100% in the testing. Results suggest that the DR-A-LSTM model could be developed for the prediction of landslide movement.

One main reason to outperform the DR-A-LSTM model could be that the autoencoder reduced the dimension, removed the noise, and provided important information. The autoencoder with the nonlinear activation function transformed the data in the nonlinear space. As a result, the autoencoder learned the nonlinear manifolds and found a better representation of the data [21]. The PCA-LSTM model was the second-best model where PCA provided the reduced dimension, but PCA transformed the data into the linear space and could not fit the nonlinear patterns in the data.

This study has numerous practical implications. For example, the DR-A-LSTM model could be developed for real-time landslide movement prediction ahead of time on the LMS recorded data and generate the warnings. In future work, we could formulate various autoencoders such as LSTM-autoencoder and prediction-autoencoder [25, 26].

Acknowledgment. We are grateful to the DST, India, and the DDMA Mandi, Kinnaur, and Kangra for providing the fund for this research grant. We are also thankful to the IIT Mandi for providing the space and computing facilities for this research work.

References

1. Parkash, S.: Historical records of socio-economically significant landslides in India. J. South Asia Disaster Stud. **4**(2), 177–204 (2011)
2. Crosta, G.: Regionalization of rainfall thresholds: an aid to landslide hazard evaluation. Environ. Geol. **35**(2), 131–145 (1998)
3. Kumar, P., et al.: Prediction of real-world slope movements via recurrent and non-recurrent neural network algorithms: a case study of the Tangni landslide. Indian Geotech. J. **51**(4), 788–810 (2021). https://doi.org/10.1007/s40098-021-00529-4
4. Kumar, P., Sihag, P., Chaturvedi, P., Uday, K.V., Dutt, V.: BS-LSTM: an ensemble recurrent approach to forecasting soil movements in the real world. Front. Earth Sci. **9**, 696–792 (2021)
5. Pathania, A., et al.: A lowcost, sub-surface IoT framework for landslide monitoring, warning, and prediction. In: Proceedings of 2020 International Conference on Advances in Computing, Communication, Embedded and Secure Systems (2020)
6. Vabalas, A., Gowen, E., Poliakoff, E., Casson, A.J.: Machine learning algorithm validation with a limited sample size. PloS One **14**(11) (2019)
7. Wang, Y., Yao, H., Zhao, S.: Auto-encoder based dimensionality reduction. Neurocomputing **184**, 232–242 (2016)
8. Lazzara, M., Chevalier, M., Colombo, M., Garcia, J.G., Lapeyre, C., Teste, O.: Surrogate modelling for an aircraft dynamic landing loads simulation using an LSTM AutoEncoder-based dimensionality reduction approach. Aerosp. Sci. Technol. **126**, 107629 (2022)
9. Wang, C., Liu, H., Sun, Y., Wei, Y., Wang, K., Wang, B.: Dimension reduction technique based on supervised autoencoder for intrusion detection of industrial control systems. Secur. Commun. Netw. **2022** (2022)
10. Boquet, G., Morell, A., Serrano, J., Vicario, J.L.: A variational autoencoder solution for road traffic forecasting systems: missing data imputation, dimension reduction, model selection and anomaly detection. Transp. Res. Part C: Emerg. Technol. **115**, 102622 (2020)
11. Nam, K., Wang, F.: An extreme rainfall-induced landslide susceptibility assessment using autoencoder combined with random forest in Shimane Prefecture Japan. Geoenviron. Disasters **7**(1), 1–16 (2020)
12. Huang, F., Zhang, J., Zhou, C., Wang, Y., Huang, J., Zhu, L.: A deep learning algorithm using a fully connected sparse autoencoder neural network for landslide susceptibility prediction. Landslides **17**(1), 217–229 (2019). https://doi.org/10.1007/s10346-019-01274-9
13. Tan, F., Yu, J., Jiao, Y.-Y., Lin, D., Lv, J., Cheng, Y.: Rapid assessment of landslide risk level based on deep learning. Arab. J. Geosci. **14**(3), 1–10 (2021). https://doi.org/10.1007/s12517-021-06616-3
14. Jiang, H., Li, Y., Zhou, C., Hong, H., Glade, T., Yin, K.: Landslide displacement prediction combining LSTM and SVR algorithms: a case study of Shengjibao Landslide from the Three Gorges Reservoir Area. Appl. Sci. **10**(21), 7830 (2020)
15. Lin, Z., Sun, X., Ji, Y.: Landslide displacement prediction model using time series analysis method and modified LSTM model. Electronics **11**(10), 1519 (2022)
16. Kumar, P., et al.: Predictions of weekly slope movements using moving-average and neural network methods: a case study in Chamoli, India. In: Nagar, A., Deep, K., Bansal, J., Das, K. (eds.) Soft Computing for Problem Solving. AISC, vol. 1139, pp. 67–81. Springer, Singapore (2020). https://doi.org/10.1007/978-981-15-3287-0_6

17. Pathania, A., et al.: Predictions of soil movements using persistence, auto-regression, and neural network models: a case-study in Mandi India. Int. J. Swarm Intell. **7**(1), 94–109 (2022)

18. Qiu, X., Sun, T., Xu, Y., Shao, Y., Dai, N., Huang, X.: Pre-trained models for natural language processing: a survey. Sci. China Technol. Sci. **63**(10), 1872–1897 (2020). https://doi.org/10.1007/s11431-020-1647-3

19. Jolliffe, I.: Principal component analysis. In: Lovric, M. (ed.) International Encyclopedia of Statistical Science, pp. 1094–1096. Springer, Heidelberg (2011). https://doi.org/10.1007/978-3-642-04898-2_455

20. Liou, C.Y., Cheng, W.C., Liou, J.W., Liou, D.R.: Autoencoder for words. Neurocomputing **139**, 84–96 (2014)

21. Wang, W., Huang, Y., Wang, Y., Wang, L.: Generalized autoencoder: a neural network framework for dimensionality reduction. In: Proceedings of the IEEE Conference on Computer Vision and Pattern Recognition Workshops, pp. 490–497 (2014)

22. Medsker, L., Jain, L.C.: Recurrent Neural Networks: Design and Applications International Series on Computational Intelligence. CRC Press, Boca Raton (1999)

23. Bengio, Y., Simard, P., Frasconi, P.: Learning long-term dependencies with gradient descent is difficult. IEEE Trans. Neural Netw. **5**(2), 157–166 (1994)

24. Hochreiter, S., Schmidhuber, J.: Long short-term memory. Neural Comput. **9**(8), 1735–1780 (1997)

25. Nguyen, H.D., Tran, K.P., Thomassey, S., Hamad, M.: Forecasting and anomaly detection approaches using LSTM and LSTM autoencoder techniques with the applications in supply chain management. Int. J. Inf. Manag. **57**, 102282 (2021)

26. Brownlee, J.: A Gentle Introduction to LSTM Autoencoders. https://machinelearningmastery.com/lstm-autoencoders/. Accessed 02 Sept 2022

Exploring the Incremental Improvements of YOLOv7 over YOLOv5 for Character Recognition

Alden Boby[✉][ID], Dane Brown[ID], James Connan, and Marc Marias[ID]

Department of Computer Science, Rhodes University, Grahamstown, South Africa
boby.alden128@gmail.com, {d.brown,j.connan}@ru.ac.za

Abstract. Technological advances are being applied to aspects of life to improve quality of living and efficiency. This speaks specifically to automation, especially in the industry. The growing number of vehicles on the road has presented a need to monitor more vehicles than ever to enforce traffic rules. One way to identify a vehicle is through its licence plate, which contains a unique string of characters that make it identifiable within an external database. Detecting characters on a licence plate using an object detector has only recently been explored. This paper uses the latest versions of the YOLO object detector to perform character recognition on licence plate images. This paper expands upon existing object detection-based character recognition by investigating how improvements in the framework translate to licence plate character recognition accuracy compared to character recognition based on older architectures. Results from this paper indicate that the newer YOLO models have increased performance over older YOLO-based character recognition models such as CRNET.

Keywords: Character Recognition · Licence Plate Recognition · Object Detection

1 Introduction

Licence plate recognition (LPR) consists of three main stages: localisation, extraction and character recognition [4,10]. While all three stages cannot work without each other, character recognition is essential. At this stage, the information from the licence plate is digitised for it to be used practically. Existing systems have explored character recognition through image processing, similar to most computer vision tasks. Deep learning models are quickly replacing these old methods, which lack extensive capabilities to generalise when solving problems [5]. Due to increased computing power at more affordable costs, deep learning has become more viable to deploy at a large scale and apply to real-world problems in real-time [2]. This extends to intelligent transport systems (ITS), which

This work was undertaken in the Distributed Multimedia CoE at Rhodes University.

aim to automate or, at the very least, alleviate the manual labour required for traffic regulation [21]. With a growing number of vehicles on the road, there has never been a better time to deploy machine learning models to analyse large sets of data programmatically.

Licence plate recognition has many practical uses that extend across many domains. The main benefactor of licence plate recognition is law enforcement, as recognition can aid with tracking stolen vehicles as well as vehicles that have broken road rules and escaped [21]. This can also enforce security [3,20]. Natural scenes or images in the wild are a persisting problem that has not adequately been solved yet [18]. This can be approached by refining the sub-systems involved in LPR. The importance of the character recognition portion of LPR makes it the focus of this paper.

Licence plate designs vary across regions and even in different provinces or states. Figure 1 shows an example of two different licence plates from the same country. These varying designs make it difficult to create a blanket solution for LPR. The lack of an international standard leads to different licence plate fonts, introducing an ambiguity problem. This speaks specifically to how different typefaces represent certain characters differently. Specific fonts use serifs to make similar characters easily distinguishable from one another.

(a)   (b)

Fig. 1. These licence plates vary in design despite belonging to the same country.

2   Object Detection

Multiple object detection models are based on convolutional neural networks (CNNs). These include Faster R-CNN, the Single Shot Detector (SSD), You Only Look Once (YOLO) [15], and others [8]. The most popular object detector amongst these is YOLO, which exists in several versions. YOLO has three versions officially worked on by the main authors, with YOLOv3 being the final release from the first authors [17]. Following this, members from the machine learning community took over to produce subsequent versions of the YOLO model. YOLOv4 was introduced following minor changes over YOLOv3 but still maintaining the same relative architecture [1].

New builds of the YOLO model were pushed out in a short space of time, leading to the credibility of the newer systems and their improvements over the previous version being questioned. The rapid development of new versions prompted whether it is necessary to change the version name or write something in as a minor improvement. Currently, the latest version of YOLO is YOLOv7 [19].

YOLOv5 through to v7 are all using PyTorch, which differs from the original implementations running from the darknet neural network framework [14]. These three versions have different authors, and all come with minor additions. YOLOv7 is very similar to YOLOv5 created by ultralytics[1]; YOLOv7 directly improves upon this version. YOLOv7 adds improved performance and pose recognition, a new feature not present in any other version of YOLO. YOLOv5, to date, does not have a formal paper written on it, hence why it is difficult to justify its performance compared to YOLOv7. Within the paper by Wang *et al.* [19], certain performance metrics for the YOLOv5 models have been omitted as the data is not yet readily available.

All YOLO models are trained and evaluated on the Common Objects in Context (COCO) image dataset [12], an extensive collection of images that have become the standard when evaluating object detectors. YOLOv5 and YOLOv7 have models aimed at different devices based on compute capability.

Table 1 shows the mean average precision (mAP) at an IoU threshold of 0.5 (mAP@0.5) for the standard versions of YOLO v5 and v7. The differences below are not incredibly significant for a two-version step-up. The major differences are in the speed of inference and computational expenses.

Table 1. mAP values for the respective YOLO models.

Model	Test Size	$\text{mAP}^{\text{val}}0.5$
YOLOv7	640	69.7
YOLOv5l	640	67.3

3   Related Studies

Some promising research has come from using YOLO, specifically in the LPR domain. The focal point has been obtaining a licence plate's location through YOLO and predicting the bounding box coordinates for the region of interest (ROI) [21]. Lee *et al.* [11] used YOLO9000 (YOLOv2) to extract licence plates from surveillance footage but did not explore its use further for character recognition.

Silvia and Jung [18] went far enough to produce a novel framework based on YOLO designed to detect licence plates specifically, including their shape. Their work introduced the concept of bounding parallelograms instead of bounding boxes, which fully encompass a licence plate from corner to corner. This has

---

[1] https://github.com/ultralytics/yolov5.

added benefits later in the LPR pipeline when corrective transformations are to be applied to an extracted licence plate.

Given this, licence plate recognition through machine learning is becoming more robust. An area less explored is applying these object detection models to character recognition specifically. Current literature has produced two YOLO-based character recognition models, CR-Net [18] and Fast-OCR [9].

Montazzolli et al. [13] have one of the earliest YOLO-based character recognition models based on the YOLO model. The authors called this model LPS/CR-Net, based on a less computationally expensive version of YOLO (Fast-YOLO). Silvia [18], a co-author of the original paper, further extended this custom character recognition model concept. They proposed a model that detects 35 classes 0–9 and A–Z, with '0' and 'O' being detected as one class. One thing common across these character recognition models is that they are fed images of licence plates that have already been cropped. Meaning they would struggle when given an entire image. This means they need to be supported by a robust licence plate extractor.

Fast-OCR is a small framework aimed at detecting only digits and was aimed at detecting small images [9]. This framework is based on Fast-YOLOv4 and YOLOv2, similar to CR-Net. Some improvements may be found by exploring character recognition with newer versions of YOLO, such as versions 5 and 7. Comparing the performance of these models against existing models discussed can give insight into how well these models can perform in real-world scenarios. YOLOv2 had a mAP@0.5 of 44 [16], which is significantly improved by over 20 by both YOLOv5 and v7 as shown in Table 1.

4   Experimental Setup

Since YOLO is an object detector, it does not use metrics specific to character recognition. The paper will test the ability to locate characters in an image and classify them as one of 36 classes. The paper will not evaluate the characters' order as that can be done perfectly mathematically, given that all the characters on the licence plate are detected correctly.

4.1   Datasets

A total of three datasets were combined to create a completely new set of data to train both the YOLOv5 and YOLOv7 models. This dataset consisted of licence plate images in the wild with characters individually labelled. The etiquetadoOlval dataset [7] contributed 306 images to this dataset and the chvaltrain-OpenIMGS [6] contributed 719 images. Extra classes were deleted from these datasets, so there were just 36 classes A–Z and 0–9. The remainder came from a new dataset containing ten images per class, comprising 1372 images with 7018 annotated bounding boxes. This combined dataset is a new contribution, the Natural Scene Licence Plate Dataset.

Figure 2 shows the distribution of the characters in the dataset.

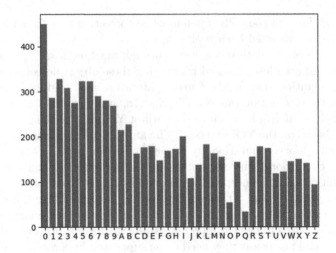

Fig. 2. The frequency of each class within the dataset.

The dataset followed an 80:20 split with 1102 training and 270 validation images. All images were augmented to fit the resolution of 416 × 416, the input size for the YOLO models. Some sample images from the dataset are presented in Fig. 3.

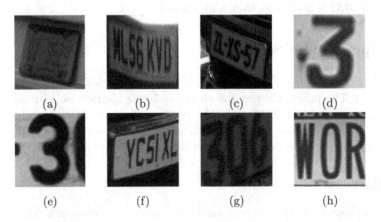

Fig. 3. Samples from the Natural Scene Licence Plate Dataset.

The datasets used for testing are defined in the sections that follow.

UFPR-ALPR Datatset

The UFPR-ALPR Dataset [10] contains 150 vehicles with multiple frames of data. The resolution of the images is 1920 × 1080 but the licence plates in the images occupy a very small region within each image. The data set is split into 40% for training and testing and 20% for validation. Only the testing images were used for this paper to evaluate the model's performance.

MakeML Dataset

The MakeML Dataset contains 433 images of vehicles from different perspectives. Fifty licence plates were extracted from this dataset to use for testing. The extracted licence plates were also corrected to eliminate any perspective distortion.

4.2   Performance Metrics

The standard object detection methods intersection over union (IoU) and mAP will be used to evaluate the performance of the YOLO models on licence plate-specific data. Moreover, precision and recall are lower-level metrics that can be used to assess per class performance of the model.

Intersection over Union

IoU represents the intersection area between a ground truth bounding box and a predicted bounding box. A greater area of intersection signifies a more accurate prediction from the model. Figure 4 demonstrates IoU visually.

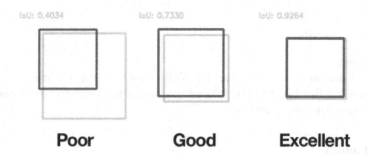

Fig. 4. Different levels of bounding box accuracies.

$$\text{Intersection over Union} = \frac{\text{Area of Overlap}}{\text{Area of Union}}. \tag{1}$$

Equation 1 shows the formula for calculating IoU. A threshold for IoU can be used to control the predictions. Suppose a prediction is below a specified threshold. In that case, the prediction is discarded due to a lack of confidence-increasing the IoU threshold results in higher recall but less precision and vice versa.

Mean Average Precision

A good object detection model has both high recall and precision. For maximum performance at any point on the precision-recall curve, precision and recall should be high regardless of the confidence score. Average precision is the area under the precision-recall curve, and mAP is the mean of the average precision across all classes calculated at different IoU thresholds. Mean average precision maximises both precision and recall finding the optimum value to minimise the trade-off between the two metrics.

4.3   Model Training

The training procedure was consistent for both YOLOv5 and YOLOv 7. Both models were trained on the Natural Scene LP Dataset with 1102 training images supplemented with 270 for validation during the training process. The models were trained for 300 epochs with a batch size of 8, which was limited to the memory of the GPU. All training was performed on an NVIDIA GeForce RTX 2080Ti with 11 GB of RAM using PyTorch. Transfer learning was used from the COCO dataset weights provided for both models. The transfer learning helps the new model not make false predictions based on the objects the old model is trained to detect and improves the model's overall performance.

4.4   Test Models

Experiment 1
The first evaluation includes testing the YOLO models using the standard evaluation metrics defined in Section. 4.2 and comparing the performance of the older model against the newer model.

Experiment 2
This experiment shows qualitative results showing the weaknesses and strengths of the YOLOv5 and v7 models. Identifying what types of licence plates and fonts made predictions for the model complex.

Experiment 3

Evaluating the performance of both the models on the UFPR-ALPR dataset and comparing the performance to CR-Net [18] which is based on a tuned version of the older YOLOv2.

5   Results and Discussion

The results from the test models are presented in this section in the order they were performed.

5.1   Experiment 1

YOLOv5 had an overall mAP@0.5 of 87.6% versus 85.6% for YOLOv7 after being trained on the same dataset. This is inconsistent with the values seen in Table 1 showing that YOLOv7 performed better on the MSCOCO dataset. The data from this experiment show that the performance of YOLOv5 for this task was more satisfactory on paper. However, the difference between the mAP values is almost negligible. Table 2 shows the performance of the models for each individual class. These low-level results enable further analysis of which specific characters performed poorly for each model.

The precision and recall for 'Q' were zero for both YOLOv5 and YOLOv 7. This is highly likely because the dataset used for training had very few instances of the 'Q' class, as seen in Fig. 2 it actually has the lowest instances amongst the classes and is severely underrepresented. Balancing a character dataset is difficult because within the licence plate domain, specific sets of characters appear more frequently, and others less so, leading to the imbalance amongst the classes in the dataset.

The character 'I' had a high recall but a low precision, likely because 'I' is one of the characters that suffers from the ambiguity problem sharing similar or, in some instances, the same features as the character '1'. This was consistent across both YOLOv5 and v7, with YOLOv7 having better performance for that class specifically. Additionally, the character 'O' had the reverse problem, high precision but low recall in comparison. This character also had a low representation in the training dataset but also shares similar features to zero. The model would benefit from more training data for these characters to allow the models to consolidate the features of those characters.

The confusion matrices in Figs. 5 and 6 show how the models performed for each class at a glance and provide visual feedback on which classes were easily mistaken for each other (Fig. 7).

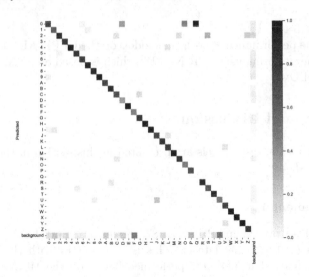

Fig. 5. Confusion matrix for the YOLOv5 model.

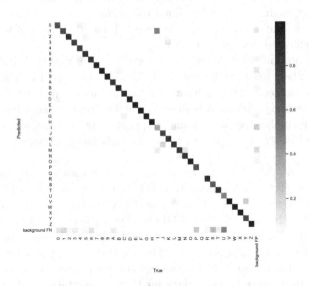

Fig. 6. Confusion matrix for the YOLOv7 model.

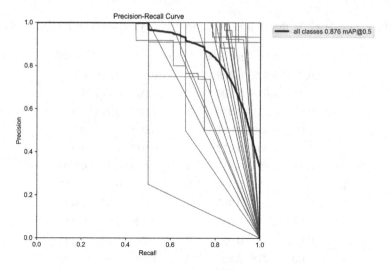

(a) Precision-recall curve for YOLOv5.

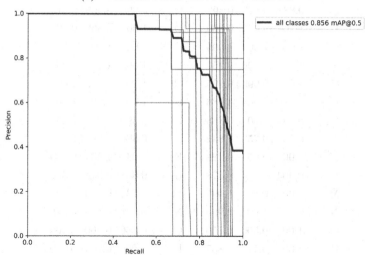

(b) Precision-recall curve for YOLOv7.

Fig. 7. Precision-recall curves for models tested on the MakeML dataset.

Table 2. Low-level results showing the mAP@0.5, precision and recall per class.

Class	P	R	mAP50	Class	P	R	mAP50
0	0.740	0.722	0.799	0	0.875	0.778	0.768
1	0.986	0.643	0.796	1	1.00	0.714	0.719
2	0.913	0.935	0.955	2	1.00	0.873	0.908
3	1.00	0.842	0.921	3	0.941	0.842	0.847
4	0.806	1.00	0.977	4	0.945	1.00	0.999
5	0.917	0.824	0.925	5	0.975	0.941	0.946
6	0.984	0.852	0.923	6	1.00	0.833	0.857
7	0.979	1.00	0.995	7	1.00	0.977	1.00
8	0.970	0.941	0.968	8	0.925	0.941	0.946
9	0.913	1.00	0.981	9	1.00	0.974	1.00
A	1.00	0.778	0.889	A	1.00	0.889	0.894
B	1.00	0.877	0.964	B	0.937	0.993	0.991
C	0.888	0.818	0.892	C	0.999	0.909	0.913
D	1.00	0.600	0.800	D	1.00	0.800	0.805
E	1.00	1.00	0.995	E	1.00	1.00	1.00
F	1.00	0.500	0.750	F	1.00	1.00	1.00
G	1.00	0.990	0.995	G	1.00	0.928	1.00
H	0.986	0.900	0.986	H	1.00	1.00	1.00
I	0.495	1.00	0.808	I	0.599	0.748	0.647
J	0.927	0.750	0.842	J	0.800	1.00	0.949
K	1.00	0.857	0.928	K	0.941	1.00	0.999
L	0.904	0.784	0.878	L	0.883	0.917	0.900
M	1.00	0.921	0.995	M	0.932	0.913	0.924
N	0.935	1.00	0.995	N	0.928	0.875	0.879
O	1.00	0.500	0.750	O	0.886	0.500	0.500
P	1.00	0.714	0.857	P	1.00	0.714	0.719
Q	0.00	0.00	0.00	Q	0.00	0.00	0.00
R	0.919	0.877	0.952	R	1.00	0.912	0.928
S	1.00	0.625	0.749	S	1.00	0.667	0.672
T	0.968	0.889	0.938	T	1.00	0.889	0.894
U	0.308	0.500	0.559	U	1.00	0.500	0.505
V	1.00	0.778	0.889	V	1.00	0.778	0.783
W	0.857	1.00	0.995	W	1.00	1.00	1.00
X	1.00	0.894	0.995	X	1.00	1.00	1.00
Y	0.75	1.00	0.995	Y	0.75	1.00	0.916
Z	1.00	0.800	0.900	Z	1.00	1.00	1.00

5.2 Experiment 2

Through qualitative examples, it is easy to spot which characters were incorrectly predicted by the models as well as what specific features caused the model to perform poorly.

Figure 8 shows an incorrect prediction from the YOLOv5 model. The model has mistaken the character 'J' for the character 'U'. The character 'J' is also a problem character and can be misidentified as an 'L' by the models. Interestingly the YOLOv7 model did not have this error, correctly predicting each character on the plate.

Fig. 8. 172TMU

Low-resolution images also affected the ability of the models to correctly predict characters, with few pixels in an image, information is lost, making it even harder to distinguish between characters such as 'C' and 'G', which is evidently shown in Fig. 9 where both the YOLOv5 and YOLOv7 models produced the same erroneous result. Upscaling the images can help to mitigate this issue by preventing the loss of information.

Fig. 9. YNTZDBC

Moreover, a more even distribution of characters will mitigate the problems faced by underrepresented characters. In addition, the dataset should be modified to have a heavier bias on weaker characters, especially those directly affected by the ambiguity problem.

Fig. 10. Predictions and confidence values from both models shown on the same licence plate YOLOv5 (a) and YOLOv7 (b)

Figure 10 compares annotations from both models and further consolidates the similarity between the performance of these models. The improvements to YOLO in version seven barely affect the model's accuracy. This paper is not currently focused on the speed of inference on images or videos, which is where most improvements may lie. The bounding boxes, as well as the confidence scores in Fig. 10 are incredibly similar and demonstrates the similar mAP@0.5 score for both the models, 85.6% (YOLOv7) and 87.6% (YOLOv5) visually.

5.3   Experiment 3

The UFPR-ALPR dataset was selected to benchmark the models trained for this paper against an already existing model in the literature. CR-Net by Laroca *et al.* [10] was evaluated using this same dataset. The comparison results are shown in Table 3.

Table 3. Each model's performance on the UFPR-ALPR dataset.

Model	Recall/Accuracy
YOLOv7	68.80%
YOLOv5l	65.30%
CR-NET	64.89%

The results from Table 3 show that both models outperformed CR-Net on the UFPR-ALPR dataset when processing individual frames from the dataset (3.91% for YOLOv7 and 0.41% for YOLOv5). The highest performance of the three came from the YOLOv7 model going towards the upper end of 60% for recall/accuracy. These results are promising showing that perhaps fine-tuning one of these YOLO models specifically to detect characters in the way that CR-Net was may open up more room for improvement.

When running inference on this dataset, both the YOLOv5 and YOLOv7 struggle to predict licence plates with light text on dark backgrounds. Figure 11 presents some examples where the licence plate has white text and a red background. The model could only predict two of the seven characters on these licence plates. This is a direct effect of the training data, which is primarily made up of licence plates with dark text and a light background. The Natural Scene LP dataset could benefit from improvements that will allow it to better train these models. More light text on dark backgrounds must be added to improve performance in detecting those characters.

(a)   (b)   (c)

Fig. 11. Licence plates that proved to be difficult to detect for the new YOLO models.

Moreover, both the YOLOv5 and YOLOv7 models had difficulties classifying characters that were rotated at an angle of about forty-five degrees and above. Figure 12 shows direct output from the YOLOv7 model on sample images from the UFPR dataset, from the figure it can be seen that the model was unable to recognise some of the characters completely. In this particular example YOLOv5 performed better but does not represent performance on all predictions as it is just one sample from the dataset. As the problem was consistent across both models one variable to consider for this problem is most likely inadequate training data, data augmentation can be used to improve the model's performance to make it invariant to rotation.

(a)Outputfrom   (b)Outputfrom
YOLOv5.   YOLOv7.

Fig. 12. Rotated characters presented a challenge for both models.

6 Conclusion

This paper has shown that object detectors are viable for LPR. These YOLO-based models should be further developed and extended to improve their performance on a more diverse data set. This promise was shown as the YOLOv5 and YOLOv7 models both outperformed CR-Net by beating its recall score on the UFPR dataset by 3.91% and 0.41%, respectively. However, the gap between performance is not exceptionally significant as CR-Net is based on the much older YOLOv2. Some extra techniques could be extrapolated from Laroca *et al.* such as temporal redundancy on multiple frames for the same vehicle, this has been proven to improve recognition rates.

The experiments in this paper have shown that YOLOv5 and YOLOv7 are almost equal regarding standard object detection methods such as mAP and IoU. Even at a low level, the per-class results were all within the same range, with only minor differences between the two. One key finding is that although the YOLOv5 model performed slightly better than the YOLOv7 model on the MakeML dataset with a 2% increase in mAP@0.5, the YOLOv7 model performed better in the UFPR-ALPR experiment, which included more images to detect. One problem noted was that in all tests, the resolution of an image affected the models' ability to make an accurate prediction. Future work should explore the use of super-resolution to improve input image quality to boost confidence scores and correct prediction for the YOLO character recognition models.

References

1. Bochkovskiy, A., Wang, C.Y., Liao, H.Y.M.: YOLOv4: optimal speed and accuracy of object detection. arXiv preprint arXiv:2004.10934 (2020)
2. Chen, R.C., et al.: Automatic license plate recognition via sliding-window darknet-yolo deep learning. Image Vis. Comput. **87**, 47–56 (2019)
3. Du, S., Ibrahim, M., Shehata, M., Badawy, W.: Automatic license plate recognition (ALPR): a state-of-the-art review. IEEE Trans. Circuits Syst. Video Technol. **23**(2), 311–325 (2012)
4. Han, J., Yao, J., Zhao, J., Tu, J., Liu, Y.: Multi-oriented and scale-invariant license plate detection based on convolutional neural networks. Sensors **19**(5), 1175 (2019)
5. He, M.X., Hao, P.: Robust automatic recognition of Chinese license plates in natural scenes. IEEE Access **8**, 173804–173814 (2020)
6. Hernandez, M.: Chvaltrainopenimgs dataset (2022). https://universe.roboflow.com/mario-hernandez/chvaltrainopenimgs. Accessed 29 Sept 2022
7. Hernandez, M.: etiquetadooival dataset (2022). https://universe.roboflow.com/mario-hernandez/etiquetadooival. Accessed 29 Sept 2022
8. Huang, J., et al.: Speed/accuracy trade-offs for modern convolutional object detectors. In: Proceedings of the IEEE Conference on Computer Vision and Pattern Recognition, pp. 7310–7311 (2017)
9. Laroca, R., Araujo, A.B., Zanlorensi, L.A., De Almeida, E.C., Menotti, D.: Towards image-based automatic meter reading in unconstrained scenarios: a robust and efficient approach. IEEE Access **9**, 67569–67584 (2021)

10. Laroca, R., et al.: A robust real-time automatic license plate recognition based on the YOLO detector. In: 2018 International Joint Conference on Neural Networks (IJCNN), pp. 1–10. IEEE (2018)
11. Lee, Y., Yun, J., Hong, Y., Lee, J., Jeon, M.: Accurate license plate recognition and super-resolution using a generative adversarial networks on traffic surveillance video. In: 2018 IEEE International Conference on Consumer Electronics-Asia (ICCE-Asia), pp. 1–4. IEEE (2018)
12. Lin, T.-Y., et al.: Microsoft COCO: common objects in context. In: Fleet, D., Pajdla, T., Schiele, B., Tuytelaars, T. (eds.) ECCV 2014. LNCS, vol. 8693, pp. 740–755. Springer, Cham (2014). https://doi.org/10.1007/978-3-319-10602-1_48
13. Montazzolli, S., Jung, C.: Real-time Brazilian license plate detection and recognition using deep convolutional neural networks. In: 2017 30th SIBGRAPI conference on graphics, patterns and images (SIBGRAPI), pp. 55–62. IEEE (2017)
14. Nepal, U., Eslamiat, H.: Comparing YOLOv3, YOLOv4 and YOLOv5 for autonomous landing spot detection in faulty UAVs. Sensors 22(2), 464 (2022)
15. Redmon, J., Divvala, S.K., Girshick, R.B., Farhadi, A.: You only look once: unified, real-time object detection. CoRR abs/1506.02640 (2015). https://arxiv.org/abs/1506.02640
16. Redmon, J., Farhadi, A.: YOLO9000: better, faster, stronger. In: Proceedings of the IEEE Conference on Computer Vision and Pattern Recognition, pp. 7263–7271 (2017)
17. Redmon, J., Farhadi, A.: YOLOv3: an incremental improvement (2018)
18. Silva, S.M., Jung, C.R.: Real-time license plate detection and recognition using deep convolutional neural networks. J. Vis. Commun. Image Represent. 71, 102773 (2020)
19. Wang, C.Y., Bochkovskiy, A., Liao, H.Y.M.: YOLOv7: trainable bag-of-freebies sets new state-of-the-art for real-time object detectors. arXiv preprint arXiv:2207.02696 (2022)
20. Xie, L., Ahmad, T., Jin, L., Liu, Y., Zhang, S.: A new CNN-based method for multi-directional car license plate detection. IEEE Trans. Intell. Transp. Syst. 19(2), 507–517 (2018)
21. Zou, Y., Zhang, Y., Yan, J., Jiang, X., Huang, T., Fan, H., Cui, Z.: License plate detection and recognition based on YOLOv3 and ILPRNET. Signal Image Video Process. 16, 1–8 (2021)

Verifiable Machine Learning Models in Industrial IoT via Blockchain

Jan Stodt[1]([✉]) [iD], Fatemeh Ghovanlooy Ghajar[2] [iD], Christoph Reich[1] [iD],
and Nathan Clarke[3] [iD]

[1] Institute for Data Science, Cloud Computing and IT Security, Furtwangen University
of Applied Sciences, Furtwangen, Germany
{Jan.Stodt,Christoph.Reich}@hs-furtwangen.de
[2] Institute of Reliable Embedded Systems and Communication Electronics (ivESK),
Offenburg University of Applied Sciences, Offenburg, Germany
fatemeh.ghovanlooy@hs-offenburg.de
[3] Centre for Security, Communications, and Networks Research (CSCAN) Plymouth
University, Portland Square, Plymouth PL4 8AA, UK
N.Clarke@plymouth.ac.uk

Abstract. The importance of machine learning (ML) has been increasing dramatically for years. From assistance systems to production optimisation to healthcare support, almost every area of daily life and industry is coming into contact with machine learning. Besides all the benefits ML brings, the lack of transparency and difficulty in creating traceability pose major risks. While solutions exist to make the training of machine learning models more transparent, traceability is still a major challenge. Ensuring the identity of a model is another challenge, as unnoticed modification of a model is also a danger when using ML. This paper proposes to create an ML Birth Certificate and ML Family Tree secured by blockchain technology. Important information about training and changes to the model through retraining can be stored in a blockchain and accessed by any user to create more security and traceability about an ML model.

Keywords: Machine learning · Verifiability · Blockchain · Poisoning · Cybersecurity

1 Introduction

Industry 4.0 has spawned a new sector in manufacturing known as Smart Manufacturing, which creates opportunities for analytics in industry. The goal is to automate manufacturing processes to optimise efficiency, promote sustainability, improve supply chain management and identify system obstacles before they arise. To do this, huge amounts of data are collected, optimised and applied [1]. Through the use of artificial intelligence (AI), companies can maximise the efficiency of individual assets and the entire manufacturing process by applying sophisticated analytics to industrial data. ML techniques, a subset of artificial intelligence, have the potential to become the primary driver for uncovering fine-grained, complex production patterns in the smart manufacturing paradigm and providing timely decision support in a variety of manufacturing

© Springer Nature Switzerland AG 2023
D. Garg et al. (Eds.): IACC 2022, CCIS 1782, pp. 66–84, 2023.
https://doi.org/10.1007/978-3-031-35644-5_6

and production applications. These include predictive maintenance, process optimisation, task scheduling, quality improvement, supply chain and sustainability, among others [2]. Despite the fact that various ML approaches have been used in a number of manufacturing applications in the past, many open questions and issues remain, such as curating big data and understanding the cybersecurity elements of smart manufacturing. In recent years, large companies have invested directly in machine learning, this in turn has created the need for general guidelines. Organisations such as ISO propose certification guidelines for assessing the security of machine learning (ML) systems [3], whose recommendations have been sought by industry in the past. The European Union has developed a detailed checklist for assessing the reliability of ML systems [4]. Finally, machine learning is increasingly becoming a company's key value proposition. One of the basic requirements mentioned in the guidelines is transparency. Traceability can make a significant contribution to transparency. The lack of traceability not only makes it difficult for internal auditors to verify quality and compliance, but also for external audits by clients or regulators in the future. Even if there is a record of the process, it can be very difficult to find a source of error hidden in poorly documented pre-processing of training data. One problem that has been noticed when reviewing pre-processing documentation is often the lack of precision. Typical phrases are "a subset of dataset X" without clearly defining the subset. One technology that is particularly suitable for traceability is the blockchain. Information recorded in the blockchain can no longer be changed and updates to the information can be traced. The decentralised storage of data also ensures that the stored data is still available even if a local copy of the data is lost, and legally independent nodes of a blockchain can control each other without the need for a central control authority. To address the traceability issues that exist in machine learning for documentation, this paper introduces two concepts: (a) ML Birth Certificates and (b) ML Family Tree. Both concepts aim to clarify the lineage of models and to document model provenance decisions unambiguously and semi-automatically.

The contribution of this paper is as follows:

- ML Birth Certificates: To store creation information of a model in a secure manner
- ML Family Tree: To store the relationship of ML models that can arise through transfer learning
- Secure storage of the ML Birth Certificate and the ML Family Tree via the blockchain, for tamper-proof, auditable and decentralised storage
- Information that makes the ML model life cycle verifiable

The paper is structured as follows: Sect. 1.1 describes the current state of the art, and Sect. 2 discusses the security challenges associated with machine learning models. In Sect. 3, we describe the new approach to maintain the security of the model, we provide security analyses and evaluation in Sect. 4 and Sect. 5 concludes the paper.

1.1 State of the Art

From a cybersecurity perspective, there are several ways to negatively impact a machine learning-based system, such as attacking data acquisition or transmission and modifying the models created. Huang et al. proposed an early taxonomy of adversarial machine learning that includes the categories of influence, security breach and specificity [5]. In addition, the proliferation of driverless cars and the expansion of deep neural networks have made visual recognition an attractive target for machine learning attacks [6,7]. McGraw et al. [8] identified 78 security risks in ML models and highlighted the top 10. Most of these attacks target the data used to train the model. There are also attacks when the model is re-trained: Online learning, where the model is trained with new data during use, and attacks that occur during transfer learning, where an existing model is trained (tuned) to new data. A detailed taxonomy of machine learning attacks was described by Pitropakis et al. [9]. In addition to the theory-focused reviews, Cheatham et al. [10] provide a detailed overview of the resulting consequences in the areas of individuals, organizations and society. In order to capture some information about the creation of the ML model and its origin, Mitchell et al. [11] introduced the concept of ML Model Report Cards. However, it must be clearly stated that the aim of Model Report Cards is to provide transparency in fairness, not traceability. Although the Model Report Cards (may) contain information about the production, the level of detail to be achieved is not specified. Furthermore, in the evolution of models through online learning, and especially in transfer learning, it is difficult to determine the 'base model' used in the process. Over several generations of transfer learning, the problem is exacerbated; in retrospect, traceability is effectively non-existent. To address some of the above problems, Arnold et al. [12] developed FactSheets 360, which gathers more information in the area of traceability and versioning of the ML model. But again, the quality/granularity of the information collected is not defined in detail. In examples of FactSheets 360, such vague statements as "The test data consists of a subset of dataset X" [13]. This coarse granularity does not allow outsiders or even internal staff to subsequently verify the creation of the model. Furthermore, there is no automatic fact collection in the area of data pre-processing. In addition to the approaches mentioned, there are now best practices and tools in the field of ML DevOps [14] that attempt to solve the traceability problem mentioned above. For example, there are model registries that record the processing steps performed [15]. Examples of tools used for this are MLFlow[1] and Comet[2]. However, one problem with these tools is the centralised storage approach of these solutions. This creates numerous data silos, which makes it difficult to keep track of the data and leads to a lack of traceability when the centralised storage approach is turned off. In contrast, the blockchain and IPFS-based solution is decentralised and distributed and therefore available as long as a node is still available. As it can be seen in the literature review, that traceability is still a gap for ML models, even though some proposed solutions. But these solutions are centralized and single point of failure might happen, and the possibility to change the data is high. Our approach focuses on providing detailed traceability for ML models, while also storing them in a decentralized environment that is tamper-proof.

In summary, it can be said that previous work has addressed the problem of the comprehensibility of ML models, but only in partial or superficial areas. ML Model Report Cards and FactSheets 360 attempt to document information about the use of the ML model, but fall short in terms of the granularity of the information. ML development tools in the area of ML DevOps inherit information about ML creation, but fall short in the area of availability of data by third parties (e.g. auditors).

---

[1] https://mlflow.org/.

[2] https://www.comet.com/.

2 Security Challenge of ML Models

Problems with ML models exist in the areas of security against attacks, insufficient documentation of model creation and tracing the lineage of ML models. This section covers the security issues that arise during the development of an ML system, as well as while the system is being attacked and prepared for deployment.

2.1 Security Attacks

Attacks on ML models can sometimes have dramatic consequences [16], as described above. ML components might be attacked with different approaches and system-specific expertise. Attacks on process optimisation models can be used to cause financial damage by slowing down or shutting down production. However, not every attack is only financially damaging. It is easy to imagine that people can also be harmed when decisions are made about people, which only makes attacks on machine learning models more critical. The most important attacks on machine learning models and software are described below.

Malicious data training model: a training model based on datasets with flawed data, a vulnerability that may occur in the ML development phase. Most ML developers are not aware that attackers can penetrate the inventory of ML training datasets. In the training phase, an attacker attempts to obtain or manipulate training data or the model itself. In data access attacks, some or all of the training data is obtained and used to create an alternative model. This alternate model can be used to evaluate the effectiveness of attacks before they are used as inputs during the testing phase. Poisoning attacks [17], also known as causative attacks, directly or indirectly alter data or models. Poisoning alters the data through data injection or modification, or directly corrupts the model through logic corruption. In this attack, injected samples are used to change the decision boundary of a centroid model or to reduce classification accuracy (in supervised learning) by gradient increase on the model's test error. In data manipulation, the output labels of the original training data and the input data are changed in an adversarial manner.

Malicious code: Normally, programmers do not start from scratch when creating a model. Instead, they use existing code. If an attacker uploads modified scripts to websites such as libraries or sample code, they can easily manipulate the model and the result. Vulnerabilities can occur at this level because there are no automated tools for secure developers and no transparency centre for machine learning systems.

Model poisoning: An attacker degrades model performance to achieve a different model decision [18]. Poisoning a model means replacing a valid model with a corrupted model. In a conventional cyber attack, this is quite simple. Once trained, a model is nothing more than a file on a computer, much like an image or a PDF document. Attackers can compromise the systems that contain these models and then either modify the model file or replace it with a corrupted file. Even if a model has been trained with a dataset that has been carefully checked and found to be uncorrupted, this model can be replaced with a corrupted model at various stages of the distribution pipeline.

Attack on Transfer Learning: In transfer learning, the majority of models are built on previously trained solution architectures derived from a larger data set. Despite the many advantages of the method, the possibility of a backdoor attack remains [19]. If someone trains an attack on the system underlying the model, it is likely that the attack will also work on the current model.

Manipulation of a running program and modification of its output: When the machine learning system is attacked and the target of the attack is something that is important to the industry's business.

2.2 Insufficient Documentation of Model Creation

As mentioned in State of The Art (Sect. 1.1), there are approaches to improve the documentation of ML model creation and its use. Model report cards [11] and FactSheets 360 [13], which still have the problem that the documentation of individual model quality determining steps (e.g. data preprocessing) is not automatically documented. Missing information about how the data set is preprocessed makes a subsequent review of the processes difficult or impossible. However, this is very important to investigate errors in the model and find the origin of the error. This could be due to faulty pre-processing or a deliberate attack on the data.

2.3 Tracing Lineage of ML Model

The lack of knowledge and information about how the model is created makes it difficult or even impossible to check the model creation process later. Model creation involves collecting a data set, transforming it according to a set of rules, and then using it to train the model; all of these processes are influenced by decisions and (un)conscious biases. Although there are approaches to versioning data in the field of data pre-processing, it is usually not possible to trace how the data has been processed, e.g. which transformation methods, which parameters, which version of tools, etc. However, this is very important to investigate errors in the model and to find the origin of the error. This could be due to faulty pre-processing or a deliberate attack on the data.

3 ML Birth Certificate and ML Model Family Tree

The method for solving the traceability problems mentioned above can be divided into two phases: The creation of a traceable model and the storage of the model. In the following, the respective steps and methods of the phase are described to show how the traceability problems are addressed.

3.1 Model Creation

The model creation phase comprises two steps: the collection of all relevant information that makes the model verifiable in the later life cycle in order to detect errors and make the model traceable, and the storage of this information in a uniform and extensible data format that can be stored on the blockchain. If a model is continuously trained, a new branch of the model is created during each training run, based on the common root.

Important Information to be Recorded. The ML model life cycle comprises 9 phases [20] (1. Model Requirements, 2. Data Collection, 3. Data Cleaning, 4. Data Labelling, 5. Feature Engineering, 6. Model Training, 7. Model Evaluation, 8. Model Deployment, 9. Model Monitoring). While CRISP-DM (CRoss Industry Standard Process for Data Mining) [21] defines 6 phases[3], this work is deliberately based on the 9 phases presented by Amershi et al. [20]. This is because this definition of the life cycle is based on the experience of a large and successful company (Microsoft) in the field of AI-based application development and reflects reality better than a process defined 22 years ago (in 2000), which is based more on theory than on insights from day-to-day business and a much changed state of the art.

To achieve traceability, comprehensive information must be collected on all phases. In the following, it is defined for each phase of the ML model life cycle which information must be recorded in order to make the respective phase traceable and thus verifiable in the future.

As an application example, the development of an AI is outlined which detects scratches on a metal surface, counts them and determines the degree of the scratch. For this purpose, pictures are taken of a metal surface with a camera. In order to ensure uniform illumination of the metal surface (important for reliable recognition of the scratches), a light system is used which guarantees this. It can happen that objects (e.g. ballpoint pens) are accidentally placed on the metal surface by the person taking these pictures.

In the following, examples are given of the information that is collected in order to make the development verifiable. Furthermore, for each phase an example (Listings) is given of how the blockchain entries (blocks) can be structured; these blocks are in JSON format. For each epoch, the block stores the corresponding phase, phase-id to identify the phase and the model-id it refers to, as well as epoch-specific information that makes it verifiable. The reference of each phase (phase-id) is entered in the Model Birth Certificate; this process is described in more detail in Sect. 3.1. These blocks of collected information can later be used in the course of an audit by ML developers, customers, users of the ML application or by an auditor to understand the development process or to get to the bottom of an error in the ML application.

Phase 1 - Model Requirements: In this phase, decisions are made about which functions must be used to achieve the goals of the ML model. The goal of the model and the decisions made must be stored in order to achieve traceability. In this area, it makes sense to record the thought processes of the model developer, not only for traceability, but also for later audits. An example of a corresponding blockchain entry of the collected information can be seen in Listing 1.1.

```
{
  "record-type": "phase",
  "phase": "1",
  "phase-id": "5016ba10-c733-4754-9e21-2d37782ae86f",
  "model-id": "8ad53dd3-4b02-4af5-a17f-e03d2fabee1c",
```

---

[3] 1. Business Understanding, 2. Data Understanding, 3. Data Preparation, 4. Modelling, 5. Evaluation and 6. Deployment.

```
"goal": "The aim is to create a ML model for the
     ↪ classification of metal surface quality. The accuracy
     ↪ should be 95% and the precision should be 90%. Metal
     ↪ surface images are taken with camera XYZ and an
     ↪ illumination of 10.000 lux",
"decisions": "Data sets in this domain do not exist, so new
     ↪ data must be collected. Synthetic data should not be
     ↪ used. At least 1000 data should be collected. The model
     ↪  architecture ResNet50 is to be used and completely
     ↪ retrained without using existing weights"
}
```

Listing 1.1. Example of blockchain block of Phase 1.

Phase 2 - Data Collection: There are a number of factors that can influence the data collection and the data collected. For example, the interviewer and his/her behaviour has a great influence on the quality of the data [22]. For example, the socio-economic background of the interviewer (e.g. race and ethnicity) affects data quality [23,24]. In the technical field, it is important to know which devices have collected data, as their properties (e.g. accuracy and resolution of the measurement of a temperature sensor or contrast of an image sensor) influence the data collected [25]. If this influence and its extent are known, it can be corrected later [26,27]. It is therefore very important to collect and store information about the factors that may influence data quality. In the case of sensor data collection, this includes other environmental data that is not necessarily used for the model but has an influence on the measured value. An example of such environmental data in the case of temperature measurement would be humidity. In the case of measuring devices/cameras, their model information and ideally their data sheet must also be stored. If measuring instruments are calibrated before use, a calibration checklist must be prepared and kept. If interviewers are trained before use, information about the training must be stored. The aim of all this additional data collection is to make this phase of the ML model's life cycle traceable and thus enable subsequent error analysis. To link the training data to the phase or model, the training-data-id and the hash are stored to guarantee the integrity of the data set. An example of the corresponding blockchain entry of the collected information can be seen in Listing 1.2.

```
{
  "record-type": "phase",
  "phase": "2",
  "phase-id": "34be7fda-d4a1-4920-8fc5-ac9dc4a902c5",
  "training-data-id": "4a0c0c0b-6012-4332-ba8e-91a5f2e37821",
  "training-data-hash": "3cf33bd19e5001e9c151fe8127632e9...",
  "model-id": "8ad53dd3-4b02-4af5-a17f-e03d2fabee1c",
  "data-collection-entity": "Camera XYZ; Resolution: 2,3 MP;
       ↪ Frame rate: 160 FPS; Dynamic range: 71,7 dB; Signal-to-
       ↪ noise ratio: 40,2 dB",
  "environment-data": "Ambient brightness: 3.500 lux; Ambient
       ↪ colour temperature: 2.500 K"
}
```

Listing 1.2. Example of blockchain block of Phase 2.

Phase 3 - Data Cleaning: The potential errors in the data mentioned in Phase 2 are cleaned up in Phase 3. The task and tools used to clean up the data must be recorded to ensure traceability of this process. Again, it may be necessary to record the thought processes of the model developer. As this phase concerns the training data set, the reference id for the data set is also saved here. An example of the corresponding blockchain entry of the collected information can be seen in Listing 1.3.

```
{
    "record-type": "phase",
    "phase": "3",
    "phase-id": "b3dbf7be-a7fb-4eff-8b51-b4186b72b1b3",
    "model-id": "8ad53dd3-4b02-4af5-a17f-e03d2fabee1c",
    "training-data-id": "4a0c0c0b-6012-4332-ba8e-91a5f2e37821",
    "task-1": "Remove images of metal surfaces that contain
        ↪ foreign objects (e.g. hand)",
    "tool-1": "Tool ABC",
    "task-2": "Remove images with signal-to-noise ratio < 25 dB",
    "tool-2": "Tensorflow 2.9; Method: tf.image.psnr"
}
```

Listing 1.3. Example of blockchain block of Phase 3.

Phase 4 - Data Labeling: After collecting the data and correcting data quality errors, Phase 4 involves labelling the data, also called data annotation: Assigning ground truths, creating segmentations, creating bounding boxes or other techniques. In this area, the annotator's training, background, understanding of training, quality and understanding of instructions, among other factors, directly affect data quality [28]. In addition, the ease of use of the labelling software has a direct impact on data quality. An extensive list of errors that can occur during labelling is shown by Kili [29]. To make this phase comprehensible, all relevant information about the annotator [30], the training material, the instructions for the labelling task and information about the labelling software must be stored. If automatic labelling methods such as reinforcement learning are used, the model that performs the labelling must also be made comprehensible. If this is not possible, the resulting hazard must be understood and documented. As this phase concerns the training data set, the reference id for the data set is also saved here. An example of the corresponding blockchain entry of the collected information can be seen in Listing 1.4.

```
{
    "record-type": "phase",
    "phase": "4",
    "phase-id": "88c63f90-254b-4154-9554-5c5891ce3b20",
    "model-id": "8ad53dd3-4b02-4af5-a17f-e03d2fabee1c",
    "training-data-id": "4a0c0c0b-6012-4332-ba8e-91a5f2e37821",
    "task": "Label scratches on the metal surface",
    "Instruction": "Draw a bounding box containing one scratch
        ↪ each. If two scratches are overlapped, draw a bounding
        ↪ box for each scratch",
    "tool": "LabelMe - \url{https://github.com/wkentaro/labelme"}
}
```

Listing 1.4. Example of blockchain block of Phase 4.

Phase 5 - Feature Engineering: Feature engineering modifies the collected and labelled data to increase model accuracy and precision and thus improve the quality of the model. The data is filtered, transformed or generated through augmentation, among other techniques [31]; either by hand or in the case of AutoML [32], by algorithms. When augmenting data, care must be taken that the truth of the data is not destroyed by the augmentation. An example of this would be the process of image augmentation, where an image is rotated by a random number of degrees and the object of interest is rotated out of the image. Therefore, it is also important at this stage to store the thought processes that lead to the feature engineering decisions. Methods, their parameters and tools in this area should also be stored. As this phase concerns the training data set, the reference id for the data set is also saved here. An example of the corresponding blockchain entry of the collected information can be seen in Listing 1.5.

```
{
    "record-type": "phase",
    "phase": "5",
    "phase-id": "4f921439-b322-4d9b-9bfa-76c608bf6d6a",
    "model-id": "8ad53dd3-4b02-4af5-a17f-e03d2fabee1c",
    "training-data-id": "4a0c0c0b-6012-4332-ba8e-91a5f2e37821",
    "augmentation": "Rotate the image randomly (+- 90 degrees) to
        ↪ the left or right.",
    "tool": "Tensorflow 2.9"
}
```

Listing 1.5. Example of blockchain block of Phase 5.

Phase 6 - Model Training: During the training of the model with the collected, cleaned and annotated data, a series of decisions are made by the ML developer or, in the case of AutoML [32], algorithms to increase the accuracy and precision of the model; this is called hyperparameter optimisation/tuning [33,34]. For optimal transparency not only the hyperparameters that are considered best must be saved, but also the evolution of the hyperparameter selection. In the case of an optimisation by AutoML, the evolution of the selection must be saved in addition to the best hyperparameters. In this way, it is also possible to draw conclusions later on whether the AutoML algorithm contains errors. As this phase concerns the training data set, the reference id for the data set is also saved here. An example of the corresponding blockchain entry of the collected information can be seen in Listing 1.6.

```
{
    "record-type": "phase",
    "phase": "6",
    "phase-id": "3767cf3f-4616-4f96-84da-eb7ce83c64db",
    "model-id": "8ad53dd3-4b02-4af5-a17f-e03d2fabee1c",
    "training-data-id": "4a0c0c0b-6012-4332-ba8e-91a5f2e37821",
    "hyperparameter-1": "Epochs",
    "value-1": "25",
    "hyperparameter-2": "Learning rate",
    "value-2": "0.0001",
}
```

Listing 1.6. Example of blockchain block of Phase 6.

Phase 7 - Model Evaluation: The model evaluation phase is a form of quality control. The performance and quality of the model is assessed against tested or validated evaluation data sets and various metrics [20]. If the results are satisfactory, it is possible to move on to the next phase; if the results are not satisfactory, improvements must be made in the previous phases. The selection of the evaluation dataset and its origin must be traceable. The same applies to the selection of metrics and thresholds set for satisfactory model performance and quality. Any necessary improvements must also be recorded. As this phase concerns the evaluation data set, the reference id for the data set is also saved here. An example of the corresponding blockchain entry of the collected information can be seen in Listing 1.7.

```
{
    "record-type": "phase",
    "phase": "7",
    "phase-id": "87328dc5-99a5-41d9-8fa5-4ef9d4137b8a",
    "model-id": "8ad53dd3-4b02-4af5-a17f-e03d2fabee1c",
    "eval-dataset-id": "b0dc2d4d-1365-4b5d-bfbb-0b7569b69887",
    "accuracy-desired": "95%",
    "accuracy-achieved": "97%",
    "precision-desired": "90%",
    "precision-achieved": "91%"
}
```

Listing 1.7. Example of blockchain block of Phase 7.

Phase 8 - Model Deployment: In this phase, the trained and evaluated model is rolled out in the target environment. In this step it is important to check again whether the expected environment and the intended use of the model still correspond to the state defined in the model requirement. If the environment (e.g. non-expected sensor characteristics) and the intended use no longer match, profound but not necessarily directly noticeable errors can occur. Monitoring (see Phase 9) can help in this case ante hoc, but post hoc actual and target state should be compared to avoid mistakes directly. Therefore, checklists should be used and their results recorded. An example of the corresponding blockchain entry of the collected information can be seen in Listing 1.8.

```
{
    "record-type": "phase",
    "phase": "8",
    "phase-id": "5863628d-4c20-4351-9c06-def48fc0da83",
    "model-id": "8ad53dd3-4b02-4af5-a17f-e03d2fabee1c",
    "equipment": "Camera XYZ; Illumination 10.000 lux",
    "environment": "Ambient brightness: 3.500 lux; Ambient colour
        ↪ temperature 2.500 K"
}
```

Listing 1.8. Example of blockchain block of Phase 8.

Phase 9 - Model Monitoring: Monitoring oversees the behaviour of the model and warns the developers when predefined limit values are exceeded. Defined limit values and the number of warnings triggered should be logged. In this way, the behaviour of the model can be made traceable. An example of the corresponding blockchain entry of the collected information can be seen in Listing 1.9.

```
{
  "record-type": "phase",
  "phase": "9",
  "phase-id": "e0944d94-e84a-48d4-befd-072432e0cd46",
  "model-id": "8ad53dd3-4b02-4af5-a17f-e03d2fabee1c",
  "Alert": "Data drift",
  "Limit": "p-value 0.0005"
}
```

Listing 1.9. Example of blockchain block of Phase 9.

Model Birth Certificate and Model Family Tree. To enable detailed traceability of the ML model, we introduce the idea of ML Birth Certificates as well as an ML Family Tree to trace the changes made to the basic ML model and the changes made. A graphical example can be seen in Fig. 1.

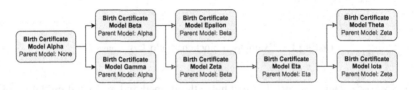

Fig. 1. ML Birth Certificates and ML Family Tree

ML Birth Certificates contain detailed information about the creation process in order to make it verifiable later in the life cycle of the model. This information is similar to the concept of ML Model Report Cards [11] and FactSheets 360 [12], our ML Birth Certificates contain a much finer granularity of information that is captured semi-automatically. For example, it records exactly which pre-processing steps and which commands were used with which software version. The advantages of using blockchain for storage are manifold, in addition to longer availability and fail-safety compared to a centralised solution. On the one hand, collaborative work is possible in which models can be exchanged with each other and their exact creation parameters are verifiably documented. On the other hand, this verifiability is an essential property for the certification of ML models in critical application areas. In other words, an auditor can verify beyond doubt how a model was created. An example can be seen in Fig. 1 Model Alpha, Beta and Epsilon. To make the descent of models from predecessor models (e.g. through transfer learning or online learning) explicit, the concept of the ML Family Tree is introduced. Here, the ML Birth Certificate refers to the parent model and the changed phases are saved. An example of the blockchain entries (in the JSON format) for the model Birth Certificates can be seen in Listing 1.10; a series of related models create the ML Family Tree. Line 3 to line 16 describe the first model Birth Certificate (root) of the

ML Family Tree. Lines 6 to 9 contain the references to the blockchain block entries for phases 1 to 9 (representation shortened for clarity). How the information is structured in these phases was described in Sect. 3.1. Lines 11 and 12 would contain the reference to the parent model (highlighted in yellow), but since this is the first model, the entry is "None". Lines 13 to 15 contain the reference, hash and IPFS URL of the dataset used. The structure of the (child) ML Birth Certificate (lines 18 to 31) contains the completed reference to the parent model (lines 21–22), references to the changed phases in lines 24–27 (in this case phase 1, 2, 7, 8) and the reference, hash and IPFS URL of the record used (lines 29–31).

```
1   [
2     {
3         "record-type": "model",
4         "model-name": "Model Alpha",
5         "model-id": "8ad53dd3-4b02-4af5-a17f-e03d2fabee1c",
6         "phases": {
7           "1": "5016ba10-c733-4754-9e21-2d37782ae86f",
8           ...
9           "9": "e0944d94-e84a-48d4-befd-072432e0cd46"
10        },
11        "parent-model-name": "None",
12        "parent-model-id": "None",
13        "training-data-id": "4a0c0c0b-6012-4332-ba8e-91a5f2e37821",
14        "training-data-hash": "3cf33bd19e5001e9c151fe8127632e9...",
15        "training-data-url": "ipfs://h199h884pkragfmn1gx1"
16    },
17    {
18        "record-type": "model",
19        "model-name": "Model Beta",
20        "model-id": "402441d4-677f-4363-84aa-6f5a400a179cc",
21        "parent-model-name": "Model Alpha",
22        "parent-model-id": "8ad53dd3-4b02-4af5-a17f-e03d2fabee1c",
23        "phase-changes": {
24          "1": "6a12d81a-14ce-4d88-83a3-2aa32cd6a03b",
25          "2": "3c192185-279f-4ecc-a840-678401f192b9",
26          "7": "fa8dd1e1-d982-4eea-b7a9-ab9b8902a02b",
27          "8": "9ed6189a-5a90-49fb-9bb7-4b97cd528f93"
28        }
29        "training-data-id": "908d2fdd-16aa-4e93-8a57-78b48daf87bb",
30        "training-data-hash": "960f0bac5d1740c8ef0924442bc31ea8...",
31        "training-data-url": "ipfs://9i0xd83ucroffgp739x4"
32    }
33  ]
```

Listing 1.10. Example of blockchain blocks of Model Family Tree consisting out of two Model Birth Certificates

This information stored in the blockchain (ML Birth Certificate and ML Family Tree) can then be retrieved at a later time by a series of actuators, a potential use case would be error fielding; a number of use cases are described in Sect. 4.2.

3.2 Model Storage

To ensure traceability, the data used for training is either stored as a hash in the Hyperledger Fabric [35] blockchain (for confidential data). The model can be hashed and the hash can be signed by the creator. The model can also be signed. The hash of the model, the signature of the model and the signature of the hash are kept as a block in the blockchain. Since the storage of data in a blockchain is immutable, the authenticity of the model can be verified and its development can be tracked. The signature of the model shows how the model was created, and the signature of the hash confirms that the same person wrote the hash. In this way, the integrity and identity of the model are guaranteed. The model is stored in the InterPlanetary File System (IPFS) [36] to ensure optimal data availability and to save storage space on the blockchain nodes. The IPFS address of the stored data and the hash of the stored data are then stored in the Hyperledger Fabric blockchain in the corresponding block. To ensure originality and address the concerns in Sect. 2.1, it is recommended to place the model in a Docker container and store it in IPFS. A smart contract is also introduced to verify and sign the output based on the model's data stored in the blockchain. The process of data verification and signing by the smart contract can be seen in Fig. 2a. An overview of the architecture can be seen in Fig. 2b. While no conclusions can be drawn about the performance of this solution, as the proposed solution will be implemented in Future Work, performance evaluation in the literature can be used. Androulaki et al. [35] points out that 3500 transactions per second can be performed and Fabric scales to more than 100 nodes. Nakaike et al. [37] speaks of 2200 transactions per second (2 reads and 2 writes per transaction).

Model Storage Process. The issues of security and privacy in the exchange and transmission of data (transactions) in such a novel network environment are naturally addressed in the architecture of the blockchain [38, 39]. The aim is to use the capacity of the blockchain to increase the trustworthiness, security, transparency and traceability of data across the network and to achieve cost savings through new efficiencies. It also aims to offer a common, immutable ledger for storing data. In this subsection, an industrial blockchain is proposed as a use case to illustrate the scenario for the storage model in the blockchain and the need for its use considering cooperative factories. This cooperation is based on the interests of factories. To pursue their common interests, they need to cooperate. Thus, they need the consent of all factory stack holders as blockchain nodes to share data, storage and computing resources. This partnership is the engine for their growth. Data sharing and transparency are essential to its mission. The security and immutability of shared data must be ensured to build and sustain this collaboration. Blockchain ensures that members share their data in a transparent way. Malicious agents can then no longer change it. Companies can make joint decisions by interacting as blockchain nodes and using consensus algorithms and blockchain services such as smart contracts. As mentioned in Sect. 1, machine learning is fast becoming the primary value proposition of an enterprise. Based on the task specifications, it makes sense for industrial companies to develop their own machine learning models. Due to the security challenges described in Sect. 2.1, stakeholders must be able to rely on the security and originality of the model. In this case, not only the engineers in the factory, but also the

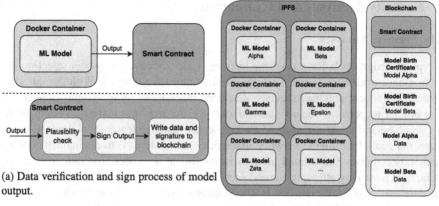

(a) Data verification and sign process of model output.

(b) Architecture.

Fig. 2. Data verification and proposed architecture.

IT security department and the factory stack owners need to be informed and in agreement about the security of the machine learning model to be used in the factory. The sequence diagram for model storage is shown in Fig. 3. It shows how the stakeholders verify the model before storing the signature, hash and hash signature of the model in the blockchain. Due to the immutability of the blockchain, it is guaranteed that they will not be changed. Afterwards, however, it is possible to compare the hash of the model with the stored hash and determine whether the original model has been changed.

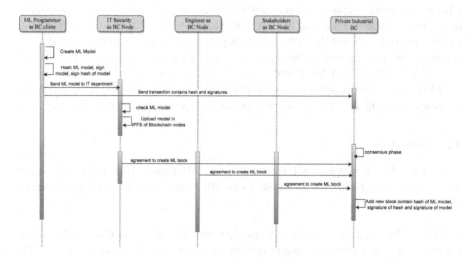

Fig. 3. Sequence Diagram of Model Storage.

4   Security Analyses and Evaluation

4.1   Security Analyses

A typical design cycle for a machine learning system focuses on model selection and performance evaluation, while security considerations are ignored. With the introduction of the above-mentioned security attacks on machine learning systems in Sect. 2.1, it is crucial to perform security assessments for the machine learning system in the design phase and to use the most up-to-date secure machine learning methods. Furthermore, the goal of intelligent network attack detection systems is to distinguish between malicious activities and normal patterns in intelligent networks. To counter the many variants of poisoning attempts, these detection systems must ensure the security risks of the data collected by the sensors. It is well known that a competent attacker can insert malicious data into the training dataset during poisoning attacks. Consequently, most existing poisoning protections provide adequate protection against relatively simple attack strategies designed to reduce model accuracy. Overall, most available countermeasures against poisoning provide adequate protection against relatively simple attack techniques designed to reduce model accuracy. In general, such countermeasures first examine the accuracy and performance of the model's loss function and then identify irregularities against a set threshold. Training data filtering, robust learning and the use of tools are the three basic defences against poisoning attacks. Training data filtering, such as input manipulation detection and gradient shaping, are not powerful enough to detect outliers. Model robustness and model checking are not robust enough to identify outliers and are only useful for backdoor attacks. Use of utilities such as GAN and robust statistics, which are only suitable for Deep Neural Networks (DNN). The ML Birth Certificate and ML Family Tree proposed in this research can address fundamental concerns about openness and traceability difficulties. While there are ways to make the training of machine learning models more visible, traceability is a key problem that can be achieved with an ML Birth Certificate proving the identification of a model as a solution to the relevant threats. However, this study aims to create a blockchain-backed ML Birth Certificate and ML Family Tree. Important information about training and model changes through retraining can be stored. An ML model should be immutable in the blockchain and available to any user to increase its security and traceability.

4.2   Evaluation

The impact of the concepts of ML Birth Certificate, ML Family Tree and the blockchain in which they are stored on the verifiability of ML models is evaluated below based on the defined use cases.

Use Case - Changed Environment: A company uses ML in a control system for a sorting machine. The model has been trained by the machine manufacturer and stored in the blockchain. The machine is maintained by an external service provider who also has access to the blockchain. The workpiece to be sorted is photographed as it passes the camera on a conveyor belt. The ML model assesses which quality category the workpiece should be sorted into based on the quality-giving areas on the workpiece. The sorting machine functioned as expected until the last maintenance, but after the maintenance the sorting machine largely sorted the workpieces into the wrong category. This led to manual re-sorting, which is labour-intensive and time-consuming. The company now wants to find out why this happens and how it can be avoided in the future. For this purpose, the machine manufacturer starts an audit. Using the stored error trigger rate, the machine manufacturer can determine that the machine has not been working as expected since the time of the last maintenance. Based on this information, the changed variables are checked. It turns out that the camera used for image capture is replaced. The camera mentioned in the ML Birth Certificate and the currently installed camera differ in one crucial point: the frame rate. The new camera is too slow to take a sharp picture of the workpiece on the conveyor belt. The result: the model no longer recognises the quality areas on the surface of the workpiece because they are out of focus.

Use Case - Wrong Model: A company places an order with an ML developer for the application of tool classification (Phillips screwdriver, slotted screwdriver and grooving tool). The developer adapts an existing model (ResNet50) in the area of tool classification to the required specifications. When the model is first tested with real images, it turns out that the desired accuracy cannot be achieved, regardless of which augmentation is used. To troubleshoot, the ML developer turns to a consulting firm that has access to the ML Family Tree and the ML Birth Certificate. An investigation shows that the parent model used contains too many parameters and is therefore too complex for the desired classification. Changing the parent model to ResNet18 brings the desired accuracy.

Use Case - Model Branching: A company uses a continuously trained ML model to optimise the production parameters of printed circuit boards (PCBs). Relearning is done to integrate knowledge gained (production process parameters) that improve the quality of the product into the model. With each relearning, a new ML Birth Certificate is created and attached to the ML Family Tree. Over a period of 12 months, the model was continuously trained, with training taking place every two days to improve the quality of the products. After 14 months, it was found that the quality of the PCBs produced had deteriorated significantly. An investigation revealed that the temperature during sintering of the ink must have been too low and therefore the conductive ink had detached from the dielectric board. Now an independent auditor has to find out why the temperature of the sintering process was not correct. The auditor consults the ML Family Tree and the ML Birth Certificates. An analysis of the training data showed a continuous change in the temperature readings, while the ambient temperature sensors showed no unusual change. It was found that sensor ageing due to the high temperatures of the sintering process caused the sensor to age faster than expected and led to an unexpected change in the readings. Based on the traceability of each model, it was determined that all models were faulty after month 10 and should no longer be used.

Use Case - Wrong Data Set: An ML model is to be developed for predicting product quality in the manufacture of turned parts made of steel. The data for the development has already been collected and a suitable model architecture identified. The development goes smoothly, but not the introduction of the model into the real environment, where it consistently gives an incorrect result. Initial troubleshooting (sensors were checked and calibrated) did not uncover the cause of the error. Both the introducing company and the ML developer verify the ML development process by inspecting the blockchain and the stored data. When comparing the collected data for training and evaluation, it turned out that the wrong data set was used for evaluation: not the data set for steel A36 as required, but steel grade 50, which has a different hardness. This was detected by the hash of the data set stored in the ML Birth Certificate.

Use Case - Faulty Data Augmentation: A contactless counting system based on ML is to be created for the production of stamped parts. For this purpose, a service provider takes pictures of the assembly line with a camera and counts the punched parts. Since the position of the ejected stamped parts varies greatly, the camera image covers a large area. However, it may happen that a punched part appears in the corner of the image. Data augmentation is used to reduce the effort of data acquisition. The model development went flawlessly. However, when the model is used in the company, it is found that the model counts incorrectly: Too few punched parts are counted compared to the samples taken by hand. The company's review of the ML Birth Certificate revealed that the increase in size was due to a rotation of the image. The rotation was supposed to cover position changes, but it rotated the stamp out of the image. This distorted the label and blank images were interpreted as images with stamped parts.

5   Conclusion

The vast majority of machine learning engineers and incident response personnel working in the sector do not have the necessary skills to protect enterprise-grade ML systems from attacks by malicious actors. Semi-automated data collection and blockchain technologies can help track the lifecycle of ML models to mitigate the risks of attacks on ML models and enable more comprehensive traceability of the development process. The blockchain and the concepts of ML Birth Certificates and the ML Family Tree presented here also help to record the lineage of models in more detail. This way, it is always clear on which data or model basis a model was trained or retrained. In addition, this approach enables retrospective checks in case of errors or mistrust in the ML life cycle by the developer, users or regulators. The performance evaluation will be a future research work and provide some ideas on possible tools etc. Proof of concept implementation of the proposed ML Family Tree and the ML Birth Certificates will be carried out. Apart from Hyperledger Fabric as the blockchain platform, MLFlow or tools compatible that can be used to manage the AI life cycle.

References

1. Leng, J., Wang, D., Shen, W., Li, X., Liu, Q., Chen, X.: Digital twins-based smart manufacturing system design in industry 4.0: a review. J. Manuf. Syst. **60**, 119–137 (2021)
2. Nagar, D., Raghav, S., Bhardwaj, A., Kumar, R., Singh, P.L., Sindhwani, R.: Machine learning: best way to sustain the supply chain in the era of industry 4.0. Mater. Today: Proc. **47**, 3676–3682 (2021)

3. ISO: ISO/IEC JTC 1/SC 42 - Artificial intelligence. https://www.iso.org/cms/render/live/en/sites/isoorg/contents/data/committee/67/94/6794475.html

4. Smuha, N.A.: The EU approach to ethics guidelines for trustworthy artificial intelligence. Comput. Law Rev. Int. **20**(4), 97–106 (2019)

5. Huang, L., Joseph, A., Nelson, B., Rubinstein, B., Tygar, J.: Proceedings of the 4th ACM Workshop on Security and Artificial Intelligence (2011)

6. Shumailov, I., Zhao, Y., Mullins, R., Anderson, R.: To compress or not to compress: understanding the interactions between adversarial attacks and neural network compression. In: Proceedings of Machine Learning and Systems, vol. 1, pp. 230–240 (2019)

7. Nguyen, A., Yosinski, J., Clune, J.: Deep neural networks are easily fooled: high confidence predictions for unrecognizable images. In: Proceedings of the IEEE Conference on Computer Vision and Pattern Recognition, pp. 427–436 (2015)

8. McGraw, G., Bonett, R., Shepardson, V., Figueroa, H.: The top 10 risks of machine learning security. Computer **53**(6), 57–61 (2020)

9. Pitropakis, N., Panaousis, E., Giannetsos, T., Anastasiadis, E., Loukas, G.: A taxonomy and survey of attacks against machine learning. **34**, 100199. https://www.sciencedirect.com/science/article/pii/S1574013718303289

10. Cheatham, B., Javanmardian, K., Samandari, H.: Confronting the risks of artificial intelligence. http://ceros.mckinsey.com/unintended-consequences-desktop

11. Mitchell, M., et al.: Model cards for model reporting. In: Proceedings of the Conference on Fairness, Accountability, and Transparency, pp. 220–229 (2019)

12. Arnold, M., et al.: FactSheets: increasing trust in AI services through supplier's declarations of conformity. http://arxiv.org/abs/1808.07261

13. IBM Research: AI FactSheets 360. https://aifs360.mybluemix.net/examples/aifs360.mybluemix.net/examples

14. Rubasinghe, I., Meedeniya, D., Perera, I.: Traceability management with impact analysis in devops based software development. In: 2018 International Conference on Advances in Computing, Communications and Informatics (ICACCI), pp. 1956–1962. IEEE (2018)

15. Kreuzberger, D., Kühl, N., Hirschl, S.: Machine learning operations (MLOps): overview, definition, and architecture. arXiv preprint arXiv:2205.02302 (2022)

16. Cheatham, B., Javanmardian, K., Samandari, H.: Unintended Consequences. http://ceros.mckinsey.com/unintended-consequences-desktop

17. Goldblum, M., et al.: Dataset security for machine learning: data poisoning, backdoor attacks, and defenses. IEEE Trans. Pattern Anal. Mach. Intell. **45**, 1563–1580 (2022)

18. Panda, A., Mahloujifar, S., Bhagoji, A.N., Chakraborty, S., Mittal, P.: SparseFed: mitigating model poisoning attacks in federated learning with sparsification. In: International Conference on Artificial Intelligence and Statistics, pp. 7587–7624. PMLR (2022)

19. Rezaei, S., Liu, X.: A target-agnostic attack on deep models: exploiting security vulnerabilities of transfer learning. arXiv preprint arXiv:1904.04334 (2019)

20. Amershi, S., et al.: Software engineering for machine learning: a case study. In: 2019 IEEE/ACM 41st International Conference on Software Engineering: Software Engineering in Practice (ICSE-SEIP), pp. 291–300. IEEE (2019)

21. Wirth, R., Hipp, J.: CRISP-DM: towards a standard process model for data mining. In: Proceedings of the 4th International Conference on the Practical Applications of Knowledge Discovery and Data Mining, Manchester, vol. 1, pp. 29–39 (2000)

22. Pannucci, C.J., Wilkins, E.G.: Identifying and avoiding bias in research. Plast. Reconstr. Surg. **126**(2), 619 (2010)

23. Davis, R.E., Couper, M.P., Janz, N.K., Caldwell, C.H., Resnicow, K.: Interviewer effects in public health surveys. Health Educ. Res. **25**(1), 14–26 (2010)

24. Hannon, L., DeFina, R.: Just skin deep? The impact of interviewer race on the assessment of African American respondent skin tone. Race Soc. Probl. **6**(4), 356–364 (2014)

25. Choi, B.C.K., Pak, A.W.P.: Bias, overview. Wiley StatsRef: Statistics Reference Online (2014)
26. Gibbons, B.C., Chambers, M.C., Monroe, M.E., Tabb, D.L., Payne, S.H.: Correcting systematic bias and instrument measurement drift with mzRefinery. Bioinformatics **31**(23), 3838–3840 (2015)
27. Zhang, X., Wang, C.: Measurement bias and error correction in a two-stage estimation for multilevel IRT models. Br. J. Math. Stat. Psychol. **74**, 247–274 (2021)
28. CloudFactory: The Ultimate Guide to Data Labeling for Machine Learning. https://www.cloudfactory.com/data-labeling-guide
29. Things that Can go Wrong During Annotation and How to Avoid Them. https://kili-technology.com/blog/things-that-can-go-wrong-during-annotation-and-how-to-avoid-them
30. Al Kuwatly, H., Wich, M., Groh, G.: Identifying and measuring annotator bias based on annotators' demographic characteristics. In: Proceedings of the Fourth Workshop on Online Abuse and Harms, pp. 184–190 (2020)
31. Zheng, A., Casari, A.: Feature Engineering for Machine Learning: Principles and Techniques for Data Scientists. O'Reilly Media, Inc. (2018)
32. He, X., Zhao, K., Chu, X.: AutoML: a survey of the state-of-the-art. Knowl.-Based Syst. **212**, 106622 (2021)
33. Feurer, M., Hutter, F.: Hyperparameter optimization. In: Hutter, F., Kotthoff, L., Vanschoren, J. (eds.) Automated Machine Learning. TSSCML, pp. 3–33. Springer, Cham (2019). https://doi.org/10.1007/978-3-030-05318-5_1
34. Akiba, T., Sano, S., Yanase, T., Ohta, T., Koyama, M.: Optuna: a next-generation hyperparameter optimization framework. In: Proceedings of the 25th ACM SIGKDD International Conference on Knowledge Discovery & Data Mining, pp. 2623–2631 (2019)
35. Androulaki, E., et al.: Hyperledger fabric: a distributed operating system for permissioned blockchains. In: Proceedings of the Thirteenth EuroSys Conference, pp. 1–15 (2018)
36. Benet, J.: IPFS-content addressed, versioned, P2P file system. arXiv preprint arXiv:1407.3561 (2014)
37. Nakaike, T., Zhang, Q., Ueda, Y., Inagaki, T., Ohara, M.: Hyperledger fabric performance characterization and optimization using GoLevelDB benchmark. In: 2020 IEEE International Conference on Blockchain and Cryptocurrency (ICBC), pp. 1–9. IEEE (2020)
38. Stodt, J., Schönle, D., Reich, C., Ghovanlooy Ghajar, F., Welte, D., Sikora, A.: Security audit of a blockchain-based industrial application platform. Algorithms **14**(4), 121 (2021)
39. Ghovanlooy Ghajar, F., Sikora, A., Welte, D.: Schloss: blockchain-based system architecture for secure industrial IoT. Electronics **11**(10), 1629 (2022)

Sentence Classification Using Quantum Natural Language Processing and Comparison of Optimization Methods

K. M. M. Rajashekharaiah[1]([⊠]) [ID], Satyadhyan Chickerur[2] [ID],
Goutam Hegde[1] [ID], Subrahmanya L. Bhat[1] [ID], and Shubham Annappa Sali[1] [ID]

[1] School of Computer Science and Engineering, K L E Technological University,
Hubballi 580 031, Karnataka, India
kmmr@kletech.ac.in
[2] Centre for High Performance Computing, K L E Technological University,
Hubballi 580 031, Karnataka, India
chickerursr@kletech.ac.in

Abstract. The natural language processing (NLP) demands high computing resourses to process language related problems. The evolution of quantum computing hardware and simulators create avenues to design and develop NLP methods to test on these platforms. This research uses quantum natural language processing (QNLP) to simulate the sentence classification and compares optimization techniques (Simultaneous perturbation stochastic approximation: SPSA and convergent optimization via most-promising-area stochastic search: COMPASS) for small dataset and simple sentence structures and the results are promising to show that with the COMPASS optimization technique the model performs better Table 1. When the ansatz depth is less and vice-versa. The research in quantum natural language processing is infancy, the simulation results are promising and the better results can be expected for large datasets with different sentence structures if real quantum computers are available in near future.

Keywords: Quantum Computing · Quantum Natural Language Processing (QNLP) · SPSA · COMPASS · Binary Classification · DISCOCAT Model

1 Introduction

Natural language processing (NLP) problems like automatic summarization, machine translation, information retrieval and sentiment analysis and few of these involve sentence classification, where they often require high computing resources to understand sentence meanings. The advent of quantum computing promises the computational speed up exponentially higher than the present classical computing. Then the apparent question is whether this model of computing

K L E Technological University.

can also be applied to natural language processing. If this becomes true, such approach may be the end of finding a computing model for speed ups matching to address the language related problems.The Quantumness of computing field is infancy in research and the majority of the effort in this computing model is theoretical or its realization is carried out as simulation on classical platform.

The research in quantum computing led to the development of quantum computers accessible are termed Noisy Intermediate Scale Quantum (NISQ) devices, assuring some success in implementation of application in various domains like text analysis, cryptography, medicine, machine learning and cloud computing. The other aspects with this new computing paradigm, the information representation and encoding of information may direct to theoretical and realistic advances in representing and dealing out language related issues beyond computational speed ups. Motivated by theses view points, the quantum natural language processing (QNLP) a new paradigm of innovation targeted to develop the NLP models to run on quantum hardware (NISQ) or simulator. Most of the work in this area is theoretical and the experiments are classically simulated. However the recent work [7] shows the implementation of QNLP model on real quantum hardware in a very small scale.

This research follow the work [15] and tests the capabilities of the QNLP model by increasing the data set size and compare the results by using the optimization techniques such as SPSA (Simultaneous Perturbation Stochastic Approximation) and COMPASS minimization techniques with different depths of ansatz (discussed in next sections). The observations are the COMPASS optimization technique give good classification accuracy in comparison with SPSA for low depth of ansatz and vice versa for higher depth of ansatz. The content of this paper is structured as: the Sect. 2 covers the related work; in the Sect. 3 we discuss the basics of quantum computing and model of meaning with the help of DisCoCat model that helps to understand the how the quantum computing is native to NLP. The methodology is explained in Sect. 4, here the pipeline of information encoding, the circuit representation, and model training and optimization techniques discussed. The results are discussed in Sect. 5 for different optimization techniques and finally conclusions are drawn in Sect. 6.

2   Related Works

The QNLP is a field of research still in its early years; however the following references embody the knowledge of general quantum computing and quantum information to understand quantum environment and natural language processing. Nelson and Isaac [1] disseminated introduction to quantum computing and quantum information that prelude for researchers in this domain. Lee J O'Riordan et al., [2] presented the idea for encoding corpus to the quantum circuit model with reference to DisCoCat formalism which is convenient and native to how the quantum information is processed. The Johannes Bausch et al., [3] designed the quantum algorithm for finding the globally optimal parse with high success probability for context sensitivity of language models, which is quadratically faster than classical methods very useful in NLP. Bob Coecke [4] discusses a very useful theoretical and arithmetical foundation for near term natural language processing with the starting point, the DisCoCat brand of natural language processing. Joachim Lambek [5] explains a computational algebraic approach to grammar.

Dea Bankova et al., [6] introduced a idea of entailment, exploiting ideas from the categorical semantics of partial know K L E Technological University ledge in quantum computing theory, this shows that entailment strength lifts compositionally the sentence level, giving a lower bound on sentence entailment. They explain the necessary properties of graded entailment such as continuity, and provide a process for calculating entailment strength. Konstantinos Meichanetzidis et al., [7] developed a QNLP model to demonstrate it is NISQ friendly and promises scalability as the feature of the quantum hardware improves over a time. Relying on the algebra of pregorups [8] proposed a mathematical framework with diagrammatic calculus which explains how the information flow among the words in a sentence in order to make up the meaning of complete sentence and which helps to compare the meaning of the words in the distributional model. Bharti et al., [9] explained many hybrid classical-quantum algorithms with Noisy Intermediate Scale Quantum (NISQ) technology which motivates to design algorithms for NISQ. The greater part of previously demonstrable quantum machine learning (QML) protocols are based on variational quantum circuit methods (VQC) (Benedetti et al., 2019) [10,11]. Ramesh and Vinay [12] present quantum speed-ups for string matching which is significant for language identification. Recently [7] implemented QNLP and optimized on a NISQ device the classifier with a small dataset size of 16 sentences. The current work presents the testing the performance of the QNLP model by increasing the data set size and compare the results by using the optimization techniques such as SPSA(Simultaneous Perturbation Stochastic Approximation) [15] and COMPASS (Convergent Optimization Via Most-Promising-Area Stochastic Search) minimization techniques with different depths of ansatz(discussed in next sections) [16].

3   Quantum Computing and Model of Meaning Framework

3.1   Quantum Computing Background

Giving the complete knowledge of quantum computing and quantum information is beyond the scope of this paper, the reader is directed to the text [1]. However, to be a self explainable manuscript, this section will describe the theory and the terminology behind quantum computing who had no experience of quantum computing and quantum information. The natural starting point is a "qubit" which is the basic component of storage unit in quantum computing and is analogous to a "bit" in classical computing. It is connected with a property of a physical system such as the roll of an electron ('up' or 'down' along some axis) or the polarization of a single photon in which the two states can be considered to be the vertical polarization and the horizontal polarization [18]. As classical bit has a state - either 0 or 1 - a qubit also has a state. Two possible states for a qubit are the states $|0\rangle$ and $|1\rangle$, which as you might guess correspond to the states 0 and 1 for a classical bit. Notation like '$|\ \rangle$' is called the Dirac notation, and we'll be seeing it frequently, as it's the standard notation for states in quantum mechanics. The difference between bits and qubits is that a qubit can be in a state(ψ) other than $|0\rangle$ or $|1\rangle$. It is also possible to form linear combinations of states; it is called superposition [1]:

$$|\psi\rangle = \alpha|0\rangle + \beta|1\rangle$$

The numbers α and β are complex numbers, even though for many purposes not much is lost by considering them as real numbers. The state of a qubit is also represented as a vector in a two-dimensional complex vector space. The states $|0\rangle$ and $|1\rangle$ are known as computational basis states, and form an orthonormal basis for this vector space. We can examine a bit to determine whether it is in the state 0 or 1. Instead, quantum mechanics tells us that we can only acquire much more restricted information about the quantum state. When we measure a qubit we get either the result 0, with probability $|\alpha|^2$, or the result 1, with probability $|\beta|^2$. The $|\alpha|^2 + |\beta|^2 = 1$, given that the probabilities must sum to one. Geometrically, we can infer this as the condition that the qubit's state be normalized to length 1. Thus, in general a qubit's state is a unit vector in a two-dimensional vector space.

Quantum theory is a probabilistic theory which predicts the probabilities for the outcomes of 0 and 1. An isolated qubit's evolution before being measured is explained by changing the state of the qubit by applying a unitary linear map U i.e. $|\psi'\rangle = U|\psi\rangle$. Figure 1 represents such evolution.

The combined state space of the q qubit is given by tensor product of individual state spaces. So the dimension is 2^q. For two uncorrelated qubits $|\psi 1\rangle = \alpha 1|0\rangle + \beta 1|1\rangle$ and $|\psi 2\rangle = \alpha 2|0\rangle + \beta 2|1\rangle$ the joint space is [15]

$$|\psi 1\rangle \otimes |\psi 2\rangle = (\alpha 1\alpha 2, \alpha 1\beta 2, \beta 1\alpha 2, \beta 1\beta 2)$$

The combination of multiple qubits that interact with each other for a particular task is described by unitary map acting on the overall state space. The diagrammatic representation from Fig. 1 then extends also to a quantum circuit, such as the example shown in Fig. 2. Quantum circuit is a model for quantum computation, it consists of quantum gates. All the nouns appear as effects in the quantum circuit. Generally effects can be generated by using Rx gate or combination of Rx and Rz gate. The cups are replaces with bell state in quantum circuit. The bell effect is generated by combining a CNOT gate and a Hadamard gate. The triangle and parallel boxes represents the tensor products of states and unitary maps respectively. The sequential connections of boxes represents composition of linear maps. The quantum circuit is designed such that it will be a function of outcome probabilities. When the quantum circuit is run on the hardware, the qubits are measured. We have to run the circuits multiple times to obtain the statistics for the outcome probabilities. In order to obtain the result for a given problem, the design of the circuit has to encode the problem such

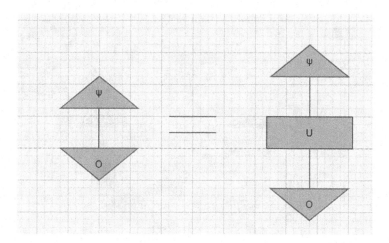

Fig. 1. Basic example of the diagrammatic representation, here of $\langle 0|\psi'\rangle = \langle 0|U|\psi'\rangle$, i.e. The evolution of a qubit in initial state $|\psi\rangle$ with unitary map U and then composed with the effect $h\langle\,0\,|$, corresponding to the (non- deterministic) outcome '0'.

that that result is a function of the outcome probabilities. Hence, the selection of circuit is important [14].

The reason for high supremacy of quantum computing is quantum parallelism. We can create exponentially huge superpositions for the solution space of a problem. With more number of qubits, quantum computers supremacy increases exponentially. Adding extra transistors to a classical computer only increases power linearly; this is not the case here. In Quantum Computing there is another important property called as Entanglement. Here a pair's two individuals exist in a single quantum state. When one of the qubits' states is altered, the other one will instantly and predictably change as well.

The qubits are prone to noise and errors from the environment. A quantum computer that will be give advantage in solving large scale problems comes with more number of fault tolerant qubits. It will be helpful for solving some algorithms that is hard to be solved using classical computer. The currently available quantum computer known as noisy intermediate scale quantum computers comes with about 100 and is useful for development of theory and applications.

3.2   DisCoCat Model

The main model used in this work is DISCOCAT of Coecke et al. (2010). The complete discussion of DisCoCat model and how the quantum computing is native of NLP is beyond the scope of this research, however it directs to the text [4]. The fact that, the quantum computing environment and natural language share the make use of vector spaces for describing states albeit for very different reasons makes those two theories (essentially) coincide. Therefore we say that quantum natural language processing is the "quantum-native". What

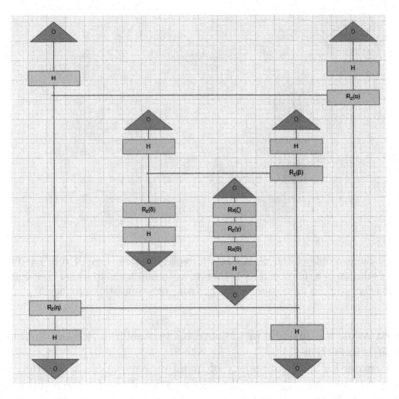

Fig. 2. The quantum circuit, which contains most of the gates related to this paper: the Hadamard H gate, the X-rotation gate $Rx(\beta)$ by angle β, the controlled Z rotation gate, a component of which is a Z-rotation gate $Rz(\delta)$ by angle δ, and the quantum CNOT gate.

this implies is that natural language fit on quantum hardware, for the obvious reason that we have adopted a quantum model for language processing [4]. This is similar to simulation of quantum systems having been identified as a problem that would require a quantum computer [19]. But this of course hasn't stopped people from doing simulation of quantum systems on classical hardware. Category composition distribution semantics (also known as DisCoCat) uses category theory to combine the advantages of two very different approaches to linguistics: category grammars and distribution semantics. DisCoCat diagram represents the sentences in terms of string diagrams. The main reason for the use of DISCO-CAT model in QNLP is that the underlying compact-closed structures provide the concept of Hilbert Space formulation of quantum theory. In this model the meaning of a word is expressed in a tensor, and the order is determined by the type of words expressed in a pregroup grammar. In this model a type p has left(pl) and right(pr) adjuncts and there are two reduction rules in the grammar [14].

$$p.p^l \rightarrow 1 \text{ and } p.p^r \rightarrow 1 \tag{1}$$

We use 'n' and 's' as atomic types to represent nouns and sentences respectively so type of transitive verb become $n^r.s.n^l$. For example sentence, Man prepares Dinner can be derived as

$$n.(n^l.s.n^r).n \rightarrow (n.n^r).s.(n^l.n) \rightarrow 1.s.1 \rightarrow s. \tag{2}$$

This indicates that the sentence is grammatically correct. The diagrammatic representation for the above sentence is

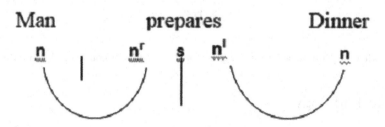

Fig. 3. Diagrammatic representation of a sentence

In Fig. 3, the "cups" (∪) denote the grammar reductions. The conversion from pregroups to vector space semantics is achieved by a mapping F that sends atomic types to vector spaces (n to N and s to S) and composite types to tensor product spaces ($n^r.s.n^l$ to N⊗S⊗N). For example, a transitive verb becomes a tensor of order 3, which can be seen as a bilinear map N⊗N → S, while an adjective (with type n.nl) can be seen as a matrix, representing a linear map N→N. Further, F translates all grammar reductions to tensor contractions, so that the meaning of a sentence s = w1w2 ... wn with a pregroup derivation α is given by:

$$s = F(\alpha)[w1 \bigotimes w2 \bigotimes ... \bigotimes wn] \tag{3}$$

Here, F turns α into a linear map that, apply to the tensor product of the word representations, by tensor-contracting that expression returns a vector for the complete sentence. As a concrete example, the meaning of the sentence "Man prepares Dinner" becomes s = m.P.d, where m, d ∈ N and L ∈ N ⊗ S ⊗ N. Above, P is a tensor of order 3, and s is a vector in S. Note that the underlying field of the vector spaces is not specified, and can, e.g., be R or C depending on the particular type of model (it is C in this work) [14]. Meaning computations like the instance above can be suitably represented by means of the diagrammatic calculus of compact closed categories [1], where the boxes refer to tensors, the order of which is determined by the number of their wires, while the cups are now the tensor contractions. Note the correspondence between the pregroup diag ram above with the one here, and how the grammatical derivation successfully dictates equally the shapes of the tensors and the contractions. These string diagrams logically are mapped to quantum circuits, as used in quantum computation [14] (Fig. 4).

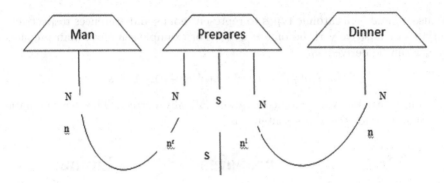

Fig. 4. Meaning computations as diagrammatic calculus of compact closed categories

4   Methodology

The previous section explained the quantum computing equivalent to classical programming involves the application of quantum gates on qubits according to a quantum circuit and the DisCoCat model. This section explains the methodology for sentence classification i.e. in particular the process of how to go from a sentence to its representation as a quantum circuit, on the basis of which the model predicts the label. Figure 2 presents the flow chart for the process of sentence classification using QNLP (Fig. 5).

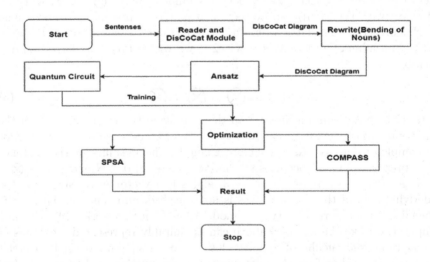

Fig. 5. Process pipeline of sentence classification in QNLP

The initial step is to obtain a syntax tree equivalent to the sentence, on the basis of which a DISCOCAT derivation is produced in a diagrammatic form.

To evade computational complications, this diagram is first optimized to yield the input into an ansatz that then determines the authentic translation into a quantum circuit [14,19]. The generated quantum circuit then executed on a simulator. These steps are described in more detail below.

Step 1: For the natural language experiments with large number of sentences (1000 and more) of different structures, the application of a pregroup parser to generate the syntax trees would be needed. However the current work considers the sentences with limited vocabulary and the small number of different grammatical structures. For example, with nouns, adjectives and transitive verbs having the respective types as n, $n.n^l$ and $n^r.n.n^l$, the sentence "person debugs useful software" is parsed as below:

$$n.(n^r.s.n^l).(n.n^l).n \rightarrow$$
$$(n.n^r).s.(n^l.n).(n^l.n) \rightarrow 1.s.1.1 \rightarrow s \qquad (4)$$

Step 2: Drawing the DISCOCAT diagram representing each word as a state and represent each reduction rule with cups. As discussed in the previous section, the following diagram represents linear-algebraic operations between tensors in vector spaces N, S and tensor products of them. For expediency, we also include the pregroup types as a reminder of the grammatical rules involved in each contraction. For the remainder of this paper, only the pregroup types will be shown since they are indicative of the vector spaces they are mapped to (Fig. 6).

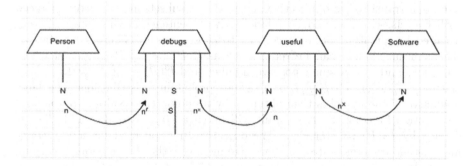

Fig. 6. DisCoCat representation of a sentence

Step 4: Mapping of DISCOCAT diagrams to quantum circuit. This is the step where abstract DisCoCat representation (Fig. 7) is mapped to specific quantum circuit. After the choice of ansatz (parameterization) every DisCoCat diagram is mapped to quantum circuit. The mapping of DisCoCat to quantum circuit is follows. Mapping of DisCoCat model to quantum circuit is determined by the choice of number of qubits qn and qs used to map n and s, choice of parameterized quantum and word states (effects) called ansatz. Each cup in DISCOCAT model is equivalent to Bell effect. Bell effect can be generated by using a CNOT gate with a Hadamard gate. The number of qubits in the circuit is determined by the number of adjectives and transitive verbs in the sentences. Adjectives are states on 2 qubits and transitive verb are states on 3 qubits. The choice for number of qubits used for sentence $q_s = 1$. All the nouns appear as effects in the quantum circuit. These effects can be generated in two ways. First ways is to use two Rx gate and one Rz gate or we can use simply one Rx gate to generate qubit effects. Single parameter gives a more economical option that is considered. Therefore choice of parameter can be $p_n \in \{3, 1\}$. The next choice is consider the number of IQP (Instantaneous Quantum Polynomial [14] layers. For a circuit containing m qubits all are initialized to zero state. Followed by IQP layers, each of this IQP layer contains a Hadamard gate on each Qubit (To bring qubits to superposition or initial state) and m-1 controlled Rz gate connects adjacent qubits. The choice of IQP layers considered here are $d \in \{1, 2\}$ to keep the circuit depth small. So totally three hyperparameters are considered $(q_s, p_n, d) q_s = 1(fixed), p_n \in \{1, 3\}, d \in \{1, 2\}$. The total number of parameters is represented using k and it depends on size of vocabulary. The below figure Fig No 8: shows the quantum circuit corresponding to the DisCoCat diagram in Fig No 7.

Step 5: Model training and Optimization

The dataset used for the experiment consists of 150 sentences. The dataset were partitioned into 3 subsets namely training (90), test (35) and development (35) sets. The sentences used in the dataset are mainly of 4 grammatical structures. They are noun_tranisitive verb_noun, noun_transitive verb_adjective_noun, adjective_noun_transitive verb_noun, adjective_noun_transitive verb_adjective_noun. All the subsets are perfectly balanced with two classes (food and IT related). Every sentence in the dataset is represented by quantum circuit according to chosen ansatz. The output state of the quantum circuits can be represented as $l_\theta^i(P) := ||\langle i|P(\theta)\rangle|^2 - \varepsilon|$ where $i \in (0, 1)$ and ε is a small positive number and $l_\theta^0(P) + l_\theta^1(P) \leq 1$, so that $l_\theta(P) := (l_\theta^0(P), l_\theta^1(P))/(\sum_i l_\theta^i(P))$ defines probability distribution. The label predicted by the model is then obtained by rounding the results of probability distribution function. So that result will be either 0 or 1(food or IT). This is defined by $L_\theta(P) := \lfloor(l_\theta(P))\rfloor$. The objective function used for model training is standard cross-entropy. If we assume L(P) the actual label according to the data. The cost function is given by $C(\theta) := \sum_{P \in T} L(P)^T .\log(l_\theta(P))$. Optimization algorithms are used for minimizing the cost function by $C(\theta)$ [15]. There are mainly two types of optimization techniques used in the experiment namely SPSA (Simultaneous Perturbation Stochastic Approximation) and COMPASS (Convergent Optimization Via Most-Promising-Area Stochastic Search).The results of both optimization techniques are compared for various parameters. Both the optimization algorithms are explained below.

Simultaneous perturbation stochastic approximation (SPSA)

SPSA is a method for minimizing differentiable multivariate functions. It is useful for those function for which calculating gradient is resource intensive or not possible. Similar to gradient descent SPSA is also iterative optimization

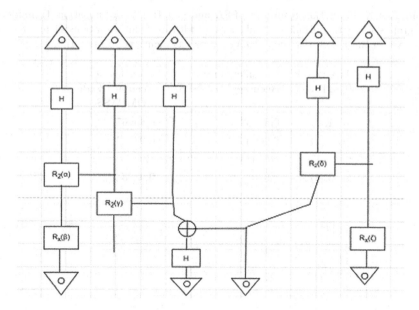

Fig. 7. Quantum circuit for a DisCoCat diagram

algorithm. The main feature of SPSA is that the objective function requires only two measurements regardless of the dimension of optimization problem. SPSA is most appropriate for high-dimensional problems where there is a requirement of determining many terms in the optimization process [13].

Compass Search Optimization (COMPASS) Compass (convergent optimiza- tion via most-promising-area stochastic search) is a optimization algorithm based on random search [16]. It is a search algorithm that does not use derivatives In this algorithm most promising region at each step is very adaptive which is chosen from a predetermined nested sets. Primarily all practical solutions are considered to be equally promising. Once some solutions have been visited, the promising index of every feasible solution is the sample mean performance of the visited solution that is closest to it. COMPASS solves a wide range of problems, including problems with very large numbers of feasible solutions, and works bet- ter than some of the existing algorithms COMPASS converges with probability 1 to a set of local optimal solutions and that it has robust finite-time performance. But the algorithm is not guaranteed to find a global minimum. It can be easily attracted to local minimum.

Step 6: Model testing After training the model, it will be used for predicting the labels for test dataset. Then the accuracy is calculated for the test data and the graphs for accuracy and cost are drawn.

5   Results and Discussions

The simulation is conducted on both Quantum IBM experience and Google colab. The libraries used for experiments are, Lambeq, Pytket (python module for interfacing with CQC (Cambridge Quantum Computing)) a set of quantum

Table 1. The Simulation results of SPSA and COMPASS optimization Techniques. The graphs for both optimization algorithms with different variations of parameters are shown in the Fig. 8. For the results obtained as mentioned in the Table 1.

Ansatz (Qs, Pn, d)	Classification Accuracy with SPSA	Classification Accuracy with COMPASS
(1, 1, 1)	0.633334	0.86667
(1, 1, 2)	0.966667	0.93334
(1, 3, 1)	0.533336	1.0
(1, 3, 2)	1.0	0.93334

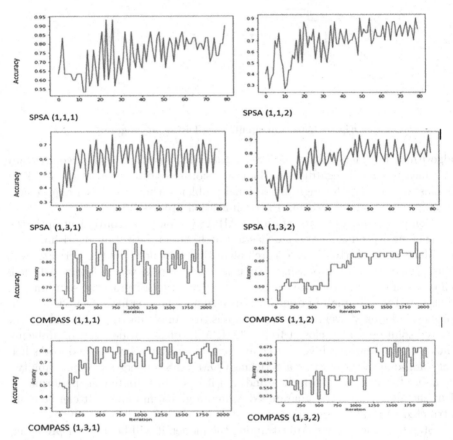

Fig. 8. The performance of model optimization Techniques SPSA and COMPASS with various parameter.

computing programming tools. The python library Noisyopt used for optimizing noisy functions. SPSA and COMPASS from Noisyopt and other supporting tools. The Table 1, shows the simulation results. The table shows that the Compass optimization algorithm gives good results for the quantum circuits with depth = 1. SPSA optimization algorithm gives good results for the circuits with depth = 2. Compass is not robust to noise but gives good results for the quantum circuits with minimum depth. SPSA is robust to noise so noises are less likely to hinder the optimization process. Quantum circuits with larger depth (large number of qubits) contains more noise and the dimension of the optimization problem is also large in this case. As SPSA is robust to noise and gives good results for high dimensional optimization problem, the SPSA algorithm gives high accuracy for quantum circuits with more depth.

6 Conclusion

In this work we have simulated the sentence classification using QNLP on classical system with moderate data set size. This work also compares two machine learning model optimization techniques namely SPSA and COMPASS. The classification accuracy obtained by using SPSA and COMPASS for the parameters $(1, 1, 1), (1, 1, 2), (1, 3, 1), (1, 3, 2)$ are 0.63334, 0.96667, 0.53336, 1.0 and 0.86667, 0.93334, 1.0, 0.93334 respectively. The results are promising to show that with the COMPASS optimization technique the model performs better Table 1 when the ansatz depth is less and vice-versa if the optimization technique is SPSA Table 1. The research in QNLP is infancy and the implementations can be realized with large data set of different sentence format if the real quantum computer is available in the near feature.

References

1. Nielsen, M.A., Chuang, I.L.: Quantum Computation and Quantum Information: 10th Anniversary Edition, 10th edn. Cambridge University Press, New York (2011)
2. O'Riordan, L.J., Doyle, M., Baruffa, F., Kannan, V.: A hybrid classical-quantum workflow for natural language processing. Mach. Learn.: Sci. Technol. 2(1), 015011 (2020)
3. Bausch, J., Subramanian, S., Piddock, S.: A quantum search decoder for natural language processing (2020)
4. Coecke, B., de Felice, G., Meichanetzidis, K., Toumi, A.: Foundations for near-term quantum natural language processing (2020)
5. Lambek, J.: From Word to Sentence. Polimetrica, Milan (2008)
6. Bankova, D., Coecke, B., Lewis, M., Marsden, D.: Graded entailment for compositional distributional semantics. J. Lang. Modell. 6(2), 225–260 (2019)
7. Meichanetzidis, K., Toumi, A., de Felice, G., Coecke, B.: Grammar-aware question-answering on quantum computers (2020)
8. Coecke, B., Sadrzadeh, M., Clark, S.: Mathematical foundations for a compositional distributional model of meaning. Linguist. Anal. 36, 345–384 (2010)
9. Bharti, K., et al.: Noisy intermediate-scale quantum (NISQ) algorithms (2021)
10. Benedetti, M., Lloyd, E., Sack, S., Fiorentini, M.: Parameterized Quantum Circuits as Machine Learning Models. Quantum Sci. Technol. 4(4), 043001 (2019)

11. Rajashekharaiah, K.M.M., et al.: Transfer learning using variational quantum circuits. In: Garg, D., Jagannathan, S., Gupta, A., Garg, L., Gupta, S. (eds.) IACC 2021. Communications in Computer and Information Science, vol. 1528, pp. 254–267. Springer, Cham (2022). https://doi.org/10.1007/978-3-030-95502-1_20

12. Ramesh, H., Vinay, V.: String matching in O(n+m) quantum time. J. Discrete Algorithms **1**(1), 103–110 (2003). Combinatorial Algorithms

13. Spall, J.C.: Implementation of the simultaneous perturbation algorithm for stochastic optimization. IEEE Trans. Aerosp. Electron. Syst. **34**(3), 817–823 (1998)

14. Lorenz,R., Pearson, A., Meichanetzidis, K., Kartsaklis, D., Coecke, B.: QNLP in practice: running compositional models of meaning on a quantum computer. arXiv:2102.12846 [cs.CL] (2021)

15. Spall, J.C.: Implementation of the simultaneous perturbation algorithm for stochastic optimization. IEEE Trans. Aerosp. Electron. Syst. **34**(3), 817–823 (1988)

16. Hong, L.J., Nelson, B.L.: Discrete optimization via simulation using COMPASS. Oper. Res. **54**(1), 115–129 (2006)

17. https://en.wikipedia.org/wiki/Qubit

18. Feynman, R.P.: Simulating physics with computers. Int. J. Theor. Phys. **21**(6/7), 467 (1982)

19. Grefenstette, E., Sadrzadeh, M.: Experimental support for a categorical compositional distributional model of meaning. In: Proceedings of the Conference on Empirical Methods in Natural Language processing, pp. 1394–1404. Association for Computational Linguistics (2011)

Dimension Reduction in the Sagittal Plane for Diagnosis of Mild Cognitive Impairment

Harsh Bhasin[1] , Vishal Deshwal[2(✉)] , and Arush Jasuja[3]

[1] Manav Rachna University, Faridabad, India
[2] International Centre for Neuromorphic Systems, MARCS Institute,
Western Sydney University, Sydney, NSW 2150, Australia
vishaldeshwal2106@gmail.com
[3] Ripik Technology Pvt. Ltd., Noida, Uttar Pradesh, India

Abstract. Dementia constitutes the major chunk of the diseases in elderly population. The preventive diagnostics of dementia may help the clinicians in handling the symptoms and delaying the progression of the disease. Mild cognitive impairment may be considered precursor to dementia. This work uses the structural-Magnetic Resonance Imaging data obtained from Alzheimer's Disease Neuroimaging Initiative to classify MCI-Converts from Non-Converts. The information from this 3-D data is difficult to handle using 2-D models, in which the correlation between the slices is lost, and the 3-D models, which are computationally expensive. The proposed model is able to find the correlation between slices of brain volume using s-MRI which grasps the correlation between the slices, is computationally efficient, uses less memory and performs better in comparison with the current state of the art. The work applies Independent Component Analysis and Principal Component Analysis to accomplish the above task. In addition to being more accurate than the state-of-the-art, the proposed model yields an accuracy of 87% with only 714 features.

Keywords: Mild Cognitive Impairment · Independent Component Analysis · Principle Component Analysis · Convolutional neural network

1 Introduction

As per the National Health Portal of India, nearly 20% of the people above the age of 80 suffer from dementia [1]. This causes immense suffering to not just the patients but also to their families. Furthermore, dementia cannot be cured but it is imperative to detect dementia early so that clinicians can treat the symptoms and delay the progression of the disease. Mild Cognitive Impairment (MCI) is a formative stage of dementia, particularly of Alzheimer's type. Cognitive abilities are impaired by MCI more so than by normal aging [2]. It is estimated that 15–20% percent of individuals with MCI progress to dementia each year [2]. There are two types of MCI patients: those who convert to Alzheimer's disease

© Springer Nature Switzerland AG 2023
D. Garg et al. (Eds.): IACC 2022, CCIS 1782, pp. 99–105, 2023.
https://doi.org/10.1007/978-3-031-35644-5_8

(MCI-C) and those who do not convert (MCI-NC). As part of this research, structural magnetic resonance imaging (s-MRI) data obtained from the Alzheimer's Disease Neuroimaging Initiative (ADNI) is used for developing the model to differentiate MCI-C from MCI-NC. This work uses the gray matter as its decrease is found responsible for dementia [3]. Owing to scarcity of specialists and resources, the diagnosis of cognitive impairment may be time consuming and expensive for a patient. The automated diagnosis of MCI not only handles these issues but also helps in better visualization. The researchers have applied conventional machine learning methods to accomplish this task [4,5]. These methods require crafting of a pipeline by choosing appropriate combinations of feature extraction and selection. This problem can be handled by using Deep learning methods which do not require explicit feature engineering [6,7]. The Convolutional Neural Networks are deep learning models specifically designed for imaging related tasks. These models may be divided into 2-D CNNs & 3-D CNNs. The former fail to grasp the correlation between the slices, whereas the latter are computationally very expensive. This work uses the s-MRI scans of the patients and the controls, which is a 3-D data. Also the structures in which the decrease in the gray matter is responsible for the impairment of cognitive abilities are 3-D, hence the model should be able to find the correlation between the slices of the volumes to accomplish this task. This problem has been earlier handled by applying PCA along the third axis of the s-MRI volume [13] and combination of PCA and t-SNE [8]. This work explores the applicability of ICA and random projection for the same. Finally, we combine the most relevant outputs of the three methods to generate the input for the CNN.

The contributions of this work is as follows:

1. The dimensionality in the 3rd axis of an s-MRI volume can be reduced while still retaining the pertinent information.
2. This work explores the possibility of combining ICA & PCA for the above task.
3. This work empirically establishes the supremacy of the proposed model vis-à-vis state of the art.

2   Materials and Method

2.1   Materials

"The datasets supporting the conclusions of this article are available in Alzheimer Disease Neuroimaging Initiative (ADNI) repository, Data used in the preparation of this article were obtained from ADNI database. The ADNI was launched in 2003 as a public-private partnership, led by Principal Investigator Michael W. Weiner, MD. The primary goal of ADNI has been to test whether Magnetic Resonance Imaging (MRI), PET, other biological markers, and clinical and neuropsychological assessment can be combined to measure the progression of MCI and early AD" [9] (Fig. 1).

In this study, we analyzed ADNI-2 subjects who had a one-year follow-up period. The patients with 3-D MRI scans and the corresponding neuropsycholog-

Fig. 1. Slices in s-MRI volume

ical assessments were selected and divided into two groups: MCI-C and MCI-NC. An assessment of dementia severity was conducted using the Clinical Dementia Rating (CDR). In the case of MCI-NC, the CDR score remains the same after one year, but in the case of MCI-C, the score has changed from 0.5 to 1. A total of 187 patients were selected, including 75 patients converted to Alzheimer's disease and 112 who did not. Participants in the study ranged from 75 to 100 years of age. During the collection of T1 weighted s-MRI images, the field strength was 1.5 T, the TE was 3.6099 ms, and the TR was 3000 ms.

2.2   Methods

The processing of data consumes considerable computing resources and storage capacity. It is difficult to determine the key features of the data when they are hidden within complex structures. This research aims to expose low-dimensional patterns in the gray matter without impairing the statistical distribution of its component. The task in hand is performed using various feature selection techniques including Independent Component Analysis (ICA), and Principal Component Analysis (PCA).

PCA was first introduced in a paper published by Pearson in 1901 [10]. It is a hierarchical coordinate system based on the statistical variation of the data that transforms the N-dimensional variables into an orthogonal coordinate system in which each coordinate is ordered from greatest variance to least variance [11]. A restructured coordinate system is employed using PCA to transform the data so that the maximum variance is located on the first coordinate, followed by the second most significant variance in the second coordinate, and so on. An uncorrelated dimension with a maximum variance is retained by PCA. An eigen decomposition is carried out on a covariance matrix, the elements of this matrix represent covariance between features. As a result of PCA, a reduced number of features is extracted. This will represent the original volume in a compressed manner whilst capturing up to a certain portion of its variance [12]. Although PCA can extract and create feature maps that can represent substantial variance in data, in some cases the nature of the problem requires maximum separation between the groups, like in this study the given groups are MCI and MCI-NC (Fig. 2).

While PCA seeks to maximize variance to determine correlation, independent component analysis (ICA) seeks to maximize independence [13]. In this method, the observed data are linearly decomposed into statistically independent components. It is predicated on the premise that the components are non-Gaussian distributed and have zero mutual information. Furthermore, all the

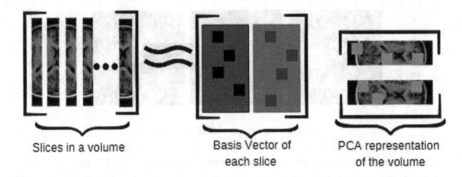

Slices in a volume   Basis Vector of   PCA representation
                            each slice   of the volume

Fig. 2. PCA on slices of volume

features are constructed in such a way that there is a high level of mutual information between them. In order to extract image features, a sparse basis function is used for applying the improved independent component analysis algorithm [14]. The algorithm is sparse and converges quickly since it does not require extensive optimization of high-level complex functions. This study aims to create a low-dimensional feature map that can represent the change in gray matter with the same statistical distribution as that of the original gray matter volume across all slices. It can facilitate the resolution of the problem of classifying MCI-C and MCI-NC using models that are less computationally expensive (Refer Fig. 3).

2.3 Proposed Method

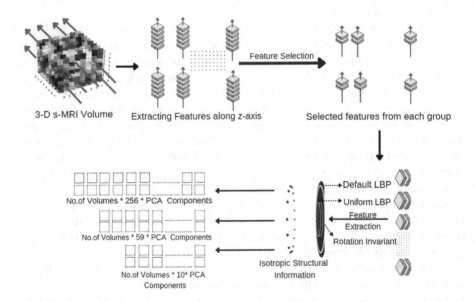

Fig. 3. Proposed Model

Figure 3 shows the pipeline used for creating efficient features for classifying MCI-C and MCI-NC. Through the application of PCA & ICA, two different sets of features are created. In the given dataset, every volume is composed of 166 slices. Consider each slice in the volume as a 2-dimensional sheet stacked along the z-axis in a three-dimensional space. Next, imagine inserting a pin through all sheets at 90 degree on the z-axis. With the pin removed, there will be 166 pixels, one from each slice. Using the feature selection technique to analyze this 1-D array of 166 pixels, two principal components are identified. The aim is to represent the slices across the volume in a way that enhances the spatial independence of contributions from individual slices within the volume and uncovers the dominating features of the respective slice. With this method, it is possible to capture changes in gray matter, as well as determine the basis projection for these changes. This not only removes the noise but also magnifies the relevant features. Similarly, repeat all steps 65536 times, as the slice dimensions are 256×256. This way we create two new slices based on the first and second principles. Instead of the 166 slices in the previous volume, the new volume consists of two slices, with the most relevant information preserved. Based on the S-MRI data provided, the following steps are performed each s-MRI volume:

1. A single pixel is extracted from each slice of the volume(256, 256, 166) along the z axis.
2. This resulted in 166 pixels being extracted total, i.e., one pixel per slice along the z axis from the same x, y coordinates.
3. PCA is applied to these selected pixels and the first two principal components are selected.
4. Repeat the step from 2 to 4 for all 256 * 256 pixels along z axis.
5. Create two new slices with first slice of 256 * 256 using 1st principal components, while a second slice is made from 2nd principles components.
6. Resultant shape of each sample - (65536, components).
7. Samples are reshaped to (256, 256, components)
8. For extracting the local spatial patterns all three variants of LBP is applied on both the newly formed slices.
9. Three feature vector of the volume is obtained from (LBP-default, Uniform and Uniform in-variant) from each slice by concatenating the feature vectors of each slice horizontally.
10. The resulting data sample is of shape (bins, components) which is then flattened.
11. The dataset formed is of shape (samples, bins * components)
12. Three types of datasets are generated for each of the three LBP methods
13. We divide the transformed features into training and testing sets.
14. Using the training data, different kernels of the SVM model are trained
15. For experiment 2, same steps are performed as above, only PCA is replaced by ICA.

Table 1. Table captions should be placed above the tables.

	PCA (components = 2)	ICA (components = 2)	PCA + Fast ICA
LBP default	0.88	0.83	0.87
LBP nri-uniform	0.85	0.85	0.85
LBP uniform	0.72	0.68	0.77

3   Results

This work used two feature transformation methods, and the feature extraction technique was applied to the results of each of these two methods. We conducted 10 sets of experiments using selected features from PCA and ICA. Three variations of LBP are applied to the selected features from PCA and ICA: Default, Rotation Invariant Uniform, and Non-Rotation Invariant Uniform. First, we applied PCA along the third axis of the s-MRI and extracted two components, thus forming two slices. On each slice so obtained, we applied variations of LBP. The features obtained were concatenated and fed to SVM. Note that with PCA, LBP default gave the most accurate results; with ICA, LBP-NRI uniform gave the best results. However, the difference between the two was not radical. Finally, we utilized the combination of the two followed by forwarding feature selection. The results are presented in the Table 1. In the experiments, an accuracy of 87% was obtained with only 714 features(Refer Fig. 4), indicating that greater accuracy can be achieved with fewer features. The technique utilizes the advantages of PCA & ICA to reduce the number of slices of 3-dimensional volume while preserving brain volume's discriminative properties. All pipelines are developed in Python using keras framework on a system that is equipped with an Intel i5 11th Gen CPU running at 2.4 GHz with 8 GB of RAM.

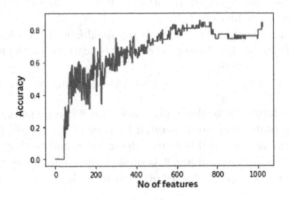

Fig. 4. Change in accuracy with increase in features

4   Conclusion

The detection of MCI and the classification of MCI-C and MCI-NC is critical, as they may help clinicians to delay the progression of dementia. In this study, the s-MRI modality is used in to assess the structural volumetric changes in the brain. Additionally, since 2-D CNNs do not take advantage of the correlation between slices and 3-D CNNs are computationally expensive, a model is developed that addresses both issues. This work suggests the application of a combination of PCA and ICA for the reduction in the number of slices. This is followed by the application of LBP to craft pertinent features. The results are encouraging. The model uses the power of PCA and ICA to reduce the dimensionality along the 3rd axis. Thus reducing the number of pertinent features, saving memory, and enhancing performance.

References

1. National Health Portal of India. https://www.nhp.gov.in/disease/neurological/dementia#::text=Prevalence%20of%20dementia%20in%20India,than%20in%20the%20developed%20countries
2. Ward, A., Tardiff, S., Dye, C., Arrighi, H.M.: Rate of conversion from prodromal Alzheimer's disease to Alzheimer's dementia: a systematic review of the literature. Dementia Geriatric Cogn. Disord. Extra **3**(1), 320–332 (2013)
3. Wu, Z., Peng, Y., Hong, M., Zhang, Y.: Gray matter deterioration pattern during Alzheimer's disease progression: a regions-of-interest based surface morphometry study. Front Aging Neurosci. **13**, 593898 (2021). https://doi.org/10.3389/fnagi.2021.593898. PMID: 33613265; PMCID: PMC7886803
4. Costafreda, S.G., et al.: Automated hippocampal shape analysis predicts the onset of dementia in mild cognitive impairment. Neuroimage **56**(1), 212–219 (2011)
5. Chincarini, A., et al.: Local MRI analysis approach in the diagnosis of early and prodromal Alzheimer's disease. Neuroimage **58**(2), 469–480 (2011)
6. LeCun, Y., Bengio, Y., Hinton, G.: Deep learning. Nature **521**, 436–444 (2015)
7. Goodfellow, I., Bengio, Y., Courville, A.: Deep Learning. MIT Press, Cambridge (2016)
8. Bhasin, H., Agrawal, R.K.: Multiple-activation parallel convolution network in combination with t-SNE for the classification of mild cognitive impairment. In: 21st International Conference on Bioinformatics and Bioengineering (BIBE) (2021)
9. Petersen, R.C., et al.: Alzheimer's disease neuroimaging initiative (ADNI). Neurology **74**(3), 201–209 (2010)
10. Pearson, K.: On lines and planes of closest fit to systems of points in space. Phil. Mag. **2**, 559–572 (1901). https://doi.org/10.1080/14786440109462720
11. Jolliffe, I.T.: Principal Component Analysis, 2nd edn. Springer, New York (2002)
12. Essay On Principal Component Analysis. https://www.ipl.org/essay/Principal-Component-Analysis-Algorithm-FJFYE9WTTU
13. Martinez, A.M., Kak, A.C.: PCA versus LDA. IEEE Trans. Pattern Anal. Mach. Intell. **23**(2), 228–233 (2001). https://doi.org/10.1109/34.908974
14. Van Hateren, J.H., Ruderman, D.L.: Independent component analysis of natural image sequences yields spatio-temporal filters similar to simple cells in primary visual cortex. Process. Biol. Sci. **265**(1412), 2315–2320 (1998). https://doi.org/10.1098/rspb.1998.0577. PMID: 9881476; PMCID: PMC1689525

Univariate, Multivariate, and Ensemble of Multilayer Perceptron Models for Landslide Movement Prediction: A Case Study of Mandi

Priyanka[1] , Praveen Kumar[1(✉)] , Arti Devi[1] , K. Akshay[1] , G. Gaurav[1] ,
K. V. Uday[2] , and Varun Dutt[1]

[1] ACS Lab, Indian Institute of Technology Mandi, Mandi 175075, Himachal Pradesh, India
`bluecodeindia@gmail.com, varun@iitmandi.ac.in`
[2] Geotechnical Engineering Lab, Indian Institute of Technology Mandi, Mandi 175075,
Himachal Pradesh, India
`uday@iitmandi.ac.in`

Abstract. The landslides are a challenging problem in the Himalayan states such as Himachal Pradesh and Uttarakhand in India and as well as in the world. Machine learning models could be developed to predict the movement of landslides in advance. In our proposed study, we developed a univariate, multivariate, and ensemble multilayer perceptron (MLP) and trained on the data collected from ten different stations in the Mandi district in Himachal Pradesh, India. The primary goal of this paper is to develop a model to predict the movement value using time series data. Recorded data was divided into the 80:20 ratio to train and test the model's performance. The root-mean-squared error (RMSE) was used to compare the model's performance. In training, the multivariate MLP was the best model with 0.012 RMSE, and ensemble MLP was the second-best model with 0.025 RMSE. In testing, the ensemble MLP was the best with 0.012 RMSE, and the univariate MLP was the second-best model with 0.013 RMSE. The analysis of the results shows that ensemble MLP is a promising method that can be used for landslide prediction using movement data.

Keywords: landslide movement · univariate · multivariate · ensemble · multilayer perceptron

1 Introduction

Landslides are a devastating problem in the Indian hilly states such as Himachal Pradesh and Uttarakhand and in the World [1]. It causes more damage to the infrastructure, such as roadblocks, buildings, bridges, and human lives [2]. The problem of the landslide could not be avoided, but it could be predicted by the machine learning (ML) models [3–6]. The ML models require the time series data of the landslide to detect the patterns of the landslides. These time series data could be recorded from the landslide monitoring station (LMS) [7]. The LMS could record the real-time univariate data of the landslide movement and multivariate data of the weather parameters. These univariate or multivariate data could pass to the ML models and predict the movement of landslides in advance.

© Springer Nature Switzerland AG 2023
D. Garg et al. (Eds.): IACC 2022, CCIS 1782, pp. 106–118, 2023.
https://doi.org/10.1007/978-3-031-35644-5_9

Several researchers in the literature survey used the univariate time series data of the landslide to predict the movement of the landslides [8–11]. For example, Bourmas and Tsakiri (2008) developed the univariate multilayer perceptron (MLP) and the autoregressive integrated moving average (ARIMA) model to predict the movement of soil mass of lignite mines in Greece [8]. Furthermore, Aggarwal et al. (2020) developed the ARIMA, dynamic neural network (DNN), and generalized autoregressive conditional heteroskedasticity (GARCH) models to predict the univariate time series data of the landslides [9]. Next, Pathania et al. (2022) developed the persistence, autoregressive (AR), MLP, and long-short-term memory (LSTM) model to predict the movement of the Gharpa landslide in Himachal Pradesh, India [10]. Similarly, Kumar et al. (2019) developed the seasonal ARIMA (SARIMA), MLP, LSTM, stacked LSTMs, bidirectional LSTMs, convolutional LSTMs, CNN-LSTMs, and encoder-decoder LSTM models to predict the movement of real-world landslides [11].

Literature surveys suggest that the multivariate data could increase the accuracy of the ML models, and multivariate ML models could be developed for the landslide movement predictions [12–15]. For example, Zare et al. (2013) developed the multivariate radial basic function (RBF) and multivariate MLP models for landslide susceptibility and hazard assessments in the Vaz Watershed area of Iran [12]. Furthermore, Ermini et al. (2005) developed the multivariate MLP and Probabilistic Neural Network (PNN) to assess landslide hazards at Riomaggiore catchment, a subwatershed of the Reno River basin in the Northern Apennines (Italy) [14]. Next, Pham et al. (2017) developed multivariate models such as Naive Bayes (NB), MLP, and Functional Trees (FT) to assess the landslide susceptibility in the Uttarakhand area (India) [15]. Results from these experiments revealed that the multivariate ML model could be developed for landslide movement prediction.

In the literature survey, several authors have also developed an ensemble of ML models in different domains to enhance one ML model's performance with another [16–21]. For example, Mali et al. (2021) developed different ensemble ML models to predict and evaluate the causal factors for slope failures [16]. Results suggested that the ensemble model increased the accuracy of the non-ensemble models. Next, Pham et al. (2017) developed an ensemble MLP model for landslide susceptibility assessment [17]. Results showed that the ensemble of MultiBoost and MLP models was the best model among other models for landslide susceptibility assessment. Next, Wichard et al. (2004) developed an ensemble model for predicting time series forecasting of two standard datasets [18]. Results showed that the developed ensemble method performed best on the standard datasets. Furthermore, Li et al. (2021) developed an ensemble of Spatial-Temporal Attention Networks and MLP (E-STAN-MLP) for weather forecasting in Beijing [20]. Results showed that the developed ensemble model performed well and achieved better accuracy.

From the literature survey, it was found that univariate and multivariate ML models could be developed for landslide movement prediction. Furthermore, the ensemble of ML models could also be developed to enhance the performance of one model with another model. Next, the literature mainly developed neural networks such as MLP for landslide movement prediction. However, these ML models' development has not been used for the Himalayan states (Himachal Pradesh and Uttarakhand) in India. Furthermore, researchers have developed the ML models mostly from the satellite data and the geotechnical data but not developed from the LMS recorded time series data. We fill this literature gap by developing the univariate, multivariate, and ensemble of MLP models and comparing their performance to predict the movement of landslides. As per the author's knowledge, this is the first kind of study to predict the movement of the landslide from the ten stations of the Mandi district in Himachal Pradesh by univariate, multivariate, and the ensemble of MLP model.

First, the background literature is detailed on various univariate, multivariate, and ensemble ML models for predicting landslide movements. Then, the data attributes and site locations are discussed. Next, the development of univariate, multivariate, and ensemble ML models for landslide movement predictions is detailed. Furthermore, in the result section, the performance of the univariate, multivariate, and ensemble ML models is evaluated by comparing their predictions for ten landslide stations. We close this study by discussing the relevance of the univariate, multivariate, and ensemble ML models for landslide movement predictions.

2 Background

In the machine learning literature on landslide movement prediction, several researchers have used univariate, multivariate, and ensemble MLP models to predict the movement in landslides [8–21]. Several researchers developed the univariate ML models for landslide movement prediction [8–11]. For example, Bourmas and Tsakiri (2008) developed the MLP model to predict the movement of soil mass of lignite mines in Greece [8]. The developed model was compared with the ARIMA model to compare the performance. Results showed that the MLP model outperformed the ARIMA model in predicting soil mass movement. Furthermore, Aggarwal et al. (2020) developed the ARIMA, DNN, and GARCH models to predict the univariate time series data of the landslides [9]. The data was collected from a 15-m real-world landslide in India to compare the performance of the models. Results showed that the DNN model was the best compared to ARIMA and GARCH models for univariate time series prediction. Next, Pathania et al. (2022) developed the persistence, AR, MLP, and LSTM model to predict the movement of the Gharpa landslide in Himachal Pradesh, India [10]. The experiment's findings suggest that a neural network-based model such as MLP and LSTM could be developed for landslide movement prediction. Similarly, Kumar et al. (2019) developed the seasonal ARIMA (SARIMA), MLP, LSTM, stacked LSTMs, bidirectional LSTMs, convolutional LSTMs, CNN-LSTMs, and encoder-decoder LSTMs to predict the movement of real-world landslides [11]. The data was recorded from the Tangni landslide in the Uttarakhand state of India. Results show that a neural network-based model such as MLP and LSTM could be considered for landslide movement prediction.

Several researchers in the literature have also developed a multivariate version of the MLP model to predict landslide movement [12–15]. For example, Zare et al. (2013) developed the multivariate RBF and multivariate MLP models for landslide susceptibility and hazard assessments in the Vaz Watershed area of Iran [12]. The multivariate data were used to train the models. Results showed that multivariate MLP outperformed the

RBF model. Next, Huang et al. (2020) developed an analytic hierarchy process (AHP), general linear model (GLM), information value (IV), back-propagation neural network (BPNN), binary logistic regression (BLR), C5.0 decision tree (C5.0 DT), support vector machine (SVM) and MLP models for landslide susceptibility prediction [13]. The multivariate data were recorded from several landslide locations in Shicheng County, China, to train the models. Results showed that the C5.0 DT was the best model for landslide susceptibility mapping. Furthermore, Ermini et al. (2005) chose a study area at Riomaggiore catchment, a subwatershed of the Reno River basin in the Northern Apennines (Italy), to assess landslide hazards [14]. For this purpose, they used two artificial neural networks MLP and the other Probabilistic Neural Network (PNN). Multivariate data was used to train models. Results showed that the MLP outperformed the PNN. Next, Pham et al. (2017) conducted a study on landslide susceptibility assessment in the Uttarakhand area (India) using three techniques: Naive Bayes (NB), MLP, and Functional Trees (FT) [15]. Various multivariate geotechnical features recorded from the landslide sites were used to train the models. Results showed that MLP performed best among other models. Findings from these literature surveys suggest that the multivariate data may increase the accuracy of the models.

Apart from the univariate and multivariate models, several researchers in the background have also developed an ensemble of different models [16–21]. For example, Mali et al. (2021) developed different ensemble MLP models to predict and evaluate the causal factors for slope failures [16]. Different ensemble ML techniques such as AdaBoost, stacking, bagging, voting, random forest (RF), decision tree (DT), support vector machine (SVM), bayesian network (BN), and MLP were compared to predict the causal factors. Results showed that the ensemble of AdaBoost, bagging, and RF with an MLP model showed better performance in evaluating the causal factor for slope failure. Next, Pham et al. (2017) developed an ensemble MLP model for landslide susceptibility assessment [17]. The model was developed using various ensemble methods (rotation forest, AdaBoost, dagging, MultiBoost, random subspace, and bagging) and the base classifier of MLP. Results showed that the ensemble of MultiBoost and MLP models was the best model among other models for landslide susceptibility assessment. Next, Wichard et al. (2004) developed an ensemble method for predicting time series forecasting [18]. Experiments were performed on two standard datasets, Chua's Circuit and the Cats dataset consisting of time series data points. The comparisons were performed using several different models, including linear and polynomial, neural networks, nearest neighbor, and perceptron radial basis net. Results showed that the developed ensemble method performed best on the standard datasets. Next, Rahman et al. (2015) developed a layered ensemble architecture (LEA) for time series data [19]. The developed model consists of two layers with an ensemble of MLP. The developed model was compared using two standard datasets, such as NN3 and NN5, forecasting competition time series datasets. Results showed that the ensemble LEA model performed well on both datasets. Furthermore, Li et al. (2021) developed an ensemble model named E-STAN-MLP (Spatial-Temporal Attention Network and MLP) for weather forecasting [20]. The experiments were performed on two years of datasets of Beijing weather stations, including temperature, wind speed, wind direction, and humidity. Results showed that the developed E-STAN-MLP model performed well and achieved better accuracy.

Similarly, Kumar et al. (2021) developed the ensemble of two LSTM models named bidirectional-stacked LSTM or BS-LSTM to predict the movement of the Tangni land-slide in Uttarakhand, India [21]. The multivariate movement data of the Tangni landslide were used to train the model. Results revealed that the ensemble model outperformed their individual models.

3   Data Attributes

For data collection, several landslide monitoring station (LMS) systems were installed in different places located in the state of Himachal Pradesh, India. The ten different locations of the landslides are illustrated in Fig. 1. The five monitoring stations are located on the national highway NH-154 from Mandi, Himachal Pradesh to Joginder Nagar, Himachal Pradesh, and the remaining five on the national highway NH-3 connect Chandigarh, Punjab to Manali, Himachal Pradesh. As shown in Fig. 1, stations 1 to station 5 on the NH-154 and stations 6 to station 10 on the NH-3. Figure 1 depicts these stations with different numbers 1-Narla Village (Lat. 31.866222, Long. 76.928889), 2-Kotropi land-slide crest (Lat. 31.913648, Long. 76.893350), 3-Kotropi landslide toe (Lat. 31.912356, Long. 76.890764), 4-Gumma village (Lat. 31.969710, Long. 76.853573), 5-Near Jogin-der Nagar (Lat. 31.973704, Long. 76.849344), 6-Pandoh dam (Lat. 31.679218, Long. 77.081109), 7-Deode village (Lat. 31.681440, Long. 77.085732), 8-Hanogi temple (Lat. 31.691740, Long. 77.129542), 9-Thalt village (31.694512, Long. 77.137235), and 10-Dwada village (Lat. 31.694718, Long. 77.146143). The LMS includes a group of sensors that collect different kinds of data such as temperature (in degrees Celsius), humidity (in percent), atmospheric pressure (in millibars), rainfall (in mm), acceleration of the soil (Ax, Ay, Az) in three directions, and moisture of the soil (in percent). These systems with several sensors were installed at the top of the real landslide active area. At a time interval of 10 min, it senses the data and sends it to cloud servers. The dataset contains three months of time series data from June to August 2019. The dataset hardly had some movement points. So, we averaged the dataset by half a day. Later, the magnitude of the movement of the landslide was calculated by the following equation (Eq. 1).

$$Movement = \sqrt{Ax^2 + Ay^2 + Az^2} \tag{1}$$

where the Ax, Ay, and Az are the acceleration of the soil in three directions.

Table 1 shows the sample data points recorded from the LMS at one station. The sta-tion ID is shown by the (S.id) column in Table 1. Similarly, the Temp column represents the temperature, the Hum column represents the humidity, the Press column represents the atmospheric pressure, the Move column represents the movement of the landslide, and the Mois column represents the soil moisture.

4   Methodology

4.1   Machine Learning Models

MLP. The MLP is a special class of neural network family mainly used for approximating the nonlinear function [22]. As shown in Fig. 2, the MLP network contains an input layer, hidden layers, and an output layer at last. All the layers contain a different number of

Table 1. Sample data points recorded by the LMS from a station.

S.id	Temp	Hum	Press	Rain	Acceleration (Ax, Ay, Az)	Move	Mois
S1	20	94	1042	0.003	−0.35, −0.34, −0.81	0.94	60
S1	20	94	1058	0.004	−0.34, −0.33, −0.80	0.93	60
S1	20	94	1054	0.004	−0.34, −0.33, −0.80	0.93	60
S1	21	92	1048	0.000	−0.32, −0.34, −0.80	0.92	60

Fig. 1. The location of ten landslide monitoring stations on Google Maps.

neurons. Each neuron is activated with an activation function. The input layer receives the information and passes the weighted input to the next hidden layer. Next, the multiple numbers of hidden layers nonlinearly transform the input information into a higher dimension and provide a good feature representation to the output layer. The output layer is the final layer that does regression tasks. The backpropagation technique reduces the error of the MLP and updates the layers' weights by gradient descent [23]. Equation 2 shows the error calculation in the nth iteration at the output layer.

$$E_n = \frac{1}{2}\left(y_n - \hat{y}_n\right)^2 \tag{2}$$

where y_n and $\hat{y}_n$ are the actual and predicted value in the nth iteration. Equation 3 shows the updating in weights using the gradient descent method.

$$\Delta w_{ji} = -\eta \frac{\partial E}{\partial w_{ji}^l} v_i \tag{3}$$

where v_i is the output of the previous layer neuron, w_{ji}^l is the weight value at the jth neuron in a layer l connected to the ith neuron in the previous layer, and η denotes the learning rate such that error minimizes faster. The $\frac{\partial E}{\partial w_{ji}^l}$ is a partial derivative of the error with respect to weight in a layer l.

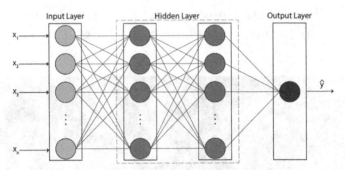

Fig. 2. An architecture of MLP algorithm.

Univariate MLP. The univariate MLP has the same architecture as the MLP model. The input feature is one in the univariate MLP model, which is the movement of the landslide. The input layer size is the number of lag values considered in the experiment. The output layer has a neuron with a linear activation function to predict the next movement value.

Multivariate MLP. The multivariate MLP has the same architecture as the MLP model. The input features are five in the multivariate MLP model, which are temperature, atmospheric pressure, rainfall, soil moisture, and movement of the landslide. The input layer size is the multiple of the lag and the features considered in the experiment. The output layer has a neuron with a linear activation function to predict the next movement value.

Ensemble MLP. The ensemble MLP has the same architecture as the MLP model. The input features are two in the ensemble MLP model, which are the predicted movement values of landslides by univariate MLP and multivariate MLP models. The input layer size is the multiple of the lag and the features considered in the experiment. The output layer has a neuron with a linear activation function to predict the next movement value.

4.2 Optimization of the Models

Univariate MLP. The univariate MLP model has three layers: input, hidden, and output. The input dimension of the input layer was multiple of the lag value and input features selected. The number of hidden layers varied from 1 to 12. The number of neurons in the hidden layer varied from 10 to 200. The activation function in the hidden layer was changed to logistic, hyperbolic tan (tanh), and rectified linear unit (ReLU). The lag value changed between 1 to 10. The output layer has a neuron with a linear activation function to predict the movement value. The batch size was varied to 32, 64, and 128. The number of epochs was set at 500 with early stopping in training. The early stopping used the loss threshold, which did not decrease below the threshold value in 10 consecutive epochs. The threshold value was set to 10e-6. The different parameters and their range for univariate MLP are shown in Table 2.

Multivariate MLP. In multivariate MLP, all the parameters were varied as in univariate MLP except the number of input features. The number of input features was 5 in the multivariate MLP. The different parameters and their range for multivariate MLP are shown in Table 2.

Ensemble MLP. In ensemble MLP, all the parameters were varied as in univariate MLP except the number of input features. The number of input features was 2 in the ensemble MLP. The different parameters and their range for ensemble MLP are shown in Table 2.

Table 2. Range of parameters in the univariate, multivariate, and ensemble of the MLP models.

Parameter	Univariate MLP	Multivariate MLP	Ensemble MLP
Input Features	1	5	2
Lags	1 to 10	1 to 10	1 to 10
Epochs	500 with early stopping	500 with early stopping	500 with early stopping
Batch Size	32, 64, and 128	32, 64, and 128	32, 64, and 128
Hidden Layers	1 to 12	1 to 12	1 to 12
Number of Neurons in Hidden Layers	10 to 200	10 to 200	10 to 200
Optimizer	Adam	Adam	Adam
Activation Function	Logistic, tanh, and ReLU	Logistic, tanh, and ReLU	Logistic, tanh, and ReLU

4.3 Error Measures

To calculate the error between actual and predicted values the root-mean-squared error (RMSE) was used. The equation of the error is as follows:

$$RMSE = \sqrt{\frac{1}{n} \sum_{i=1}^{n} (y_i - \hat{y}_i)^2} \qquad (4)$$

where y_i is the actual data point and $\hat{y}_i$ is the predicted value by the ML algorithm. The variable n represents the total number of data points.

5 Results

The dataset collected from different stations were divided into 80% and 20%. The developed univariate, multivariate, and ensemble of multilayer perceptron models were trained on the training dataset and later tested on the test dataset. The parameters of the models were optimized in the training of the models. Table 3 shows the optimized parameters of the different models. For example, the univariate MLP showed the best performance with a lag value of 3, batch size was 30, and the number of neurons were 128. Similarly, the multivariate MLP showed the best performance with a lag value of 5, the number of hidden layers was 8, and the number of neurons in each hidden layer was 100. Furthermore, the ensemble MLP model showed the best performance with lag value 3, the number of hidden layers was 10, and the number of neurons in each hidden layer was 128.

The training results of the models are shown in Table 4 across the ten stations. As seen in Table 4, the multivariate MLP was the best model with a 0.012 average RMSE. Furthermore, the ensemble MLP was the second-best model with a 0.025 average RMSE. Next, Table 5 shows the results of the MLP models in the testing across ten stations. As seen in Table 5, the ensemble of MLP models was the best, with a 0.012 average RMSE. The univariate MLP was the second-best model with a 0.013 average RMSE. Figure 3 shows the fitting of actual and predicted values by the best-performing ensemble MLP model in the training and testing for the ten stations. As seen in Fig. 3, the actual values are shown in the red curve and predicted values by the model are shown in the blue curve.

Table 3. Optimized parameters of the univariate, multivariate, and ensemble of the MLP.

Parameter	Univariate MLP	Multivariate MLP	Ensemble MLP
Input Features	1	5	2
Lags	3	5	3
Input Size	3	25	6
Epochs	100	400	350
Batch Size	32	128	32
Hidden Layers	1	8	10
Number of Neurons in Hidden Layers	128	100 in all hidden layers	128 in all hidden layers
Optimizer	Adam	Adam	Adam
Activation Function	ReLU	ReLU	ReLU

Table 4. The performance of the univariate, multivariate, and ensemble of the MLP in training.

Station	RMSE		
	Univariate MLP	Multivariate MLP	Ensemble MLP
S1	0.019	0.015	0.019
S2	0.033	0.025	0.036
S3	0.065	0.029	0.064
S4	0.031	0.000	0.031
S5	0.001	0.000	0.002
S6	0.035	0.007	0.034
S7	0.008	0.005	0.000
S8	0.022	0.015	0.022
S9	0.032	0.009	0.031
S10	0.011	0.013	0.011
Average RMSE	0.026	0.012	0.025

Table 5. The performance of the univariate, multivariate, and ensemble of the MLP in testing.

Station	RMSE		
	Univariate MLP	Multivariate MLP	Ensemble MLP
S1	0.007	0.059	0.008
S2	0.004	0.025	0.010
S3	0.065	0.051	0.060
S4	0.011	0.000	0.013
S5	0.018	0.016	0.000
S6	0.003	0.041	0.004
S7	0.006	0.004	0.007
S8	0.005	0.086	0.006
S9	0.001	0.054	0.001
S10	0.008	0.074	0.009
Average RMSE	0.013	0.037	0.012

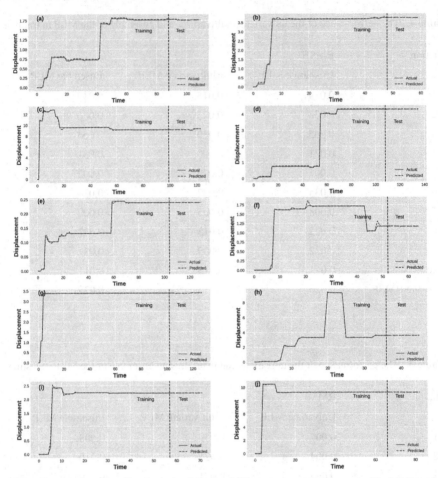

Fig. 3. The actual and predicted curve of the landslide movement by the ensemble MLP model for ten stations. (a) Station one. (b) Station two. (c) Station three. (d) Station four. (e) Station five. (f) Station six. (g) Station seven. (h) Station eight. (i) Station nine. (j) Station ten.

6 Discussion and Conclusions

The primary focus of this research was to predict the movement of the landslide from the ten stations of the Mandi district of Himachal Pradesh in India. The univariate, multivariate, and ensemble MLP models have been developed to compare the performance to predict landslide movement. Two months of univariate and multivariate data were used from the ten stations to train the models. The univariate data consisted only of movement values, whereas the multivariate data also consisted of the weather parameters. The data was divided into the 80:20 ratio to train and test the MLP models. The univariate MLP model was trained with univariate data, and the multivariate MLP model provided the multivariate data as input. Furthermore, the ensemble MLP model provided the outputs of univariate MLP and multivariate MLP as input. Later the univariate, multivariate performance was tested on the test data. In training, the multivariate MLP was the best model with 0.012 RMSE, and ensemble MLP was the second-best model with 0.025 RMSE. In testing, the ensemble MLP was the best with 0.012 RMSE, and the univariate MLP was the second-best model with 0.013 RMSE.

The findings of this study revealed that the ensemble MLP model outperformed the other models. The study's results matched the literature, suggesting that the ensemble models enhance the performance of one model with another model. One of the reasons could be that the ensemble MLP provided the output of both univariate and multivariate MLP models, and ensembling techniques reduced the variation in the output results.

The study has some implications that the univariate, multivariate, and ensemble MLP models could be developed to predict the landslide's movement. These MLP models could also be implemented to generate the real-time movement prediction of the landslides. The real-time warnings could also be generated based on predefined thresholds set on the movement.

Future work could develop different types of neural networks, such as transformers [24] and prediction autoencoders [25], to predict and warn about the landslide's movement.

Acknowledgment. We are grateful to the DST, India, and the DDMA Mandi, Kinnaur, and Kangra for providing the fund for this research grant. We are also thankful to the IIT Mandi for providing the space and computing facilities for this research work.

References

1. Nayek, P.S., Gade, M.: Seismic landslide hazard assessment of central seismic gap region of Himalaya for a Mw 8.5 scenario event. Acta Geophys. **69**(3), 747–759 (2021)
2. Parkash, S.: Historical records of socio-economically significant landslides in India. J. South Asia Disast. Stud. **4**(2), 177–204 (2011)
3. Kumar, P., et al.: Landslide debris-flow prediction using ensemble and non-ensemble machine-learning methods. In: The International Conference on Time Series and Forecasting (2019)
4. Kumar, P., et al.: Predictions of weekly soil movements using moving-average and support-vector methods: a case-study in Chamoli, India. In: Correia, A.G., Tinoco, J., Cortez, P., Lamas, L. (eds.) ICITG 2019. SSGG, pp. 393–405. Springer, Cham (2020). https://doi.org/10.1007/978-3-030-32029-4_34
5. Kumar, P., Sihag, P., Pathania, A., Chaturvedi, P., Uday, K. V., Dutt, V.: Comparison of moving-average, lazy, and information gain methods for predicting weekly slope-movements: a case-study in Chamoli, India. In: Casagli, N., Tofani, V., Sassa, K., Bobrowsky, P.T., Takara, K. (eds.) WLF 2020. ICL Contribution to Landslide Disaster Risk Reduction, pp. 321–330. Springer, Cham (2020). https://doi.org/10.1007/978-3-030-60311-3_38
6. Kumar, P., et al.: Predictions of weekly slope movements using moving-average and neural network methods: a case study in Chamoli, India. In: Nagar, A., Deep, K., Bansal, J., Das, K. (eds.) Soft Computing for Problem Solving 2019. Advances in Intelligent Systems and Computing, vol. 1139, pp. 67–81. Springer, Singapore (2020). https://doi.org/10.1007/978-981-15-3287-0_6
7. Pathania, A., et al.: A lowcost, sub-surface IoT framework for landslide monitoring, warning, and prediction. In: Proceedings of 2020 International Conference on Advances in Computing, Communication, Embedded and Secure Systems (2020)

8. Bourmas, G., Tsakiri, M.: Comparing a univariate time series approach with neural networks to predict deformation of soil mass. In: Measuring the Changes, A Joint Symposium of FIG and IAG (2008)

9. Aggarwal, A., Alshehri, M., Kumar, M., Alfarraj, O., Sharma, P., Pardasani, K.R.: Landslide data analysis using various time-series forecasting models. Comput. Electr. Eng. **88**, 106858 (2020)

10. Pathania, A., et al.: Predictions of soil movements using persistence, auto-regression, and neural network models: a case-study in Mandi, India. Int. J. Swarm Intell. **7**(1), 94–109 (2022)

11. Kumar, P., et al.: Prediction of real-world slope movements via recurrent and non-recurrent neural network algorithms: a case study of the Tangni landslide. Indian Geotech. J. **51**(4), 788–810 (2021). https://doi.org/10.1007/s40098-021-00529-4

12. Zare, M., Pourghasemi, H.R., Vafakhah, M., Pradhan, B.: Landslide susceptibility mapping at Vaz Watershed (Iran) using an artificial neural network model: a comparison between multilayer perceptron (MLP) and radial basic function (RBF) algorithms. Arab. J. Geosci. **6**(8), 2873–2888 (2013)

13. Huang, F., Cao, Z., Guo, J., Jiang, S.H., Li, S., Guo, Z.: Comparisons of heuristic, general statistical and machine learning models for landslide susceptibility prediction and mapping. CATENA **191**, 104580 (2020)

14. Ermini, L., Catani, F., Casagli, N.: Artificial neural networks applied to landslide susceptibility assessment. Geomorphology **66**(1–4), 327–343 (2005)

15. Pham, B.T., Tien Bui, D., Pourghasemi, H.R., Indra, P., Dholakia, M.B.: Landslide suscepti-bility assesssment in the Uttarakhand area (India) using GIS: a comparison study of prediction capability of naïve bayes, multilayer perceptron neural networks, and functional trees meth-ods. Theoret. Appl. Climatol. **128**(1–2), 255–273 (2015). https://doi.org/10.1007/s00704-015-1702-9

16. Mali, N., Dutt, V., Uday, K.V.: Determining the geotechnical slope failure factors via ensemble and individual machine learning techniques: a case study in Mandi, India. Front. Earth Sci. **9**, 701837 (2021)

17. Pham, B.T., Bui, D.T., Prakash, I., Dholakia, M.B.: Hybrid integration of multilayer perceptron neural networks and machine learning ensembles for landslide susceptibility assessment at Himalayan area (India) using GIS. CATENA **149**, 52–63 (2017)

18. Wichard, J.D., Ogorzalek, M.: Time series prediction with ensemble models. In: 2004 IEEE International Joint Conference on Neural Networks (IEEE Cat. No. 04CH37541), vol. 2, pp. 1625–1630. IEEE (2004)

19. Rahman, M.M., Islam, M.M., Murase, K., Yao, X.: Layered ensemble architecture for time series forecasting. IEEE Trans. Cybern. **46**(1), 270–283 (2015)

20. Li, Y., et al.: Weather forecasting using ensemble of spatial-temporal attention network and multi-layer perceptron. Asia-Pac. J. Atmos. Sci. **57**(3), 533–546 (2021)

21. Kumar, P., Sihag, P., Chaturvedi, P., Uday, K.V., Dutt, V.: BS-LSTM: an ensemble recurrent approach to forecasting soil movements in the real world. Front. Earth Sci. **9**, 696–792 (2021)

22. Rosenblatt, F.: Principles of neurodynamics. Perceptrons and the theory of brain mechanisms. Cornell Aeronautical Lab Inc., Buffalo (1961)

23. Rumelhart, D.E., Hinton, G.E., Williams, R.J.: Learning internal representations by error propagation. In: Rumelhart, D.E., Mcclelland, J.L. (eds.) Parallel Distributed Processing: Explorations in the Microstructure of Cognition, vol. 1. pp. 318–362 (1985)

24. Han, K., Xiao, A., Wu, E., Guo, J., Xu, C., Wang, Y.: Transformer in transformer. Adv. Neural Inf. Process. Syst. **34**, 15908–15919 (2021)

25. Liou, C.Y., Cheng, W.C., Liou, J.W., Liou, D.R.: Autoencoder for words. Neurocomputing **139**, 84–96 (2014)

An Effective Approach for Identification of Multivariate Global Outlier Using Min, Average and Max Linkage Methods of Agglomerative

Vijay Kumar Verma[✉] [ID]

Computer Science and Engineering Department, Shri Vaishnav Institute of Information Technology, Shri Vaishnav Vidyapeeth Vishwavidyalaya, Indore, Ujjain Road Gram Baroli, Indore, Madhya Pradesh, India
drvijaykumarverma20@gmail.com

Abstract. Outliers are normally defined as piece of data which is extremely faraway as of the remaining of dataset. Presently no unbending or any of mathematical description which describe an outlier. Defining for a data point whether it belongs to an outlier category or not, is at last the matter of subject. Data points could be outlier, can be defined as piece of dataset which departs extremely faraway with y the remaining data set. Present of Outliers indicates irregularities in a measurement or in experimental. Take a real work example, the average height of a person is between 5 to 6 feet tall. However, if it has been that a person has height 8 feet. Then the person with height 8 feet would be considered as outliers in comparison to the height of other persons. There are several methods are available to detect outliers present in a data set, but the main problem is Difficult to decide the method or tools for founding outliers in the data set, outlier affects the mean, variance and standard deviation, outliers are reducing the power of statistical tests, they can decrease normality of data set. In this paper we used hierarchical clustering technique to find out the global outlier. In hierarchical clustering there are three method Min, Max and Average linkage used to create clusters. In this paper we used real life data set of car sales in which we have taken 29 models of four famous brand Maruti Suzuki, Hyundai. Tata and Land Rover. There is a total of 9 attributes are taken are and we want to find that how the clusters are formed using these three methods and is there any outlier is present in the dataset based on these attributes. We have implemented these three-approach using R language. We found that the clusters forming is different, but the outlier is detected by three approaches are same.

Keywords: Outliers · Min · Max · Average · Global · Clusters

1 Introduction

Outliers are normally defined as piece of data which is extremely faraway as of the remaining of dataset. Presently no unbending or any of mathematical description which describe an outlier. Defining for a data point whether it belongs to an outlier category

© Springer Nature Switzerland AG 2023
D. Garg et al. (Eds.): IACC 2022, CCIS 1782, pp. 119–139, 2023.
https://doi.org/10.1007/978-3-031-35644-5_10

or not, is at last the matter of subject. Data points could be outliers, can be defined as piece of dataset which departs extremely faraway with y the remaining data set. The present of Outliers indicates irregularities in a measurement or in experimental. Take a real work example, the average height of a person is between 5 to 6 feet tall. However, if it has been that a person has height 8 feet. Then the person with height 8 feet would be considered as outliers in comparison to the height of other persons. The presence of an outlier shows some sort of problem. Detecting outliers might be a well-defined procedure in which correctly detect and at the same time provides a way to exclude the detected outliers from a specified dataset. Methods for detecting outliers are mostly reliant on nature of the dataset that's why no standard method are available for handling outliers. Outlier discovery is an integral part of data analysis, data preprocessing and are used in variety of applications. During data preprocessing, data analysts need to find outliers in the "dirty" data. After detecting, either removing them from the dataset completely or handling them properly by replacing them with suitable values using some another way [12, 13].

In Data analytics process there are two important reasons for giving special attention to outliers.

1. Analysis of the data give negative result when the outliers are present
2. Outliers provides important information to the data analyst which he/she requires from the analysis process

Outlier are classified based

- Univariate outlier: - This type of outlier has extreme value and is related with only one factor. For example, height of Mohan is 8 feet and is a tallest alive man. We can consider it as univariate outlier because related to only one factor height.
- Multivariate outlier: - This type of outlier has a combination of extreme values and is related with two or more than two factors. For example, taking both the height and weight of one person in dataset is 8 feet with weight 110 kg is a surprising combination and a multivariate outlier (Fig. 1).

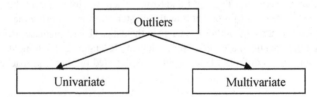

Fig. 1. Types of outliers based on number of factors

There is one another categorization of outliers are given below:

- **Global outliers:** - It is a single data point or more than one data points that very far from the rest of points of dataset.
- **Contextual outliers:** - The object in dataset which deviate from remining part of the dataset respect to same situation.

- **Collective outliers:** - The point of dataset which are the subset (group of points) of whole dataset that are completely different with respect to the whole dataset (Fig. 2).

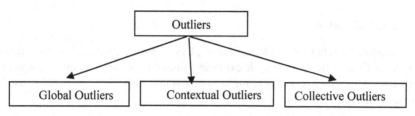

Fig. 2. Types of outliers-based context and distance

2 Issue Related with Outlier Detection

Some of the important issue related with outliers' detection are [14, 15].

2.1 Real Identification

Definition of outliers are highly subjective and varies on the domain and application scenarios. The difference between usual observations and outliers are very small. Therefore, we need to take cautious while choosing the outlier detection approach.

2.2 Specific Challenges Related to Application

Selecting similarity or distance measure to define data objects is very important in outlier detection. The similarity or distance measure are dependent on application type. Different applications might have different requirements. For example, detecting an outlier in the medical dataset is totally different form detecting an outlier form purchasing dataset. Sometimes outlier detection methods must be dedicated to specific applications that need to develop.

2.3 Dealing with Noise

Noise present in the dataset may be like the outliers and therefore is tough to differentiate and eliminate them from outliers. We must carefully understand that outliers and noise are two different entities. The noises are often invariably and can be present in all kinds of data set. It is a big challenge to detect outliers by obscuring the difference between usual observations and outliers.

2.4 Understandability

We must clear that why a particular object has become an outlier and therefore we must be a precise condition, criterion and reason to differentiate the normal objects from the outliers. The justification needs to be well formulated. And should be understandable.

3 Methods for Outlier Detection

There are three main classifications of outlier detection [17, 18].

3.1 Statistical Methods

Statical methods include Box plots, Scatter plots, Whisker plots, etc. these methods can help in finding the outlier with extreme values in the data. Assuming a normal distribution, Methods like z-score, mean and standard deviation (σ) are also used to detect extreme value outliers.

3.2 Proximity Methods

Proximity methods basically used clustering techniques to identify the clusters in the data. These approaches follow a fixed threshold and calculate the distance of each object from the cluster centroid and then remove the outlier. These methods include DB Scan, k-means, and hierarchical clustering. These methods are utilized and find out the centre of each cluster. The disadvantages of these approaches are that some specific problems can be a challenge to find the correct distance measure.

3.3 Projection Methods

These methods utilize advanced techniques such as the Principal Components Analysis to create model and the data reduce into a lower-dimensional subspace. The extent between every data object fitting to a space and reduce it to the sub-space. Methods of projection are easy to understand and simple to apply and also highlight irrelevant values. The PCA based approach has a problem that analyzing existing features to define and constitutes a "normal" space (Fig. 3).

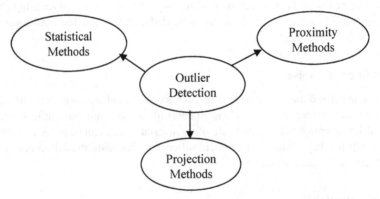

Fig. 3. Methods for Outlier Detection

4 Hierarchical Clustering and Linkage Function

It is based on the decomposition of the given data set into hierarchical structure. It produces a hierarchical sequence of nested clusters. Dendrogram is used to merge or splits clusters which is a tree-like diagram. Dendrogram represents hierarchy which an inverted tree that describes the order to merged clusters. It is divided into two types [13, 15, 16].

1. **Agglomerative:**

    In this approach individual data object is considered a distinct cluster and, in every stage, merge the nearest pairs to form a cluster this process is repeated until one cluster is formed.

2. **Divisive:**

    It is just opposite of agglomerative, in these techniques initially we take all object as single clusters and separate objects based on neatest distance in every iteration, In the end, we are left with N clusters.

The linkage function is used to calculate the distance between clusters. There are three linkage functions used in hierarchical clustering (Table 1).

Table 1. Linkage function

Name of function	Value used to update row and column
Min linkage	$\min(d(x, y))$
Average linkage	$\max(d(x, y))$
Max linkage	$\text{average}(d(x, y))$

5 Literature Survey

In 2015 Usman, Gerhard et al. proposed "Outliers Detection Method Using Clustering in Buildings Data". They applied the algorithm of expectation maximization and by using this algorithm showed the result for regression and interpolation which in petite epochs with explained. They applied automatic detection of chiller states. They employed a layered K-Means approach. The layered approach of K-Means algorithm gives various states [1]. In 2016 Monowar H. et al. proposed "A multi-step outlier-based anomaly detection approach to network-wide traffic". They used the modules with mutual information and entropy for selection of relevant subsection of features. They applied a technique which is based on a tree structure and created a set of position points. They designed a framework which is fast and extracts features efficiently and accurately from network traffic [2]. In 2017 Rasim M. et al. "An Anomaly Detection Based on Optimization". They proposed an enhanced optimization-based technique for clusters acknowledgment. They assigned weight to each data point. Their objective is to demonstrate increment of every object and progress the result of clustering. They compared to the k-means clustering algorithm and estimated the quality of the clustering with the help of clustering assessment metrics. They proposed a new technique to only detect abnormal values but also detect anomaly in huge data. The object of the proposed approach in the paper is to advance the process of the detection. [3]. In 2018 Victoria J. et al. proposed "An Evaluation of Classification and Outlier Detection Algorithms". They focused on training algorithms and classified rapidly to combine frequently new data. Comparability they check accuracy for six algorithms and applied a limit for time series-based data. They examined and demonstrated algorithm tasks for specific data. They appraised procedures for classification and discovery of outlier for on-line system which regularly integrates new data. They developed a heuristic for the best algorithms [4]. In 2019 Yue Zhao et al. proposed "PyOD: A Python Toolbox for Scalable Outlier Detection PyOD: A Python Toolbox for Scalable Outlier Detection". The proposed toolbox is open source which is scalable for detection of outlier with multivariate features. In this toolbox there are several other components like coverage, checks, and parallelization. The presented toolbox was constructed using scalable Python approach for detection of outlier. This toolbox contains more than 20 algorithms for outliers of detection. This toolbox can be used for used in academic and commercial purposes [5]. In 2019 Agnieszka Duraj et al. proposed "Detection of outliers in data streams using grouping methods". They showed that to process data streams efficiently at the initial stage we need to detect removal of anomalies, these are caused measuring errors. These errors may affect misconception of the spectacles which being analyzed. They describe several existing methods for detecting exceptions in data streams. These methods require proper selection of effective parameters. They also presented that the efficiency of methods may vary and depend on various factors of he data set being analyzed. They describe a few methods for detecting exceptions present in data stream. They also analyzed their operation for consumption data [6]. In 2020 Atiq ur Rehman et al. proposed "Unsupervised outlier detection in multidimensional data". They proposed an idea and proposed an approach which is better and more accurate for better performance and easy implementation. The proposed approach also has no computational complexity. They presented two more techniques which transform data into single dimensional space and for detection of outliers. They reduce high dimension and reduce computational inexpensive and increase feasibility [7]. In 2020 Shahrooz Abghari et al. "Data Mining Approaches for Outlier Detection Analysis". They focused on domains of three applications named maritime surveillance, district heating, and online media dataset. They presented the significance of preprocessing for data and the importance of selecting feature in building appropriate approach for data modeling. They acquired advantage form supervised and unsupervised learning to design hybrid method. They presented a new system to detect anomaly which is rule based system, they applied this system for the maritime surveillance domain [8]. In 2020 Afrah Yahya et al. proposed "Effect of outliers on the coefficient of determination in multiple regression analysis with the application on the GPA for student". They presented an algorithm based on determination of coefficients. They also calculate sum of averages to approximation multiple outliers. They presented an algorithm for understanding a solution to this inconsistency. The proposed algorithm was evaluated with some strong regression techniques. With the help of results, they demonstrated that proposed technique is better for estimation of outliers [9]. In 2021 Saima Afzal proposed "A Novel Approach for Outlier Detection in Multivariate Dat". They applied Principal Components Analysis (PCA) with three-sigma limits to design new approach. They successfully employed PCA and reduced dimension by restoring objects and close-fitting from the unique interpretations. Superiority of the proposed method is confirmed with mentioned datasets. They applied F-measure in real life data for the proposed method and for two existing approaches. They also observed by the tests to execute of the proposed method to achieve best growing sample size [10]. In 2021 Ishani Chatterjee et al. "Statistics-Based Outlier Detection and Correction Method for Amazon Customer Review". They used real life example and proposed outlier detection and correction method by using statistics-based approach They absorbed scraped datasets to achieve which contain customer analyses regarding various products [11].

6   Proposed Approach

Proposed approach includes steps given below

1. Assume each objects as separate clusters and denote them as $C_1, C_2, C_3, ...C_n$ where n denotes total number of objects
2. Used Euclidean distance method to calculate the distance matrix and denotes as D, similarity measure.
3. Search the object pair with smallest distance and let take pair (p), (q), conferring that d (p, q) = min distance (i, j) {where cluster p contain i and cluster q contain j}.
4. Combine and create clusters with p and q. Denote combined objects with single clusters using Dendrogram distance.
5. Modify matrix contain distance value, D, remove row and column related to p and q. Update the values based on the approach (Min, Max, Average). For remaining rows and columns do not change corresponding matrix contain distance value.
6. When total number of objects came into one cluster, stop the procure. If not, move to step 3.
7. After creating Dendrogram check the number of clusters creating for each approach (Min, Max, Average). Now find the global cluster created by these approaches and find the number of objects in each cluster.

7   Illustrate with an Example

Consider a data set with six objects shown in Table 2 with coordinate value. Each object is represented in two-dimensional number from D1 to D6 (Table 3).

Table 2. Two-dimensional data set with 6 objects

Object	X	Y
D1	4	4
D2	5	5
D3	7	9
D4	10	6
D5	11	6
D6	15	14

Table 3. Distance matrix

Object	D1	D2	D3	D4	D5	D6
D1	0	1.41	5.83	6.32	7.28	14.86
D2	1.41	0	4.47	5.09	6.08	13.45
D3	5.83	4.47	0	4.24	5	9.43
D4	6.32	5.09	4.24	0	1	9.43
D5	7.28	6.08	5	1	0	8.06
D6	14.86	13.45	9.43	9.43	8.06	0

Apply Min Linkage to Create Dendrogram

Use the same process which is used in Min linkage but replacement of value in column and row are based minimum value (Tables 4, 5, 6, 7 and 8).

Table 4. Combined objects D4 and D5 with minimum distance 1

Object	D1	D2	D3	D4	D5	D6
D1	0	1.41	5.83	6.32	7.28	14.86
D2	1.41	0	4.47	5.09	6.08	13.45
D3	5.83	4.47	0	4.24	5	9.43
D4	6.32	5.09	4.24	0	1	9.43
D5	7.28	6.08	5	1	0	8.06
D6	14.86	13.45	9.43	9.43	8.06	0

Table 5. Combined objects D1 and D2 with minimum distance 1.41

Object	D1	D2	D3	D4, D5	D6
D1	0	1.41	5.83	6.32	14.86
D2	1.41	0	4.47	5.09	13.45
D3	5.83	4.47	0	4.24	9.43
D4, D5	6.32	5.09	4.24	0	8.06
D6	14.86	13.45	9.43	8.06	0

Table 6. Combined objects (D1, D2) and (D4, D5) with minimum distance 4.24

Object	D1, D2	D3	D4, D5	D6
D1, D2	0	4.47	5.09	13.45
D3	4.47	0	**4.24**	9.43
D4, D5	5.09	**4.24**	0	8.06
D6	13.45	9.43	8.06	0

Table 7. Combined objects (D1, D2) and (D4, D5) with minimum distance 4.24

Object	D1, D2	((D4, D5), D3)	D6
D1, D2	0	**4.47**	13.45
((D4, D5), D3)	**4.47**	0	8.06
D6	13.45	8.06	0

Table 8. Combined to form single cluster at 8.06

	(D1, D2), ((D4, D5), D3)	D6
(D1, D2), ((D4, D5), D3)	0	8.06
D6	8.06	0

Apply Average Linkage to Create Dendrogram

Use the same process which is used in Min linkage but replacement of value in column and row are based average of both column (Tables 9, 10, 11 and 12).

Table 9. Combined objects D1 and D2 with minimum distance 1.41

Object	D1	D2	D3	D4, D5	D6
D1	0	**1.41**	5.83	6.63	14.86
D2	**1.41**	0	4.47	6.105	13.45
D3	5.83	4.47	0	4.62	9.43
D4, D5	6.63	6.105	4.62	0	8.74
D6	14.86	13.45	9.43	8.74	0

Table 10. Combined objects D3 and D4, D5 with minimum distance 4.62

Object	D1, D2	D3	D4, D5	D6
D1, D2	0	5.15	6.36	14.15
D3	5.15	0	**4.62**	9.43
D4, D5	6.36	**4.62**	0	8.74
D6	14.15	9.43	8.74	0

Table 11. Combined objects (D1, D2) and ((D4, D5) D3) with minimum distance 5.57

Object	(D1, D2)	(D4, D5) D3	D6
(D1, D2)	0	**5.75**	14.15
(D4, D5) D3	**5.75**	0	9.08
D6	14.15	9.08	0

Table 12. Combined D6 to form single cluster at 11.61

Object	(D1, D2), ((D4, D5) D3)	D6
(D1, D2), ((D4, D5) D3)	0	11.61
D6	11.61	0

Apply Max Linkage to Create Dendrogram

Use the same process which is used in Min linkage but replacement of value in column and row are based Maximum value (Tables 13, 14, 15 and 16).

Table 13. Combined objects D1 and D2 with minimum distance 1.41

Object	D1	D2	D3	D4, D5	D6
D1	0	**1.41**	5.83	7.28	14.86
D2	**1.41**	0	4.47	6.08	13.45
D3	5.83	4.47	0	5	9.43
D4, D5	7.28	6.08	5	0	9.43
D6	14.86	13.45	9.43	9.43	0

Table 14. Combined objects D3 and D4, D5 with minimum distance 5

Object	D1, D2	D3	D4, D5	D6
D1,D2	0	5.83	7.28	14.86
D3	5.83	0	**5**	9.43
D4, D5	7.28	**5**	0	9.43
D6	14.86	9.43	9.43	0

Table 15. Combined objects (D1, D2) and ((D4, D5) D3) with minimum distance 7.28

Object	D1, D2	(D4, D5), D3	D6
D1, D2	0	**7.28**	14.86
(D4, D5), D3	**7.28**	0	9.43
D6	14.86	9.43	0

Table 16. Combined D6 to form single cluster at 14.86

Object	(D1, D2) ((D4, D5), D3)	D6
(D1, D2) ((D4, D5), D3)	0	14.86
D6	14.86	0

8 Implementation Environment

We have taken real life data set of car sales which has total 9 attributes. Data set contains 3 brand Maruti Suzuki, Hyundai and Tata of cars. There is total 29 models are taken for experiment. First attribute is average per liter, seconds attribute is number of cylinders, third attribute is dispersant, fourth attribute is Horsepower, fifth attribute is drat, sixth attribute is weight, seventh attribute number of sales, eight attribute is Fuel Type and ninth attribute is no of Seats. Total number of sales are more 1000 (Table 17).

Table 17. Car sales data set

model	APL	Cylinders	Dispersant	Horsepower	Drat	Weight	Fule Type	Seats	Sales
Suzuki Brezza	21	6	160	110	3.9	2.62	2	5	46
Maruti Suzuki	21	6	160	110	3.9	2.875	2	5	77
Suzuki Baleno	22.8	4	108	93	3.85	2.32	2	5	38
Maruti Suzuki Ertiga	21.4	6	258	110	3.08	2.215	1	7	39
Maruti Suzuki Dzire	18.7	6	360	175	3.15	2.44	1	5	77
Hyundai Venue	18.1	6	225	105	2.76	2.46	1	5	30
Hyundai Creta	15.3	6	360	245	3.21	2.57	1	5	28
Hyundai i20	24.4	4	146.7	62	3.69	3.19	2	5	40
Tata Nexon	22.8	4	140.8	95	3.92	3.15	2	5	32
Tata Punch	19.2	6	167.6	123	3.92	3.44	2	5	38
Tata Altroz	17.8	6	167.6	123	3.92	3.44	2	5	38
Tata Safari	16.4	6	275.8	180	3.07	2.07	3	7	37
Tata Harrier	17.3	6	275.8	180	3.07	3.73	2	7	32
Maruti Suzuki Alto K10	15.2	6	275.8	180	3.07	3.78	2	5	38
Maruti Suzuki Wagon	15.4	4	472	205	2.93	2.25	1	5	37

(*continued*)

Table 17. (*continued*)

model	APL	Cylinders	Dispersant	Horsepower	Drat	Weight	Fule Type	Seats	Sales
Maruti Suzuki Alto 800	16.4	4	460	215	3	2.424	2	5	34
Tata Winger	16.7	4	440	230	3.23	2.345	2	5	27
Tata Nano Diesel	28.4	4	78.7	66	4.08	2.2	1	5	39
Maruti Suzuki Grand Vitara	24.4	4	75.7	52	4.93	2.615	2	5	38
Hyundai New Kona	24.9	4	71.1	65	4.22	1.835	2	5	39
Maruti Suzuki Celerio	21.5	4	120.1	97	3.7	2.465	3	5	30
Maruti Suzuki Eeco	15.5	6	318	150	2.76	3.52	3	5	16
Hyundai Alcazar	15.2	6	304	150	3.15	3.435	3	5	37
Hyundai Tucson	14.3	4	350	245	3.73	3.84	3	5	35
Hyundai Santro	19.2	4	400	175	3.08	3.845	3	5	47
Hyundai Verna	27.3	6	79	66	4.08	1.935	2	5	38
Maruti Suzuki Ignis	26	4	120.3	91	4.43	2.14	3	5	36
Hyundai Aura	24.4	4	95.1	113	3.77	1.513	3	5	33
Land Rover Defender	10	8	301	335	3.54	5.57	1	7	8

First, we have calculated distance matrix using Euclidean distance formula.

$$d(p, q) = \sqrt{(x1 - x2)^2 + (y1 - y2)^2}$$

The matrix contains distance value shown in Fig. 5 (Figs. 4, 6, 7, 8, 9, 10).

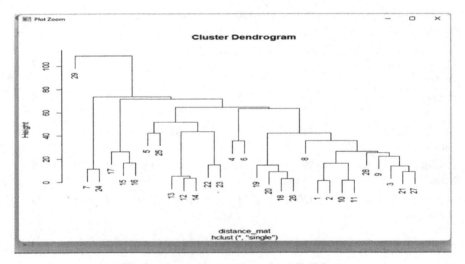

```
in dist(data1, method = "euclidean") : NAs introduced by coercion
> distance_mat
        1          2          3          4          5          6          7          8          9         10
2    1.087824
3   57.776701  57.749945
4  103.381690 103.356277 159.169944
5  221.692692 221.690579 279.386857 127.559770
6   68.934230  68.878975 124.120451  35.434641 160.327833
7  254.433944 254.427591 310.321915 178.485458  73.881140 205.039440
8   52.839579  52.763554  52.345354 127.854139 254.543675  94.433856 296.419963
9   26.607461  26.372461  34.905170 124.643402 246.072589  89.582685 280.132370  35.440474
10  16.147680  16.031900  70.477572  96.345479 210.094166  63.484696 240.183335  68.255772  41.302194
11  16.386743  16.272664  70.572416  96.392290 210.095647  63.474894 240.162609  68.390102  41.463828   1.475730
12 142.742158 142.739611 199.380905  76.375251  88.994839  95.602058 112.176050 184.615061 168.413674 128.981822
13 142.848992 142.804256 199.395438  76.346762  89.120832  95.550970 112.254697 184.553202 168.289793 129.016177
14 142.786999 142.773278 199.416761  76.476063  89.011185  95.573639 112.136493 184.644350 168.420372 128.983539
15 343.846603 343.845397 401.521566 246.912094 122.288250 280.929732 125.384700 374.702180 367.991531 332.342187
16 335.082093 335.080709 392.754791 240.062608 113.579697 273.540468 110.087215 367.635014 359.561420 323.138221
17 321.150734 321.149359 378.640250 229.877091 102.382808 262.183553  85.848775 356.398818 346.103668 308.515595
18  97.835797  97.808986  42.438417 194.771919 318.178326 159.991632 351.738845  71.950077  72.569492 111.775634
19 107.966615 107.951525  55.056571 201.714519 326.593834 167.155599 362.347685  75.622368  82.373650 122.562232
20 105.183113 105.159160  48.892082 202.702036 325.938237 167.796081 358.953619  79.775567  80.092441 118.866900
21  44.501236  44.415564  13.709021 146.055039 265.959799 110.997766 297.221767  46.457815  22.103233  57.227995
22 171.908760 171.910719 229.525884  76.402555  51.699543 109.045778 109.535103 203.275603 195.847482 161.139008
23 157.666549 157.661790 215.330478  64.703884  64.792318  95.965924 116.269619 190.281317 181.804761 146.638455
24 245.803461 245.808982 301.390435 172.467302  74.786039 197.976669  11.541389 288.575667 271.594883 231.401446
25 262.120441 262.117135 319.732316 164.696680  42.298265 198.732737  85.152494 292.437517 286.016294 251.043665
26  97.417724  97.402977  42.090526 194.419045 317.838324 159.612928 351.422759  71.627331  72.280256 111.389510
27  46.757071  46.772631  13.779969 148.690446 267.864204 111.790435 300.555510  41.622244  23.208480  60.722320
28  68.636015  68.633017  25.202020 171.824778 286.856030 137.423178 312.141796  76.567898  52.108352  77.409631
29 280.503183 280.553803 326.995580 242.384973 180.648951 256.144253 114.751901 331.428787 305.170045 264.707136
```

Fig. 4. Distance matrix for car sales data set

Fig. 5. Dendrogram creating using Min linkage

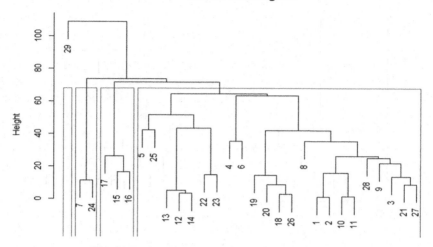

Fig. 6. Total 4 clusters are created using Min linkage

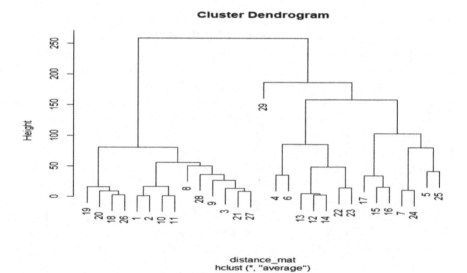

Fig. 7. Dendrogram creating using Average linkage

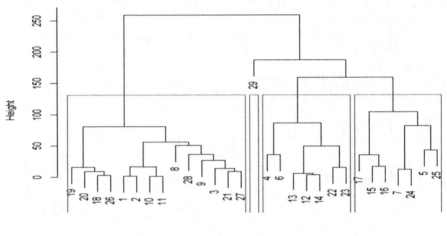

Fig. 8. Total 4 clusters are created using Average linkage

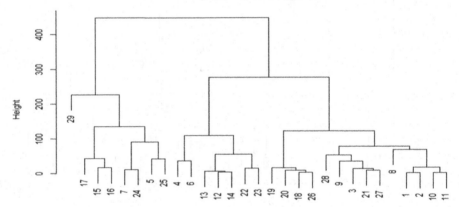

Fig. 9. Dendrogram creating using Max linkage

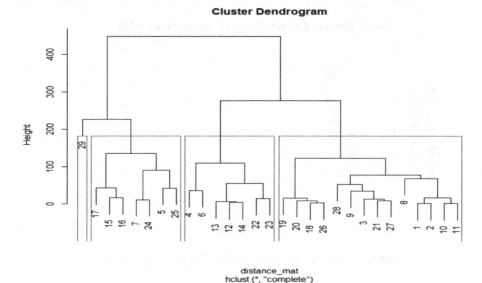

Cluster Dendrogram

distance_mat
hclust (*, "complete")

Fig. 10. Total 4 clusters are created using Max linkage

9   Comparative Analysis

We have compared these three-approach based on number of clusters and number of objects in each cluster.

1. **Number of objects present in each clusters using Min Linkage** (Fig. 11 and Graph 1)

```
Console   Terminal ×   Background Jobs ×
  R  R 4.2.1 · ~/
> # Plotting dendrogram
> plot(Hierar_cl)
> # Cutting tree by no. of clusters
> fit <- cutree(Hierar_cl, k = 4 )
> fit
 [1] 1 1 1 1 1 1 2 1 1 1 1 1 1 1 3 3 3 1 1 1 1 1 1 2 1 1 1 1 4
> table(fit)
fit
 1  2  3  4
23  2  3  1
> rect.hclust(Hierar_cl, k = 4, border = "red")
>
>
>
>
>
>
>
```

Fig. 11. Total 4 clusters with 23, 2, 3 and 1 objects with Min linkage

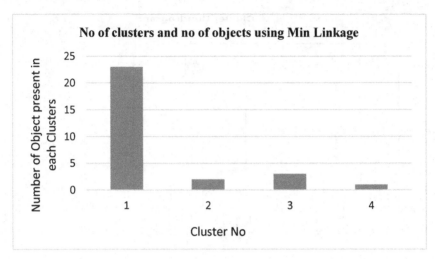

Graph 1. Total 4 clusters with 23, 2, 3 and 1 objects with Min linkage

2. **Number of objects present in each clusters using Average Linkage** (Fig. 12 and Graph 2)

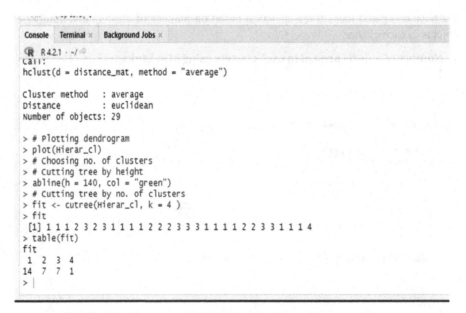

Fig. 12. Total 4 clusters with 14, 7, 7 and 1 object with Average linkage

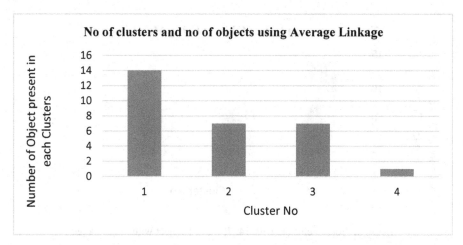

Graph 2. Total 4 clusters with 14, 7, 7 and 1 object with average linkage

3. **Number of objects present in each clusters using Max Linkage** (Fig. 13 and Graph 3)

```
Console    Terminal    Background Jobs

R  R 4.2.1 · ~/
> Hierar_cl <- hclust(distance_mat, method = "complete")
> Hierar_cl

Call:
hclust(d = distance_mat, method = "complete")

Cluster method   : complete
Distance         : euclidean
Number of objects: 29

> # Plotting dendrogram
> plot(Hierar_cl)
> # Cutting tree by no. of clusters
> fit <- cutree(Hierar_cl, k = 4 )
> fit
 [1] 1 1 1 2 3 2 3 1 1 1 1 2 2 2 3 3 3 1 1 1 1 2 2 3 3 1 1 1 4
> table(fit)
fit
 1  2  3  4
14  7  7  1
> |
```

Fig. 13. Total 4 clusters with 14, 7, 7 and 1 object with Max linkage

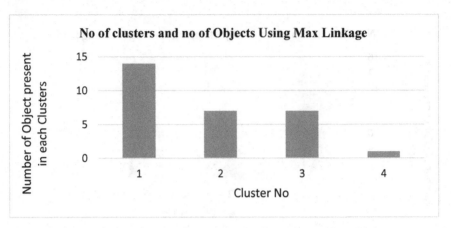

Graph 3. Total 4 clusters with 14, 7, 7 and 1 object with Max linkage

10   Conclusion

From the above implementation of all three approaches of Agglomerative hierarchical clustering we found that in each method the shape of dendrogram is different and also the number of objects in each cluster are also different, especially in average linkage. From the dendrogram we can identify that the three are clusters which contain only one object and the merging value of this cluster is also very high. We used real life data set with 29 car model of four famous brand Maruti Suzuki, Hyundai, Tata and Land Rover. There is total 9 attribute are used in the data set. In the data set there are more 1000 models sold but we found that the selling of the model Land Rover is very low as compared to all other three model. All 9 attributes of Land Rover of are much different from the other model. Using Agglomerative hierarchical it is clear that the global outlier can easily see in the dendrogram. One more important thing is that there no need to give number of clusters. In future we can use the approach for finding groups of outliers. In future we also compare the proposed approach with other existing methods.

References

1. Habib, U., Zucker, G., Blöchle, M., Judex, F., Haas, J.: Outliers detection method using clustering in buildings data. In: IECON2015-Yokohama, 9–12 November 2015. IEEE (2015). 978-1-4799-1762-4/15
2. Bhuyana, M.H., Bhattacharyya, D.K., Kalita, J.K.: A multi-step outlier-based anomaly detection approach to network-wide traffic. Inf. Sci. **348**, 243–271 (2016).
3. Alguliyev, R.M., Aliguliyev, R.M., Imamverdiyev, Y.N.: An anomaly detection based on optimization I.J. Intell. Syst. Appl. **12**, 87–96 (2017). http://www.mecs-press.org/, https://doi.org/10.5815/ijisa.2017.12.08
4. Hodge, V.J., Austin, J.: An evaluation of classification and outlier detection algorithms. Digital Creativity Labs, Department of Computer Science, University of York, UK (2018). arXiv: 1805.00811v1 [stat.ML]

5. Zhao, Y., Nasrullah, Z.: PyOD: a python toolbox for scalable outlier detect. J. Mach. Learn. Res. **20**, 1–7 (2019). Submitted 1/19; Revised 4/19; Published 5/19, arXiv:1901.01588v2 [cs.LG] (2019)

6. Duraj, A., Chomątek, Ł.: Politechnika Łódzka, Instytut Informatyki, Wydział Fizyki Detection of outliers in data streams using grouping methods Przegląd Elektrotechniczny (2019). ISSN 0033-2097

7. ur Rehman, A., Belhaouari, S.B.: Unsupervised outlier detection in multidimensional data. J. Big Data **8**(1), 1–27 (2021). https://doi.org/10.1186/s40537-021-00469-z

8. Abghari, S.: Data mining approaches for outlier detection analysis. Blekinge Institute of Technology Doctoral Dissertation Series No 2020:09 2020 Department of Computer Science Publisher: Blekinge Institute of Technology SE-371 79 Karlskrona, Sweden Printed by Exakta Group, Sweden (2020). ISBN 978-91-7295-409-0, ISSN 1653-2090, urn:nbn:se:bth-20454

9. Al Rezami, A.Y.: Effect of outliers on the coefficient of determination in multiple regression analysis with the application on the GPA for student. Int. J. Adv. Appl. Sci. **7**(10), 30–37 (2020). http://www.science-gate.com/IJAAS.html

10. Afzal, S., Afzal, A., Amin, M., Saleem, S., Ali, N., Sajid, M.: A novel approach for outlier detection in multivariate data. Hindawi Math. Probl. Eng. **2021**, 12 (2021). https://doi.org/10.1155/2021/1899225. Article ID 1899225

11. Chatterjee, I., Zhou, M.: Abdullah Abusorrah statistics-based outlier detection and correction method for amazon customer reviews. Entropy **23**, 1645 (2021). https://doi.org/10.3390/e23121645. Academic Editor: Ernestina Menasalvas Received: 23 October 2021 Accepted: 30 November 2021 Published: 7 December 2021

12. Dominguesa, R., Filipponea, M., Michiardia, P., Zouaouib, J.: A comparative evaluation of outlier detection algorithms: experiments and analyses. Department of Data Science, EURECOM, Sophia Antipolis, France (2018)

13. Pamula, R., Deka, J.K., Nandi, S.: An outlier detection method based on clustering. In: 2011 Second International Conference on Emerging Applications of Information Technology (2011)

14. Ishaq, N., Howard, T.J.: III clustered hierarchical anomaly and outlier detection algorithms. Department of Computer Science and Statistics University of Rhode Island Kingston, RI. arXiv:2103.11774v1 [cs.LG], 9 February 2021

15. Bakar, Z.A., Mohemad, R., Ahmad, A.: A comparative study for outlier detection techniques in data mining. University College of Science and Technology 21030 Kuala Terengganu, Malaysia (2006)

16. Masciari, E., Mazzeo, G.M., Zaniolo, C.: A New, fast and accurate algorithm for hierarchical clustering on euclidean distances. In: Pei, J., Tseng, V.S., Cao, L., Motoda, H., Xu, G. (eds.) PAKDD 2013. LNCS (LNAI), vol. 7819, pp. 111–122. Springer, Heidelberg (2013). https://doi.org/10.1007/978-3-642-37456-2_10

17. Malitsky Y., Sabharwal, A., Samulowitz, H., Sellmann, M.: Algorithm portfolios based on cost-sensitive hierarchical clustering. In: Proceedings of the Twenty-Third International Joint Conference on Artificial Intelligence IBM Watson Research Center Yorktown Heights, NY 10598, USA (2013)

18. Chandola, V., Banerjee, A.: Outlier detection: a survey. University at Buffalo, The State University of New York ACM Computing Surveys (2009)

Prediction of Heat Energy Consumption by LSTM Sequence-to-Sequence Models

Mazen Ossman, Rozina Mohaideen, and Yaxin Bi[✉]

School of Computing, Ulster University, Belfast, UK
{ossman-m,mohaideen-r,y.bi}@ulster.ac.uk

Abstract. The accurate estimation of heat energy performance in buildings is critical for optimizing energy demand and supply. Non-residential properties have predictable operating patterns in principle, incorporating these patterns into simulations of energy consumption can help estimate building energy use. In this work we develop Long-Short Term Memory (LSTM) Sequence to Sequence and Gated Recurrent Unit (GRU) architectures, which are composed of Dropout, Repeat Vector, Time-distributed and Graph Convolution layers. We have conducted a rigor comparative study on the structures and hyper parameters using the national grid data, then use the learnt models for the energy demand site management undertaken in a laboratory environment.

Keywords: LSTM · GRU · energy consumption prediction · time series data analysis

1 Introduction

Recurrent Neural Networks (RNN) are subsets of deep networks, which lately showed remarkable potentials in solving a variety of applications with complex sequential models, including automatic voice commands, language processing, and the creation of linguistic descriptions for pictures. RNNs are characterized by cyclic interconnections with a hidden layer wherein stimulation at each temporal step relies on the activity of the preceding time, rendering RNNs fundamentally deep around the major axis in contrast to forward propagation models like multi-perceptron neural networks. Nevertheless, because of the very well-known high derivative and expanding gradient difficulties, the complexity of RNNs makes it challenging to train a RNN, this pitfall restricts their ability to understand long-term spatio-temporal features. From the standpoint of types of networks and evolutionary algorithms, researchers have devised a variety of solutions to overcome these issues, the most effective of which is a customized RNN framework known as LSTM.

The LSTM model makes use of a memory module that can preserve its condition over a period and a filtering mechanism that generally includes three non-linear gateways to manage the flow of data through and out of the zones. This technique has been discovered to be very capable of capturing and utilizing long-range interconnections embedded in data without experiencing the instructional difficulties that are a problem for traditional

D. Garg et al. (Eds.): IACC 2022, CCIS 1782, pp. 140–153, 2023.
https://doi.org/10.1007/978-3-031-35644-5_11

RNNs. For forecast timeseries problems Arima and machine learning algorithms could be used as well. In [1] a logistic regression model combined by Arima was used to predict CO2, temperature, and humidity from sensors. Numerous enhancements or structural changes have been proposed to LSTMs for increasing its performance since it was first developed [2]. LSTM model was used with attention mechanism to provide forecasting for solar assisted water heating systems and a comparison of the numbers of layers and neurons were made [3]. Another paper discussed LSTM with attention mechanism to create a system that forecasting the heating, ventilation, and air conditioning systems and compared it to different models [4]. A different paper has addressed the GRU architecture combined with CNN, and made a comparison of the performance between GRU and CNN separately, for instance, combining them together to forecast Electricity of Wuwei and Gansu provinces [5]. LSTM was compared with support vector machine to forecast landslide displacement by analyzing the geological environment in China [6].

This work presents the development of a LSTM Sequence to Sequence model and its application for forecasting electricity consumption along with a comparative study with GRU. The requirement for electricity consumption over the short, moderate, and term period must be accurately forecasted in order for process control in the energy demand site management. There are several other methods that can be for predicting the usage of energy, including conventional machine learning algorithms, statistical models with nonlinear systems and classic approaches. The contribution of our work is that we have studied four separate LSTM and GRU configurations with different layers and evaluate their capability for predicting the electricity consumption behavior of a laboratory environment using the lab electricity consumption data monitored.

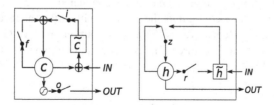

Fig. 1. LSTM (left) and GRU (right) [7]

1.1 LSTM Models

LSTM networks are typically employed as links to retain responses of occurrences throughout the form of inputs. They have been applied to sequence-to-sequence learning tasks, such as for machine translation, speech recognition, time series analysis, etc. An LSTM memory command's streamlined design is shown in Fig. 1 (left), where i, f and o are the input, forget and output gates, respectively. c and $\tilde{c}$ denote the memory cell and the new memory cell content. This model, like some of the others, really does have a unique three-dimensional structure that depends on the training dataset that it already has. It features a simple design that allows reading a given input series and anticipates the power consumption with only a vector result. By utilizing memory units c and $\tilde{c}$ really can adjust the prior concealed configuration, preserving their better ability. Every cell receives feedback from it. LSTM output is influenced by past neural contributions in addition to the current column input as well as weight of the different gates. It is feasible to comprehend interrelations on a continuous series because of this feature.

1.2 Gru Models

GRU works like LSTM, however it has less complex structure as illustrated graphically in Fig. 1(right), where r and z are the reset and update gates, and h and $\tilde{h}$ are the activation and the candidate activation. The reset gate will decide how to aggregate the new input with the previous memory cell, and the update gate determines how much of the previous memory cell to keep around. The basic idea is to use a gating mechanism to learn long-term dependencies as an LSTM does. However, there are no output layers that determines the outputs like LSTM as shown in Fig. 1 (left), the output is the full state vector.

2 The Architectures of the Models

We designed the model architectures to evaluate the capability of LSTM and GRU, in addition to those memory architectures. The models have included a Repeat Vector layer, a Time Distribution layer, and a Graph Convolution layer, respectively. The aim of adding these layers is to compare their effectiveness and choose the best suited architecture in terms of time of the training, and the accuracy of the models. 2 experiments on each of the models (GRU and LSTM models) have been conducted.

The experiments have configured the models with different layers, for example removing a layer either Repeat Vector, Time Distribution layer, or Graph convolution layer from the network architectures. The architecture components of the two models are presented in Table 1.

Table 1. Model architecture

Layer/Model	Model A	Model B
Layer 1	Graph Conv 5 Nodes 8 Edges	Graph Conv 5 Nodes 8 Edges
Layer 2	Time Distribution layer	Time Distribution layer
Layer 3	LSTM 32 Neurons	GRU 32 neurons
Layer 4	Repeat vector	Repeat Vector
Layer 5	Drop out 50%	Drop out 50%
Layer 6	LSTM 64, Neurons	GRU 64, Neurons
Layer 7	Drop out 40%	Drop out 40%

(*continued*)

Table 1. (*continued*)

Layer/Model	Model A	Model B
Layer 8	Dense 16 neurons Activation Relu	Dense 16 neurons Activation Relu
Layer 9 (Output Layer)	Dense Activation Relu	Dense Activation Relu

In first experiment we used 20 timesteps to forecast 3 timesteps ahead. In the second experiment the timesteps were 300 to forecast 10 timesteps ahead. In each of the experiments we removed from the model one of the following layers Layer 1, Layer 2, and Layer 4 which are described in Table 1 to test the impact of each layer on the model. The model output layer size depends on the experiment.

3 Evaluation

The benchmark dataset initially used for hyperparameter tuning is called Historic2 Day Ahead Demand Forecasts [8]. It contains all historic 2 day ahead demand forecasts from 2018 till now. After attaining initial results with that, a real-time dataset was used for training and testing the models, which was acquired from the laboratory room for June 22–30th, 2022 as shown in Fig. 2. The dataset consists of the time stamps, temperature, plus electricity meter along with about 25000 entries. We treat the forecasting of energy consumption as a problem of sequence-to-sequence prediction and aim to forecast the power usage for the subsequent M inspections using the prior N samples (that include whole columns mentioned before). That means we consider M (Forecasting ahead) and N (the timesteps) to be hyperparameters.

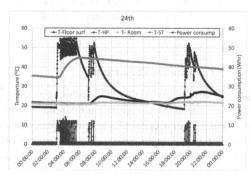

Fig. 2. Heat Pump for charging the storage and underfloor heating system on 24th Jun 2022

Three losses are employed in the training process:

- Mean Absolute Error – The difference between the forecasted value and the actual value.

- Mean Squared Error – Average of the square of the difference between actual and estimated consumption demand.
- Huber Loss – Another crucial metric for loss calculation.

The dataset was normalized first and divided into 80% of the dataset for training and 20% of the dataset for validation. The training dataset is further split into training and test, and then shuffled in a way that they are in sequences, each sequence is fed to the network in a mini batch. The mini batch is composed of 30 samples that are fed during the training process. For example, a mini batch starts from 00:00:00 and ends at 00:15:00, and another mini batch starts from 00:13:00 and ends at 00:28:00, and so forth.

4   Experimental Results

The 2 experiments are Experiment A and Experiment B. In Experiment A timesteps used is 20, forecasting timesteps ahead is 3 and epochs are 20. In Experiment B the timesteps is 300, forecasting is 10 timesteps ahead, and the epochs are 20. We used two different experiments to test our models in different environments and a comparison of the models were provided in terms of time consumed for training and the results accuracy. In the experiment part we used Tensorflow 2.0, because it is easy to implement and has a body of practical resources [10–12].

4.1   Experiment A

The training set shape was (30, 20, 5) where the 30 is the mini batches, the 20 is the timesteps, and the 5 features are T floor, T room upper, T room, Electric Meter, and Power Consumption. The output was (30, 3) which are the 3 timesteps ahead forecasted of the Power Consumption.

The negative time-steps in the graphs presents the time-steps that were passed to the model (past time-steps). The positive time-steps represents the model forecasted time-steps.

4.1.1   Analysis of the LSTM Models Performance

When working using time series data and image elements, the Time Distributed layer is quite helpful, since it allows the network to apply a layer each timesteps, which makes the shape of the output (batch, timesteps, output dimensions) instead of (batch, output dimensions) [9]. We may employ a layer with each input to improve the predictability of our approach, we may try adding a Time Distributed layer as illustrated in Fig. 5.

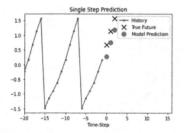
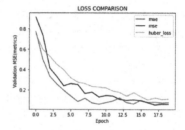

Fig. 3. LSTM Model prediction (left) and Loss Comparison plot MAE, MSE, Huber for the models (right) over the national grid datasets

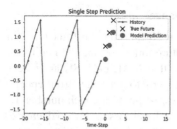
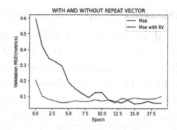

Fig. 4. LSTM Without Repeat Vector Layer MSE predictions (left) and LSTM with and without Repeat Vector Layer MSE (right) on validation set.

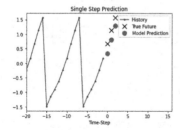
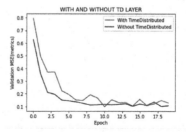

Fig. 5. LSTM with and without Time Distributed Layer prediction (left) and LSTM with and without Time Distributed Layer MSE performance (right) on validation set

Then we added the GraphConv type layer as the first level to our network and run additional tests to compare the output with the results of the present model as Fig. 6.

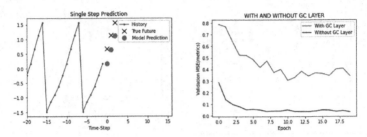

Fig. 6. LSTM with and Without Graph convolution layer prediction (left) and LSTM with and without Graph convolution layer MSE on Validation set.

4.1.2 Analysis of the GRU Models Performance

We conducted an evaluation of GRU model on 20 timesteps to forecast 3 timesteps. Figure 7 (left) shows the model predicted 3 future timesteps and the real timesteps. In Fig. 7 (right), the loss function Huber starts lower than MAE and MSE, and it keeps going down until MAE loss function decreases as it starts to get better from epoch number 3 and then keeps going down until it reaches lowest point in epoch number 18. That's because MAE takes more epochs than MSE and Huber loss to start to decrease.

From Fig. 8, it can be seen that GRU performance has drastically improved, when Repeat vector exists.

From Fig. 9, it can be observed that GRU model had done much better without Time distributed.

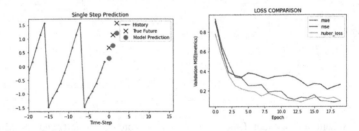

Fig. 7. GRU model prediction (left) and GRU Model loss functions (right)

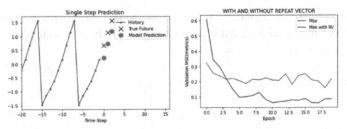

Fig. 8. GRU without Repeat Vector Model prediction (left) and GRU with and MSE without Repeat Vector Layer (right) on validation set.

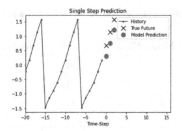
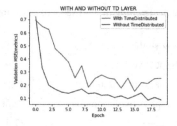

Fig. 9. GRU without Repeat Vector Model predictions (left) and GRU with and without Time distributed performance (right) on validation set.

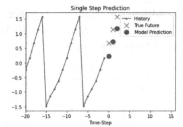
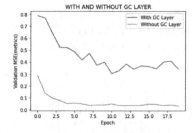

Fig. 10. With and without Graph convolution layer prediction (left) and MSE performance with and without Graph convolution layer (right) on validation set

Table 2. Comparison between LSTM and GRU performance on the validation set using MSE metric

Experiment/Model	LSTM Model MSE	GRU Model MSE
Without Repeat vector	0.0577	0.1575
Without Time distribution layer	0.1025	0.0840
Without Graph convolution layer	0.0224	0.0343
With every layer	0.0537	0.2116

Generally, both models perform good for the task. From the results, it can be noticed that LSTM outperformed GRU models, but GRU took less training time than LSTM when we removed convolution layer, and when we removed the Time-distributed layer as shown in Tables 2, 3. It is also noticed that in all tests MSE loss function did not work well with GRU illustrated in Fig. 7 (right), However, MSE loss function worked well for LSTM as shown in Fig. 3 (right).

Table 3. Training time in seconds consumption comparison between LSTM and GRU

Experiment/Model	LSTM Model MSE	GRU Model MSE
Without Repeat vector	38.9	58.7
Without Time distribution layer	40.8	37.3
Without Graph convolution layer	52.80	51.11
With every layer	37.4	37.7

4.2 Experiment B

In this subsection the LSTM architecture and the GRU architecture are evaluated on 300 timesteps. The input shape in this case is (30, 300, 5) and the labels are (30, 10), because the model is receiving the 5 features, and outputs 10 timesteps forecasts.

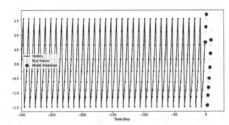 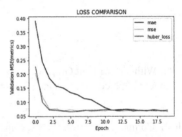

Fig. 11. LSTM model prediction (left) and Loss Comparison plot of MAE, MSE, Huber for the model (right)

As seen from Fig. 11 (right), that the Huber Loss gets less than the MAE and the MSE, since it is a combination of both. Huber is apparently better when the timesteps are high.

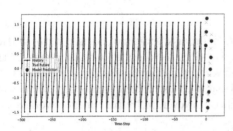 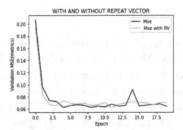

Fig. 12. LSTM without Repeat Vector Model predictions (left) and LSTM with and without Repeat Vector Layer Model performance on validation set (right)

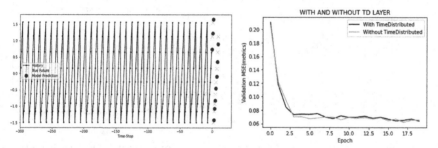

Fig. 13. LSTM without Repeat Vector Model predictions (left) and LSTM with and without Time distributed performance (right) on validation set.

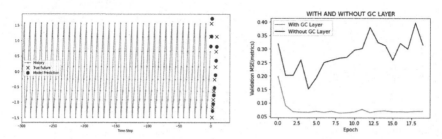

Fig. 14. Without Graph convolution layer prediction (left) and With and without Graph convolution layer (right)

4.2.1 Analysis of the GRU MODel's Performance

The following shows that the GRU model is trained and tested on datasets of 300 timesteps to forecast 10 timesteps ahead. In Fig. 16 (right) the GRU model predictions against the labels. Figure 15 (right) shows the model performance when trained with MAE, MSE, and Huber loss.

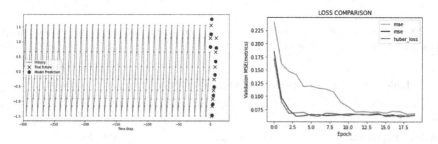

Fig. 15. GRU model prediction for $N = 10$ (left) and GRU Model loss functions (right)

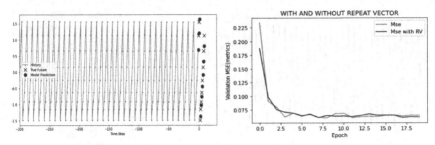

Fig. 16. GRU without Repeat Vector Model prediction (left) and GRU with and without Repeat Vector Layer on validation set (right)

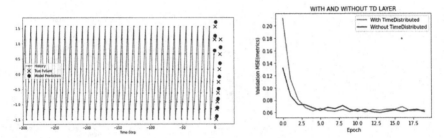

Fig. 17. Without Time distributed layer prediction (left) and GRU with and without Time distributed layer Model performance on validation set (right).

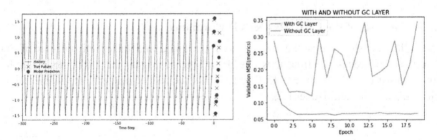

Fig. 18. Without Graph convolution layer prediction (left), and with and without Graph convolution layer (right) on validation set.

Table 4. Comparison between LSTM and GRU performance on the validation set.

Experiment/Model	LSTM Model MSE	GRU Model MSE
Without Repeat vector	0.0620	0.0604
Without Time distribution layer	0.0620	0.0597
Without Graph convolution layer	0.1508	0.1195
With every layer	0.0656	0.0663

Table 5. Training time in seconds consumption comparison between LSTM and GRU.

Experiment/Model	LSTM Model MSE	GRU Model MSE
Without Repeat vector	124.1	100.9
Without Time distribution layer	114.8	110.1
Without Graph convolution layer	711.0	557.1
With every layer	108.6	102.1

5 Discussion

From the previous figures and tables, we have observed the following findings for LSTM:

- When timesteps are 20 and forecast is 3 timesteps, MSE and MAE are good with LSTM and quickly reach the lowest error as shown in Fig. 3 (right), while timesteps are 300, Huber quickly goes to the lowest point and so as MSE, then after few epochs MAE starts to get to the lowest point with the rest at some point, because MAE takes time to reach the lowest point as shown in Fig. 11 (right).
- LSTM perform better with Repeat vector, but it takes more time to achieve the lowest error when timestep is 20 and the timestep of forecasts is 3 as shown in Fig. 4 (right). On the other side, when timesteps are 300 with 10 timesteps forecasts, the Repeat vector layer does not have much change as shown in Fig. 12 (right).
- LSTM performs better with Time distribution in conjunction with the flatten layer when the timesteps are 20 as shown in Fig. 5 (right), but the model takes almost the same time as training does. While with 300 timesteps the model does not perform much difference Fig. 13 (right), but it saves a small amount of time as illustrated in Table 5.
- For Graph convolution layer the LSTM model does not perform well in 20 timesteps as shown in Fig. 6 (right) but saves so much time as shown in Table 3. That is because the Graph convolution layer extracts the features of each node, which are initialized from the inputs and each of the features of the nodes are averaged with the neighbor nodes, which take the important features of the inputs, such as the Convolution neural network and max pool [13]. On the other hand when the model is with 300 timesteps, it obtains pretty much high accuracy as shown in Fig. 14 (right), and the training time is reduced from 711 s to 108 s as shown in Table 5.
- The LSTM models outperform the GRU models in some cases in terms of training time in 20 timesteps since the input is too small ($20 \times 30 \times 3$). When input small, it affects the size of the neural network since the dot product requires that the row or column of the input to be the same size as the column or row of the neural network, therefore the training time increases. For 20 timesteps the time consumed for training is less compared when using 300 timesteps ($20 \times 300 \times 10$), that is why LSTM has outperformed GRU in some cases because the time consumed is small in both models, due to the small size, and the ability of the GRU of fast training time won't be apparent when timesteps are low, unlike when the timesteps are 300, the GRU

performs much faster, but the accuracy is very similar to LSTM. The more the input is the more time the LSTM requires shown in Tables 3, 5.

Additionally, from the previous figures and tables we have the findings for GRU models as follows:

- When timesteps are 20 the GRU does not perform much better with the MSE loss for training, but the model performs better with both Huber and MAE losses as shown in Fig. 7(right). When timesteps are 300 the MSE and Huber also tend quickly to go to the lowest point, and after few epochs the MAE starts to go back to the same level as shown in Fig. 15 (right).
- When timesteps is 20 the model with the Repeated Vector speeds up the training drastically as shown in Fig. 8 (right), saving 21 s approximately as shown in Table 3, also achieving high accuracy. It does not change much using Repeated Vector when the timesteps are 300 as illustrated in Fig. 16 (right).
- When timesteps are 20, the model with the Time distributed and the flatten layer does not perform better, and the model gets worse in the training efficiency as shown in Fig. 9 (right). When it is 300 timesteps the model has quick training, but the accuracy of model does not change much compared with not using the layer as presented in Fig. 17 (right)..
- The model with the Graph Convolutional layer performs worse in 20 timesteps as shown in Fig. 10 (right), but it has decreased the training time. On the other hand, when timesteps are 300 the model achieves the high accuracy as shown in Fig. 18 (right), meanwhile saving training time from 557 s to 102 s as shown in Table 5. And error decreases from 0.1 to 0.06 in validation set as given in Table 4.
- The GRU model performs well in 300 timesteps in terms of accuracy and training time. The LSTM is 0.0007 better than GRU in terms of error rate as presented in Tables 2, 4.

6   Conclusion

In this study, we have developed the LSTM-based and GRU-based models for predicting the energy consumption of heat pumps in premises. The two models have been evaluated with 2 experiments, where Experiment A has 20 timesteps input and 3 timesteps forecasting ahead, and Experiment B has 300 timesteps and 10 timesteps forecast. For experiment A, both models take 37 s to be trained. For experiment B, the training time of LSTM is 108 s and GRU is 102. Our study suggests the Graph convolution layer is preferred as part of the architecture, it speeds up the training process in Experiment B which reduces the training time by 600 s for LSTM, and 400 s for GRU. However, this layer is not suggested to be used when the timesteps are low for LSTM models, since the performance of the model has lower accuracy. The GRU performs better with the Huber loss function, but the LSTM performs better when using the MSE loss. The Time distribution with flatten layer is not effective in the case of Experiment B. The Repeat vector decreases the time of the training and increases the accuracy for GRU models in Experiment A. While for Experiment B the repeat vector was not very effective.

Acknowledgement. This work is supported by the project of "Novel Building Integration Designs for Increased Efficiencies in Advanced Climatically Tuneable Renewable Energy Systems (IDEAS)" (Grant ID: 815271), which is funded by the EU Horizon 2020 programme.

References

1. Cao, T.D., Delahoche, L., Marhic, B., Masson, J.B.: Occupancy forecasting using two ARIMA strategies. In: Proceedings of the ITISE 2019: International Conference on Time Series and Forecasting, vol. 2. Granada, Spain, 25–27 September 2019 (2019)
2. Chen, K.: APSO-LSTM: an improved LSTM neural network model based on APSO algorithm. In: Journal of Physics: Conference Series, p. 012151. IOP Publishing, Bristol, UK (2020)
3. Heidari, A., Khovalyg, D.: Short-term energy use prediction of solar-assisted water heating system: Application case of combined attention-based LSTM and time-series decomposition. Sol. Energy **207**, 626–639 (2020)
4. Xu, Y., Gao, W., Qian, F., Li, Y.: Potential analysis of the attention-based LSTM model in ultra-short-term forecasting of building HVAC energy consumption. Front. Energy Res. **9**, 463 (2021)
5. Wu, L., Kong, C., Hao, X., Chen, W.: A short-term load forecasting method based on GRU-CNN hybrid neural network model. Math. Probl. Eng. **2020**, 1428104 (2020)
6. Yang, B., Yin, K., Lacasse, S., Liu, Z.: Time series analysis and long short-term memory neural network to predict landslide displacement. Landslides **16**(4), 677–694 (2019). https://doi.org/10.1007/s10346-018-01127-x
7. Denny's Blog. Recurrent Neural Network Tutorial, Part 4 Implementing a GRU and LSTM RNN with Python and Theano. https://dennybritz.com/posts/wildml/recurrent-neural-net works-tutorial-part-4
8. https://data.nationalgrideso.com/demand/2-day-ahead-demand-forecast
9. Géron, A., Demarest, R.: Hands-on Machine learning with Scikit-learn and TensorFlow, 2nd ed. Sebastopol (Clif.) [Etc.], p. 510, 69 O'Reily (2019)
10. https://towardsdatascience.com/energy-consumption-time-series-forecasting-with-python-and-lstm-deep-learning-model-7952e2f9a796
11. https://github.com/VeritasYin/STGCN_IJCAI-18
12. https://towardsdatascience.com/forecasting-the-future-power-consumption-of-germany-using-lstm-rnn-and-dnn-d8e05e7fdc0a
13. Wu, F., Souza, A., Zhang, T., Fifty, C., Yu, T., Weinberger, K.: Simplifying graph convolutional networks. In: International Conference on Machine Learning, pp. 6861–6871. PMLR (2019)

A Chi-Square Dissimilarity Measure for Clustering Categorical Datasets

Luis Ariosto Serna Cardona[1,2(✉)] ⓘ, Kevin Alejandro Hernández[1,2] ⓘ,
Gina Marcela Barreto[2] ⓘ, Piedad Navarro González[1] ⓘ,
and Álvaro Ángel Orozco Gutiérrez[1] ⓘ

[1] Department of Electrical Engineering, Universidad Tecnológica de Pereira,
Pereira, Colombia
{luarserna,kevin_loco,pinago,aaog}@utp.edu.co
[2] Department of Engineering, Corporación Instituto de Administración y finanzas
(CIAF), Pereira, Colombia
gina.barreto@ciaf.edu.co

Abstract. Currently, there has been a high use of databases of large proportionalities. In addition, in using these data, there has been an enormous increase in using categorical data, specifically in using new alternatives to identify the most relevant items. In this order of ideas, cluster analysis is a relevant approach for the processing of categorical data. However, different machine learning models that have been proposed in the literature have problems to interpret categorical variables because of their high dimensionality and data overlapping, which can cause high computational cost or low performance in the algorithms. For this reason, we propose an unsupervised method using the C-S (Chi-Square) dissimilarity measure mapping from a categorical to a continuous Euclidean space, allowing an adequate interpretation of the k-means algorithm with the squared Euclidean distance. Furthermore, the proposed method was compared with other state-of-the-art techniques in unsupervised learning for categorical data such as: k-means, Mkm-nof, weighted dissimilarity, Mkm-ndm and structure-based clustering (SBC) algorithms; evaluated the accuracy (AC), adjusted rand index (ARI) and normalized mutual information (NMI). The results we present in the proposal outperform the clustering methods in the different evaluation methods on the 9 databases worked, for example, the (AC) of our Kmeans (C-S) method presented on the whole dataset is 0. 8090, in SBC1 of 0.7907, SBC2 of 0.7820, k-modes of 0.6979, W-D of 0.6949, Mkm-not of 0.6906 and Mkm-ndm of 0.7254 demonstrating superiority not only in the AC, but also in NMI and ARI. On the other hand, computational time was an issue of great relevance in our proposal because of the results got, in them it can be interpreted that the Kmeans (C-S) method in 8 of the 9 databases takes less than half the time of the other algorithms executing its model.

Keywords: Categorical Data · Chi-square · Cluster · Dissimilarity · K-means

© Springer Nature Switzerland AG 2023
D. Garg et al. (Eds.): IACC 2022, CCIS 1782, pp. 154–166, 2023.
https://doi.org/10.1007/978-3-031-35644-5_12

1   Introduction

The augment of available datasets and integration of meta-data provide to the research community new resources to achieve scientific discoveries, optimizing industrial processes and it grants to find relations or characteristic patterns in data. For this reason, some research works have developed methods and algorithms for processing huge amount of data (data mining), allowing to compress the relevant information into a smaller set. The above is done preserving the data structure and highlighting the most significant features [15].

A successful framework employed to describe and find patterns in datasets is the unsupervised learning or clustering. This learning methodology categorizes the data in groups called clusters as [16], by finding relations among features from samples or directly from the raw data [6]. For example, a clustering method assigns a label for each sample depending on a similarity measure with other grouped data.

The K-means algorithm is the most common and efficient method (in terms of computational cost) for clustering [2,4,21]. Nevertheless, the selection of a similarity measure (metric) is often done depending on the application, type of dataset, number of clusters, dimensionality, among others. This is explained because there are categorical, nominal, qualitative and quantitative variables, so, it is not correct to apply directly a numeric metric in all type of data [15].

Moreover, the high demand for categorical data in the global market requires different clustering models to provide solutions to the problems presented in this type of data. Therefore, one of the first approaches developed is that of Ralambondrainy clustering categorical data with K-means. Specifically, he used a method of transforming categorical data to binary (1 presence and 0 absence of the category), and the binary data were considered as numerical descriptors in K-means. However, this approach presents a major problem of computational cost and memory storage for databases with large numbers of samples and categories, since coding would considerably increase the amount of data to be processed by the [25] algorithm. Another approach is that of Gower with his dissimilarity measures [14], Kaufman's method based on PAM algorithms [19], another relevant method in the literature is that of Seshadridesing with the hierarchical clustering for categorical data [27], Woodbury with his fuzzy statistical algorithms [29] and Michalski interpreting different conceptual clustering methods [22]. However, all the aforementioned methods present computational cost and performance problems when applied to large amounts of categorical data.

Also, in the same way, many clustering methodologies specifically k-means have been making different types of contributions for categorical or mixed data as Andrew Lithio [20] argues, where he developed an algorithm that locally minimizes the objective function of k-means using partial distances. However, the many repetitions required by the methodology are very costly computationally. Similarly, Eugene Demidenko [5] implemented an algorithm based on the Maximum Likelihood (ML) developed by Banfield and Raftery [10]. They are transforming the classification method into clustering using the distribution of Laplace in a k-means algorithm, obtaining excellent results and easy identification of the clusters. However, this method is only normally applicable to data distributions with the same variance, a big problem since most data are of different scales. Therefore they have different variances.

There are methods such as Kaufman's, Ahmad's and Jain's that perform cluster analysis discussing the application of different clustering approaches on categorical data. However, all the presented works do not give an adequate solution to the existing problem on categorical data since the main recommendation given by each author is to use binary similarity measures, but the large amount of memory storage becomes a tangible problem. Also, Wilson et al. developed a study based on distances related to heterogeneous data (quantitative and qualitative variables - mixed data) and focused on supervised algorithms that had the sample and its respective class, but, this types of methods cannot be generalized to unlabeled databases [28]. Nowadays, different authors such as Qian, have developed clustering algorithms that allow the mapping of categorical data to a Euclidean space [24]. These methods display the configuration scheme in structure-based clustering (SBC), which allows excellent results in identifying samples and labels, and have even improved the performance of other clustering methods using unsupervised learning techniques: is that of Gower with his dissimilarity measures [14], Kaufman's method based on PAM algorithms [19], is that of Seshadridesing with the hierarchical clustering for categorical data [27], Woodbury with his fuzzy statistical algorithms [29] and Michalski interpreting different conceptual clustering methods [22]. However, there are distinct disadvantages to SBC methods, the first being based on the high computational cost and the second on the performance of the algorithms for high dimensional data.

According to the previously established in the literature, there are important drawbacks related to the clustering of categorical data. In this work, we introduce a methodology for clustering categorical data sets, where the samples are mapped using the Chi-Square dissimilarity distance adapted to a K-means algorithm. We compare our proposal with state-of-the-art methods: SBC [24], K-modes [17], weighted dissimilarity [9], Mkm-nof and Mkm-ndm algorithms [3]. We evaluate the adjusted rand index (ARI) and accuracy (AC). Results show that our proposal outperforms comparison methods on nine different categorical datasets. Also, the computational time is lower for our approach than the other algorithms.

The rest of the paper is organized as follows: in Sect. 2 we describe the materials and methods. In Sect. 3, we show and discuss the experimental results. Finally, in Sect. 4, we give the conclusions of this work.

2   Materials and Methods

Let $\mathbf{X} \in \mathbb{Z}^{N \times P}$ a categorical data set with N inputs and P features, our aim is to find k groups (clusters) using the standard K-means method and the Chi-Square distance as dissimilarity measure, which is similar to the Euclidean, but in this case it is weighted. This distance is a suitable metric for analysis of qualitative, categorical, nominal and redundant data. Also, it compares the counting of corresponding categorical variables to two or more independent features [23]. Accordingly, we consider this distance as a dissimilarity metric for mapping categorical data to the Euclidean space. We construct the distance matrix with the following expression:

$$d_{ij} = \sqrt{\sum_{n=1}^{P} \frac{1}{\widetilde{w}_n} \left(\widetilde{x}_{in} - \widetilde{x}_{jn} \right)^2},$$

where: $\widetilde{x}_{in} = \frac{x_{in}}{\sum_{n=1}^{P} x_{in}}$, $a_n = \sum_{i=1}^{N} x_{in}$ and $\widetilde{w}_n = \frac{a_n}{\sum_{i=1}^{P} a_n}$. In this case $x_{in} \in \mathbb{Z}$ and $\mathbf{x}_i = \{x_{i1}, ..., x_{iP}\} \in \mathbb{Z}^P$ represents the initial form of the categorical sample, and $\mathbf{d}_i = \{d_{i1}, ..., d_{iN}\} \in \mathbb{R}^N$ is the new sample in the Euclidean space, $\widetilde{w}_i \in \mathbb{R}$ can be interpretate as a i-th feature weight, in this way the original dataset $\mathbf{X}$ is transform in a new data set $\mathbf{D} \in \mathbb{R}^{N \times N}$. Then we use the K-means algorith applying on $\mathbf{D}$, this is method commonly used for partitioning a dataset in k groups (clusters). This is done by minimizing the distance among samples of the same cluster and it is maximized the distance among objects belonging to other groups [12]. The cluster assignation is based on the distance matrix, which is calculated with a similarity measure $\nu (\mathbf{d}_n, \boldsymbol{\mu}_k)$, and its form depends on the employed metric, being $\mathbf{d}_n \in \mathbb{R}^N$ the n-th sample and $\boldsymbol{\mu}_k \in \mathbb{R}^N$ the k-th centroid [7,8,26].

Algorithm 1. The basic algorithm for K-means is given as follows:

1. Initialize cluster centroids $\boldsymbol{\mu}_1, \boldsymbol{\mu}_2, ..., \boldsymbol{\mu}_k \in \mathbb{R}^N$, randomly.
2. Repeat until convergence:
For every i, set:
$$c^{(i)} = \text{argmin}_j \left\| \mathbf{d}^{(i)} - \boldsymbol{\mu}_j \right\|^2$$

For each j, set:
$$\mu_j = \frac{\sum_{i=1}^{m_k} 1\{c^{(i)}=j\} \mathbf{d}^{(i)}}{\sum_{i=1}^{m_k} 1\{c^{(i)}=j\}}$$
Being m_k the number of data points belonging to the k-th group c_k

---

2.1   Datasets and Experimental Setup

First, we select the suitable metric for finding the clusters. To do this, we assess two typical metrics: squared Euclidean (Sqeuclidean) defined by the expression $d_{ij} = \sum_{n=1}^{P} (x_{in} - x_{jn})^2$ similar to the Euclidean distance, but does not take the squared root, for improve time consuming in cluster task, respect to the regular Euclidean distance. And Cosine distance defined by $d_{ij} = 1 - \cos(\mathbf{x}_i, \mathbf{x}_j)$, where $\cos(\mathbf{x}_i, \mathbf{x}_j) = \frac{\mathbf{x}_i \cdot \mathbf{x}_j}{|\mathbf{x}_i||\mathbf{x}_j|}$, which compute the distance based on the angle between two vectors. We applied these distances over two categorical data sets:

Balance-scale and Tic-Tac-Toe [11]. Next as we pointed out before, we compare the proposed K-means (C-S) with other benchmark clustering methods: SBC [24], K-modes [17], weighted dissimilarity [9], Mkm-nof and Mkm-ndm algorithms [3]. We test nine public datasets downloaded from UCI repository [11] (see Table 1), evaluating the accuracy (AC), adjusted rand index (ARI), normalized mutual information (NMI) and the time demanded for each algorithm. We validate all methods under the same conditions: we repeat the experiments 100 times for each dataset, and we report the average values of AC, ARI and NMI with their corresponding standard deviations. The simulations were performed using Matlab software on a server Intel(R) Xeon(R), CPU E5-2650 v2 - 2.60 GHz, 2 processors with 8 cores, and 280 GB-RAM.

We describe the categorical databases used in this approach in Table 1, we downloaded the 9 databases from UCI Repository Machine Learning [11]. The table shows the samples, characteristics, number of classes and the distribution of classes in each of the 9 categorical databases.

Table 1. Description of UCI public datasets [11]

Dataset	# of samples	# of features	Classes	Class Distribution
Fitting contact lenses (FTL)	24	4	3	$\{4, 5, 15\}$
Ballon (B)	20	4	2	$\{8, 12\}$
Space Shuttle Autolanding (SSA)	15	6	2	$\{6, 9\}$
Soybean-small (SS)	47	35	4	$\{10, 10, 10, 17\}$
Hayes-Roth-Hayes-Roth (HRHR)	132	4	3	$\{51, 51, 30\}$
Lymphography Domain (LD)	142	18	2	$\{81, 61\}$
Vote (V)	435	16	2	$\{168, 267\}$
Breast Cancer (BC)	699	9	2	$\{458, 241\}$
Promoters (P)	106	57	2	$\{53, 53\}$

3   Experimental Results and Discussion

In order to define a distance for cluster stage. We observe in Fig. 1 and 2 that Sqeuclidean obtains better results than Cosine. Then, we employ the Sqeuclidean for all comparison methods including the proposed K-means Chi-Squared (C-S). Figure 3 and 4 shows the funtion of the (S-C) metric, which aims to increase the dimensionality of the database, this to make it more visibly separable and obtain better results.

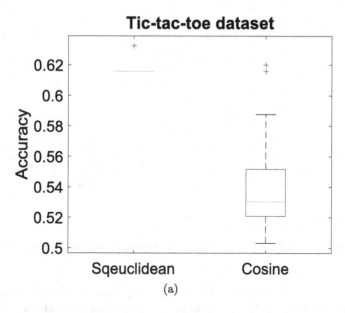

Fig. 1. Accuracy levels for Sqeuclidean and Cosine metrics. (a) Tic-Tac-Toe.

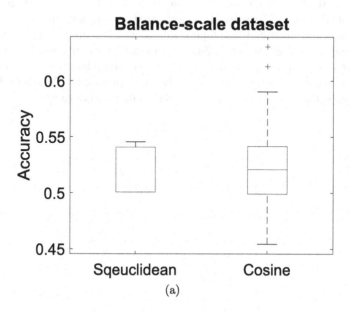

Fig. 2. Accuracy levels for Sqeuclidean and Cosine metrics.(b) Balance-scale.

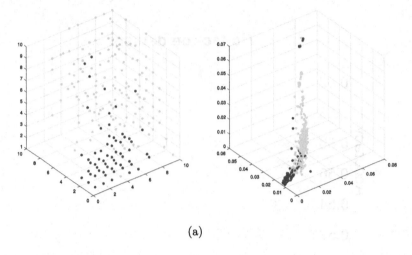

(a)

Fig. 3. Separability of the breast cancer databases with distance C-S.

Table 2 shows the accuracy results for comparison methods tested on nine public datasets from the UCI repository. The proposed method obtains the best accuracy results in most of the databases. Overall, the average value for k-means (C-S) is clearly higher than the achieved by K-modes, W-D, Mkm-nof and Mkm-ndm, and we can say there is a statistically significant difference. Regarding SBC framework, our proposal is slightly better, but there is not a considerable disparity. Categorical datasets are the complex type of data because their attributes are codified as integers values, which generate high overlapping. Hence, the groups or classes are difficult to identify with an acceptable precision. The Chi-square distance allows mapping the categorical features to the Euclidean space with a higher dimensionality, but a better separability. Therefore, K-means (C-S) reduces the undesirable effect of overlapping and outliers.

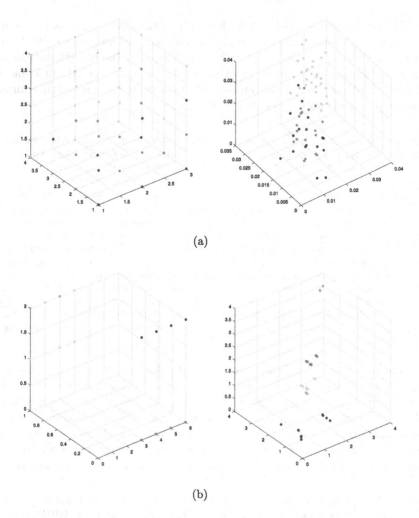

Fig. 4. Separability of the (a) Hayes-Roth, (b) Space Shuttle Domain databases with distance C-S.

Table 2. Accuracy results for comparison methods tested in nine UCI public datasets. K-means(C-S) refers to our proposal, W-D corresponds to weighted dissimilarity. The datasets: FTL, B, SSA, SS, HRHR, LD, V, BC, and P are defined in Table 1.

Datasets	K-means(C-S)	SBC-1	SBC-2	K-modes	W-D	Mkm-nof	Mkm-ndm
FTL	0.6083±0.1046	0.7288±0.0016	**0.7458±0.0005**	0.6417±0.0013	0.6588±0.0016	0.6813±0.0026	0.6587±0.0020
B	**1.0000±0.0000**	0.7940±0.0034	0.8485±0.0001	0.6910±0.0083	0.7045±0.0080	0.7310±0.0070	0.6710±0.0071
SSA	0.6309±0.0959	**0.7140±0.0074**	0.6720±0.0007	0.6240±0.0010	0.6293±0.0011	0.6140±0.0007	0.6367±0.0040
SS	0.8936±0.0000	**0.9660±0.0061**	0.9589±0.0079	0.9185±0.0087	0.8353±0.0096	0.7626±0.0051	0.9483±0.0078
HRHR	**0.7144±0.0788**	0.4566±0.0004	0.4630±0.0009	0.4256±0.0004	0.4782±0.0020	0.4550±0.0019	0.4329±0.0026
LD	**0.8902±0.0125**	0.7618±0.0009	0.7217±0.0008	0.6252±0.0030	0.5808±0.0007	0.5801±0.0000	0.6589±0.0046
V	**0.8852±0.0172**	0.8783±0.0001	0.8759±0.0000	0.8604±0.0001	0.8094±0.0088	0.8715±0.0027	0.8715±0.0027
BC	0.9288±0.0000	0.9293±0.0000	0.9413±0.0000	0.8608±0.0112	0.7717±0.0022	0.7697±0.0026	**0.9464±0.0000**
P	0.7302±0.0520	**0.8878±0.0023**	0.8106±0.0001	0.6335±0.0057	0.7865±0.0028	0.7500±0.0026	0.7043±0.0121
Average	**0.8090±0.0401**	0.7907±0.0024	0.7820±0.0012	0.6979±0.0044	0.6949±0.0040	0.6906±0.0025	0.7254± 0.0047

Table 3 exhibits the ARI results for each method. Our proposal does not outperform SBC-1 method. However, it has a similar performance to SBC-2, and achieves better ARI results than the other comparison methods, with statistically significant differences, according to a Kruskal-Wallis test. Although the K-means (C-S) and SBC framework have similar performances, the demanded time for our approach is considerably lower than SBC.

Table 3. ARI results for comparison methods tested in nine UCI public datasets. K-means(C-S) refers to our proposal, W-D corresponds to weighted dissimilarity. The datasets: FTL, B, SSA, SS, HRHR, LD, V, BC, and P are defined in Table 1.

Datasets	K-means(C-S)	SBC-1	SBC-2	K-modes	W-D	Mkm-nof	Mkm-ndm
FTL	0.1442±0.0557	0.2897±0.0347	**0.3582±0.0207**	0.0169±0.0088	0.1009±0.0232	0.1232±0.0198	0.0621±0.0118
B	**1.0000±0.0000**	0.3262±0.0215	0.4590±0.0010	0.1356±0.0247	0.1536±0.0253	0.1987±0.0234	0.0981±0.0209
SSA	0.0256±0.0214	**0.1556±0.0248**	0.0566±0.0028	-0.0050±0.0017	0.0064±0.0020	-0.0155±0.0014	0.0262±0.0110
SS	0.7477±0.0000	0.9400±0.0193	**0.9410±0.0159**	0.8247±0.0288	0.6959±0.0214	0.6330±0.0038	0.9111±0.0233
HRHR	**0.2954±0.0566**	0.0133±0.0001	0.0369±0.0005	-0.0018±0.0001	0.0377±0.0010	0.0240±0.0007	0.0071±0.0011
LD	0.0629±0.0141	**0.2721±0.0020**	0.1934±0.0015	0.0627±0.0053	0.0106±0.0011	0.0080±0.0000	0.1109±0.0106
V	0.4470±0.0343	**0.5715±0.0001**	0.5641±0.0000	0.5187±0.0005	0.4123±0.0455	0.5599±0.0127	0.5599±0.0127
BC	0.7369±0.0000	0.7331±0.0001	0.7780±0.0000	0.5395±0.0792	0.2636±0.0126	0.2487±0.0000	**0.7959±0.0000**
P	0.1495±0.0458	**0.6072±0.0082**	0.3802±0.0003	0.0859±0.0065	0.3334±0.0061	0.2545±0.0060	0.2084±0.0310
Average	0.3953±0.0253	**0.4343±0.0123**	0.4186±0.0048	0.2419±0.0172	0.2238±0.0153	0.2261±0.0075	0.3089±0.0136

Table 4 we show the percentages of the NMI index, which is a decisive measure to calculate the quality of the grouping made by our method. As we can see, our method surpasses in most of the databases the SBC methods demonstrating a high quality at the moment of making the grouping, as we can observe in Fig. 5. This figure illustrates the execution time diagrams for all methods with one iteration, and we can observe our algorithm is always executed in the lowest time, no matter the dataset. For some datasets, the difference in execution times is very

Table 4. NMI results for comparison methods tested in nine UCI public datasets. K-means(C-S) refers to our proposal. The datasets: FTL, B, SSA, SS, HRHR, LD, V, BC, and P are defined in Table 1.

Datasets	K-means(Chi-square)	SBC-1	SBC-2
FTL	**0.2387±0.1073**	0.2102±0.0327	0.2355±0.0924
B	**0.4324±0.3050**	0.3602±0.1648	0.1962±0.0762
SSA	**0.0391±0.0213**	0.0362±0.0047	0.0379±0.0079
SS	0.7949±0.0816	0.7996±0.0668	**0.8330±0.0661**
HRHR	**0.3907±0.0781**	0.0071±0.0149	0.0180±0.0311
LD	**0.0339±0.0229**	0.0283±0.0232	0.0264±0.0309
V	0.4357±0.1381	0.4880±0.0052	**0.4898±0.0490**
BC	0.4590±0.0049	0.5552±0.0060	**0.7073±0.0000**
P	**0.0733±0.0586**	0.0728±0.0649	0.0761±0.0629
Average	0.3220	0.2842	0.2911

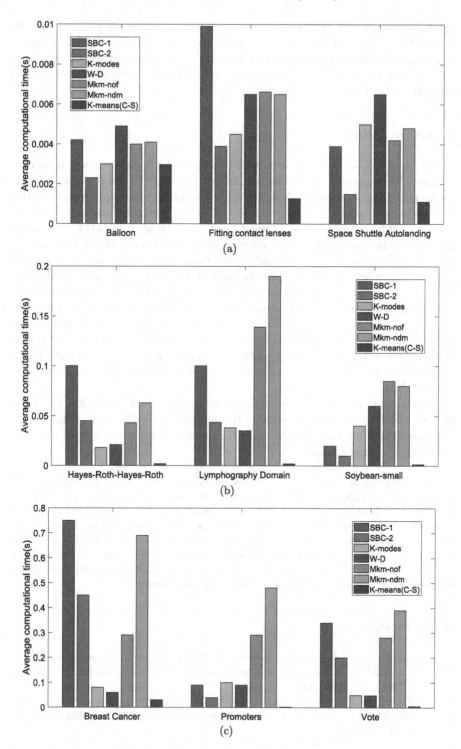

Fig. 5. Algorithms execution time diagrams. (a) Balloon, Fitting contact lenses y Space Shuttle Autolanding. (b) Hayes-Roth-Hayes-Roth, Lymphography Domain y Soybean-small. (c) Breast Cancer, Promoters y Vote.

significant. In general, these outcomes are relevant, because our proposal may be applied to any type of dataset, either categorical or quantitative. Furthermore, we can achieve similar results to the robust SBC, nevertheless, the computational cost of K-means(C-S) is very low compared to similar methods for clustering categorical databases.

4   Conclusion

In this work, we introduced an alternative approach for clustering categorical datasets. We adapted a chi-square dissimilarity distance to the K-means method for mapping the categorical features to a Euclidean space, allowing a better separability of the groups or classes. We call to this method K-means (C-S). Our proposal improved the results obtained for state of the art methods for clustering (K-modes, Mkm-nof, Mkm-ndm) on nine public datasets from UCI repository, and it obtains a similar performance to the robust SBC, when we evaluated the accuracy, adjusted rand index and normalized mutual information. In addition, the K-means (C-S) has a lower computational cost than the comparison methods, as we demonstrated in execution time diagrams of Fig. 5.Thus, K-means (C-S) can be considered as a competitive method for clustering categorical datasets. In addition this work has limitations in the sense of we did not compared the Chi-Squared embedding whit some traditional embedding algorithms like stochastic neighbor embedding, and others categorical-continuous codifications like one-hot-encoding.

As future work, we propose a relevance analysis and dimension reduction for categorical features, through stochastic neighbor embedding. The idea is to project the data to a 2D-3D space for augmenting separability or reducing overlapping among groups.

Acknowledgement. This research is developed under the project financed by Minciencias and ICETEX with title: "Desarrollo de una metodología para la identificación de perfiles de consumo sostenible de los usuarios de agua en la ciudad de Pereira utilizando técnicas de aprendizaje de máquina". It under the program: Fortalecimiento de CTeI en Instituciones de Educación Superior - Convocatoria 890-2020. We also thank to Corporacion Instituto de Administracion y Finanzas (CIAF). Also, we acknowledge to the Vicerrectoría de investigaciones, innovación y extensión and the Maestría en ingeniería eléctrica of the Universidad Tecnológica de Pereira.

References

1. Ahmad, A., Dey, L.: A method to compute distance between two categorical values of same attribute in unsupervised learning for categorical data set. Pattern Recogn. Lett. **28**(1), 110–118 (2007)
2. Anderberg, M.R.: Cluster Analysis for Applications: Probability and Mathematical Statistics: A Series of Monographs and Textbooks, vol. 19. Academic press, Cambridge (2014)

3. Bai, L., Liang, J., Dang, C., Cao, F.: The impact of cluster representatives on the convergence of the k-modes type clustering. IEEE Trans. Pattern Anal. Mach. Intell. **35**(6), 1509–1522 (2013)
4. Ball, G.H., Hall, D.J.: A clustering technique for summarizing multivariate data. Behav. Sci. **12**(2), 153–155 (1967)
5. Banfield, J.D., Raftery, A.E.: Model-based Gaussian and non-gaussian clustering. Biometrics **49**, 803–821 (1993)
6. Bishop, C.M.: Pattern Recognition and Machine Learning (Information Science and Statistics). Springer, Heidelberg (2006)
7. Cardona, L.A.S., Gómez, K.A.H., Gutiérrez, Á.Á.O.: The characterization of high school students in the department of Risaralda using the chi-square metric. Scientia et Technica **26**(2), 119–126 (2021)
8. Cardona, L.A.S., Vargas-Cardona, H.D., Navarro González, P., Cardenas Peña, D.A., Orozco Gutiérrez, Á.Á.: Classification of categorical data based on the chi-square dissimilarity and t-SNE. Computation, **8**(4), 104 (2020)
9. Chan, E.Y., Ching, W.K., Ng, M.K., Huang, J.Z.: An optimization algorithm for clustering using weighted dissimilarity measures. Pattern Recogn. **37**(5), 943–952 (2004)
10. Demidenko, E.: The next-generation k-means algorithm. Stat. Anal. Data Min. ASA Data Sci. J. **11**(4), 153–166 (2018)
11. Dheeru, D., Taniskidou, E.K.: UCI machine learning repository (2017)
12. Ghosh, S., Dubey, S.K.: Comparative analysis of k-means and fuzzy c-means algorithms. Int. J. Adv. Comput. Sci. Appl. **4**(4) (2013)
13. Gowda, K.C., Diday, E.: Symbolic clustering using a new dissimilarity measure. Pattern Recogn. **24**(6), 567–578 (1991)
14. Gower, J.C.: A general coefficient of similarity and some of its properties. Biometrics **27**, 857–871 (1971)
15. Hand, D.J.: Principles of data mining. Drug Saf. **30**(7), 621–622 (2007)
16. Huang, J., Yang, D., Gao, C., Fu, C.: A PCA and Mahalanobis distance-based detection method for logical hardware trojan. Concurrency Comput. Pract. Experience **31**, e4724 (2019)
17. Huang, Z.: A fast clustering algorithm to cluster very large categorical data sets in data mining. DMKD **3**(8), 34–39 (1997)
18. Jain, A.K., Dubes, R.C.: Algorithms for Clustering Data. Prentice-Hall Inc, Upper Saddle River (1988)
19. Kaufman, L., Rousseeuw, P.J.: Finding Groups in Data: An Introduction to Cluster Analysis, vol. 344. Wiley, Hoboken (2009)
20. Lithio, A., Maitra, R.: An efficient k-means-type algorithm for clustering datasets with incomplete records. Stat. Anal. Data Min. ASA Data Sci. J. **11**(6), 296–311 (2018)
21. MacQueen, J., et al.: Some methods for classification and analysis of multivariate observations. In: Proceedings of the Fifth Berkeley Symposium on Mathematical Statistics and Probability, vol. 1, pp. 281–297. Oakland (1967)
22. Michalski, R.S., Stepp, R.E.: Automated construction of classifications: conceptual clustering versus numerical taxonomy. IEEE Trans. Pattern Anal. Mach. Intell. **4**, 396–410 (1983)
23. Mohanavalli, S., Jaisakthi, S.M.: A precise distance metric for mixed data clustering using chi-square statistics. Res. J. Appl. Sci. Eng. Technol. **10**(12), 1441–1444 (2015)
24. Qian, Y., Li, F., Liang, J., Liu, B., Dang, C.: Space structure and clustering of categorical data. IEEE Trans. Neural Netw. Learn. Syst. **27**(10), 2047–2059 (2016)

25. Ralambondrainy, H.: A conceptual version of the k-means algorithm. Pattern Recogn. Lett. **16**(11), 1147–1157 (1995)
26. Ariosto Serna, L., Alejandro Hernández, K., Navarro González, P.: A k-means clustering algorithm: using the chi-square as a distance. In: Tang, Y., Zu, Q., Rodríguez García, J.G. (eds.) HCC 2018. LNCS, vol. 11354, pp. 464–470. Springer, Cham (2019). https://doi.org/10.1007/978-3-030-15127-0_46
27. Seshadri, K., Iyer, K.V.: Design and evaluation of a parallel document clustering algorithm based on hierarchical latent semantic analysis. Concurrency Comput. Pract. Experience **31**, e5094 (2019)
28. Wilson, D.R., Martinez, T.R.: Improved heterogeneous distance functions. J. Artif. Intell. Res. **6**, 1–34 (1997)
29. Woodbury, M.A., Clive, J.: Clinical pure types as a fuzzy partition. J. Cybern. **4**(3), 111–121 (1974)

System Security and Communication using AI

DDoS Attacks Detection Using a Deep Neural Network Model

Meenakshi Mittal[1]([⊠]) [iD], Krishan Kumar[1] [iD], and Sunny Behal[2] [iD]

[1] Department of IT, UIET, Panjab University, Chandigarh, India
meenakshi.cup@gmail.com, k.salujauiet@gmail.com
[2] Department of Computer Science and Engineering, Shaheed Bhagat Singh State
University Ferozepur, Firozpur, India
sunnybehal@sbsstc.ac.in

Abstract. In today's world of globalization, with the exponential increase in the use of Internet-based services, there is also an increase in network traffic and a huge risk of hacking and cyber-attacks. One of the cyber-attacks is the Distributed Denial of Service (DDoS) attack which simply sends the requests to the target for the denial of service for the legitimate users. To detect the DDoS attacks from the vast volume of network traffic, there is a need of a deep learning model. Also, there is the requirement for a lightweight model for today's high-volume traffic and time critical applications. Therefore, in this paper, a deep neural network (DNN) model has been proposed and validated over the CICD-DoS 2019 and PVAMUDDoS-2020 datasets with all features and reduced (important) features. The hyperparameters of the DNN model have been tuned and the best model has an input layer, five hidden layers, and an output layer. The proposed DNN model with the same hyperparameters values performed well over the CICDDoS 2019 and PVAMUDDoS-2020 datasets with all features and reduced features. The results are comparable in both cases and the evaluation with reduced features shows less training and testing time which would be helpful in the time-critical applications and the large volume of network traffic.

Keywords: Deep neural network · Deep learning · CICDDoS 2019 dataset · PVAMU-DDoS-2020 dataset · DDoS attack · Cyber attacks

1 Introduction

In today's era, Internet has become an indispensable part of modern human society. It has completely changed the way how people and organizations used to share information and communicate. The Internet is a system of interconnected networks that connects a huge number of private, public, business, academic, and governmental networks to enable global communication and access to data resources [1]. Therefore, in today's information society, no one can imagine this world without the Internet. In the last decade, there has been an exponential

© Springer Nature Switzerland AG 2023
D. Garg et al. (Eds.): IACC 2022, CCIS 1782, pp. 169–182, 2023.
https://doi.org/10.1007/978-3-031-35644-5_13

increase in the use of Internet-based services. Every single human comfort service, including social media sites like Facebook and Twitter and e-commerce websites, is accessible online. There were 5 billion Internet users worldwide as of April 2022, making up 63% of the world's population [2]. The rise in Internet users has led to an increase in demand for adequate bandwidth, advanced types of equipment, and secure networks. Vulnerabilities in the network systems pose a huge risk to data in the form of hacking and cyber-attacks. So, the major challenge is to develop and implement new technologies which can secure the data from hacking and cyber-attacks. The most significant kind of cyber attack, known as a DDoS attack, can seriously harm enterprises and governments by causing massive system and network disruptions, losing revenue, and decreasing legitimate traffic. The aim of a DDoS attack is to prohibit users from accessing target services by flooding a server with internet traffic [3]. DDoS attacks have the potential to target the most valuable customers and put the infrastructure necessary to maintain the network and services for subscribers and clients at risk [4]. With the increase in Internet-based services and Internet users, the number of DDoS attacks have also been increased. DDoS attacks are being used as a lethal weapon by the hackers, therefore defending the network systems from such hackers have become inevitable [4]. In recent times, there has been a sudden upsurge in the number of DDoS attacks. The COVID-19 shutdown, which caused a rapid move to the internet for everything, from medical care, and teaching to office work, provided attackers with more targets than ever before [4]. Some of the recent DDoS attacks have been explained below:

- Amazon Web Services announced that a DDoS attack by a throughput of 2.3 Tbps occurred in 2020 [5].
- Microsoft stopped what is believed to be the largest DDoS attack in the past, which was cast against an Azure customer in November 2021 and had a throughput of 3.45 Tbps and a packet rate of 340 million packets per second [4].
- DDoS attacks are now synonymous with the ongoing conflict between Russia and Ukraine since the beginning of the year 2022. Both nations have been attacking one another's railways, media, financial, and telecommunications systems [6]. The Russian government's websites are the target of DDoS attacks carried out by the Ukrainian government's "IT army" by sending junk requests to a list of web resources [6].
- North Korean websites also became inaccessible after conducting a series of missile tests in January 2022, in addition to those of Ukraine and Russia [6].

There are many existing techniques and solutions to detect DDoS attacks but most of the existing solutions have not been evaluated over a reduced number of features as selected by [7–9] and also most of the evaluation parameters (like training time, testing time, etc.) are not computed. As the less number of features (important features) and evaluation parameters are important in time-critical applications to prevent denial of services, therefore, in this paper both factors have been considered. DNN model has been proposed and the hyperparameters of this model are tuned using Talos. The best model has an input layer, five hidden layers, and an output layer. This model has been evaluated over reduced (important) features as well as all features. The structure of the proposed model is shown in Fig. 1. In this paper, the following are contributed:

- A Deep Neural Network (DNN) deep learning approach has been proposed.
- The hyperparameters of the proposed DNN have been tuned using the Talos tool.
- The proposed DNN has been validated over the CICDDoS 2019 and PVAMU-DDoS-2020 datasets using all and reduced features.
- All results have been analyzed and compared.

The rest of the paper has been organized as follows: Sect. 2 describes the related work; Sect. 3 talks about the proposed methodology; Sect. 4 describes the experimental setup and results; Sect. 5 explicates the conclusion of this paper.

2   Related Work

Several researchers have conducted experiments using DNN deep learning approach. These papers have been reviewed and described as below:

A network intrusion detection solution for the internet of things (IoT) based on deep learning has been proposed by the authors [10]. The model comprises a custom-made feed-forward neural network (FNN). The authors have used the BoT-IoT dataset. They used 344 original pcap files in the feature extraction phase, extracted 29 packet header fields of each packet from the pcap files, labeled the packets, and saved them in the csv files. The schema in the csv files have been unified then and converted into an Apache Parquet file, and only 2% of the processed dataset has been taken. The feature preprocessing has been done over the extracted features. Thereafter, the redundant rows have been removed in testing and training data and finally worked on 9163751 records/packets. The network embedding and transfer learning are also used to encode high-dimensional categorical features. The two FNN models used are, mFNN (multi-class FNN model) and bFNN (binary categorization model) to identify legitimate and attack traffic. The FNN model with embedding layers is used for the multi-class categorization. Then transfer learning has been applied as the second FNN model (i.e. bFNN) has been built for the binary categorization by extracting the weights from the embedded layers of the multi-class categorization model. The results showed good performance of both the models with good accuracy and low misclassification. The accuracy of models mFNN and bFNN is 99.79% and 99.99% respectively. The classification accuracy and runtime of the mFNN model have been compared with Support Vector Machine (SVM). The feature pre-processing, and settings of the model, have been done, and then evaluated the results in the multi-class categorization using SVM. The mFNN model is acceptable over a large dataset and has more accuracy as compared to the Support Vector Classifier (SVC) in the multi-class categorization problem.

In [7] a composite and effective DDoS attack detection architecture has been used for 5G and B5G. The model is the concatenation of two differently designed deep neural network models which was paired with an effective feature extraction technique (Pearson correlation coefficient (PCC)) to detect the different DDoS attacks encountered. The proposed architecture has been evaluated over four different scenarios using the CICDDoS2019 dataset. Results showed that scenario 1 is better than other scenarios with the accuracy rate of 99.66% and 0.011 loss. The results of the detection architecture are also compared with the existing techniques i.e. K-Nearest Neighbor (KNN), SVM, and deepsense and Convolutional Neural Network (CNN) ensemble. The proposed architecture performed well all over than the CNN ensemble. The CNN ensemble has enhanced recall and precision as compared to the proposed architecture.

In [11] the deep learning model has been proposed which consists of both feature extraction and categorization methods in its design. The dataset CICD-DoS2019 has been divided into Dataset 1 and Dataset 2. Dataset 1 is labeled as two category of traffic that include legitimate and attack. Dataset1 has training and testing Dataset ratios of 292,379 and 73,095 respectively. Dataset2 was created to identify the different DDoS attacks. Dataset2 contains training and testing datasets ratios of 291,904 and 72,977 respectively. On Dataset1, DNN model detects DDoS attacks with approximately 100% accuracy and is able to accurately classify the different DDoS attack kinds with a rate of close to 95% on Dataset2.

In [12], a deep neural categorization model using flow data has been used to identify slow DoS attacks on HTTP. The categorization model used a fully connected feed-forward deep neural network. The model is assessed using the DoS attacks from CICIDS2017 dataset. The kind of DoS attack can be determined by the classifier. According to the results, the model can categorise an attack with the overall accuracy of 99.61%.

3   Proposed Methodology

In this section the proposed model, datasets used and preprocessing of datasets, dataset splitting and hyperparameter tuning are explained:

3.1   Proposed Model

In this paper, the DNN model, which is made up of a collection of feedforward neural networks [11], has been used. DNN is made up of an input layer, hidden layers, and the output layer [7]. The structure of the proposed model is shown in Fig. 1. The hyperparameters of the proposed DNN approach have been chosen using the Talos tool [13] from the set of parameter space boundaries as shown in Table 2. The final DNN model has an input layer, 5 hidden layers, and an output layer. The other parameters of the proposed DNN model have 160 neurons in the first hidden layer, 60 neurons in the remaining hidden layers, the dropout rate is 0, 1000 batch size, the optimizer is adam, uniform kernel initializer, no. of epochs are 50 and activation function used in hidden and output layers are relu and sigmoid respectively.

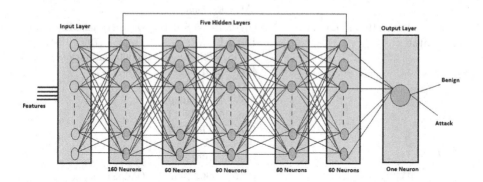

Fig. 1. Structure of the proposed DNN

3.2 Dataset Description

The two DDoS datasets have been used to evaluate the proposed DNN model. These two datasets are CICDDoS 2019 and PVAMU-DDoS-2020.

CICDDoS 2019 Dataset: The CICDDoS dataset was generated by Sharafaldin et al. [8] in 2019. Authors have generated DDoS attacks using TCP/UDP-based protocols. The attacks are divided into two types, that are, exploitation-based and reflection-based attacks. Authors have executed 12 DDoS attacks on the training day which include NTP, WebDDoS, DNS, SYN, Net-BIOS, LDAP, MSSQL, SNMP, SSDP, UDP, TFTP, and UDP-Lag and 7 attacks were executed on the testing day that are NetBIOS, UDP-Lag, LDAP, PortScan, MSSQL, UDP and SYN. This dataset has 86 features. In this paper, the attacks used are DNS, LDAP, MSSQL, NetBIOS, SSDP, UDP, NTP, Syn, TFTP, Web-DDoS and UDP-lag from the training day dataset. The benign records are also considered. The details of records for attacks and benign traffic are shown in Table 1.

PVAMU-DDoS-2020: This dataset was generated by Alam et al. [9]. Authors have developed the PVAMU-DDoS-2020 realistic DDoS dataset using Spirent's CyberFlood-CF20 emulator. The authors have focused mainly on flood attacks. The attack traffic included ICMP Type 11, 8, and 3 floods, TCP SYN flood using ports 25, 80, and 443, UDP Flood Port 53, and XMAS Tree flood Port 80. The normal traffic included HTTP1.0, Telnet, SSH-Login, HTTPs, HTTP1.1, FTP, POP3, SMTP, SIP, RTSP, BitTorre, IMAP4, Exchange, CIFS/SMB, SSH, Facebook traffic. The authors have extracted 83 features and used 76 features. Details of records for DDoS attacks and legitimate traffic are shown in Table 1.

Table 1. Details of Records

Dataset and no. of features	Attack types	Records Distribution (Attacks, Benign)	Dataset Splitting Details
CICDDoS2019 and 69 Features	11	UDP: 49775 SSDP: 49762 LDAP: 49045 MSSQL: 48931 UDP-lag: 48001 NetBIOS: 46777 DNS: 46492 Syn: 45722 TFTP: 44791 NTP: 37375 WebDDoS: 142 Benign: 16517	Dataset: 483330 Train: 347997 Test: 96666 Validation: 38667
CICDDoS2019 and 24 Features	11	UDP: 49997 Syn: 49995 TFTP: 49995 LDAP: 49980 SSDP: 49891 NetBIOS: 49839 MSSQL: 49352 DNS: 48298 UDP-lag: 48247 NTP: 37653 Benign:16612 WebDDoS: 142	Dataset: 500001 Train: 360000 Test: 100001 Validation: 40000
CICDDoS2019 and 10 Features	11	UDP: 49775 SSDP: 49762 LDAP: 49045 MSSQL: 48931 UDP-lag: 48001 NetBIOS: 46777 DNS: 46492 Syn: 45722 TFTP: 44791 NTP: 37375 Benign: 16517 WebDDoS: 142	Dataset: 483330 Train: 347997 Test: 96666 Validation: 38667
PVAMU-DDoS-2020 and 76 features	1	DDoS: 1554227 Benign: 1499506	Dataset: 3053733 Train: 2198687 Test: 610747 Validation: 244299
PVAMU-DDoS-2020 and 14 features	1	DDoS: 1554227 Benign: 1499506	Dataset: 3053733 Train: 2198687 Test: 610747 Validation: 244299

Table 2. Hyperparameter space boundaries

S. No.	Hyperparameters	Values
1.	First hidden neuron	10, 40, 50, 69, 160, 640
2.	Remaining Hidden neurons	10, 20, 30, 40, 50, 60
3.	No. of hidden layers	3, 5
4.	Dropout rate	0, 0.25, 0.5
5.	Batch size	1000, 1024, 5000,10000
6.	Optimizer	adam
7.	Kernel initializer	Uniform
8.	Epochs	50
9.	Last activation	sigmoid

3.3 Preprocessing of Datasets

The .csv files have been used for both datasets i.e. CICDDoS 2019 and PVAMU-DDoS-2020. In the preprocessing phase, the rows which contain NaN and infinity values are deleted for both the datsets.

As per in paper [11] six features (Flow ID, Source IP, Destination IP, Source Port, Destination Port, Protocol) that makes the flow in csv file from the pcap file are not considered for the CICDDoS2019 dataset. Also, the features that either do not contribute or contain zero value are removed and these are 11 features (Timestamp, Fwd Bulk Rate Avg, Bwd PSH Flags, Bwd URG Flags, Fwd URG Flags, Bwd Packet/Bulk Avg, Bwd Bytes/Bulk Avg, Fwd Packet/Bulk Avg, Fwd Bytes/Bulk Avg, Bwd Bulk Rate Avg, and SimillarHTTP) [11]. In addition to the above, the CICDDoS2019 dataset has also been evaluated using important 24 [8] and 10 [7] reduced features.

For the PVAMU-DDoS-2020 dataset, 76 features are used from 83 features. Seven features (Flow ID, source IP, SourcePort, DestinationIP, DestinationPort, Protocol and Timestamp) are not considered. The PVAMU-DDoS-2020 dataset has also been evaluated over important 14 reduced features taken from [9].

Then values in both datasets have been normalized using the MinMax scaler() [14]. In the label, Benign is replaced with 0 and other attacks are replaced with 1.

3.4 Dataset Splitting

Firstly, the dataset has been split into test and train data by the split ratio of 80:20. Secondly, the training data is further split into train and validation data by the ratio of 90:10. The train and validation data are used to train and evaluate the model. Then, the trained model is used to predict the target of the test data.

Table 3. Results of Existing Studies

Refer-ences	No. of features used	Approach used	Classification: Binary/ Multiclass	Dataset used	Results
[11]	69	DNN	Binary as well as multiclass classification	The CICDDoS2019 dataset converted into two different formats i.e. Dataset1 and Dataset2. Dataset1: was labeled as two types of traffic that include normal and attack. Dataset2: was created to determine the types of DDoS attacks	Dataset1: Accuracy= 0.9997, Precision= 0.9999, Recall= 0.9998, Fscore= 0.9998. Dataset2: Accuracy= 0.9457, Precision= 0.8049, Recall= 0.9515, Fscore= 0.8721
[7]	Extracted top 10 features using PCC	DNN	Multiclass: 10 types of attacks and one benign class	Took 180,000 samples from CICDDoS 2019 consisting of both benign and the various other DDoS attack classes	Accuracy: 99.66, Recall: 99.30, Precision: 99.52, F1 score: 99.99
[12]	80	DNN	Multiclass classification: Benign, Slowloris, SlowHTTP, Hulk, GoldenEye	CICIDS2017: selected only DoS samples	Overall accuracy: 99.61%

3.5   Hyperparameter Tuning

The best prediction model has been obtained by the hyperparameter tuning using the Talos tool [13]. Firstly, the DNN Keras model has been prepared and tested to check whether it is working properly or not. Secondly, a set of hyperparameter space boundaries in the parameters dictionary of Talos has been defined. The set of parameter space boundaries is shown in Table 2. Thirdly, the experiment has been configured and hyperparameters are run with scan(). Fourthly, the result is evaluated with Evaluate() against k-fold cross-validation.

Then, the best model (the hyperparameters values which gives best result) is obtained. The optimized and trained model for the prediction of the target value of the test data is then used and result is thus analyzed.

4   Experimental Setup and Results

4.1   Experiment Environment

The system used in the experiments includes Windows 10 operating system (OS), Intel Core i7-7700 CPU @ 3.60 GHz processor, and 8 GB RAM. Python 3.9.7 programming language has been used with TensorFlow and Keras libraries for the deep learning model for the experimental environment.

4.2   Results

The proposed DNN model has been validated over CICDDoS 2019 and PVAMU-DDoS-2020 datasets. Tables 4 and 5 show the comparison of results for training and testing datasets respectively. They also show the results for all and less number of features for both datasets. The important (reduced) features of the CICD-DoS2019 and PVAMU-DDoS-2020 datasets have been used. The performance of the proposed DNN model on the PVAMU-DDoS-2020 dataset outperformed the CICDDoS2019 dataset because the PVAMU-DDoS-2020 dataset is focused on critical flood attacks.

As shown in Table 5, if the no. of features is reduced, the values of some of the performance metrics (like AUC and specificity) are also decreasing because if a model is getting fewer features, then that model can infer less information but the difference is comparable. This trend is noticed for both the datasets that are CICDDoS 2019 and PVAMUDDoS-2020. The values of other performance metrics (like accuracy, recall, and precision) are nearly the same in the different number of features for both datasets. The results of existing related work have been shown in Table 3. The samples of DDoS attacks taken in the existing work are fewer as compared to the records taken in this paper. Also, the proposed DNN model (with the same hyperparameters values) has been evaluated over the different no. of features compared to the existing work. The confusion matrix of results is shown in Table 6.

As shown in Tables 4 and 5 with the fewer number of features, it takes less time for testing and training which produces a lightweight model for critical applications.

The receiver operating characteristic (ROC) curve for the proposed model over both the datasets has been shown in Figs. 2 and 3. ROC curve is a graph that shows the performance of a model at all possible thresholds [15]. This curve is plotted between the true positive rate (TPR) and the false positive rate (FPR) [15]. AUC is the area under the ROC curve. The model performed well for both datasets.

Table 4. Comparison of Results (Training)

Dataset	No. of features used	Training Accuracy	Validation Accuracy	Training Time with preprocessing	Training time without Pre-processing
CICDDoS 2019	69	0.99792	0.99842	44.9347	40.4365
CICDDoS 2019	24	0.99663	0.99680	38.4779	35.8140
CICDDoS 2019	10	0.99101	0.99105	37.3532	35.31520
PVAMU-DDoS-2020	76	1	1	493.2247	405.7275
PVAMU-DDoS-2020	14	0.99999	1	273.8172	253.3554

Table 5. Comparison of Results (Testing)

Dataset	No. of features used	Accuracy	Precision	Recall	AUC	Specificity	Testing Time
CICDDoS 2019	69	0.9985	0.9995	0.9989	0.9934	0.9880	3.16
CICDDoS 2019	24	0.9970	0.9989	0.9979	0.9844	0.9708	2.82
CICDDoS 2019	10	0.99170	0.9983	0.9930	0.9731	0.9532	2.17
PVAMU-DDoS-2020	76	1.0	1.0	1.0	1.0	1.0	20.27
PVAMU-DDoS-2020	14	0.9999	0.9999	1.0	0.9999	0.9999	14.15

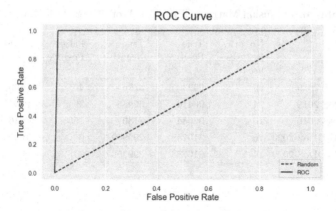

(a) CICDDoS2019 dataset with 69 features

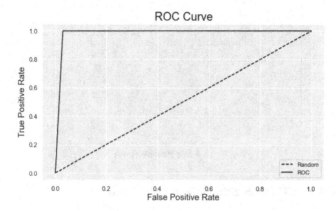

(b) CICDDoS2019 dataset with 24 features

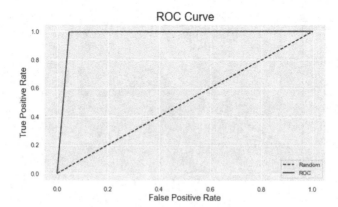

(c) CICDDoS2019 dataset with 10 features

Fig. 2. ROC Curve for the CICDDoS 2019 Dataset

Table 6. Confusion Matrix of Proposed Work Over Both Datasets

Dataset	No. of features used	True Positive	True Negative	False Positive	False Negative
CICDDoS 2019	69	93230	3296	40	100
CICDDoS 2019	24	96410	3298	99	194
CICDDoS 2019	10	92684	3180	156	646
PVAMU-DDoS-2020	76	310788	299959	0	0
PVAMU-DDoS-2020	14	310788	299956	3	0

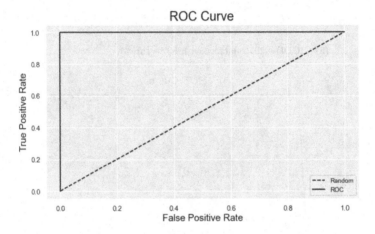

(a) PVAMU-DDoS-2020 dataset with 76 features

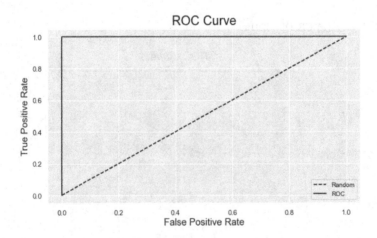

(b) PVAMU-DDoS-2020 dataset with 14 features

Fig. 3. ROC Curve for the PVAMU-DDoS-2020 Dataset

5   Conclusion

In this paper, the proposed DNN model has been used for the detection of DDoS attacks over CICDDoS2019 and PVAMU-DDoS-2020 datasets using all and reduced features. The hyperparameters of the DNN model have been tuned to get the best model using Talos tool. The trained DNN model classifies the traffic of the test data and the model is validated over the CICDDoS2019 and PVAMU-DDoS-2020 datasets using all and reduced features. The proposed DNN model with the same hyperparameters values performed well over the CICDDoS 2019 and PVAMUDDoS-2020 datasets with all features and reduced features. Testing and training time is also reduced in the case of fewer features which would be helpful in time-critical applications. In this paper, multiclass classification hasn't been done using the proposed DNN model. In the future, the multiclass classification would be done to detect the types of DDoS attacks.

Acknowledgements. We would like to thank Alam et al. [9] for providing us with the PVAMU-DDoS-2020 dataset and features reduction method.

References

1. "What is the Internet? - Definition from Techopedia" (2022). https://www.techopedia.com/definition/2419/internet
2. "Internet users in the world 2022 | Statista" (2022). https://www.statista.com/statistics/617136/digital-population-worldwide/
3. "What is a DDoS Attack? DDoS Meaning, Definition & Types | Fortinet" (2022). https://www.fortinet.com/resources/cyberglossary/ddos-attack
4. "Five Most Famous DDoS Attacks and Then Some | A10 Networks" (2022). https://www.a10networks.com/blog/5-most-famous-ddos-attacks/
5. "AWS hit by Largest Reported DDoS Attack of 2.3 Tbps | A10 Networks" (2022). https://www.a10networks.com/blog/aws-hit-by-largest-reported-ddos-attack-of-2-3-tbps/
6. "Kaspersky DDoS report, Q1 2022 | Securelist" (2022). https://securelist.com/ddos-attacks-in-q1-2022/106358/
7. Amaizu, G.C., Nwakanma, C.I., Bhardwaj, S., Lee, J.M., Kim, D.S.: Composite and efficient DDoS attack detection framework for B5G networks. Comput. Netw. **188**, 107871 (2021)
8. Sharafaldin, I., Lashkari, A.H., Hakak, S., Ghorbani, A.A.: Developing realistic distributed denial of service (DDoS) attack dataset and taxonomy. In: Proceedings - International Carnahan Conference on Security Technology, vol. 2019 (2019)
9. Alam, S., Alam, Y., Cui, S., Akujuobi, C., Chouikha, M.: Toward developing a realistic DDoS dataset for anomaly-based intrusion detection. In: Digest of Technical Papers - IEEE International Conference on Consumer Electronics, vol. 2021 (2021)
10. Ge, M., Syed, N.F., Fu, X., Baig, Z., Robles-Kelly, A.: Towards a deep learning-driven intrusion detection approach for Internet of Things. Comput. Netw. **186**, 107784 (2021)
11. Cil, A.E., Yildiz, K., Buldu, A.: Detection of DDoS attacks with feed forward based deep neural network model. Expert Syst. Appl. **169**, 114520 (2021)

12. Muraleedharan, N., Janet, B.: A deep learning based HTTP slow DoS classification approach using flow data. ICT Express **7**, 210–214 (2021)
13. "GitHub - autonomio/talos: Hyperparameter Optimization for TensorFlow, Keras and PyTorch" (2022). https://github.com/autonomio/talos
14. "Sklearn.preprocessing.MinMaxScaler — scikit-learn 1.1.1 documentation" (2022). https://scikit-learn.org/stable/modules/generated/sklearn.preprocessing.Min-MaxScaler.html
15. "Classification: ROC Curve and AUC | Machine Learning | Google Developers" (2022). https://developers.google.com/machine-learning/crash-course/classification/roc-and-auc

A Large Scale IoT Botnet Attack Detection Using Ensemble Learning

B. Jwalin and S. Saravanan$^{(\boxtimes)}$

Department of Computer Science and Engineering, Amrita School of Computing, Bengaluru,
Amrita Vishwa Vidyapeetham, Banglore, India
s_saravanan@blr.amrita.edu

Abstract. The escalation of the newer technology called Internet of Things (IoT), introduced numerous benefits to people. However, it has also raised the risk of cybercriminal attacks. For instance, it has allowed criminals to access confidential information and launch Distributed Denial of Service (DDoS) attacks. Most frequent type of attacks that are carried out is botnets, which are designed to take over a device's memory and computation. The shortfall of security platform for these devices, can make them vulnerable to exploitation. As connected devices and huge network traffic data rocket in number, it has become more challenging for companies to concentrate on safeguards. In this paper, we propose to implement ensemble algorithms specifically Random Forest and Gradient Boosted Decision Tree (GBDT) that can identify botnet attacks. The research is conducted on a complete N_BaIoT dataset as more data leads to better decisions. We deployed an Apache Spark, a big data technology platform, five nodes cluster to process the complete N_BaIoT dataset. Through the experiments, both the GBDT and Random Forest can produce impressive results. With respect to accuracy, GBDT and Random Forest resulted in 99.24% and 99.8% respectively. However, in terms of time elapsed, GBDT can outperform Random Forest by 12 s. Overall, the GBDT model proved effective in finding malicious data from diverse IoT devices with astounding accuracy and a noteworthy time.

Keywords: Big data · N_BaIoT dataset · Apache Spark · IOT · Ensemble · Botnet

1 Introduction

With the growth in IoT, it has created numerous technological advancements. These devices, which are often referred to as IoT, collect vast amounts of data. They also establish connections with their users through various networks. It is widely believed that by 2025, over a trillion devices shall be linked to the internet [1]. The amplitude of connected devices on the Internet and the rise of IoT have led to an increase in the frequency of DDoS Attacks. These attacks are usually done through a combination of device, usually end up consuming a huge number of resources. One of the main reasons why these attacks are continuously launched is due to the presence of a group of devices

© Springer Nature Switzerland AG 2023
D. Garg et al. (Eds.): IACC 2022, CCIS 1782, pp. 183–193, 2023.
https://doi.org/10.1007/978-3-031-35644-5_14

known as botnets. These are computers or IoT devices that are infected with malware. The active bots can perform various tasks, such as scanning and sending spam emails. They can also consume internal storage and perform other tasks, which can degrade the services of the network. One of the biggest hazards to the Internet is botnets. These botnets have become a growing concern for network administrators [2–4]. The advancing in the magnitude of internet connected devices has in turn multiplied the DDoS attacks with increasing frequency [5]. It is therefore important that network administrators take the necessary steps to prevent these attacks from happening. Hence, this paper aims to use ensemble machine learning algorithms to identify botnet attacks that are generated by IoT network. Previous experiments on the detection of IoT network intrusions were utilizing only the partial dataset of N_BaIoT [6]. The value of studying the entire dataset is that more data leads to better conclusions. Hence, this study takes a different approach by using the entire dataset generated from machines infiltrated with two separate botnets, notably BASHLITE and MIRAI. Besides the usual devices, such as the doorbell, the researchers also collected data from other commercial IoT devices, such as the Webcam, Baby Monitor, and Security Camera. The proposed system uses Apache Spark to process the entire dataset of N_BaIoT.

Apache Spark [7] is a data processing framework that can handle processing on exceptionally huge data sets and can also organize these processing tasks among many machines. These benefits are key to the worlds of big data and machine learning, as they need massive power to process large data. The presented system holds two machine learning models. The first model used is Random Forests Classifier and it creates a set of decision trees, The program randomly chooses the trees that it will use for its predictions. It then gets the votes from these trees to produce a final prediction. Second model used in the experiment is the Gradient Boost Decision Tree classifier, homogeneous to Random Forest classifier in the aspect of making many decision trees and makes predictions. However, GBDT uses boosting as supposed to bagging in Random Forest and it does not need bootstrapping. Since the decision trees are all fit to the residuals of the previous one, we do not need to worry about having them correlated. This paper attempts to create a machine learning model with methodology that involves the concept of an ensemble where multiple trained models are then combined to achieve the best decision for classification. These models are then trained using the complete dataset, the experimental assessments are carried out using traffic data from devices infected with two botnet families: Mirai and BASHLITE. The use of complete dataset has benefited us as massive volumes of data result in better judgments, which lead to higher performance. We also leverage the Apache Spark platform, a big data technology, to boost computing power and shorten the time it takes to analyze and comprehend data. This paper's significant contributions are listed below.:

- The use of the entire N_BaIoT dataset with a total of 7062606 instances
- The use of Apache Spark to allocate the tasks among five nodes
- The proposed system can detect attacks in a large-scale network traffic data

The rest of this paper is organized as follows: An overview of the literature is included in Sect. 2 along with a synopsis of the most recent studies surveyed. The system model and architecture, together with a thorough explanation of each underlying subsystem, are presented in Sect. 3. In-depth experimental results and performance trajectories are reported in Sect. 4, along with a comparison to current models. The presented work is concluded in Sect. 5.

2 Related Work

Due to an increasing number of botnet attacks on IoT, many researchers have been looking into this issue. To provide with a greater perspective of how to prevent these attacks, in [8], the authors have developed a cloud based deep learning framework that can be used to detect and mitigate these threats. The framework is composed of two main security mechanisms: a distributed CNN and a cloud-based LSTM network model. After retaining top seventy-five features, and creating the model, it was backed by the LSTM model, to produce an accuracy of 94.80%.

In [9], the authors created a framework to detect botnets by machine learning and deep learning model. It was composed of a N_BaIoT dataset, a detection model, and a training model. The training model was built using five ML models: Naive Bayes, KNN, Random Forest, Decision Tree, and Logistic Regression. The researchers used the training model to develop a botnet detection model. It was designed to perform well in binary and multiclass classification. The tests' outcomes showed that the ML models excelled in binary and multiclass categories. However, the F1 score of the Logistic Regression was lower than that of the other models and Naive bayes had low F1 Score for Multiclass classification. To untangle, the experimental evaluation found that CNN outperforms all other deep learning models.

The goal of this study [10] is to analyze the data of the Provision PT 737E security cameras, a part of the N_BaIoT dataset. Through machine learning, its goal is to discern between legitimate and malicious network data. To minimize the computational complexity of the study, the dimension of the study was reduced to ten from 115. The dataset was trained using unsupervised learning method and supervised learning model. The Decision Tree J48 algorithm was used for training, and the accuracy percentage was 99.95%. While the unsupervised learning method uses an Expectation Maximization algorithm to gain an accuracy rate of 76.73%.

In [11] the authors goal was to find an efficient machine learning algorithm that can detect anomalous traffic from the N_BaIoT dataset. Through a combination of four models, the researchers were able to produce a result that is highly accurate and recallable. The dataset used for this study consisted of only four unique devices. Out of the nine devices in the database, only four of them were used to train and test the models. It was discovered that the machine learning algorithms utilized in the study worked effectively in recognizing the different types of assaults. When trying to predict the vulnerabilities that will affect an unrelated device, such as a smartphone, these methods tend to have a lower efficiency. On the other hand, the Random Forests classifier was able to detect vulnerabilities on an unrelated device with a high F1 score.

The paper [12] presents a framework that aims to provide a comprehensive analysis of the most challenging attacks that can be carried out on the IoT. The machine learning algorithms used were Classification and Regression Trees algorithm (CART) and Naive Bayes algorithm to identify and detect botnets. The proposed system was analyzed using the N_BaIoT dataset, which contains nine kinds of records related to the IoT devices,

Home XCS7_1002_WHT Security Camera is selected for this paper. The results show that the Naive bayes detection accuracy is 58% and that of CART is 99%. The paper concludes that the CART system is the ideal tool for identifying and preventing botnets from operating in the IoT environment.

In [13], the researchers present a multiclassification framework that uses three ML algorithms to analyze the performance of Provision PT 737E Security Camera in the N_BaIoT dataset. They analyzed the performance of these algorithms in both time complexity and metrics. The framework uses multiple classification metrics such as the confusion matrix, Macro F1, Micro F1, MCC, Weighted F1, and Cohen Kappa to assess the execution of the three ML algorithms. The stability of the ANN and RF algorithms was confirmed by the metrics. Although the NB algorithm can achieve good outcomes, it does not perform well in terms of time complexity and multiclassification metrics. The ANN algorithm has a robust performance when it comes to both time complexity and training.

In this paper [14], they present a framework that aims to provide an IDS for Internet of Things. The methodology includes detection techniques such as Random Forest, Naive Bayes, REPTree, Random Tree and Decision Tree. They tested the system against Apache Flink and Spark Streaming. The datasets used consists of a total of 113,103 instances of the N_BaIoT dataset and 10% of the KDDcup dataset, a sample of over 494,021 records. The paper shows that in terms of accuracy, Random Forest gave the highest score when it comes to KDDcup and N_BaIoT datasets with 99.95% and 99.96% respectively. The results reveal that the Apache Flink streaming engine outperformed Spark Streaming in terms of throughput.

The paper [15] presents a framework that can be used to detect and secure IoT botnets using network flows, Their DL based method outperforms the classical methods when it comes to analyzing the data collected from network traffic flows. It considers the various features extracted from the traffic flows and then provides a comprehensive view of the activity. It can also be used for analysis and training. To summarize, with the increase in attacks on the Internet of Things, Unusual behavior in the network and surroundings has been identified using machine learning. All the studies on N_BaIoT dataset have not used the entire dataset of N_BaIoT dataset.

Hence, this paper focuses on two main aspects: first, to use the entire data collected by the N_BaIoT dataset to identify potential threats and second, to perform experiments on the Big Data platform using Apache Spark.

3 Proposed Methodology

3.1 Dataset

The N_BaIoT dataset contains 115 attributes which comprises many statistics like weight of the stream, magnitude of two streams variances, covariance between two streams and so on. This dataset is generated by infecting nine IoT devices which are Doorbell Danmini, Doorbell Ennio, Thermostat Ecobee, Baby monitor Philips B120N/10, Security camera Provision PT_737E, Security camera Provision PT_838, Security camera Simple Home XCS7_1002_WHT, Security camera Simple Home XCS7_1003_WHT, Webcam Samsung SNH 1011 N with Mirai and Bashlite malwares [16].

There are many flooding attacks, including TCP and UDP assaults. Mirai botnet uses several types of attacks, such as ACK, Syn, and UDP, while the Bashlite botnet uses diverse types of attacks, such as TCP, junk. Table 1. illustrates the ten attacks of Mirai and Bashlite. The instances are divided into eleven classes, with the former containing regular traffic and the latter ten containing attack traffic. The number of attack instances are shown in Table 2. and that of benign in Table 3..

Table 1. Various attacks launched by Bashlite and Mirai botnet malwares.

Botnet	Attack
Bashlite	Scan
	Junk
	UDP
	TCP
	COMBO
Mirai	Scan
	Ack
	Syn
	UDP
	Plain UDP

Table 2. Count of instances for each attack type.

Type of attack	Instances
Combo	515156
Junk	261789
Scan	255111
TCP	859850
UDP	946366
M_ACK	643821
M_SCAN	537979
M_SYN	733299
M_UDP	1229999
M_UDPPLAIN	523304

Table 3. Count of benign instances.

Type of attack	Instances
Benign	555932

3.2 Environment Setup

An Apache Spark cluster using Spark 3.3.0 software was setup to run machine learning algorithms on the entire 7062606 instances N_BaIoT dataset. The cluster consists of five nodes, one node is used as Master node and the rest are used as worker nodes. Specifications of the node is detailed in Table 4.. The default values are used for environment variables such as executor memory and executor code.

Table 4. System requirements of workers and master.

Processor	12th Generation Intel® Core™ i5-12500T (6 Cores/18 MB/12T/2.0 GHz to 4.4 GHz/35 W)
Memory	16 GB DDR4
Hard Drive	M.2 2230 256 GB PCIe NVMe Class 35 SSD

3.3 Data Preprocessing

Figure 1 displays the suggested approach's process. The first step is to add class labels to the dataset. For instance, the benign class is first labeled as zero, followed by the other classes with a one. In the next step, we are going to combine the files of the same class, and then merge them into a single file, which then acts as a data set. Shuffle is conducted to make the dataset more complex and balanced.

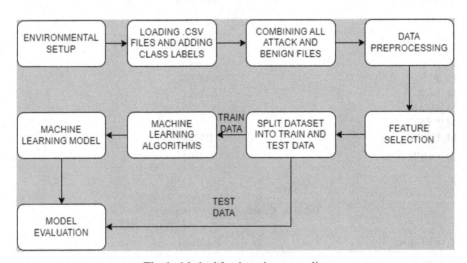

Fig. 1. Method for detecting anomalies

Feature Selection

In paper [17], the researchers found that out of 115 features only nineteen features were most prominent by adding features with greater coefficient values to the ROC graph after logistic regression, Once the ROC value is closer to 100%, it means that incorporating additional features no longer significantly affects the accuracy. Table 5. shows the various features that were most prominent. We have used these nineteen features to train the models.

Table 5. Prominent features.

Feature name
Ml_dir_L5_weight, Ml_dir_L5_mean, Ml_dir_L5 variance, MI_dir_L3_weight, MI_dir_L3_mean, MI_dir_L3_variance, MI_dir_L1_weight, Ml_dir_L1_mean, MI_dir_L1_variance, MI_dir_L0.1_weight, HpHp_L0.1_pcc, HpHp_L0.1_covariance, HpHp_L0.01_weight, Hp Hp_L0.01_mean, Hp Hp_L0.01_std, HpHp_L0.01magnitude, HpHp_L0.01_radius, HpHp_L0.01_covariance, HpHp_L0.01_pcc

Standard Scaler

Due to the complexity of the dataset, there are a lot of outliers that can affect the machine learning models. To overcome this issue, we used the standard scalar framework to transform the data distribution curve into a representation whose mean attributes to zero and standard deviation of one. After which a String Indexer was used so that the records with class labels in maximum number are changed to zero and that of minimum number are changed to one.

3.4   Random Forest

A random forest classifier's objective is to simultaneously train a number of decision trees with the aggregation and bootstrapping procedure. The success of this model depends on the type of decision trees that are used. For instance, if we use a single decision tree with a similar set of characteristics, then the overall result will not be different from that of a different model. Bootstrapping helps in creating uncorrelated decision trees. It ensures that individual decision tree is unique. This ensures that the overall variance in the random forest's classification is minimized. Compared with other methods, the random forest classifiers are more accurate. They do not have to overfitting issues, and they can perform better than other models.

3.5 GBDT

Like Random Forest Classification, GBDT is an ensemble model which means it combines many weak learners to get a strong one, they are highly different algorithms. GBDT uses a boosting technique to create an ensemble learner. It then uses a sequence of decision trees to generate a strong learner. Although the decision trees are connected to a series, they are not necessarily fit to the entire dataset. To minimize the errors of the past tree, each tree fits to its residuals. The GBDT does not need to be run bootstrapping. Since the decision trees are always fit to their residuals, they do not need to be correlated with the previous ones. The model's overall accuracy and robustness are also improved by adding new trees. This eliminates the need for subsamples.

3.6 Metrics

We use the following metrics to describe to assess machine learning algorithms performance on N_BaIoT dataset.

Confusion Matrix
When the model displays a positive value, the idea of true positive (TP) is introduced. While true negative (TN) is indicated when the model shows a negative value, which is matching the actual value. False positive (FP), refers to when the model shows a positive value, but it is not actually positive. Finally, false negative (FN), is when the model shows a negative value, but it is positive.

Accuracy
One of the most common measurements used in binary classification is accuracy. It is division of the TN and TP elements by the total number of FP, FN, TN, and TP elements.

$$ACCURACY = (TN + TP)/(FP + FN + TN + TP) \tag{1}$$

Precision
The precision of this calculation is division of the true positives (TP) and the combination of false negative (FP) and true positives (TP).

$$PRECISION = TP/(FP + TP) \tag{2}$$

Recall
Recall is the division of true positives (TP) to the cluster of false negative (FN) and true positives (TP).

$$RECALL = TP/(FN + TP) \tag{3}$$

F1 Score
The harmonic combination of the recall and the precision of a classifier is said to be F1 Score. It is useful to compare the performance of two different classifiers. For instance, if one of the classifiers has a higher recall, then the other one has a higher precision. The two F1 scores can then be used to determine which one is better.

4   Evaluation and Results

80% of the dataset is used to develop the model and the rest 20% to assess the model. We then run the Random Forest model with the default settings. We record its confusion matrix, accuracy, and F1 score. Then, the same is recorded after we run GBDT model with default settings. Table 6 illustrates the confusion matrix of Random Forest while the confusion matrix for GBDT is presented in Table 7.

Table 6. Confusion matrix of Random Forest

	Attack class	Benign class
Attack class	1300963	10387
Benign class	339	100832

Table 7. Confusion matrix of GBDT

	Attack class	Benign class
Attack class	1300840	1059
Benign class	584	110038

Table 8 presents a comprehensive summary of all metrics, including recall, precision, accuracy, and F1 score. Table 8 shows that the Random Forest model is at 99.24% accuracy, which is below the GBDT's accuracy of 99.8%. On the other hand, when we compare the F1 scores with the model, it yields a value of 0.9959 and 0.9994. Although the accuracy and F1 scores of the random forest and the GBDT are similar. It is vital to remember that training times are different. The training time of Random Forest and GBDT are shown in Table 9. Taking time and accuracy into consideration we can conclude that GBDT is a better option when compared to Random Forest.

Table 8. Model analysis using mentioned metrics

	Recall	Precision	Accuracy	F1_Score
Random forest	0.9997	0.9921	0.9924	0.9959
GBDT	0.9996	0.9992	0.9988	0.9994

Table 9. Time taken to train the models

	Random Forest	GBDT
Time	144 s	130 s

5 Conclusion

As the amount of the Internet connected devices is only going to explode in the coming years, there is also going to be an explode in potential vulnerabilities that will be exploited by hackers. It is an at most requirement to protect these devices from being infected by these vulnerabilities. To address these vulnerabilities, we need to use newer technologies such as big data and machine learning. This research has proposed to apply ensemble machine learning algorithms like Random Forest and GBDT. And used entire N_BaIoT dataset to train machine learning models as more data leads to better decisions. While dealing with vast amount of data we need huge computational power, to solve the issue of limited system settings, we used big data technology, which split the tasks among the four worker nodes using Apache Spark. GBDT, has produced amazing results in a short span of time. Our method primarily uses binary classification at the moment. We intend to concentrate on multiclass classification in our upcoming work.

References

1. Vinayakumar, R., Alazab, M., Srinivasan, S., Pham, Q.V., Padannayil, S.K., Simran, K.: A visualized botnet detection system based deep learning for the internet of things networks of smart cities. IEEE Trans. Ind. Appl. **56**(4), 4436–4456 (2020)
2. Vysakh, S., Binu, P.K.: IoT based Mirai vulnerability scanner prototype. In: 2020 Third International Conference on Smart Systems and Inventive Technology (ICSSIT), pp. 97–101. IEEE (2020)
3. Tulasi Ratnakar, P., Uday Vishal, N., Sai Siddharth, P., Saravanan, S.: Detection of IoT botnet using recurrent neural network. In: Hemanth, D.J., Pelusi, D., Vuppalapati, C. (eds.) Intelligent Data Communication Technologies and Internet of Things. LNDECT, vol. 101, pp. 869–884. Springer, Singapore (2022). https://doi.org/10.1007/978-981-16-7610-9_63
4. Pranav, P.R.K., Verma, S., Shenoy, S., Saravanan, S.: Detection of botnets in IoT networks using graph theory and machine learning. In: 2022 6th International Conference on Trends in Electronics and Informatics (ICOEI), pp. 590–597. IEEE (2022)
5. Chunduri, H., Gireesh Kumar, T., Charan, P.V.S.: A multi class classification for detection of IoT botnet malware. In: Chaubey, N., Parikh, S., Amin, K. (eds.) COMS2 2021. CCIS, vol. 1416, pp. 17–29. Springer, Cham (2021). https://doi.org/10.1007/978-3-030-76776-1_2
6. Meidan, Y., et al.: N_baiot—network_based detection of iot botnet attacks using deep autoencoders. IEEE Pervasive Comput. **17**(3), 12–22 (2018)
7. Zaharia, M., et al.: Apache spark: a unified engine for big data processing. Commun. ACM **59**(11), 56–65 (2016)
8. Parra, G.D.L.T., Rad, P., Choo, K.K.R., Beebe, N.: Detecting internet of things attacks using distributed deep learning. J. Netw. Comput. Appl. **163**, 102662 (2020)
9. Kim, J., Shim, M., Hong, S., Shin, Y., Choi, E.: Intelligent detection of IoT botnets using machine learning and deep learning. Appl. Sci. **10**(19), 7009 (2020)

10. Celil, O.K.U.R., DENER, M.: Detecting IoT botnet attacks using machine learning methods. In: 2020 International Conference on Information Security and Cryptology (ISCTURKEY), pp. 31–37. IEEE (2020)
11. Joshi, S., Abdelfattah, E.: Efficiency of different machine learning algorithms on the multivariate classification of IoT botnet attacks. In: 2020 11th IEEE Annual Ubiquitous Computing, Electronics & Mobile Communication Conference (UEMCON), pp. 0517–0521. IEEE (2020)
12. Htwe, C.S., Thant, Y.M., Thwin, M.M.S.: Botnets attack detection using machine learning approach for IoT environment. In: Journal of Physics: Conference Series, vol. 1646, no. 1, p. 012101. IOP Publishing (2020)
13. Tran, T.C., Dang, T.K.: Machine learning for multi_classification of botnets attacks. In: 2022 16th International Conference on Ubiquitous Information Management and Communication (IMCOM), pp. 1–8. IEEE (2022)
14. Yahyaoui, A., Lakhdhar, H., Abdellatif, T., Attia, R.: Machine learning based network intrusion detection for data streaming IoT applications. In: 2021 21st ACIS International Winter Conference on Software Engineering, Artificial Intelligence, Networking and Parallel/Distributed Computing (SNPD_Winter), pp. 51–56. IEEE (2021)
15. Sriram, S., Vinayakumar, R., Alazab, M., Soman, K.P.: Network flow based IoT botnet attack detection using deep learning. In: IEEE INFOCOM 2020_IEEE Conference on Computer Communications Workshops (INFOCOM WKSHPS), pp. 189_194. IEEE (2020)
16. Marzano, A., et al.: The evolution of bashlite and mirai IoT botnets. In: 2018 IEEE Symposium on Computers and Communications (ISCC), pp. 00813–00818. IEEE (2018)
17. Abbasi, F., Naderan, M., Alavi, S.E.: Anomaly detection in Internet of Things using feature selection and classification based on logistic regression and artificial neural network on N_BaIoT dataset. In: 2021 5th International Conference on Internet of Things and Applications (IoT), pp.1–7. IEEE (2021)

Neural-Network-Based OFDM-SNM Detection: Emerging Technique of Future Data Communication

Jagadeshwaran Ramasamy$^{(\boxtimes)}$ (ID) and Dhandapani Samiappan

Saveetha Engineering College, Saveetha Nagar, Chennai, India
Jagadeshwaran231@gmail.com, dhandapani@saveetha.ac.in

Abstract. Neural Network-based Orthogonal Frequency Division Multiplexing–Subcarrier Number Modulation (OFDM-SNM) bit detector is developed for exploiting the signals at the receiver. Fully connected layers of Neural networks are employed with deep learning to recover the signals in the OFDM-SNM. The pre-processed data is essential to map the received signal with the estimated signal with known channel state information. The channel vectors are formulated with the knowledge of the channel characteristics. Data sets are randomly generated using Pseudo Random Sequence Generator (PRSG) and simulated OFDM-SNM data sets are taken as samples. The system is trained with 10^3 data samples with 20 batch to optimize the Bit Error Rate. Simulation optimizes the BER rate more equivalent to conventional Maximum Likelihood (ML) detector and outperform OFDM Greedy Detector (GD). Simulation shows BER perform better with ML in 10 dB and 15 dB SNR with different data rates of 1 and 2 bps respectively.

Keywords: OFDM-SNM · Neural Network · Bit Error Rate · Multi-carrier modulation

1 Introduction

5G supports a wide range of uses satisfying high data rates, spectrum efficiency, computational complexity, and reliability targets [1, 2]. Orthogonal Frequency Division Multiplexing (OFDM) was the everlasting multicarrier system used for massive growth to sustain the demand of the spectrum resource. To combat multipath fading the OFDM techniques adopt various standards in wireless technology [3]. Conventional OFDM have certain limitations and necessitate the optimal variants of the OFDM schemes considering the metrics of reliability, energy efficiency, and spectrum efficiency [4], etc., Some promising OFDM technologies were OFDM -IM and OFDM-SNM such as the index and subcarrier number modulation of OFDM technologies respectively. In Index based techniques the ratio of active subcarriers was fixed per subblock. Though Index modulation has performance excellence in comparison with conventional OFDM, complexity of hardware detection design become the great impact.

A technique based on the number modulation of OFDM was proposed [5, 6] to map the adaptive active subcarriers per subblock offers high signal-to-noise (SNR) with

D. Garg et al. (Eds.): IACC 2022, CCIS 1782, pp. 194–204, 2023.
https://doi.org/10.1007/978-3-031-35644-5_15

improved spectral efficiency. The OFDM-SNM, convey certain bits of information via index bits of number of subcarriers and it was no longer fixed for any subblock of the OFDM-SNM [6]. The length conveying the message bits also varied which improve the spectral efficiency with nominal BER performance [7]. On other hand, the communication receiver plays a wider significance for detecting the data symbols. Received energy-based detection aimed with low complexity Greedy Detector (GD) was presented [8]. The detectors to achieve optimal BER performances on exploit search of the transmitted symbols based on Maximum Likelihood (ML) detection was proposed [9]. The noise model characteristic is well defined to the receiver with that behavior of the signal noise power spectral density also defined at receiver to achieve a approximate ML performance in Log-Likelihood ratio (LLR) detector [10].

Recently, Deep Learning (DL) techniques combined with the Neural Network (NN) layers provide successful implementation in the Data Communication Technologies [11]. A Machine Learning approach to spectrum sensing techniques was proposed that includes the OFDM design configuration. Features of the OFDM considered for the learning algorithm were the energy of the received signal, and relevant channel state information. The complexity of the hardware transmitter and receiver encoder was reduced by replacing conventional encoder block with the DL encoder [12]. The channel prediction based Neural Network was proposed [13], to improve the full-duplex millimetre wave communication with MIMO (multiple-input multiple-output) users. Research present [14] a technique to explore the channel knowledge prior to detect the symbols in OFDM was proposed. To estimate the challenging time varying characteristics of the channel state information using the gradient descent algorithm was proposed to exploit the channel impulse response [15].

OFDM-SNM based Neural Network was proposed to improve the existing complexity in the hardware detectors maintaining the BER performance and spectrum efficiency [5]. The input fed to the Neural Network has prior information of Channel state information and pre-processed with the features of the OFDM-SNM signal signifies the Deep Learning techniques in the next generation OFDM wireless communication standards [16]. OFDM Neural Network need two fully connected layers to detect the signals under the channel state information of Rayleigh models. The trade-off between the complexity and BER performance adaptively maintained with the adjusting of the number of optimized nodes in the hidden layer. Neural Network trained with the simulated OFDM-SNM signals to reduce the BER and improve the performance. Finally, the network is deployed in the state of art communication technologies to greatly optimize the performance of the hardware OFDM-SNM under any circumstance of the channel state information.

The paper presented as follows. Section 2 deals the background of OFDM-SNM model. Neural Network based OFDM-SNM structure is presented in the Sect. 3. Simulation results are discussed and comparison of the BER with OFDM technologies are explained in the Sect. 4. At the end, the paper concludes the OFDM-SNM.

2 Background

Consider an OFDM-SNM model as shown in Fig. 1 with total N_t available subcarriers equally fractioned into G of N_g subcarriers each. Each group independently processes the information to transmit the signal with the assigned subcarriers and follows the same throughout the group. In each group out of N_g subcarrier OFDM-SNM activates only out of N_g available subcarriers of each independent group. The message bits (total m-bits in each independent group) split into m_1 and m_2 -bits are mapped to the selected active subcarriers in each group where $m = m_1 + m_2$ bits respectively. The m_1 carries the bit length of the M-ary modulation size mapped with K complex data symbols stated as Eq. (1) and m_2 represents Eq. (2) state the total number of active subcarriers and m_2 varied based on the different groups and different symbols of m_1.

$$m_1 = K \log_2 M \text{ bits} \tag{1}$$

$$m_2 = \left[\log_2 C \binom{N_g}{K} \right] \text{bits} \tag{2}$$

The bit mapping of m_1 bits with the K active subcarriers carried out either using combinational methods or Look-up table method. The transmitted vector is formed $X = [x1, x2, \ldots, xN_t]$ based on the number of message bits m with the combination of K non-zero message symbols correspond to K active subcarriers. Equation (3) shows that the non-zero samples are assigned to the active subcarriers and data samples becomes zero for the case of active subcarriers.

$$xi = \begin{cases} non-zero, & when \ i \ is \ active \\ zero, & otherwise \end{cases} \tag{3}$$

Bit to symbol mapping of OFDM-SNM is denoted as a function of $X = f_{OFDM-SNM}(m)$, where m-represents incoming sequence bits from one group. At the reception, the signal in frequency domain is denoted as Eq. (4).

$$Y = h \odot X + n \tag{4}$$

where, elementwise multiplication denotes as $\odot$, h is the model of the Rayleigh fading channel assumed to be the channel state information vector $h = [h1, h2, \ldots, hN_t]$ and n denotes the AWGN with the parameters $n_i \sim N(0, \sigma^2)$, $i = 1, 2, \ldots, N$ represents the gaussian distribution with the mean and variance. The transmitted OFDM signal with the E_s average energy M-ary symbol, received with the signal-to-noise ratio (SNR) given as $\gamma = E_s/\sigma^2$.

The essential performance characteristics of the ODFM-SNM are Spectral efficiency, Power efficiency was discussed. The spectral efficiency of the scheme formulated by the number of symbols carried by the OFDM-SNM in comparison with the conventional OFDM is given in Eq. (5).

$$\eta_{OFDM-SNM} = \frac{m_1 + m_2}{N_t + N_{cp}} \tag{5}$$

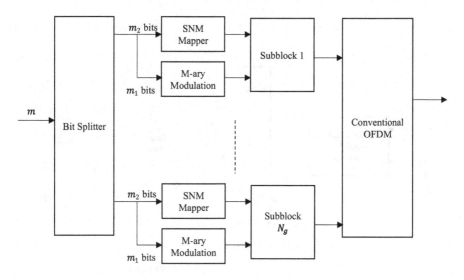

Fig. 1. Architecture of OFDM-SNM

where m_1, m_2 is the conveying bits in OFDM-SNM, especially m_2 signifies the efficiency, as observed number of the active subcarriers per subblock varied that improve the efficiency. In case of power efficiency, SNM performs better than conventional OFDM and OFDM-IM techniques. In conventional OFDM, transmitted power (P_t) is equally distributed to all subcarriers, then the average power carried by each subcarrier is P_t/N_t. Equation (6) shows number of active subcarriers distributed in the subblock of OFDM-SNM is P_c/N_t observed to follow a binomial distribution.

$$P(K) = \binom{N_t}{N_g} p_{true}^{N_g} (1 - p_{true})^{N_t - N_g} \tag{6}$$

where, N_g represents number of active subcarriers per subblock among the assigned subcarriers to each subblock. Also, p_{true} is the probability of the event of transmitting N_g active subcarriers per subblock. The total power is equally distributed to each subblock of OFDM-SNM, now the power consumption of OFDM-SNM subblock is equated as shown in Eq. (7).

$$P_{c=} \frac{P_t}{GN_t} \sum_{g=1}^{G} K(g) P(K(g)) \tag{7}$$

where $K(g)$ and $P(K(g))$ represent the number of active subcarriers per subblock and probability of active subcarriers per subblock respectively. As Sect. 1, explains the state of art method of the OFDM, next section deals with the architecture of the proposed method.

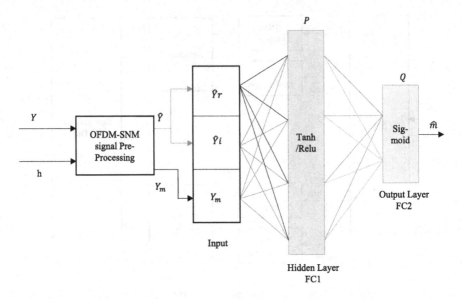

Fig. 2. Structure of Neural Network Based OFDM-SNM

3 Proposed OFDM-SNM Detector

The section deals with the structure of the OFDM-SNM detector and is followed by the training of the Neural Network with OFDM signal with randomly generated sets of the message bits.

3.1 Structure

The OFDM-SNM is shown in Fig. 2 detection schemes assume the Channel State Information (CSI) is known at the receiver to train Neural Network. The input to the Neural Network is the received OFDM-SNM signal and the CSI pre-processed to extract the parameters of the signal detection. The input of the network model is pre-processed with knowledge of the OFDM signal to significantly optimize the efficiency of the Neural Network. With the channel state information, the received signal is intuitively applied to the inverse response of the frequency response analyzer known as Zero Forcing equalizer. The pre-processed signal equalized as follows in Eq. (8).

$$\overline{Y} = Y \odot h^{-1} \tag{8}$$

The equalized signals improve the reconstruction of symbols from the active subcarriers. Also, the received signal energy is computed as Eq. (9) and collective with the equalized signal fed as input to the Neural Network. Figure 1 shows Neural Network of OFDM-SNM structure, the pre-processed received signals are fed into the network to get comparatively improved detection using the coarse inputs. The equalized signal has real and imaginary parts of $\overline{Y}r$ and $\overline{Y}i$ respectively. The received energy vector and equalized signal vector concatenated as the input for the fully connected networks of three nodes $[\overline{Y}r, \overline{Y}i, Y_m]$.

$$Y_m = \left[|y1|^2, |y2|^2, \ldots, |yN_t|^2\right] \tag{9}$$

The Neural Network has full connected two layers includes hidden layer of P nodes, another output layer of Q nodes. The activation function of the layers effectively identified to exploit the message signals at the output. At the first layer or hidden layer, activation function used is either the Rectifier Linear unit (Relu) or the hyperbolic tangent function (Tanh) as provided in Eq. (10).

$$P(x) = \max(0, x) \, or \, \frac{1 - e^{-2x}}{1 + e^{-2x}} \tag{10}$$

In the second layer or output layer, the Sigmoid Function is applied to exploit the transmitted message bits $\widehat{m}$, where $f_{sigmoid}(x) = \frac{1}{1+e^{-x}}$. The sigmoid function output lies between 0 to 1, so the message bits of digital information can effectively decide with the deciding parameter. Also, the weights and biases of the hidden and output layer are $\{W_1, b_1\}$, $\{W_2, b_2\}$ respectively. Final output of the Neural Network model given as Eq. (11).

$$\widehat{m} = f_{sigmoid}\left(W_2 f_{Tanh/Relu}(W_2[\overline{Y}r, \overline{Y}i, Y_m] + b_1) + b_2\right) \tag{11}$$

The insights of the proposed OFDM-SNM derived from the $N_t, K, M - ary$, it determines the hidden and output layer lengths. The Length of the hidden layer P, need to selection appropriately to attain the desired performance of the system model. Probably, the number of transmitted bits m increases then the hidden layer nodes need to increase selectively to reach the determined performance and also, the trade-off exist between accuracy and the system model complexity by increasing nodes of the hidden layer.

3.2 OFDM -SNM Training Network

The proposed OFDM-SNM is trained with the data from simulations and apply for the real time experimentation. The message bits m is generated randomly using the PRSG and the input vectors for the corresponding OFDM-SNM are obtained as $x = OFDM - SNM (m)$. The input vectors subject to the Channel fading effects and AWGN noise in real-time are incorporated into the vectors and OFDM-SNM was generated. Channel noise effect of Rayleigh fading is considered to model the non-line of sight distribution of the signal with Probability Distribution Function with σ is the parameter of distribution scale as Eq. (12). The channel and noise models are related to one another with the domain knowledge of the statistical models. The channel vectors and OFDM-SNM signal are pre-processed to attain the datasets z, relations with the message bits m. The training samples large enough to fit the clerical identifications between the pre-processed data and the message bits (z, m) respectively.

$$f(x, \sigma) = \frac{x}{\sigma^2} e^{-x^2/2\sigma^2} \tag{12}$$

The BER is the performance analysis for the proposed model carried out to achieve marginalized improvement in the performance in the domain of the Neural Network. The minimum mean square error (MMSE) trained the network model with the function of the measured and observed signal with the same dimension vector variable to minimize the loss function between the estimated $\{m\}$ and predicted $\{\hat{m}\}$ value. The mean square loss functions for the trained model adopt with the weight and biases of the Network model is given Eq. (13), where W_i, b_i are the weights, biases of the trained model respectively.

$$\mathcal{L}(m, \hat{m}, \delta) = ||m - \hat{m}||^2, \ \delta = \{W_i, b_i\}_{i=1,2} \tag{13}$$

The parameter of the weight and biases proportionally update for any randomly picked message symbols with the appropriate consideration of the stochastic gradient descent algorithm, motive to reduce the difference in loss function as Eq. (14), where η is the step size of the learning rate. The adaptive moment estimation (Adam) optimizer effectively optimizes the function with moment generating function is adopted to compute the learning rates.

$$\delta^+ := \delta - \eta \nabla \mathcal{L}(m, \hat{m}, \delta) \tag{14}$$

The effectiveness of the training also depends on the SNR level parameter and proper selection of SNR level is achieved to maintain the sensitive of the model. In occurrence, when SNR is very small, the conception of the noise model taken slightly into consideration leads to poor performance. For cases, SNR is too high, signal source dominant the model and training consider the signal with less dominant of the noise model. SNR need to be appropriate in the trained model will provide better performance.

The optimized trained model with parameters δ, η deployed on the signal detection of OFDM-SNM with the signal received with the CSI, SNRs and the noise. In real-time, the channel conditioned with arbitrary estimate, the scheme reveals the data the same level of training parameters. The proposed scheme necessitates the received signal along with the channel state information to estimate the symbols or bits within the computation runtime. OFDM-SNM outperforms the maximum likelihood detector, with the perfection of the known channel state information with the adequate training.

4   Simulation and Results

The proposed OFDM-SNM simulation results compared with the existing schemes in terms of the BER and computational run time is discussed. Rayleigh fading channel model is considered in our experiment and extend to any other channel models. Table 1 shows the network hyper parameter to simulate the proposed technique. Batch size of 20 with the 10^3 data samples overall considered for training the data models. The learning rate of the stochastic gradient descent for the Adam optimization η, is considered as 0.001. Other parameters are considered based on the OFDM-SNM experiment.

The data sets to train the model are simulated in the MATLAB with varying the parameter of the N, K, M of the OFDM techniques with the complex data symbols. The input to the neural network is preprocessed based on the real and imaginary of the received time domain samples as well as energy and noise variance of the symbols. Now, the simulated OFDM-SNM signal is trained in the Neural Network designed in the MATLAB with the parameter in the Table 1 and results are discussed in this section.

Table 1. Neural Network Parameters

Parameter	Values
Learning Rate	$1e^{-3}$
Batch size	20
Train size	1000
Optimizer	Adam
Testing SNR	0,5,10,15,20,25 dB
N,K,M	[4, 1, 4], [4, 3, 4]

4.1 BER Performance

Figure 3 shows comparison among some OFDM technologies like OFDM-SNM, GD and ML based detections with known Channel state information effectively pre-processed and fed as input of the Neural Network with the parameters (N_g, K, M) assumed to (4,1,4). As mentioned, the two-activation function Relu and Tanh in the hidden layer are analyzed and signals are plotted. The hidden layer with different values for P nodes is created and particularly for the larger P nodes Relu unit is preferred to provide higher model capacity, while for smaller P nodes, the Tanh unit is preferred in the Network model which have unperfect model capacity for detection task. Figure 3 shows that activation function of Relu with $P = 128$, achieves a BER rate significantly outperforms GD based detection and very close with little surge on coarse with ML based signal detection. By decreasing the hidden layer nodes P to 32 performance surges optimally 1 db to 1.5 db on comparison with ML detection and outperform than GD. On comparison, the hidden nodes $P = 32$ for Relu and Tanh activation function, the hyperbolic tangent function provide better BER performance than the Relu unit.

Figure 4 represents comparison of same techniques with higher data rates with increase of 1bps and parameters (N_g, K, M) assumed to (4, 3, 4). Whenever, the data rate increased the complexity of the hidden layer nodes increases to marginalize the BER performance and have improved capacity than previous case of $K = 1$. The hidden nodes increase to $P = 256$ for Relu and $P = 64$ for Tanh function and perform comparison with the conventional OFDM detection techniques. Result shows that ML outperforms GD based detection. Relu unit have improved BER performance compare to GD based detection. Tanh activation function-based detection performs well in comparison with Relu unit. Comparing Fig. 3 & Fig. 4 represents trade-off exist between the BER performance and hardware complexity of conventional OFDM which reduced in the Neural based detection, however number of nodes P has to adjust to gain the performance.

Figure 5 observes the comparison of the conventional scheme and proposed with imperfect channel state information condition. BER performance competing with unknown channel condition and parameters (N_g, K, M) assumed to (4, 1, 4). Comparison shows BER performance of OFDM-SNM with Neural Network deployment achieved identical to the OFDM conventional detection with imperfect CSI. The trained model remembers the familiar characteristic of the OFDM-SNM signal and performs the learning in the real time implementation.

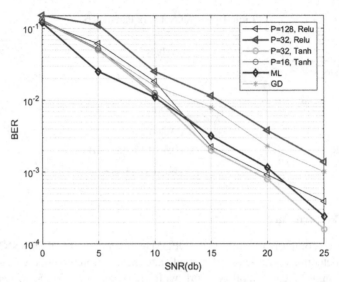

Fig. 3. BER comparison of OFDM-SNM with conventional detector with known CSI

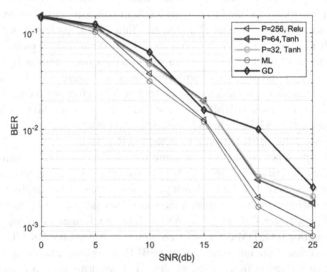

Fig. 4. BER comparison of OFDM-SNM with conventional detector with known CSI and increased data rate

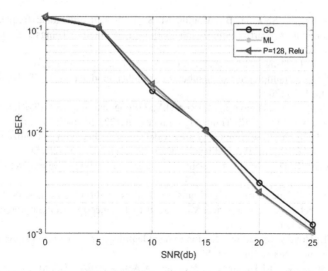

Fig. 5. BER comparison of OFDM-SNM with conventional detector with imperfect CSI

5   Conclusion

The effectiveness of the OFDM-SNM illustrated in the Neural Network with optimized error performance was presented. The proposed model results the experimentation of known characteristics of the channel and also tested the imperfect CSI. The output layer node was fixed based on the data symbols; the experiment result shows detection of two symbols and detection outperforms with the sigmoid function. The hidden layer nodes were varied according to the data rate, Symbol energy, complex received symbols and total active subcarriers of the subblock with the adaptive learning rate 0.001. Increase in data rate, results in increase in number of active subcarriers in each block and proportional increase in the nodes of the hidden layers. Trade-off between nodes and BER exist while increasing the data rate. Subsequently, trained results stable with the ML detector with SNR and data rates of 10 dB, 15 dB and 1and 2 bps respectively. In future, hyper parameter analysis will be carried to optimize the trade-off to increase the data rate.

References

1. Zaidi, A., et al.: 'Waveform and numerology to support 5G services and requirements.' IEEE Commun. Mag. **54**(11), 90–98 (2016)
2. Ankarali, Z.E., Pekoz, B., Arslan, H.: 'Flexible radio access beyond 5G: a future projection on waveform, numerology, and frame design principles.' IEEE Access **5**, 18295–18309 (2017)
3. Li, Y., Stüber, G.: Orthogonal Frequency Division Multiplexing for Wireless Communications. Springer, Boston (2006)
4. Jaradat, M., Hamamreh, J.M., Arslan, H.: Modulation options for OFDM-based waveforms: classification, comparison, and future directions. IEEE Access **7**, 17263–17278 (2019)
5. Jaradat, M., Hamamreh, J.M., Arslan, H.: OFDM with subcarrier number modulation. IEEE Wirel. Commun. Lett. **7**(6), 914–917 (2018)

6. Dang, S., Ma, G., Shihada, B., Alouini, M.-S.: Enhanced orthogonal frequency-division multiplexing with subcarrier number modulation. IEEE Internet Things J. **6**(5), 7907–7920 (2019)

7. Wen, M., Li, J., Dang, S., Li, Q., Mumtaz, S., Arslan, H.: Joint-mapping orthogonal frequency division multiplexing with subcarrier number modulation. IEEE Trans. Commun. **69**(7), 4306–4318 (2021)

8. Başar, E., Aygölü, Ü., Panayırcı, E., Poor, H.V.: Orthogonal frequency division multiplexing with index modulation. IEEE Trans. Sign. Process. **61**(22), 5536–5549 (2013)

9. Crawford, J., Ko, Y.: Low complexity greedy detection method with generalized multicarrier index keying OFDM. In: Proceedings IEEE PIMRC, pp. 688–693 (2015)

10. Schmidhuber, J.: Deep learning in neural networks: an overview. Neural Netw. **61**, 85–117 (2015)

11. O. P. Awe, "Machine learning algorithms for cognitive radio wireless networks," Ph.D. dissertation, Mechanical and Electrical Manufacturing Engineering, Loughborough University, Loughborough, U.K. (2015)

12. O'Shea, T., Hoydis, J.: An introduction to deep learning for the physical layer. IEEE Trans. Cogn. Commun. Netw. **3**(4), 563–575 (2017)

13. Satyanarayana, K., El-Hajjar, M., Mourad, A.A.M., Hanzo, L.: Multiuser full duplex transceiver design for mmWave systems using learning aided channel prediction. IEEE Access **7**, 66068–66083 (2019)

14. Ye, H., Li, G.Y., Juang, B.-H.: 'Power of deep learning for channel estimation and signal detection in OFDM systems.' IEEE Wirel. Commun. Lett. **7**(1), 114–117 (2018)

15. Jebur, A., Alkassar, S.H., Abdullah, M.A.M., Tsimenidis, C.C.: Efficient machine learning-enhanced channel estimation for OFDM systems. IEEE Access **9**, 100839–100850 (2021)

16. Yi, X., Zhong, C.: Deep learning for joint channel estimation and signal detection in OFDM systems. IEEE Commun. Lett. **24**(12), 2780–2784 (2020)

Anomaly Detection in Time Series Data by Forecasting Using Facebook Prophet

Sangeeta Oswal[✉], Shubham Hadawle, and Atharva Khangar

AI & Data Science, Vivekanand Education Society's Institute of Technology (VESIT), Mumbai, India
{sangeeta.oswal,2020.shubham.hadawle,
2020.atharva.khangar}@ves.ac.in

Abstract. The process of finding data points, observations, or occurrences that differ from typical behaviour is known as anomaly detection. Time-series data analysis would aid in identifying the root cause of various trends or patterns that have emerged throughout time. This is crucial since the subsequent value in time-series data is dependent on the prior value's input. Currently, we are detecting anomalies in time-series data with Facebook Prophet, an open-source library for forecasting in R or Python. Prophet is a method for forecasting time series data based on an additive model in which nonlinear trends are fitted with annual, weekly, and daily seasonality, as well as holiday impacts. To find anomalies, this study utilizes the Real Ad Exchange dataset, which displays online advertisement click-through rates, where the metrics are cost-per-click (CPC) and cost-per-thousand impressions (CPM).

1 Introduction

Identifying anomalous data can help indicate unusual incidents in a system, business or organisation. It can also provide us ways to use potential opportunities, which can greatly enhance the decision-making process. Time series data shows information of data over a set time period. In analysis and pre-processing of time series data, we can split and create samples according to randomness, unlike in normal data analysis. But as all the values are related to each other in a hierarchical order of time, the pre-processing should be done with care. [10] Hidden patterns in data can be identified with different visualisation techniques like graphs, histograms, pie charts, etc., whereas to identify anomalies in a time series data, there are different models and algorithms.

The occurrence of anomalies in the data may be caused by numerous reasons such as Natural Variation, Data Measurement and Collection Errors, Data belonging to different Classes, etc. These anomalies are majorly categorised into three types; Point anomaly, Collective anomaly and Contextual Anomaly.

1. *Point Anomaly -*
   A single data point may deviate or differ significantly from the remnant of the data. Such an instance is referred to as Point Anomaly.

© Springer Nature Switzerland AG 2023
D. Garg et al. (Eds.): IACC 2022, CCIS 1782, pp. 205–220, 2023.
https://doi.org/10.1007/978-3-031-35644-5_16

2. *Collective Anomaly* -

At times, we come across cases where individual data points are not anomalous, rather we find a sequence of points that can be labelled as an Anomaly.

3. *Contextual Anomaly* -

The values of some data points may seem suitable in some scenarios, while the same values may seem anomalous in other contexts.

The process of picking out or identifying such anomalies from the conventional data is called Anomaly Detection. There are three prime approaches for identifying anomalies: unsupervised, semi-supervised, supervised. Detecting Anomalies becomes substantive because anomalies help to either recognise a problem, a technical glitch, a potential opportunity or a new phenomenon that could influence the current business model [3, 4].

1.1 Time Series Modelling

Time Series is a collection of numeric values of the same entity, obtained by repeatedly measuring it at equal intervals of time. Time series data can be gathered yearly, quarterly, monthly, weekly, daily, hourly or even biennial or decennial. Example: For meteorological analysis, the rainfall of a particular geographical location needs to be noted at regular time periods.

Time Series Analysis attempts to acknowledge the underlying patterns in the time series data, to be able to make predictions for future events. Time Series Models are extensively used in statistics, economics, business, applied sciences to foretell the seasonal variability of a target entity, by using the previous values as input variables for the model [5].

The Time Series Model has four key components:

1. **Trend** - gives the overall long-term direction of the series
2. **Seasonality** - occurs when there is repetition in the behaviour of the data, which occurs at regular intervals.
3. **Cycles** - occurs when the series follows some kind of an up-and-down pattern that isn't seasonal.
4. **Irregularity** - gives information about strange dips, jumps, fluctuations or non-seasonal patterns.

Time Series Data can be grouped into two classes:

1. **Univariate -**

This time series consists of sequential measurements of a single variable over time. Example: We track a person's body weight on a daily basis.

2. **Multivariate -**

Multivariate time series consists of regular measurements of multiple variables that are interrelated over time. Example: Say, along with the body weight, we measure the person's height, body mass index and calorie intake, which are all interconnected.

Anomaly Detection in Multivariate Time Series is more complex than in Univariate Time Series. This is because, as the number of random variables increases, the prospects of making prediction errors increases. [3, 10] Here, we would be working to detect anomalies in Multivariate Time-Series Data using the Prophet Model.

1.2 Prophet Model

Facebook Prophet is an open-source tool launched by Facebook (now Meta) in 2017, used for forecasting and goal setting, which can be implemented in Python and R. It is the predecessor to NeuralProphet. Prophet is an additive regression model. It identifies the seasonality and trend from the given data and then combines them to get the forecast. FB Prophet finds the best fitting curve by using a linear/logistic curve component for external regressor. Prophet is a favourable toolkit as it has easily understandable parameters and does not require a lot of data to automatically identify seasonal trends.

The Prophet's Algorithm incorporates four vital ingredients:

1) A piecewise linear or logistic growth curve trend.
   (The model selects changepoints from the data and thus detects changes in the trends.)
2) A yearly seasonal component that has been modelled using Fourier Series.
3) A weekly seasonal component modelled using dummy variables.
4) A record of holidays that has been provided by the user.

Ergo, the algorithm can be mathematically represented as follows -

$$y(t) = g(t) + s(t) + h(t) + \varepsilon_t \qquad (1)$$

where,

- $g(t)$ is called the growth function that gives the trends in the data
- $s(t)$ is the seasonality function
- $h(t)$ gives the holiday effect
- εt is the error term [6]

- **Growth Function**

  The growth function, also referred to as the trend factor, tries to acclimate the patterns or trends shown by the data. The Prophet Algorithm, by default, uses a 'Linear Model' to model its growth (signifies a constant rate in the growth). However, with the use of this function, we can apply either of two trend models; Piecewise Linear Model and Logistic Growth Model.

  1) Piecewise Linear Model -

     At times, only a single linear model isn't sufficient. This is because the time-series happens to have some abrupt changes in their trajectories. The algorithm identifies changepoints where the graph's slope changes, and uses different linear equations for different slopes, combining them to model the growth function. These changepoints can be specified by the user or else, Prophet recognises them automatically if they haven't been specified explicitly. [6, 7] Mathematically, it can be formulated as:

$$g(t) = \beta_0 + \beta_1 x + \beta_2(x - c)^+ + \varepsilon \qquad (2)$$

  2) Logistic Growth Model -

     This trend function is used to model non-linear growths with saturation limits. These saturations help to set an upper or lower bound (cap or floor) and limit the values of the trend. Thus, ensuring that the growth does not surpass a specific maximum or minimum value, we happen to formulate the trend into an S-Curve. Say 'L' gives the cap or floor, 'k' gives the growth rate, 't' time and 'm' the offset, then the mathematical formulation would be:

$$g(t) = L/1 + e^{-k(t-m)} \beta_0 \tag{3}$$

We can also choose to set the growth to be flat. In such a flat trend, there is no growth over time and the growth function is a constant value [7, 9].

- **Seasonality Function.**

    For this component, a Fourier series is used to account for seasonal patterns. It was mainly designed to model yearly, weekly and daily seasonal effects. Although, apart from this, one can also use conditional seasonality. We make use of a partial Fourier sum (also referred to as the order), which is a parameter to discover how quickly the seasonality changes. Increasing the order allows the seasonality to fit faster-changing cycles. [1, 2, 6, 7, 9] The function can be represented as:

$$s(t) = \sum_{n=1}^{N} \left(a_n \cos\left(\frac{2\pi nt}{P}\right) + b_n \sin\left(\frac{2\pi nt}{P}\right) \right) \tag{4}$$

- **Holiday Effect or Event Function**

    The Holiday Effect component allows the Prophet model to adjust the forecasting when a holiday or major occasion may tend to affect the forecast. The function takes a matrix list of dates as input and adds or subtracts values from the growth, the seasonality terms and the forecast for those particular days, according to the historical data [2, 6, 7, 9].

    Suppose Z(t) is a matrix of regressors with D as the set of holiday dates and k ~ Normal (0, v2) where v is the smoothing parameter, then:

$$Z(t) = [1(t \in D_1), \ldots, 1(t \in D_L)] \tag{5}$$

$$h(t) = Z(t)k \tag{6}$$

- **Additive and Multiplicative Regressors.**

    Prophet allows us to add additive or multiplicative regressors to the usual linear regression model. The additive model in regression is given as the arithmetic summation of the individual effects of the predictor variables. The additive model can be represented as:

$$y = \beta_0 + \beta_1 x_1 + \beta_2 x_2 + \ldots + \beta_n x_n \tag{7}$$

Likewise, the multiplicative model would be given by the arithmetic multiplication of the predictor variables' individual effects.

$$y = \beta_0 * x_1^{\beta_1} * x_2^{\beta_2} * \ldots * x_n^{\beta_n} * \varepsilon \tag{8}$$

These additive and multiplicative regressors make the linear model more flexible [8] (Fig. 1).

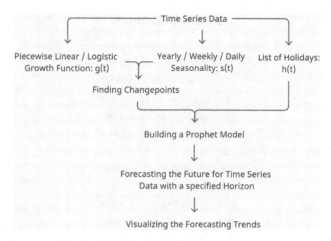

Fig. 1. Work Flow Diagram of Prophet Model

1.3 Perquisites of Modelling with Prophet

Using Facebook Prophet is advantageous for the following reasons:

- Prophet makes fast and accurate predictions all by itself.
- It allows the user to adjust parameters and thus customise the seasonality or growth components in order to improve the forecast.
- Any person, without prior knowledge or experience in analytics or forecasting, can circumvent the modelling with Prophet.

Thus, Prophet is able to help both experts and non-experts to make high quality forecasts that keep up with demands as well.

2 Methodology

2.1 Setting up the Environment

We shall be using Facebook Prophet to detect the anomalies in time-series data. So, we first install the same. Then we import all the libraries required for the project. We are including the Pandas library for working with data frames and Plotly Express for data visualisation. The model creation for the study has been performed in Python using a Google Colab Notebook.

2.2 Dataset

The NAB (Numenta Anomaly Benchmark) is a standard, open-source framework to evaluate and compare various anomaly detection algorithms. It contains a dataset with real-world and artificial, labelled time series data files across various platforms and a unique scoring mechanism that rewards early detection, penalises late or false results, and gives credit for on-line learning. Here, we are using the realAdExchange dataset from NAB, which shows online advertisement clicking rates, where the metrics are cost-per-click (CPC) and cost-per thousand impressions (CPM) (Table 1).

Table 1. NAB Dataset

	timestamp	value
0	2011-07-01 00:00:01	0.081965
1	2011-07-01 01:00:01	0.098972
2	2011-07-01 02:00:01	0.065314
3	2011-07-01 03:00:01	0.070663
4	2011-07-01 04:00:01	0.102490
...	...	...
1619	2011-09-07 11:00:01	0.094662
1620	2011-09-07 12:00:01	0.097657
1621	2011-09-07 13:00:01	0.096201
1622	2011-09-07 14:00:01	0.085386
1623	2011-09-07 15:00:01	0.109327

1624 rows × 2 columns

2.3 Pre-processing

Data pre-processing is a technique that involves transforming raw data into an understandable conformation. In Machine Learning processes, data pre-processing is critical to encode the dataset in a form that could be interpreted and parsed by the algorithm.

Here, we shall apply 'Feature Engineering' for the same, so as to convert the unrefined raw data into some meaningful features that the model can understand better and provide a better decision boundary. Using Feature Engineering, we shall generate more variables from date-time data; since we wish to deal with 'Multivariate Time Series Data'. These newly generated variables, like 'day', 'week_of_year', 'hour' and others, will be considered as factors affecting the model. The data can also be 'Resampled' to change the frequency at which the time series data is reported. In this case, we have resampled the data to an 'hourly' basis for our convenience (Table 2).

Table 2. Resampling & Feature Engineering

timestamp	value	day	day_name	day_of_year	week_of_year	hour	is_weekday
2011-07-01 00:00:00	0.081965	1	Friday	182	26	0	5
2011-07-01 01:00:00	0.098972	1	Friday	182	26	1	5
2011-07-01 02:00:00	0.065314	1	Friday	182	26	2	5
2011-07-01 03:00:00	0.070663	1	Friday	182	26	3	5
2011-07-01 04:00:00	0.102490	1	Friday	182	26	4	5

Any further variables required for 'Regression' can also be added. We shall add a 'month' column, that gives the number of the particular month and Reset the Indexing of the data frame (Table 3).

Table 3. Creating anymore required Variables

	ds	y	day	day_name	day_of_year	week_of_year	hour	is_weekday	month
0	2011-07-01 00:00:00	0.081965	1	Friday	182	26	0	5	7
1	2011-07-01 01:00:00	0.098972	1	Friday	182	26	1	5	7
2	2011-07-01 02:00:00	0.065314	1	Friday	182	26	2	5	7
3	2011-07-01 03:00:00	0.070663	1	Friday	182	26	3	5	7
4	2011-07-01 04:00:00	0.102490	1	Friday	182	26	4	5	7

2.4 Data Visualisation

For visualising or representing the data, we plot a line graph with: the 'timestamp' on the x-axis and the 'values' on the y-axis. We shall use the 'px.line' method, from Plotly Express, where each data point is represented as a vertex of a polyline mark in two dimensional space (Fig. 2).

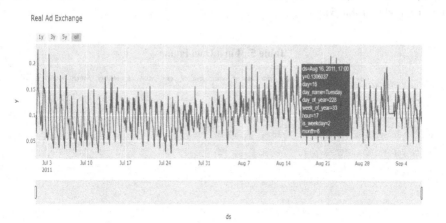

Fig. 2. Plotting 'Line Graph' to represent the Data

2.5   Creating the Prophet Model

Now, we analyse the graph, so as to select various features as variables for our model. For e.g.: Let us consider how these values change for each hour of the day. Let's do so by grouping the value and the hour data by 'hour' and finding the maximum, minimum and average values (Table 4).

Table 4. Analysing Data by Hours

hour	min	mean	max
0	0.040555	0.076766	0.126895
1	0.036329	0.070469	0.115210
2	0.029836	0.062447	0.104638
3	0.026843	0.055901	0.104638
4	0.039034	0.072798	0.136761
5	0.051258	0.091418	0.161497
6	0.049853	0.099622	0.183986
7	0.061923	0.121641	0.191602
8	0.104638	0.159612	0.218536
9	0.098608	0.141139	0.226598
10	0.093615	0.127746	0.181725
11	0.094026	0.122838	0.159902
12	0.089616	0.122931	0.176341

Here, we notice that values normally range somewhere between 0.05 to 0.19. So, we define a function to segregate the values that might lie outside this range, and add another column called 'hourly_analysis', which can be used as a regressor or variable for our model (Table 5).

Table 5. Final Data Frame

	ds	y	day	day_name	day_of_year	week_of_year	hour	is_weekday	month	hourly_analysis
0	2011-07-01 00:00:00	0.081965	1	Friday	182	26	0	5	7	0
1	2011-07-01 01:00:00	0.098972	1	Friday	182	26	1	5	7	0
2	2011-07-01 02:00:00	0.065314	1	Friday	182	26	2	5	7	0
3	2011-07-01 03:00:00	0.070663	1	Friday	182	26	3	5	7	0
4	2011-07-01 04:00:00	0.102490	1	Friday	182	26	4	5	7	0

Separating the data into 'train' and 'test'. We notice that the data ranges from 1st of July, 2011 to 7th of September, 2011 on hourly basis. So, let's split the dataset from "01-07-2011 to 31-08-2011" into 'train' and the rest into 'test'. That is, we shall be considering about 90% of our data for training and 10% for testing. If the time series is more than two cycles long, Prophet will fit the weekly and yearly seasonality, by default. It also fits the daily seasonality for a sub-daily time-series. One can also add other seasonality like hourly, monthly, quarterly using the 'add_seasonality' method. Here, while initiating the model, we shall explicitly set the daily, weekly and yearly seasonality to True.

The Prophet algorithm gives results according to the 'confidence interval', a range of values you expect your estimate to fall between. This would give us the predictions (yhat) and the upper & lower levels of uncertainty (yhat_upper & yhat_lower). The default confidence interval is set to 80%. However, here, we set it to 95%. One can add additional regressors to the model using the 'add_regressor' method. The column of the regressor value must be present in both the fitting and prediction dataframes. These extra regressors that are added must be known for both the history and future dates. Let's use the 'hourly_analysis' column, that we constructed earlier, and the 'day_of_year' column to be added as regressors in the additive fashion. We shall use the 'month' column in the multiplicative model. These will form the prime hyperparameters for our study. Along with seasonality_mode, Prophet supports a few other hyperparameters like n_changepoints, changepoint_prior_scale, changepoint_range, holidays, holiday_prior_scale, to optimise the model. One can also tune these hyperparameters by defining a 'parameter-grid'. This enables to create all possible combinations of the parameters and test using each one of those combinations (Fig. 3).

```
model = Prophet(interval_width=0.95, yearly_seasonality=True,
                weekly_seasonality=True, daily_seasonality=True)
model.add_regressor('hourly_analysis', standardize=False)
model.add_regressor('day_of_year', standardize=False)
model.add_regressor('month', standardize=False, mode='multiplicative')
```

Fig. 3. Creating the Model and Adding Regressors

We can now train the model using the 'fit' method by passing the Training Data Frame to it. We shall use this model to forecast for the future. The 'test' dataset, as we saw earlier, includes 183 rows and 10 columns. Therefore, we shall forecast the next 183 periods using the 'make_future_dataframe' method. We shall create a 'future' data frame that only consists of dates of the 'test data' as timestamps. According to our 'test' data, our data frame must include hourly frequency. By default, the method creates predictions on daily basis. Hence, we specify the frequency to predict for each hour. In multivariate forecasting, when we are predicting our target data points, we must know the future values of the regressors that we have given. Hence, we add the regressor columns containing their future values from the final data frame to our future data frame (Table 6).

Table 6. Added the Regressor Columns to the Future Data Frame

future

	ds	hourly_analysis	day_of_year	month
0	2011-07-01 00:00:00	0	182	7
1	2011-07-01 01:00:00	0	182	7
2	2011-07-01 02:00:00	0	182	7
3	2011-07-01 03:00:00	0	182	7
4	2011-07-01 04:00:00	0	182	7
...	...	...	...	...
1643	2011-09-07 11:00:00	0	250	9
1644	2011-09-07 12:00:00	0	250	9
1645	2011-09-07 13:00:00	0	250	9
1646	2011-09-07 14:00:00	0	250	9
1647	2011-09-07 15:00:00	0	250	9

1648 rows × 4 columns

Now, we take the model and try to predict the target values for these dates from the 'future' data frame to get the forecast. This forecast will then include:

1. **yhat** - Predicted value for the particular time
2. **yhat_lower** - Lower value of the confidence interval
3. **yhat_upper** - Upper value of the confidence interval (Table 7).

Table 7. Final Predictions

```
forecast = model.predict(future)
forecast[['ds', 'yhat', 'yhat_lower', 'yhat_upper']].tail()
```

	ds	yhat	yhat_lower	yhat_upper
1643	2011-09-07 11:00:00	0.194851	0.164599	0.224416
1644	2011-09-07 12:00:00	0.192848	0.162800	0.224523
1645	2011-09-07 13:00:00	0.196892	0.166847	0.225783
1646	2011-09-07 14:00:00	0.200424	0.169981	0.233106
1647	2011-09-07 15:00:00	0.197537	0.166180	0.229367

2.6 Analysing Forecasted Data

Let us now plot the actual values and the predicted values together to check the difference between the two. We'll use the 'concat()' function from the Pandas library to do so (Fig. 4).

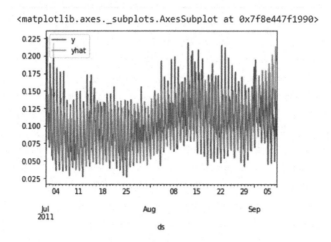

Fig. 4. Plotting the difference between Actual & Predicted values

Let us also visualise our 'forecasted' values to better understand these predictions (Fig. 5).

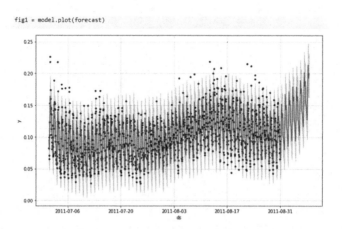

Fig. 5. Visualising the Forecasted Values

Here, the 'black points' represent the Actual Values, whereas the 'dark blue' part of the graph shows the Predicted Data Points. The upper and lower shades of 'light blue' represent the Upper and Lower Confidence Intervals.

fig2 = model.plot_components(forecast)

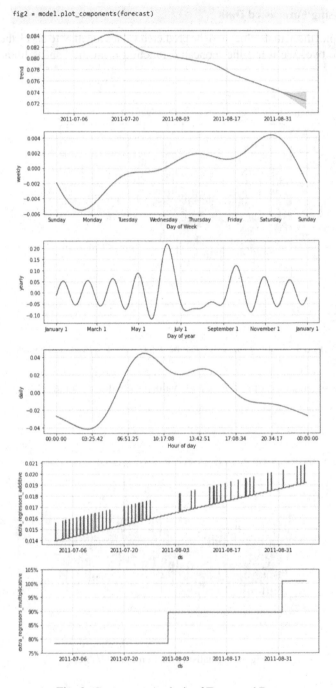

Fig. 6. Component Analysis of Forecasted Data

We can also check out the seasonality components of this forecasted time-series and visualise its trends (Fig. 6).

The first graph shows the trend in the predicted values. The data shows a rise for the first 15 days and then shows a gradual decline. The second, third and the fourth graphs represent the weekly, yearly and daily trends respectively. And finally, the last two graphs show the effects of the 'additive' and 'multiplicative' regressors.

2.7 Cross Validation

Cross Validation is a model validation technique in which we divide the dataset into two segments: one for training the model and one for evaluating our performance. We will use a diagnostic package provided by Facebook (Meta) that includes cross_validation() function to accomplish this. Next, we import the 'performance metrics' utility and pass it the results of our cross validation to get various statistical computations of prediction performance, such as mean squared error (MSE), mean absolute percent error (MAPE), median absolute percent error (MDAPE), coverage of the yhat lower and yhat upper estimates, and so on (Table 8).

Table 8. Performance Metrics of our Model

	horizon	mse	rmse	mae	mape	mdape	smape	coverage
0	0 days 18:30:00	0.000268	0.016374	0.011806	0.104078	0.075586	0.104345	0.945205
1	0 days 19:00:00	0.000266	0.016297	0.011709	0.103583	0.073404	0.103789	0.945205
2	0 days 19:30:00	0.000258	0.016073	0.011449	0.101807	0.073139	0.101923	0.945205
3	0 days 20:00:00	0.000275	0.016574	0.011805	0.103440	0.073404	0.103868	0.931507
4	0 days 20:30:00	0.000302	0.017364	0.012459	0.108257	0.081131	0.109160	0.917808
...	...	...	...	...	...	...	...	...
325	7 days 13:00:00	0.002426	0.049259	0.040070	0.378875	0.423473	0.509075	0.452055
326	7 days 13:30:00	0.002561	0.050606	0.041395	0.392778	0.425393	0.537306	0.438356
327	7 days 14:00:00	0.002553	0.050522	0.041355	0.391205	0.423473	0.533903	0.438356
328	7 days 14:30:00	0.002758	0.052512	0.042906	0.403462	0.425393	0.559270	0.424658
329	7 days 15:00:00	0.002672	0.051694	0.042103	0.397450	0.423473	0.550449	0.438356

330 rows × 8 columns

The performance metrics of our cross validation can be visualised using 'plot_cross_validation_metric' function. Let's plot the Mean Absolute Percent Error (MAPE). The dots represent the absolute percent error for each prediction made in our cross-validation result, and the blue line shows the mean of all these absolute percent errors (MAPE) (Fig. 7).

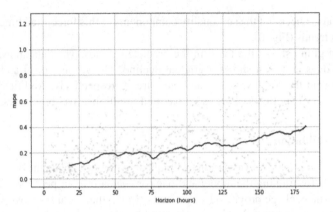

Fig. 7. Plotting MAPE of our Cross Validation

2.8 Detecting Anomalies

Lastly, let's identify the anomalous data points in the dataset. The difference between the true values and the prophesied values would give us the errors. Similarly, the difference between the upper and lower confidence intervals would give us a value of the uncertainty range. We shall calculate the same for further processing. The error can be both positive and negative, hence we first take its absolute value and then compare it with the uncertainty. For an anomalous entity, the value of the absolute error would be greater than the upper bound or less than lower bound. We can mark such a point as an Anomaly (Table 9).

Table 9. Resultant Data Frame marked with the Anomalies

	ds	y	yhat	yhat_lower	yhat_upper	error	uncertainty	anomaly
0	2011-07-01 00:00:00	0.081965	0.095440	0.061795	0.125739	-0.013476	0.063944	No
1	2011-07-01 01:00:00	0.098972	0.089232	0.057544	0.119782	0.009740	0.062238	No
2	2011-07-01 02:00:00	0.065314	0.082826	0.051985	0.113853	-0.017512	0.061869	No
3	2011-07-01 03:00:00	0.070663	0.079461	0.047724	0.109995	-0.008798	0.062271	No
4	2011-07-01 04:00:00	0.102490	0.084377	0.053256	0.116714	0.018113	0.063458	No
...	...	...	...	...	...	...	...	...
1643	2011-09-07 11:00:00	0.094662	0.194851	0.163252	0.226650	-0.100188	0.063398	Yes
1644	2011-09-07 12:00:00	0.097657	0.192848	0.163964	0.225074	-0.095192	0.061110	Yes
1645	2011-09-07 13:00:00	0.096201	0.196892	0.161876	0.228125	-0.100691	0.066249	Yes
1646	2011-09-07 14:00:00	0.085386	0.200424	0.167179	0.232360	-0.115037	0.065180	Yes
1647	2011-09-07 15:00:00	0.109327	0.197537	0.163236	0.228637	-0.088211	0.065400	Yes

Ultimately, let's visualize the Anomalies in our data by generating a scatter plot with the timestamp on the x-axis and the values of the data points on the y-axis. Here, we have colour coded the Anomalies with 'red', whereas the typical data values are marked with 'blue' (Fig. 8).

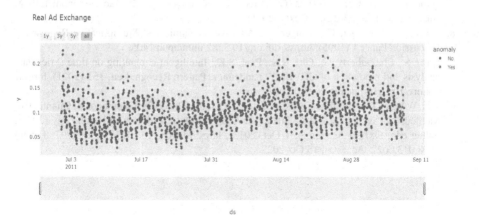

Fig. 8. Visualisation of Anomalies

3 Conclusion and Further Work

This study is set out to implement Facebook's (Meta) Prophet Algorithm for anomaly detection in a Multivariate Time-Series Dataset. To do this, we developed a forecasting model in Prophet and compared our predictions to actual data to identify outliers. With the help of the 'prophet' library's modules and functionalities, we were able to reach our objective. The NAB Real Ad Exchange datasets were also investigated and analysed.

In our further studies, we aim to investigate forecasting sequence of values using deep learning and training an LSTM or convolution model to a data set, and then visualize the model's performance.

References

1. Khayyat, M., Laabidi, K., Almalki, N., Al-Zahrani, M.: Time series facebook prophet model and python for COVID-19 outbreak prediction. Comput. Mater. Contin. **67**(3), 3781–3793 (2021). Artigo I ProQuest Central I ID: covidwho-1112965
2. Taylor, S.J., Letham, B.: Forecasting at scale. PeerJ Preprints, vol. 5, p.e3190v2; Facebook, Menlo Park, California, United States (2017). https://doi.org/10.7287/peerj.preprints.3190v2
3. Braei, M.: Technische Universität Darmstadt, Master thesis; Advisor: Prof. Max Mühlhäuser, Dr. Sebastian Wagner, December 2019. https://doi.org/10.13140/RG.2.2.17687.80801
4. Madhuri, G.S., Rani, M.U.: Anomaly detection techniques causes and issues. Int. J. Eng. Technol. https://doi.org/10.14419/ijet.v7i3.24.22791
5. Time Series. In: The Concise Encyclopedia of Statistics. Springer, New York, NY (2008). https://doi.org/10.1007/978-0-387-32833-1_401

6. Almazrouee, A.I., Almeshal, A.M., Almutairi, A.S., Alenezi, M.R., Alhajeri, S.N.: Long-term forecasting of electrical loads in Kuwait using prophet and holt-winters models. Appl. Sci. **10**(16), 5627 (2020). https://doi.org/10.3390/app10165627

7. Hyndman, R., Athanasopoulos, G.: Forecasting: Principles and Practice. Econometrics & Business Statistics, 3rd ed. OTexts (2021)

8. Fahrmeir, L., Gieger, C., Klinger, A.: Additive, Dynamic and Multiplicative Regression. Discussion Paper 1 (1995). https://doi.org/10.5282/ubm/epub.1405

9. Dash, S., Chakraborty, C., Giri, S.K., Pani, S.K.: Intelligent computing on time-series data analysis and prediction of COVID-19 pandemics. Pattern Recogn. Lett. **151** (2021). https://doi.org/10.1016/j.patrec.2021.07.027

10. Wei, W.W.S.: Time series analysis. In: Little, T.D. (ed.), The Oxford Handbook of Quantitative Methods in Psychology, vol. 2: Statistical Analysis, Oxford Library of Psychology (2013). online edn, Oxford Academic, 1 Oct. 2013), https://doi.org/10.1093/oxfordhb/9780199934898.013.0022. Accessed 15 Oct 2022

A Survey of Statistical, Machine Learning, and Deep Learning-Based Anomaly Detection Techniques for Time Series

Sangeeta Oswal[2]($\boxtimes$) (iD), Subhash Shinde[2] (iD), and M. Vijayalakshmi[1] (iD)

[1] AI and Data Science, VESIT, Mumbai, India
m.vijayalakshmi@ves.ac.in
[2] Computer Engineering, LTCE, Navi Mumbai, India
sangeeta.oswal@ves.ac.in, skshinde@ltce.in

Abstract. Anomaly detection, also known as outlier detection, has been a persistent yet active subject of study in a number of research areas for several decades. This study provides a complete taxonomy of the research on anomaly detection in time series related to types of time series data, types of anomalies, detection methods, and the dataset of time series. This taxonomy simplifies the understanding of the procedures related to each group. In addition, we detail the benefits and drawbacks of each type of approach under each respective category. Recent work based on deep learning has made significant strides in this sector. They are capable of discovering data abnormalities and learning unsupervised representations of large-scaled sequences. This survey aims to facilitate a better understanding of the many research approaches taken on this topic since the research community lacks a comprehensive comparison of statistics, machine learning, and deep learning techniques. Despite substantial progress in this area of research, there is no one anomaly detector that has been demonstrated to be effective across several datasets. Current anomaly detection methods struggle to detect anomalies related to system actions or context.

Keywords: Anomaly Detection · Outlier Detection · Machine Learning · Deep Learning · Time series · Taxonomy

1 Introduction

In a variety of research fields, time series data refers to a large volume of data indexed in a sequential form through time. Time series archives are growing rapidly in size and complexity due to the proliferation of data collected by a wide variety of sensors. Consequently, despite the fact that time series analysis has been the subject of a great deal of research, the latter's importance continues to grow.

To identify data anomalies, we examine the time series data for patterns of behavior that deviate from what would be deemed normal. Fraud detection, network intrusion detection, medical anomaly detection, log anomaly detection, Industrial Internet of Things, manufacturing, logistics, etc. are just a few of the areas where this topic can be

© Springer Nature Switzerland AG 2023
D. Garg et al. (Eds.): IACC 2022, CCIS 1782, pp. 221–234, 2023.
https://doi.org/10.1007/978-3-031-35644-5_17

explored [1, 2]. For industrial applications, the ability to detect anomalies in unlabeled time series data is vital for taking prompt corrective action and minimizing downtime-related losses. Having a system that can identify and highlight anomalies would be helpful for administrators in preventing or mitigating losses. Anomaly detection will become more common as the cost of collecting data through sensors goes down and as devices become more connected.

1.1 Organization

This survey is organized into three parts, and its structure is as follows Sect. 2 of the paper introduces a taxonomy. We examine the literature on categories of input data, outlier types, and detection methods as shown in Fig. 1. We provide a categorization of anomaly detection techniques based on the research area to which they belong: statistical techniques, classification-based, clustering-based, and deep learning-based. In Sect. 3, we present the deep learning-based techniques used for anomaly detection. We present some discussion and relative performance of various existing techniques in a tabular manner. In subsequent sections, we will identify and discuss the research challenges. Section 5 contains publicly available datasets, and Sect. 6 contains concluding remarks.

2   Taxonomy for Time Series Anomaly Detection

This study presents a literature review for anomaly detection in time series (see Fig. 1) based on three regimes: type of time series data; anomaly type; and detection method.

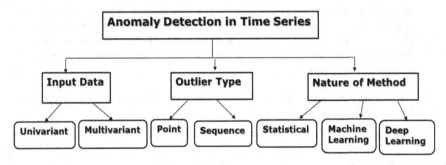

Fig. 1. Taxonomy for the Detection of Anomalies in Time Series

2.1   Input Data

The first regime the types of input data that a detection method can process (i.e., a univariate or a multivariate time series)

- A univariate time series will only have one feature, or column, and would also include a column containing timestamps linked with it.
- A multivariate time series will have more than one feature, each of which will also have a timestamp column associated with it.

2.2 Outlier Type

The second regime shows what kind of outliers the method tries to find (i.e., a point or a sequence)

- Point Outlier: Traditional heuristic techniques for anomaly detection establish thresholds using past data. When the value of a point exceeds or falls below the threshold, it is referred to as a point anomaly. The majority of current research focuses on identifying anomalous points.
- Sequence Outlier: is a continuous anomalous pattern in data points over a continuous time interval [3].

2.3 Nature of Methods

The third regime discusses the technique employed for anomaly detection.

2.3.1 Statistical Methods

The initial models for identifying anomalies were statistical models. When the discrepancy between the data and the statistical distribution exceeds a predetermined value or range, an anomaly is considered to exist. Statistical methods begin by fitting a statistical model to the available data (generally for normal behavior), and then they employ a statistical inference test to figure out whether or not an unknown occurrence fits this model. An instance is considered to be anomalous when it has a low probability of being created by the trained model, as determined by the test statistic that is applied [4]. It can be broken down into two distinct groups.

- Parametric Statistical Model: Data is sampled(drawn) from a known distribution, i.e., the data is derived from the probability density function. For example, Gaussian Model-Based- The anomaly score for a data instance is derived from the distance between that instance and its estimated mean. This distance serves as the basis for the anomaly score. The $\mu \pm 3\sigma$ region contains 99.7% of the data instances [18].
- Nonparametric techniques: model structure is not predetermined, but rather is determined by the data presented, i.e. make no assumptions about the distribution of the data. Histogram-based and kernel-based examples are examples.

To quantitatively analyze time-series data, a statistical model can be created by calculating statistical measures such as mean, variance, median, quantile, kurtosis, and skewness. Newly added timeseries data can be analyzed using the developed model to determine whether or not they are normal data.

2.3.2 Machine Learning Methods

Anomalies in time series can be found with supervised, unsupervised, and semi-supervised machine learning techniques. Since the majority of data sets lack labels, unsupervised approaches are more common than supervised ones. The semi-supervised method assumes that the data set is normal and tries to figure out its pattern so that it can decide whether new test data is normal or not.

The taxonomy for machine learning is classified as shown in the figure below (Fig. 2).

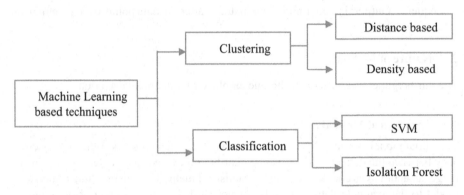

Fig. 2. Machine Learning based Taxonomy for Anomaly Detection

2.3.2.1 Clustering

The capacity to recognize abnormalities is one of the "subsidiary products" of cluster analysis. The technique takes into account the deviation from the normal distribution of data points in order to project them into the vector space. Density or distance metrics could explain the dissimilarity in distribution. While typical data records form big, dense clusters, outliers either do not cluster at all or form very small ones. Anomalies discovered by clustering-based approaches may include: –

- Data records that do not fit into any cluster (clustering residuals)—Distance-based measure
- Low density clusters: Density based measure

- **Density based:** Using density-based anomaly detection algorithms, the neighborhood density of each data instance is approximated. A location in a low-density neighborhood is classified as anomalous, while a location in a dense neighborhood is labelled as normal. The prevalent method for density-based measures is DBSCAN, which categorizes datapoints into three groups: boundary points, core points, and anomalous points. To classify the points, the user needs to provide two parameters: $\in$ and μ, where $\in$ is the distance and μ is the minimum number of points required for each normal cluster. Celik et al. [5] used DBSCAN to find abnormalities in a univariate time-series containing daily average temperature records. They began by segmenting the dataset into monthly sequences. The data set was first divided into monthly segments. The sequence's mean and variance are then used to standardize the data. Following this, DBSCAN is run on each sequence to detect the anomalies. The main difficulty lies in determining what values to give the parameters $\in$ distance and the minimum number of points in each cluster.

- **Distance based:** A point O in a dataset DB(p,d) is said to be anomalous if at least p other points in the dataset are situated at greater distances than d from point O. This is the definition of an anomaly. The K nearest neighbor approach computes the distance (dk) between each data point (d) and the Kth nearest neighbor. Sort the data points by distance, with anomalous data points being those that have the greatest distance and are located in a sparse area. The Euclidean distance is the most common type of measurement that is based on distance, and it determines the distance by calculating the length of a line segment that connects two points. Dynamic Time Wrapping (DTW) is used as the distance metric to figure out how far apart two sequences of different lengths are.

In contrast to DBSCAN, the popular algorithm is local outlier factor (LOF). LOF's original intent was for spatial information. Breuning et al. [6] broadened the use of the method to time-series data. Calculate the distance from q to the kth nearest neighboring data point (k -distance).

For each data set q, get the reach-dist between it and p by using the formula:

$$reach\text{-}dist(q,\ p) = \max\{k\text{-}distance(p),\ d(q,\ p)\} \tag{1}$$

local reachability density (lRD) is calculated by taking the inverse of the average reachability distance between each pair of nodes in the dataset, using the data example's minimum possible pairwise distance between its neighbors as the starting point.

$$IRD(Q) = MinPts/ \sum reach - dist(q, p) \tag{2}$$

To find LOF(q), divide the local reachability density of q by the local reachability density of q's k nearest neighbours.

$$LOF(Q) = \frac{1}{MinPts} \sum_{P} \frac{IR\,d(P)}{IR\,d(Q)} \tag{3}$$

Oehmcke [21] used a sliding window with a length of w in order to locate sequences of length w that did not follow the expected pattern.

The drawbacks of clustering-based techniques include:

- The method may mislabel regular occurrences if they are too far from their neighbors, or anomalous examples if they are too close to their neighbors.
- The complexity is $O(N^2)$ because each instance requires finding a distance/density measure. Several strategies have directly enhanced the anomaly detection method based on the concept that only the most significant few abnormalities are of importance, hence an anomaly score for each data instant is unneeded.
- The $O(N^2)$ complexity problem is tackled by sampling methods, which identify nearest neighbors within a reduced data set. However, if the sample size is extremely small, erroneous anomaly ratings may result from the sampling process.

- In high-dimensional domains, data is sparse, and the concept of similarity may no longer be useful.

2.3.2.2 Classification

Classification-based techniques discover the characteristics of normal data points in either supervised or semi-supervised environments. On the basis of the training data, a model is fitted to classify normal and abnormal data instances. Techniques for rule-based anomaly detection discover the rules that characterize a system's normal behavior. An anomaly is a test instance that is not covered by any of these rules. Both multivariate and univariate contexts have incorporated rule-based approaches. Anomaly detection also employs widely adopted models like neural networks, Bayesian networks, and decision trees. Since the number of anomalous data points is less compared to the number of normal data points, techniques such as up sampling and down sampling are used to generate artificial or synthetic data in scientific research.

SVM: SVM is the most prevalent supervised method for anomaly identification. The initial attempt to support vector machines was a linear supervised algorithm by [Vapnik, 1995]. By adopting the kernel approach, Boser et al. made SVM capable of nonlinear classification. As one class configuration for spotting anomalies in time series, SVM has been utilized, with the model learning the training instance region (all normal in-stance). OC-SVM is a semi-supervised method in which the training set contains only normal data from a single class. The fundamental method determines whether or not each test case falls within the learned region. If a testing instance falls within the learning region, it is considered normal otherwise, it is classified as abnormal.

For anomaly detection, most studies advise projecting the time series into a vector set, since this was the only form in which the original OC-SVM algorithm could operate. Zhang et al. [4] propose dividing the time-series dataset into windows of length w, so that for a given time-series, $\{X_T\} = (x_1, x_2,..., x_T)$, a window length w and $W \subseteq R^{p \times w}$, the dataset is first converted into:

$$(W_1, W_2, \ldots, W_p) = \left((x_1, \ldots, x_w)^T, (x_2, \ldots, x_{w+1})^T, \ldots, (x_p, \ldots, x_{w+p-1})^T\right) \tag{4}$$

The time series is then projected onto a two-dimensional space by a function p. OC-SVM gives biased results for time series points with large values, it is best to normalize the data.

Isolation Forest: It builds a set of binary trees that separate out individual data points. Because anomalous points tend to be outliers compared to typical data points, they tend to cluster near the Tree's origin. Consequently, this technique considers points with shorter journey lengths as candidates with a high probability of being anomalies. The technique of anomaly identification using Isolation Forests typically involves two steps:

- To get started with training, all you have to do is generate n iTrees using the data in the training set.

- To evaluate a case, one would run it through a series of isolation trees to determine how unusual it is.

Using sliding windows and accounting for the idea drift phenomena Ding et al. adapted streaming data anomaly detection method based on the iForest algorithm, called iForest ASD.

Issue with ML based techniques:

- Model based on Machine Learning learn a simple model to classify normal and anomalous data points in time series. As the features increase, it becomes difficult to learn the model.
- Data complexity: Traditional approaches generally suffer from the curse of dimensionality when dealing with large numbers of dimensions.
- Temporal dependency: Machine learning techniques do not take into account temporal dependency which is very crucial in time series anomaly detection.

2.3.3 Deep Learning Methods

The taxonomy for anomaly detection using deep learning is classified into prediction-based techniques and reconstruction-based techniques (Fig. 3).

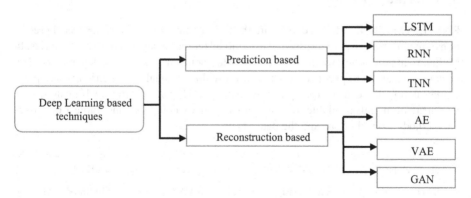

Fig. 3. Deep Learning based Taxonomy for anomaly detection

Prediction-based techniques utilize previous time series data, and they forecast future time steps (values). The projected and actual time series values are compared, and thresholding-based methodologies for locating anomalous data points are proposed. Long-short term memory (LSTM) recurrent neural networks (RNN) are used to automatically extract features in order to represent temporal dependence and predict future sample instances. The problem with prediction-based models is that they are primarily concerned with learning short-term temporal dependencies and are incapable of learning global anomalies.

Reconstruction based techniques learn low-dimension representation in semi supervised setup (trained on normal data). Anomalies are identified on the basis of reconstruction error. Reconstruction-based approaches are predicated on the premise that reconstruction errors for normal data sets are smaller than those for anomalous data sets.

With the configuration of LSTM, RNN, etc., deep learning models such as auto encoder, variational auto encoder, and adversarial network are utilized [19].

In addition to reconstruction error, the hidden representation in the latent space is an active field of research that can be utilized for probability estimation [12]. Gaussian Mixture Model (GMM).

Major challenge in implementing reconstruction-based techniques is the issue of

- Overfitting hence, regularization or additional constraints are required to reduce this issue.
- Reconstruction error-trained models are insensitive to small perturbations.

In the field of deep learning-based time series anomaly detection, reconstruction-based models are more prevalent than prediction-based ones. Reconstruction-based models are linked to other learning algorithms to improve their robustness and performance. Taking into account both the discriminator's inaccuracy in its predictions and the generator's error in its reconstructions, GAN-based approaches are increasingly used to identify anomalies in time data. Mode collapse and non-convergence are obstacles for GAN-based research methodologies.

3   Literature Review

RNN, LSTM, CNN, GRU, and TCN are the most common deep learning-based prediction or reconstruction models used today to model temporal dependency in time series. In Multivariant time series, we must include both temporal and intermetric dependence. The primary concept is to produce a systematic low-dimensional intermetric and temporal representation that can accurately capture typical MTS patterns. Figure 4 illustrates the vast array of models available for time series anomaly detection, and Table 1 discusses the methods' contributions and the datasets used.

Auto Encoder	LSTM/RNN/CNN	GAN	VAE/GRU
USAD	Stacked LSTM	MADGAN	Multimodal AD
DAEMON	DeepAnT	TAnoGAN	VAECGAN
GMM	MCRAAD	TadGAN	OmniAnomaly
MSCRED	LSTM-GAN-XGBoost	GAN-AD	MSCRED

Fig. 4. Survey for Modelling Temporal dependency using Deep Learning models

In this survey we reviewed the papers using AE, LSTM, GAN and VAE to model time series. Most of the papers have been published in IEEE conference and KDD (Knowledge Discovery and Data Mining) conference which is and active research community for time series research.

We examined the F1-scores of models trained on SWaT, WADI, and MSL datasets (Fig. 5) and found that WADI, a high-dimensional testbed with 126 features, had

Table 1. A review of the literature on Deep Learning-based Anomaly Detection Models

Paper	Method	Dataset	Contribution and Issues Discussed in Paper	Anomaly Score
USAD: Unsupervised Anomaly Detection on Multivariate Time Series [7]	Auto Encoders and GAN	SWaT, WADI, SMAP, MSL	Model Scalability Performance drop with dimensionality Weakness for non-gaussian anomalies	Reconstruction Based $A(Wb) = \alpha\|Wb - AE1(Wb)\|^2 + \beta\|Wb - AE2(Wb)\|^2$
Robust Anomaly Detection for Multivariate Time Series through Stochastic Recurrent Neural Network Omni anomaly [8]	GRU and VAE/RNN	SMAP/MSL and SMD	Critical to obtain robust latent representations and opportunity to interpret the anomalies with physical significance and localization	Reconstruction Based Anomaly Score $S_t = $ Reconstruction probability of X_t
A Novel Multivariate Time-Series Anomaly Detection Approach Using an Unsupervised Deep Neural Network [9]	Multilayer convolutional recurrent autoencoder anomaly detector (MCRAAD)	Synectic Data	Adding attention mechanism to model to build a noise insensitive framework	Thresholding based
Anomaly Detection with Generative Adversarial Networks for Multivariate Time Series [10]	Generative Adversarial Networks-based Anomaly Detection (GAN-AD)	Secure Water Treatment (SWaT) system	Feature selection for multivariate anomaly detection, and investigate principled methods for choosing the latent dimension	• Anomaly Detection with Discrimination • Anomaly Detection with Residuals
DAEMON: Unsupervised Anomaly Detection and Interpretation for Multivariate Time Series [11]	DAEMON (Adversarial Autoencoder Anomaly Detection Interpretation)	SMD, SMAP MSL and SWaT	Reconstruction error for each dimension and Top K dimension as root cause anomaly	$Sxt = \|xt - x't\|$
Deep autoencoding gaussian mixture model for unsupervised anomaly detection [12]	Autoencoder and GMM(estimator)	kdd cup, thyroid, Arrhythmia, KDD-cup rev	Reconstruction error is feed to GMM uses compression and estimation network	Reconstruction Based
LSTM-GAN-XGBOOST Based Anomaly Detection Algorithm for Time Series Data [13]	LSTM-GAN-XGBOOST	Ball Bearing time series data, Western Reserve University	Integration and threshold adjustment as per dataset, parameter optimization	Threshold
SALAD: Self-Adaptive Lightweight Anomaly Detection for Real-time Recurrent Time Series [14]	LSTM	NAB	Threshold adjustment Handling large scale time series	Thresholding

(continued)

Table 1. (*continued*)

Paper	Method	Dataset	Contribution and Issues Discussed in Paper	Anomaly Score
TAnoGAN: Time Series Anomaly Detection with Generative Adversarial Networks [15]	stacked LSTM in Generator and single LSTM in Discriminator	NAB	Determining optimal window length GAN based AD is sensitive to epoch	Reconstruction based
One-Class Predictive Autoencoder Towards Unsupervised Anomaly Detection on Industrial Time Series [16]	LSTMEncoder-decoder with prediction and one class branch	SWaT, WADI, MSL, SMAP	3 Framework: • Reconstruction(AE) • Prediction: short temporal • One-class: global pattern	Reconstruction and prediction-based formula
Practical Approach To Asynchronous Multivariate Time Series Anomaly Detection And Localization	Auto Encoders	SMD, SWaT	Transfer Asynchronicity in MTS to synchronous MTS by adding embedding layer	Reconstruction based

the lowest score compared to the other two. It is important to stress the difficulty of studying and subsequently modeling high-dimension time series. The OCPAE [16] and RANSynCoders [17] have a significant performance improvement on these dataset. Also, to achieve standardization, assessing the models on the same dataset to assess their performance will enable comparisons across various methodologies for modeling timeseries.

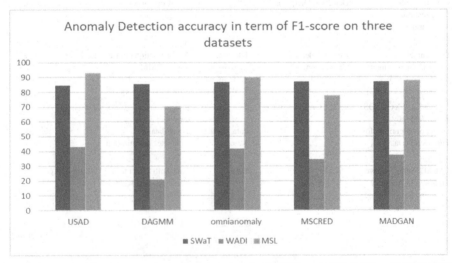

Fig. 5. F1-score for USAD, DAGMM, Omnianomaly, MSCRED and MADGAN on SWaT, WADI and MSL datasets.

4   Research Challenges

Research challenges identified after reviewing the literature for time series anomaly detection include:

1. It is critical to obtain robust latent representation: Some of the work done in the literature includes connecting two different learning algorithms. The deep autoencoding Gaussian mixture model (DAGMM) [12] combines an autoencoder and a Gaussian mixture model in order to discover the normal patterns in the latent representation space. USAD [7] combines adversarial training with autoencoders to learn to reconstruct the training set's instances.
2. Feature selection for multivariant time series data: Unsupervised methods are constructed using linear projection and transformation, but the hidden fundamental correlation of MTS is nonlinear. Methods such as
   a. Dimensional reduction reduces the amount of computation by extracting the primary characteristics.
   b. Matrix: A matrix directly represents the morphological similarity and relative scale of individual variables. In addition, it simultaneously evaluates multivariate variables.
   c. GRAPH can be used to describe an explicit hierarchical architecture and find out how different variables are related to each other [20].
3. Model scalability and performance: anomalies reside in a low probability density area. In higher dimension, it is difficult to perform density estimation in the original feature space.
4. Anomaly localization and interpretation: the lack of human interpretable information makes it hard to tell why an anomaly is abnormal, especially in high-dimensional time series data or long input sequences. Various interpretable techniques have lately gained popularity in domains that require high transparency and human-understandability in order to address the black-box problem. The top K dimension with the highest reconstruction error was proposed by DAMEON as the underlying cause of anomalies.
5. Regarding the nature of the detection approach, it should be highlighted that complicated relationships between variables in a multivariate time series are ignored when univariate techniques are extended to multivariate time series. It's possible that as a result of this, we won't be able to recognise data that seems regular for each variable taken on its own but runs counter to the correlation structure across variables.

Other challenges include Integration and threshold adjustment as per dataset, selection of the network architecture and the corresponding hyperparameters, determining optimal window length and handling large scale time series.

5 Datasets

The datasets SWaT, WADI[1], SMD[2], NAB[3], SMAP and MSL[4] are used in most of the research papers (Table 2).

Table 2. Dataset with anomaly ratio

Data Set Name	Dimension	Anomaly Ratio
SWaT	51	11.98%
WADI	126	5.99%
SMAP	25	13.3%
MSL	55	10.72%
SMD	38	4.16%

6 Conclusion

This review tries to sum up the research on anomaly detection in time series data, in a way that is complete and comprehensive. Existing techniques have been categorized into a few different groups based on the respective methodologies that they were developed from. The first regime consists of input data, for which it should be noted that applying a univariate technique independently to each variable in a multivariate time series could be computationally costly if there are many variables. The second regime discusses anomaly kinds; it ought to be highlighted that the detection of sequence anomalies is a significantly more difficult task than the detection of point anomalies.

In conclusion, the horizon of future study encompasses

- Most research has modelled offline historical data, whereas real-time data is dynamic. So, incremental learning, adding new data, and changing model parameters at the same time are all new ways to study.
- New research areas include reasoning anomalies and unlocking the black box of Deep Learning-based techniques.

References

1. Chalapathy, R., Chawla, S.: Deep learning for anomaly detection: a survey (2019). http://arxiv.org/abs/1901.03407

---

[1] https://itrust.sutd.edu.sg/.
[2] https://github.com/NetManAIOps/OmniAnomaly.
[3] https://github.com/numenta/nab.
[4] https://github.com/khundman/telemanom.

2. Chandola, V., Banerjee, A., Kumar, V.: Anomaly detection : a survey, vol. 41, no. 3, pp. 1–58 (2009). https://doi.org/10.1145/1541880.1541882
3. Blázquez-García, A., Conde, A.: Review on outlier/anomaly detection in time series data. ACM Comput. Surv. **54**(3), 1–33 (2021). https://doi.org/10.1145/3444690
4. Choi, K., Yi, J., Park, C., Yoon, S.: Deep learning for anomaly detection in time-series data: review, analysis, and guidelines. IEEE Access **9**, 120043–120065 (2021). https://doi.org/10.1109/ACCESS.2021.3107975
5. Çelik, M., Dadaşer-Çelik, F., Dokuz, A.Ş.: Anomaly detection in temperature data using DBSCAN algorithm, undefined, pp. 91–95 (2011). https://doi.org/10.1109/INISTA.2011.5946052
6. Breunig, M.M., Kriegel, H.P., Ng, R.T., Sander, J.: LOF: identifying density-based local outliers. In: SIGMOD 2000 - Proceedings of the 2000 ACM SIGMOD International Conference on Management of Data, pp. 93–104 (2000). https://doi.org/10.1145/342009.335388
7. Audibert, J., Michiardi, P., Guyard, F., Marti, S., Zuluaga, M.A.: USAD: unsupervised anomaly detection on multivariate time series. In: Proceedings of the ACM SIGKDD International Conference on Knowledge Discovery and Data Mining, pp. 3395–3404, August 2020. https://doi.org/10.1145/3394486.3403392
8. Su, Y., Zhao, Y., Niu, C., Liu, R., Sun, W., Pei, D.: Robust anomaly detection for multivariate time series through stochastic recurrent neural network. https://doi.org/10.1145/3292500.3330672
9. Zhao, P., Chang, X., Wang, M.: A novel multivariate time-series anomaly detection approach using an unsupervised deep neural network (2021). https://ieeexplore.ieee.org/stamp/stamp.jsp?tp=&arnumber=9503373. Accessed 17 Dec 2021
10. Li, D., Chen, D., Goh, J., Ng, S.-K.: Anomaly detection with generative adversarial networks for multivariate time series. https://github.com/LiDan456/GAN-AD
11. Chen, X., et al.: DAEMON: unsupervised anomaly detection and interpretation for multivariate time series. In: 2021 IEEE 37th International Conference on Data Engineering (ICDE), vol. 2021-April, pp. 2225–2230, April 2021. https://doi.org/10.1109/ICDE51399.2021.00228
12. Zong, B., et al.: Deep autoencoding Gaussian mixture model for unsupervised anomaly detection.
13. Xu, X., Zhao, H., Liu, H., Sun, H.: LSTM-GAN-XGBOOST based anomaly detection algorithm for time series data. IEEE Conference. https://doi.org/10.1109/PHM-Jinan48558.2020.00066
14. Lee, M.-C., Lin, J.-C., Gran, E.G.: SALAD: self-adaptive lightweight anomaly detection for real-time recurrent time series. In: 2021 IEEE 45th Annual Computers, Software, and Applications Conference (COMPSAC), pp. 344–349, April 2021. https://doi.org/10.1109/COMPSAC51774.2021.00056
15. Bashar, A., Nayak, R.: TAnoGAN: time series anomaly detection with generative adversarial networks. https://github.com/mdabashar/TAnoGAN
16. Zhang, H., Cheng, F., Pandey, A.: One-Class Predictive Autoencoder Towards Unsupervised Anomaly Detection on Industrial Time Series (2022)
17. Abdulaal, A., Liu, Z., Lancewicki, T.: Practical approach to asynchronous multivariate time series anomaly detection and localization. In: Proceedings of the 27th ACM SIGKDD Conference on Knowledge Discovery & Data Mining, pp. 2485–2494, August 2021. https://doi.org/10.1145/3447548.3467174
18. Shaukat, K., et al.: A review of time-series anomaly detection techniques: a step to future perspectives. In: Arai, K. (ed.) FICC 2021. AISC, vol. 1363, pp. 865–877. Springer, Cham (2021). https://doi.org/10.1007/978-3-030-73100-7_60
19. Malhotra, P., Ramakrishnan, A., Anand, G., Vig, L., Agarwal, P., Shroff, G.: LSTM-based Encoder-Decoder for Multi-sensor Anomaly Detection, July 2016. https://arxiv.org/abs/1607.00148v2

20. Han, S., Ai, S.H., Seoul, R., Korea, S., Woo, S.S.: Learning sparse latent graph representations for anomaly detection in multivariate time series. In: Proceedings of the 28th ACM SIGKDD Conference on Knowledge Discovery and Data Mining, vol. 1, pp. 2977–2986, August 2022. https://doi.org/10.1145/3534678.3539117
21. Oehmcke, S., Zielinski, O., Kramer, O.: Event detection in marine time series data. In: Hölldobler, S., Krötzsch, M., Peñaloza, R., Rudolph, S. (eds.) KI 2015. LNCS (LNAI), vol. 9324, pp. 279–286. Springer, Cham (2015). https://doi.org/10.1007/978-3-319-24489-1_24

An Analysis Employing Various Machine Learning Algorithms for Detection of Malicious URLs

Fizza Rizvi[✉], Saika Mohi ud din, Nonita Sharma, and Deepak Kumar Sharma

Department of Information Technology, Indira Gandhi Delhi Technical University for Women, Kashmere Gate, Delhi, India
{fizza006mtit21,saika017mtit21,nonitasharma, deepaksharma}@igdtuw.ac.in

Abstract. Currently, there are millions and trillions of webpages online. Therefore, in order to protect their data, users must be able to distinguish between trustworthy and dangerous websites. Since they are on the rise, malicious URLs (Uniform Resource Locators) are one of the most common cybersecurity concerns nowadays. They host free content (like malware, ransomware, trojans, password sniffers, etc.), and by clicking on this free content, especially the links found in emails, messages, and other formats, unwary users become the targets of these scams, have their personal information compromised, or have their system infected with malware, resulting in the loss of billions of rupees. There are more threats to cybersecurity than ever before, so a quick fix is required. In this study, we investigate how well different machine learning methods work in spotting potentially dangerous URLs. To identify both dangerous and benign URLs, this study employs a variety of machine learning methods. Decision Tree classifier, Random Forest classifier, AdaBoost classifier, K-Nearest Neighbors classifier, Gaussian Nave Bayes classifier, and XGB classifier are just a few of the machine learning methods that are used. Finding the most effective algorithm for accurately detecting fraudulent URLs is the main objective of this project. The accuracy metric was utilised as the evaluation tool to determine the accuracy of the various algorithms, with Random Forest having the highest accuracy (92.6%) of all of them.

Keywords: Machine learning · Malicious URLs · Trojans · Password sniffers · Decision Tree classifier · Random Forest classifier · AdaBoost classifier · K-Nearest Neighbors classifier · Gaussian Nave Bayes classifier · XGB classifier

1 Introduction

Technology breakthroughs have ushered in a brand-new era in which routine tasks like banking, socialising, learning, and shopping can all be done online. However, this advancement has also made it simpler for other forms of cybercrime, such as malware, phishing, link spamming, and other forms of spoofing. During the COVID-19 epidemic, online activities like as e-banking, e-commerce, social networking, and other things

D. Garg et al. (Eds.): IACC 2022, CCIS 1782, pp. 235–241, 2023.
https://doi.org/10.1007/978-3-031-35644-5_18

[1] expanded abruptly and significantly, which increased the number of cybercrimes targeted at taking advantage of consumers. Typically, these assaults feature malicious URLs that can steal all the user's private information, which a hacker can then access by just clicking on the bad link. Regular expression and signature matching procedures are difficult [1] in conventional methods of hazardous URL identification like blacklisting due to the enormous datasets and technical improvements. We therefore applied machine learning methods for malicious URL detection to solve these problems. Our dataset is composed of URLs and is derived from the publicly accessible Kaggle dataset. The prior techniques employed by researchers were as follows:

1.1 URL Blacklist Based Method

This blacklisting technique was previously researched and used [2–4]. The majority of the research has been done using lists of known harmful URLs. Blacklists are collections of URLs that have caused harm in the past. Some PhishTank.com websites maintain a blacklist, a list of harmful websites. If the website's URL is on the blacklist, the application software will recognise it as a dangerous site and promptly block it. Sadly, the blacklist can only be used to identify bad URLs that already exist; it cannot detect new malicious URLs. The workload is increased since we must continuously update and maintain the list of harmful URLs.

1.2 URL Signature Based Method

For a very long period [5–7], this blacklisting methodology has been researched and applied. Most studies have made use of lists of known hazardous URLs. A database query is made from a database of URLs each time a new URL is requested. If the URL is blacklisted because it is thought to be dangerous, a warning is produced; otherwise, it is thought to be benign. This method's drawback is that it can't detect recently found dangerous URLs that aren't already on the list.

2 Research Methodology

This study uses classification algorithms as its technique. When deciding which classes or groups to assign new observations based on training data, a model learns from the dataset or observations presented. The dataset is loaded, prepared, and trained before the model's output is categorised into new classes or groups. Binary Classifier and Multi-class Clasifier are the two fundamental classification techniques. In this work, we will employ a binary classifier, which can only yield two outcomes. The classification algorithms used in this study are listed below:

2.1 Decision Tree Classifier

Decision Tree Classifier falls under the class of Supervised learning. The goal of this classifier is to create a training model and it can be utilised to forecast the category or value of the target variable by generating a set of rules.

2.2 Random Forest Classifier

The Random Forest classifier falls under the class of supervised learning. It is an ensemble classifier that integrates numerous decision trees from various dataset subsets. To improve the expected accuracy of dataset, the final result is based on the mean of numerous trained decision trees. This classifier makes use of the bagging method, which turns a group of decision trees into a forest.

2.3 K-Nearest Neighbours Classifier

The classifier, which employs supervised learning, is one of the most simple machine learning techniques. It uses the nearest neighbours in K. KNN determines the distance between the experimental data and all of the learning points, then selects the K number of points that are closest to the experimental data to predict the result for the experimental data. The class with the highest likelihood of being picked The KNN determines how likely it is that the experimental data will correspond to the K learning data classes. This model performs well when trained on large datasets.

2.4 Naive Bayes Classifier

The Naive Bayes Classifier is a heuristic model built on the Bayes theorem. It is utilised for classification issues. Naive Bayes models come in three different varieties: Multinomial, Gaussian, and Bernoulli. This study uses the Gaussian Naive Bayes model. The independent variables in this classifier are assumed to have very low correlations with one another, meaning that changing the value of one variable does not affect the value of the others. However, there are very few situations where variables are independent in the real world.

2.5 AdaBoost Classifier

AdaBoost Classifier, which may also be employed as an ensemble method, is also known as the Adaptive Boosting methodology in machine learning. The decision tree is the most popular one-level AdaBoost classifier, which indicates that there is only one split in a decision tree. Decision Stumps is another name for these trees. To improve classifier accuracy, it additionally combines several weak classifiers. This classifier creates a model, gives all the data values identical weights, and gives higher weights to the values that are incorrectly classified. For the following model, values with greater weights are assigned more significance.

2.6 XGBoost Classifier

The Extreme Gradient Boosting classifier, often known as XGBoost, is a decision tree-built machine learning technique that makes use of boosting to enhance model performance. For tasks involving regression, classification, and ranking, it is the most successful and well-known machine-learning library. Decision trees are built consecutively in this classifier. The influential component of this classifier are the weights. All predictor variables are given weights in this, which are eventually input into the decision tree to produce output. If the decision tree predicts a variable's weight incorrectly, the decision tree's weight is increased and the variable is then passed into the second decision tree.

3   Data Visualization

3.1   Data Collection

The public dataset is collected from the Kaggle repository and consists of 651,191 URLs. The dataset is used to learn and evaluate machine learning models and to produce the best outcomes. Figure 1 depicts the data which comprises of two features: URL and type.

] :	url	type
0	br-icloud.com.br	phishing
1	mp3raid.com/music/krizz_kaliko.html	benign
2	bopsecrets.org/rexroth/cr/1.htm	benign
3	http://www.garage-pirenne.be/index.php?option=...	defacement
4	http://adventure-nicaragua.net/index.php?optio...	defacement

Fig. 1. URL dataset

The Fig. 2 depicts the count of types of URLs in the dataset that begins with phishing, malware, and defacement.

3.2   Feature Extraction

Feature extraction is a strategy for minimising the number of features in a dataset that involves producing new features from the original dataset and then eliminating the original features. Additionally, it offers quicker processing because of dimensionality reduction. Figure 3 depicts the features which are taken from the URL [8–10] for classification procedure.

4   Results

The experiment was carried out using an AMD Ryzen 5 5500U CPU, which runs a 64-bit operating system, and Python Collaboration software, which enables the use of Python libraries for data analysis and visualisation to produce the best results. The experiment's Kaggle dataset is primarily partitioned according to the 80/20 rule. 80% of the data is used to train the various machine learning algorithms, while the remaining

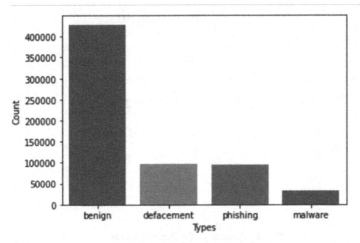

Fig. 2. Types of URLs

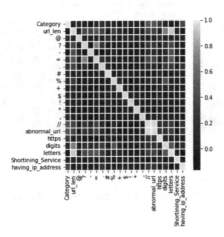

Fig. 3. Number of features extracted

20% is used to test their performance. The experiment employed the confusion matrix as a measurement instrument to categories several machine learning models, and the accuracy metric [10, 11] was calculated from it. Utilizing the confusion matrix, the accuracy of the model is evaluated together with the efficacy of the classification model performance. The Random Forest model provides the maximum level of accuracy when using the accuracy metric, as seen in the Fig. 4. As shown in Fig. 5, the image also features a bar graph depiction.

	Model	Accuracy
0	Decision Tree Classifier	0.920600
1	Random Forest Classifier	0.926159
2	AdaBoost Classifier	0.827310
3	KNeighbors Classifier	0.903577
4	Gaussian NB	0.789418
5	XGBClassifier	0.903370

Fig. 4. Accuracy of different models

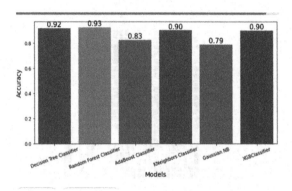

Fig. 5. Different models outcomes displayed in a bar plot.

5 Conclusion

Cybersecurity relies heavily on the detection of malicious URLs, and machine learning techniques are utilised to address this issue. Here, we undertake an investigation using different machine learning techniques that have been shown to produce the highest levels of accuracy. As demonstrated in Fig. 5, the Random Forest method, out of all the ones utilised, provides the most accuracy, whereas Gaussian Nave Bayes provides the lowest accuracy. By giving the model more data, the accuracy of the model can be improved. The future involves more accurate outcomes through the use of balanced data and more efficient methods, such as feature selection using deep learning [12].

Catak, Ferhat Ozgur & Şahinbaş, Kevser & Dortkardes, Volkan. (2020) found that random forest classifier provided the best accuracy, which was 98.6%, in their investigation [13].

Patil, Dharmaraj R., and Jayantro B. Patil. according to the findings of their experiments, all decision tree learning classifiers have successfully attained a good detection rate of between 98 and 99% with extremely low False Positive Rate (FPR) and False Negative Rate (FNR) [14].

References

1. Janet, B., Kumar, R.J.A.: Malicious URL detection: a comparative study. In: 2021 International Conference on Artificial Intelligence and Smart Systems (ICAIS), pp. 1147–1151. IEEE, March 2021
2. Sahoo, D., Liu, C., Hoi, S.C.: Malicious URL detection using machine learning: a survey (2017). arXiv preprint arXiv:1701.07179
3. Khan, F., Ahamed, J., Kadry, S., Ramasamy, L.K.: Detecting malicious URLs using binary classification through ada boost algorithm. Int. J. Electr. Comput. Eng. 10(1), 2088–8708 (2020)
4. Lekshmi, R.A., Thomas, S.: Detecting malicious URLs using machine learning techniques: a comparative literature review. Int. Res. J. Eng. Technol. (IRJET) 6(06) (2019)
5. Hoa Do Xuan, C., Nguyen, H.D., Tisenko, V.N.: Malicious URL detection based on machine learning. Int. J. Adv. Comput. Sci. Appl. 11(1) (2020)
6. Sheng, S., Wardman, B., Warner, G., Cranor, L., Hong, J., Zhang, C.: An empirical analysis of phishing blacklists (2009)
7. Li, K., Chen, R., Gu, L., Liu, C., Yin, J.: A method based on statistical characteristics for detection malware requests in network traffic. In: 2018 IEEE Third International Conference on Data Science in Cyberspace (DSC), pp. 527–532. IEEE, June 2018
8. Chen, Y.-C., Ma, Y.-W., Chen, J.-L.: Intelligent malicious URL detection with feature analysis. In: 2020 IEEE Symposium on Computers and Communications (ISCC), pp. 1–5 (2020). https://doi.org/10.1109/ISCC50000.2020.9219637
9. Rupa, C., Srivastava, G., Bhattacharya, S., Reddy, P., Gadekallu, T.R.: A machine learning driven threat intelligence system for malicious URL detection. In: The 16th International Conference on Availability, Reliability and Security, pp. 1–7, August 2021
10. Kumi, S., Lim, C., Lee, S.-G.: Malicious URL detection based on associative classification. Entropy 23(2), 182 (2021)
11. Sharma, N., Mangla, M., Mohanty, S.N., Satpaty, S.: A stochastic neighbor embedding approach for cancer prediction. In: 2021 International Conference on Emerging Smart Computing and Informatics (ESCI), 2021, pp. 599–603 (2021). https://doi.org/10.1109/ESCI50559.2021.9396902
12. Bu, S.-J., Kim, H.-J.: Optimized URL feature selection based on genetic-algorithm-embedded deep learning for phishing website detection. Electronics 11(7), 1090 (2022)
13. Catak, F.O., Sahinbas, K., Dörtkardeş, V.: Malicious URL detection using machine learning. In: Artificial Intelligence Paradigms for Smart Cyber-Physical Systems, pp. 160–180. IGI Global (2021)
14. Patil, D.R., Patil, J.B.: Malicious URLs detection using decision tree classifiers and majority voting technique. Cybern. Inf. Technol. 18(1), 11–29 (2018)
15. Dataset. https://www.kaggle.com/datasets/sid321axn/malicious-urls-dataset

Channel Estimation of mmWave Massive MIMO Systems Using Large Intelligent Surfaces

Divya Udataneni$^{(\boxtimes)}$ ⓘ and Vijayalakshmi Maddala ⓘ

G. Narayanamma Institute of Science and Technology (for Women), Hyderabad, India
udatanenidivya@gmail.com

Abstract. The abstract should summarize the contents of the paper in short terms, i.e. 150–250 words. Massive MIMO and mmWave communications are utilized in 5G and 6G cellular networks to boost system capacity. In this article, a DL (Deep Learning) approach for mm-Wave massive MIMO systems based on LIS is proposed. The proposed technique was evaluated, and the results showed that it outperformed 10^{-1} than existing techniques such as Spatial Frequency CNN and Least Square.

Keywords: Massive MIMO · mmWave · Deep Learning · ChannelNet · SF-CNN

1 Introduction

One of the major technologies for 5G and 6G is massive MIMO (Multiple-Input and Multiple-Output). In contrast to the traditional MU (Multi-User) MIMO systems, Massive MIMO is a unique kind of MIMO system with hundreds of antennas mounted at the BS to concurrently serve tens of users in their cells. The mmWave (Millimeter Wave) frequency refers to the spectrum between 30 GHz to 300 GHz; however, traditionally, the mmWave category also includes a spectrum above 20 GHz, such as the local multipoint distribution service (LMDS) band at 28 GHz [1]. The combination of Massive MIMO with mm-Wave transmission comes at a high cost in terms of energy consumption as well as hardware complexity, even when using hybrid beamforming.

Millimeter wave massive MIMO technique may greatly increase data transmission rate with broader bandwidth & improved spectral efficiency [2]. To reduce the cost and complexity in mm-Wave Massive MIMO systems, LIS (Large Intelligent Surface) is proposed with a greater number of passive reflecting elements. LIS serves as a reflecting surface in the users and Base Station (BS) that may be controlled by outside signals, like a backhaul control connection from the BS, to increase the received signal energy and coverage [3].

A new framework that incorporates DL technology into the massive MIMO systems for DOA estimation and signal detection is considered when it comes to channel estimation in mmWave massive MIMO systems [4]. A DNN (Deep Neural Network) is adopted and considered a black box, i.e., the DNN encompasses the whole massive MIMO system, with distinct levels of the network capable of processing specialized

© Springer Nature Switzerland AG 2023
D. Garg et al. (Eds.): IACC 2022, CCIS 1782, pp. 242–250, 2023.
https://doi.org/10.1007/978-3-031-35644-5_19

operations. In [5], a CNN ("Convolutional Neural Network") for MIMO (CNN-MIMO) is designed, which receives the channel matrix of users as input and outputs the analog precoder and combiners. A DL-based strategy is suggested for the hybrid precoding in a MU massive MIMO system [6]. Beixion Zheng presents a transmission technique for an IRS-enhanced OFDM system that sequentially executes reflection optimization along with channel estimation. A new reflection pattern at the IRS is created using the user-received pilot signals to make channel estimation easier by always taking into account the complete reflection of the IRS.

[7] proposes efficient solutions by using techniques from DL and compressive sensing. A new LIS architecture is introduced where few LIS elements are active. Two solutions i.e., compressive sensing and DL are developed that construct the LIS reflection matrices with low training effort. Deep learning technique is studied [8]. The channel matrices at neighboring sub-carriers are concurrently fed into the CNN in SF-CNN ("Spatial-Frequency CNN") based on channel estimation. Peihao Dong and Hua Zhang developed a mmWave Massive MIMO system with transmitters and receivers. Phase shifters are used to link multiple antennas with a considerably smaller number of RF chains on BS and user sides.

This paper proposes a DL method for channel estimation in "LIS-assisted mm-Wave massive MIMO" systems. Here, a CNN pair for the prediction of BS-user (direct) as well as BS-LIS-user (cascaded) channels, assuming that every consumer has accessibility to the network to predict its channel. The pilot signals are supplied to CNN, which creates a non-linear connection between the channel data and signals. The deep network i.e., Channel Net trained by different channel estimations to estimate the performance.

The remainder of the paper is arranged as follows. In Sect. 2, the mmWave big mimo systems model is examined and channel estimate is carried out in Sect. 3. The simulation's results are presented in Sect. 4, and Sect. 5 comes to a conclusion by recommending more research.

2   MmWave Massive MIMO System Model

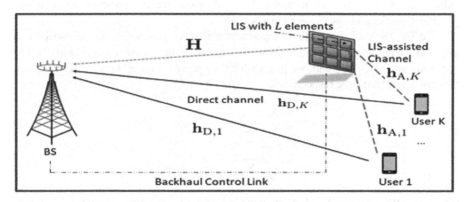

Fig. 1. A scenario for mm-Wave massive MIMO with LIS assistance

As seen in Fig. 1, we investigate the mm-Wave massive MIMO system with LIS assistance. Suppose that the base station has M antennas to support K single-antenna consumers with the aid of L passive reflecting components in the LIS. Every LIS element in a LIS-aided communication system contributes a phase difference to the receiving signal from the BS. Every LIS element's phase may be modified using PIN diodes controlled with the LIS controller linked to the base station via the backhaul connection (Fig. 2).

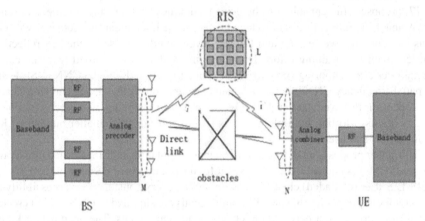

Fig. 2. Block diagram of LIS-aided mmWave MIMO system

The Base Station transmits 'K' data symbols from the baseband precoder "F = $[f_1, ..., f_K]$" $\in C^{MxK}$ to users. The signal that was sent from the k-user consists of 2 components, i.e., the BS may be reached directly, and a second path through LIS can be given.

$$y_k = (h_{D,K}^H + h_{A,K}^H \Psi^H H^H)\bar{s} + n_k \tag{1}$$

where $h_{D,K} \in C^M$ is a direct channel between the k-th user and BS, $h_{A,K} \in C^L$ are LIS aided channel LIS and the kth user, Ψ indicates diagonal matrix represents LIS elements, $\underline{s}$ is transmitted signal and n_k is a noise signal.

The SV ("Saleh-Valenzuela") model, which adopts a geometric channel model with minimal scattering, can be used to depict the channel in mm-wave transmission [6]. The contributions of N_D, N_A and N_H paths which are represented by $h_{D,K}$, $h_{A,K}$ and H, in the mm-Wave channels, respectively.

$$h_{D,K} = \sqrt{\frac{M}{N_D}} \sum_{n_D=1}^{N_D} \alpha_{D,k}^{(n_D)} a_D(\theta_{D,k}^{(n_D)}) \tag{2}$$

$$h_{A,K} = \sqrt{\frac{L}{N_A}} \sum_{n_A=1}^{N_A} \alpha_{A,k}^{(n_A)} a_A(\theta_{A,k}^{(n_A)}) \tag{3}$$

where **M** is BS antennas, **L** is LIS antennas, α is complex channel gains, θ is path angles, and **a** is steering vectors for path angles. The "mm-Wave" channel H between the LIS &

BS is presented by

$$H = \sqrt{\frac{M\,L}{N_H}} \sum\nolimits_{n_D=1}^{N_D} \alpha^{n_H} a_{BS}(\theta_{BS}^{(n_H)}) a_{LIS}(\theta_{LIS}^{(n_H)}) \tag{4}$$

where $\theta_{BS}^{(n_H)}$, $\theta_{LIS}^{(n_H)}$ represent the AOD ("Angle-of-Departure") and AOA ("Angle-of-Arrival") angles of the paths. The main goal is to assess the $h_{D,K}$ (Direct Channel Estimation) and G_k ("Cascaded Channel Estimation") in downlink transmission. In this scenario, we suppose that every user sends the "received pilot" signals to the ChannelNet deep neural network to predict their channel.

3 Channel Estimation Using DL

In the downlink case, the BS sends the "orthogonal pilot" signals $x_P \in C^M$, with p = 1..., P and P ≥ M. There are P total channels used to predict the direct channel. The "received signal" may be provided to the k-th user by

$$y_k = (h_{D,K}^H + \Psi^H G_K^H)X + n_k \tag{5}$$

where $G_K = \mathbf{H}\,\Gamma_k$ is the cascaded channel matrix, $\Gamma_k = \text{diag}\{h_{A,K}\}$, "X = [X_{,1}, \ldots \ldots, X_{,P}]" $\in C^{MXP}$ indicates the pilot signal matrix whereas $y_k = [y_{k,1}, \ldots \ldots, y_{k,P}]$ and $n = [n_{k,1}, \ldots \ldots, n_{k,P}]$ are row vectors of $1 \times P$. There are two stages of pilot training i.e., $h_{D,K}$ and G_k. In direct channel estimation ($h_{D,K}$), utilizing BS backhaul connection, assuming that all the PIN diodes in LIS elements are turned off, such that it does not depend on Ψ. Therefore, the baseband signal received by the kth user becomes,

$$y_D^{(k)} = (h_{D,K}^H)X + n_{D,k} \tag{6}$$

Once estimated channel $h_{D,k}$ is determined, the cascaded channel G_k may be calculated in the 2nd step of the training stage. This may be attained by 2 techniques. In the 1st technique, "P = M" pilot signals are broadcast when every LIS element is switched on individually. In this instance, the BS instructs the LIS to switch on one LIS element at a time by sending a request over the backhaul link's microcontroller device. The signal that the k-th user receives from the "cascaded channel" for the l-th frame becomes

$$y_C^{(k,l)} = (h_{D,k}^H + g_{k,l}^H)X + n_{k,l} \tag{7}$$

where $g_{k,l}$ presents the l-th column of G_K. The least-square error estimation is $\hat{g}_{k,l}$ = $(y_C^{(k,l)}X^H(XX^H)^{-1})^H$-$h_{D,k}$. In the 2nd technique, "channel estimation" is performed when every element of LIS are turned on. In this instance, $\underline{X} \in C^{MLxML}$ pilot signal matrix is used to jointly estimate the L columns of G_K. The received signal is given as

$$\underline{y}_C^{(k)} = (\underline{h}_{D,k}^H + \underline{g}_k^H)\underline{X} + \underline{n}_k \tag{8}$$

The least-square error estimation is $\hat{g}_k = (\underline{y}_C^{(k)}\underline{X}^H(\underline{XX}^H)^{-1})^H$- $\underline{h}_{D,k}$. Two approaches are used to estimate the channel when pilot signals are corrupted.

Training Data Generation for ChannelNet

1. Initialize the input parameters such as K, M, SNR, Ψ.

2. Generate the $h_{D,k}$ and G_K.

3. Using $h_{D,k}$ and $g_{k,l}$, generate $y_D^{(k)}$ and $y_C^{(k,l)}$.

4. Using $y_D^{(k)}$ and $y_C^{(k,l)}$, design $X_{DC}^{(t)}$ and $X_{cC}^{(t)}$.

5. Using $h_{D,k}$ and G_K, design output $Z_{DC}^{(t)}$ and $Z_{cC}^{(t)}$

6. $D_{DC}^{(t)} = "(X_{DC}^{(t)}, Z_{DC}^{(t)}), D_{CC}^{(t)} = (X_{CC}^{(t)}, Z_{CC}^{(t)})"$ using CNN.

7. End.

Channel Net Model

The received signals are fed as input to the convolutional neural network. ChannelNet is made up of two identical CNNs with nine layers each. The direct & cascaded channels are represented by the deep network's input a X_{DC} and X_{CC} respectively. Each entry must have "real", "imaginary", and "absolute" values to feed the deep network.

For 2 dimensional convolutional filters, constructing the matrix quantity X_{DC} from the vector using partitioning $y_D^{(k)}$ into sub-vectors and organized into columns. The 1st and 2nd "channels" of X_{DC} are vec $\{[X_{DC}]_1\} = \text{Re}\{y_D^{(k)}\}$ & vec$\{[X_{DC}]_2\} = \text{Im}\{y_D^{(k)}\}$ and the 3rd channel is vec$\{[X_{DC}]_3\} = |y_D^{(k)}|$. Similarly, X_{CC} is partitioned. The network's output is the vectored type of the channel matrices, "$Z_{DC} = \left[Re\{h_{D,k}\}^T, Im\{h_{D,k}\}^T\right]^T$ and $Z_{CC} = \left[Re\{vec\{G_K\}^T, Im\{vec\{G_K\}\}^T\right]^T$."

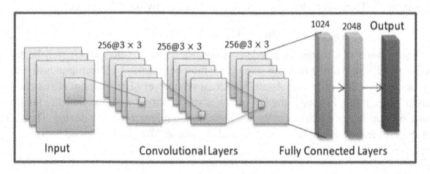

Fig. 3. Proposed deep neural network architecture

As seen in Fig. 3, ChannelNet is made up of two identical CNNs, each of which has nine layers. The input layer, which is the initial layer, is where the pilot signals are received. The size of the input varies as stated above because the same network is utilized for direct as well as cascaded channels. CLs ("Convolutional Layers") with 256 filters having a size of 3 × 3 make up the second, third, and fourth layers. Fully linked layers (FCLs) are present in the fifth and seventh levels, with 1024 & 2048units. There are "dropout" layers with a fifty percent possibility after every FCL and the final layer is the "regression" layer. After the training is finished, new pilot data that wasn't included in the training is created and utilized in the prediction phase, the NMSE for G_k is described as

$$\mathrm{NMSE} = \frac{1}{J} \sum\nolimits_{j=1}^{J} \frac{\left\| G_k - \hat{G}_k^{(j)} \right\|_F}{\|G_k\|_F}$$

Here $J = 100$ "Monte Carlo" tests

4 Simulation Results

The proposed ChannelNet performance is assessed using Matlab and compared the results with SF-CNN and LS. The simulation parameters used throughout the process are $M = 100$, $K = 40$, $L = 100$, SNR 0:10:60 dB. The prediction stage is carried out by receiving data other than training data once the channel training phase has been completed.

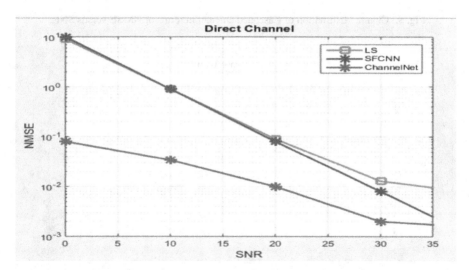

Fig. 4. Channel Estimation of Direct channel in terms of NMSE vs SNR.

In Fig. 4 and 5, the finding of the proposed method in terms of NMSE vs SNR are shown. In Fig. 4, ChannelNet has better NMSE than SF-CNN and LS. For the Direct channel, at 30dB the NMSE of ChannelNet is 10^{-3}. In Fig. 5, ChannelNet1 and ChannelNet2 have superior performance to SF-CNN and LS. The performance of ChannelNet is better because of the joint use of convolutional layers and fully connected layers, while SF-CNN uses only convolutional layers.

In Fig. 6 and Fig. 7, the influence of corrupted pilot data is evaluated and the effectiveness of direct and cascaded channels is obtained. In Fig. 6, the ChannelNet has less NMSE than SF-CNN and LS. In Fig. 7, the performance of ChannelNet1 has better NMSE because more pilot signals are corrupted in ChannelNet2. Among all methods, ChannelNet1 has a better performance compared to others.

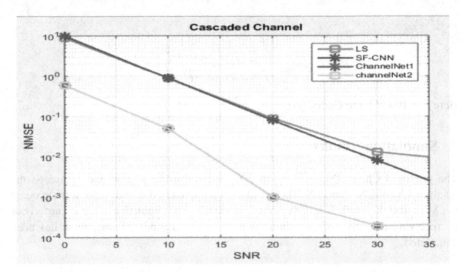

Fig. 5. Channel Estimation of Cascaded channel in terms of NMSE versus SNR.

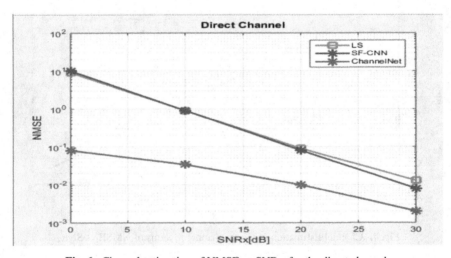

Fig. 6. Channel estimation of NMSE vs SNR_X for the direct channel.

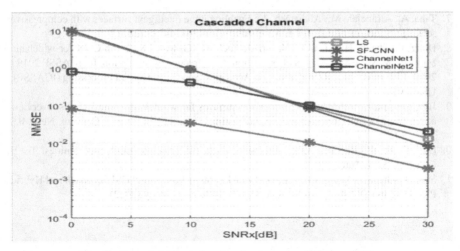

Fig. 7. Cascaded Channel estimation in terms of BER vs SNR_X.

5   Conclusion

A DL-based channel estimation approach for mm-Wave massive MIMO systems based on LIS is suggested. Every user in the proposed work has a similar deep network, that is trained by the "received pilot" signals in order to predict the direct & cascaded channels. The performance of deep learning ChannelNet is evaluated and compared the results with existing techniques. Results shows that ChannelNet has 10^{-1} better NMSE than existing techniques. The finding indicates that the suggested technique has superior performance to SF-CNN and LS. In the future, innovative channel estimation algorithms and other approaches may be used to improve NMSE performance in mmWave Massive MIMO systems. Complexity reduction in the system is possible as well.

References

1. Busari, S.A., Huq, K.M.S., Mumtaz, S., Dai, L., Rodriguez, J.: Millimeter-wave massive MIMO communication for future wireless systems: a survey. IEEE Commun. Surv. Tutor. **20**, 836–869 (2018)
2. Khwandah, S.A., Cosmas, J.P., Lazaridis, P.I., Zaharis, Z.D., Chochliouros, I.P.: Massive MIMO systems for 5G communications. Wirel. Pers. Commun. **120**(3), 2101–2115 (2021). https://doi.org/10.1007/s11277-021-08550-9
3. He, M., Xu, W., Zhao, C.: RIS-assisted broad coverage for mmWave massive MIMO system. In: IEEE International Conference on Communications Workshops (ICC Workshops), Montreal, QC, Canada (2021)
4. Huang, H., Gui, G.: Deep learning for super-resolution channel estimation and DOA estimation based massive MIMO system. IEEE Trans. Veh. Technol. **03**(01), 1–12 (2018)
5. Elbir, A.M., Papazafeiropoulos, A.: Hybrid precoding for multi-user millimeter wave massive MIMO systems: a deep learning approach. IEEE Trans. Veh. Technol. **61**(09), 552–563 (2019)
6. Zheng, B., Zhang, R.: Intelligent reflecting surface-enhanced OFDM: channel estimation and reflection optimization. IEEE Wirel. Commun. Lett. **09**(04), 518–522 (2020)

7. Taha, A., Alrabeiah, M., Alkhateeb, A.: Enabling large intelligent surfaces with compressive sensing and deep learning. IEEE Access **09**(04), 44304–44321 (2021)
8. Dong, P., Zhang, H., Li, G.Y., NaderiAlizadeh, N., Gaspar, I.S.: Deep CNN for wideband Mmwave Massive Mimo channel estimation using frequency correlation. In: ICASSP 2019 - 2019 IEEE International Conference on Acoustics, Speech and Signal Processing (ICASSP), UK (2019)
9. Jian, M., et al.: Reconfigurable intelligent surfaces for wireless communications: overview of hardware designs, channel models, and estimation techniques. Intell. Converg. Netw. **03**, 1–32 (2022)
10. Liu, Y., et al.: Reconfigurable intelligent surfaces: principles and opportunities. IEEE Commun. Surv. Tutor. (2021)
11. Sun, Q., Zhao, H., Wang, J., Chen, W.: Deep Learning-Based Joint CSI Feedback and Hybrid Precoding in FDD mmWave Massive MIMO Systems, Entropy (2022)

Malware Detection in URL Using Machine Learning Approach

Rajesh Kumar[1], Rachit Talwar[2], Manik Sharma[2], Suchi Kumari[3(✉)],
Shivani Goel[3], Kanika Malhotra[2], and Faiz Ahmed[2]

[1] College of Engineering and Design, Alliance University Bangalore,
Bengaluru, India
`rajeshkumar.k@alliance.edu.in`
[2] Department of CSE, Bharati Vidyapeeth's College of Engineering, New Delhi, India
[3] School of Computer Science Engineering and Technology, Bennett University,
Greater Noida, India
`suchi.singh24@gmail.com`, `shivani.goel@bennett.edu.in`

Abstract. The most common technique to host fraudulent or harmful
content, such as spam, malicious ads, etc., is using a Uniform Resource
Locator (URL). Malicious URLs hold harmful contents that cause loss
of information, malware installation, and monetary loss of the victims.
Hence, it is necessary to detect such URLs and take some action on such
threats. Earlier, one database is maintained to blacklist such URLs and
a URL is compared with the available database of blacklisted URLs.
If the URL is found in the database then the browser considers the
URL suspicious and blocks it. But, this method is ineffective in finding newly discovered URLs. By suggesting a solution based on machine
learning, this problem can be resolved. This research aims to investigate
how machine-learning techniques can be used to identify harmful URLs.

Keywords: Malware Detection · Malicious URLs · Machine
Learning · Black Listing

1 Introduction

Over the past few years, the importance of the World Wide Web (WWW)
[10,12,17] is continuously increasing with the advancement of technology. The
resources of WWW can be accessed using a global address named Uniform
Resource Locator (URL). Thus, it is essential to use URLs to operate a business,
to carry out financial transactions to process online orders, etc. [11,13,18]. The
huge dependence on technology cause users to stuck in a scam such as financial
fraud, loss of sensitive information, and installation of malware in the user's
system. The user is attacked using various ways like social engineering, SQL
injection, phishing, malicious URL, and many more. Malware is currently one
of the biggest risks to the digital world. Nowadays, there are a lot of devices
online, making it simple and quick for malicious code to spread. According to

© Springer Nature Switzerland AG 2023
D. Garg et al. (Eds.): IACC 2022, CCIS 1782, pp. 251–263, 2023.
https://doi.org/10.1007/978-3-031-35644-5_20

data shown in [2], among the top 10 most popular attack strategies for 2019 are attacks that use malicious URLs. The malware is propagated through various ways such as malicious URLs, botnet URLs, and phishing URLs. According to data, there has been a rise in the prevalence of malicious URLs over time. Therefore, it is crucial to keep Internet-connected computers safe from malware by detecting viruses in URLs.

An Internet website can be found using a Uniform Resource Locator (URL), which is a special identification. A URL is nothing more than the Internet address of a specific unique site. It has two components namely, protocol identifier and resource name (shown in Fig. 1). Both components are differentiated by using a semicolon which is followed by two forward slashes. One can write the resource name either as an IP address or domain name. An IP address is made up of numbers and letters, in order for computer networks and servers to "speak" to one another. Each internet-connected gadget has its own IP address. Thus, it is quite difficult for the user to navigate the web by simply entering their IP address. As a result, domain names were developed to replace IP addresses with names that were more appropriate. We may think of a domain name as an IP address's "nickname".

There are two ways to identify a fraudulent URL: blacklisting (heuristic) and machine learning methods. The blacklist method is the most popular technique for identifying fraudulent URLs. Blacklists are repositories of harmful URLs that have previously been verified. Over time, this database has been assembled. This method is quick thanks to a straightforward query and is very simple to use. The drawback of employing blacklists is that attackers can alter the URLs and new malicious URLs appear every day, making it exceedingly challenging to keep the blacklists current. Consequently, it is almost crucial to have a detailed list of malicious URLs. Therefore, to identify malicious URLs, machine learning methods: Decision Trees, Random Forests, and Logistic regression are used.

The rest of the manuscript is organized as follows: Sect. 2 discusses the related work, Sect. 3 describes the methodology, Sect. 4, the results of the simulation are provided, and finally, in Sect. 5, the conclusion and future scope are given.

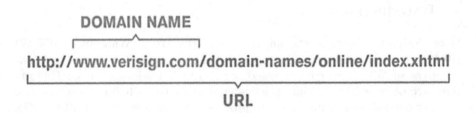

Fig. 1. URL structure

2   Related Work

In the existing literature, the researchers have mainly emphasized two methods to detect malicious URLs. These are: (i) Blacklisting (Heuristics) and (ii) Machine Learning.

Blacklisting or Heuristic Approach

Signature sets has been widely used over a long time fro the detection of malicious URLs. Details of this method and related issues are provided in INTRODUCTION section.

Blacklisting is a well-known and traditional method to detect malicious URLs. A database (blacklist) containing the suspicious is maintained. On visiting a new URL, the database entries are looked up to verify whether the visited URL is harmful or not. If the visited URL appears in the database, it is classified as malicious. The blacklisting method is inefficient for harmful URLs which are new or have not been added to the blacklist database [20]. To address the issue with the blacklisting technique, a heuristic method is adopted where each attack has a signature attached to it and a flag is raised if any suspicious activity is reported ([9,21]). This approach must be used in a controlled setting. If an attack is not launched right away after a visit, it won't be detected.

Machine Learning Based Approach

To address the issues blacklisting, the researchers have adopted a machine-learning approach to detect malicious URLs. Here, a specified fraction of the total number of URLs is taken as training and testing data. On the basis of statistical characteristics, a function is defined to predict the class of a URL as malignant [18]. In a research work, the authors exploited big data technology along with machine learning to detect the malicious URLs. The authors noticed that the proposed method improved the ability to detect malicious URLs [5]. In Machine learning approaches, good features of the URLs are extracted, prediction model is trained against malicious and benign URLs training data. The extracted features may be explicitly categorized into two types: static and dynamic. In static analysis, it is not needed to execute the URL to test its malicious behavior [6,15] instead the features are extracted through lexical features of the URL. Dynamic analysis technique monitors the system call sequence of the URL to check the anomalous behavior of the URL [23].

In a research work, the authors proposed a malicious URL detection framework using machine learning and exploiting big data technology to detect malicious URLs based on anomalous behaviors. The authors noticed that the proposed method improved the ability to detect malicious URLs significantly. Wang et al. designed a method for malicious URLs based on a dynamic convolutional neural network (DCNN) by introducing a folding layer to the existing convolution network. The authors proposed a new embedding method to learn the vector representation of a URL. Their investigations showed that word embedding could achieve higher accuracy [24].

In related work, the authors proposed a framework named as DeepURLDe-tect (DURLD) where the encoding of the raw URLs takes place with the help of character-level embedding. They employed the hidden layers to extract features from the character level embedding in order to comprehend the various forms of information in the URL, and then they used a non-linear activation function to determine whether or not the URL is likely to be malignant. Their findings demonstrated that DURLD could identify variants of malicious URLs [22]. The authors suggested a phishing detection approach using SVM in their article [25]. They were accurate to the tune of 95.80%. Only six URL characteristics are taken into account by the suggested framework: the length of the URL, the number of dots and hyphens, the amount of numeric characters, the number of dots, a variable relating to the IP address in the URL, and the similarity index. Similarly, the authors in [19] employed the SVM approach and achieved an accuracy of 95.66% and a very low false-positive rate. They demonstrated that the proposed method could identify new temporary phishing sites and minimize the damage caused by phishing attacks. In [3], the authors introduced a reinforcement learning-based approach for automated malicious URL detection. The authors used only lexical features of the URLs. The authors of [16] identified malicious URLs using association rule mining algorithms feature ranking approach to rank the importance of features. The authors in [4,14] employed logistic regression models to discover malicious URLs. In the research work, the authors used a machine learning approach to extract 19 functions to differentiate the malicious URLs [8]. In related work, researchers extracted features from abstract syntax trees using a random forest classifier to identify the malicious JavaScript instances [7].

There exist multiple tools for detecting malicious URLs [5]. Some of them are provided as follows:

- **URL Void:** A URL checking program that utilizes a few engines and domain blacklists is called URL Void. Examples of URL Void include Norton Safe-Web, My-WOT, and Google Safe-Browsing.
- **UnMask Parasites:** It parses Hypertext Markup Language (HTML) codes, specifically those for external links, iframes, and JavaScript, as well as downloads provided links. This tool has the advantage of being able to quickly and precisely observe iframes. However, this tool is only helpful if the user has reason to believe that a suspicious activity is taking place on their websites.
- **Dr.Web Anti-Virus Link Checker:** It is a Chrome, Firefox, Opera, and Internet Explorer add-on that automatically detects and scans harmful content on download hyperlinks on all social networking sites, including Facebook, Vk.com, and Google+.
- **Comodo Site Inspector:** a programme for finding security holes and malware. This can be used by users to view URLs, and by webmasters to set up daily testing by downloading all the specified websites and running them in a sandbox browser environment.

In addition to the typical tools mentioned above, there is a variety of URL checking programs, including UnShorten.it, VirusTotal, Norton Safe Web, SiteAdvisor (by McAfee), Sucuri, Browser Defender, Online Link Scan, and Google Safe Browsing Diagnostic. After the comparative analysis done on all the detection algorithms, it is found that signature-based URL detection systems are the best among all the approaches. Most of the discussed URL detection tools are working on the principle of signature-based URL detection and they have their own challenges. Hence, in the following section, a model is proposed to address all the issues related to the signature-based approach.

3   Proposed Methodology

Our main focus in this research is to analyze the features extracted from the URLs. Inputs are fed along with some labels mimicking whether the URL is harmful or not. The machine learning algorithms determine if a URL is malicious or simply benign by taking advantage of the attributes that may be extracted from the set of URLs. To aim this task, the following steps have been taken:

i. Data collection
ii. Data Filtration and Pre-processing

3.1   Data Collection and Description

The dataset of URLs is collected from GitHub [1] containing both malicious and benign data. There is a total of 450176 samples, out of which 104438 are malware file samples and 345738 are benign samples (Fig. 2).

```
urldata.head()
```

	url	label	result
0	https://www.google.com	benign	0
1	https://www.youtube.com	benign	0
2	https://www.facebook.com	benign	0
3	https://www.baidu.com	benign	0
4	https://www.wikipedia.org	benign	0

Fig. 2. Original dataset

The percentage of malicious URLs is 23.20% and the percentage of benign URLs is 76.80%.

3.2 Data Filtration and Pre-processing

In this step, noise from the dataset is eliminated. Noise is unwanted, useless characters in the text data and repetitive words. Dataset cleaning enables the model to consider only the most crucial information in the dataset. This process not only increases the model performance but also enhances the accuracy of the predictions. Firstly, length features, count features, and binary features represented in Table 1 are added to the dataset.

Table 1. Different Features and Attributes

Features	Attributes
Length Feature	Length Of URL, Hostname, Path, First Directory, Top Level Domain
Count Feature	Count Of '−', '@', '?', '%', '.', '=' Digits, Letters, 'http', 'www', count of directories
Binary Feature	Use of IP or not Use of Shortening URL or not

After adding all the features our dataset looks like this (Fig. 3):

	url	label	result	url_length	hostname_length	path_length	fd_length	tld_length	count-	count@
0	https://www.google.com	benign	0	22	14	0	0	3	0	0
1	https://www.youtube.com	benign	0	23	15	0	0	3	0	0
2	https://www.facebook.com	benign	0	24	16	0	0	3	0	0
3	https://www.baidu.com	benign	0	21	13	0	0	3	0	0
4	https://www.wikipedia.org	benign	0	25	17	0	0	3	0	0

5 rows × 22 columns

Fig. 3. Final dataset

3.3 Experimental Setup

The pre-processed data set is then split into a training set and a testing set respectively. For the training set, nearly 80% of the dataset is used while for testing 20% of the dataset is used. The experiment is repeated 20 times and the sizes of training and testing sets are varied to get different results. The following three supervised machine learning algorithms have been employed: We used the three supervised machine-learning algorithms listed below:

i Logistic Regression

ii Decision Tree

iii Random Forest

Logistic Regression. Logistic Regression is a widely used machine-learning method to detect Malicious URLs. It is a kind of statistical model (a.k.a logit model) that is frequently used for predictive analytics and classification. In this model, the probability of occurring an event is estimated. For example, to predict whether an e-mail is spam (1) or not (0) for a dataset. The outcome of the analysis is a probability, therefore dependent variable lies between 0 and 1. It is a discriminative model that evaluates the conditional probability of a feature vector x to be classified as a class $y = 1$ by

$$P(y = 1|x; w, b) = \sigma(wx + b) = \frac{1}{(1 + e^{-(wx+b)})} \tag{1}$$

Using the maximum-likelihood estimation, the logistic regression can be formulated as an optimization problem given by,

$$(w, b) \longleftarrow argmin \frac{1}{T} \sum_{t=1}^{T} -logP(y_t x_t; w, b) + \lambda R(w) \tag{2}$$

where the regularization term can be either $L2 - normR(w) = ||w||_2$ or $L1 - normR(w) = ||w||_1$ to achieve a sparse model for high-dimensional data.

Decision Tree Algorithm. This algorithm falls under the category of supervised machine learning. It can be applied to regression problems as well as classification problems. The goal of this strategy is to develop a model that estimates the value of a target variable. To accomplish this, a decision tree is employed, where the leaf nodes represent a class label while the internal nodes indicate characteristics. There is a statistic called Entropy that measures the degree of uncertainty in the dataset and can be used to determine the decision node and when to cease splitting. The following is a formula for entropy:

$$E(S) = -p(c)log\, p(c) - n(c)log\, n(c) \tag{3}$$

where

$$p(c) \text{ represents positive class probability}$$
$$n(c) \text{ represents negative class probability}$$
$$S \text{ is the subset of the training example.}$$

Random Forest Algorithm. This machine-learning algorithm can be used to address issues involved in regression as well as classification. It uses a technique called ensemble learning that combines several classifiers to overcome challenging problems and improves the model performance. To improve the accuracy, of the input dataset, the Random Forest classifier calculates the average of results from several decision trees applied to various subsets of the input dataset. This algorithm makes use of predictions from every decision tree and forecasts the result majority votes of the projections rather than relying completely on a single decision tree. The higher number of trees in the forest leads to greater accuracy. While using the Random Forest Algorithm to overcome regression issues, one must use the mean squared error (MSE) to show how the data points deviate from each node.

$$MSE = \frac{1}{N} \sum_{i=1}^{N} (f_i - y_i)^2 \tag{4}$$

where,

N is the number of data points,
f_i is the estimated value returned by the model and
y_i is the actual value for data point i.

This algorithm determines each node's distance from the expected real value, allowing you to choose the best branch for your forest. We must apply the "Entropy" formula, which determines how the nodes on a decision tree branch when employing Random Forests to handle classification data problems.

Evaluation Metrics. It is a metric used to evaluate the proposed model. The metrics are given as follows:

A. Confusion Matrix: A matrix used to evaluate the performance of a classification model which indicates how many samples are classified in accordance with the labels. Table 2 represents the confusion matrix for the proposed work.

The confusion matrix of the proposed work is as follows: In the matrix (in Table 2), True Positive represents the count of accurately labeled URLs, False Negative shows the count of safe URLs as malicious (incorrectly labeled), False Positive is the number of safe URLs which are incorrectly labeled as malicious, and True Negative represents the count of safe URLs that accurately labeled as safe.

Table 2. Confusion Matrix for the proposed work

	Predicted Suspicious URLs	Predicted Safe URLs
Actual Suspicious URLs	True Positive	False Negative
Actual Safe URLs	False Positive	True Negative

B. Accuracy: It represents the proportion of accurate choices made across all test samples.

$$Accuracy = \frac{(TP+TN)}{(TP+TN+FP+FN)} \times 100\% \tag{5}$$

where TP = True Positives, TN = True Negatives, FP = False Positives, and FN = False Negatives, respectively.

C. Precision: It is the proportion of malicious URLs that the classifier accurately identified (TP) out of all the malicious URLs (TP + FP).

$$Precision = \frac{(TP)}{(TP+FP)} \times 100\% \tag{6}$$

D. Recall: It is used to find the proportion of correctly identifies URLs over the actual malicious URL. In other words, it can be identified as the fraction of True positive cases over the actual malicious testing data (True Positive+False Negative). It provides accuracy over the predicted as well as missed positive malicious URLs.

$$Recall = \frac{TP}{TP+FN} \times 100\% \tag{7}$$

E. F1-Score: It is used to measure the actual performance of the classification model. It considers both precision and recall and provides balanced results in the output. The F1 score is calculated by taking the harmonic mean of both the parameters; precision and recall. Sometimes a model provides good precision but a very bad recall score and vice-versa. A higher F1- score can be observed for a higher score of precision as well as recall. The formula for the F1 score is provided in Eq. (8).

$$F1 = \frac{(2 \times Precision \times Recall)}{(Precision + Recall)} \tag{8}$$

F. False Prediction Rate (FPR). It is the proportion of false positive predictions of malicious URLs to all positive predictions of malicious URLs.

$$FPR = \frac{FP}{(FP+TN)} \times 100\% \tag{9}$$

4   Results and Analysis

In this section, the performance evaluation of the considered machine learning algorithm is discussed. The results obtained for the Logistic regression are shown in Table 3 (confusion matrix). Here, out of 241952 samples of actual safe URLs, the algorithm predicts the 241387 samples as safe URLs, and 565 samples are predicted as malicious URLs. Whereas, out of 73172 samples of actual malicious

Table 3. Confusion Matrix for Logistic Regression

	Classified Safe URL	Classified Malicious URL
Actual Safe URLs	241387	565
Actual Malicious URLs	767	72405

Table 4. Confusion Matrix for Decision Tree

	Classified Safe URL	Classified Malicious URL
Actual Safe URLs	241245	707
Actual Malicious URLs	704	72468

URLs, the algorithm predicts 72405 samples as malicious and 767 samples as non-malicious URLs.

The results obtained for the Decision Tree algorithm are shown in Table 4 (confusion matrix). Here, out of 241952 samples of actual safe URLs, the algorithm predicts the 241245 samples as safe URLs and 707 samples are predicted as malicious URLs. Whereas, out of 73172 samples of actual malicious URLs, the algorithm predicts 72468 samples as malicious and 704 samples as non-malicious URLs (Table 5).

Table 5. Confusion Matrix for Random Forest

	Classified Safe URL	Classified Malicious URL
Actual Safe URLs	241673	279
Actual Malicious URLs	575	72597

The results obtained for the Random Forest algorithm are shown in Table 6 (confusion matrix). Here, out of 241952 samples of actual safe URLs, the algorithm predicts the 241673 samples as safe URLs, and 279 samples are predicted as malicious URLs. Whereas, out of 73172 samples of actual malicious URLs, the algorithm predicts 72597 samples as malicious and 575 samples as non-malicious URLs.

Overall performance in terms of parameters, accuracy, precision, and recall for the considered algorithms are shown in Table 6. It is evident that the Random Forest algorithm performs the best with an accuracy of 99.72% followed by Logistic Regression with 99.57% accuracy and the Decision Tree algorithm with 99.52% of accuracy.

In addition to the research work presented in the paper, we have also created the API for the detection of malicious URLs. A snapshot of the API is shown in Figs. 4 (a) and (b) respectively.

Table 6. Confusion Matrix for Random Forest

Classification Algorithms	Accuracy	Precision	Recall	F1-score	FPR
Logistic Regression	99.57%	99.68%	99.76%	99.73	1.04%
Decision Tree	99.52%	99.70%	99.70%	99.70	0.96%
Random Forest	99.72%	99.76%	99.88%	99.82	0.79%

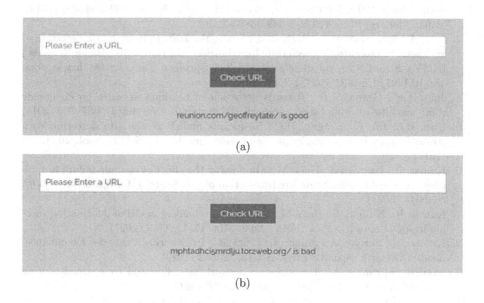

(a)

(b)

Fig. 4. Screenshot of the Web App

5 Conclusion and Future Scope

In this research work, machine learning-based models are used to detect malicious URLs based on the features of the URLs. It is observed that the Random Forest algorithm outperforms with an accuracy of 99.72%. The proposed model can accurately predict whether the particular URL is good or bad. However, the proposed mechanism does not provide any information about the family from which the URLs malware is derived. For future reference, Deep learning models can be used for predictive analysis.

References

1. https://github.com/iosifache/DikeDataset/tree/main/files
2. Internet security threat report (istr) 2019-symantec. https://www.symantec.com/content/dam/symantec/docs/reports/istr-24-2019-en.pdf. Accessed October 2019
3. Chatterjee, M., Namin, A.S.: Deep reinforcement learning for detecting malicious websites. arXiv preprint arXiv:1905.09207 (2019)

4. Chiramdasu, R., Srivastava, G., Bhattacharya, S., Reddy, P.K., Gadekallu, T.R.: Malicious URL detection using logistic regression. In: 2021 IEEE International Conference on Omni-Layer Intelligent Systems (COINS), pp. 1–6. IEEE (2021)
5. Do Xuan, C., Nguyen, H.D., Tisenko, V.N.: Malicious URL detection based on machine learning. Int. J. Adv. Comput. Sci. Appl. **11**(1) (2020)
6. Eshete, B., Villafiorita, A., Weldemariam, K.: BINSPECT: holistic analysis and detection of malicious web pages. In: Keromytis, A.D., Di Pietro, R. (eds.) SecureComm 2012. LNICST, vol. 106, pp. 149–166. Springer, Heidelberg (2013). https://doi.org/10.1007/978-3-642-36883-7_10
7. Fass, A., Krawczyk, R.P., Backes, M., Stock, B.: JaSt: fully syntactic detection of malicious (Obfuscated) JavaScript. In: Giuffrida, C., Bardin, S., Blanc, G. (eds.) DIMVA 2018. LNCS, vol. 10885, pp. 303–325. Springer, Cham (2018). https://doi.org/10.1007/978-3-319-93411-2_14
8. Jain, A.K., Gupta, B.B.: Towards detection of phishing websites on client-side using machine learning based approach. Telecommun. Syst. **68**(4), 687–700 (2018)
9. Kim, B.I., Im, C.T., Jung, H.C.: Suspicious malicious web site detection with strength analysis of a JavaScript obfuscation. Int. J. Adv. Sci. Technol. **26**, 19–32 (2011)
10. Kumar, R., Kumari, S., Bala, M.: Minimizing the effect of cascade failure in multilayer networks with optimal redistribution of link loads. J. Complex Netw. **9**(6), cnab043 (2021)
11. Kumar, R., Kumari, S., Bala, M.: Quantum mechanical model of information sharing in social networks. Soc. Netw. Anal. Min. **11**(1), 1–12 (2021)
12. Kumari, S., Saroha, A., Singh, A.: Efficient edge rewiring strategies for enhancement in network capacity. Phys. A **545**, 123552 (2020)
13. Kumari, S., Singh, A.: Time-varying network modeling and its optimal routing strategy. Adv. Complex Syst. **21**(02), 1850006 (2018)
14. Lee, S., Kim, J.: Warningbird: a near real-time detection system for suspicious URLs in twitter stream. IEEE Trans. Dependable Secure Comput. **10**(3), 183–195 (2013)
15. Ma, J., Saul, L.K., Savage, S., Voelker, G.M.: Learning to detect malicious URLs. ACM Trans. Intell. Syst. Technol. (TIST) **2**(3), 1–24 (2011)
16. Manjeri, A.S., Kaushik, R., Ajay, M., Nair, P.C.: A machine learning approach for detecting malicious websites using URL features. In: 2019 3rd International Conference on Electronics, Communication and Aerospace Technology (ICECA), pp. 555–561. IEEE (2019)
17. Muhuri, S., Kumari, S., Namasudra, S., Kadry, S.: Analysis of the pertinence of Indian women's institutions in collaborative research. IEEE Trans. Comput. Soc. Syst. (2022)
18. Sahoo, D., Liu, C., Hoi, S.C.: Malicious URL detection using machine learning: a survey. arXiv preprint arXiv:1701.07179 (2017)
19. Shahrivari, V., Darabi, M.M., Izadi, M.: Phishing detection using machine learning techniques. arXiv preprint arXiv:2009.11116 (2020)
20. Sheng, S., Wardman, B., Warner, G., Cranor, L., Hong, J., Zhang, C.: An empirical analysis of phishing blacklists (2009)
21. Shibahara, T., et al.: Malicious URL sequence detection using event de-noising convolutional neural network. In: 2017 IEEE International Conference on Communications (ICC), pp. 1–7. IEEE (2017)
22. Srinivasan, S., Vinayakumar, R., Arunachalam, A., Alazab, M., Soman, K.: DURLD: malicious URL detection using deep learning-based character level rep-

resentations. In: Stamp, M., Alazab, M., Shalaginov, A. (eds.) Malware Analysis Using Artificial Intelligence and Deep Learning, pp. 535–554. Springer, Cham (2021). https://doi.org/10.1007/978-3-030-62582-5_21

23. Tao, Y.: Suspicious URL and device detection by log mining. Ph.D. thesis, Applied Sciences: School of Computing Science (2014)

24. Wang, Z., Li, S., Wang, B., Ren, X., Yang, T.: A malicious URL detection model based on convolutional neural network. In: Xiang, Y., Liu, Z., Li, J. (eds.) SocialSec 2020. CCIS, vol. 1298, pp. 34–40. Springer, Singapore (2020). https://doi.org/10.1007/978-981-15-9031-3_3

25. Zouina, M., Outtaj, B.: A novel lightweight URL phishing detection system using SVM and similarity index. HCIS **7**(1), 1–13 (2017)

Use of AI in Human Psychology

Importance of Feature Extraction in Sentiment Analysis Implementation

Priyanka Tyagi[1]([✉]), Suveg Moudgil[1]([✉]), and Garima Saini[2]

[1] IMSEC, Ghaziabad, India
{priyanka.tyagi,suveg.moudgil}@imsec.com
[2] Lingayas Vidyapeeth, Faridabad, India

Abstract. Twitter is a major online social networking website that has grown in popularity among millions of users. Sentiment analysis was employed by a number of companies to discover their customers' mentalities and feelings regarding their products. Sentiment analysis is a technique for determining the intended meaning or polarity of tweets sent by Twitter users. As a result of the high volume of sentiment tweets, it is impossible to discern people's overall perceptions without automatic sentiment analysis and classification. Numerous classifications of sentiment are emerging, with study concentrating on tweets. Five steps are used to analyse the sentiment data. The first phase is to collect data using the Twitter API, and the second step is to analyse and classify the dataset's unique text data using natural language processing and text analytics. It's a necessity because the dataset is so vast and includes so many slang terms and phrases. The second process is text preparation, which involves examining and extracting specific material as well as cleaning out non-textual components such as emoticons and numerical figures. Finally, sentiment analysis is performed on the extracted tweets, identifying emotion and inspecting the opinions. There is no objective communication, but individual expressions remain. Positive and negative sentiments are classified in the fourth phase of the algorithm. Sentiment analysis primary purpose is to turn unstructured text into useful information. The study's tweets were subjected to sentiment analysis.In our dataset, the above five steps are handled by extracting a specific text feature and analysing it. Finally, we apply our suggested hybrid algorithm, which is based on ACO-PSO with SVM to classify sentiment in extracted data.

Keywords: Sentiment Analysis · Ant Colony Optimization · Particle Swarm Optimization · SVM · Kernel Functions

1 Working of Sentiment Analysis

Using social media as a data source, Fig. 1 illustrates how sentiment analysis is used during the extraction phase. Twitter, for example, updates its data on a regular basis. Consequently, it creates the appearance of real-time sentiment representation. A web crawler is used to collect real-time data. To index web pages, this crawls the World Wide Web sequentially. The retrieved data is cleaned because it contains a lot of noise before

© Springer Nature Switzerland AG 2023
D. Garg et al. (Eds.): IACC 2022, CCIS 1782, pp. 267–281, 2023.
https://doi.org/10.1007/978-3-031-35644-5_21

being sent for analysis. Grammatical errors are evident in the retrieved text because of its short length. The study examines the attitudes contained in the data, the amount of repetitions found in tweets, and their location. To get opinions from people about a given occurrence during the Knowledge Discovery phase, it is critical to preserve data on the event. Once the polarity of sentiments is determined, it provides statistical graphs and charts. In sentiment analysis, four categories are used:

1.1 Syntactic Feature

It makes use of POS tickets, N grams, punctuation, and phrase patterns to enhance readability. "patterns such as n + aj (positive adjective) reflect the direction of good sentiment, whereas n + dj (negative adjective) denotes the direction of negative feeling". Semantic feature: Semantic features are concerned with the relationship between signifiers such as phrases and words, and the score-base method classifies these associations based on whether they include positive or negative semantic features. Indexing web pages on the World Wide Web in an ordered method. The retrieved data is cleaned because it contains a lot of noise before being sent for analysis. Grammatical errors are evident in the retrieved text because of its short length. The study examines the attitudes contained in the data, the amount of repetitions found in tweets, and their location [10]. To get opinions from people about a given occurrence during the Knowledge Discovery phase, it is critical to preserve data on the event. Once the polarity of sentiments is determined, it provides statistical graphs and charts.

Link Base Feature.   The classification of link base samples is based on the relationships between relations and relations.

Stylistic Feature.   Artists use this to communicate with us.

Use of Symbolism.   Authors and artists often utilise symbols to convey meaning, convey meaning through a character's actions, and identify a place or object.

The envisioned system will be developed in stages. Electronic brand reviews are included in the dataset created from tweets. Everybody knows that tweets are filled with slang and misspelt words. A sentiment analysis of tweets is carried out as a consequence. Parts one, two, and three make up this technique. Preprocessing is performed in the initial stage. Then, using the suitable features, a feature vector is constructed. Finally, tweets are sorted into good, negative, and neutral categories using disparate classifiers.

1.2 Algorithm of Working of Sentiment Analysis

Input: Training and Testing Datasets

Step 1: Take a training dataset as a input to machine model
Step 2: In preprocessing step we will delete stop words from training dataset.
Step 3: Tokenization of training dataset.
Step 4: Stemming of training dataset.
Step 5: Use the testing dataset in machine model
Step 6: Delete stop words from testing dataset.

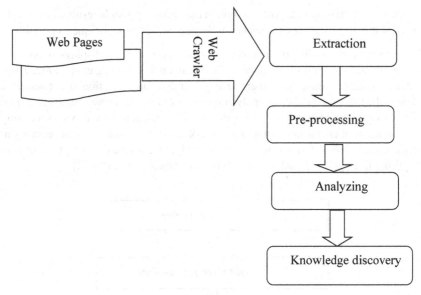

Fig. 1. Working of Sentiment Analysis

Step 7: Tokenization of testing dataset.
Step 8: Stemming of testing dataset.
Step 9: Extract special keywords by using feature extraction process.
Step 10: Extract positive and negative keywords.
Step 11: Extract positive and negative tags.
Step 12: Form 8-features based vector using regression in case of linear dataset.
Step 13: Perform Classification in case non linear dataset.
Step 14: Form Bow (bag of words) vector used feature extraction and text for use in modeling.
Step 15: Form Hybrid Vector by fusion of vector 1 and 2.
Step 16: Measure the present and suggested method's Precision, Recall, and Accuracy Performances. To execute sentiment analysis, you'll need to obtain data from the source you've chosen (here Twitter).

There are a number of ways this data has been preprocessed to make it more machine-readable. Among the exciting aspects of machine learning is overfitting, which allows an algorithm to remember the data and then fail when applied to new data. To get around this problem, I use a test-driven approach. We randomly partition each dataset and each component into three equal pieces, resulting in a total of nine datasets.

2 Different Levels of Analysis

Hybrid systems are those that employ both rule-based and machine learning-based problem resolution techniques. To begin, by analysing a large number of tagged examples, the model is trained to recognise sentiment. The results are then compared to a lexicon to ensure accuracy. The ultimate goal is to obtain the greatest possible result while avoiding as many of the disadvantages associated with each particular technique as possible.

- **Document level.** Finding out if a piece of writing consistently displays an optimistic or pessimistic viewpoint is the goal at the document level (Pang et al., 2002; Turney, 2002). Thus, the phrase "document-level sentiment categorization" has been coined to describe this process. When analysing a product review, the system assesses if it is generally good or negative. Assuming that each document represents views on a single thing is an implicit assumption at this level of analysis, which is not necessarily true (e.g., a single product or service). Consequently, large-scale document comparisons requiring finer-grained analysis cannot be performed with it (Fig. 2).

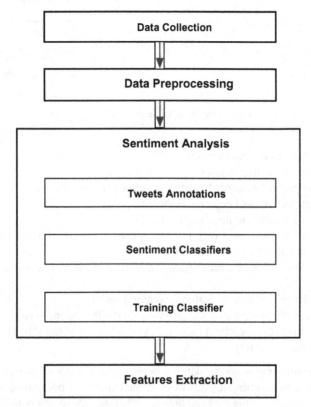

Fig. 2. Methodology for Sentiment Analysis

- **Sentence level.** Each sentence should be analysed to see whether it represents a good, negative, or neutral point of view before advancing. To avoid misunderstandings, "neutral opinion" is often used to mean "no opinion". The subjectivity classification (Wiebe et al., 1999), which distinguishes between phrases that convey factual information (referred to as objective sentences) and sentences that represent subjective ideas and opinions (referred to as subjective statements), is essential to this level of analysis (called subjective sentences) [5]. As previously said, subjectivity is not the same as sentiment or opinion, as many objective statements can indicate sentiments or opinions, such as "We acquired the automobile last month and the windshield wiper has fallen off". However, subjective phrases like "I imagine he went home after lunch" may not convey any kind of sentiment or point of view in the first place.

- **Aspect level.** Contrary to popular belief, neither a document level nor a sentence level analysis can give us a comprehensive picture of what individuals like and dislike. Instead of defining what each position is about, they leave it open to interpretation. Just knowing that the statement "I like the iPhone 5" is positive limits our ability to use that statement until we know that the good attitude is directed toward the iPhone 5. There is a school of thought that holds that anything that is positive must likewise be positive. Because a phrase can have multiple points of view, such as "Apple is doing incredibly well in this challenging economy", this won't work. In order to classify this sentence as either positive or negative, it would be irrational to do so. We must go all the way down to the aspect level in order to get such fine-grained results. The term "aspect-based sentiment analysis" has replaced the term "feature-based opinion mining and summarization" (Hu and Liu, 2004; Liu, 2010).

Rather than focusing on language units, aspect-level analysis explores the relationship between an opinion and its intended audience (also known as the opinion target). Our grasp of sentiment analysis has improved greatly once we realised the importance of opinion targets. Despite the restaurant's shoddy service, I still enjoy dining there. "We cannot, however, conclude that this statement is entirely satisfactory because the tone is inconsistent throughout. To summarise, the line is complimentary to the restaurant (as highlighted), but is critical of the establishment's service (not emphasized). If a customer sees a negative review on the service, they are unlikely to dine there. If you're writing an application, it's common to use entities (like the restaurant in the prior example) and/or their multiple features (like the restaurant) to specify opinion targets (e.g., service of the restaurant). Consequently, this level of investigation aims to uncover people's viewpoints on a variety of subjects and/or their qualities. It is feasible to build a summary of concepts about entities and their numerous constituents on the basis of this level of study [8]. In some apps, the user may only care about their own thoughts of entities, thus it's vital to remember that. There are times when a system may choose to ignore features that it does not like. All commercial sentiment analysis systems are built on this level of analysis when it comes to their applications. Traditional and comparative viewpoints (Jindal and Liu, 2006b) are distinct from one another.

3 Research Methodology

Data collection: The data is given as input in the initial step. The twitter data is either collected on an excel sheet or the real-time data is collected with the help of tweppy, kaggle and Tweet Binder application to be provided as input.

Pre-processing: The data to be given as input is pre-processed in this phase. The tokenization of data is done and the stop words are eliminated from it using N-gram algorithm.

Feature Extraction: The algorithm for feature extraction is supplied with the pre-processed data. The optimised dataset is generated using the hybrid ACO-PSO algorithm.

Classification: In order to perform sentiment analysis, the classification technique is applied in the final step of sentiment analysis. In this step, the hybrid classifier will be designed with the combination of ACO-PSO-SVM. The sentiment analysis will be much enhanced by the hybrid classifier.

Data Collection. Regardless of the range of methodologies used in different sectors, accurate data collecting is a fundamental concern in this form of research. There should always be an emphasis on gathering high-quality data that can quickly and accurately be analysed to provide solid answers to the questions being asked. This is the case. The process of collecting tweets involves compiling a collection of relevant tweets on a specific topic. The tweets are collected via an API. These APIs help us obtain the data we need for the input. So it basically acts as an intermediary between the user's tweets and a website that can retrieve that user's data. A number of websites were used instead of Twitter in order to acquire data for this study because the process was so lengthy. Pre-sing of data is a critical stage in the same way that it determines the effectiveness of subsequent phases. It entails correcting the tweets' syntactical structure as desired.

3.1 Statistics About the Dataset

Table 1. Statistic about the dataset

Total No. of Data	*413840*
Positive Reviews	156123
Negative Reviews	123395
Neutral Reviews	134322
Total no. of Features after Extraction	61023
Word occurrences list of multiple times like go used 499 times in the tweets list	77828

The dataset is comprised of Positive Reviews, Negative Reviews, and Neutral Reviews, as detailed in Table. Following the extraction of the dataset, statistical analysis explains the features, which include Positive Reviews, Negative Reviews, and Neutral Reviews (Table 1).

4 Data Pre-processing

This procedure is mostly concerned with eliminating stop words and stemming. The views' real verbs and adverbs were derived from stemming by removing stop words. The stop word removal technique eliminates unnecessary numbers, punctuation, and words (an, the, a, and, is...) [13]. Stemming reduces derivative words to their root form ("smoothly", "smoother" to the base or root word "smooth"). We pre-process the data and remove irrelevant information using the N-Gram technique.

4.1 Feature Extraction

ACO and PSO are used in this research to optimise the process. The term 'combinatory optimization' refers to this phenomena. Searching for beginning values with the intention of decreasing our function's end outcomes may be necessary in some multi-objective functions. In this method, the most important features are selected from a large array of features [11]. Using an algorithm that is better at optimization, this can be accomplished. Insect swarms, such as ants and bees, provide inspiration for both ant colony and particle swarm optimization. In order to find the ants' most direct routes, this method was applied. Analyzing the data reveals that the optimise approach not only reduces the number of possible routes, but it also identifies the shortest route to take in that particular place, as seen in the graph [12]. Ant-like in their approach, these algorithms provide us with the best possible results.

4.2 Particle Swarm Optimization (PSO)

Specifically, PSO is taken from animal behaviour, such as a group of birds or fish swimming together. When it comes to the behaviour of a group, individuals' actions and the impacts of their fellow members make up social behaviour (as measured by intelligence) [13]. Another way of saying this is that a herd's behaviour depends on the actions of its members individually and collectively. Afterwards, the PSO method is reworked to incorporate the group's habits.

The following are the terms used to refer to the PSO algorithm:

Population. A collection of candidate solutions that are evaluated in a single time step using m particles.

Particle. Vector v velocity and vector x position in dimension are used to indicate possible solutions.

Evaluation Range. The time span for evaluating each prospective solution in a single step.

Fitness Function. Determining the efficacy of candidate solutions offered during the review period.

Population Manager. Updating the velocity and position of each particle in accordance with the PSO's main loop.

4.3 Ant Colony Optimization (ACO)

Ant colonies work together to determine which path from their nest to their food source is the most efficient, which is the basis for this model. Because they are blind, ants rely on pheromones to locate the quickest route from their nest to a food source [36]. Ant pheromones are chemical compounds found on the ants' bodies. These pheromones serve as a means of communication between ants and colonies. When ants discover food, they follow randomly targeted pathways toward the food source, leaving pheromones in their wake. Once the ants have finished the trail, the pheromones will be refreshed. ACO is used to assist the feature selection process and is particularly useful for generating a candidate subset of optimal features. It improves the data's quality.

5 ACO-PSO Hybrid Approach for Optimal Features Selection

Three distinct stages comprise the hybrid PSO-ACO algorithm procedure. The fundamental algorithm is a hybridization of the PSO and ACO algorithms. The following are the stages involved in the PSO-ACO hybrid process.

First Stage. The ant algorithm function allows you to specify the number of particles and their size, as well as the inertia weight used to set the particle velocity for scheduling.

Second Stage. Set the ACO parameter and initialise the ant by performing permutations with the random and optimal1 functions. The function "random" is used to build a schedule that adheres to rigorous specifications, ensuring that no conflicts between course subjects, lecturers, and classrooms occur during the lecture scheduling preparation process. Meanwhile, the function "optimum1" is utilised to optimise the schedule that was obtained previously using standard deviation computation.

Third Stage. Revert to the PSO algorithm and use it to optimise the ACO method's parameters automatically (Figs. 3 and 4).

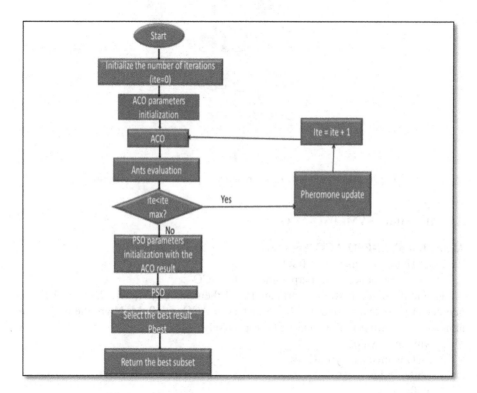

Fig. 3. ACO-PSO Hybrid Approach for optimal features selection

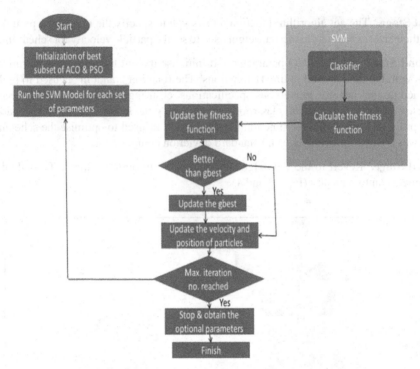

Fig. 4. ACO-PSO Hybrid Approach for optimal features selection

5.1 Algorithm: SVM- PSO-ACO

Algorithm SVM-PSO-ACO Approach:

Input:Hyper parameters of PSO;

Output:A sequence of Hyperparameters for ACO.

1: InitializeD-dimensional particles Piand their velocityVi(i¼1, 2, …, I, I is the number of particles) related withDparameters of ACO; m¼0; M, N are the maximum numbersof iterations in PSO and ACO respectively;

2: whilem < Mdo.

3: ACO is invoked by PSO, i¼0;

4: whilei < Ido

5: n¼0;

6: whilen < Ndo

7: ACO deals as (1)–(5) withPi;

8: n¼nþ1;

9: Clear the pheromones;

10: The achieved result is used to evaluatePi;

11: Update the velocity of SVM, PSO, Vi, as (6);

12: Update the location ofSVM, PSO, Pi, as (7);

13: i¼iþ1;

14: m¼mþ1;

15: returnThe optimal solution of the relatedPi.

6   Classification Approaches

Sentiment analysis concludes with a classification strategy that is applied. In this step, the hybrid classifier will be designed with the combination of ACO-PSO-SVM. The hybrid classifier will give high accuracy for the sentiment analysis.By first creating an isolated hyper plane, the SVM aims to maximise the "margin" between two classes. SVM uses this margin to create two parallel hyperplanes on either side of the first. They are then "pushed" in opposite directions until they collide with the nearest examples of each class. You'll see what's known as "SVM examples". (1) Figure: Machine with Support Vectors: Classification Functions of the Kernel: The following are various SVM kernel functions that were utilised categorization. The following four fundamental kernels are detailed in research.Kernel Functions: The SVM kernel functions utilised in the categorization process are listed below in detail. According to research, there are four fundamental kernels:

6.1   Kernel Functions

SVM piece capabilities used in this arrangement are listed below. The four following essential bits are depicted in study.

Liner kernel: $k(x, y) = X^T Y + C$
Polynomial kernel: $k(x, y) = (X^T Y + C)$
Radial basis kernel: $k(x, y) = \exp(\frac{-IIx-yII^2}{2\sigma^2})$
Sigmoid Kernel k (X_i, Y): $\tan h\ (Yx^T y + C)$

Kernel function provides the window to manipulate the data. The kernel's purpose is to take in data and turn it into the desired format. Radial basis function kernel is default kernel for SVM.

7   Accuracy Comparison

Methods like NB and SVM for text categorization are widely used as a starting point, although their performance varies greatly depending on the model version, features used, and the task/dataset involved. Using this data, you can identify basic NB and SVM improvements that outperform the majority of previously published results on text datasets, achieving previously unattainable levels of performance. Consequently, a new system must be developed that can accurately and quickly classify emails or texts (Fig. 5).

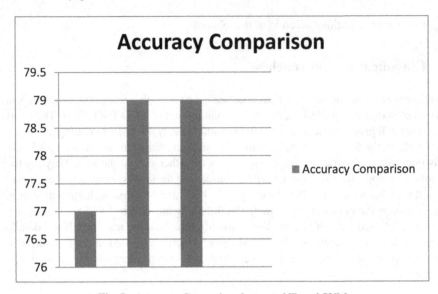

Fig. 5. Accuracy Comparison between NB and SVM

7.1 SVM, ACO-PSO

It is crucial to emphasise that a sizable amount of the SVM and **ACO-PSO** algorithms' exploitative and exploratory capabilities can be controlled by modifying their implementation parameters. We should emphasise, however, that for each dataset analysed, we obtained our results using the same **ACO-PSO** and SVM control parameters. Thus, whereas the accuracy of PSO classification is strongly dependent on the SVM parameters customised for each dataset investigated, the APS-SVM or PSO control parameters specified were valid for each dataset analysed. Once recognised, these implementation parameters should remain consistent for newly discovered datasets. Correlation between

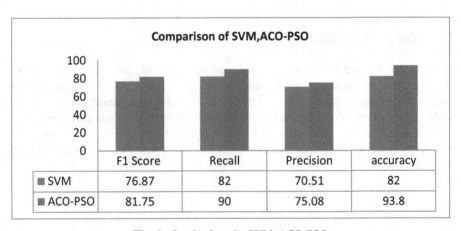

Fig. 6. Graph of results SVM, ACO-PSO

SVM, SVM-PSO, and ACO results in a bar diagram with an x-hub including exactness, review, and precision and a y-hub containing percentages (Fig. 6):

8 Conclusion

Sentiment analysis, a major application of Text Analytics, aims to know about collective sentiment of people about the entity under discussion.The feature extraction algorithm is provided with the pre-processed data. We used N-Gram algorithm for pre-processing. The hybrid ACO-PSO algorithm is applied to this data to generate the optimized dataset. The effective weight of PSO and ACO, as well as a discriminative classifier of SVM, are used to analyse the data in this text. Because SVM-ACO-PSO repeatedly changes the edge if the weight is diverse for different boundaries, the outcomes exhibit that SVM-KNN and SVM-PSO perform well, but not as good as SVM-ACO-PSO, which has a 94.7% accuracy. There is also a scope to make bigger the domain of our experiments and run the classifiers on multiple dataset considering number of different languages so as will have more representative inputs and thus better generalizable results. Audio and Vedio sentiment analysis are an area that is still being explored by researchers and hence new techniques of deep neural network can utilize in this area.

References

1. Aggarwal, C.C.: Opinion Mining and Sentiment Analysis. In: Machine Learning for Text. Springer, Cham (2018)
2. Alsaleh, M., Alarifi, A., Al-Quayed, F., Al-Salman, A.: Combating comment spam with machine learning approaches. In: 2015 IEEE 14th International Conference on Machine Learning and Applications (ICMLA), pp. 295–300. IEEE (2015)
3. Anbananthen, K.S.M., Elyasir, A.M.H.: Evolution of opinion mining. Aust J. Basic Appl. Sci. 7(6), 359–370 (2013)
4. Ficamos, P., Liu, Y., Chen, W.: A Naive Bayes and maximum entropy approach to sentiment analysis: capturing domain-specific data in Weibo. In: 2017 IEEE International Conference on Big Data and Smart Computing (BigComp) (2017)
5. Bouazizi, M., Ohtsuki, T.: A pattern-based approach for multi-class sentiment analysis in twitter. IEEE Access 5, 20617–20639 (2017)
6. Binder, M.: Explaining the stars: Aspect-based sentiment analysis of online customer reviews (2019)
7. Blei, D.M., Ng, A.Y., Jordan, M.I.: Latent Dirichlet allocation. Mach. Learn. Res. 3, 993–1022 (2003)
8. Pal, D., Verma, P., Gautam, D., Indait, P.: Improved optimization technique using hybrid ACO-PSO. In: 2016 2nd International Conference on Next Generation Computing Technologies (NGCT), pp. 277–282 (2016). https://doi.org/10.1109/NGCT.2016.7877428
9. Catal, C., Nangir, M.: A sentiment classification model based on multiple classifiers. J. Appl. Soft Comput. 50, 135–141 (2017)
10. Chakraborty, K.: Comparative sentiment analysis on a set of movie reviews using deep learning approach. In: Hassanien, A., Tolba, M., Elhoseny, M., Mostafa, M. (eds.) AMLTA 2018. Advances in Intelligent Systems and Computing, vol. 723, pp. 311–318. Springer, Cham (2018). https://doi.org/10.1007/978-3-319-74690-6_31

11. Fong, S., Wong, R., Vasilakos, A.V.: Accelerated PSO swarm search feature selection for data stream mining big data. IEEE Trans. Serv. Comput. **9**(1), 33–45 (2016)

12. Jianqiang, Z., Xiaolin, G.: Comparison research on text pre-processing methods on twitter sentiment analysis. IEEE Access **5**, 2870–2879 (2017)

13. Dey, A., Jenamani, M., Thakkar, J.J.: Senti-N- Gram: An n-gram lexicon for sentiment analysis. Expert Syst. Appl. **103**, 92–105 (2018)

14. Menaria, H.K., Nagar, P., Patel, M.: Tweet sentiment classification by semantic and frequency base features using hybrid classifier. In: Luhach, A.K., Kosa, J.A., Poonia, R.C., Gao, X.-Z., Singh, D. (eds.) First International Conference on Sustainable Technologies for Computational Intelligence. AISC, vol. 1045, pp. 107–123. Springer, Singapore (2020). https://doi.org/10.1007/978-981-15-0029-9_9

15. Meda, C., Bisio, F., Gastaldo, P., Zunino, R.: A machine learning approach for twitter spammers detection. In: 2014 International Carnahan Conference on Security Technology (ICCST), pp. 1–6. IEEE (2014)

16. Liu, M., Song, Y., Zou, H., Zhang, T.: Reinforced training data selection for domain adaptation. In: Proceedings of the 57th annual meeting of the association for computational linguistics, pp. 1957–1968 (2019)

17. Ducange, P., Fazzolari, M., Petrocchi, M., Vecchio, M.: Engineering applications of artificial intelligence an effective decision support system for social media listening based on cross-source sentiment analysis models. Eng. Appl. Artif. Intell. **78**, 71–85 (2019). https://doi.org/10.1016/j.engappai.2018.10.014

18. Xu, L.: Twitter sentiment analysis using machine learning and optimization techniques. In: 2018 2nd IEEE International Conference on Computer and Communications (2018)

19. Hassan, F., Usman, K., Saba, Q.: Enhanced cross-domain sentiment classification utilizing a multi-source transfer learning approach. Soft Comput. (2018) https://doi.org/10.1007/s00500-018-3187-9

20. Gulati, A.N., Sawarkar, S.D.: A novel technique for multi-document Hindi text summarization. In: 2017 International Conference on Nascent Technologies in the Engineering Field (ICNTE-2017) (2017)

21. Tyagi, P., Chakraborty, S., Tripathi, R.C., Choudhury, T.: Literature review of sentiment analysis techniques for microblogging site (March 15, 2019). In: International Conference on Advances in Engineering Science Management & Technology (ICAESMT) (2019)

22. Tyagi, P., Tripathi, R.C.: A review towards the sentiment analysis techniques for the analysis of twitter data (February 8, 2019). In: Proceedings of 2nd International Conference on Advanced Computing and Software Engineering (ICACSE) (2019)

23. Tyagi, P., Javalkar, D.: Sentiment analysis of twitter data using hybrid classification methods and comparative analysis Turkish. Online J. Qual. Inq. (TOJQI) **12**(3), 322–341 (2021)

24. Tyagi, P., Javalkar, D., Chakraborty, S.: Enhanced twittersentiment analysis using hybrid classification methods and result analysis. Jilin Daxue Xuebao (Gongxueban)/J. Jilin Univ. (Eng. Technol. Edn.). ISSN 1671-5497

25. Hua, W., Wang, Z., Wang, H., Zheng, K., Zhou, X.: Understand short texts by harvesting and analyzing semantic knowledge. IEEE (2016)

26. Wilson, T., Kozareva, Z., Nakov, P., Rosenthal, S., Stoyanov, V., Ritter, A.: Semeval 2013 task 2: Sentiment analysis in twitter. In: Proceedings of the International Workshop on Semantic Evaluation, SemEval', vol. 13 (2013)

27. Wickramaarachchi, W.U., Kariapper, R.K.A.R.: An approach to get overall emotion from comment text towards a certain image uploaded to social network using latent semantic analysis. In: 2017 2nd International Conference on Image, Vision and Computing with maximum margin learning. Natural Language Engineering, vol. 18, no. 2, pp. 263–289 (2017)

28. Wu, Y., Ren, F.: Learning sentimental influence in twitter. In: 2011 International Conference on Future Computer Sciences and Application, pp. 119–122. IEEE (2011)

29. Chen, Y., Hao, Y.: A distributed algorithm for function optimization based on artificial life. In: proc. The 2002 International Conference on Control and Automation, pp. 698–702. IEEE, Xiamen (2002)
30. Sun, Y.: Iterative RELIEF for feature weighting: algorithms, theories and applications. IEEE Trans. Pattern Anal. Mach. Intell. 29(6), 1035–1051 (2007)

ACDNet: Abusive Content Detection on Social Media with an Effective Deep Neural Network Using Code-Mixed Hinglish Data

Rohit Kumar Kaliyar[1]([✉]), Anurag Goswami[1], Ujali Sharma[2], and Kanika Kanojia[2]

[1] Bennett University, Greater Noida, India
{rohit.kaliyar,anurag.goswami}@bennett.edu.in
[2] Indira Gandhi Delhi Technical University for Women, New Delhi, India

Abstract. In linguistically open geographic regions around the world, the amazing growth of social media platforms like Twitter, Facebook, and Instagram has led to the blending of native languages or regional tongues with English for the purpose of improving communication. Holocaust denial is a significant social problem that has the potential to escalate violence in a number of ways, from violent attacks to compassionate purging. A fundamental challenge in the categorization and tracking of extremely toxic lexical features is differentiating between language that incites hatred and language that is disparaging. Our study concentrates on locating abusive tweets written in Hinglish, a combination of Hindi and Roman Script. In this paper, we propose an approach for classifying tweets into three categories: hate speech, non-offensive speech, and abusive speech. Using the Hindi-English offensive tweet dataset, which includes tweets in the Hindi-English code transferred language and is divided into three categories: non-offensive, abusive, and hate speech. We utilized transfer learning to conduct research on the abusive and hate speech datasets and pre-trained the proposed model on English tweets that have been pre-processed using Hinglish Tweets. We were able to achieve 98.92% accuracy using the proposed model.

Keyword: Hate Speech Social Media Deep Neural Network Classification Fake News

1 Introduction

In the world of technology, people spend an exorbitant amount of time [4] on social media. Potentially harmful online content has become a subject of great concern because of the explosive growth in internet accessibility by people of different ethnicities and socioeconomic backgrounds. Social media organizations like Facebook and Twitter, which are cracking down on hate speech, are working to address concerns about encroaching on free speech rights. These online communication platforms are being pressed to deal with a variety of international norms and legal systems, as well as government inquiries. As a result, the responsibility of choosing what to broadcast and what

© Springer Nature Switzerland AG 2023
D. Garg et al. (Eds.): IACC 2022, CCIS 1782, pp. 282–293, 2023.
https://doi.org/10.1007/978-3-031-35644-5_22

not to was placed on the shoulders of the social media goliaths. The need for limitations led to the creation of baseline content, which explores the definition of hate speech and how it differs from other types of abusive language. Social media frequently posts offensive stuff, which is harmful to a liberal society. Several instances of hate speech on social media are illustrated in Fig. 1. Documents related to hate speech in the Scopus database are presented with the help of Fig. 2.

Hinglish, which is made up of Hindi words written in the Roman script rather than the Devanagari script, is a major contributor to the vast volume of offensive web content. Hinglish is a bilingual language [5] with no accent-dependent grammar rules [13]. Due to regional impact, Hinglish expands its grammatical structure from native Hindi, with a profusion of obscenities, jargon, and morphosyntactic changes. The automatic classification of Hinglish is exceedingly challenging due to randomized spelling variants and several alternative interpretations of Hinglish terms in various contexts [10].

1.1 Contribution

In this paper, we tried to resolve the main issue of detecting offensive In this paper, we propose an effective classification method to resolve the main issue of detecting offensive Hinglish tweets by creating an effective deep learning model that examines the textual data and categorizes it as either non-offensive, abusive, or hate-inducing. The proposed framework's effectiveness is evaluated using a set of validation data with Hinglish tweets. The method is divided into two stages. Primarily, we examined the semantic relationship between the Hindi- English code-switched language and the native English language and offered a lexicon translation of the Hinglish text into Roman English words. Subsequently, employing an effective deep neural network to transfer previously learned information, we evaluated the performance of semantically comparable but syntactically distinct tweets obtained via transliteration and translation. Utilizing different performance parameters, we have evaluated the performance the proposed model, achieved state-of-the-art results utilizing traditional hate speech detection methodology.

2   Related Work

2.1   Hate Speech Detection

For the past 20 years, the problem of recognizing hateful speech and abusive language on the internet has always been a contentious issue in the scientific world. "Smokey," a decision tree-based classification with 47 semantic and syntactic textual features, was created [41]. When "Smokey" was trained on a diverse handful of 720 dynamic web postings (manually marked (as "okay" "maybe," or "flame") and then analyzed on 502 additional messages, it did a good job of categorizing non-inflammatory communications but entirely failed to recognize flame texts, achieving accuracy of just 88.20% on an assignment with an 86.10% baseline. Gradually shifting from characteristics based purely on the language used in user-generated content, [5] proposed an approach that additionally considers the individuals' publishing behaviors in addition to identifying people who are abusive.

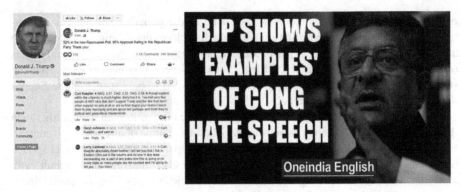

Fig. 1. Examples of hate speech on Social Media (Source: Facebook)

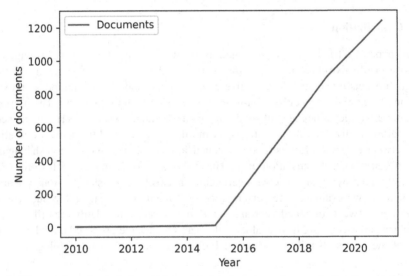

Fig. 2. The number of scholarly articles related to hate speech news in the Scopus database between 2010 and 2021.

Buckels et al. (2014) [34], on the other hand, tried to derive destructive personality characteristics from digital user activity. Yin et al. (2009) [33] and Papegnies et al. (2017) [35] point out, with the aforementioned proposing a few descriptors (at the morphometric, idiomatic expressions, and predictive analysis stages) which can be used to distinguish when players on a French Massively Multiplayer Online gaming website switch from describing competitive match issues to making ridiculous offensive statements. Specific diagnostics samples, including the HATECHECK test scenarios, were used to evaluate models together in a variety of NLP activities, including language processing interpretation [2], computational linguistics [3], and language processing [4]. Yet, they've only been used sporadically in hate speech identification.

Neural networks have been deliberately programmed to anticipate approval ratings in certain preliminary studies (Lawrence et al., 1996; Allen and Seidenberg, 1999) [36]; Post (2011). Warstadt et al. (2018) [37] employ transfer learning whereby an unsupervised model is fine-tuned based on acceptance prognostication. The labeled datasets have not been really shared publicly, which has become a recurring issue with some of this research. Ross et al. (2016) [38] analyzed 541 German tweets, focusing on topics such as observer and descriptor dependability, and what data should be offered to observers. Waseem (2016) [39] addresses great similarities while presenting a sample of 6,909 English tweets labeled by CrowdFlower users and expanding on a subsequent dataset (Waseem and Hovy, 2016) [40].

Several scholars [6–9, 11, 12] have investigated text vocabulary recognition for various linguistic pairings and accent variants over the last decades [1, 14, 15]. The FIRE team works together to develop a series based on language recognition of code-mixed web searches for information extraction in English and Indian dialects [16, 17]. The First and Second Concurrent Tasks on Text Recognition in Code-Switched Data [43, 44] demonstrate the need for automated code-switched encoding and give comparisons of various language recognition systems. The preferred method from the second version among these task interdependence employs a logistic regression model, with SPAENG scoring 97.30 %on token- level F1-score.

A comparison of monolingual and multilingual BERT models was undertaken. In five distinct intermediate fine-tuning studies, Marathi monolingual models outperformed multilingual BERT versions [42]. Through freezing the BERT encoder layers, we were able to examine sentence embeddings [18–21] among these models. It demonstrated how monolingual MahaBERT-based models produce rich interpretations, particularly in comparison to multilingual sentence embeddings [22–24]. Conversely, such embeddings are therefore not a fairly straightforward process and therefore do not perform effectively with out of-domain social network datasets. To effectively categorize tweets [45], the authors implemented a comprehensive text mining method and the Naive Bayes machine learning classification algorithm on two sets of data (tweets Num1 and tweets Num2) acquired from Twitter. The proposed method performed well enough in terms of many metrics [25–32] depending on the confusion matrix, including those of the accuracy metric, which attained 87.23% and 93.06%, respectively.

In this paper, we propose a novel method for assessing hate speech articles on social media based on a robust deep learning architecture. This method will be described in detail and evaluated in Section III. Our proposed method has the following advantages:

- It automatically extracts the useful features with the architecture of deep learning.
- It provides more accurate results as compared to existing benchmarks.

3 Methodology

In this section, the methodology and architecture of our proposed model are discussed.

3.1 Dataset

In this subsection, the dataset used in this research is discussed.

HASOC2019 Dataset. The HASOC2019 dataset[1] was developed to assist in the detection of derogatory and vile terms in Indo-European languages. The goal of HASOC is to advance the linguistic characterization of hate speech through study and technology. Twitter and Facebook are used to build the dataset, which is then made available in the tab-separated form. There are three languages for the datasets (German, English, and code-mixed Hindi). For each language, the Training data corpus has a size of about 8000 posts. For exploration, we used a dataset that was code-mixed. The data enables the development and evaluation of machine learning systems under close supervision.

The prevalence of harmful and undesirable content online creates a significant problem for civilizations. Objective debates are undermined by offensive language, such as insulting, harmful, disparaging, or obscene material targeted at yet another individual and viewable to others. This kind of rhetoric is becoming even more prevalent online and, therefore, can cause conversations to turn more extreme. To influence public sentiment, intelligent and critical debate is necessary. The democratic process may be threatened by objectionable content. Open societies must simultaneously come up with a suitable response to such content that avoids enforcing strict surveillance laws. Therefore, as a result, several social networking sites keep an eye on user posts. As a result, there is an urgent provision of tools that can detect dubious content automatically. In order to eradicate abusive behavior in specific media, online communities, social media businesses, and technology firms have already significantly leveraged technology and procedures to recognize objectionable language.

3.2 Pre-processing

Text preprocessing is the cleansing and preparation of text data. Preprocessing, in its most fundamental form, refers to the modifications made to raw data before feeding it to a machine learning or deep learning algorithm. Examples of such alterations include eliminating HTML elements, extra white space, special characters, lowercase text overall, converting number words to numeric form, and removing numerals.

3.3 ACDNet: Architecture of Our Proposed Deep Learning Model

In this study, experiments were conducted using real-world fake news datasets and our proposed deep learning network. In this approach, the HASOC dataset was used, and we employed a very deep convolutional neural network to recognize abusive text. After preprocessing the data, we divided it into train and test sets in an 80:20 ratio, and then we divided the test set into a test and validation set in a 50:50 ratio. The layered architecture of our deep neural network is depicted in Fig. 3. Our sequential model receives an embedding layer as input that has a dimension of 100 and an input length of 2000. First, two onedimensional convolutional layers are generated, each with 1024 filters, a kernel

---

[1] https://hasocfire.github.io/hasoc/2019/.

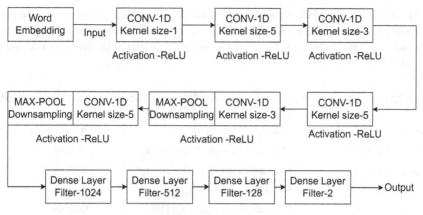

Fig. 3. Proposed Model

Table 1. Optimal Hyper-parameters for our proposed Model

Hyperparameter	Value
Number of Convl. Layer	6
Number of Max-pooling layer	2
Number of Kernel-sizes	1, 3, and 5
Number of Dense layer	4
Number of filters in convl-layers	1024,512,256,128,64,32
Number of filters in dense-layers	1024,512,128,2
Loss function	binary crossentropy
Activation function	ReLU
Optimizer	Adam
Metrics	Accuracy
Batch-size	256, 32
Batch-Normalization	Yes
Number of Epochs	10
Dropout	0.1

size of 1, and a Relu activation function applied. These layers are then standardized using BatchNormalization after activation function application. Then two one-dimensional convolutional layers with 1024 filters, a kernel size of 1, and the application of the Relu activation function are standardized using batch normalization and then added. In the model with 32 filters and a kernel size of 5, five further 1-D convolutional layers are added after that. These layers are standardized using BatchNormalization, and Relu Activation is applied once more after normalization. The model now has five more 1-D convolutional layers with 64 filters, three kernel sizes, and the Relu Activation function. These layers are standardized using BatchNormalization, and Relu Activation is applied once more after normalization. The outputs from this layer are then fed into the subsequent 1-D convolutional layer, which uses the Relu activation function, a kernel size of 5, and 64 filters (Tables 1 & 2).

Table 2. Comparison with Existing Classification Outcomes Utilizing Public Dataset-PHEME

Author	Model	Accuracy (%)
Spertus et al. [41]	Machine Learning [Features-BOW]	87.20%
Alaoui et al. [45]	Machine Learning [Naive Bayes]	88.20%
Velankar et al.[42]	BERT-based approach	93.06%
Solorio et al. [43]	Featured-based Approach [ML]	96.20%
Molina et al. [43]	Logistic Regression [ML]	97.30%
Our proposed model	**ACDNet**	**98.92%**

To standardize this layer BatchNormalization technique is used and then again Relu activation is applied, then outputs from this layer are fed as input to the next 1-D convolutional Layer with 128 filters, kernel size as 3, and relu activation following Batch-Normalization and applying MaxPooling1D with pool size as 2 to downsize the layer, here strides will be default taken as pool size. The MaxPooling Relu activation function is further applied. This type of layer is again made two more times, then seven more 1-D convolutional layers are added to the model with 128 filters, kernel size of 5, and relu activation following BatchNormalization to standardize the layer and applying relu activation after standardization. Five more 1-D convolutional layers are added to the model with filters set to 256, and kernel size set to 3 following the Relu activation function, further standardizing the layer using BatchNormalisation and again applying Relu activation. Then the output from the latest layer will be fed to the next 1-D convolutional layer having 256 filters, kernel size 5, and Relu activation function, further following BatchNormalisation. This type of layer is added two more times in the model.

With a small amount of dropouts, the accuracy will progressively increase and the loss will gradually decrease. Dropout was chosen as a parameter because it makes the classification model simpler and prevents over-fitting. The activation function has been determined to be ReLU (Rectified Linear Unit). Increased nonlinear properties of the decision-making function enable it to eliminate negative values from an activation map by setting them to zero in a specific network without affecting the convolution layer fields of other networks. We can define the equation of ReLU as:

$$\sigma = max(0, z) \tag{1}$$

As a loss function for evaluating the performance of a classification model, we have employed binary cross-entropy. In addition, it increases as the estimated probability moves away from the label. In binary classification (number of classes M equals 2), cross-entropy can be calculated as:

$$L = -(y log(p) + (1 - y) log(1 - p)) \tag{2}$$

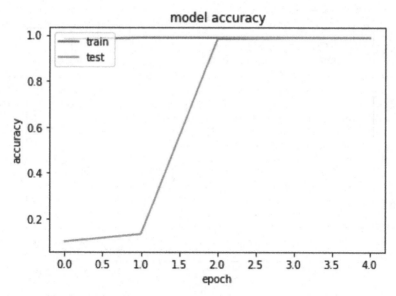

Fig. 4. Accuracy utilizing training and test samples with ACDNet

We have chosen Adam to be an optimizer in our network. For our suggested model, we have thought about the ideal hyper-parameters (see Table 1 for additional information). A model that minimizes a predetermined loss function is produced through hyperparameter optimization, which locates a tuple of hyperparameters.

NVIDIA DGX-1 V100 hardware was used to conduct the research in this study. The computer has 128 GB of RAM, 1000 TFLOPS speed, 5120 tensor cores, and 40600 CUDA cores.

4   Results and Discussion

The real-world fake news dataset HASOC2019 was used to tabulate the experimental and evaluation results. Experimental findings show that when compared to other available detection models for detecting hate speech, our proposed model provides state-of-the-art results.

The accuracy and cross-entropy loss using the HASOC dataset are displayed in Figs. 4 and 5. We can see that our suggested model performs quite admirably over a period of 20 epochs. Classification results show that after the three epochs, accuracy becomes saturated at some point in time. In our classification results, if we increase the number of epochs, it is providing almost the same value (refer to Fig. 4 for the same). Classification results also indicated that after the three epochs, loss almost becomes saturated at validation dataset. In our approach, if we increase the number of epochs, it is providing almost the same value (refer to Fig. 5 for the same).

In the case of HASOC, cross-entropy loss is hardly noticeable. Using HASOC, our suggested model performed well, with an accuracy of 98.92%. Our suggested model has significantly increased the accuracy of hate speech detection using social media

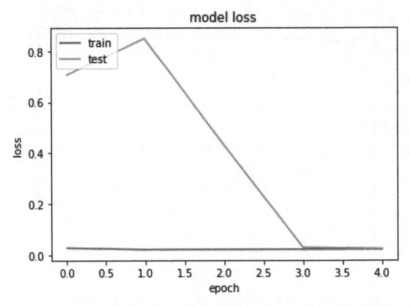

Fig. 5. Cross Entropy loss utilizing training and test samples with ACDNet

data, according to classification results. With the help of additional real-world fake news datasets, we have verified our proposed model. With other datasets as well, we have produced results that are compelling.

5 Conclusion and Future Work

With the help of our suggested deep learning model, we were able to get excellent results because it was able to capture both phrase-level representations and temporal semantics while maintaining optimum accuracy. The experimental results demonstrated empirically how well the suggested approach addressed the challenge of detecting hate speech. We have achieved state-of-the-art results.

In our upcoming study, we'll use different metadata for more precise classification and graph-based analysis to determine the precise path that hate speech news pieces take as they spread. In the upcoming research, we will also focus on merging different types of semantic features to get more accurate results.

References

1. Mathur, P., Sawhney, R., Ayyar, M., Shah, R.: Did you offend me? classification of offensive tweets in hinglish language. In: Proceedings of the 2nd Workshop on Abusive Language online (ALW2), pp. 138–148 (2018)
2. Bohra, A., Vijay, D., Singh, V., Akhtar, S.S., Shrivastava, M.: A dataset of Hindi-English code-mixed social media text for hate speech detection. In: Proceedings of the Second Workshop on Computational Modeling of People's Opinions, Personality, and Emotions in Social Media, pp. 36–41 (2018)

3. Gambäck, B., Sikdar, U.K.: Using convolutional neural networks to classify hatespeech. In: Proceedings of the First Workshop on Abusive Language Online, pp. 85–90 (2017)
4. Warner, W., Hirschberg, J.: Detecting hate speech on the world wide web. In: Proceedings of the Second Workshop on Language in Social Media, pp. 19–26 (2012)
5. Yuvaraj, N., et al.: Automatic detection of cyberbullying using multi-feature based artificial intelligence with deep decision tree classification. Comput. Electr. Eng. **92**, 107186 (2021)
6. Sowmya, V.B., Choudhury, M., Bali, K., Dasgupta, T., Basu, A.: Resource creation for training and testing of transliteration systems for Indian languages. In: Proceedings of the Seventh International Conference on Language Resources and Evaluation (LREC), vol. 39, no. 10 (2010)
7. Sreelakshmi, K., Premjith, B., Soman, K.P.: Detection of hate speech text in Hindi-English code-mixed data. Procedia Comput. Sci. **171**, 737–744 (2020)
8. Kumari, K., Singh, J.P., Dwivedi, Y.K., Rana, N.P.: Bilingual Cyber-aggression detection on social media using LSTM autoencoder. Soft. Comput. **25**(14), 8999–9012 (2021). https://doi.org/10.1007/s00500-021-05817-y
9. Kumar, R., Ojha, A.K., Malmasi, S., Zampieri, M.: Benchmarking aggression identification in social media. In: Proceedings of the First Workshop on Trolling, Aggression and Cyberbullying (TRAC-2018), pp. 1–11 (2018)
10. Veerasamy, S., Khare, Y.K., Ramesh, A., Adarsh, S., Singh, P., Anjali, T.: Hate speech detection using mono BERT model in custom content- management-system. In: 2022 4th International Conference on Smart Systems and Inventive Technology (ICSSIT), pp. 1681–1686. IEEE (2022)
11. Mandl, T., et al.: Overview of the hasoc track at fire 2019: hate speech and offensive content identification in indo-european languages. In: Proceedings of the 11th Forum for Information Retrieval Evaluation, pp. 14–17 (2019)
12. Davidson, T., Warmsley, D., Macy, M., Weber, I.: Automated hate speech detection and the problem of offensive language. In: Proceedings of the International AAAI Conference on Web and Social Media, vol. 11, no. 1, pp. 512–515 (2017)
13. ElSherief, M., Nilizadeh, S., Nguyen, D., Vigna, G., Belding, E.: Peer to peer hate: hate speech instigators and their targets. In: Proceedings of the International AAAI Conference on Web and Social Media, vol. 12, no. 1 (2018)
14. Ousidhoum, N., Lin, Z., Zhang, H., Song, Y., Yeung, D.Y.: Multilingual and multi-aspect hate speech analysis. arXiv preprint arXiv:1908.11049 (2019)
15. Basile, V., et al.: Semeval-2019 task 5: multilingual detection of hate speech against immigrants and women in twitter. In Proceedings of the 13th International Workshop on Semantic Evaluation, pp. 54–63 (2019)
16. Vashistha, N., Zubiaga, A.: Online multilingual hate speech detection: experimenting with Hindi and English social media. Information **12**(1), 5 (2020)
17. Islam, T., Ahmed, N., Latif, S.: An evolutionary approach to comparative analysis of detecting Bangla abusive text. Bull. Electr. Eng. Inf. **10**(4), 2163–2169 (2021)
18. Park, H., Kim, H.K.: Verbal abuse classification using multiple deep neural networks. In: 2021 International Conference on Artificial Intelligence in Information and Communication (ICAIIC), pp. 316–319. IEEE (2021)
19. Ahuja, R., Banga, A., Sharma, S.C.: Detecting abusive comments using ensemble deep learning algorithms. In: Stamp, M., Alazab, M., Shalaginov, A. (eds.) Malware Analysis Using Artificial Intelligence and Deep Learning, pp. 515–534. Springer International Publishing, Cham (2021). https://doi.org/10.1007/978-3-030-62582-5_20
20. Haoxiang, W.: Emotional analysis of bogus statistics in social media. J. Ubiq. Comput. Commun. Technol. (UCCT) **2**(03), 178–186 (2020)

21. Gr¨ondahl, T., Pajola, L., Juuti, M., Conti, M., Asokan, N.: All you need is "love" evading hate speech detection. In: Proceedings of the 11th ACM Workshop on Artificial Intelligence and Security, pp. 2–12 (2018)

22. Waseem, Z., Hovy, D.: Hateful symbols or hateful people? predictive features for hate speech detection on Twitter. In: Proceedings of the NAACL Student Research Workshop, pp. 88–93 (2016)

23. Ayo, F.E., Folorunso, O., Ibharalu, F.T., Osinuga, I.A.: Machine learning techniques for hate speech classification of twitter data: State-of-the-art, future challenges and research directions. Comput. Sci. Rev. **38**, 100311 (2020)

24. O'Keeffe, G.S., Clarke-Pearson, K.: The impact of social media on children, adolescents, and families. Pediatrics **127**(4), 800–804 (2011). https://doi.org/10.1542/peds.2011-0054

25. Ravi, K., Ravi, V.: Sentiment classification of Hinglish text. In: 2016 3rd International Conference on Recent Advances in Information Technology (RAIT), pp. 641–645. IEEE (2016)

26. Vidgen, B., Harris, A., Nguyen, D., Tromble, R., Hale, S., Margetts, H.: Challenges and frontiers in abusive content detection. Association for Computational Linguistics (2019)

27. Kuss, D.J., Griffiths, M.D.: Online social networking and addiction—a review of the psychological literature. Int. J. Environ. Res. Public Health **8**(9), 3528–3552 (2011)

28. Srivastava, A., Hasan, M., Yagnik, B., Walambe, R., Kotecha, K.: Role of artificial intelligence in detection of hateful speech for Hinglish data on social media. In: Choudhary, A., Agrawal, A.P., Logeswaran, R., Unhelkar, B. (eds.) Applications of Artificial Intelligence and Machine Learning. LNEE, vol. 778, pp. 83–95. Springer, Singapore (2021). https://doi.org/10.1007/978-981-16-3067-5_8

29. Sinha, R., Mahesh, K., Thakur, A.: Machine translation of bi-lingual hindi- english (hinglish) text. In: Proceedings of Machine Translation Summit X: Papers, pp. 149–156 (2005)

30. Bassignana, E., Basile, V., Patti, V.: Hurtlex: a multilingual lexicon of words to hurt. In: 5th Italian Conference on Computational Linguistics, CLiC-it 2018, vol. 2253, pp. 1–6. CEUR-WS (2018)

31. Mathur, P., Shah, R., Sawhney, R., Mahata, D.: Detecting offensive tweets in hindi-english code-switched language. In: Proceedings of the Sixth International Workshop on Natural Language Processing for Social Media, pp. 18–26 (2018)

32. Thakur, V., Sahu, R., Omer, S.: Current state of hinglish text sentiment analysis. In: Proceedings of the International Conference on Innovative Computing & Communications (ICICC) (2020)

33. Yin, D., Xue, Z., Hong, L., Davison, B.D., Kontostathis, A., Edwards, L.: Detection of harassment on web 2.0. In: Proceedings of the Content Analysis in the WEB, vol. 2, pp. 1–7 (2009)

34. Buckels, E.E., Trapnell, P.D., Paulhus, D.L.: Trolls just want to have fun. Pers. Individ. Differ. **67**, 97–102 (2014)

35. Papegnies, E., Labatut, V., Dufour, R., Linarès, G.: Impact of content features for automatic online abuse detection. In: Gelbukh, A. (ed.) Computational Linguistics and Intelligent Text Processing: 18th International Conference, CICLing 2017, Budapest, Hungary, April 17–23, 2017, Revised Selected Papers, Part II, pp. 404–419. Springer International Publishing, Cham (2018). https://doi.org/10.1007/978-3-319-77116-8_30

36. Allen, J., Seidenberg, M.S.: The emergence of grammaticality in connectionist networks. In: The Emergence of Language, pp. 115–151 (1999)

37. Warstadt, A., Singh, A., Bowman, S.R.: Neural network acceptability judgments. Trans. Assoc. Comput. Linguist. **7**, 625–641 (2019)

38. Ross, B., Rist, M., Carbonell, G., Cabrera, B., Kurowsky, N., Wojatzki, M.: Measuring the reliability of hate speech annotations: the case of the european refugee crisis. arXiv preprint arXiv:1701.08118 (2017)

39. Waseem, Z.: Are you a racist or am i seeing things? annotator influence on hate speech detection on Twitter. In: Proceedings of the First Workshop on NLP and Computational Social Science, pp. 138–142 (2016)

40. Waseem, Z., Hovy, D.: Hateful symbols or hateful people? predictive features for hate speech detection on twitter. In: Proceedings of the NAACL Student Research Workshop, pp. 88–93 (2016)

41. Spertus, E.: Smokey: automatic recognition of hostile messages. In: AAAI/IAAI, pp. 1058–1065 (1997)

42. Solorio, T., et al.: Overview for the first shared task on language identification in code-switched data. In: Proceedings of the First Workshop on Computational Approaches to Code Switching, pp. 62–72 (2014)

43. Molina, G., et al.: Overview for the second shared task on language identification in code-switched data. arXiv preprint arXiv:1909.13016 (2019)

44. Velankar, A., Patil, H., Joshi, R.: Mono vs multilingual BERT for hate speech detection and text classification: a case study in marathi. arXiv preprint arXiv:2204.08669 (2022)

45. Alaoui, S.S., Farhaoui, Y., Aksasse, B.: Hate speech detection using text mining and machine learning. Int. J. Decis. Supp. Syst. Technol. (IJDSST) **14**(1), 1–20 (2022)

Prediction of Face Emotion with Labelled Selective Transfer Machine as a Generalized Emotion Classifier

Dipti Pandit[1,2]([⊠]) [iD] and Sangeeta Jadhav[3] [iD]

[1] Vishwakarma Institute of Information Technology, Pune, India
dppandit@gmail.com
[2] DY Patil College of Engineering, Pune, India
[3] Army Institute of Technology, Pune, India

Abstract. Emotion prediction and classification using facial expressions still remains as the utmost thought-provoking activity in the computing arena. The most traditional approaches largely depend on pre-processing and feature extraction techniques. This paper factually represents the implementation and evaluation of learning algorithms like SVM, Random Forest, KNN, CNN and LSTM for recognition and predicting emotions of 2D facial expressions based on recognition rate as well as effect of unbalanced datasets. The projected structure in this paper has targeted two datasets, CK+ and JAFFE for two different feature extraction and classification techniques like supervised and unsupervised techniques. Fusion of histogram equalization, PCA and LBP are used for pre-processing. LSTM technique which is normally used with textual or vocal is used for 2D images which is also evaluated with a self modelled CNN algorithm. The recognition rate with LSTM was 76.59% and 98.43% respectively on the CK+ and JAFFE datasets. CNN also showed 70.58% of recognition rate on JAFFE where as 71.56% on CK+ dataset.

Keywords: Face Emotion Prediction · LBP · LSTM · CNN · 2D facial dataset

1 Introduction

Face is an authoritative biometric aspect of humans, and its contribution to the research of face emotion prediction has fully-fledged interest from scholars in the computational learning areas. Emotional face, or nonverbal communication [1–3], is intercepted and interpreted in an assortment of contexts, straddling biology, neuroscience, commercial, cultural anthropology and numerous other disciplines. Different models for emotion classification have been defined by emotion theorists and psychologists, ranging from commonly revealed basic emotions to customarily distinctive complicated emotions [4]. Ekman's basic emotional spectrum [5] and Russell's affect circumflex model [6] have dominated facial expression research in psychology. Russell's circumflex model in Fig. 1 illustrates the emotions in four quadrants as intense, pleasant, mild and unpleasant. Despite decades of research in Human Computer Interaction (HCI), many questions

© Springer Nature Switzerland AG 2023
D. Garg et al. (Eds.): IACC 2022, CCIS 1782, pp. 294–307, 2023.
https://doi.org/10.1007/978-3-031-35644-5_23

like, the most important indications and expressions to be evaluated for communication meaning encoding is yet unanswered. The problem persists because it is critical to generalize classifiers to unknown subjects that differ in actions and facial structures such as brows, wrinkles due to ageing can miss or offer false expressions, and so on [5, 6]. Enough training data for individual classifiers is a potential solution which is not always available or feasible. Other hurdles in involuntary emotion recognition include non-accurate computation, impulsive affective behavior, illumination alteration owing to head movements, registration strategies causing registration flaws, and wearables or camera movements causing occlusions.

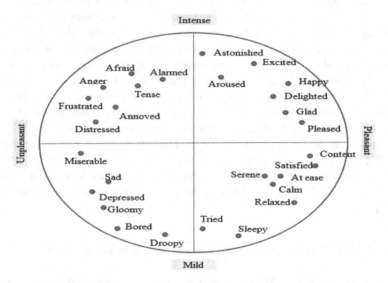

Fig. 1. Human Emotions in Russell's Circumflex Model

Emotion classification always has been a measure concern, and it is handled using a variety of traditional and innovative techniques. Face detection and tracking can be accomplished using the Viola-Jones method [7–9] and Subspace Constrained Mean-shifts [10, 11]. The Viola-Jones [7] methodology for object and face detection, which uses the Harr technique, is the technique most frequently employed for face detection. Several models [12–17] addressed issues such as predicting moment expression variation, conceptual understanding, emotion aspects, and personalization of current models. The more details survey is mentioned in the [18], for different methods of face recognition, feature extraction as well as recognition with different data base. Blends different methods are utilized based on the feature selection; for example, the SIFT algorithm is used for color photos, whilst the Local Binary feature might be used for grey scale data. Principal Component Analysis [19, 20] is the most often used adaptive transform. A general model, such as SVM, is used by the majority of emotion identification systems [21, 22]. The SVM works on the principle of maximal margin classifier, where the best separating points in the variable space, hyperplane is selected by their class.

Other classifiers used are K-NN [23] and Random forest [24]. K-Nearest Neighbours (k-NN) [25, 26] is the lethargic technique in computing which is also known as instant space learning. It works very easily by taking into consideration the proximity of the k-neighbours, and then with the most common points, classifying the unknown. Random Forest is meta estimator which takes another estimator as a parameter, that fits no of decision tree classifiers. Using averaging, improves the predictive accuracy and control overfitting. It is one of the bagging techniques using bootstrap aggregation with multiple combination of models. Modelling of predicting moment expression variation, conceptual understanding, emotion aspects, and personalization of current models were all handled by several models. By attenuating individual unique mismatches, Selective Transfer Machine [27] allows to configure a basic categorizer without the test subjects' external labels. By concurrently training a classifier and re-weighting the training examples that are most relevant to the test data, STM is able to produce this effect. Labelled Selective Transfer Machine is an extension of STM that significantly improved when introduced to available labelled test data. By attenuating individual unique mismatches, STM [27] allows to configure a basic classifier without the test subjects' external labels. LSTM is an RNN that can learn sequence dependence in pattern time series prediction. Neural network with multiple hidden layers has better learning characteristics. CNN [28, 29], model was then used for Face Emotion Recognition using EmotiW 2015 (Emotion Recognition in the Wild Challenge). Mostly researchers prefer CNN over deeper models for FER due to many reasons like large dataset, high resolution images required, and generalization of the model is difficult. Adding more to this the increase in number of layers are not the only solution to increase the accuracy as it leads to vanishing gradient problem.

Table 1. FER (Face Emotion Recognition) analysis for different algorithms.

Pre-processing Technique	Feature Extraction Technique	Classification Method	Author
Histogram Equalization	–	CNN	[30]
Cropping, Normalization	DWT, HOG	SVM	[31]
Harr Face Detection	Gabor filter and anisotropic texture, Local histogram	SVR	[32]
SQI, Sobel filter	Gabor filter	ART, DCT	[22]
Face Detection	Gabor filter, Gentle boost algorithm	DWT, SVM	[33]
Face Detection	Intensity normalization, Gaussian weighted average	CNN	[34]
Haar-like features, Histogram Equalization	–	CNN, KNN	[26]
Viola and Jones, Intra-Face library Normalization	–	AlexNet, VGG	[35]

Table 1 presents an analysis of various strategies and algorithms for facial emotion recognition based on pre-processing, feature extraction, and classification methods. This paper provides an approach to determine and compare some major classifiers used to classify face emotion recognition like K-NN, SVM, Random Forest, CNN and L-STM. The paper is structured in sections as 2 reviews on proposed work, the implemented system overview with pre-processing and feature extraction is covered in section. It also describes the structure of classifiers, K-NN, SVM, Random Forest, CNN and L-STM. Section 3 Experiments and evaluates the performance of all the classifiers. The paper concludes with the remark and potential work in Sect. 4.

2 Proposed Work

Human-computer interaction has become more sophisticated with artificial intelligence and advances in deep learning technology. The overall flow of the proposed model implemented in this paper described in Fig. 2, consists of input module, detection of ROI (Reason of Interest), here face detection and pre-processing module, feature extraction, and prediction components or different classifiers, and output module.

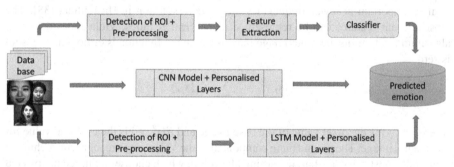

Fig. 2. Flow diagram for the complete system implemented

The input module obtains the input image that includes the Extended Cohn-Kanade Dataset [36] and the Japanese Female Facial Expression Database [37], which are facial emotion database widely used posed and unposed datasets. These databases have data classified in 7 basic sentiments: neutral, disgust, anger, fear, surprise, sadness and happiness as shown in Fig. 3. To enhance the database size for enormous training, testing and validation, new images are generated synthetically by rotation, shifting and flipping actions from image augmentation. In our experiments on CK+ database, we used 1522 images in total: neutral (231), happy (240), disgust (253), sad (211), fear (205), angry (126) and surprise (256). Whereas for JAFFE database, we used 848 total images: neutral (120), happy (124), disgust (116), sad (120), fear (128), angry (120) and surprise (120).

With featuring 14 action units and some updated intensity labels, the expanded CK dataset provides image-by-image action unit intensity annotations for the entire CK dataset. The subsequent phase is pre-processing module which involves face detection using Viola Jones algorithm. In several feature selection algorithms, picture pre-processing is identical to mathematical normalization. The input from the two different

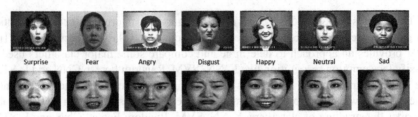

Fig. 3. Database CK+ and JAFFE faces cropped and sorted according to the emotions

datasets is given to the pre-processing module, where the face is detected and cropped to a definite size. For Face detection; Viola-Jones [7, 14] is implemented which is the most popular algorithm used to recognize objects as the training is slow but easy to detect. Later, the image is pre-processed with image enhancement technique called as Histogram equalization. Histogram equalization is one of the most popular techniques to adjust intensities of the input images. The technique enhances the distinct features in the image and also works on illumination normalization. The viola-Jones algorithm makes advantage of Alfred Haar's, Haar basis feature filters in 1909. Time resolution is important at higher frequencies than frequency resolution, while frequency resolution is more important at lower frequencies than time resolution in Haar filters [38]. The most relevant features can be represented using Haar features. Viola-Jones detection algorithm firstly turns the input image into an where the function is orthogonal i.e. sum is zero.

$$ii(x, y) = \sum_{x' \leq x, y' \leq y} i(x', y') \qquad (1)$$

where, $i(x, y)$ is the pixel value of the base image and $ii(x', y')$ is the essential value for the integral image. The second main component of the Viola-Jones recognition technique is the AdaBoost classifier-based learning algorithm, which chooses a limited no. of vital image features from a collection that produces an effective classifier and then cascades more complex classifiers that help to discard the image's context regions and detect the face region promisingly.

The very next category is feature extraction, which is a cluster of techniques which enables a framework to eliminate unnecessary deviations from the database while also assisting in the learning of representations essential for feature detection and recognition. Dimensionality reduction is commonly projecting data to a lower dimensional space that is strongly associated, similar to clustering the data, although the goals might vary like, eliminate light variation, registration mistakes, and identification bias, among other things. In emotion recognition, the most common techniques like Principal Component Analysis [19] and LBP are used. By thresholding the area around each pixel and then considering the result as a binary integer, the LBP [39, 40] texture operator labels the pixels in a picture. The most notable feature of the LBP [39, 41] in practical applications is its resistance to monotonic alterations in the grey scale brought on, for example, by changes in lighting. Ojala et al. in 1996 proposed LBP operator that shapes image pixel labels by thresholding the center value of 3×3 neighborhood of every pixel and treating the result as a binary number. As a texture descriptor, the histogram of these $28 = 256$

distinct labels can then be used.

$$LBP = \sum_{n=0}^{7} s(i_n - i_c)2^n \tag{2}$$

There's an issue with directly using a classifier to larger images as it might affect the speed and as they are high dimensional, it might have a ton of noise and comparing each and every single pixel using matrix subtraction and Euclidean distance might give us a high error and misclassification. This is the reason, high-dimensional images are scaled down to a smaller dimensionality while retaining the essence or important parts of the image. Principal component analysis (PCA) [19], chooses the hyperplane so that they are maximally spaced out when all the points are projected onto it. The high-dimensional data is reduced to a lower resolution by picking the prime eigenvectors [42] of the covariance matrix and projecting on eigenvectors. Assume that, $\{x_n\}$ is the arbitrary n-dimensional records of input data with mean data (μ), where n = 1, 2,..., N. The following equation describes it:

$$\mu = \frac{1}{N} \sum_{t=1}^{N} x_n \tag{3}$$

The covariance matrix of xn is defined as

$$C = \frac{1}{N} \sum_{t=1}^{N} (x_n - \mu)(x_n - \mu)^T \tag{4}$$

The covariance matrix C's eigenvalue problem is solved by PCA:

$$C_{v_i} = \lambda_i v_i \tag{5}$$

where the λ_i, eigenvalues and the corresponding eigenvectors, v_i are (i = 1, 2, 3,..., n). The variance in the main direction of the estimates of the input data is well known to be greater than that of any other direction. We compare the performance of several classifiers based on output module recognition accuracy in the classifier's module.

2.1 Classifiers

After feature extraction and dimension reduction using LBP and PCA respectively, different classifiers like SVM [43], k-NN, Random forest, CNN and LSTM model, performance are evaluated.

Support Vector Machine (SVM): is used in machine learning for regression analysis and classification [43]. Data objects are represented in n-dimensional space as a point where n is a no. of characteristics with the values of each characteristic. On the basis of hyper-plane, that distinguish the classes, w * x − b = 0, classification is performed. 'w' is the normal vector to the hyperplane which not necessaryily a unit vector. The region bounded by the hyperplanes is called the margin, and the half way between lies the maximal margin hyperplan which is seperates without error. The decision band is from w * x + b ≥ 1 to w * x + b ≥ −1 and maximal margin w * x + b ≥ 0. Best separation of data is done by the hyperplane when it is minimized. The decision surface will have a equation as:

$$f(x) = \sum_{i=1}^{l} y_i \propto_i k(x, x_i) + b \tag{6}$$

where, $\propto_i$ are Lagrange multipliers which has t be min with respect to w and b. This leads to lagrange duality problem which can be solved as below:

$$\propto = \arg \min_{\propto} \sum_{i=1}^{l} \propto_i -\frac{1}{2} \sum_{i=1}^{l} \sum_{j=1}^{l} \propto_i \propto_j y_i y_j x_i x_j \tag{7}$$

where, $\propto_i \geq 0, i = 1$ *to* l. Above equations where restricted to linearly seperable trainning data. For nonlinear separating surfaces, each point is mapped to a point $z = \emptyset(x)$, called as feature space. So, $\emptyset(x) * \emptyset(y)$ can be written as a kernel function $k(x, y)$.

K-Nearest Neighbors (KNN): is a univariate learning method in which the role is projected locally as well as computation is delayed till the function is analyzed. Accuracy significantly increases by normalizing the training data as the algorithm relies on distance for classification. An object is recognized via a popular referendum by its neighbours, with the object assigned to its most basic category of its nearest neighbours. Attributing weights to the inputs of neighbours so that the closest neighbours contribute to the median rather than the farthest neighbours is a useful strategy for classification and regression. Neighbours are chosen from an object category defined by the object's class or its property value [24].

Random Forest: A group of decision trees are hypothesised by the supervised algorithm Random Forest, which is often trained using bagging technique. The basic principle of this approach is a mixture of erudition models that rises the cumulative performance. By aggregating or combining the outcomes of various decision trees, it solves the error of overfitting and is very flexible and highly accurate [24, 44] by adjusting hyperparameters like number of features, trees and levels in each decision tree. Random forest construction is much more complex and time consuming than decision-making trees.

CNN: When developing a DCNN for an assigned purpose, numerous configurations and parameters must be determined to ensure that the network is well adapted for the task at hand. Complex models, such as CNNs, with a small dataset (CK+ and JAFFE images) based on static facial expression recognition challenge, which have mixed i.e. posed and non-posed type data. The fully connected convolution layer with dense connection 128 neurons is followed by batch normalization layer and LeakyRelu activation function with alpha = 0.1. A dropout layer of 0.2 is used to connect to the next layer with same configuration as first layer. The configuration for LeakyRelu and dropout remains the same with all fully connected layers. The third and fourth layer with dense connection, 64 neurons followed the last layer of final layer with SoftMax as the activation function. The CNN is trained for up to 500 epochs using an Adam optimizer and a categorical cross-entropy loss function.

Labelled Selective Transfer Machine (L-STM): Both the sampling weights and classifier parameters are jointly optimized by (STM) Selective Transfer Machine (STM)

[27], and thus retains the new decision boundary's discriminant property. STM requires no labels in target subject or in personalized generic classifier whereas in LSTM use of labelled data for training which is done in this paper.

$$S^{tr} = \{x_i, y_i\}_{i=1}^{n_{tr}} \tag{8}$$

where, x_i = column vector of ith column of the matrix X; and $y_i \in \{+1, -1\}$. To compensate for the offset, stacking one in each data vector x_i denotes the column vector as $x_i \in \mathbb{R}^{d+1}$. The STM is further formulated for minimizing the objective as

$$g(f, s) = \min_{f,s} R_f(S^{tr}, s) + \lambda \Omega_s(X^{tr}, X^{te}) \tag{9}$$

where,

$R_f(S^{tr}, s)$ = On the decision function f, SVM experimental risk is specified. S^{tr} = training set in relation to time by selection coefficients $s \in \mathbb{R}^{n_{tr}}$, for training sample x_i, each s_i reacts to positive weight. $\Omega_s(X^{tr}, X^{te})$ = dispersal mismatch as feature of s. When Ω_s is smaller, training and test distribution are nearer and the trade-off between mismatch of risk and distribution is when $\lambda > 0$. The choice characteristic f, and also the selection coefficient s, are optimised using STM. The linear penalized SVM in the form $f(x) = w^T x$ has the goal decision function and minimizes:

$$R_w(S^{tr}, s) = \frac{1}{2}\|w\|^2 + C \sum_{i=1}^{n_{tr}} s_i L^p(y_i, w^T x_i) \tag{10}$$

where,

$$L^p(y, \cdot) = \max(0, 1 - y \cdot)^p \tag{11}$$

Here, L can be any loss function as hinge loss and quadratic loss for p = 1 and 2 respectively. The second term in STM, $\Omega_s(X^{tr}, X^{te})$, copies mismatch region and the objectives are to find a re-weighting function that reduces the difference among the dispersals of train and test. Kernel means matching is used to reweight the function, which reduces the empirical mean distance between t_r and t_e in Kernel Hilbert Space $\mathfrak{H}$.

$$\Omega_s(X^{tr}, X^{te}) = \left\| \frac{1}{n_{tr}} \sum_{i=1}^{n_{tr}} s_i \varphi(x_i^{tr}) - \frac{1}{n_{te}} \sum_{j=1}^{n_{te}} \varphi(x_j^{te}) \right\|_{\mathcal{H}}^2 \tag{12}$$

Let, $k_i := \frac{n_{tr}}{n_{te}} \sum_{j=1}^{n_{te}} k(x_i^{tr}, x_j^{te})$, where, i = 1,.........,n_{tr}, which will collect the proximity among a training and each test sample. It is possible to accept such labels as the only reference to the target topic and to help in deciding the personalized classifier. In L-STM, which is the extension of STM, by adding regularization term $\lambda_L \Omega_L(S^L)$, a customized classifier is developed to adapt the target labels, where, $S^L = \{x_j^L, y_j^L\}_{j=1}^{n_L}$, as target data and their labels with, $y_j^L \in \{+1, -1\}, 0 \leq n_L \leq n_{te}$ and $\lambda_L > 0$, is used as a trade-off parameter. The objective of this additional parameter is to normalize the excellence of classification on the targeted labelled data, which is specified as, $\Omega_L(S^L) = \sum_{j=1}^{n_L} L^p(y_j^L, f(x_j^L))$.

3 Experimentation and Results

The classifier algorithms are evaluated for its facial emotion recognition on the JAFFE [37] and CK+ [36]. The CK+ and JAFFE database complies of more than 2000 image sequences from over 200 models ranging from 18 to 30 years together and are unique on the bases of size as well as models' origin. The dataset includes African-American, Japanese as well as Asian or Latino students. Digitalized images from neutral to target in the dimension of 640 by 480-pixel arrays are arrayed with grayscale values of 8-bit. The database also includes color images and some images vary in size of 240 by 240.

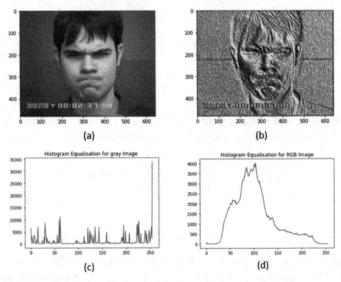

Fig. 4. Image applied with LBP on, (a) RGB, (b) Gray, Histogram equalization on (a) and (b) in figure (c) and (d) respectively.

Detected faces are applied LBP for feature extraction and histogram to scale all with 256 features as shown in Fig. 4. The performance of all the classifiers were evaluated on OpenCV platform using Core i5 9th generation 16 GB memory device. The 7-fold cross validation was used as the experimental paradigm was randomly divided into 7 groups of approximately equal size and cross-validated by 'leaving one group out'. The total samples are divided into two sets as testing and training set. The training and test sets are used to fit the models and for evaluation of the error of the chosen model. The validation set is used to assess prediction error for the model where validation score is calculated which should be high and loss value should be less. The loss function, evaluates the algorithm over the dataset. If prediction is less, loss function will be a high value and vice-versa.

The most common and efficient classifiers have been evaluated, such as KNN, SVM, Random Forest and compared with CNN model as well as LSTM. KNN and SVM's performed well on small datasets with 90.69 and 95.34 accuracy of recognition, but it seems to be much lower with big datasets with 53.58 and 66.66 respectively. Accuracy

Table 2. Overall performance of CNN method on JAFFE and CK+ dataset

Dataset	Accuracy	ROC	Precision	Recall	Loss
JAFFE	70.58	70.58	79.56	79.56	1.0722
CK+	71.56	76.24	68.22	68.22	0.5293

with random forest was almost same for both the datasets as 61.5 and 55.29. To train the CNN model, we used input shape of 256 × 256, and used the Adam optimizer with learning rate of 0.001 with loss function as categorical cross entropy. We tried different batch sizes learning rate and epochs in order to determine the best setup for the model training and finalized with epoch of 500 and batch size of 16. We also used dropout with p = 0.2 for all layers to normalize the network. The overall performance of the CNN is demonstrated in the Table 1.

Table 3. Performance Evaluated with accuracy for different classifier techniques on JAFFE and CK+ datasets

Sr. No.	Methodology	JAFFE Dataset	CK+ Dataset
1	KNN	90.69	53.58
2	SVM	95.34	66.66
3	Random Forest	61.5	55.29
4	CNN	70.58	71.56
5	Our Method using LSTM*	**98.43**	**80.91**
6	LSTM [27]	–	76.6

Compared to all other classifiers, the recognition accuracy, significantly improved with LSTM using 27495 learning parameters. The combination of feature extraction method using LBP + Normalization + PCA and then using LSTM for classification improved the overall performance. Total learning loss of 0.2479 and 0.1909 for JAFFE and CK+ dataset respectively, the overall accuracy of 98.43 and 80.91 described in the Table 2. The Fig. 5 shows the learning curve on JAFFE and CK+ dataset respectively (Table 3).

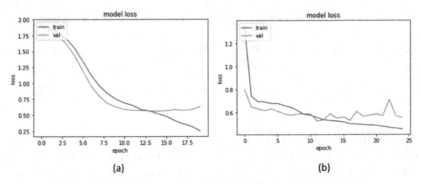

Fig. 5. Learning Curve on (a) JAFFE, (b) CK+ for LBP with LSTM

4 Conclusion

The performance of different techniques for facial emotion recognitions are evaluated in this paper. The complete structure includes input database, pre-processing unit, feature extraction, and prediction component or different classifiers and output module. The input images are obtained from the JAFFE database and Extended CK+ database, with posed and unposed individuals. Viola-Jones technique is used for face detection and histogram equalization is used for pre-processing. While for feature extraction and dimensionality reduction is done using LBP and PCA respectively. Different classifiers like SVM, k-NN, Random Forest, CNN and LSTM are evaluated. Compared to all the others, LSTM outperformed the classifiers on holistic expression detection. Experiments revealed insights such as (1) the efficacy of LSTM scales increases with the increase in number of training subjects. It can also be concluded that with convex verdict functions and the losses, STM can be generalized to other classifiers like logistic regression. (2) A local minimum could result in worse performance in case of non-convex categories like random forests. (3) Increasing the training pace for LSTM may be a path for future work due to the QP for solving s.

Acknowledgement. The authors appreciate the help they received from the research center (D Y Patil college, Pune) and affiliated colleges (Vishwakarma Institute of Information Technology and Army Institute of Technology).

References

1. Altamura, M., et al.: Facial emotion recognition in bipolar disorder and healthy aging. J. Nerv. Ment. Dis. **204**(3), 188–193 (2016). https://doi.org/10.1097/NMD.0000000000000453
2. Ricciardi, L., et al.: Facial emotion recognition and expression in Parkinson's disease: an emotional mirror mechanism? PLoS ONE **12**(1), 1–16 (2017). https://doi.org/10.1371/journal.pone.0169110
3. Harms, M.B., Martin, A., Wallace, G.L.: Facial emotion recognition in autism spectrum disorders: a review of behavioral and neuroimaging studies. Neuropsychol. Rev. **20**(3), 290–322 (2010). https://doi.org/10.1007/s11065-010-9138-6

4. Benitez-Quiroz, C.F., Wilbur, R.B., Martinez, A.M.: The not face: a grammaticalization of facial expressions of emotion. Cognition **150**, 77–84 (2016). https://doi.org/10.1016/j.cognit ion.2016.02.004

5. Lou, Z., Alnajar, F., Alvarez, J.M., Hu, N., Gevers, T.: Expression-invariant age estimation using structured learning. IEEE Trans. Pattern Anal. Mach. Intell. **40**(2), 365–375 (2018). https://doi.org/10.1109/TPAMI.2017.2679739

6. Shreve, M.: Automatic macro- and micro-facial expression spotting and applications. Grad. Theses Diss. no. January (2013)

7. Fang, W.M., Aarabi, P.: Robust real-time audiovisual face detection. Multisensor, Multisource Inf. Fusion Archit. Algorithms Appl. **5434**, 411 (2004). https://doi.org/10.1117/12.545934

8. Nicolle, J., Rapp, V., Bailly, K., Prevost, L., Chetouani, M.: Robust continuous prediction of human emotions using multiscale dynamic cues. In: Proceedings of the ACM International Conference on Multimodal Interaction (ICMI 2012), pp. 501–508 (2012). https://doi.org/10.1145/2388676.2388783

9. Kamarol, S.K.A., Jaward, M.H., Parkkinen, J., Parthiban, R.: Spatiotemporal feature extraction for facial expression recognition. IET Image Process. **10**(7), 534–541 (2016). https://doi.org/10.1049/iet-ipr.2015.0519

10. Saragih, J.M., Lucey, S., Cohn, J.F.: Face alignment through subspace constrained mean-shifts. In: Proc. IEEE Int. Conf. Comput. Vis., pp. 1034–1041 (2009). https://doi.org/10.1109/ICCV.2009.5459377

11. Xiong, X., De La Torre, F.: Supervised descent method and its applications to face alignment. In: Proc. IEEE Comput. Soc. Conf. Comput. Vis. Pattern Recognit., pp. 532–539 (2013). https://doi.org/10.1109/CVPR.2013.75

12. Zhang, L., Tjondronegoro, D.: Facial expression recognition using facial movement features. IEEE Trans. Affect. Comput. **2**(4), 219–229 (2011). https://doi.org/10.1109/T-AFFC.2011.13

13. Ding, X., Chu, W.S., La Torre, F.D., Cohn, J.F., Wang, Q.: Facial action unit event detection by cascade of tasks. In: Proc. IEEE Int. Conf. Comput. Vis., pp. 2400–2407 (2013). https://doi.org/10.1109/ICCV.2013.298

14. Cruz, A.C., Bhanu, B., Thakoor, N.S.: Vision and attention theory based sampling for continuous facial emotion recognition. IEEE Trans. Affect. Comput. **5**(4), 418–431 (2014). https://doi.org/10.1109/TAFFC.2014.2316151

15. Çeliktutan, O., Ulukaya, S., Sankur, B.: A comparative study of face landmarking techniques. EURASIP J. Image Video Process. **2013**(1), 1–27 (2013). https://doi.org/10.1186/1687-5281-2013-13

16. Yang, M., Zhang, L.: Gabor feature based sparse representation for face recognition with Gabor occlusion dictionary. In: Daniilidis, K., Maragos, P., Paragios, N. (eds.) ECCV 2010. LNCS, vol. 6316, pp. 448–461. Springer, Heidelberg (2010). https://doi.org/10.1007/978-3-642-15567-3_33

17. Tian, Y., Kanade, T., Cohn, J.F.: Recognizing upper face action units for facial expression analysis. In: Proc. IEEE Comput. Soc. Conf. Comput. Vis. Pattern Recognit., vol. 1, no. 2, pp. 294–301 (2000). https://doi.org/10.1109/cvpr.2000.855832

18. Pandit, D., Jadhav, S.: A comprehensive survey of different phases for involuntary system for face emotion recognition. In: Santosh, K.C., Gawali, B. (eds.) RTIP2R 2020. CCIS, vol. 1380, pp. 169–182. Springer, Singapore (2021). https://doi.org/10.1007/978-981-16-0507-9_15

19. Calder, A.J., Burton, A.M., Miller, P., Young, A.W., Akamatsu, S.: A principal component analysis of facial expressions. Vision Res. **41**(9), 1179–1208 (2001). https://doi.org/10.1016/S0042-6989(01)00002-5

20. Ahonen, T., Hadid, A., Pietikäinen, M.: Face description with local binary patterns: application to face recognition. IEEE Trans. Pattern Anal. Mach. Intell. **28**(12), 2037–2041 (2006). https://doi.org/10.1109/TPAMI.2006.244

21. Sikka, K., Dykstra, K., Sathyanarayana, S., Littlewort, G., Bartlett, M.: Multiple kernel learning for emotion recognition in the wild. In: Proceedings of the 15th ACM on International Conference on Multimodal Interaction, pp. 517–524 (2013)

22. Tsai, H.-H., Chang, Y.-C.: Facial expression recognition using a combination of multiple facial features and support vector machine. Soft. Comput. **22**(13), 4389–4405 (2017). https://doi.org/10.1007/s00500-017-2634-3

23. Trabelsi, A., Frasson, C.: The emotional machine: a machine learning approach to online prediction of user's emotion and intensity. In: Proceedings - 10th IEEE International Conference on Advanced Learning Technologies (ICALT 2010), pp. 613–617 (2010). https://doi.org/10.1109/ICALT.2010.174

24. Al Amrani, Y., Lazaar, M., El Kadirp, K.E.: Random forest and support vector machine based hybrid approach to sentiment analysis. Procedia Comput. Sci. **127**, 511–520 (2018). https://doi.org/10.1016/j.procs.2018.01.150

25. Institute of Electrical and Electronics Engineers: 2017 International Conference on Networks & Advances in Computational Technologies (NetACT): 20–22 July 2017, Trivandrum, Kerala, India (2017)

26. Bacon, L., et al.: Proceedings, 2017 15th IEEE/ACIS International Conference on Software Engineering Research, Management and Applications (SERA): 7–9 June 2017, The University of Greenwich, London, UK (2017)

27. Chu, W.S., De La Torre, F., Cohn, J.F.: Selective transfer machine for personalized facial expression analysis. IEEE Trans. Pattern Anal. Mach. Intell. **39**(3), 529–545 (2017). https://doi.org/10.1109/TPAMI.2016.2547397

28. Yu, Z., Zhang, C.: Image based static facial expression recognition with multiple deep network learning. In: Proceedings of the 2015 ACM International Conference on Multimodal Interaction (ICMI 2015), pp. 435–442 (2015). https://doi.org/10.1145/2818346.2830595

29. Fernández-Caballero, A., et al.: Smart environment architecture for emotion detection and regulation. J. Biomed. Inform. **64**, 55–73 (2016). https://doi.org/10.1016/j.jbi.2016.09.015

30. Clawson, K., Delicato, L.S., Bowerman, C.: Human centric facial expression recognition. In: Proc. 32nd Int. BCS Hum. Comput. Interact. Conf. HCI, pp. 1–12 (2018). https://doi.org/10.14236/ewic/HCI2018.44

31. Nigam, S., Singh, R., Misra, A.K.: Efficient facial expression recognition using histogram of oriented gradients in wavelet domain. Multimed. Tools Appl. **77**(21), 28725–28747 (2018). https://doi.org/10.1007/s11042-018-6040-3

32. Institute of Electrical and Electronics Engineers and IEEE Signal Processing Society: 2013 IEEE International Conference on Image Processing: ICIP 2013: proceedings: 15–18 September 2013, Melbourne, Victoria, Australia (2013)

33. Wu, Q., Shen, X., Fu, X.: The machine knows what you are hiding: an automatic microexpression recognition system. In: D'Mello, S., Graesser, A., Schuller, B., Martin, J.-C. (eds.) ACII 2011. LNCS, vol. 6975, pp. 152–162. Springer, Heidelberg (2011). https://doi.org/10.1007/978-3-642-24571-8_16

34. Lopes, A.T., de Aguiar, E., De Souza, A.F., Oliveira-Santos, T.: Facial expression recognition with convolutional neural networks: coping with few data and the training sample order. Pattern Recognit. **61**, 610–628 (2017). https://doi.org/10.1016/j.patcog.2016.07.026

35. Ng, H.W., Nguyen, V.D., Vonikakis, V., Winkler, S.: Deep learning for emotion recognition on small datasets using transfer learning. In: Proceedings of the 2015 ACM International Conference on Multimodal Interaction (ICMI 2015), pp. 443–449 (2015). https://doi.org/10.1145/2818346.2830593

36. Lucey, P., et al.: IEEE Computer Society Conference on Computer Vision and Pattern Recognition Workshops. In: IEEE Comput. Soc. Conf. Comput. Vis. Pattern Recognit. Work. 4(July), pp. 94–101 (2003)

37. Wang, P.S.P.: Performance comparisons of facial expression recognition in JAFFE database. Int. J. Pattern Recognit. Artif. Intell. **22**(3), 445–459 (2008)
38. Zhou, J., et al.: Biometric recognition. http://www.springer.com/series/7412
39. Zhao, G., Pietikäinen, M.: Dynamic texture recognition using local binary patterns with an application to facial expressions. IEEE Trans. Pattern Anal. Mach. Intell. **29**(6), 915–928 (2007). https://doi.org/10.1109/TPAMI.2007.1110
40. Ahonen, T., Hadid, A., Pietikä, M.: Face description with local binary patterns: application to face recognition. http://www.ee.oulu.fi/research/imag/texture/lbp/bibliography/
41. Shan, C., Gong, S., McOwan, P.W.: Facial expression recognition based on local binary patterns: a comprehensive study. Image Vis. Comput. **27**(6), 803–816 (2009). https://doi.org/10.1016/j.imavis.2008.08.005
42. De, A., Saha, A., Pal, M.C.: A human facial expression recognition model based on eigen face approach. Procedia Comput. Sci. **45**, 282–289 (2015). https://doi.org/10.1016/j.procs.2015.03.142
43. Li, W., Li, M., Su, Z., Zhu, Z.: A deep-learning approach to facial expression recognition with candid images. In: 2015 14th IAPR International Conference on Machine Vision Applications (MVA), pp. 279–282. IEEE (2015)
44. Jotheeswaran, J., Koteeswaran, S.: Feature selection using random forest method for sentiment analysis. Indian J. Sci. Technol. **9**(3), 1–7 (2016). https://doi.org/10.17485/ijst/2016/v9i3/86387

Study of Bitcoin Price Prediction Based on Sentiment Scores of Influencer Tweets with Experimental Validation

Abhishek Gandhi, Mukund Shinde, Rajendra Kulkarni, Shubham Chavan, Arshadali Sayyed, Dhanalekshmi Yedurkar$^{(\boxtimes)}$, and Shraddha Phansalkar

Department of Computer Science and Engineering, MIT School of Engineering, MIT ADT University, Pune, India
dhanalekshmipy2013@gmail.com,
shraddha.phansalkar@mituniversity.edu.in

Abstract. Although Bitcoin is the most popular cryptocurrency, it is very unstable even today. As the number of newsfeeds, articles, comments, trends, and opinions of influencers on popular social media platforms like Twitter is exponentially growing, they have a significant impact on the price of Bitcoin. People are often influenced by people who inspire them, events that impact their lives, or products and services they use. Therefore, an analysis of sentiments of people or investors triggered by social events becomes important for predicting the future of Bitcoin and its value. This paper forecasts Bitcoin prices by analyzing the sentiment scores of tweets and newsfeeds and their history. A large number of opinions on Twitter and other social media have drawn researchers to study public sentiment. We applied sentiment analysis to extract tweets from Twitter and analyzed the news blogs and historical bitcoin price data to improve our results' accuracy. The presented work have achieved 82.87% accuracy to predict the sentiment score.

Keywords: Artificial Intelligence model · Bitcoin · Blockchain · cryptocurrency · Natural Language Processing · sentiment analysis · Tweet Analysis

1 Introduction

In this technological era, easy access to the internet has triggered many new ideas and concepts [1] emerging due to the enormous growth of internet users. Digital cryptocurrency, one such concept, works as a medium of exchange based on strong cryptography and secures financial transactions. It is a decentralized system built using blockchain technology. After Bitcoin was released in 2009 as the first decentralized cryptocurrency, a slew of other cryptocurrencies has been released. The increasing value of bitcoin has attracted many people because they consider it an investment opportunity [2]. According to investing.com, there are more than 10,000 cryptocurrencies with a total market capitalization of $1,330,521,965,284 [3]. As bitcoin prices fluctuate wildly, they should be monitored closely before investing. Bitcoin prices are unpredictable as cryptocurrencies

© Springer Nature Switzerland AG 2023
D. Garg et al. (Eds.): IACC 2022, CCIS 1782, pp. 308–318, 2023.
https://doi.org/10.1007/978-3-031-35644-5_24

do not function like traditional currencies. As detecting a pattern is difficult, predicting a cryptocurrency's future price is a challenge [2].

The blockchain system records information in a specific format to prevent anyone from altering it. It is a digital ledger of transactions, with duplicates distributed across the Blockchain network. Whenever a new transaction occurs in blockchain that will be added to the participant ledger and multiple participants manage this decentralized database and are known as distributed ledger technology (DLT) [4].

Cryptocurrency is a form of payment separate from real-world currency and works on blockchain technology spread across a network of computer systems that manage transactions. For example, Litecoin, Bitcoin, and Ethereum currently in use today are centralized currencies. Unlike cryptocurrency, decentralization provides more security [5].

A mysterious person called Satoshi launched Bitcoin in 2009 as he was concerned about banks and governments using their power over money for their self-interest. Unlike the price of a normal currency, Bitcoin prices cannot be controlled by central banks or any government. It can also be sent across the world without any charge (decentralized). Bitcoin is based on a peer-to-peer network system [6]. Since Bitcoin was introduced, investors have increased in number, and the price has undergone massive fluctuations. As the number of users and capitalization grew, so did the amount of research done in this field on price prediction using various machine learning and lexicon-based approaches (Fig. 1).

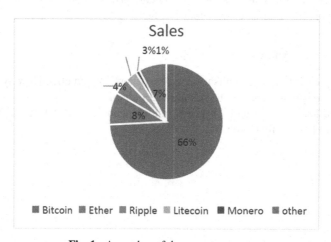

Fig. 1. A number of documents per year.

Organization of the paper is as follows: Sect. 2 discuss about related work and models. In Sect. 3 the proposed framework using the twitter data from social media platforms in real time for the sentiment analysis. Section 4 concludes the paper.

2 Related Work

The prospect theory of behavioral economics developed by Amos Tversky and Daniel Kahneman states that financial decisions are influenced by emotions, which further proves that fluctuations in bitcoin prices are due to the opinions of influencers and the masses [7].

Authors of [8] used two different approaches, one lexicon-based with nine lexicons and one machine learning-based approach with 22,610 judgments of an experienced user. Also, they used the best indicators in different ARIMAX models to calculate the daily returns of bitcoin-based on their prediction and concluded that sentiment regression is beneficial for the forecasting model and can give higher returns.

Authors of [9] built KryptoOracle in the Apache ecosystem that used Apache Spark. This system aims to predict cryptocurrency trends based on sentiment while the model learns, predicts, and updates itself in real-time. They used this system on Twitter sentiments and cryptocurrency prices, which gave good results. The prospect of this study was to generalize the engine for real-time changing market trends (stock prices, loyalty towards company/product, election results).

Authors of [10] used the TextBlob polarity model for sentiment analysis. They considered Twitter and historical bitcoin price data as the dataset and counts the number of tweets in two hours and the polarity of only those tweets, after finding predictor scores of bitcoins and Bitcoin 44% and 59%. They concluded that bitcoin prices are not affected much by tweet sentiment as compared to Litecoin prices. Also, the fluctuations depend on other factors like mining costs, economic factors, etc.

2.1 Bibliometric Analysis

It is a strategic evolution of published articles, papers, and an effective way to measure the influence of publications in the scientific community [7].

Searched Keywords: Bitcoin, VADER sentiment analysis, Blockchain, price prediction, Random Forest, Text Blob.

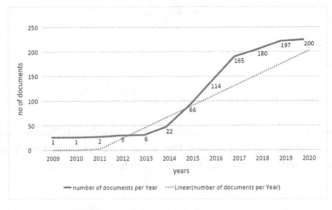

Fig. 2. A number of documents per year.

Figure 2 provides detailed information on the rise of papers in sentiment analysis in the IEEE database.

Subject areas: As per the various subject areas, there is a total of 1000 documents of which 415 are from computer science field showing majority researches are from this field, 17 documents out of 1000 are from economic field, 373 documents registered from the engineering field, 20 documents registered from telecommunications field, 1 registered as psychology, 60 documents as communication.

Figure 3 show the performance of the existing research works in the field of sentiment analysis and opinion mining.

Fig. 3. Performance indicator of all authors

3 Proposed Framework

Bitcoin Historical Price data obtained from Yahoo Finance was extracted in CSV format. The file contained the date, open price, close price, high price, low price, close, adjusted closing price, and volume per day. Twitter data was obtained from the python-based library TweePy that compiles tweets from Twitter.

We created a comprehensive price prediction system by calculating polarity scores of Bitcoin-related posts on Twitter, news articles, and blogs from the websites that were aggregated by the News API using VADER and TextBlob algorithms. Figure 4 shows the overall system architecture used for the proposed system.

To make a valid prediction about the prices of cryptocurrencies that have gained popularity in recent years [11], Twitter is the best platform to understand the sentiments of people. The amount of data generated on different social media platforms is shown in Table 1.

Table 1. Post Count per Second.

S.No.	Social Media Platform	Post count per second
1	Facebook	21 Million
2	Twitter	4 Million
3	Skype	1 Million
4	Instagram	454 Thousand

In the first phase, Twitter data was collected in JSON format and historical data in CSV format. After analyzing the polarity scores of the tweets, news articles, and blogs, they were grouped into three categories: negative, positive, and neutral as per the polarity score. Finally, all of the gathered data were converted to CSV format for synchronizing and were correlated with that day's closing price.

In the second phase, we did feature extraction on the preprocessed data using the Word2Vec 1-g method and calculated the sentiment score using the TextBlob and Vader algorithms with the extracted features. After calculating the sentiment scores, we correlated them with the real-time prices of Bitcoin. Data collected in the first phase were used to determine predictions using the TextBlob scores [12]. It starts with data gathering from Twitter, news/blogs, historical data, processing and analyzing gathered data for the final prediction phase. The presented work is carried out using python as a software.

3.1 Data Collection

Collection of Tweets Data in Real-Time

We also collected data on specific influential people by their Twitter handles and tags and measured their impact by correlating the bitcoin prices and their sentiment score Table 2 shows the selected influencers who were chosen based on popularity.

Collection of Bitcoin Prices

We collected historical bitcoin prices with the help of the python-based library "yFinance," which is capable of aggregating bitcoin prices accurately [13].

It is a strategic evolution of published articles, papers, and an effective way to measure the influence. Table 2 shows the selected influencers who were chosen based on popularity.

3.2 Gathering and Pre-processing Tweets

As mentioned previously, the Twitter API with the Python framework, Tweepy gathers and filters data using definitive words related to Bitcoin as keywords for filtering, including only bitcoin-related words (BTC, bitcoin), and also avoids the collection of irrelevant data, which saves storage. Also, individual tweets were collected and saved in a folder named "unprocessed file". They were further loaded into a Python object.

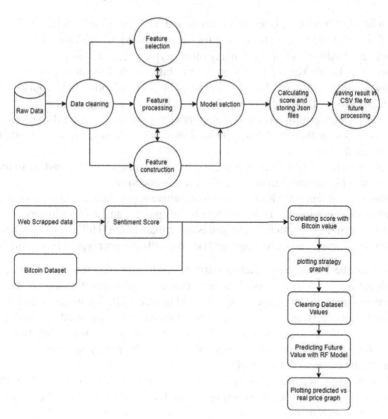

Fig. 4. System architecture

Table 2. A collection of Tweets.

Twitter Handler	Source	Time Period	Tweet Counts
@charlielite	Twitter	24 Months	3204
@elonmusk	Twitter	24 Months	120
@aantonop	Twitter	24 Months	524
@rogerkver	Twitter	24 Months	3194
@APompliano	Twitter	24 Months	1781
@ VitalikButerin	Twitter	24 Months	61

Prominent Twitter Influencers

- Charlie Lee: Charlie Lee is the creator of LiteCoin, and has more than 1 million followers on Twitter. He is considered one of the most impactful influencers for bitcoin prices.

- Elon Musk: Elon Musk is an entrepreneur and has more than 77.5 million followers on Twitter. Elon Musk is also known for his "The Musk Effect", Not only in bitcoin, investors consider his impact in many other cryptocurrency coins.
- Roger Ver: Roger Ver is an early investor in bitcoin and bitcoin-related startups. He is also known as "Bitcoin Jesus", because of his early adoption of bitcoin as a digital currency vision. He has more than 742 thousand followers on Twitter.
- Andreas Antonopoulos: Andreas Antonopoulos is a British-Greek Bitcoin advocate, educator, and author of 8 books related to cryptocurrency. He has 715 thousand followers on twitter.
- Vitalik Buterin: Vitalik buterin is a Canadian programmer, writer, and co-founder of Ethereum. He has more than 3.5 million followers on twitter.
- Anthony Pompliano: He is one of the more active crypto influencers across a number of platforms, not just on Twitter, where he has more than 1,6 M followers
- Ben Horowitz: On Twitter, where he has more than 629,900 followers, he talks about business, finance, and technology, and occasionally covers crypto and Bitcoin issues.

We used the Word2Vec model to learn embedding from raw texts. It contains two algorithms: the Skip-Gram model, which tries to predict words related to the given center word, and the Continuous Bag Of Word model (CBOW), which is an inverse of the former model as it predicts the center word based on the surrounding words [14].

With the help of tokenization, we divided large sentences into small blocks, i.e., tokens. Tokenization removes the unnecessary words and punctuation that are not relevant in the context of a given phrase.

Also, we used an apostrophe dictionary to search for contractions like "didn't" and "can't" and convert them into their original form. It also serves as an emoticon dictionary for defining emojis in word format.

After collecting data by using keywords related to bitcoin, we got the most used keywords. Litecoin was the most used keyword, followed by Bitcoin, and LTC, because the influencer Charlie Lee has posted more tweets as compared to other influencers with tags for Bitcoin.

3.3 Sentiment Analysis Processing

We used the VADER (Valence Aware Dictionary for Sentiment Reasoning) algorithm based on natural language processing (NLP) in our model to calculate the polarity scores. VADER returns the probability of input text as positive, negative, or neutral using a list of words that are labeled according to semantic orientation (positive, negative) [15]. Research shows that VADER accuracy is as good as manual rates. As per the results of F1 scores, the VADER score was 0.96 and the human score was 0.84 in the aspect of correctly labeling sentiments [16].

VADER works in three different phases:

1. Analyzing tweets by finding individual sentiment scores, and then calculating compound scores.
2. All collected tweets in the range of 2600–3600 are cleaned by removing unnecessary data from the tweets. Cleaning function removes unwanted characters and words such as hyperlinks, non-alphabetic symbols. Then it removed the Twitter handles from the

tweets if it is available in tweets. By doing this process we achieved a substantially reduced size of tweets dataset. We have preserved emojis and possible emoticons characters for use in sentiment analysis.
3. In the last phase, all gathered data (such as polarity score, compound score, positive/negative labels) are aggregated by adding columns [17, 18].

Figure 5 shows that the polarity score of tweets is nearly linear between 0.00 and 0.15, i.e., the neutral score pertaining to the sentiments of the tweet.

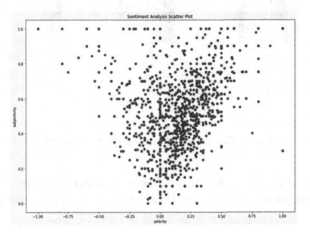

Fig. 5. Sentiment analysis scatter graph

We used the TextBlob library to analyze the sentiment of the tweets and news articles. TextBlob is a Python-based library for processing textual data. This type of operation is performed on text data to extract relevant information from the text and pass it to a machine learning model.

After importing the TextBlob library, we selected the text data for processing and passed it to the TextBlob function. Using the sentiment function, we calculated the polarity (whether the test is positive/negative/neutral) and subjectivity (checking whether the text is objective or subjective).

3.4 Data Prediction

Polarity results were classified into: positive (if the score was more than zero); negative (if the score was less than zero); and neutral (if the score was equal to 0).

With the help of TPOT (Tree-based Pipeline Optimization Tool), we found the best pipeline from various options that fit our model. TPOT is an automated machine-learning open-source tool built on a sci-kit learn library based on Python.

We applied decision tree, logistic regression, and random forest machine learning classifiers as suggested by TPOT. The random forest classifier method gave the most precise results for the F1 score. Figure 6 shows the comparison of the 3 machine learning classifiers.

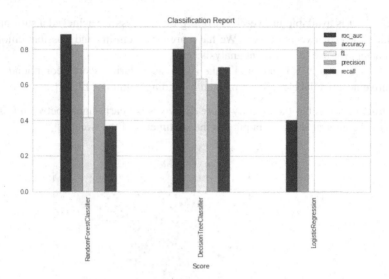

Fig. 6. Comparison of machine learning classifiers

As displayed in Fig. 7, the Random Forest classifier has more ROC Score and accuracy as compared to other models. Hence, it was chosen for the prediction analysis.

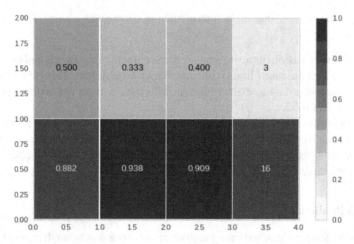

Fig. 7. Classification Report of Random Forest Classifier f1 score, precision score, recall score

3.5 Analysis of the Variance in Bitcoin Prices with Sentiment Scores

Table 3 shows the Bitcoin price fluctuation concerning the tweet sentiments of the influencer Charlee Lee. This helps in understanding the pattern of rising and falling of bitcoin's last closing price with respect to the positivity, neutrality, or negativity of the tweet.

Table 3. A collection of Tweets.

Twitter Handle	Tweet Samples	Bitcoin Opening Price	Positive Sentiment Score	Negative Sentiment Score	Price Difference	Tweet Sentiment Flag
Charlie	"really need usdc trading pair considering litecoin"	465.864013671875	0	0	−8	2

4 Conclusions

We collected data from social media platforms like Twitter to analyze the sentiments of influencers regarding Bitcoin. These data can also be used to learn and predict sentiment for future tweets. Also, these predictions may be useful in determining Bitcoin prices and the impact of a Tweet on price variation in the future. We achieved 82.87% accuracy with the Random Forest Classifier, and this model was able to predict the sentiment score. The impact of a tweet on Bitcoin prices was studied by sentiment scores and the history of prices with an accuracy of 72.1%.

References

1. Jain, A., Tripathi, S., Dwivedi, H.D., Saxena, P.: Forecasting price of cryptocurrencies using tweets sentiment analysis. In: 2018 Eleventh International Conference on Contemporary Computing (IC3), pp. 1–7. IEEE (2018)
2. Mohapatra, S., Ahmed, N., Alencar, P.: KryptoOracle: a real-time cryptocurrency price prediction platform using Twitter sentiments. In: 2019 IEEE International Conference on Big Data (Big Data), pp. 5544–5551. IEEE (2019)
3. Stenqvist, E., Lönnö, J.: Predicting Bitcoin price fluctuation with Twitter sentiment analysis. Ph.D. Dissertation (2017)
4. Pant, D.R., Neupane, P., Poudel, A., Pokhrel, A.K., Lama, B.K.: Recurrent neural network based bitcoin price prediction by twitter sentiment analysis. In: 2018 IEEE 3rd International Conference on Computing, Communication and Security (ICCCS), pp. 128–132. IEEE (2018)
5. Sattarov, O., Jeon, H.S., Oh, R., Lee, J.D.: Forecasting bitcoin price fluctuation by twitter sentiment analysis. In: 2020 International Conference on Information Science and Communications Technologies (ICISCT), pp. 1–4. IEEE (2020)

6. Aggarwal, A., Gupta, I., Garg, N., Goel, A.: Deep learning approach to determine the impact of socio economic factors on bitcoin price prediction. In: 2019 Twelfth International Conference on Contemporary Computing (IC3), pp. 1–5. IEEE (2019)

7. Hassan, M.K., Hudaefi, F.A., Caraka, R.E.: Mining netizen's opinion on cryptocurrency: sentiment analysis of Twitter data. Stud. Econ. Finance **39**(3), 365–385 (2022)

8. Raju, S.M., Tarif, A.M.: Real-time prediction of BITCOIN price using machine learning techniques and public sentiment analysis. arXiv preprint arXiv:2006.14473 (2020)

9. Pano, T., Kashef, R.: A complete VADER-based sentiment analysis of bitcoin (BTC) tweets during the era of COVID-19. Big Data Cogn. Comput. **4**(4), 33 (2020)

10. Ibrahim, A.: Forecasting the early market movement in bitcoin using twitter's sentiment analysis: an ensemble-based prediction model. In: 2021 IEEE International IOT, Electronics and Mechatronics Conference (IEMTRONICS), pp. 1–5. IEEE (2021)

11. Kaur, S., Mohana, R.: A roadmap of sentiment analysis and its research directions. Int. J. Knowl. Learn. **10**(3), 296–323 (2015)

12. Kilimci, Z.H.: Sentiment analysis based direction prediction in bitcoin using deep learning algorithms and word embedding models. Int. J. Intel. Syst. Appl. Eng. **8**(2), 60–65 (2020)

13. Sánchez-Núñez, P., Cobo, M.J., De las Heras-Pedrosa, C., Pelaez, J.I., Herrera-Viedma, E.: Opinion mining, sentiment analysis and emotion understanding in advertising: a bibliometric analysis. IEEE Access **8**, 134563–134576 (2020)

14. Ahuja, R., Chug, A., Kohli, S., Gupta, S., Ahuja, P.: The impact of features extraction on the sentiment analysis. Procedia Comput. Sci. **152**, 341–348 (2019)

15. Kasri, M., Birjali, M., Beni-Hssane, A.: A comparison of features extraction methods for Arabic sentiment analysis. In: Proceedings of the 4th International Conference on Big Data and Internet of Things, pp. 1–6 (2019)

16. Jianqiang, Z., Xiaolin, G.: Comparison research on text pre-processing methods on twitter sentiment analysis. IEEE Access **5**, 2870–2879 (2017)

17. Korkontzelos, I., Nikfarjam, A., Shardlow, M., Sarker, A., Ananiadou, S., Gonzalez, G.H.: Analysis of the effect of sentiment analysis on extracting adverse drug reactions from tweets and forum posts. J. Biomed. Inform. **62**, 148–158 (2016)

18. Liu, R., Shi, Y., Ji, C., Jia, M.: A survey of sentiment analysis based on transfer learning. IEEE Access **7**, 85401–85412 (2019)

Modeling Human Performance in Complex Search and Retrieve Environment Using Supervised and Unsupervised Machine Learning Techniques

Shashank Uttrani$^{(\boxtimes)}$ ⓘ, Sakshi Sharma ⓘ, Mahavir Dabas ⓘ, Bhavik Kanekar ⓘ, and Varun Dutt ⓘ

Applied Cognitive Science Lab, Indian Institute of Technology Mandi, Kamand, Mandi, HP 175075, India
shashankuttrani@gmail.com

Abstract. Prior research has evaluated human performance in complex search-and-retrieve environment. However, little is known about how supervised and unsupervised machine learning techniques could account for human performance in such complex scenarios. The primary objective of this research is to develop supervised and unsupervised machine learning models to account for human actions in a complex search-and-retrieve environment. A total of 50 participants were recruited to participate in the study to perform as human agents in a simulation developed using Unity 3D. The environment consisted of four building with targets (having positive reward) and distractors (having negative reward) present inside those buildings. Participants were tasked to explore the environment and maximize their score by collecting as many target items while avoiding distractor items present in the environment. The experiment consisted of training and test phases which differed in the availability of feedback, items present in the environment, and the duration. Next, machine learning models were developed to account for human actions using supervised and unsupervised techniques such as Decision Tree, Random Forest, Support Vector Classifier (SVC), Multilayer Perceptron (MLP), and K-nearest neighbor (KNN). These models were trained using data collected in the training phase of the experiment and their performance was evaluated on data collected in the test phase. Results revealed that KNN, an unsupervised learning model, performed better in predicting human actions on the test dataset compared to supervised learning models such as decision tree, random forest, MLP, and SVC. We highlight the main implications of our findings for the human factors research community.

Keywords: Search-and-Retrieve task · Multilayer Perceptron · Support Vector Classifier · K-nearest neighbor · Human Performance

© Springer Nature Switzerland AG 2023
D. Garg et al. (Eds.): IACC 2022, CCIS 1782, pp. 319–327, 2023.
https://doi.org/10.1007/978-3-031-35644-5_25

1 Introduction

Prediction of human action in complex and high demand cognitive tasks has been a topic of great interest in the neuroscience, psychology, and machine learning community [1]. In simple terms, the problem of predicting human actions can be looked as a n-class classification problem [2]. Numerous classification algorithms have been developed and enhanced to cater to the problem of n-class classification such as decision tree [3], random forest [4], support vector classifier (SVC) [5], multilayer perceptron (MLP) [6], and K-nearest neighbor [7]. These machine learning algorithms are either supervised learning or unsupervised learning in nature.

Decision trees have been employed to recognize human actions using smartphone sensor data [8]. Authors showed that human behavior and action data can be capture using accelerometer present in the smart phones [8]. This data can be used the recognize the orientation and actions of human such as standing, sitting, sleeping, walking, and running. [8] used the decision tree algorithm to recognize and predict human actions with high accuracy using the accelerometer data.

Similarly, support vector machines have been used to recognize human actions in a video using spatio-temporal feature descriptor [9]. The authors used surveillance and sports videos to capture and label human actions and trained the support vector classifier to recognize human action from those videos [9]. This technique provided a faster method to recognize human actions than decision trees [9].

Various state-of-the-art reinforcement learning and cognitive models have also been developed to account for human actions in complex scenarios [10]. Recent developments have shown that deep reinforcement learning algorithms such as Deep Q-learning network (DQN) [11] have been successful in defeating human in video games like Atari [12]. Also, sophisticated models like Soft-Actor Critic [13] have been used to play highly complex and strategic games like DOTA [14] and Call of Duty [15]. Research has also demonstrated the use of cognitive models developed using cognitive architectures like ACT-R [16] in modeling human actions in aviation such as air-refueling and aircraft maneuvering [17].

Such developments in the field of computational modeling have led to an increase in the interest of modeling human actions in complex search-and-retrieve environments such as an on-going military operation [10]. Researcher have evaluated human performance in simple and complex cognitive tasks; however, little is known about how machine learning algorithms would account for human actions in complex cognitive tasks.

Although prior research has evaluated human performance in various cognitive-demand tasks and developed machine learning models to predict human agent's actions [10], however, little is known how these machine learning models would account for human actions in complex search-and-retrieve simulated environments. The primary objective of this research is to develop computational models to predict human actions in a complex search-and-retrieve environment using supervised and unsupervised machine learning techniques such as decision tree, random forest, SVC, MLP, and KNN.

In what follows, we detail the experiment design, participant demographic, and models used to account for human actions in the search-and-retrieve environment. Next, we present the model results and discuss the implication of our findings in the discussion section. Finally, we close the paper by defining the limitations of our study and future scope of this research.

2 Methodology

2.1 Participants

Fifty participants were recruited from the Indian Institute of Technology Mandi to perform as human agents in the search-and-retrieve simulation experiment. Participants' age ranged between 18 and 31 years and the mean age of the recruited participants was 25.5 years with a standard deviation of 3.4 years. Out of fifty recruited participants, 70% were males and the rest were females. More than 90% of the participants were pursuing postgraduate degrees while the rest were pursuing bachelor's degrees. About 90% of the participants had a major in STEM related subjects while the rest belonged to Arts and Humanities. Upon successful completion of the study, participants were thanked and renumerated a base payment of INR 40 (USD 0.22) for their participation in the study. The top three scorers of the experiment were provided a bonus of INR 20 each.

2.2 Experiment Design

The search-and-retrieve simulation environment was developed using Unity 3D [18], a professional game development engine, to collect human data. The simulation consisted of four under construction buildings with target and distractor items available in the environment. The objective of the simulation game was to maximize the score by collecting as many target items present in the environment while avoiding distractor items. Upon collecting each target item, human agent received a positive reward of + 5 points whereas upon collecting each distractor item, a negative reward of −5 points was awarded. The experiment was divided into training and test phase which differed on the availability of feedback, number of items present in the environment (target or distractor), and the duration of the phase. In the training phase, feedback was present in the form of score whereas, in the test phase, feedback was absent. Moreover, there was difference in the number of target items (14 in training and 28 in test) and distractor items (7 in training and 14 in test). Furthermore, the training phase was 15 min long whereas the test phase was 10 min long.

2.3 Procedure

The search-and-retrieve environment was developed to collected human data in a cognitive challenging and complex search-and-retrieve task. Later, human participants were recruited to participate in the study to perform as human agents in the search-and-retrieve environment. The collected data along with recorded gameplay video across the training phase was used to train machine learning models and data collected in the test phase was used to evaluate the performance of trained models.

2.4 Dataset

Upon completion of data collection, the dataset of the gameplay of all participants was prepared consisting of timestamps, actions, coordinates, and 1000 principal component values of screen grab. The recorded gameplay videos of each participant were divided into frames corresponding to timestamps against each action. Next, each captured frame was converted into its vectorized form, and its dimensions were reduced by taking 1000 major components using Principal Component Analysis (PCA) technique [19]. Thus, the final training and test datasets had 1005 features, namely, timestamp, x-coordinate, y-coordinate, z-coordinate, and 1000 PCA values against each timestamp. The training dataset corresponds to data collected during the training session of the gameplay for all the participants. Similarly, the test dataset corresponds to data collected during the test session of the gameplay for all the participants.

2.5 Evaluation Metrics

The purpose was this research was to develop machine learning algorithms to predict actions (Left, Right, or Forward) of an agent in a simulated search-and-retrieve environment using the human activity dataset recorded during empirical study. Thus, the research problem boils down to a three-class classification using different machine learning techniques. Therefore, to evaluate the performance of each model, we trained the models using the training dataset, i.e., the dataset recorded during the training phase of the gameplay, and evaluated the performance using the test dataset, i.e., the dataset recorded during the test phase of the gameplay. Thus, the accuracy of each model was calculated using Eq. 1.

$$Accuracy = \frac{Correctly\ Predicted\ Classes}{Total\ Number\ of\ classes} * 100 \tag{1}$$

3 Models

3.1 Decision Tree

Decision tree algorithm is a supervised machine learning technique that builds a hierarchical model using a tree structure [3]. The tree contains decision nodes having an attribute (or feature) associate to each node. Each decision node can have two or more branches associated to a value or a range of value of the attribute [3]. However, the leaf node has no branches, and it contains the target value. The training data is split into smaller subsets to maximize the homogeneity at each decision node [3]. The execution of the algorithms starts from the root node and the model traverses down the tree based on the decision rules at each node [3]. The accuracy of the model may vary on the following hyperparameters: criterion of the split, maximum depth of the tree, and the number of the samples for a split at each decision node. The splitting criterion can either be Gini Impurity or Entropy method [20]. The maximum depth of the tree is the number of edges from the root node to the decision leaf [3].

3.2 Random Forest

The random forest algorithm is also a supervised machine learning technique [4]. It extends on the on the works of decision tree algorithm and develops an ensemble of many individual decisions trees [4]. The main concept behind using an ensemble of different tree lies in the fact that relatively uncorrelated decision trees combined together as an ensemble can outperform any individual tree [4]. Bootstrap aggregation is employed to ensure low correlation between individual tree by making each tree to sample from the dataset with replacement [4]. Also, a major difference between a decision tree and a random forest is that in a decision tree all features are considered before making a decision node [4]. However, in a random forest each individual tree has to pick only a random subset of available feature set. All the hyperparameters of a random forest remain the same except one, i.e., the number of individual trees in the forest.

3.3 Support Vector Machine

Support Vector Classifier (SVC) is also a supervised machine learning algorithm based on the support vector machines [5]. The objective of the SVC algorithm is to classify the dataset by mapping the input to a higher dimensional feature space and fit a hyperplane in that feature space in such a way that the margin between each class is maximum [5]. The objective function penalizes the model for each misclassification [5]. The accuracy of this model may vary due to the following hyperparameters: kernel, gamma, and degree of regularization [5]. The shape of the hyper-plane is determined by the kernel and the gamma is the kernel coefficient [5]. The overfitting is controlled by the degree of regularization.

3.4 Multilayer Perceptron

A multilayer perception or MLP is another supervised machine learning which builds on the biological neural network responsible for mammalian intelligence [6]. It is a fully connected feed forward neural network consisting of a minimum of three layers, namely, the input layer, the hidden layer, and the output layer. In each layer, a collection of computational nodes (or perceptron) are present to perform simple weight aggregation operation [6]. Also, a non-linear activation function is used at the output each neuron to produce and forward the response to next layer. All the weights are initially assigned a random value between 0 and 1 and later updated using the backpropagation algorithm [21] to minimize the error in prediction. Thus, number of layers, number of units in each layer, and the activation function are the hyperparameters of the MLP for calibration [6].

3.5 K-Nearest Neighbor

K-nearest neighbor (KNN) is an unsupervised machine learning algorithm which works by storing all the training data and makes a prediction for the test the data by using a target value "k" for its nearest neighbors [7]. The calculation of nearest neighbor among the training dataset is made using the distance from the test data point [7]. Any one of the distances among several distance metrics such as Euclidean distance,

Manhattan distance, and Minkowski distance can be used for this algorithm [7]. Thus, distance metric and the number of nearest neighbors are the two hyperparameters for this algorithm [7].

3.6 Model Evaluation

All the models, supervised and unsupervised, were trained using the training dataset, and their performance was evaluated using the test dataset. During model training, different hyperparameters associated with respective models were calibrated using the grid search algorithm [22]. Upon calibration using the training dataset, the calibrated parameters were fixed and test data were used to evaluate the accuracy of each model using Eq. 1.

For the decision tree algorithm, Gini impurity and Entropy criterion were used while ranging the maximum depth of the decision tree between 1 and 50. Also, the minimum number of samples for a split at each decision node were varied between 2 and 10. Similarly, for the random forest algorithm, both Gini impurity and Entropy criterion were used while the number of estimators were ranged between 2 and 512 (in the steps of 2i, where i = 1, 2, 3,..., 9). Moreover, for calibrating the support vector classifier, linear, poly, and rbf kernels were used with different values of gamma and degree of regularization. Also, we calibrated the MLP for different number of hidden layers and number of nodes in each layer along with different activation functions such as sigmoid, tanh, and ReLu. Furthermore, the KNN algorithm was calibrated using different values of nearest ranging between 1 to 100 and different distance metrics.

4 Results

All the machine learning models (decision tree, random forest, SVC, MLP, and KNN) were trained using the training dataset and calibrated using the hyperparameters as discussed above. Table 1 shows the performance (accuracy) of each model along with their best calibrated hyperparameters. In the decision tree model, entropy criterion produced better results compared to Gini impurity and the accuracy stagnated at the maximum depth of 6. Similarly, for the random forest algorithm, entropy criterion produced higher accuracy with 256 estimators. Thus, random forest model performed better than decision tree model. However, the support vector classifier could not perform accurately compared to the decision tree or random forest models. Moreover, the best results produced by the MLP model had an accuracy of 60.02% with 3 hidden layers and tanh activation function. The first, second, and third layers had 10, 30, and 10 neuron units, respectively. The best performance was shown by KNN algorithm using Euclidean distance metric and K = 49. The KNN algorithm produced an accuracy of 61.43% in predicting the actions using the calibrated hyperparameters.

Therefore, the rank of the machine learning as per their performance would be KNN, random forest, decision tree, MLP and SVC.

5 Discussion and Conclusion

Although prior research has evaluated human performance in complex search-and-retrieve tasks using simulated environments, however, little was known about how machine learning algorithms (supervised and unsupervised) would account for human

Table 1. Performance of different models and their optimal hyperparameters.

Model	Optimal Hyper-parameters	Accuracy
Decision Tree	*Criterion* = Entropy, *maximum depth* = 6, *minimum sample split* = 6	60.98%
Random Forest	*Criterion* = Entropy, *number of estimators* = 256	61.28%
Support Vector Classifier	*Kernel* = linear, *gamma* = "auto", *C* = 2000	48.20%
Multilayer Perceptron	5 layers = [1004, none], [10, tanh], [30, tanh], [10, tanh], [3, ReLu]	60.02%
K-nearest neighbor	*Distance* = Euclidean, *K* = 49	0.6143

actions in such complex and cognitive demanding tasks. The primary objective of this research was to develop machine learning models using decision tree [3], random forest [4], SVC [5], MLP [6], and KNN [7] algorithm to predict human actions in complex search-and-retrieve simulated environments. The collected human data of fifty participants during the training phase was used to training different machine learning algorithms and calibrate the hyperparameters using grid search. Subsequently, test data obtained from the test phase data collection was used to evaluate the performance of machine learning models with their calibrated parameters.

Results show that KNN, an unsupervised machine learning algorithm outperformed all the supervised machine learning algorithms. Also, algorithms like decision tree and random forest performed slightly better than MLP. However, SVC could not account for human actions in test scenario compared to other machine learning models. One reason for such poor performance of SVC might be due to methodology to project the original dataset onto a higher dimensional hyper-plane. Since our dataset was already consisting of 1005 features, SVC would have failed to classify (find a hyperplane) human actions properly.

This paper contributes to the computational modeling community by developing supervised and unsupervised machine learning models to predict human actions in complex search and retrieve environments. These models can be deployed in physical robots to mimic human strategies and decision-making skills in an on-ground military operation.

Although the machine learning models have produced promising results that can be translated to real world implementations, however, there are few limitations of our research. Being a lab-based simulated study, the data collection was done on computer systems using simulated games and not in real arenas. However, the simulation was developed using a professional game development engine, Unity 3D [18] to give immersive and real-world experience to the participants. All the recruited participants were students at the Indian Institute of Technology Mandi with no real experience of search-and-retrieve missions. To overcome this limitation, we provided a 15-min training session of the game to participants to make them accustomed to the simulated environment.

Numerous ideas can be taken forward as future scope of this research. First, computational cognitive models such as instance-based learning [23] can be developed to account for human actions in complex search-and-retrieve environments. Second, an ensemble of cognitive and machine learning model can be developed to combine the best of both the world and account human actions such scenarios. Also, these models can be used as a second agent to understand how humans perform as a team with machines [24] in high demand cognitive tasks such as search-and-retrieve scenarios.

References

1. Fong, R.C., Scheirer, W.J., Cox, D.D.: Using human brain activity to guide machine learning. Sci. Rep. **8**, 1–10 (2018)
2. Vrigkas, M., Nikou, C., Kakadiaris, I.A.: A review of human activity recognition methods. Front. Robot. AI **2**, 28 (2015)
3. Quinlan, J.R.: Learning decision tree classifiers. ACM Comput. Surv. **28**(1), 71–72 (1996)
4. Pal, M.: Random forest classifier for remote sensing classification. Int. J. Remote Sens. **26**(1), 217–222 (2005)
5. Lau, K., Wu, Q.: Online training of support vector classifier. Pattern Recognit. **36**(8), 1913–1920 (2003)
6. Rosenblatt, F.: The perceptron: a probabilistic model for information storage and organization in the brain. Psychol. Rev. **65**(6), 386 (1958)
7. Keller, J.M., Gray, M.R., Givens, J.A.: A fuzzy k-nearest neighbor algorithm. IEEE Trans. Syst. Man Cybern. **4**, 580–585 (1985)
8. Fan, L., Wang, Z., Wang, H.: Human activity recognition model based on decision tree. In: 2013 International Conference on Advanced Cloud and Big Data, pp. 64–68. IEEE (2013)
9. Chathuramali, K.M., Rodrigo, R.: Faster human activity recognition with SVM. In: International Conference on Advances in ICT for Emerging Regions (ICTer2012), pp. 197–203. IEEE (2012)
10. Vohra, I., Uttrani, S., Rao, A.K., Dutt, V.: Evaluating the efficacy of different neural network deep reinforcement algorithms in complex search-and-retrieve virtual simulations. In: Garg, D., Jagannathan, S., Gupta, A., Garg, L., Gupta, S. (eds.) Advanced Computing (IACC 2021). CCIS, vol. 1528, pp. 348–361. Springer, Cham (2022). https://doi.org/10.1007/978-3-030-95502-1_27
11. Hester, T., et al.: Deep q-learning from demonstrations. In: Proceedings of the AAAI Conference on Artificial Intelligence, vol. 32, no. 1 (2018)
12. Mnih, V., et al.: Playing Atari with deep reinforcement learning. arXiv preprint arXiv:1312.5602 (2013)
13. Haarnoja, T., et al.: Soft actor-critic algorithms and applications. arXiv preprint arXiv:1812.05905 (2018)
14. Berner, C., et al.: Dota 2 with large scale deep reinforcement learning. arXiv preprint arXiv:1912.06680 (2019)
15. Serafim, P.B.S., Nogueira, Y.L.B., Vidal, C., Cavalcante-Neto, J.: On the development of an autonomous agent for a 3D first-person shooter game using deep reinforcement learning. In: 2017 16th Brazilian Symposium on Computer Games and Digital Entertainment (SBGames), pp. 155–163. IEEE (2017)
16. Anderson, J.R., Matessa, M., Lebiere, C.: ACT-R: a theory of higher level cognition and its relation to visual attention. Hum.-Comput. Interact. **12**(4), 439–462 (1997)
17. Stevens, C., Fisher, C.R., Morris, M.B.: Toward modeling pilot workload in a cognitive architecture. In: 85th International Symposium on Aviation Psychology, p. 293 (2021)
18. Xie, J.: Research on key technologies base Unity3D game engine. In: 2012 7th International Conference on Computer Science and Education (ICCSE), pp. 695–699. IEEE (2012)

19. Abdi, H., Williams, L.J.: Principal component analysis. Wiley Interdiscip. Rev. Comput. Stat. **2**(4), 433–459 (2010)
20. Grabmeier, J.L., Lambe, L.A.: Decision trees for binary classification variables grow equally with the Gini impurity measure and Pearson's chi-square test. Int. J. Bus. Intell. Data Min. **2**(2), 213–226 (2007)
21. Van Ooyen, A., Nienhuis, B.: Improving the convergence of the back-propagation algorithm. Neural Netw. **5**(3), 465–471 (1992)
22. Liashchynskyi, P., Liashchynskyi, P.: Grid search, random search, genetic algorithm: a big comparison for NAS. arXiv preprint arXiv:1912.06059 (2019)
23. Gonzalez, C., Dutt, V.: Instance-based learning: Integrating sampling and repeated decisions from experience. Psychol. Rev. **118**(4), 523–551 (2011)
24. Lyons, J.B., Wynne, K.T., Mahoney, S., Roebke, M.A.: Trust and human-machine teaming: a qualitative study. In: Artificial Intelligence for the Internet of Everything, pp. 101–116. Academic Press (2019)

Virtual Reality and Artificial Intelligence in e-Commerce

Grzegorz Chodak[1]([⊠]) [iD] and Edyta Ropuszyńska-Surma[2] [iD]

[1] Department of Operational Research and Business Intelligence, Wroclaw University of Science and Technology, Wybrzeże Wyspiańskiego 27, 50-370 Wroclaw, Poland
grzegorz.chodak@pwr.edu.pl
[2] Department of Management Systems and Organizational Development, Wroclaw University of Science and Technology, Wybrzeże Wyspiańskiego 27, 50-370 Wroclaw, Poland

Abstract. Virtual reality (VR) applied in e-commerce is undoubtedly the technology of the future, but it also brings with it many challenges and risks. The first part of the paper presents state of art concerning application of VR in e-commerce. Among others we showed the typology of VR devices as well as discussed models which were used to evaluate the potential v-commerce proliferation. In the next part of the paper we presented main advantages and threats which may be met in v-commerce (e-commerce with virtual reality). We also highlight the potential application of Artificial Intelligence techniques in v-commerce to better analyze customer behavior patterns. In the next part of the paper we present results of survey research which presents customers attitude to v-commerce, considering the advantages and disadvantages, which they believe are the most significant.

Keywords: Virtual Reality · V-Commerce · Artificial Intelligence · E-commerce

1 Introduction

Virtual reality was widely popularized by Oculus in recent decade. The previous attempts to supply satisfactory level of immersion was only partially successful. Developed by Palmer Luckey and his team Oculus Rift gained considerable publicity and then a major investor - Mark Zukenberg, who invested about 2 bln $ in this project [7].

Virtual reality has great potential in many aspects of our life, however in this paper we will concentrate only on e-commerce aspects. As usual, when a new technology is implemented and becomes more and more popular, many questions arise as to whether it is safe, whether it carries any risks that may not be apparent at first. Especially when a new technology seems to be very attractive to use (and this is the case with virtual reality), the analysis of such risks is extremely important. Using e-commerce, artificial intelligence techniques combined with virtual reality make it possible to manipulate consumer behavior and purchasing decisions. Therefore, the aim of this article is to analyze not only the advantages but also the risks of using virtual reality and artificial intelligence in e-commerce. The second purpose of the paper is to analyze customers attitude to virtual commerce. As a research tool, the literature analysis as well as surveys,

D. Garg et al. (Eds.): IACC 2022, CCIS 1782, pp. 328–340, 2023.
https://doi.org/10.1007/978-3-031-35644-5_26

which were conducted by CAWI (Computer Aided Web Interviewing) method was applied.

In the following text we will use v-commerce (virtual commerce) term, which refers to the buying and selling of goods and services with using virtual and augmented reality technology [10]. V-commerce requires the use of specialized tools for the customer's perception of virtual reality, which will be listed later in the article. We will also use v-shop term which is defined as internet shop in which customers can use virtual reality staff to do shopping.

The structure of this paper is the following. In the first part we present short literature review with selected areas concerning VR and V-commerce. Then we present the main advantages and threats of v-commerce. Then we shortly discuss connection of Virtual Reality and artificial intelligence techniques in e-commerce context. The next part of this paper presents results of survey research. A brief summary is provided at the end of the paper.

2 State of Art

Application of VR in e-commerce was analyzed in the previous decades in many aspects. In doing a brief literature review for this publication, we used Google Scholar databases and keywords: v-commerce, virtual reality in e-commerce. Most papers concern technical issues as hardware and software, however there are also other areas which analyze the social context [19]. The shopping in reality takes place in social environment therefore an electronic commerce in virtual reality application should take into consideration such aspects from the social context, as trust which is one of the most important social aspects of shopping [6, 15].

Comparing to traditional e-commerce, virtual marketplaces have advanced features such as stereoscopic 3D visualization, immersion and multisensory feedback [21].

Billewar et al., [2] presented how virtual reality and augmented reality can provide more enhanced product information in 3D e-commerce environment. The e-store in virtual reality experience can be also improved by an AR (augmented reality) assistant who supports the customers by providing them all needed information concerning the products in offer.

The typology of VR devices by Meißner, Pfeiffer, Pfeiffer [18] categorizes them by their human–machine interfaces: 1) computer monitors; 2) powerwalls – huge, ultra-high resolution screens, 3) smartphones connected to virtual reality headsets, such as the Samsung Gear VR; 4) HMDs (Head-Mounted Displays), for example: the Oculus Rift or HTC Vive; (5) immersive cubes as CAVE [1]. This typology can be enhanced by the content that can be displayed by very realistic and high resolution images and video presented in 360° or 3D (three-dimensional) representations [16]. Martínez-Navarro et al. [16] analyzed also the efficiency of different VR formats as well as devices in a virtual shop environment.

In the literature there are some studies of differences between virtual and traditional physical commerce. The presented comparisons between these two shopping models show that attitudinal measurements of cognition and intention are comparable [17].

Luna-Nevarez, C., & McGovern [14] provide an abstract framework, which enables recognizing the antecedents and consequences of client attitudes toward v-commerce.

This framework enhances the TAM (technology acceptance model) by incorporating immersion, enjoyment, trust and virtual reality self-efficacy as the potential antecedents. Subsequently they analyzed clients' intention to purchase, as well as intention to visit the online shop, and also customers' intention to recommend v-commerce to other customers as potential consequences.

Peukert et al. [20] developed and experimentally validated a theoretical model, that enlightens the influence of immersion into adoption of v-commerce. They discovered that immersion does not influence the users' intention to use again the virtual shopping environment, since extremely immersive shopping environments positively impact on a hedonic path through telepresence. However they negatively impact on a utilitarian path through familiarization with products. In our opinion the last result of Peukert et al. [20] is very disputable and need to be wider investigated.

Summarizing the literature analysis, it can be concluded that a significant part of the considerations are related to hardware issues, while there are still few analyses on the use of virtual reality in e-commerce.

3   V-commerce – Development, Advantages and Threats

3.1   Perspectives for V-commerce

The popularity of v-commerce will increase with the number of devices that allow the use of virtual reality such as VR goggles. Ownership of such equipment is a barrier to consumers and therefore limits the number of potential consumers of an e-store providing v-commerce. This raises the question of how large a percentage of consumers need to own VR devices in order for it to be worthwhile for e-stores to invest in software and other resources to enable VR shopping. The number of statistics in Internet concerning v-commerce is not large yet, however on the webpage [12] authors gathered some. One of them shows that the number of worldwide consumers who are interested in using VR to do shopping increased from 17% in 2021 to 19% in 2022 [8]. Another data show that Virtual Reality in Retail Market reach value of over 5 Bln US $ by 2028, whereas in 2021 it was less than 2 Bln US $ [11]. On the other hand, one can ask how large a percentage of shops must offer v-commerce in order for customers to be willing to invest in VR hardware just because of shopping in VR. These are interesting research questions for much wider research, however in our surveys we concentrated on the opinions of customers concerning v-commerce and customers fear of being manipulated in a virtual environment of v-commerce.

3.2   Selected Advantages of v-commerce

The main advantage of v-commerce is real time interaction with products, the ability to view them in a realistic way There are some additional gains of v-commerce like:

– ability to present products in their typical environment, for example costumer can see the furniture or decor presented in v-shop in his own room or try on a tennis outfit while on the tennis court (e.g. model of Arthur Ashe Stadium);

- the opportunity to see a product that is geographically far away. This advantage is particularly important in the travel industry when selling tours abroad. The customer can, using VR googles, view the hotel and the place where he or she intends to go on holiday or on a business trip.
- possibility to "face to face" talk with shop assistant or people hired by v-shop to present products. Using deepfake technique, which enables that a person in an existing image or video is replaced with someone else's likeness [5, 9], the avatar of shop assistant in v-shop can look and talk as well-known celebrity like movie or sports star (e.g. Roger Federer in tennis v-shop).
- V-commerce also represents an opportunity for people with disabilities. Virtual reality can allow them to forget about their problems such as physically moving around in a shop.
- with additional equipment as VR-gloves or VR suits there is possibility to touch products and feel interaction with customer body. Such facilities remove one of the biggest downsides of e-commerce - the inability to touch the products being bought.

3.3 Selected Threats of v-commerce

Despite the existence of the many advantages of v-commerce and the great visual appeal of this technology, it is important to be aware of the many risks it brings. Below we present a selection of the risks and issues facing v-commerce:

- some VR customers may experience side effect termed as motion sickness as nauseated feeling, vomiting, dizziness, headache and others. Some authors claim that motion sickness may limits the VR community in the full proliferation and adaptation of this immersive technology [3].
- being in a virtual world can lead to addiction and, in the case of shopping, to VR shopaholism. The control of time flow is very weak in VR, therefore customers may spend a lot of time in v-shops without being aware of how much time they spent there. This may be dangerous especially for children and youths.
- V-shopping may lead to an increase in unjustified expenditure due to less control over one's behavior in a virtual environment. Aforementioned deepfake technology applied in v-shop may provide an increase of money spending due to an extremely persuasive salesman, who may be the avatar of a well-known celebrity. We can hypothesize that the more immersive the environment of v-shop is created, the less control the consumer will have over their purchasing decisions. In extreme cases, the consumer may lose control of his or her decisions completely and only a restriction on the credit card will put a barrier to further purchase.
- V-commerce may enable to collect the data about customer. Some of the data can be gathered by the software which records all activities done by a customer as all kind of movement in the v-shop. Also the voice of customer can be recorded and analyzed. In the next paragraph some other possible ways of gathering data about customer are mentioned.

4 Connection of Virtual Reality and Artificial Intelligence Techniques

It seems extremely interesting to combine virtual reality with artificial intelligence techniques, allowing a better understanding of the customer's preferences, depending on their behavior in the shop. It should be noted that the amount of metadata that can be analyzed for a customer using VR goggles and additional VR devices is much greater than for traditional e-commerce. It is possible to track eyeballs using VR goggles. For example the HTC VIVE Pro Eye with built-in Tobii eye tracking is available on the market at the webpage https://www.tobiipro.com/fields-of-use/immersive-vr-research/. Eye tracking supplies huge amount of data, which should be analyzed with AI techniques to obtain customer behavioral patterns. Also the additional staff like VR gloves and VR suits (e.g. Teslasuit) allow a large amount of additional data on consumer behavior to be collected.

As early as 2000, Luck & Aylett wrote about applying artificial intelligence in VR describing the environments providing knowledge to lead or help the customer rather than relying completely on the customer's knowledge and expertise [13]. Such solutions we will probably meet in v-shops in which shop assistants will be replaced by intelligent avatars able to advise customers on the basis of all their data and metadata.

Artificial intelligence is widely used in e-commerce processes [4], however virtual reality opens new application possibilities for AI techniques. The steering of avatars and the creation of a virtual environment in which the consumer moves in the v-store offer extensive opportunities of AI appliance.

5 Research

5.1 Research Methodology

In order to determine the attitude of online shoppers towards v-commerce, a survey was conducted among customers of online shops. The research was conducted electronically with Google Forms tool, using CAWI methodology. The data was collected according to the snowball method. The respondents received a link to the questionnaire by Facebook, LinkedIn and other social media platforms. Respondents shared the link to the survey on their social networks.

The survey was conducted from 4th August to 7th September 2022. In this paper we present the results of survey research concerning applying virtual reality in e-commerce. The main aim of our study was focused on collecting basic opinions of the users of e-commerce on applying the VR (e.g. VR goggles) during e-shopping. The questionnaire contained basic information about the respondents such as their age, sex, education, place of residence, and their status on the labor market. The following questions were related to their behavior and attitudes as e-consumers. The final part of the survey was dedicated to applying VR in e-commerce and its advantages and disadvantages in e-commerce. Our study is the first step of deeper and wider research which we are going to carry out in the future. Therefore, we would like to know the general opinion on VR among this consumer group. This research process will allow us to formulate hypotheses for subsequent studies.

5.2 Characteristics of Research Sample

The questionnaire was fully completed by 110 respondents. There were no surveys that we had to reject (uncompleted etc.). The structure of the sample according to demographic criteria is presented on Fig. 1 (the sex of respondents), Fig. 2 (the status on a labor market of respondents), Fig. 3 (the education level of respondents), Fig. 4 (the age of respondents), Fig. 5 (the residence of respondents).

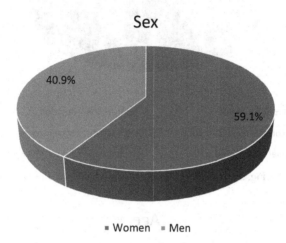

Fig. 1. The sample structure according to the respondents' sex

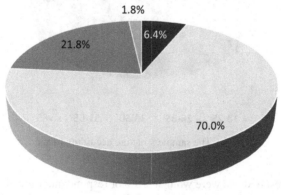

Fig. 2. The sample structure according to the status on the labor market

Education

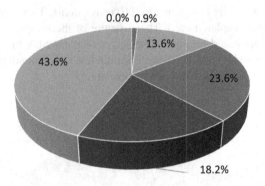

- Primary education
- Secondary technical education
- higher technical education
- Professional education
- Non-technical secondary education
- higher non-technical education

Fig. 3. The sample structure according to education

Age

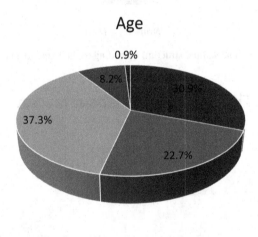

- 18-25 ■ 26-35 ■ 36-50 ■ 51-65 ■ >65

Fig. 4. The sample structure according to age

Most of the respondents were women. 70% of respondents were employed (Fig. 2). The pupils and students constituted 22% of the survey sample (Fig. 2). The majority of the respondents has non-technical education (less than 44% of the respondents had higher and almost 24% - on the secondary level). Almost 22% of the sample were respondents with secondary or technical education. The largest group of respondents were 36–50 years old. The second largest group were young people who were either

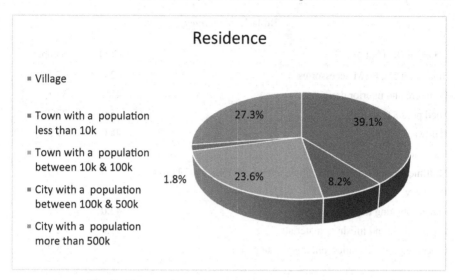

Fig. 5. The sample structure according to place of residence

pupils or students (almost 31%). More than 66% of the survey population lives in a village or city of 10,000 to 100,000 inhabitants.

5.3 Results of Research and Discussion

Considering the percentage of consumers buying selected goods according to our studies compared to the data provided by the Report Gemius [22] (the most comprehensive and representative report on e-commerce in Poland) (Table1) we can point out strong similarities. Alike percentages in many categories indicate the representativeness of the survey sample.

Table 1. The comparison between the percentage of e-consumers buying selected goods online in Poland according to the Report Gemius and our research sample [%]

Criterion (Kind of good)	CSO	Sample
Clothes and footwear	79.0	75.5
Cosmetics	65.0	51.8
Books, records, films	57.0	60.0
Consumer electronics and household appliances	52.0	54.5
Pharmaceuticals	55.0	39.1
Children's goods, toys	44.0	40.0

(continued)

Table 1. (*continued*)

Criterion (Kind of good)	CSO	Sample
Smartphoness, GSM accessories	42.0	42.7
Furniture and interior design	41.0	37.3
Food products	45.0	22.7
Hardware	34.0	17.3
Insurance	37.0	44.5
Multimedia, software/games, applications, e-books, audiobooks	36.0	29.9
Jewellery	34.0	45.5
Travel (booking trips, hotels, etc.)	43.0	8.2
Constructing and finishing materials	27.0	62.7
Others (e.g. numismatics, philately, bike parts)		2.7

The respondents in our research buy mainly 3 types of goods online: clothes and footwear (75.5%), constructing and finishing materials (62.7%), books, records and films (60%). More than half of the respondents buy consumer electronics and household appliances on the Internet. Almost 23% buy food products. Consumers buy mainly durable goods online. Therefore it is not be surprising that most respondents shop several times per month on the Internet (59 people). Over 22 people were the most active purchasers – they shop more than once a week. A similar number of people admitted they generally like and dislike buying online approximately 43 respondents.

Taking into consideration the aim of this paper, we focus on the advantages and disadvantages of using the VR appliances when shopping. The control question of the survey was if the respondents have VR goggles. Only two people living in a city with population more than half million with technical background have VR goggles. This fact suggests that the respondents' opinions are declarative and that they do not have experience using VR-commerce. The small percentage of respondents owning VR goggles was not surprising given the still low popularity of such devices, as well as their relatively high price.

The next question was 'If you had VR goggles and shops allowed you to make purchases using such goggles, would you shop online using them?'. The respondents could choose one from five options (always; often; sometimes; not likely; definitely no). Answers 'not likely' or 'definitely no' were chosen by 43 people. Therefore, it can be assumed that the willingness to use the VR-commers equals 60.9%. Almost 40% were more critical, but only 2 respondents had a strongly negative attitude.

The next two questions should be analyzed together. They were related to the advantages (Fig. 6) and disadvantages (Fig. 7) of using VR tools such as VR-goggle and VR-gloves. They were multiple choice questions and semi-open one.

Fig. 6. The percentage of the respondents' answers to the question: 'What do you see as the advantages and benefits of shopping online in virtual reality using VR tools (goggles, VR gloves)?'

According to the respondents, seeing a product in three dimensions (60% of the respondents) is one of the main advantages of using VR tools when they do online shopping. More than 50% of the sample chose the possibility of seeing the product in its original environment. It is not surprising since the respondents pointed out that they buy constructing and finishing materials (62.7%) as well as furniture and interior design products (37.3%). Considering that more than 75% respondents declared buying clothes and footwear, the fact that only 32% of them indicated as advantage of v-commerce the ability to touch the product is more than surprising. 20% of the respondents does not see the pros and cons of VR shopping, which is another aspect worth considering in the future, showing that the awareness of these consumers in the field of v-commerce is low.

The majority of the respondents fear surveillance and gathering information about them (almost 40%). They are afraid of manipulation (37.3%) and spending too much time on shopping.

Before conducting this research we expected that people are afraid of being manipulated. The last question in the questionnaire addressed this issue. The question was: 'Are you concerned that you would be more susceptible to manipulation by artificial

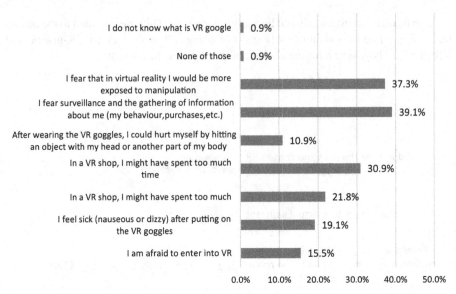

Fig. 7. The percentage of respondents answers to the question: 'What do you see as the downsides and risks of shopping online in virtual reality simply using VR tools (goggles, VR gloves)?'

intelligence (AI) software used in online shops when shopping in VR?' The structure of the answer is presented in Fig. 8.

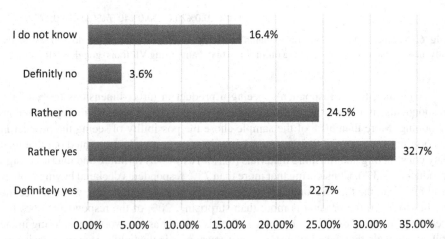

Fig. 8. The percentage of respondents considering that the AI in VR-shopping poses a threat of manipulation

The received feedback confirms that 55% of the respondents are afraid of higher level of manipulation in VR-shops than in traditional ones. This result is in line with our expectations, as the possibilities for manipulating the consumer using artificial intelligence techniques in a virtual environment are considerable.

6 Summary

Virtual reality commerce is in the initial stage, though with great potential of growth in the following years. The respondents still have no experience with using VR-commerce. However are interested in the use of the VR google in the future. It shows that the potential market of VR-commerce could develop in the upcoming years.

While the development of the v-commerce market offers consumers many benefits, it also carries a number of risks and threats. Identifying these risks is important for consumer safety.

The greatest benefit of online shopping supported by VR-tools is seeing a product in three dimensions as well as the possibility to see the product in its original environment. Also the ability of touching the product with tools as VR gloves was indicated by almost one third of respondents. But we need more extensive research in this area to verify for which consumer segments this aspects is the most important and what the consumers' profiles are.

Similar research question should be asked about the risk. The collection of data about the users and the threat of manipulation are seen as the biggest risks of shopping in an VR environment, especially when the trader may use sophisticated artificial intelligence tools. Customers are also afraid of gathering information about them by the v-commerce software. In this situation the education of people in this area and new social competences could be especially helpful.

The future directions of research in v-commerce domain will include analyzes of environments of real v-stores, which will hopefully be created in the coming years, giving consumers the opportunity to immerse themselves in virtual reality shopping.

Acknowledgements. This work was partially supported by the National Science Centre (NCN) in Poland under grant number: 2018/29/B/HS4/02857 (Logistics, Trade and Consumer Decisions in the Age of the Internet).

References

1. Bigne, E., Llinares, C., Torrecilla, C.: Elapsed time on first buying triggers brand choices within a category: a virtual reality-based study. J. Bus. Res. **69**(4), 1423–1427 (2016). https://doi.org/10.1016/j.jbusres.2015.10.119
2. Billewar, S.R., Jadhav, K., Sriram, V.P., Arun, A., Abdul, S.M., Gulati, K., Bhasin, N.K.K.: The rise of 3D E-Commerce: the online shopping gets real with virtual reality and augmented reality during COVID-19. World J. Eng. (2021). https://doi.org/10.1108/WJE-06-2021-0338
3. Chattha, U.A., Janjua, U.I., Anwar, F., Madni, T.M., Cheema, M.F., Janjua, S.I.: Motion sickness in virtual reality: an empirical evaluation. IEEE Access **8**, 130486–130499 (2020)
4. Chodak, G., Chawla, Y.: Artificial Intelligence in Online Stores' Processes. In: Garg, D., Jagannathan, S., Gupta, A., Garg, L., Gupta, S. (eds.) Advanced Computing, Communications in Computer and Information Science, IACC 2021, vol. 1528, pp. 214–228. Springer, Cham (2022). https://doi.org/10.1007/978-3-030-95502-1_17
5. Drobyshev, N., Chelishev, J., Khakhulin, T., Ivakhnenko, A., Lempitsky, V., Zakharov, E.: MegaPortraits: One-shot Megapixel Neural Head Avatars. arXiv preprint arXiv:2207.07621. (2022)

6. Fang, H., Zhang, J., Şensoy, M., Magnenat-Thalmann, N.: Reputation mechanism for e-commerce in virtual reality environments. Electron. Commer. Res. Appl. **13**(6), 409–422 (2014)

7. Harris, B.,J.: The history of the future: oculus, facebook, and the revolution that swept virtual reality, Dey Street Books (2019)

8. https://business.yougov.com/content/42775-global-appetite-vr-activities-falling-around-world. Accessed 14 Sept 2022

9. https://en.wikipedia.org/wiki/Deepfake. Accessed 09 Sept 2022

10. https://rechargepayments.com/glossary/v-commerce/. Accessed 06 Sept 2022

11. https://www.prnewswire.com/in/news-releases/virtual-reality-in-retail-market-to-reach-usd-5455-million-by-2028-at-a-cagr-of-13-82-valuates-reports-829447207.html. Accessed 14 Sept 2022

12. https://www.stylight.com/insights/news/50-v-commerce-statistics-you-need-to-know/. Accessed 14 Sept 2022

13. Luck, M., Aylett, R.: Applying artificial intelligence to virtual reality: intelligent virtual environments. Appl. Artif. Intell. **14**(1), 3–32 (2000). https://doi.org/10.1080/088395100117142

14. Luna-Nevarez, C., McGovern, E.: The rise of the virtual reality (VR) marketplace: exploring the antecedents and consequences of consumer attitudes toward V-commerce. J. Internet Commer. **20**(2), 167–194 (2021). https://doi.org/10.1080/15332861.2021.1875766

15. Maamar, Z.: Commerce, e-commerce, and m-commerce: what comes next? Commun. ACM **46**(12), 251–257 (2003). https://doi.org/10.1145/953460.953508

16. Martínez-Navarro, J., Bigné, E., Guixeres, J., Alcañiz, M., Torrecilla, C.: The influence of virtual reality in e-commerce. J. Bus. Res. **100**, 475–482 (2019)

17. Massara, F., Liu, S.S., Melara, R.D.: Adapting to a retail environment: modeling consumer–environment interactions. J. Bus. Res. **63**(7), 673–681 (2010). https://doi.org/10.1016/j.jbusres.2009.05.004

18. Meißner, M., Pfeiffer, J., Pfeiffer, T., Oppewal, H.: Combining virtual reality and mobile eye tracking to provide a naturalistic experimental environment for shopper research. J. Bus. Res. **100**, 445–458 (2019)

19. Papadopoulou, P.: Applying virtual reality for trust-building e-commerce environments. Virtual Reality **11**(2), 107–127 (2007). https://doi.org/10.1007/s10055-006-0059-x

20. Peukert, C., Pfeiffer, J., Meißner, M., Pfeiffer, T., Weinhardt, C.: Shopping in virtual reality stores: the influence of immersion on system adoption. J. Manag. Inf. Syst. **36**(3), 755–788 (2019). https://doi.org/10.1080/07421222.2019.1628889

21. Price, S., Jewitt, C., Brown, B.: The Sage handbook of digital technology research. Sage (2013)

22. Report Gemius. https://www.gemius.pl/wszystkie-artykuly-aktualnosci/raport-e-commerce-2022-juz-dostepny.html. Accessed 10 Oct 2022

Critical Review on Machine Reading Comprehension (MRC) Developments: From High Resource to Low Resource Languages

Bechoo Lal[✉] , G. Shivakanth , Arun Bhaskar , M. Bhaskar , Ashish, and Deepak Kumar Panda

Department of CSE, Koneru Lakshmaiah Education Foundation (KLEF), KL Deemed University, Vaddeswaram, AP, India
bechoolal@kluniversity.in

Abstract. In Natural Language Processing (NLP), the significant role of Machine Reading Comprehension (MRC) is introduced the different dimension of task by asking the machine to asking a question on given context. This is one of the revolutionize way of thinking by the human and machine interactions with each other's. The MRC technique can directly return the correct answer to the questions which are posed by the human in a natural language manner. The MRC system can read taking support s from the documents and provide users with high quality communication services. In this research paper the researcher trying to review different phases of machine learning comprehension model (MRC) to analyze that critical thinking by the human and machine interactions are with each other's or not. The researcher focused on the different published and unpublished research articles from the different research portal and summarizes a review report based on MRC and its predictive model with high accuracy. The machine reading comprehension (MRC) is the advance technological approach based on machine learning approach to communicate to the real word and solve specific problem that are unaware of the technology and subject issues in the real world.

Keywords: MRC · Machine Learning · NLP

1 Introduction

Machine Reading Comprehension (MRC) is a challenging research field to teach machines and comprehend into high resource to low resource languages. It is based on natural language process (NLP) which is having a wide area research field to understand and answer the questions using unstructured text datasets (Liu et.al., (2020)). There are different level of reading comprehension using literal meaning, inferential meaning and finally evaluating the meaning [2]. Machine Learning Comprehension (MRC) is divided into four category (Fig. 1 and Table 1).

© Springer Nature Switzerland AG 2023
D. Garg et al. (Eds.): IACC 2022, CCIS 1782, pp. 341–352, 2023.
https://doi.org/10.1007/978-3-031-35644-5_27

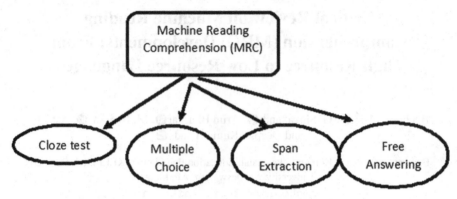

Fig. 1. Categories of Machine Learning Comprehensive (MRC)

Table 1. Description of Categories of Machine Learning Comprehensive (MRC)

MRC Categories	Description
Cloze Test	Provides emperical evidence of how easy text to read and understand for aspecific audience and mesure reading comprehension and not justify the reading score
Multiple Choice	Multiple choice MRC provides task due to conveience of evaluation and flexibility of the answer format
Span Extraction	Predicting a span in a documents that grounds an agent turn and generating an agent response based a dialog and grouding documents
Free Answering	Search free answering machine message ringtone on Zedge and personalie your phone to suit you

2   Background of the Research Study

The categoris of the Machine Reading Comprehesion (MRC) task is having a signfi-
cant contribution towards A survey of MRC Developments: from high resource to low
resource languages and limitations with rspect to constructions, understatning, flexibility,
evaluation and applications [3]. In each dimension the Machine Reading Comprehension can score then a ranming manners. In analysis way high score shows the significant
contribution and least score defines the worst performance of the reading and understanding habits. In case of similar score it is very hard to judge which one is better in
the dimension [4] (Fig. 2 and Table 2).

2.1   For Each Category Such as Cloze Style, Free Form, MCQs Provide Examples

The researcher stated that Cloze testing requires a process to understand the context and
vocabulary to be able to identify the correct words for deleted parts of text. Example: A
language interpreter may give learners the following piece: "Today, I went somewhere

Table 2. Description of MRC Dimension

MRC-Dimension	Description
Construction	It define the dimension measures and construct dataset for the tasks
Understanding	This dimension evaluates how well the task can test the machine
Flexibility	The flexibility of the answer can measure the quality of the task
Evaluation	It is a necessary part of MRC tasks to determine its quality and evaluates get high score in the dimension
Application	It is supposed to be close to real world application

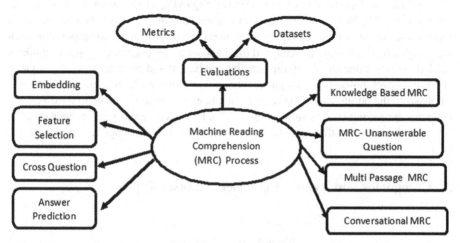

Fig. 2. Machine Reading Comprehension Process

to buy bread and peanut butter. Explain the differences between geometric shapes and free forms. Give examples one by one., powder, cloud Multiple choice question type questions/research questions asked by responders Provides many options for answers [8].

2.2 Sources of Corpus like Wikipedia, News Articles

The researcher stated that a description of a corpus or collection of texts of a particular type or subject for MRC developments: from high resource to low resource languages. An example of a corpus is a dead animal. A corpus example is a set of examples of ten sentences of the same word. The total length of the violin. One of the first requirements for natural language processing (NLP) activities is corpus. In languages and NLP, corpus (literally Latin means body) refers to a collection of texts. Such collections may be multilingual or may be multilingual - there are many reasons why a multilingual corpus (corpus plural) can be useful. Corpora may also have thematic texts (historical, biblical, etc.) [8]. Corpus is often used only to analyze language statistics and to test the hypothesis. A corpus is a collection of basic computer archive documents that can be used to obtain information about a language that may not have been fully understood by the individual [9].

There are many different types of corpus forMRC developments: from high resource to low resource languages. They may contain written or spoken language (written), modern or old texts, monolingual or minority texts. Texts can be complete books, newspapers, journals, lectures, etc., or contain quotations of various lengths. In this context the good thing is that the internet is full of text, and in most cases this text is well-organized and well-organized, even if you need to immerse yourself in a workable, well-defined format. Wikipedia is a rich source of well-organized text data. It is also a vast collection of information, and the unaffected mind can dream of all sorts of uses of such a text body [10].

The Stanford Question Answering Dataset (SQuAD), a new comprehensive data set that includes 100,000 + questions asked by many staff members in a Wikipedia article set, in which the answer to each question is a text segment from the corresponding reading paragraph. The researcher analyzed the database to understand the types of thinking needed to answer questions, relying heavily on adjacent and circular trees for designing and MRC developments: from high resource to low resource languages. The researcher emphasized the building a robust regression model, reaching F1 points of 51.0%, a significant improvement over a simple base (20%). However, human performance (86.8%) is very high, indicating that the database presents a positive challenge for future research [13].

3   Categories and Types of Datasets Dataset Types

Table 3. Types of Datasets

Dataset Type	Characteristics	Example
File	a single file	AutoCAD DXF
Folder	a set of files in a single folder	Esri Shapefile
Database	a database	Oracle Spatial
Web	an Internet site	Web Feature Service (WFS)

The above tabular data are showing the datatypes of datasets which can be used in MRC: machine reading comprehension. The data are generally categorized into file, folder, databases and web datasets which played a significant role for the Machine Reading Comprehension (MRC) (Table 3).

The below Venn-diagram represent the general phases of machine reading comprehension(MRC), the researcher emphasized that how MRC can handle the questions and answering as possible assumptions. It is specified that only one thing: how Question and Answering and Machine Reading Comprehension are linked [3].

The researcher given a fundamental approach on QA and MRC which are two different things but, sometimes, they converge. Just to resume the image:, MRC tasks are a group of tasks which to solve them you need the ability to read some text, QA tasks are a group of tasks which to solve them you must answer a question, QA tasks can be solved in different ways, as we saw before (Retriever Generator, Retriever Extractor, Generator, and other) [13, 14]. Sometimes a QA task is solved with a MRC technique, this is the reason for the convergence. Retriever Extractor and retriever Generator, for example, are solutions that fall in this case because they required the ability to read a text. Instead, the solution that is made up only of the Generator solves a QA problem without requiring this skill (so without using an MRC solution) [10] (Fig. 3).

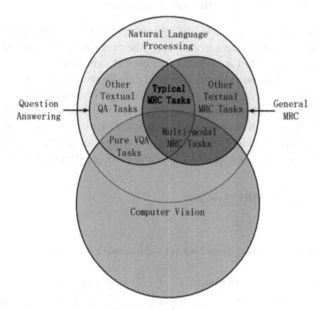

Fig. 3. MRC vs. QA

4   Research Design and Methodology

In research design and methodology, this research article is based on the secondary data which are collected from the different research portal and published and unpublished work on "A survey of MRC Developments: From High Resource to Low Resource Languages". The MRC criteria are characteristics that the prospective subjects must have if they are to be included in the research study. Exclusion criteria are those characteristics that disqualify prospective subjects from inclusion in the study. Inclusion criteria is everything a study must have to be included. Exclusion criteria are the factors that would make a study ineligible to be included [16, 17]. Criteria that should be considered include.

The researcher specifies that the process to select articles with an appropriate study design for the research question. What are the criteria for exclusion from literature review? Exclusion criteria are elements of an article that prevent one study from being included in the literature review [17]. The researcher used all possible phases to design the structural framework of Machine Reading Comprehension (MRC) system and its specification based on the previous research work. The above table specifies the data sources used to search for MRC Systems with details of, Year, Tasks, Corpus Type, Question Type, Answer Source, and Answer Type. These all data are collected from 2013 to 2018 for the machine reading comprehension (MRC) and its controlling operations (Table 3).

4.1 Publications of MRC in Difference Languages

In this segment of research article the researcher specifies publications of MRC in difference languages and structural elements when preparing a report manuscript, the researchers are responsible for including the correct structural elements where appropriate. When enabled, these elements appear in the following order [18]: The researcher specifies the some of the criteria to give the structured form of entire data and its specification for MRC: machine reading comprehension with respect to A survey of MRC Developments: From High Resource to Low Resource Languages. The researcher given the details of writing procedure and rules for title design, main cover pages, heading and subheading, funding sources pages MRC receives and copyright information.

4.2 Existing English MRC Systems

Table 4. Existing Open- Domain and Closed-Domain MRC Systems

Year	Direction		Dimension		Number of steps		
	One direction	Two direction	One dimension	Two dimension	Single	Multi-fixed	Multi-dynamic
2016	89%	11%	78%	22%	89%	22%	0%
2017	58%	42%	10%	90%	83%	12%	5%
2018	51%	49%	21%	83%	76%	22%	2%
2019	12%	89%	2%	98%	44%	56%	4%
2020	23%	77%	18%	82%	55%	46%	0%
All	35%	65%	15%	86%	61%	36%	3%

The above table shows that Open- Domain and Closed-Domain MRC Systems for English Language(Table) with all possible movement of data with respect to direction, dimension and number of steps taken by the MRC: Machine Reading Comprehension on From High Resource to Low Resource Languages (Table 4).

The above table specifies the MRC: machine reading comprehension model structure, its datasets, task specifications and evaluation measure. The model structure of MRC varies in between 50% to 61% from the year 2016 to 2020 to all. The specification usage

Table 5. Existing Open- Domain and Closed-Domain MRC Systems- Model Structure

Year	Model structure	Dataset	Other tasks	Evaluation measure
2016	50%	50%	21%	7%
2017	54%	14%	23%	6%
02018	71%	31%	14%	5%
2019	68%	20%	24%	11%
2020	57%	20%	29%	31%
All	61%	23%	21%	12%

Table 6. Categorization by Type of datasets, language

Dataset	#Gloss	#Videos	#Signers	Type	Sign Language
LSA64 [52]	64	3,200	10	RGB	Argentinian
PSL Kinect 30 [34]	30	300	–	RGB, depth	Polish
PSL ToF [34]	84	1,680	–	RGB, depth	Polish
DEVISIGN [3]	1,000	24,000	8	RGB, depth	Chinese
GSL [24]	20	840	6	RGB	Greek
DSG Kinect [3]	40	3,000	15	RGB, depth	German
LSE-sign [27]	2,400	2,400	2	RGB	Spanish

of datasets for MRC varies from 23% to 50%. The evaluation criteria that measure by the MRC system in between 7% to 31% (Table 5).

The above table showing the specification of categorization by type of datasets, language with different categories of data types including audio and video and color specification. The machine reading comprehension (MRC) is capable to handle different languages interpreter and identify the semantic meaning of that statement, textual data (Table 6).

The above data table showing that categorization of MRC by techniques such as Machine Reading Comprehension (PRC), STTC and OSTBC, and the techniques which are used by this MRC system are known as MRC, 4-state,8 state, 16 state,32 state, Orthogonal and Quasi orthogonal STBC (Table 6).Sanjeev Kumar et al. (2013) specified the some of the operations on MRC system to show that, due to the time-varying nature of radio channels and the availability of limited resources for signal transmission, path loss, delay spreading, Doppler spreading, shadowing and interference, and achieving sufficient data rates are very difficult. [20]. To avoid the effects of multipath fading, a diversity combining mechanism has been introduced in wireless communication systems (Table 7).

Table 7. Categorization of MRC by Techniques

	Technique	BER achieved $= 10^{-2}$
MRC	MRC (Tx = 1, Rx = 2)	5.9 dB
	MRC (Tx = 1, Rx = 2)	1 Db
STTC	4-state	17.8 dB
	8-state	15 dB
	16-state	14.5 dB
	32-state	13.5 dB
OSTBC	Orthogonal STBC	6 dB
	Quasi Orthogonal STBC	11 dB

5 Discussion

In this section the researcher focused on Existing MRC systems for low-resource languages language with respect to type of datasets, techniques and different languages which would be read by MRC system to perform from high resource to low resource languages. Mubarak Alkhatnai et al. (2007) emphasized that machine reading comprehension (MRC) is an important task in natural language understanding and its goal is to teach machines to understand text. Machine comprehension can be accessed through a question-and-answer approach. Studies on Arabic reading comprehension have been limited. This research study provides an overview survey of MRC developments: from high resource to low resource languages. [21].

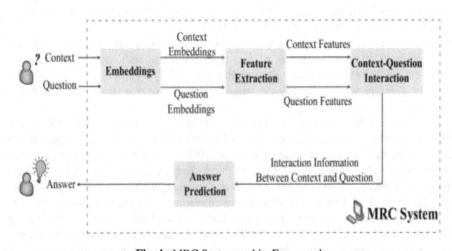

Fig. 4. MRC System and its Framework

The above Fig. 4 shows that MRC system and its framework and its controlling all possible operation behind the system. The MRC system accepted context in the form of embedding questions and send to the feature extraction to select the meaningful data and pass to the context questions interaction to the MRC system for further answering based on the semantics meaning of questions (Fig. 4). Liu et.al., (2019) stated that machine reading comprehension (MRC), which requires a machine to answer questions based on a given context, has attracted increasing attention with the incorporation of various deep learning techniques over the past few years. Although research on MRC based on deep learning is flourishing, there remains a lack of a comprehensive survey summarizing existing approaches and recent trends, which motivated the work presented in this article.

5.1 Rule Based Approaches

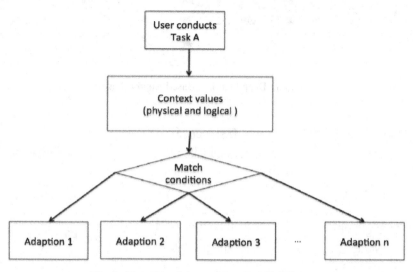

Fig. 5. Rule Based Approaches for MRC System

The above Fig. 5 showing the Rule Based Approaches for MRC System to identify the context value of physical and logical categories of data and passed to the rule-based approach to specify that what would be ethe exact semantic meaning of data.

5.2 Deep Learning Based Approaches

In this research section the researcher specifies the Deep Learning Based Approaches to control the basic operation of data conversion based on artificial neurons. Turing, A. M. (2009). Artificial neural networks (ANNs) are also called connected systems. ANNs are inspired by the brain neural networks of living organisms. ANNs are a framework of different machine learning algorithms that work together to process complex data sets. As shown in Fig. 5, each ANN can be divided into three layers: an input layer, a hidden layer, and an output layer. A hidden layer can have multiple layers. Each layer is a set of nodes called artificial neurons. Each artificial neuron connects with the artificial neuron in the next layer. The connections between these neurons are called the ribs. This edge sends information as a signal from one neuron to another, which then processes the information and passes it on to the next neuron (Fig. 7) (Fig. 6).

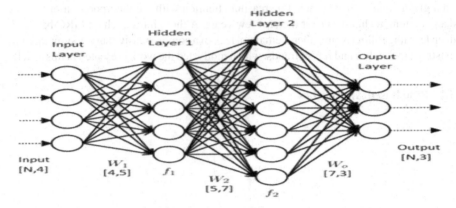

Fig. 6. Deep Learning Based Approaches

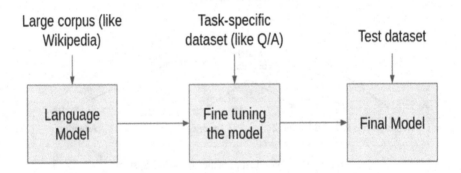

Fig. 7. Pre-Trained Language Modeling

Prakhar Ganesh (2019) specifies the Pre-Trained Language Modeling first receives a large amount of uncommented data (eg full Wikipedia dumps). This allows the model to learn how different words are used and how those languages are usually written. The model is now sent to an NLP job, where a smaller job-specific dataset is provided, which is used to fine-tune and create a final model capable of performing the above operations [19].

6   Summary and Conclusion

Finally the researcher summarized that Machine Reading Comprehension (MRC) is a challenging research field to teach machines and comprehend into high resource to low resource languages. It is based on natural language process (NLP) which is having a wide area research field to understand and answer the questions using unstructured text datasets (Liu et.al., (2020)). There are different level of reading comprehension using literal meaning, inferential meaning and finally evaluating the meaning. However, these word representations are learned in a generalized context and do not represent task specific information. This is where the fine-tuning part of a language model comes into account. Directly using the pretrained embeddings can decrease the overall model size but forces us to only utilize generalized word representations. Pre-Trained Language Modelingfinetuning on the other hand allows the user to fine-tune these word embeddings/representations by training on the task specific dataset.

References

1. Zeng, C., Li, Q., Hu, J.: A survey on gadget studying comprehension—responsibilities. Evaluation metrics and benchmark datasets. Appl. Sci. **10**(21), 7640 (2020). https://doi.org/10.3390/app10217640
2. Baradaran, R., Ghiasi, R., Amirkhani, H.: A survey on machine reading comprehension systems. Nat. Lang. Eng. **28**(6), 683–732 (2022). https://doi.org/10.1017/S1351324921000395
3. Alkhatnai, M., Amjad, H.I., Amjad, M., Gelbukh, A.: Methods and trends of machine reading comprehension in the Arabic language. Computación y Sistemas **24**(4), 1607–1615 (2020). https://doi.org/10.13053/cys-24-four-3878
4. Baradaran, R., Ghiasi, R., Amirkhani, H.: A survey on system studying comprehension systems, laptop and facts era branch. University of Qom, Qom, Iran (2017)
5. Jing, Y., Xiong, D.: Effective techniques for low resource studying comprehension. In: IALP 2020, Kuala Lumpur, 4–6 December (2020)
6. Baradaran, R., Ghiasi, R., Amirkhani, H.: A survey on system analyzing comprehension systems, posted on-on online with the aid of Cambridge college Press 19 January 2022 (2022)
7. Liu, J., Shou, L., Pei, J., Gong, M., Yang, M., Jiang, D.: Move-lingual gadget reading comprehension with language department expertise distillation Junhao. In: Complaints of the Twenty Eighth International Convention on Computational Linguistics, pp. 2710–2721, Barcelona, Spain (online online), 18 December (2020)
8. Hedderich, A., Lange, L., Adel, H., Strötgen, J., Klakow, D.: A survey on latest techniques for herbal language processing in low-aid scenarios Michael. In: Complaints of the 2021 Convention of the North American Chapter of the Association for Computational Linguistics: Human Language Technology, pp. 2545–2568 June 6–11, 2021. Association for Computational Linguistics (2021)
9. Zhou, M., Shujie, N.D., Heung-Yeung, S.: Progress in neural NLP: modeling, mastering, and reasoning engineering, quantity 6, and difficulty 3, pp. 275–290 (2020)
10. Liu, S., Zhang, X., Zhang, S., Wang, H., Zhang, W.: Neural machine reading comprehension: Methods and trends. Appl. Sci. **9**(18), 3698 (2019). https://doi.org/10.3390/app9183698
11. Papineni, K., et al.: Bleu: a method for automatic evaluation of machine translation. In: Proceedings of the 40th Annual Meeting of the Association for Computational Linguistics, pp. 311–318 (2002)
12. Sugawara, S., Kido, Y., Yokono, H., Aizawa, A.: Assessment metrics for system analyzing comprehension: prerequisite competencies and readability. In: Court Cases of the 55th Annual meeting of the Affiliation for Computational Linguistics (quantity 1: long Papers), Vancouver, Canada, pp. 806–817
13. The MRC Writing, booklet and fashion manual, Mekong River fee, pp. 2789–7656 (2021). https://doi.org/10.52107/mrc.qx5yo4. ISSN: 2789–7664

14. Kumar, S., Gupta, P., Chauhan, D.: Overall Performance Comparison of Numerous Diversity Techniques the usage of Matlab Simulation. International Magazine of Records Era and Pc Technology, posted 1 October 2013 (2013). https://doi.org/10.5815/IJITCS.2013.11.06C orpus. Id: 27606440

15. Guzmán, F., et al.: The FLORES assessment datasets for low-resource device translation: Nepali–English and Sinhala–English. EMNLP (2019)

16. Awadalla, H.H.: Bringing low-aid languages and spoken dialects into play with semi-supervised generic neural machine translation. Published may additionally 17 (2018)

17. Karczewski, J.: How gadget gaining knowledge of models can outperform rule totally based structures, defined. MRC | service provider hazard Council through | gadget getting to know engineer | nethone, may additionally 06 (2021)

18. Turing, A.M. : Computing equipment and intelligence. In: Parsing the Turing Test, pp. 23–65. Springer, Dordrecht (2019)

19. Ganesh, P.: Pre-trained language fashions: simplified, posted in towards facts technological know-how (2019)

20. Lin, B.: Investigating the device reading comprehension hassle with deep gaining knowledge of, posted in in the direction of statistics technological know-how (2019)

21. Blohm, M., Jagfeld, G., Sood, E., Yu, X., Vu, N.T.: Comparing attention-based totally convolutional and recurrent neural networks: success and obstacles in gadget reading comprehension. In: Proceedings of the 22nd Conference on Computational Natural Language Learning, Brussels, Belgium, pp. 108–118. Affiliation for Computational Linguistics (2018)

Generative Adversarial Network for Hand-Writing Detection

Vimal Kumar$^{(\boxtimes)}$ ⓘ, Rajesh Kumar Shrivastava ⓘ, and Simar Preet Singh ⓘ

Bennett University, Noida, UP, India
{Vimal.Kumar,rajesh.shrivastava,Simarpreet.Singh}@bennett.edu.in

Abstract. This paper introduces a Generative Adversarial Network (GAN) for producing images of handwritten numbers from 0–9. This approach generates whole random images of digits in generation phase of GAN. The Detection phase, algorithm tries to detect handwritten image of digits. The GAN algorithm produces variable-sized images by calculating character widths from style vectors. The generator network is trained using GAN, employs a trained handwriting recognition network to make writing understandable. Here we experimented with generator and discriminator oven MNIST dataset and train the model using deep learning to map an image with correct digits.

Keywords: GAN · Deep Learning · Keras · Generator · Discriminator

1 Introduction

In this paper we discussed the building of the concepts offered in [2,8] and makes use of the strength of generative adversarial networks to generate handwritten text images in an adversarial manner (GANs [9]). This model is basically based on two player game. Player one is a generator, which produces fake images. Player two is a discriminator which is try to predict real images. Generator doesn't have access to real image but discriminator can access both fake and real image. This game or GAN model training will continue until discriminator is nat able to detect real image from the dataset. Although the research community has paid a lot of attention to GANs, particularly cGANs [3] and variations, very little work has so far been done on picture generation conditioned on sequences (not to be confused with text to image learning tasks such as [12] or [11]). A clean comparison is challenging since it is not always evident which component has contributed to an improvement in more recent works [2,8].

This paper apply GAN model on MNIST dataset. Figure 1 shows the sample dataset. In this dataset we have 60,000 images of digits in hand-written format. Our objective is to train our GAN model to identify these handwritten image correctly. Earlier various researchers applied different machine learning and deep learning methods. In this paper we use different approach i.e. GAN. The images on dataset are quite pixelated because the size of the images are 28×28. This

D. Garg et al. (Eds.): IACC 2022, CCIS 1782, pp. 353–359, 2023.
https://doi.org/10.1007/978-3-031-35644-5_28

Fig. 1. Sample dataset for digital numbers stored in database

small size images makes MNIST dataset more useful and ideal for experiments. All these images are represented as binary by nature i.e. black-and-white so only one dimension is needed to represent them. This paper mainly focuses on:

1. Building the GAN model with generator and discriminator to train MNIST dataset.
2. Evaluate GAN's generator and discriminator loss functions.
3. Compare results with other Deep Learning model with same dataset.

GANs are among the most effective and well-liked generating models. The generator and discriminator of the GAN's models must be optimised in order for it to perform well. For complicated datasets, they also use more memory and computing time. Therefore, it is necessary to discuss these issues and suggest remedies in further research. Additionally, since accuracy begins to decline in large and complicated datasets, this review can be expanded by including more current GAN variations on large and dynamic datasets. Future research should delve considerably deeper into GANs and its uses. Rest of the paper is organize as follows: Sect. 2 discusses about related work. Section 3 discussed about proposed work, dataset and algorithms. Section 4 discussed the outcome of the algorithms. Section 5 ends the paper with final note and future work plan.

2   Related Work

There are numerous research papers on handwriting recognition that may be found in the literature. Support Vector Machine (SVM) is the one of the most common method to train the machine learning models. SVM was originally employed for handwritten digit OCR in 1995 [7]. Later, SVM classifiers have been the go-to solution for a variety of supervised classification issues, including character recognition [6], face identification, and object recognition. Boukharouba and Bennia [4] created a handwritten digit recognition system based on Support Vector Machines and proposed a Freeman Chain Code technique for feature extraction.

Convolution Neural Network (CNN) is the most common method to apply Neural Network (NN). CNN is mostly used for visualization using feed-forward artificial neural networks. CNN used for multiple object detection and visualization [14]. In the year 1998, LeCun proposed the LeNet-5 model [15], the author provided a way to use CNN in combination with different layers. In Lenet-5 model CNN consists of more then one convolutional layers with different weight and pooling layers.

Convolutional neural networks have been successfully applied in recent years for handwritten digit recognition for the benchmark MNIST handwritten digit dataset, in particular. The majority of the tests were highly regarded. more than 98% or 99% accuracy [13]. On the MNIST dataset, a high recognition accuracy of 99.73% is attained. While attempting to create an ensemble network by integrating numerous CNNs using the well-known committee technique [10]. From the initial 7-net committee, the study was subsequently expanded into a 35-net committee, and very high quality results were published. 99.77% accurate [10]. Three-layer Deep Belief Networks (DBN) with a greedy algorithm were investigation for the MNIST dataset revealed a 98.75% accuracy rate [5].

To extract and transform features, deep learning employs a cascade of numerous layers of nonlinear processing units. Higher layers learn more complex features derived from lower layer features, whereas lower layers adjacent to the data input learn simpler features. A hierarchical and effective feature representation is created by the architecture [1].

3   Proposed Work

The proposed model is shown in Fig. 2. This model divides in two step. Step 1 is generating fake images. For this purpose generative step add some noise in image and produces fake images which is look like the original. In the step 2, Gan produces these fake images along with original image to discriminator model. The job of the discriminator is to identify the real images. The training of the model will continue until discriminator correctly identifies real images.

3.1   Dataset

The MNIST dataset is available with National Institute of Standards and Technology (NIST). This dataset is a collection of 250 peoples handwritten numbers, out of 250 50% are school students and 50% are from the others. As we mentioned this datset contains 60,000 different images. Out of them 10,000 is used for testing purposes and rest is used in training and validation. This dataset is already availbale with keras.

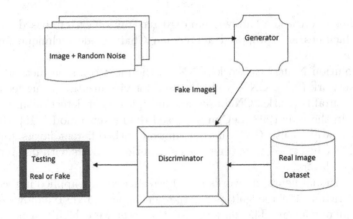

Fig. 2. Working model of GAN

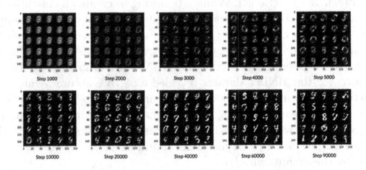

Fig. 3. Epoch wise Experimental Result

3.2 Implementation

1. We used Tensor for fast processing and extension of matrices. Tensors will be used to represent the data. We used Pytorch library to implement tensor.
2. Batch processing is used to get better result.

Next step is to create the generator class. Three values are required to build generator class:

1. The image dimension
2. The noise vector dimension
3. The initial secret dimension

The generator will create a neural network with five layers using these variables. The generator will use the block function to apply non-linear transformations starting with the noise vector until the tensor is mapped to the size of the resulting image (the same size as the real images from MNIST). The last layer has a different code than the others. The final layer requires scaling with a sigmoid function but neither a normalization nor an activation function. At the end, a forward pass function uses which develop a neural network to generates an image of the output dimension from a noise vector.

The discriminator is the second element that must build. The Algorithm 1 develop a function that creates a neural network block for the discriminator, much as we did with the generator component.

You must develop method to compute the discriminator loss and the generator loss before training your GAN. The discriminator and generator will be able to assess their performance and make improvements as a result. You must dial since the generator is required to determine the discriminator's loss. Make sure that only the discriminator is modified by calling detach() on the generator result!

4   Result

Developing a function to create a single layer or block for the generator's neural network will be the first step. Each block should have a linear transformation to translate to a different shape, a batch normalisation to stabilise the output, and then a non-linear activation function (such as ReLU) to allow for complex output transformations.

Figure 3 provide results of GAN model. It shows clearly that if we increase epoch level at certain point the loss will be minimum.

The Algorithm 1 processed the complete dataset in batches for each epoch. It used loss value to update the discriminator and generator for each batch. Before the loss functions are determined, a set of photos is forecasted in a batch (instead of calculating the loss function after each image). Be aware that a loss greater than 1 may appear, but this is OK because a sufficiently confident incorrect prediction can cause a binary cross entropy loss of any positive amount.

Algorithm 1: Generative Adversarial Network

Data: MNIST Image dataset
Result: Trained GAN Model
$loss = 0$; $threshold \leftarrow 97\%$; $y \leftarrow input\ image$;
$y \leftarrow Add\ noise$;
/* adding Noise to generate fake data */
Train discriminator on real data;
Generate fake inputs for the generator;
$N \leftarrow Real\ Image$;
while $loss$ ¡ $Treshhold$ **do**
| Train discriminator on fake data;
| Train generator with the output of the discriminator;
| Calculate loss;

---

5   Conclusion

The most promising generative techniques in the field of computer vision are generative adversarial networks (GANs) and its variations. Overall, the concept of GAN is quite intriguing, which is why numerous researchers are working on it and presenting various GAN-based models. In this study, we reviewed a few GAN variations and ran experiments on the MNIST benchmark dataset. We gave a thorough analysis of GAN and its many models and demonstrated how useful they are for picture synthesis. Despite the publication of countless GAN-based publications, we remained thorough. We simply briefly discussed a few common GAN for picture synthesis variations. We delineated the design and operation of these models and assessed them using several metrics. We also looked into the GAN's limitations and difficulties in the area of picture synthesis. It is clear that the most recent GAN variants are unsupervised and more stable than the older models. They are also applicable in a wide range of fields, including drug discovery, picture categorization, and translation from one image to another.

References

1. Agarwal, M., Gupta, S.K., Biswas, K.K.: Development of efficient CNN model for tomato crop disease identification. Sustain. Comput.: Inf. Syst. **28**, 100407 (2020)
2. Alonso, E., Moysset, B., Messina, R.: Adversarial generation of handwritten text images conditioned on sequences. In: 2019 International Conference on Document Analysis and Recognition (ICDAR), pp. 481–486. IEEE (2019)
3. Antipov, G., Baccouche, M., Dugelay, J.L.: Face aging with conditional generative adversarial networks. In: 2017 IEEE International Conference on Image Processing (ICIP), pp. 2089–2093. IEEE (2017)
4. Boukharouba, A., Bennia, A.: Novel feature extraction technique for the recognition of handwritten digits. Appl. Comput. Inf. **13**(1), 19–26 (2017)
5. Chandra, B., Sharma, R.K.: Fast learning in deep neural networks. Neurocomputing **171**, 1205–1215 (2016)
6. Choudhary, A., Rishi, R.: A fused feature extraction approach to OCR: MLP vs. RBF. In: Satapathy, S., Avadhani, P., Udgata, S., Lakshminarayana, S. (eds.) ICT and Critical Infrastructure: Proceedings of the 48th Annual Convention of Computer Society of India-Vol I. Advances in Intelligent Systems and Computing, vol. 248, pp. 159–166. Springer, Cham (2014). https://doi.org/10.1007/978-3-319-03107-1_19
7. Cortes, C., Vapnik, V.: Support-vector networks. Mach. Learn. **20**(3), 273–297 (1995)
8. Fogel, S., Averbuch-Elor, H., Cohen, S., Mazor, S., Litman, R.: Scrabblegan: semi-supervised varying length handwritten text generation. In: Proceedings of the IEEE/CVF Conference on Computer Vision and Pattern Recognition, pp. 4324–4333 (2020)
9. Goodfellow, I., et al.: Generative adversarial networks. Commun. ACM **63**(11), 139–144 (2020)
10. Li, Y., Lu, S., Luo, J., Pang, W., Liu, H.: High-performance convolutional neural network accelerator based on systolic arrays and quantization. In: 2019 IEEE 4th International Conference on Signal and Image Processing (ICSIP), pp. 335–339. IEEE (2019)

11. Qiao, T., Zhang, J., Xu, D., Tao, D.: Mirrorgan: learning text-to-image genera-tion by redescription. In: Proceedings of the IEEE/CVF Conference on Computer Vision and Pattern Recognition, pp. 1505–1514 (2019)

12. Reed, S., Akata, Z., Yan, X., Logeswaran, L., Schiele, B., Lee, H.: Generative adver-sarial text to image synthesis. In: International Conference on Machine Learning, pp. 1060–1069. PMLR (2016)

13. Seo, J., Park, H.: Object recognition in very low resolution images using deep collaborative learning. IEEE Access **7**, 134071–134082 (2019)

14. Wang, C., Bai, X., Wang, S., Zhou, J., Ren, P.: Multiscale visual attention networks for object detection in VHR remote sensing images. IEEE Geosci. Remote Sens. Lett. **16**(2), 310–314 (2018)

15. Wei, G., Li, G., Zhao, J., He, A.: Development of a LeNet-5 gas identification CNN structure for electronic noses. Sensors **19**(1), 217 (2019)

Study and Analysis of Deep Learning Models for the Recognition of Sign Language

Naima Azim[(✉)], Shamsia Afrin Jamema[ID], and Naznin Sultana

Daffodil International University, Dhaka, Bangladesh
{naima15-1015,shamsia15-1004,naznin.cse}@diu.edu.bd

Abstract. A population of 430 million people and above, or over a population of 5% of the world's population, needs therapy to treat their "disabled" hearing and speaking condition. These people have the option to learn sign language to communicate with others. Hence, our project mainly targets the deaf and mute community. Around 5000 images of hand gestures have been used and divided into 10 categories for live detection. The categories are mainly American Sign Language (ASL) and are consisted of the first 10 numbers. Our model can detect these ten hand motions and categorize them correctly. We used the You Only Look Once Version 5 algorithm. The algorithm consists of a backbone namely CSPDarknet53, in which an SPP block is accustomed to accelerating the speed of the receptive field responsible to set apart prime traits and confirming that network operation speed is inclining in speed. The neck of the algorithm, PAN, is added to aggregate the parameters from different backbone levels. This model is very easy to use and understand and gives an accuracy above 98%. That is why we chose YoloV5 as our model for object detection due to its simplicity in usage. Therefore, an artificial sign language detection system has been suggested in this study which incorporates deep learning and image processing method. This study also gives a comparison between the two models to give a better understating of why we marked YoloV5 as a better algorithm even though both models gave an accuracy of above 98%. We believe that making a hand gesture detection system will encourage individuals to communicate with people who cannot hear or speak. That being the case, we aim to make the lives of the disabled better.

Keywords: Sign Language Detection · Deep Learning · YoloV5

1 Introduction

Communication is an important part of people's daily routines. It helps people to express many emotions and interact with others. Communication is also a vital way to educate people, learn from others, enlighten people with information, etc. This makes it very difficult for the deaf or mute to converse with others as they are unable to speak or listen to others. [1] Hence, sign language is learned by the disabled. Unfortunately, not everyone knows the sign language for which these disabled people need to hire a professional interpreter which can be very costly. Also, not all deaf or mute people know all the sign language as there are different sign languages for different countries

© Springer Nature Switzerland AG 2023
D. Garg et al. (Eds.): IACC 2022, CCIS 1782, pp. 360–373, 2023.
https://doi.org/10.1007/978-3-031-35644-5_29

for which we decided to make a sign language detecting system. [1, 2] Our system can be helpful for the deaf and mute to easily communicate face-to-face with people who do not know sign language. Our system is cost-free and suitable for everyone as it contains different language options for sign language. People who are interested to learn sign language can also use our application.

The YoloV5 algorithm from the You Only Look Once (YOLO) series has been used which is a sophisticated Convolutional Neural Network (CNN) in performing object detection in real-time object detection in real-time for identifying as well as predicting hand and body gesture language. It is a single-stage object detector that analyzes as well as forecasts photos as input by applying 3 key parts: The Backbone Model, The Neck Model, and The Head Model. It is an object detection technology that breaks down an image and uses a system in which every grid can recognize an item on its own. [1] We have also used the Convolutional Neural Network, also used for image processing and artificial intelligence (AI) instruments, to compare the results made of 3 layers: an input layer, an output layer, and a hidden layer that contains various layers. [2] The reason we chose YoloV5 is that it consists of simple codes which can give all the necessary results such as graphs, confusion matrix, etc. after the training process on its own. But in the case of CNN, it does not give graphs and another necessary results after the training process. We had to go through more complex codes to get those results.

2 Literature Review

This section discusses the various other papers we went through to help us understand more about sign language and the different algorithms used in making an application for sign language detection.

Risk factors observed repeatedly for loss of hearing included toxemia preterm, low birth weight, consanguinity, and birth asphyxia. According to the inspection, the major sources of loss of hearing are hyperbilirubinemia, pneumonia, meningitis, as well as ototoxicity. Furthermore, parents lack acknowledgment and guidance regarding the risk factors of deafness making it part of the reason why children suffered from this issue. [3] HSV model can be used for feature extraction of images which mainly relies on the pigmentation of the human skin. Segmentation has been done on the images and then edge detection has been used where the edges of high-contrast images to find the boundary of objects in the images. After normalizing the images, features are extracted from a black-and-white image. [4] In this study, a robustly estimated autoencoder (SAE) pattern instruction technique has been used and is a fundamental element examination to direct the identification of human gestures using RGB-D data. The results after testing on the ASL dataset show that related features of Active Learning significantly improve accuracy from 75% to 99.05%. [5] In this study, HOG has been used as a feature descriptor to extract features of images that were first segmented using YCbCr. The result showed an accuracy of 88%. [6] An average detection percentage of 92.4% has been observed by using the k-curvature algorithm that allocates the tips of fingers and dynamic time wrapping was used to recognize gestures. [7] This research proposes a new fusion of improved attributes for the categorization of sign language's static signs. It starts by describing how depth information can be used to distinguish the hand from the scenery and a combined edge detection approach is presented to obtain several pertinent features of an image. [8] An efficient deep attention network enabling concurrent identification and detection of hand gestures on static RGB-D pictures using a CNN framework that is based on a delicate attention mechanism in a holistic manner. [9] Videos have been used where hand motions in successive video sequences are represented by fused features. On various extracting features from the ISL dataset, the ANN Based classifier is evaluated against state-of-the-art classifiers including Adaboost, support vector machine (SVM), and other ANN approaches giving an accuracy of 92.79%. [10] Another approach using the ANN classifier shows the evaluation and comparison of two extraction methods namely hand contour-based ANN and complex moments-based ANN. [11] In another study, using NATOPS datasets, an authorized lexicon of aircraft flight control movements, they evaluated their approach in a simulation of real-world nonverbal communication. This gave an accuracy of 75.37%. [12] The ethical issues regarding sign language claim that computer scientists need to be aware of the history of sign language and must learn the language beforehand making a system for recognition. [13].

The dataset was created using data-gathering processing which included the use of the webcam. Furthermore, we collected additional images from online sources to create a variety of hand shapes and sizes. The photos are cropped into the same size and converted to grayscale to get a more accurate output result. The images are then labeled in respective classes using LabelImg software. The model is then trained to recognize signs.

3   Methodology

This section has an explanation of our dataset, the methodology of our design, and the result we achieved.

3.1   Dataset Analysis

In this section, we have described how we prepared our dataset for the training process.

Below are the tables to show the structure of our dataset which has been labeled using LabelImg and made into two divisions for training and testing the YoloV5 model But for the CNN Model, we divided the dataset into each category of classes and used code to combine the images into one folder and separate them for training and testing.

The following table represents the total images for all classes with the format of the image we used as well as the size length and width of the images (Table 1).

Table 1. Details of the dataset

Class Name	Image Numbers	Format of Image	Size of Image
0	500	JPG	400 × 400

(continued)

Table 1. (*continued*)

Class Name	Image Numbers	Format of Image	Size of Image
1	517	JPG	400 × 400
2	499	JPG	400 × 400
3	498	JPG	400 × 400
4	511	JPG	400 × 400
5	507	JPG	400 × 400
6	491	JPG	400 × 400
7	495	JPG	400 × 400
8	491	JPG	400 × 400
9	489	JPG	400 × 400

The dataset comprises 10 types of hand signs which has a total of 4998 images. The division of the dataset for training and testing is roughly 90% and 10% respectively.

The table below contains information on the size of the batch and epoch used for training. It also represents the percentage of training and testing images divided from the entire dataset. It further shows the number of classes, total training samples, total test samples, as well as the input shape of the images (Table 2).

Table 2. Training Specifications

Size of Batch	32
Number of Epoch	300
Training	90%
Testing	10%
Output Label	10
Input Shape	416 × 416 × 3
Training Images	4206
Testing Images	792

This table represents how many training and testing pictures are used for distinct classes. Total training and testing images are kept roughly the same for all the classes (Table 3).

After we evaluate the two models, we concluded that both models give the same accuracy. We chose YoloV5 because it was easy to understand and with a few simple codes we can get all the necessary graphs and results as in the case of the CNN model it was the opposite. But both the models gave similar and high accuracy after testing which was suitable for usage.

Table 3. Number of training and testing pictures of the individual label for YoloV5

Class Name	Number of Training Images	Number of Testing Images
0	421	79
1	437	80
2	412	87
3	421	77
4	422	89
5	422	85
6	417	74
7	424	71
8	412	79
9	418	71

3.2 Proposed Methodology

The design of our model that described our procedure has been described in this section.

The model given below shortly describes the procedure we followed for the training process and other steps we took for the entire project (Fig. 1).

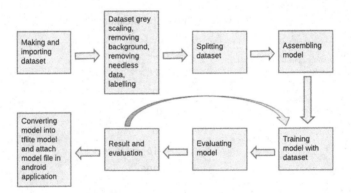

Fig. 1. Proposed Methodology Design

Input Image. The dataset consists of ten classes created using a webcam. The pictures are then taken while keeping a hand gesture for each gesture in multiple positions to increase the accuracy of real-time detection. [14].

Pre-processing. It is a method applied to acquire pictures that must be anomalous in some respects. The main purpose of this step is to eliminate unwanted sections of the pictures or the backdrop to expand features. The entire dataset is produced in grayscale which means the images are in black and white to enhance accuracy. [2] The images were then made into two divisions for testing and training, after labeling them using LabelImg. [1] We trained YoloV5 and CNN models in Google Colaboratory using the same dataset except in the CNN model, labeled images were not used.

Conversion. We have converted the trained model file of YoloV5 into a TensorFlow Lite which is supported by the Android application. This is also done in Google Colaboratory. After converting the file, it is attached to the Android application using the right specifications to make the model in the application. [15].

Here are some samples of the images used in the dataset (Fig. 2).

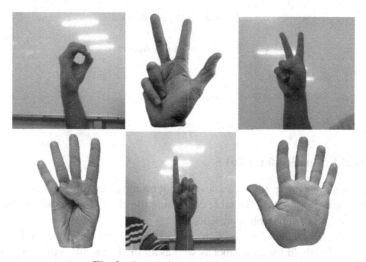

Fig. 2. Sample images of our dataset

4   Result and Analysis

This section contains the details of the accuracy we got from training both YoloV5 and CNN models using the same dataset and keeping all the necessary input the same for a fair test.

Below is a description of the training parameters used for both YoloV5 and CNN (Table 4).

Table 4. Training Specification for both YoloV5 and CNN

Size of Batch	32
Number of Epoch	300
Training	90%

(*continued*)

Table 4. (*continued*)

Testing	10%
Output Label	10

These are the accuracy we received from training the two models. It shows that the accuracy between the two models has a difference of less than 1% (Table 5).

Table 5. Accuracy Result

Model Name	Model Accuracy
YoloV5m	98.60%
CNN	99.40%

4.1 Model Evaluation for YoloV5

This section shows the result we achieved from training the YoloV5 model.

In the following images, the table containing the class numbers shows which class each colored line in the graph represents.

This graph shows the F1 curve, Formula One, which expresses the top F1 value with a confidence threshold for each label as well as all the labels altogether (Fig. 3).

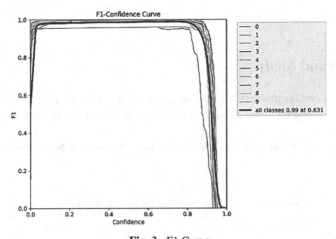

Fig. 3. F1 Curve

P Curve or Precision-Confidence Curve computes the possibility of a predicted bounding box having similarity to the actual ground truth box, called a positive predictor (Fig. 4).

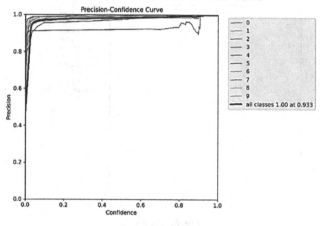

Fig. 4. P Curve

Below the R curve or Recall-Confidence Curve expresses a positive rate, also alluded to as sensitivity (Fig. 5).

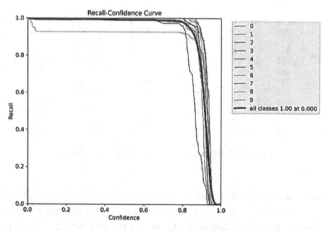

Fig. 5. R Curve

Here, the PR Curve or Precision-Recall Curve is a plot of precision and recall. This is used to evaluate the performance of object recognition models (Fig. 6).

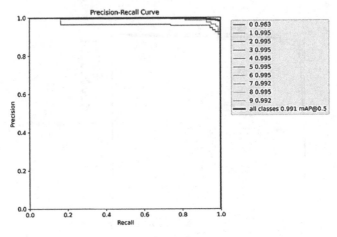

Fig. 6. PR Curve

This shows the Precision (P) score, Recall (R) score, mAP values from 0.5 to 0.95 over various IoU thresholds for the labels distinctively and altogether as well for the YoloV5 model (Fig. 7).

Class	Images	Instances	P	R	mAP@.5	mAP@.5:.95: 100% 25/25
all	792	791	0.986	0.986	0.987	0.826
0	792	73	0.921	1	0.946	0.69
1	792	80	0.995	1	0.995	0.808
2	792	87	0.995	1	0.995	0.783
3	792	77	0.996	1	0.995	0.871
4	792	90	0.978	0.973	0.993	0.87
5	792	85	0.995	0.965	0.994	0.892
6	792	74	0.994	1	0.995	0.868
7	792	70	0.986	1	0.99	0.825
8	792	74	1	0.992	0.995	0.85
9	792	81	1	0.926	0.973	0.801

Fig. 7. Performance Report for YoloV5 Model

A confusion matrix is defined as a method to compute the execution of the Classifier model. The x-axis gives out the label for the images that the model detected and the y-axis gives out the predicted labels made by our trained model. The deeper the color goes following the color range on the right side of the confusion matrix, the better the accuracy (Fig. 8).

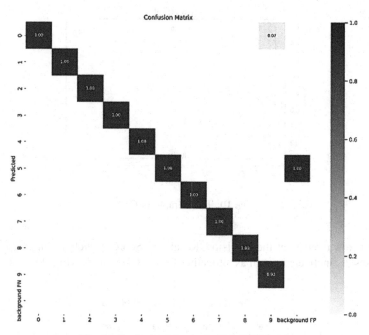

Fig. 8. Confusion Matrix for YoloV5 Model

4.2 Model Evaluation for CNN

This section shows the result we achieved from training the YoloV5 model.

Below shows accuracy graphs that measure the model's prediction performance for training in blue lines and validation in orange lines (Fig. 9).

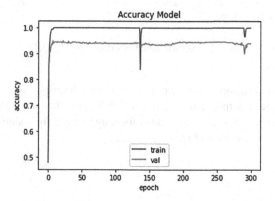

Fig. 9. Accuracy Graph for CNN

Next, the loss graphs measure the model errors it is making in training in blue lines and validation in orange lines. The fewer errors, the better the model is (Fig. 10).

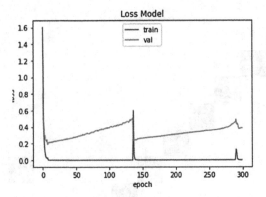

Fig. 10. Loss Graph for CNN

The below table gives the Precision, Recall, F1-Score, as well as Support values for all classes distinctively as well as altogether for the CNN model (Fig. 11).

	precision	recall	f1-score	support
0	1.00	0.99	1.00	501
1	1.00	0.99	1.00	519
2	1.00	0.99	1.00	502
3	0.99	1.00	0.99	493
4	1.00	1.00	1.00	510
5	0.99	1.00	1.00	506
6	0.99	1.00	0.99	487
7	0.99	0.98	0.99	499
8	1.00	0.99	0.99	494
9	0.99	1.00	1.00	487
accuracy			0.99	4998
macro avg	0.99	0.99	0.99	4998
weighted avg	0.99	0.99	0.99	4998

Fig. 11. Performance Report of CNN Model

Below is the confusion matrix we achieved from training our CNN model. This matrix has the same structure as the matrix of YoloV5, but the only difference is that the higher the color chart goes following the color range on the right side of the confusion matrix, the better the accuracy (Fig. 12).

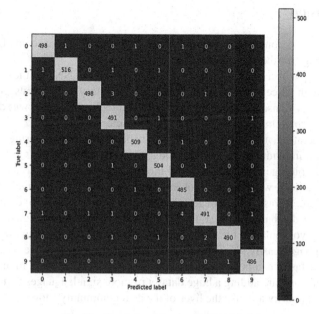

Fig. 12. Confusion Matrix of CNN Model

4.3 Results of Working Camera

Below are given some results to show how our device can recognize and predict the gestures accurately. In the bounded box, we can see on the upper left side of the box that some values are showing. The first part of the value shows the sign, or the class of the gesture predicted, and the second part of the value shows the accuracy percentage (Fig. 13).

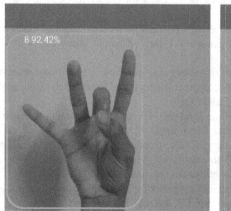

Fig. 13. Camera Results

5 Conclusion

Lastly, this section concludes with the background of sign language and how research on sign language has been established.

We ended up with a result showing that both YoloV5 and CNN give the same accuracy and were in high percentages as well. This is a satisfactory value for usage. Moreover, YoloV5 was easy to use as we got all the results right after the model was done training on the dataset which made it easy for us and was time-saving as well.

In this generation, many new technologies are being developed to bring more comfort to life and help individuals struggling through multiple issues in their everyday life. In this fast-developing generation, more and more ways are being made for the deaf and mute to communicate with ease, cutting down boundaries between normal people and the disabled. Before, it was difficult to get an idea of the sign languages of certain countries due to a lack of databases or research. But now databases are being made to include a large range of vocabularies for different sign languages to help others trying to learn new sign languages easily. With the new technologies and studies, we wish to improve our system for faster and better detection. Moreover, we are inclined to make a variety of devices and software adding a huge dataset of more sign languages that are yet to be known by the majority to make the lives of the deaf community a lot easier and simpler.

References

1. Ali, S.M.: Comparative analysis of YoloV3, YoloV4, and YoloV5 for sign language detection. Department of Information Technology, Rajagiri School of Engineering and Technology, Kerala, India (2021)
2. Barbhuiya, A.A., Kash, R.K., Jain, R.: CNN-based feature extraction and classification for sign language. Multimed. Tools Appl. **80**, 3051–3069 (2021)
3. Singh, S., Jain, S.: Factors associated with deaf-mutism in children attending special schools of rural central India: a survey. J. Fam. Med. Primary Care **9**(7), 3256 (2020)
4. Hasan, M.M., Misra, P.K.: HSV brightness factor matching for gesture recognition system. IJIP **4**(5), 456–467 (2011)
5. Nagarajan, S., Subashini, T.S.: Static hand gesture recognition for sign language alphabets using edge-oriented histogram and multi-class SVM. Int. J. Comput. Appl. **82**(4), 28–35 (2013)
6. Vedak, O., Zavre, P., Todkar, A., Patil, M.: Sign language interpreter using image processing and machine learning. Department of Computer Engineering, Datta Meghe College of Engineering, Mumbai University, Airoli, India (2019)
7. Plouffe, G., Cretu, A.M.: Static and dynamic hand gesture recognition in-depth data using dynamic time warping. IEEE Trans. Instrum. Meas. **65**(2), 305–316 (2015)
8. Jadooki, S., Mohamad, D., Saba, T., Almazyad, A.S., Rehman, A.: Fused features mining for depth-based hand gesture recognition to classify blind human communication. Neural Comput. Appl. **28**(11), 3285–3294 (2016). https://doi.org/10.1007/s00521-016-2244-5
9. Li, Y., Wang, X., Liu, W., Feng, B.: Deep attention network for joint hand gesture localization and recognition using static RGB-D images. Inf. Sci. **441**, 66–78 (2018)
10. Sign language recognition with multi-feature fusion and ANN class
11. Badi, H.: Recent methods in vision-based hand gesture recognition. Int. J. Data Sci. Anal. **1**(2), 77–87 (2016). https://doi.org/10.1007/s41060-016-0008-z

12. Archana, S., Gajanan, K.: Hand segmentation techniques to hand gesture recognition for natural human-computer interaction. ACM Trans. Interact. Intell. Syst. **3**, 15 (2012)

13. Braffort, A.: Research on computer science and sign language: ethical aspects. In: Wachsmuth, I., Sowa, T. (eds.) Gesture and Sign Language in Human-Computer Interaction, GW 2001, vol. 2298, pp. 1–8. Springer, Berlin (2002). https://doi.org/10.1007/3-540-47873-6_1

14. Dabre, K., Dholay, S.: Machine learning model for sign language interpretation using webcam images. Department of Computer Engineering Sardar Patel Institute of Technology Student of M.E. (Computer) Mumbai, India (2014)

15. Suharjitoa, R.A., Wiryanab, F., Ariestab, M.C., Kusumaa, G.P.: Sign language recognition application systems for deaf-mute people: a review based on input-process-output. Comput. Sci. **116**, 441–448 (2017)

Novel Taxonomy for E-learning Recommender System Using Opinion Mining

Kalpana[1]($\boxtimes$) , Shardul Singh Chauhan[1] , Mahesh Kumar Singh[1] ,
and Renu Bagoria[2]

[1] Department of Computer Science, ABES Engineering College, Ghaziabad, India
kalpana.artofcreatinglife@gmail.com
[2] Department of Computer Science and Engineering, Jagannath University, Jaipur, India
renu.bagoria@jagannathuniversity.org

Abstract. People constantly seek development to maintain their competitiveness in their careers in this time when every element of society is advancing. E-learning platforms adapt to the always changing environment and offer learners numerous learning resources and remote learning opportunities. Users want assistance in using the myriad resources available online. Choosing a course to enroll in might be difficult, thus recommender systems are used in online learning to give students individualized advice by automatically detecting their preferences, services are provided. This paper thoroughly examines the key E-learning uses recommendation systems to identify new areas for research. This paper reviews the following techniques: collaborative filtering-based, content-based, and knowledge-based recommendations. The paper also talks about the fundamental workings of these methods and how they're applied to meet the particular requirement. The findings in this research could confirm researchers and practitioners to better comprehend the present state and potential futures of recommender electronic learning systems.

Keywords: E-learning · E-learning Platforms · Learner · Opinion Mining · Recommender System · Data Mining · Filtering Techniques

1 Introduction

The style of life changed when the globe transitioned to an Expression has undergone significant modification, with the widespread use of smileys and symbols while texting might be perceived as emotion. Social interaction can be seen on the internet and in new word has been created for a number of communication channels. People prefer to contact with one another by texting, tweeting, publishing, etc. They desire to communicate their feelings, interests, and opinions with others through the dislikes, views, evaluations, feelings, and other characteristics of people.

To showcase popularity of recommendation system for e learning platforms we conducted a survey on some of the popular websites like IEEE, Springer, etc. We took data from 2017 to 2021. The results have been shown in Fig. 1. More than 20000 papers have been published in this field in the past 5 years.

© Springer Nature Switzerland AG 2023
D. Garg et al. (Eds.): IACC 2022, CCIS 1782, pp. 374–385, 2023.
https://doi.org/10.1007/978-3-031-35644-5_30

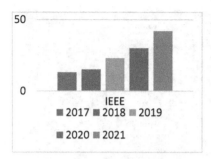
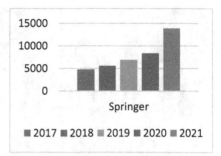

Fig. 1. Survey results to show popularity of the topic

1.1 Opinion Mining

Building a database for sentiment analysis or opinion mining mechanism refers to examining the comments/views of people, Finding the views of others is what opinion mining is all about. Recommender systems were created as a solution to the information overload issue with the purpose of offering customized services to the right people at the right time [3]. Two crucial elements of recommender systems are: the users, first people the system offers services to; and (2) the products or services that should be recommended to Users enjoy things like movies, novels, or mobile plans [4]. Typically, a recommender system aids a user in making a choice from available set of options. To save users' time and effort, a list of items for a candidate is provided in place of a huge number of things. Nowadays, Recommender systems are widely utilized in a variety of practical applications and have emerged as portal websites [5].

The term "opinion mining" refers to sentiment analysis since it mines the data from other types of content, such reviews and news & blogs categorizes them according to their polarity as neutral, positive, negative. It concentrates on classifying the text that balances being subjective and objective. Subjectivity states, the text contains or bears opinion content.

For example, "The Course Content of Coursera is good". (This phrase contains considering Coursera and demonstrating a favorable (good) opinion; hence it is subjective.

Let us now look at the second. "The Course content of Coursera is really good." (This statement is true, basic knowledge as opposed to a viewpoint or an opinion individual, and thus its goal) (Fig. 2).

Generally speaking, research into sentiment analysis has focused mostly at three. levels that are as follows:

- Document level: This level's assignment is to categorize whether a whole opinion piece provides a favorable or unfavorable opinion/sentiment. For instance, if the system is provided a product review it judges whether the review is generally favorable or negative assessment of the product This job is frequently analyzed at the document level.
- Sentence level: At this level, the entire sentences is evaluated for the expression of a positive, negative or neutral viewpoint. Neutral typically denotes a lack of viewpoint.
- Entry Level and Aspect Level-These level perform the analysis at more fine level.

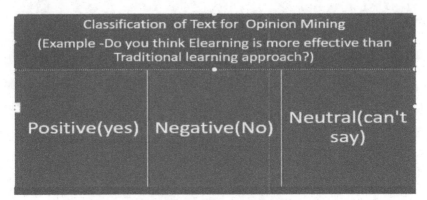

Fig. 2. Text Classification for Opinion Mining

2 Literature Survey

Building a recommendation system that incorporates both user clustering and association rules techniques has been the subject of extensive research. Al-Badarenah and Alsakran [23] proposed a Recommender System based on Collaborative Techniques that's Recommend Elective Course based on resemblance between students. Another Recommender System that suggests the webpages based on clustering time-framed navigation sessions using Hierarchical Bisecting Medoids algorithm [24]. As a result, their technology successfully enhances the recommendation service. Cognitive strategies are important for facilitating various cognitive processes throughout to access information process, such as analysis, assessment, and decision-making. These procedures include easy and quick access for people to accurate and reliable information.

Users found it more and more challenging to navigate this medium, which is made up of the vast amount of information published, altered, and shared worldwide, as the Internet expanded and became more widely used. When looking for information on a certain topic, a user frequently encounters a lot of unreliable, erroneous, and irrelevant information related to search query. This leads to information pollution which is termed as "infollution". In order to understand the suitability of a particular e learning platform for a learner we have to consider a number of factors about a learner such as background, interaction, prior experience of using e learning platforms, analyzing ability, understanding, academic background etc. Thus, this suggests that before using platforms for online learning, first it is to be determined that whether learner was able to complete study needs or that using such platforms is important to their study process. The table below summarizes the various Data Mining objectives and their corresponding Data Mining Approaches used which includes Clustering, Statistical analysis, visualization etc (Table 1).

Students are the users of the E-learning recommender systems who are lifelong learners seeking useful talents or those who are university students pursuing their degrees their career. Learning styles, learning resources, and other factors like learning pathways, or even learning activities can be included in the E-learning recommender systems.

Table 1. Evaluation of Learning Content using Data Mining Applications

Sno	Data Mining Objective	Data Mining Approach	Reference
1	SOM	Clustering	12
2	Basic statistical methods	Statistical Analysis	13
3	Naïve Bayes	Classification	14
4	Fuzzy rules	Classification	15
5	Software agents and Association Rules	Classification	16
6	Bisection K-Means	Visualization	18
7	Fuzzy set theory	Classification	19
8	Software agents and Association Rules	Classification	20
9	Metadata Analysis	Statistical analysis	21
10	ADT Tree	Classification	22

Compared to traditional e-commerce advice, Recommender systems in the context of e-learning have certain qualities:

- The information in the learning activities and the requirements for students is hazy and ambiguous. For instance, learners may not be aware of the courses or skills they require, but they are aware of the they are looking for a job. Different classifications can apply to the same educational activity [2].
- The context of learning, such as the reason for enrolling in the course and the learning objectives, is crucial to learner's style. There should be distinctions between suggestions for full-time students and those who study part-time.
- The learning activities, resources, and courses need to be set up so that the prerequisites are met. For instance, if the prerequisite for the course is "Basics of Programming" and If a student is searching for the course "Advance Java," it would not be appropriate to suggest that they take " Basics of Programming." In case they have not completed it.
- Learners require a path to adaptive learning that enables them to constantly acquire knowledge. The lifelong learners require a learning path that includes a package rather than just one lesson, exercises, and resources in a suitable sequence.

2.1 Key Concerns in E Learning

- Classification of students based on learning performance
- Identification of Unusual learning habits
- Navigation of e-learning systems
- Clustering based on similar e-learning system utilization
- Optimization, and systems' capacity to change in order to meet the needs and abilities of students.

3   Methodology

In order to understand the requirement of the learner based on the content generated by the learner, the following steps have to be performed:

Step 1: Pre-processing of Content

Data for user-generated content may come from company databases or from open sources. Following this, the material is divided into sentences, the stop-words, digits, and punctuation are deleted, and then frequently used words are concatenated using corresponding functions.

Step 2: Training of Embedding Words

Once the pre-processing of content is performed, the next step is to perform training of word embeddings using skip-gram model. To determine the context word for a given target word, skip-gram is employed. It is the CBOW algorithm inverted. Here, the target word is entered and the surrounding words are produced. This problem is challenging since there are multiple context words that must be predicted (Fig. 3).

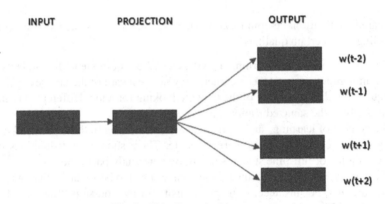

Fig. 3. Skip Gram Architecture

Step 3: Recognition of informative data-Based upon the user generated content, the next step to perform is the training of the CNN (Convolutional neural network) is trained and then filtering is done in order to get the informative and non-informative content.

Step 4: Sampling of diverse content-Sampling is done based upon data from different clusters in order to better understand the requirement of the learner.

Step 5: Conventional mining of learner's needs-The various instructive information can be reviewed for professional analysis to pinpoint the needs of the learner (Fig. 4)

4   Challenges in Opinion Mining

The main challenge in conducting research is gathering the necessary data. Tasks like sentiment analysis and opinion mining are particularly challenging because there is a wealth of information available online, making it tough to collect that information and

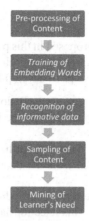

Fig. 4. Capturing of User Requirements

extract opinions from it. So, in this section, we've spoken about a few data sources that are available as well as several techniques for extracting opinions and feelings from texts. The following are some of the difficulties in opinion mining:

- Domain-independence: The greatest difficulty that Opinion mining and sentiment analysis depends on the subject matter character of the words' sentiment. One feature set could result in very good well in one domain, but also performing very well inadequate in another area [5].
- Inequality in opinion mining software accessibility: The cost of opinion mining software is now very high, hence only large corporations and the government can afford it. It is beyond what the average person would expect. This ought to be accessible to everyone, ensuring that everyone benefits from it [6].
- Spotting spam reviews: Both are present on the internet, spam and genuine material. Spam material has to be removed before processing. From available Data Sources for Opinion
- mining. On the internet, there are numerous data sources, including Blogs, Online postings, Forums, News Feeds, Microblogs, and Review Sites etc.
- Blogs: A blog is simply a user's personal journal or place where they can express their views and opinions online about subjects they choose.
- Online reviews: There are several review websites on the Internet through which you may look for internet evaluations of any product before making a purchase.
- Microblogging: Users can share brief messages on microblogs, parts of text like brief sentences, single connections to videos or photographs," which can be the main cause of their acceptance.
- Online postings: individuals express their own thoughts, views, likes, dislikes, and comments on particular issues, etc.
- Forums: An online discussion board

5 Proposed Model

Let us know understand the model proposed in this paper that talks about the generation of the recommender system. The diagram shown below discusses the methodology used in the research and the sequence of steps to develop the recommender system.

Step 1 -Data gathering and dataset preparation. To do this, information is collected from reliable resources. We are suggesting to collect the information about the "review "of the course and analyze it.

Step 2 -Opinion Spam Detection dataset is utilized for analysis. It involves pre-processing-characteristics are derived from the data based on the dataset. Filtering of Data is done at this step only.

Step 3-Classification of Data to be Performed. In addition, the data is split into two pieces a) Training Data and b) Testing Data-This selection has to be made wisely. Samples haves to be collected and analysis has to be made that which data can be selected for training the system on the other hand which data has to be tested.

Step 4 -Opinion Mining.to extract information. Now since the system is ready with the Training data based upon the review of different courses, the next step is to perform the opinion mining of the different courses offered by various E-learning platforms. The diagram below explains the components of Opinion Mining (Fig. 5).

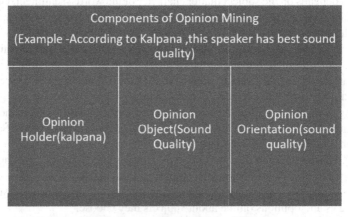

Fig. 5. Components of Opinion Mining

Step 5- Creating an RNN (LSTM) Let us know discuss the model which will perform the Functionality for opinion mining. A feedforward neural network with an internal memory is known as a recurrent neural network. The result of the current input depends on the previous computation, making RNNs recurrent in nature because they carry out the same function for every data input. The output is created, copied, and then delivered back into the recurrent network. It takes into account both the current input and the output that it has learned from the prior input when making a decision. A RNN model with an incorporated LSTM is created in this step to carry out the opinion mining.

Step 6- Development of Recommender systems-

Once the system is trained based upon different types of review, the recommender system is now ready to be used by various learners. Depending upon the requirement of the user, best E learning platform can be recommended (Fig. 6).

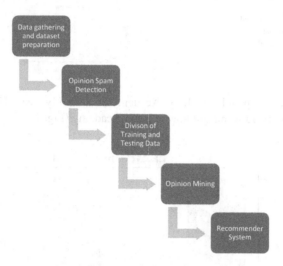

Fig. 6. Proposed Recommender Model

Let us know discuss the Dataset that we have taken which is a very popular dataset used by various researchers. The Taiwan-based non-profit Junyi Academy Foundation is pleased to support our learning community during this pandemic of Covid-19, whose mission is to educate all students with an equal and high-quality education through technology. They haves published a dataset made up of more than 16 million exercise attempt logs from more than 72,000 students collected over the course of one year (from 2018/08 to 2019/07). In addition to encouraging wider engagement for advancing the future of online learning from interdisciplinary specialists, this dataset will facilitate research aimed at improving and personalizing the learning experience for students. The fundamental building block for teaching kids a concept is an exercise. A single exercise has several problems that are all related to the same idea [25].

Number of Problem Attempts = 16,217,311
Number of Students = 72,630
Learning Stages: Elementary, Junior, and Senior
Level of difficulty = Easy, Hard, Unset and Normal (Table 2)

Significance: Junyi Academy, which was founded in 2012, is an online learning platform that offers more than 50,000 activities and 10,000 videos for students in grades ranging from elementary school to senior high school. There are many topics, such as science, technology, math, and language. All classes are free for all kids in order to achieve educational equity. Over 1.7 million people have registered as of 2019/11,

Table2. Important Measures and Factors

Ucid	Content_Pretty_Name	Content Kind	Difficulty Level	Subject	Learning Stage
133	The Chinese Display name of the content having 1320 unique values that can be sorted on the basis of names (ascending/descending values)	Unique value = 1, since type of question is only "Exercise"	Easy = 63% Normal = 23% Other = (190)14%	Maths	Elementary Junior and Senior

and over 67 thousand people use Junyi Academy on a weekly basis. The largest online learning platform in Taiwan right now is Junyi Academy (Fig. 7).

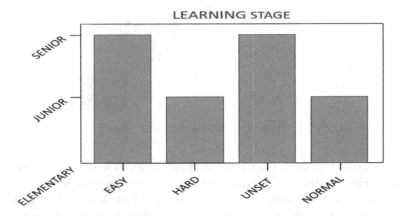

Fig. 7. Analysis of Performance

Motives for Directions

- Estimate each student's performance on each activity, which demonstrates how well they understand a certain idea.
- By using the activity prerequisites or related exercises, this prediction may be made before the learner even began the exercise.
- This can be used to forecast future student performance on a particular activity, such as whether they will improve or deteriorate.
- Check to see if we can validate a student's proficiency for a particular activity or chapter with fewer complications.

The details of the level of Difficulty were observed as follows (Fig. 8):
Easy = 835
Normal = 305
Hard = 149
Unset = 41

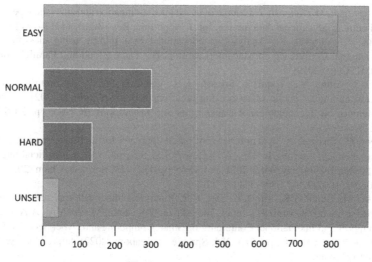

Fig. 8. Level of Difficulty

6 Conclusion

E-learning recommender systems are similar to well-known recommenders' systems used in e-commerce, like the one Amazon employs, still fall into four general categories: hybrid, content-based, CF-based, and knowledge-based. E-learning recommender systems are really very helpful to the learner since it helps them choose the best e learning platform depending upon the review. In order to get the correct feedback about the course people often check the review. In this paper we suggest performing the opinion mining of the review received about a particular course of an e learning platform. Recommender System can suggest the best course/e learning platform to a learner subject to the availability of the correct review about a particular course on an e learning platform.

References

1. Zhang, Q., Lu, J., Zhang, G.: Recommender systems in E-learning. J. Smart. Environ. Green. Comput. **1**, 76–89 (2021). https://doi.org/10.20517/jsegc.2020.06
2. Kurt, A.A., Emiroglu, B.G.: Analysis of students' online information searching strategies, exposure to internet information pollution and cognitive absorption levels based on various variables. Malays. Online J. Educ. Technol. **6**(1), 18–29 (2018)
3. Saleh, M.A., Palaniappan, S., Abdalla, N.A.A.: Education is an overview of data mining and the ability to predict the performance of students. Edukasi **15**(1), 19–28 (2021). https://journal.unnes.ac.id/nju/index.php/edukasi,
4. Ahmed, A.M., Rizaner, A., Ulusoy, A.H.: Using data mining to predict instructor performance. Procedia Comput. Sci. **102**, 137–142 (2016)
5. Angeli, C., Howard, S.K., Ma, J., Yang, J., Kirschner, P.A.: Data mining in educational technology classroom research: can it make a contribution? Comput. Educ. **113**, 226–242 (2017)

6. Anoopkumar, M., Rahman, A.: Model of tuned j48 classification and analysis of performance prediction in educational data mining. Int. J. Appl. Eng. Res **13**(20), 14717–14727 (2018)
7. Jalota, C., Agrawal, R.: Analysis of educational data mining using classification. In: International Conference on Machine Learning, Big Data, Cloud and Parallel Computing (COMITCon) (2019)
8. Singh, P., Singh, Y.P., Kapil, S., Srivastava, S., Vishwakarma, V.: An improved model for opinion mining of public reviews using recurrent neural network. In: 2021 International Conference on Technological Advancements and Innovations (ICTAI), pp. 20–25. IEEE (2021)
9. Dubey, G., Sharma, P.: A neural network based approach for text-level sentiment analysis using sentiment lexicons. In: Dev, A., Agrawal, S.S., Sharma, A. (eds.) Artificial Intelligence and Speech Technology, AIST 2021, vol. 1546, pp. 134–150. Springer, Cham (2022). https://doi.org/10.1007/978-3-030-95711-7_12
10. Khatter, H., Gupta, A.K., Singh, P., Garg, R.R.: Smart recommendation system for hollywood movies using cosine similarity index. In: Pattnaik, P.K., Sain, M., Al-Absi, A.A. (eds.) Proceedings of 2nd International Conference on Smart Computing and Cyber Security, SMART-CYBER 2021, vol. 395, pp. 283–294. Springer, Singapore (2022). https://doi.org/10.1007/978-981-16-9480-6_27
11. Abuhassna, H., Al-Rahmi, W.M., Yahya, N., Zakaria, M.A.Z.M., Kosnin, A.B.M., Darwish, M.: Development of a new model on utilizing online learning platforms to improve students' academic achievements and satisfaction. Int. J. Educ. Technol. High. Educ. **17**, 1–23 (2020)
12. Platforms to improve students' academic achievements and satisfaction. Int. J. Educ. Technol. High. Educ.
13. Drigas, A., Vrettaros, J.: An intelligent tool for building e-learning contend-material using natural language in digital libraries. WSEAS Trans. Inf. Sci. Appl. **1**(5), 1197–1205 (2004)
14. Pahl, C., Donnellan, D.: Data mining technology for the evaluation of web-based teaching and learning systems. In: World Conference on e-Learning in Corporate, Government, Healthcare, and Higher Education, pp. 747–752 (2002)
15. Singh, S.P.: Hierarchical classification of learning resources through supervised learning. In: World Conference on e-Learning in Corporate, Government, Healthcare, and Higher Education, pp. 178–183 (2004)
16. Hwang, G.J., Judy, C.R., Wu, C.H., Li, C.M., Hwang, G.H.: Development of an intelligent management system for monitoring educational web servers. In: 10th Pacific Asia Conference on Information Systems, PACIS 2004, pp. 2334–2340 (2004)
17. Zaïane, O.R.: Building a recommender agent for e-learning systems. In: The International Conference on Computers in Education, ICCE 2002, vol. 99, pp. 55–59 (2002)
18. Zaïane, O.R., Luo, J.: towards evaluating learners' behavior in a web-based distance learning environment. In: IEEE International Conference on Advanced Learning Technologies, ICALT 2001, 6–8 August, Madison, WI, pp. 357–360 (2001)
19. Tane, J., Schmitz, C., Stumme, G.: Semantic resource management for the web: an E-learning application. In: Fieldman, S., Uretsky, M. (eds.) The 13th World Wide Web Conference 2004, WWW2004, pp. 1–10. ACM Press, New York (2004)
20. Tsai, C.-J., Tseng, S.S., Lin, C.-Y.: A two-phase fuzzy mining and learning algorithm for adaptive learning environment. In: Alexandrov, V.N., Dongarra, J.J., Juliano, B.A., Renner, R.S., Tan, C.J.K. (eds.) ICCS 2001. LNCS, vol. 2074, pp. 429–438. Springer, Heidelberg (2001). https://doi.org/10.1007/3-540-45718-6_47
21. Croock, M., et al.: State-of-theArt. ALFanet/IST-2001–33288 Deliverable D12. Open Universiteit Nederland (2002)
22. Abe, H., Hasegawa, S., Ochimizu, K.: A learning management system with navigation supports. In: The International Conference on Computers in Education, ICCE 2003, Hong Kong, pp. 509–513 (2003)

23. Yoo, J., Yoo, S., Lance, C., Hankins, J.: Student progress monitoring tool using treeview. In: The 37th Technical Symposium on Computer Science Education, SIGCSE 2006, 1–5 March, Houston, USA, pp. 373–377. ACM Press (2006)
24. Al-Badarenah, A., Alsakran, J.: An automated recommender system for course selection. Int. J. Adv. Comput. Sci. Appl. **7**(3), 166–175 (2016). https://doi.org/10.14569/ijacsa.2016. 070323
25. Wang, F.H., Shao, H.M.: Effective personalized recommendation based on time-framed navigation clustering and association mining. Expert Syst. Appl. **27**(3), 365–377 (2004). https:// doi.org/10.1016/j.eswa.2004.05.005
26. Chen, P.J., Hsieh, M.E., Tsai, T.Y.: Junyi online learning dataset: a large-scale public online learning activity dataset from elementary to senior high school students (2020). https://www. kaggle.com/junyiacademy/learning-activity-public-dataset-by-junyi-academy

Predicting Student Performance in Blended Learning Teaching Methodology Using Machine Learning

Vallampatla Nanda Kishore[1]([✉]) [iD] and B. Vikranth[2] [iD]

[1] Data Sciences, IT Department, CVR College of Engineering, Hyderabad, India
vnandakishor23@gmail.com
[2] IT Department, CVR College of Engineering, Hyderabad, India
b.vikranth@cvr.ac.in

Abstract. Blended learning is a hybrid teaching methodology comprising flipped classrooms and Massive Open Online Courses (MOOCs). It is an effective teaching methodology that can improve student academic performance. In view of supporting such an innovative teaching approach, the assessment of students plays an important role. This paper proposes a machine learning model to predict the performance of students in the blended learning environment. This prediction can be used for the student final exams. The data set used in this work is collected from online education platforms. The data set can be divided into two parts 1) Spring Semester Dataset, and 2) Fall Semester Dataset. The Four different Machine Learning Models used are LGBM, Xg Boost Regressor, Gradient Boosting Decision Trees, and KNN. The models used the performance evaluation metrics of the R2 Score. For the spring and fall semester datasets, the Xg boost Regressor achieved the highest R2 Score of 0.99.

Keywords: Blended Learning · Flipped classroom · Machine Learning · MOOC · student performance

1 Introduction

Traditional teaching methods may not be more effective for the new era of the education system as students are aware of technology and can easily learn more things by using technology [1]. Teaching techniques in the new era had to change as technology advanced and traditional teaching methods may no longer be effective for these students [2]. Most of the students know how to use technology. It will be easy for them to learn through technology [3]. As a result, teachers must also adapt to new ways of learning that result in improved student performance.

The use of blended learning in the new era may result in better student performance [4]. Blended learning is a combined approach that uses the flipped classroom and MOOC online courses together [5]. Predicting the offline final exam results of the students based on their performance in the MOOC course. The data is collected in different forms, such

© Springer Nature Switzerland AG 2023
D. Garg et al. (Eds.): IACC 2022, CCIS 1782, pp. 386–394, 2023.
https://doi.org/10.1007/978-3-031-35644-5_31

as assessment submissions, course registration time, and assessment results. Based on the data, we predict the performance of the students on final exams.

Blended learning can be applied to the students of the new era so that teachers can expect more effective results from them [6] As blended learning is a combination of the flipped classroom and MOOC online courses, students can easily learn academics, resulting in increased student performance [7].

2 Literature Survey

Fahd et al. [8] Employed a Learning Management System to predict the performance of students in blended learning. Applying student LMS interaction data created a dimensional vector that was later converted to incorporate response attributes. An algorithm to detect students at risk is then developed using this altered dataset. Then they employed 5 tree-based classifiers (J48, random forest, OneR, NBTree, and decision stump) to provide extremely precise, understandable predictions to identify students who are at risk. Data was gathered from logs of LMS, cleaned up & translated into a format that was suitable for public transmission. The disadvantage is that identifying the students at risk is a time-consuming and manual process that can be skewed by personnel involvement. Different algorithms like Random Forest, Decision Stump, NB Tree, J48, and OneR are applied to the dataset. Random Forest got the best accuracy among all those algorithms. The data is collected from students' Learning Management System interaction activities. Random Forest achieved an accuracy of 79.4%. The evolution metrics are accuracy, recall, precision, RMSE, and F-measure.

Chen et al. [9] Introduced a blended learning model from multiple sources of data to predict the grades of students. There are four different types of data sets for which data integration is performed. The multiple classification problem is often divided into multiple double classifications. By integrating the results, multiple classifications are accomplished. An ensemble learning technique for multi-class classification is the ECOC algorithm. It can use a classifier to do the error-correcting function. The next method is feature selection. It is the primary method of data processing. Then they designed an ECOC Framework that is based on TBC and GA. A TBCGA-ECOC algorithm is proposed. These three different methods, namely Random Forest, Xgboost, and a new algorithm, were introduced under the name TBCGA-ECOC. The new algorithm got higher accuracy when compared with traditional ensemble learning algorithms and classical ECOC. There are four different datasets, like Rain classroom cnblogs, Rain classroom PTA, MOOC Rainclassroom PTA, and Rainclassroom PTA (2020–21). The accuracy of the model is 78%. The evolution measure is precision. The disadvantage is that its adaptability is less with hybrid binary classifier selection.

Buschetto Macarini et al. [10] Proposed a model for predicting student success in blended learning and evaluating different interactions inside an LMS. There are thirteen different datasets for each of the four semesters for detecting at-risk students early. There are four steps present in the process. In the first step, the data is gathered from the Moodle logs that record student interactions. The next step is generating the datasets that have different attributes and comparing and verifying them to achieve the best results. In the next step, preprocessing techniques like oversampling can be employed to increase the performance of the model. The next step is the generation and evaluation of the models and then comparing the results. The different algorithms used are Adaboost, Random Forest, KNN, and MLP. Adaboost is the best-performed algorithm, as it is the most present algorithm. The interactions of LMS count from week 0 to week 8, which is the middle of the semester. This data can be used as a dataset. Then they calculated the mean and median of the ROC values of the dataset and sorted them in descending order. The most repeated classifier among all the classifiers is Adaboost. So it is the best suite algorithm. The limitation of the work lies in the small number of cases included in each dataset.

Le et al. [11] Proposed a model. By using Factors of Interactive Activities to Predict the Student's Results in Blended Learning, they examined the models that predict learning outcomes for students. Using the R tool, I created a model that is based on the regression machine. The final course grade serves as the predictor in our model, while the selected interacting factors are treated as independent variables. There are several models used, including linear regression, KNR (Regression B based on KNN), SVM, and Bayesian Ridge. The ridge is a more accurate model as its learning curve shows the overfitting of the model. The data is taken from the system's log databases. The R2_loss of the model is 0.890. The performance evaluation measures are Mean Square Error, Mean Average Error, and R2_loss. The disadvantage is that model selection based on these factors is a detrimental issue.

Van Goidsenhoven et al. [12] Implemented a blended learning environment to predict student success. The data can be taken from the online learning system and then two detection methods are applied to the data to ensure that the results will not be impacted by outliers and anomalies. They are removed if found. Then the data preparation can be done for the predictive modeling of the data. They further process the data for that. Then the data is ready for predictive modeling. It is to decide the most appropriate predictive modeling technique by taking a few concerns. The appropriate predictive modeling techniques are logistic regression and random forest classification. Those are compared among which Logistic Regression got higher accuracy. The data was collected from a course at KU Leuven. They didn't collect data related to students' doubts and attendance, which is the limitation of this paper. The accuracy of the model is 84%. The different performance evaluation measures are precision, recall, accuracy, f1 score, macro average, cross-validation, and weighted average.

Guo et al. [13] Applied sentiment analysis to predict the attitude of students towards blended learning. The data is collected from the blended class from an online teaching platform website and mobile app. Then it can be divided into training and testing parts. In the next stage, the data is processed as categorical or numeric, textual. The categorical data is directly fed into the final classifier or regressor, but the textual data can be employed with word embedding from NLP. It maps textual content into vectors as a classifier or regressor only receives categorical data. Here, the existing review corpus is converted to vectors that are fed to a sentiment analyzer to get numerical sentiment scores. The average score is to be treated as another numerical feature that is incorporated into the learning process. Two different tasks, classification, and regression are performed. For classification tasks, the models used are Naive Bayes, Linear Regression, SVM, and Random Forest. In contrast, in the regression task, models like Linear Regression,

Lasso Regression, Polynomial Regression, and Support Vector Regression are used. In classification, SVM shows better performance, whereas, in regression, SV Regression shows better performance. The source of data is from a Blended Learning platform with a website and mobile app. The F1-score of SVM is 75.1 and the Root Mean Square Error of SVR is 7.68. The features of the text are hard to feed into the final classifier. The performance evaluation metrics for classification are precision, recall, and F1-Score, and for regression, Root Mean Square Error.

Akram et al. [14] Implemented a method using the homework submission data to predict an academic delay in blended learning. Clustering is mostly used to distinguish between procrastinators and non-procrastinators among students who turn in their assignments late or not at all. More precise clusters that clearly demarcate the difference between procrastinators and other students emerge as the value of k is raised. OneR, ZeroR, J48, ID3, NBTree, Decision Stump, Random Forest, PART, JRip, and Prism are among the ten classification techniques that are employed. The dataset was collected from the logs of SCHOLAT, which is from a course called ACM Programming. NB Tree is the most consistent of all the ten algorithms. The next consistent algorithm is the Random Forest. The OneR and ZeroR algorithms show the worst performance. The evaluation measures are Root Mean Square Error, the performance of correctly and incorrectly classified instances, and Kappa statistics.

Salma et al. [15] Tested the effectiveness of project-based learning on student achievement in online blended learning. A posttest control design was used in this study's research methodology, and individuals were split into two sections or groups: the control class and the experimental class. Project-based blended learning is used in the experimental group, whereas virtual synchronous learning is used in the control group. Due to the extremely huge number of populations, cluster random sampling was applied in this research, and the populations were then randomly sorted into classes or groups. The tests (i.e., pretest and posttest) are mostly used to collect data. Both the control class and the experimental class are given 30 multiple-choice questions. The Hypothesis Test Model is used for the dataset. The results show that there is an increase in the post-test results with the hypothesis test. The data was collected from 72 students by dividing them into two equal groups and conducting a test. Performance on the pretest and posttest is counted. The disadvantage of this paper is that researchers were unable to create an effective platform for project-based learning. Here, the performance evaluation is based on the performances of students in the pretest and posttest.

These studies show that Boosting algorithms have achieved more R2 scores in predicting the performance of students. Different Boosting algorithms are used in this paper. R2 Score is the best evaluation metric for measuring performance. The MOOC dataset is vast. So, the dataset is used for accurate model prediction.

3 Methodology

The dataset is collected from an online Educational Platform. The Massive Open Online Course dataset contains attributes of students' activities like Semester, viewed, explored, Completed or Not, grade, n_events, ndays_act, and n_chapters, etc. These attributes are used to predict the performance of the students. The Data set contains 13 attributes and 54520 Records. The Dataset is very large as it is having more Records (Fig. 1).

	semester	viewed	explored	Completed_or_Not	YoB	gender	grade	nevents	ndays_act	nchapters	e_value	Pa	normalized_Pa
0	Fall	1.0	0.0	0.0	1993.0	m	1329.0	12.0	6.0	0.024991	1.936746	0.189636	0.05
1	spring	1.0	1.0	0.0	1991.0	m	3018.0	27.0	9.0	0.056751	1.883158	0.174007	0.27
2	spring	0.0	0.0	0.0	1986.0	m	1.0	1.0	0.0	0.000019	1.920072	0.184773	0.00
3	spring	0.0	0.0	0.0	1972.0	m	3.0	2.0	0.0	0.000056	1.846533	0.163326	0.00
4	Fall	1.0	0.0	0.0	1988.0	f	14.0	1.0	1.0	0.000263	1.920220	0.184816	0.00
...	...	...	...	...	...	...	...	...	...	...	...	...	...
54515	Fall	0.0	0.0	0.0	1984.0	m	1.0	1.0	0.0	0.000019	1.920072	0.184773	0.00
54516	spring	1.0	0.0	0.0	1972.0	m	153.0	3.0	2.0	0.002877	1.921960	0.185324	0.00
54517	spring	1.0	0.0	0.0	1985.0	m	309.0	7.0	2.0	0.005810	1.782386	0.144618	0.01
54518	spring	0.0	0.0	0.0	1986.0	m	7.0	1.0	0.0	0.000132	1.920147	0.184795	0.00
54519	Fall	1.0	0.0	0.0	1982.0	m	1319.0	12.0	5.0	0.024803	1.936620	0.189599	0.01

Fig. 1. Massive Open Online Course Dataset

3.1 Data Preprocessing

The Data can be preprocessed Before it is deployed to the models in this process the data can be cleaned and noise data can be removed. Some of the Features can be selected from the dataset to overcome the overfitting of data. The data can be divided into two parts and all the models are applied to Two datasets and compared.

3.2 Work Flow

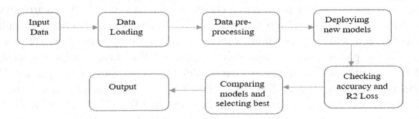

Fig. 2. Proposed workflow

The flow of the project starts with Loading the Input Dataset. The dataset is from a Massive open online course. In which log time, course start time, and all other activities within the course are recorded. After loading the data Pre-processing is performed. In Pre-processing data cleaning and removing noise data are performed. After cleaning the data and removing the noise data. Deployed the models to the cleaned data. Here dataset is divided into 2 parts: Spring Semester and Fall Semester (Fig. 2).

Deployed the models to the Two datasets separately. After loading models Initialize the Training of the model. Train the model with the dataset.

After Training the model checks the R2 Score of the models. Then compare the models and select the best one of them. A model with the highest R2 score is the best model of all.

3.3 Experimental Setup

The data collected from an online educational platform is pre-processed to remove noise and clean the data. The Models are deployed to cleaned data. Here the data can be divided into two parts Spring semester and the Fall semester. The models deployed into the two datasets separately. The models used in this experiment were Light Gradient Boosting Machine, XG Boost Regressor, Gradient Boosting Decision Trees, and K-Nearest Neighbor. The evaluation metric considered in this approach is the R2 score. XG Boost Regressor got the highest R2 Score in the experiment.

The following hardware and software are supported to use the proposed machine learning techniques: Nvidia GPU; 8.00 GB of RAM; 476 GB of storage. Windows 10 OS, Google Collab, and other required python Libraries.

4   Result Analysis

The data can be divided into 2 parts.

1. Spring Semester Dataset
2. Fall Semester Dataset

4.1   Spring Semester Dataset

The Four different Machine Learning models are used for predicting the performance of students using the Spring Semester Dataset. The performance metric used is the R2 Score (Table 1 and Fig. 3).

Table 1. R2 Score of Spring Semester Dataset

S.NO	MODEL	R2 Score
1	LGBM	0.98
2	Xg Boost Regressor	0.99
3	GBDT	0.83
4	KNN	0.78

4.2   Fall Semester Dataset

The Four different Machine Learning models are used for predicting the performance of students using the Fall Semester Dataset. The performance metric used is the R2 Score (Table 2).

When all the models of the Spring Semester and Fall semesters are compared Xg Boost Regressor got high Accuracy. Hence we conclude that Xg Boost works more accurately than other algorithms (Fig. 4).

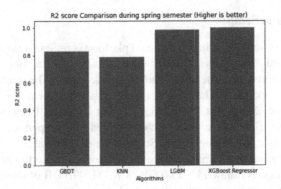

Fig. 3. R2 Score Comparison of Spring Semester Data

Table 2. R2 Score of Fall Semester Dataset

S.NO	MODEL	R2 Score
1	LGBM	0.98
2	Xg Boost Regressor	0.99
3	GBDT	0.92
4	KNN	0.75

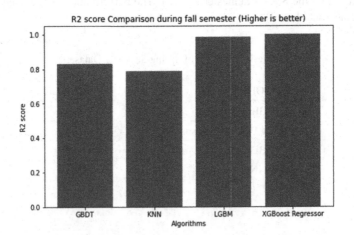

Fig. 4. R2 Score Comparison of Fall Semester Data

5   Conclusion

This paper aims to predict the performance of students in a MOOC online course. The online course is about the academics of the students. There, the students can learn the subject clearly and submit their assignments. Based on the assignment submission data, The performance of students can be predicted in the final offline exams. The data is collected from an online learning platform and then went on to predict their performance in offline classes using that data. Machine learning algorithms are applied to the collected data and predicted the performance of the students in the Final Semester Exam. There are Four different Machine learning algorithms are applied to datasets to predict the performance of the students. Finally, The Xg boost regressor has the highest R2 score of 0.99 for the spring and fall semester datasets. This prediction can also be helpful for students who are at risk of failing the exams.

References

1. Xu, Z., Yuan, H., Liu, Q.: Student performance prediction based on blended learning. IEEE Trans. Educ. **64**(1), 66–73 (2021)
2. Ozerova, G.P., Pavlenko, G.F.: Prediction of student performance in blended learning by utilizing learning analytics data. Sci. Educ. Today **9**(6), 73–87 (2019)
3. Perach, S., Alexandron, G.: A blended-learning program for implementing a rigorous machine-learning curriculum in high-schools. In: Proceedings of the Ninth ACM Conference on Learning @ Scale (2022)
4. Kintu, M.J., Zhu, C., Kagambe, E.: Blended learning effectiveness: the relationship between student characteristics, design features and outcomes. Int. J. Educ. Technol. High. Educ. **6**(1) (2017)
5. Chango, W., Cerezo, R., Romero, C.: Predicting the academic performance of university students from multi-sources data in blended learning. In: Proceedings of the Second International Conference on Data Science, E-Learning and Information Systems - DATA '8, 12 (2019)
6. Ganesh, D., Devasia, J., Mujgule, N.: Our experiments with MOOCs: a study on using blended learning pedagogy in faculty development programs at IIMBx; pilot project: strategy and the sustainable enterprise for teachers. In: ICSD 2021 (2022)
7. Nespereira, C.G., Elhariri, E., El-Bendary, N., Vilas, A.F., Redondo, R.P.D.: Machine learning based classification approach for predicting students performance in blended learning. In: Gaber, T., Hassanien, A.E., El-Bendary, N., Dey, N.. (eds.) The 1st International Conference on Advanced Intelligent System and Informatics (AISI2015), November 28–30, 2015, Beni Suef, Egypt. AISC, vol. 407, pp. 47–56. Springer, Cham (2016). https://doi.org/10.1007/978-3-319-26690-9_5
8. Fahd, K., Miah, S.J., Ahmed, K.: Predicting student performance in a blended learning environment using learning management system interaction data. Appl. Comput. Inform. **8**(2) (2021)
9. Chen, L., Wu, M., Pan, L., Zheng, R.: Grade prediction in blended learning using multisource data. Sci. Program. **2021**, 1–15 (2021)
10. Buschetto Macarini, L.A., Cechinel, C., Batista Machado, M.F., Ramos, F.C., V., Munoz, R.: Predicting student's success in blended learning—evaluating different interactions inside learning management systems. Appl. Sci. **7**(24), 5523 (2019)
11. Le, M., Nguyen, H., Nguyen, D., Nguyen, V.A.: How to forecast the students' learning outcomes based on factors of interactive activities in a blended learning course. In: Proceedings of 2020 The 6th International Conference on Frontiers of Educational Technologies, 6 (2020)
12. Van Goidsenhoven, S., Bogdanova, D., Deeva, G., Broucke, S. V., De Weerdt, J., Snoeck, M.: Predicting student success in a blended learning environment. In: Proceedings of the Tenth International Conference on Learning Analytics & Knowledge, p. 8 (2020)

13. Guo, C., Yan, X., Li, Y.: Prediction of student attitude towards blended learning based on sentiment analysis. In: Proceedings of the 2020 9th International Conference on Educational and Information Technology, 8 (2020)
14. Akram, A., et al.: Predicting students' academic procrastination in blended learning courses using homework submission data. IEEE Access **7**, 102487–102498 (2019)
15. Salma, W.A., Basori, B., Hatta, P.: The effectiveness and effect of project-based blended learning on student achievement in online learning at Surakarta, Indonesia. IJIE (Indonesian J. Inform. Educ.) **5**(1), 1 (2021)

Using OMR for Grading MCQ-Type Answer Sheets Based on Bubble Marks

Yalmar Ponce Atencio[1]([⊠]) [iD], Jhon Huanca Suaquita[1] [iD],
Joab Maquera Ramirez[2] [iD], Jesus Cabel Moscoso[1] [iD],
and Freddy Marrero Saucedo[1] [iD]

[1] Universidad Nacional de Juliaca, Puno, Peru
{ytponcea.doc,jrhuancas.doc,jesus.cabel,freddy.marreros}@unaj.edu.pe
[2] Universidad Nacional Amazonica de Madre de Dios, Puerto Maldonado, Peru
joab.maquera@unamad.edu.pe

Abstract. Currently have been many application proposals of computer vision in task automatizing. One of them is the evaluation of questionnaires based on optical mark sheets. Frequently, existing methods are depending of specific devices, resources and supplies provided by some companies like SCANTRON. On the other hand, it also requires enter parameters to work with a given template. Then, developing on low-cost solutions for optical mark recognition (OMR) is still an interesting field for researching. The need for using OMR is wide, from simple scholar tests to complex questionnaires like to used in universities admission. However, it's necessary to use a computationally efficient method that works fast and provides enough accuracy in order to be used in serious tests. To address these problems, a computationally efficient and reliable OMR method is proposed in this research. The background idea is to use a general optical marks distribution in a piece of sheet which could be printed by anyone, using a simple general template, in contrast with many other approaches where implement complex algorithms to detect where the optical marks are. Accuracy is achieved by tuning some general features like piece of sheet size and marks size, since that is possible the user could print sheets with different sizes. Marked regions are accurately detected by identifying global margins, since here la main goal is detect where the marks group are. Depending of the sheet size, configurations from one to many groups or columns are considered. Tests with different number of columns were conducted successfully, with no errors, showing the efficiency of the proposed method when the scanned images are clear and no damaged.

Keywords: Optical mark recognition · Bubble sheet scanner · Multiple choice questions

---

Universidad Nacional de Juliaca - UNAJ

© Springer Nature Switzerland AG 2023
D. Garg et al. (Eds.): IACC 2022, CCIS 1782, pp. 395–404, 2023.
https://doi.org/10.1007/978-3-031-35644-5_32

1   Introduction

The optical mark recognition system consists of evaluating optical mark sheets that normally contain a grid of circles, where each row corresponds to the options of each question. These labeled regions are detected and compared to key answers, which have been input previously to the system or also have could scanned from a single optical sheet with the correct answers. Automated OMR system finds a wide range of applications such as exam evaluation based on multiple-choice-question (MCQ) patterns, user survey data collection, opinion polls, etc. Most existing systems assume that the regions of the marking circles are known in advance. Therefore, the grade sheet reference template is required as an input parameter, which could be a limitation. So, developing a low cost and reliable solution for these tasks remains a challenge and of great interest. To develop an efficient OMR system, tagging region identification methods are used. For this purpose the most commonly used programming tool is OpenCV. Then, the region of interest is identified, using image processing and pattern recognition techniques, more specifically, by segmenting the area where the groups of circles of the optical chip meet. The obtained region of interest is processed individually by means of a optical mark (bubble) detection algorithm. The accuracy of mark detection depends on some image enhancement techniques, such as local thresholding along rows of bubbles (marks). The proposed implementation allows evaluating grading sheets with different bubble configurations, more precisely, sheets with several columns and rows, depending on the need for the number of questions to be evaluated. The main contribution of this research work is to present a simple an easy way to process multiple choice question sheets based on bubble marks, being all the step are done at low-cost, from make the design and print by self the bubble mark sheets until to scan the answered sheets with an conventional scanner and finally grade the evaluation using image processing techniques. The document is organized in sections as follows: Sect. 2 presents previous research works in the literature, Sect. 3 describes the methodology. Section 4 presents the implementation details. Section 5 shows the results of the conducted experiments. Finally, the conclusion and future works are presented.

2   Related Work

Optical Mark Recognition (OMR) tools have became popular in the last two decades, mainly they are used to automate the scoring of a large number of exams. However, commonly are used specialized mechanical equipment with practical and cost limitations [4]. Although, currently, there are image processing techniques that could provide ways to mitigate the difficulties and requirements for scoring answers of exams based on optical mark sheets. Many approaches to OMR have been proposed by using image processing techniques. For example, in [8] is presented a interesting automated parameter-less OMR system, where it doesn't depends of any prior input parameters to detect the regions with answer bubbles in a optical mark sheet. In [5] also has used OMR for processing surveys. As in the most of works, first, the edges of the answer sheets are detected with an algorithm like the Hough transform, as a reference for generalized processing, and in this way the marks can be recognized by locating the coverage of the answer areas [3]. Loke et.al. [7] In [11] was proposed a scoring algorithm for a grid-type answer sheet, which uses image enhancing and thresholding techniques. Rakesh et al. proposed a system consists of an ordinary printer, a scanner and a computer to carry out the entire process from the design of the forms, and in this way, the marked forms are scanned and processed to recognize the source format, which gives as result a spreadsheet [10]. Similarly Castro et al. [2] presented a integral system for grading exams of School Competitions. Most of them have used the OpenCV library [6,9]. On the other hand, Marakeby presents a low-cost OMR solution that takes advantage of the multiprocessing computational architecture. In this approach, the answer sheets are digitized with a regular camera. Initially the borders are located and then the bubbles with the response categories, without correcting the rotation of the image. This method uses adaptive binarization to mitigate the effects of light in images taken with normal cameras [1]. Thus, in this article is presented a simplified procedure based on image processing techniques, which are applied to scanned images acquired by an regular scanner and, therefore, with good quality.

3   Proposed Method

Many of the optical mark recognition systems have proven to be efficient and suitable in real time with some limitations. However, these limitations in some cases are impractical and require even more appropriate systems. Although many users of these systems have continued its use adopting out of habit and fear of switching to another technology, many other users do not have access to them due to high costs. So, to address a specific processing system for optical cards, hardware components are traditionally used, which already recognize the marks and report in files the readings of the optical cards that are made in blocks of up to 200 sheets. However, these systems are very expensive since the hardware is specific for that purpose. Even so, the hardware in its most expensive version can process up to 90 pages per minute, not to mention that most of the time the reading stops because the cards may be slightly bent, so the best time is reduced to less than the half, due to the sheet must fixed and then the reading process is relaunched. In addition to the specific hardware, the cards are also special, and in sheets of greater thickness and weight (120gr), and must be pre-printed in advance, in addition to that, the shipping and transfer costs of this material are also considered. And on the other hand, systems based on image processing do not depend on specific hardware, which makes them more versatile, however, a scanner is also required to digitize the optical sheets into images. This can be done by any low-cost multifunctional printer that also has a built-in scanner, although on cheap machines the speed is 20 to 30 pages per minute, there are faster multifunctional printers with up to 150 pages per minute, which can be quite useful when many sheets (>1000) have to be scanned. In these systems, a fundamental aspect is also the printing of the cards, since as they do not depend on a specific hardware, they can be designed and printed. However, after having reviewed the implementation of many of these systems, some authors consider imitating the cards of traditional optical mark recognition systems, which makes these systems unnecessarily complicated in their processing. Our proposal is to simplify the bubble marks recognition process as much as possible, then our system recognize a global region with bubble marks, which is distributed on a regular grid. Later, as an example could be considered in rows of 5 alternatives, and several columns to admit an appropriate amount of questions for all kinds of purposes. Exams of up to 90 questions are usually taken, which is quite simple to generate and then process.

The scanned images of the optical cards are processed in several steps: First, correction tilt is performed. It is done by identifying the paper sheet orientation, put the scanned image on a different color background (see Fig. 4-left).

Then, the circle marking region is identified to locate the position of the circles that must be evaluated, in this step is known how many columns have been used, since this data is entered as a parameter when executing the application. We consider that it is not necessary to spend time and effort implementing an automated dynamic recognition system (see Fig. 1).

The bubble recognition algorithm identifies the number of bubbles per row, and since the number of columns is known, the system separates them into groups that are read sequentially and incrementally (see Fig. 2).

Once the rows and columns of all the marks have been identified, the qualification is made by verifying the correspondence between the marked value and that of the scanned master optical sheet containing the correct answers (or simply to input the answer keys as an list of values).

4   Implementation Details

This stage describes the implementation of the system and will cover the most important details of how the system works.

- **Step 1**: The images on the answer sheets are scanned. This can be done by any conventional scanner or even use a cell phone camera or web camera and then the images are saved in a specific directory.
- **Step 2**: In a next step there is no need for special marks on the scanned images. Only the answer sheet with a reasonable resolution is needed, however, to ensure detection of the region where the marks are located we put the scanned image on a fixed color background.
- **Step 3**: After generating the final image, the next step is to convert the image to grayscale, as this will be helpful in easily detecting the edges of user-made marks/highlights. Then a high blur is applied to the image so that we can reduce high-frequency noise, which means distortion in the image.
- **Step 4**: After converting to grayscale, the next step will be to extract the region of interest from the given image, that is, where the marks are actually located, as said before, it does not depend on the marks always being in a

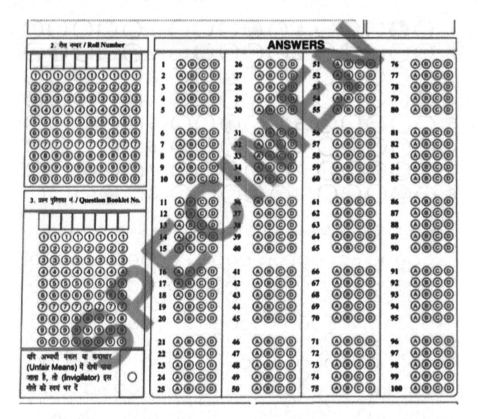

Fig. 1. This images shows an optical marks sheet paper with complex distribution .

same place, the system is able to recognize where the marks are located. For this, the Canny Edge Detection technique is applied which helps to find all the edges within the image. This algorithm is a multi-stage algorithm that goes through several steps and produces an image that has all the edges (horizontal and vertical) within it.

– **Step 5**: After obtaining the contours, an orientation transformation is applied in such a way as to provide an image aligned with the x and y axes. Then the "cv.findContours()" function is used, and also the Canny Edge Detection technique. At this stage, the goal is to search for a white block from a black background and such a transformation is possible to get using the previous step. So, to get only important points from the edges such as corners instead of continuous lines that form a rectangle (region where the marks are), the "cv.CHAIN_APPROX_SIMPLE" parameter is passed, which only extracts the corner points, eliminating the rest of the points.

– **Step 6**: After the outlines are obtained, they are sorted according to size, from large to small. Thus, the first contour is the rectangular region covering all the bubbles.

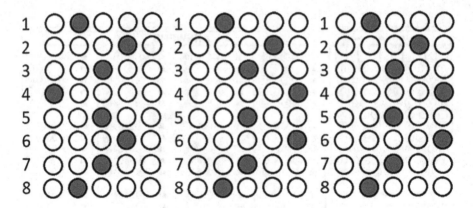

Fig. 2. This images shows an optical marks sheet paper with three columns.

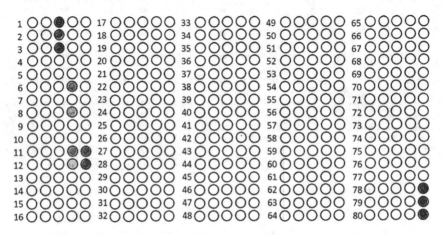

Fig. 3. This images shows a scanned sheet image, where the some bubbles were painted. Notice that the image has good quality, since it was scanned by a conventional scanner.

- **Step 7**: To achieve a proper view, the function "four_point_transform()" is used. This function allows a geometric transformation to extract only the image where the marks are located (Fig. 4).
- **Step 8**: Then the binarization of the image obtained in step 7 is performed, applying a short conversion of the image in black and white format. This is used as pre-processing before any OCR or OMR techniques are applied. This can be done using Otsu's transformation. As you can see below, a black and white image is generated, this binarization is done using OpenCV's threshold function passing to it the Otsu parameter.
- **Step 9**: The next step is to extract the options bubbles present on the answer page. So, again perspective transformation and binarization is used. To find bubbles inside the image, there are many possible ways. Here we use opencv's

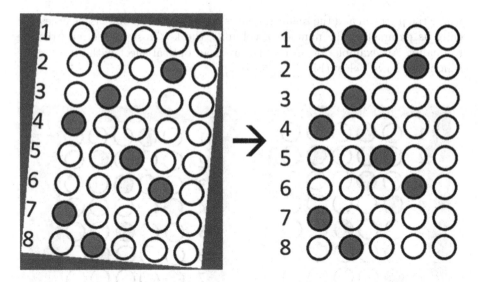

Fig. 4. This figure shows how the orientation of the scanned images is corrected in order to align with the coordinate axes.

HoughCircle() function which allows to highlight circle area inside the image. It then loops to find all the circles from the focus from left to right from top to bottom. This will save it to an array where each array index makes up four options/bubble outlines, meaning each row is saved at each array index, so you get a 2D array (Fig. 4).

- **Step 10**: Finally, the next step is to compare the highlighted, painted or marked answer is correct or not. Initially, the answer key must be in an array or a list, and this could either be entered as a parameter to the system or obtained under this same brand detection process (steps 1 to 9). But the initial step only discovered the outline of the bubble, it is not yet known which option is the correct one inside them. After looking at the image from step 6, you can see that the user highlights or marker bubble option is white, while other options are black with a white border. To find the white bubble is done using opencv's thresh() function using its parameter 1, this can define if the next bubble is a marker or not.

5   Discussion and Results

Tests were carried out with OMR sheets of different sizes and with variable distributions, from one column to five columns, which does not complicate the process of reading the marks in the scanned images at all. In all cases, satisfactory results were obtained, even when the marks are unclear, or have been smudged or marked twice in the same row, which invalidates the answer in all these cases. The tests carried out are executed from the console of some operating system where the program and the scanned images are available. In our case is necessary enter as parameters the number of columns, the key answers file, and the file to qualify. An example for an evaluation of an optical sheet with an only one column is shown below (Fig. 5):

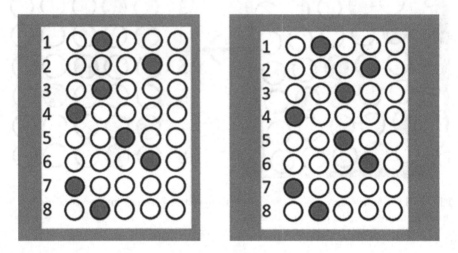

Fig. 5. The first example shows the resolution of a case of a bubble sheet paper with only one column. The Left image is the key answers sheet, and the right image is the user answers sheet.

The corresponding result and score is shown in the Fig. 6.

```
question   0 correct
question   1 correct
question   2 incorrect
question   3 correct
question   4 correct
question   5 correct
question   6 correct
question   7 correct
[INFO] score: 87.50%
[INFO] Correct  7 Incorrect  1
```

Fig. 6. Here is shown the qualification, and here no errors were reported.

Another more complex example, with five columns, was conducted showing the robustness of the technique.

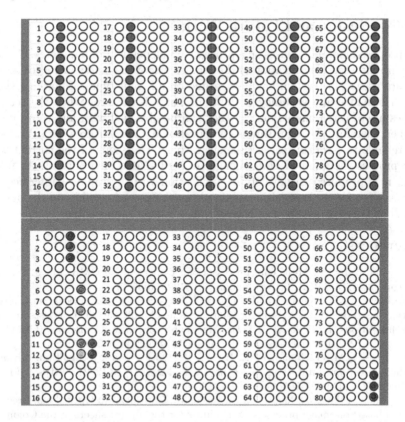

Fig. 7. This figure shows a large piece of paper containing five columns of bubble marks. The top image corresponds to the key answers and the bottom image corresponds to an user answers which was scanned by a conventional scanner.

The corresponding result and score, for the example with five columns is shown in the Fig. 8.

```
question  0 incorrect   question 16 incorrect   question 32 incorrect   question 48 incorrect   question 64 incorrect
question  1 incorrect   question 17 incorrect   question 33 incorrect   question 49 incorrect   question 65 incorrect
question  2 incorrect   question 18 incorrect   question 34 incorrect   question 50 incorrect   question 66 incorrect
question  3 incorrect   question 19 incorrect   question 35 incorrect   question 51 incorrect   question 67 incorrect
question  4 incorrect   question 20 incorrect   question 36 incorrect   question 52 incorrect   question 68 incorrect
question  5 incorrect   question 21 incorrect   question 37 incorrect   question 53 incorrect   question 69 incorrect
question  6 incorrect   question 22 incorrect   question 38 incorrect   question 54 incorrect   question 70 incorrect
question  7 incorrect   question 23 incorrect   question 39 incorrect   question 55 incorrect   question 71 incorrect
question  8 incorrect   question 24 incorrect   question 40 incorrect   question 56 incorrect   question 72 incorrect
question  9 incorrect   question 25 incorrect   question 41 incorrect   question 57 incorrect   question 73 incorrect
question 10 incorrect   question 26 incorrect   question 42 incorrect   question 58 incorrect   question 74 incorrect
question 11 incorrect   question 27 incorrect   question 43 incorrect   question 59 incorrect   question 75 incorrect
question 12 incorrect   question 28 incorrect   question 44 incorrect   question 60 incorrect   question 76 incorrect
question 13 incorrect   question 29 incorrect   question 45 incorrect   question 61 incorrect   question 77 correct
question 14 incorrect   question 30 incorrect   question 46 incorrect   question 62 incorrect   question 78 correct
question 15 incorrect   question 31 incorrect   question 47 incorrect   question 63 incorrect   question 79 correct
[INFO] score: 3.75%
[INFO] Correct  3 Incorrect  77
```

Fig. 8. The results for the five columns optical sheet example show the robustness of the technique. The accuracy is perfect.

6   Conclusion and Future Work

The proposed method focuses on a processing independent of templates. Contour recognition based identification of the regions where the marks or response bubbles are used. This system has been tested on different types of marking sheets for performance and accuracy evaluation. There is no error when the scanned images are of a reasonable quality that can be obtained with any conventional scanner, therefore the algorithm is computationally efficient to work in real time and reliable to perform real assessment ratings. The scope of the current work is to process the scanned OMR images in a PC-based environment. As future work, it is proposed to develop an application with a graphical interface and with support for the recognition of simple markings such as lines on the bubbles as well as the incorporation of other types of marks than bubbles.

References

1. AL-Marakeby, A.: Multi core processors for camera based OMR. Int. J. Comput. Appl. **68**, 1–5 (2013). https://doi.org/10.5120/11636-7116
2. Buleje, C.Y.C., Atencio, Y.T.P., Tinoco, E.E.C.: System with optical mark recognition based on artificial vision for the processing of multiple selection tests in school competitions. In: 2020 XLVI Latin American Computing Conference (CLEI), pp. 172–177 (2020). https://doi.org/10.1109/CLEI52000.2020.00027
3. de Elias, E.M., Tasinaffo, P.M., Hirata, R.: Optical mark recognition: advances, difficulties, and limitations. SN Comput. Sci. **2**(5), 1–13 (2021). https://doi.org/10.1007/s42979-021-00760-z
4. Espitia, O., Paez, A., Mejia, Y., Carrasco, M., Gonzalez, N.: Optical mark recognition based on image processing techniques for the answer sheets of the Colombian high-stakes tests. In: Figueroa-García, J.C., Duarte-González, M., Jaramillo-Isaza, S., Orjuela-Cañon, A.D., Díaz-Gutierrez, Y. (eds.) WEA 2019. CCIS, vol. 1052, pp. 167–176. Springer, Cham (2019). https://doi.org/10.1007/978-3-030-31019-6_15
5. Ha, T., Thu, N.: An application of image processing in optical mark recognition. Vietnam J. Agric. Sci. **3**, 864–871 (2020). https://doi.org/10.31817/vjas.2020.3.4.09
6. Itseez, D.E.: Open source computer vision library (2015). https://github.com/itseez/opencv
7. Loke, S., Kasmiran, K., Haron, S.: A new method of mark detection for software-based optical mark recognition. PLOS ONE **13**, e0206420 (2018). https://doi.org/10.1371/journal.pone.0206420
8. Dayananda, N.C.K., Suresh, K.V., Dinesh, R.: Automated parameter-less optical mark recognition. In: Nagabhushan, P., Guru, D.S., Shekar, B.H., Kumar, Y.H.S. (eds.) Data Analytics and Learning. LNNS, vol. 43, pp. 185–195. Springer, Singapore (2019). https://doi.org/10.1007/978-981-13-2514-4_16
9. Raundale, P., Sharma, T., Jadhav, S., Margaye, R.: Optical mark recognition using open CV. Int. J. Comput. Appl. **178**, 9–12 (2019). https://doi.org/10.5120/ijca2019919093
10. Rakesh, S., Atal, K., Arora, A.: Cost effective optical mark reader. Int. J. Comput. Sci. Artif. Intell. **3**, 44–49 (2013). https://doi.org/10.5963/IJCSAI0302002
11. Tümer, A., Küçükkara, Z.: An image processing oriented optical mark recognition and evaluation system. Int. J. Appl. Math. Electron. Comput. **6**, 59–64 (2018). https://doi.org/10.18100/ijamec.2018447788 https://doi.org/10.18100/ijamec.2018447788

Use of AI in Music and Video Industries

Human-Centric Cross-Domain Transfer Network for Music Recommendation

Bojun Liu[1]([✉]) and Bohong Liu[2]

[1] Middlebury College, Middlebury, VT 05753, USA
bojun.liu9216@gmail.com
[2] University of Cambridge, Cambridge CB2 1TN, UK

Abstract. Music is an important part of emotional and cultural expression, and music recommendation systems based on big data technology have been widely commercialized, but there is still a need to provide more personalized user recommendations. This paper proposes a human-centric cross-domain transfer network music recommendation, which simultaneously obtains potential user background knowledge relationships from two domains through a joint sentence attention layer, and uses cross-domain representation mapping for cross-domain representation mapping learning. Experiments on the dataset illustrate this structure would accomplish better mean absolute error for users with certain musical knowledge.

Keywords: Music Recommendation · Human-centric Cross-domain Transfer · Cross-domain Representation Mapping · MAE

1 Introduction

Music exists in all known human societies, and continues to evolve and develop over time as an essential part of emotional and cultural expression, regardless of country, region, or nation. Music in modern society has developed into an important manifestation of civilization, and music carries important elements of politics, economy and technology in society. Music recommendation systems based on big data technology have been widely commercialized, and music recommendation apps such as Spotify (https://www. spotify.com) already have huge commercial benefits and a wide range of user groups. Using this type of APP, listeners can easily find and obtain the music and songs they are interested in, or after simple data collection, the APP can try to recommend music tracks to the owner, who will select and listen to it.

Research on music recommender systems started more than ten years ago. For example, the paper [1] proposes Foafing the Music, which uses the FOAF and RSS vocabularies by close tastes. The FOAF vocabulary records information about people, including their name, nick, mailbox, interest, etc. As people's music taste conducted with personal traits and backgrounds, the system relies on FOAF descriptions to gather personal information, by finding out each user's specific musical interest. Then it uses RSS feeds to filter music-related information. Different from the collaborative filtering, which find other listeners who have similar tastes, and then recommend artists to the user based on

© Springer Nature Switzerland AG 2023
D. Garg et al. (Eds.): IACC 2022, CCIS 1782, pp. 407–414, 2023.
https://doi.org/10.1007/978-3-031-35644-5_33

other listener's taste, the Foafing the Music system uses content-based filtering, together with FOAF profiles, for music recommendation.

the way multimodal information sources were investigated by including users 'personality traits and physiological signals contribute to the music recommendation system (MRS) in paper [2]. The dataset was collected by conducting 23 participants with 628 records from Hong Kong University. During the experiment, users' personality, physiological signals, music acoustic features, and their implicit ratings of the music were collected. Specifically, the physiological signal features were extracted and personality features were extracted and music acoustic features were extracted through LibROSA. By comparing the four regression algorithms, with the dependent variable being the ratings given by the users, the DT regression model performs the best, indicating that personalities were useful in MRS as feature groups.

The authors of paper [3] propose a better music recommendation system which overcome the limitations of the previous systems including the representation of music objects and the method to derive user interests and behaviors for music objects. The authors perform experiments to show the effectiveness of the track selector and feature selection, as well as the precision of music recommendation on the three methods. The track selector method is shown to be effective, which achieves an 83% correctness rate. Moreover, the feature selection is effective if it represents a music object with multiple perceptual properties, which also applies to CB recommendation method. Finally, by calculating the precision of the three recommendation methods, the CB methods achieves a better result. But it should also be noted that the COL method provides more surprising music for users, which may be interesting.

Different approaches to recommend personalized music to human listeners included [4]: Metadata Information Retrieval: uses editorial information for music recommendation, which included: Collaborative Filtering: recommend music based on "nearest neighbors" (relevant users), grouping users based on their rating; Memory-Based CF: predict items based on entire collections of users' ratings; Model-based CF: with known data, to train the system to construct a prediction model for real-world data. Hybrid CF: a combination of different CF models. Content Based Music Information Retrieval: listened the past, which included: Emotion-based Model: recommend music based on users expected perceived emotion in a 2D space; Context-based Information Retrieval: uses social information to recommend music; Hybrid Model Information Retrieval: combining two or more models.

The traditional music recommendation system focuses on the information related to music content and its evaluation, and the relatively novel music recommendation system is gradually developing towards more personalized recommendation. Existing music recommendation methods have their own advantages, but still lack a human-centric perspective. This paper proposes a Human-centric cross-domain transfer network music recommendation, which forms a unique Human-centric latent music knowledge relationship based on the music preferences of listeners and performs cross-domain representation mapping learning between music and movie domains to form a meaningful music recommendation method. Experiments on the dataset illustrate the proposed structure would accomplish better mean absolute error results for users with certain musical knowledge.

The rest of this paper includes: the second part introduces related work on music recommendation; the third part introduces the human-centric cross-domain transfer network music recommendation; the fourth part presents the experimental results; The last is the conclusion.

2 Related Work

Music recommending technology have been studied and researched for many years. Before the advent of deep learning, music recommendation systems mainly used the basic acoustic features of music, such as rhythm, frequency, MFCC coefficients and other audio features. These features are relatively low-level, which are not same as the user's auditory perception and music understanding, resulting in the inability to greatly improve the accuracy. With the emergence of deep learning, the music recommendation system has gradually formed a personalized recommendation method, which is to automatically obtain personalized music according to the user's behavior, so as to meet the user's immediate music listening needs.

The general music recommendation system has the limitations of focusing too much on accuracy and user trapped in a self-reinforcing cycle. A music recommender named Auralist was proposed in [5], which considers the improvement of novelty, diversity, and serendipity in addition to accuracy. The quantitative evaluation of Auralist based on the following three genres: Diversity, Intra-List Similarity metric; Novelty: novelty metric, measure how much globally unexplored items are recommended. The algorithms used in Auralist are: cluster users with similar preferences; each artist topic vector represents the listener base of an artist. Auralist is proven to be practical and adding users' initial history data can improve the accuracy. The majority of users prefer full Auralist, despite the reduce in accuracy, users express increased satisfaction in the recommendation.

The content-based recommendation model, which uses deep belief networks (DBN), a deep learning technique, and probabilistic graphical model to enable simultaneous feature extraction and recommendation was introduced in [6]. They also develop a new hybrid model that combines collaborative filtering with music content, using the features learnt by HLDBN. The hybrid methods using HLDBN performs better than hybrid models using traditional features (AM). The new recommendation method that incorporates social influence into music recommendation measure the similarity. The Mining social influence in the network was to use topological potential approach with three factors: mass, distance (WPC measure), social influence [7]. The paper [8] gave two questions are raised to be answered. The result for first question was: users with larger profile size tend with smaller profile size tend to listen to more popular music. By using group average popularity metric to measure the average popularity of artists in the user profile, they found that the lower mainstream users receive worse recommendations. The paper [9] aims at making music recommendation and music genre classification using acoustic features extracted from raw music. They extracted the feature by CNN classifier on the GTZAN database.

3 Human-Centric Cross-Domain Transfer Network Music Recommendation

With the popularity of the Internet, the data generated every day in the world continues to increase, bringing unprecedented heterogeneity and complexity of data processing. Faced with massive amounts of data, it is no longer possible to perform basic tasks such as cleaning and retrieving it manually. In response to this phenomenon, recommender systems are introduced to deal with such big data problems, such as recommending information such as web pages or images and audios, to help users improve the efficiency of information retrieval and filtering [10].

There was a recommend music based on user's activities [11]: Develop a music player based on its tempo; Classify six activities from time-series accelerometer data using Deep Residual Bidirectional GRNN; Apply an ensemble music classification (tempo-oriented music classification) that combines dynamic classification and sequence classification. The experiments evaluated the tempo-oriented music recommendation framework by 2000 songs with different speed and genre. The participants were 12 users aging from 18–40 years old and subjective evaluation based on mean opinion score MOS rated by the participants. The system implemented ensemble classification model and user preference model had the highest recommendation accuracy.

Most recommendation systems are used in e-commerce and video websites to help users reduce the burden of information processing. These recommendation systems are all single. For example, in e-commerce systems, they mainly recommend specific users for commodity items, while video websites mainly recommend products. Recommend videos that users may be interested in. On the other hand, there are many users who use these two recommendation systems at the same time, so recommendation information from different fields can be used to improve the system's performance.

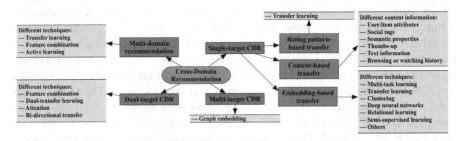

Fig. 1. The categorization of CDR approaches [12].

Under real application conditions, there is a problem that the user's ratings or evaluation data are sparse in the existing recommendation, so that the method relying on collaborative filtering cannot improve the accuracy. The cross-domain recommendation that introduces more rich information from other fields has been studied. The purpose is to introduce data and analysis from more other fields to solve the above-mentioned problems caused by data sparseness. The basic principle is that the same user Different domains may have close stylistic similarities. The categorization of CDR approaches is shown in Fig. 1.

Knowledge transfer can occur by introducing multi-source data from other fields, but the prior assumption that other data sources are similar to the data distribution in this field may not always be correct [13]. Figure 2 shows the principle of the transfer learning with multiple sources.

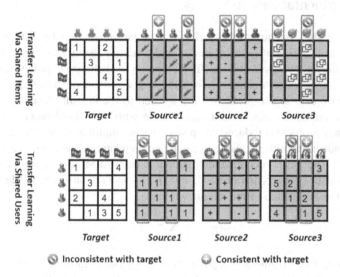

Fig. 2. The transfer learning with multiple sources [13].

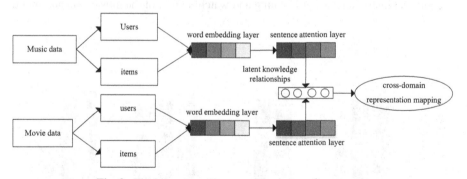

Fig. 3. The human-centric cross-domain transfer network.

In this paper, we propose a cross-domain human-centric transfer music recommendation, which is shown in Fig. 3, to forms unique human-centric latent music knowledge relationships through the user's music appreciation taste, and performs cross-domain representation mapping learning between the music and movie domains. Figure 3 shows the structure of the human-centric cross-domain transfer network. After obtaining the user data and item data of the two fields, the word-level dimension reduction is first processed by the word embedding layer, and then the sentence is encoded by the joint sentence attention layer, in order to obtain the potential user background from the two fields at the same time. Knowledge relationship, and finally use cross-domain representation mapping to build a joint model for inconsistent knowledge from different source domains.

4 Experimental Results

For example, the evaluation and scoring of popular videos may be different from the evaluation and scoring of classical music, and there are also great differences between users of different levels and abilities. Therefore, it is a challenge to judge these different levels of ratings and evaluations. When the target domain of the research and other domains have data sparse problems, it may lead to the inability to make correct and effective recommendations in the target domain with the help of other domains. This inconsistency problem is reduced when statistics of empirical errors are introduced.

We conduct experiments using music recommendation data and movie recommendation data. The music recommendation data is from LFM-1b, and the movie recommendation data is from MovieLens [14, 15]. Our evaluation index is Mean absolute error, and the calculation formula is shown in Eq. 1.

$$MAE = \frac{1}{N} \sum_{i=1}^{N} |y_i - \hat{y}_i| \tag{1}$$

Due to the lack of annotations about the user's personal musical background knowledge in the dataset, we use manual methods for manual annotation. The participants were 6 annotators, all of whom had a background knowledge of music and mastered at least one musical instrument. After listening and watching part of the music data and movie

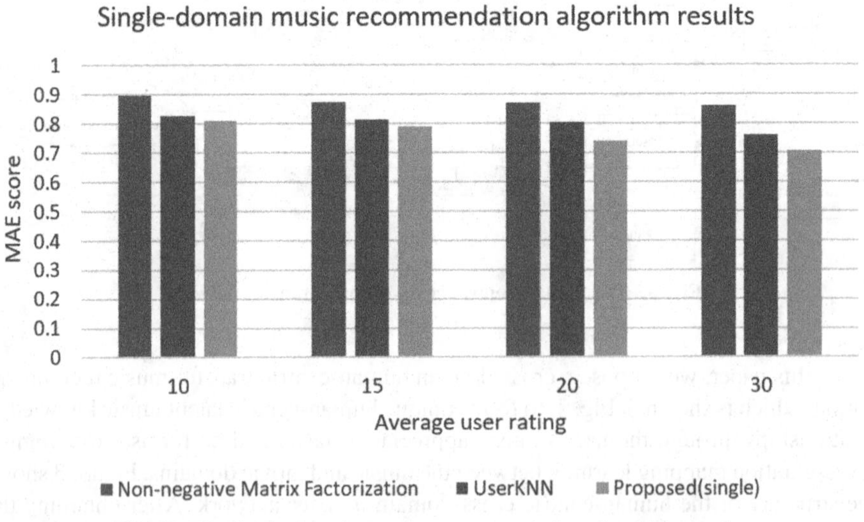

Fig. 4. The single-domain music recommendation algorithm results.

data, these participants selected the data that they thought needed music background knowledge to keep, and divided them by the different ratio. The baseline system adopts non-negative matrix factorization and compares our method with UserKNN method, and the results are shown in Fig. 4 and Fig. 5.

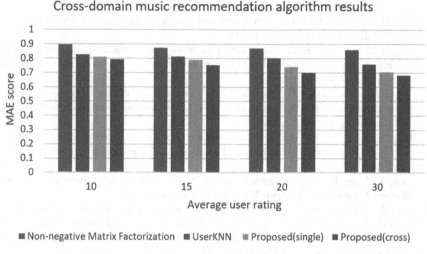

Fig. 5. The cross-domain music recommendation algorithm results.

From the Fig. 4, under the condition of single-domain music recommendation, with the increase of Average user rating, the MAE on non-negative matrix factorization, UserKNN and proposed methods all decrease. When Average user rating reaches 30, UserKNN of the three methods achieves the largest drop. In Fig. 5, compared with single-domain music recommendation, with the increase of Average user rating, the MAE of cross-domain music recommendation on proposed method decreases in different Average user ratings, where Average user rating is equal to 20 when the largest decline. It can be considered that the proposed structure performs good MAE indicator on the two domain datasets with background knowledge.

5   Conclusion

Existing music recommendation systems need more personalized recommendation content and methods. This paper proposes a human-centered cross-domain transfer network music recommendation. Sentence is encoded through a joint sentence attention layer, in order to obtain the potential user background knowledge relationship from two domains at the same time; The inconsistent knowledge of the source domain is used for joint model construction, which aims to perform cross-domain representation mapping learning and form a meaningful music recommendation method. Experiments on the dataset illustrate the proposed structure would accomplish good mean absolute error results for users with certain musical knowledge.

References

1. Celma, Ò., Ramírez, M., Herrera, P.: Foafing the music: a music recommendation system based on RSS feeds and user preferences. In: ISMIR, pp. 464–467 (2005)
2. Liu, R., Hu, X.: A multimodal music recommendation system with listeners' personality and physiological signals. In: Proceedings of the ACM/IEEE Joint Conference on Digital Libraries in 2020, pp. 357–360 (2020)
3. Chen, H.C., Chen, A.L.P.: A music recommendation system based on music and user grouping. J. Intell. Inf. Syst. **24**(2), 113–132 (2005)
4. Song, Y., Dixon, S., Pearce, M.: A survey of music recommendation systems and future perspectives. In: 9th International Symposium on Computer Music Modeling and Retrieval, vol. 4, pp. 395–410 (2012)
5. Zhang, Y.C., Séaghdha, D.Ó., Quercia, D., et al.: Auralist: introducing serendipity into music recommendation. In: Proceedings of the fifth ACM International Conference on Web Search and Data Mining, pp. 13–22 (2012)
6. Wang, X., Wang, Y.: Improving content-based and hybrid music recommendation using deep learning. In: Proceedings of the 22nd ACM International Conference on Multimedia, pp. 627–636 (2014)
7. Chen, J., Ying, P., Zou, M.: Improving music recommendation by incorporating social influence. Multimed. Tools Appl. **78**(3), 2667–2687 (2019)
8. Kowald, D., Schedl, M., Lex, E.: The unfairness of popularity bias in music recommendation: a reproducibility study. In: Jose, J.M., Yilmaz, E., Magalhães, J., Castells, P., Ferro, N., Silva, M.J., Martins, F. (eds.) ECIR 2020. LNCS, vol. 12036, pp. 35–42. Springer, Cham (2020). https://doi.org/10.1007/978-3-030-45442-5_5
9. Elbir, A., Çam, H.B., Iyican, M.E., et al.: Music genre classification and recommendation by using machine learning techniques. In: 2018 Innovations in Intelligent Systems and Applications Conference (ASYU), pp. 1–5. IEEE (2018)
10. Fernández-Tobías, I., Cantador, I., Kaminskas, M., et al.: Cross-domain recommender systems: a survey of the state of the art. In: Spanish Conference on Information Retrieval, vol. 24. sn (2012)
11. Kim, H.G., Kim, G.Y., Kim, J.Y.: Music recommendation system using human activity recognition from accelerometer data. IEEE Trans. Consum. Electron. **65**(3), 349–358 (2019)
12. Zhu, F., Wang, Y., Chen, C., et al.: Cross-domain recommendation: challenges, progress, and prospects. arXiv preprint arXiv:2103.01696 (2021)
13. Lu, Z., Zhong, E., Zhao, L., et al.: Selective transfer learning for cross domain recommendation. In: Proceedings of the 2013 SIAM International Conference on Data Mining. Society for Industrial and Applied Mathematics, pp. 641–649 (2013)
14. Schedl, M.: The LFM-1b dataset for music retrieval and recommendation. In: Proceedings of the 2016 ACM on International Conference on Multimedia Retrieval, pp. 103–110 (2016)
15. Harper, F.M., Konstan, J.A.: The movieLens datasets: history and context. ACM Trans. Interact. Intell. Syst. (TIIS) **5**(4), 1–19 (2015)

Improving Signer-Independence Using Pose Estimation and Transfer Learning for Sign Language Recognition

Marc Marais[✉][iD], Dane Brown[iD], James Connan, and Alden Boby[iD]

Department of Computer Science, Rhodes University, Grahamstown, South Africa
marcmarais07@outlook.com, {d.brown,j.connan}@ru.ac.za

Abstract. Automated Sign Language Recognition (SLR) aims to bridge the communication gap between the hearing and the hearing disabled. Computer vision and deep learning lie at the forefront in working toward these systems. Most SLR research focuses on signer-dependent SLR and fails to account for variations in varying signers who gesticulate naturally. This paper investigates signer-independent SLR on the LSA64 dataset, focusing on different feature extraction approaches.

Two approaches are proposed an InceptionV3-GRU architecture, which uses raw images as input, and a pose estimation LSTM architecture. MediaPipe Holistic is implemented to extract pose estimation landmark coordinates. A final third model applies augmentation and transfer learning using the pose estimation LSTM model. The research found that the pose estimation LSTM approach achieved the best performance with an accuracy of 80.22%. MediaPipe Holistic struggled with the augmentations introduced in the final experiment. Thus, looking into introducing more subtle augmentations may improve the model. Overall, the system shows significant promise toward addressing the real-world signer-independence issue in SLR.

Keywords: Sign Language Recognition · Pose Estimation · Recurrent Neural Networks · Transfer Learning · Deep Learning

1 Introduction

Communication between deaf and mute people and the hearing requires using sign language, which incorporates a range of hand and body gestures. The linguistics behind sign language is as complex as any natural spoken language. Therefore, communication between both hearing and hearing disabled people requires mastering sign language recognition. Sign Language Recognition (SLR) aims to alleviate hearing enable people needing to master sign language, and bridges the communication gap.

This work was undertaken in the Distributed Multimedia CoE at Rhodes University.

SLR forms part of computer vision and involves developing machine learning algorithms to translate sign language to text. It is important to note that there is no universal sign language and that sign languages differ between regions; they do not mimic spoken languages and utilise their own syntax using sign glosses[1] [8]. SLR consists of two categories, isolated and continuous recognition. Isolated SLR focuses on recognising individual words or letters through dynamic and static gestures. In contrast, continuous SLR aims at recognising a sequence of sign language glosses, which involves identifying temporal boundaries between signs and ordering sign glosses [2].

Sign language signers tend to gesticulate naturally, which results in variations between signers. This results in the problem known as signer-independence. The majority of SLR research has focused on signer-dependent SLR. The variations consist of several different possibilities, namely:

- difference in hand shape, movement and location
- signing speed due to intra/inter-personal variability and,
- fluent vs native signers

These variations present a more realistic, real-world setting for implementing a robust SLR system.

This paper notably contributes towards:

- The application of pose estimation in SLR for addressing the signer-independence problem.
- The application of the InceptionV3-GRU architecture for SLR.

In this paper different approaches toward signer-independence isolated SLR are investigate, focusing on pose estimation on the LSA64 dataset. The dataset was chosen for its smaller size and simplicity in running various experiments to evaluate signer-independence.

The structure of the rest of the paper is as follows Sects. 2 and 3 analyses existing studies and architectures. Sections 4 and 5 explain the methodology behind the proposed systems and the experimental setup. The results and discussion are presented in Sect. 6, and Sect. 7 concludes the paper and elaborates on future work.

2   Related Work

Al-qurishi et al. [1] explored current deep learning trends relating to the problem of sign language recognition (SLR) through analysing SLR studies from 2014–2021, covering aspects from data collection, current computer vision techniques, benchmarks and open issues for both machine learning and deep learning techniques. Traditional machine learning methods predominately involve combining feature extraction techniques such as Principal Component Analysis (PCA), Linear Discriminant Analysis (LDA) or Histogram of Oriented Gradients

---

[1] A sign gloss is a label associated with each sign or a sequence of signs [21].

(HOG) with a classification algorithm, namely support vector machines (SVMs). However, the machine learning approach disregards temporal information, thus affecting video-based systems and the application of CSLR. Therefore, there has been a shift towards deep learning algorithms that include temporal and spatial information. Commonly implemented deep learning algorithms for SLR include convolutional neural networks (CNNs) and recurrent neural networks (RNNs).

Konstantinidis et al. [14] implemented a system that isolated the extraction of body and hand skeletal landmarks. Body skeletal landmarks were detected using the first ten layers of a pre-trained ImageNet VGG-19 network, and hand skeletal points utilised up to conv4_4 of the network. Spatial features were created by calculating joint-line distances from the hand and body landmark coordinates. The features were subsequently fed into a four-stream stacked Long Short-Term Memory (LSTM) Network. A 98.09% accuracy was achieved using signer-dependent splits on the LSA64 dataset by the system.

OpenPose pose estimation was compared to MediaPipe Holistic pose estimation architecture for isolated SLR in a study by [19]. The Ankara University Turkish Sign Language (AUTSL) SLR dataset was the signer-independent SLR dataset used to compare the architectures. The OpenPose system was combined with an SLR transformer [4] whereas a two-layer Bidirectional LSTM was employed by the MediaPipe system. The systems achieved 79.99% and 82.14% for OpenPose and MediaPipe, respectively. However, the authors did note that a significant amount of information is lost through skeletal representation, which needs to be represented by the image domain.

Marais et al. [18] evaluated the different feature extraction algorithms for hand-based SLR, comparing hand skeletal data, segmentation and raw image approaches. The authors noted that utilising skeletal landmark coordinates as feature inputs is a more computationally efficient approach compared to using CNNs as feature extractors on raw image data. However, this study only focused on the spatial domain and did not incorporate temporal information.

3   Architectures

Pose estimation and deep learning form a vital part of the computer vision field and are often utilised for action recognition tasks. Human pose estimation localises body keypoints or landmarks for posture recognition in an image [20]. Through multiple processing layers within computational models, deep learning learns representations in data without the need for prior feature extraction as utilised in traditional machine learning approaches [15].

Action recognition, specifically SLR, encompasses both a spatial and a temporal domain. Therefore, Recurrent Neural Networks (RNNs), which form part of deep learning, is implemented to process the temporal domain. RNNs are typically combined with pose estimation algorithms or Convolutional Neural Networks (CNNs) to form a hybrid architecture.

Therefore, two hybrid approaches are considered for this research: a pose estimation-RNN and a CNN-RNN.

3.1   Pose Estimation

Human pose estimation is the process of determining the spatial location of body keypoints, the usual parts and joints, of a person from an image or video [20]. MediaPipe is a recently introduced framework that utilises perception pipelines as a graph of reusable calculators to build different pose estimation solutions [17]. MediaPipe includes a range of object detection, body landmark extraction and segmentation solutions.

MediaPipe Holistic simultaneously includes human pose, face landmarks and hand landmark solutions to generate a holistic human pose estimation, as seen in Fig. 1.

Fig. 1. MediaPipe Holistic landmarks annotation.

MediaPipe Pose is better suited to real-time SLR when compared to other pose estimation architectures such as OpenPose [5]; owing to MediaPipe being tailored towards real-time pose estimation through its lightweight CNN architecture. In comparison, OpenPose uses a two-branch multistage CNN to predict confidence maps and part affinity fields to perform pose estimation.

MediaPipe Pose

The MediaPipe Pose solution utilises BlazePose, a lightweight CNN architecture for human pose estimation [3]. The architecture is implemented in two stages an initial encoder-decoder framework to predict heatmaps for all joints, which is passed to the second stage encoder that directly regresses the joint coordinates. To overcome the limitations of the Non-Maximum Suppression (NMS) algorithm, BlazePose assumes that the head of the person is always visible, thus focusing on initially detecting the bounding box area of the human face. BlazePose outputs 33 points on the human body, as shown in Fig. 2a. Each point coordinates with x, y and z values, with z representing relative depth.

MediaPipe Hands

MediaPipe Hands utilises RGB image input to predict and track hand skeletal data [28]. The solution incorporates two models, a palm detector model followed by a hand landmark model. Partially visible hands and self-occlusions are taken into account in the MediaPipe hands model. The palm detector consists of a single shot detector, BlazePalm, and an oriented hand bounding box to localise and crop out the initial hand locations. Subsequently, the 21 hand landmark coordinates are localised and extracted by the hand landmark model, as depicted in Fig. 2b. Each hand landmark coordinate consists of x, y and z coordinates.

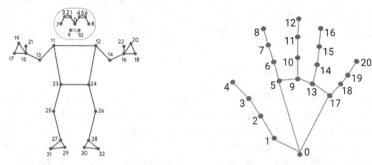

(a) BlazePose landmark topology [3].   (b) MediaPipe Hands topology [28].

Fig. 2. MediaPipe Pose and Hand topologies.

3.2   Convolutional Neural Networks: InceptionV3

CNNs are a favoured deep learning architecture for image pattern recognition tasks combining a variety of convolutional, pooling and fully connected layers to process input images, learn features and perform predictions [13]. A 22-layer Deep CNN, referred to as GoogLeNet [23] or InceptionV1, won the ILSVRC 2014 challenge by using a sub-network of inception modules. The inception module incorporates multi-scale convolutional transformations using split, transform and merge ideas. Spatial information is captured at different scales in each module through different filter sizes (1×1, 3×3, and 5×5). These inception modules replace the conventional convolutional layers and allow for higher accuracies with a reduced computational cost.

In InceptionV1, the auxiliary classifiers failed to contribute significantly at the end of the training, with the authors arguing that they act as regularises. InceptionV3 [24] was introduced to overcome this issue through integrating batch normalisation, label smoothing, and an RMSProp Optimizer in the auxiliary classifiers alongside the InceptionV2 upgrades.

3.3   Recurrent Neural Networks: LSTM

RNNs form part of deep learning and are designed to work with temporal data generally involving sequences [16]. Compared to feed-forward networks, RNNs differ as they contain internal memory and feedback connections.

3.4 Long Short-Term Memory

A popular RNN network is the Long Short-Term Memory (LSTM) network, a gradient-based algorithm that deals with sequence prediction problems with the capability of learning order dependence. LSTMs were introduced by Hochreiter and Schmidhuber [11] to solve the exponentially blowing up and vanishing gradient problems present in Back-Propagation Through Time (BPTT) and Real-Time Recurrent Learning (RTRL) [26, 27] algorithms. A series of 'gates' are utilised to control information flow in a data sequence in an LSTM. The three gates included a forget gate, input gate and output gate, which act as filters.

3.5 Gated Recurrent Units

An alternative to LSTMs is Gated Recurrent Networks (GRUs), an encoder-decoder framework that also addresses the vanishing gradient problem [7]. The GRU unit consists of two gating units, an update and reset gate, to control the flow of information. Compared to LSTMs, GRUs are more computationally efficient due to their less complex structure and do not need a memory unit.

4 Methodology

This section covers an in-depth review of the proposed hybrid architectures for sign-independent SLR. Two architectures are proposed for signer-independent SLR, the first implementing an InceptionV3-GRU model on raw image data and the second combining pose estimation landmarks with an LSTM model.

4.1 InceptionV3-GRU

Inference is performed on the video frames of the LSA64 dataset using the InceptionV3 architecture. The InceptionV3 model is pre-trained using ImageNet weights [9]. Video frames at 224×224 dimensions are fed into the InceptionV3 feature extractor. The final pool layer outputs a 2048-dimensional feature vector containing the features from the video frame.

RNNs require a fixed length sequence. Therefore, a 150-frame sequence was chosen based on the average video length of 127 frames across all the videos.

The feature vector is subsequently fed into two GRU layers with 100 unit dimensionality. A 20% dropout layer follows each GRU layer. The final output dense layer comprises 64 units and utilises a softmax activation function. Figure 3 provides a high-level overview of the proposed InceptionV3-GRU model.

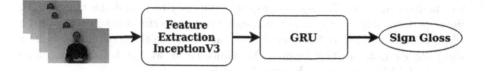

Fig. 3. High-level overview of the proposed InceptionV3-GRU system.

(a) Original Image from LSA64 dataset.

(b) Original image annotated with MediaPipe Holistic landmarks.

(c) MediaPipe Holistic landmarks only.

Fig. 4. MediaPipe Holistic visualisation of landmarks.

4.2 MediaPipe-LSTM

The skeletal based model utilises the MediaPipe Holistic framework, as discussed in Sect. 3.1 to extract body landmarks. As SLR only requires pose points from the torso and upper extremities, the lower extremities are subsequently excluded. Therefore, 21 landmarks from each hand are combined with 17 pose landmarks from the body to create a total of 59 landmarks, as visualised in Fig. 4.

The video frame landmarks are subsequently saved to a CSV file. The landmark coordinates are fed into an LSTM model. The LSTM model consists of 3 LSTM layers a 20% Dropout layer follows each layer. The final dense layer consists of 64 units and a softmax activation function.

5 Experimental Setup

This paper evaluates signer-independence on the LSA using isolated SLR and a combination of hybrid pose estimation, CNN and RNN models. Three experiments are conducted to determine the best model for sign-independent SLR. All experiments isolate two of the ten signers and reserve these signers as the test split. The two isolated signers were kept consistent for all experiments. A Nvidia RTX 3090 GPU was used for training and evaluation of the models.

5.1 LSA64 Dataset

The LSA64 dataset is an Argentinian isolated SLR dataset [22]. The dataset comprises 64 different sign classes with a total of 3200 videos. All videos in the dataset were recorded using a single RGB camera. The dataset consists of 42 one-handed and 22 two-handed signs; only the right hand was utilised for one-handed signs. Ten signer subjects were used to record the videos; each signer performed five iterations of each sign. Subjects performed signing against a white backdrop and wore fluorescent gloves and black clothing to allow for easier segmentation from the background. One-handed and two-handed sign snapshots from the LSA64 dataset can be seen in Fig. 5.

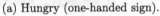

(a) Hungry (one-handed sign).   (b) Appear (two-handed sign).

Fig. 5. LSA64 dataset sample video frames.

5.2   Model Evaluation Metrics

SLR has multiple metrics to gauge model performance in machine learning. The most common metrics for SLR are word error rate (WER) [25] and accuracy. Accuracy and F-score were the chosen metrics for comparison of the proposed experiments. Accuracy is the ratio of the number of correct predictions to the total number of input samples as given by Eq. 1 [12].

$$Accuracy = \frac{\text{number of correct classifications}}{\text{total number of classifications attempted}} \tag{1}$$

F-score uses both precision and recall scores to represent a harmonic mean between the two, providing a more balanced measure for model performance [12]. F-Score is given by Eq. 2.

$$F\text{-}score = 2 \times \frac{Precision \times Recall}{Precision + Recall} \tag{2}$$

5.3   Parameter Tuning

Parameter tuning was applied to all models. Experiment 1 utilised early stopping to determine the best epoch during training. Experiments 2 and 3 utilised KerasTuner[2] with the RandomSearch algorithm to determine the optimal learning rate, LSTM layer units and best epoch.

5.4   Test Models

Three experiments were conducted to compare different approaches toward improving signer-independence on the LSA64 dataset:

---

[2] https://github.com/keras-team/keras-tuner.

- Experiment 1: Utilises the raw video frames as input fed into the InceptionV3-GRU architecture, discussed in Sect. 4.1.
- Experiment 2: Extracts pose landmarks using MediaPipe holistic and feeds these into an LSTM network, as discussed in Sect. 4.2.
- Experiment 3: Utilises augmentation and transfer learning using the same approach and architecture as Experiment 2.

For Experiment 3, each video was augmented three times using random augmentations according to the following parameters: ±15% video rotation angles, video resizing between 50% and 150 and random horizontal video flips. Transfer learning was implemented using the pre-trained weights from Experiment 2.

6   Results and Discussion

6.1   Parameter Tuning

Parameter tuning was applied to each model. A maximum of 1000 epochs were used to find the best epoch using early stopping. Experiments 2 and 3 went through a maximum of five trials to determine the best learning rate and the optimal number of units in the LSTM layers. Table 1 gives the optimal parameters for each experiment.

Table 1. Parameters for each Experiment.

Experiment	Architecture	Parameters		
		Batch Size	Learning rate	Epoch
Experiment 1	InceptionV3-GRU	128	$1e-4$	56
Experiment 2	Pose-LSTM	128	$1e-3$	74
Experiment 3	Pose-LSTM	128	$1e-3$	114

For the LSTM architecture, the optimal number of units in all layers and both experiments was 100 units.

6.2   Experiment 1

The InceptionV3-GRU model that used the raw video images from the LSA64 dataset achieved a test accuracy of 74.22%. The training and validation can be seen in Fig. 6. There is a sudden drop in accuracy at epoch 55, which can be attributed to a bad batch that adversely affected training weights at that epoch.

6.3   Experiment 2

Experiment 2 implemented the MediaPipe-LSTM architecture as explained in Sect. 4.2 training on the eight signers reserved for training. The unaugmented LSA64 dataset was used for this experiment. The MediaPipe-LSTM architecture yielded a test accuracy of 80.92%. Training and validation accuracies can be seen in Fig. 7a. The model struggled with the Skimmer, Food, Argentina and Find classes achieving F-scores ranging between 37.66% and 46.70% for these classes.

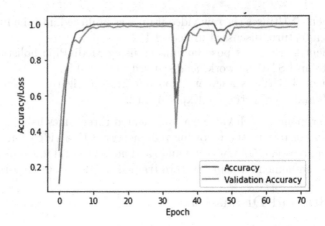

Fig. 6. Training and Validation Accuracy for Experiment 1.

6.4 Experiment 3

The MediaPipe-LSTM architecture was also implemented in Experiment 3; however, transfer learning was applied to the model using the training weights from Experiment 2. Augmentation was applied to the LSA64 dataset per Sect. 5.4. Through transfer learning and augmentation, Experiment 3 achieved a test accuracy of 81.22%. Experiment 3 struggled with the Skimmer, Food and Argentina, yielding F-scores of 30.73%, 28,44% and 44.43%, respectively. Figure 7b shows the training and validation accuracies for Experiment 3.

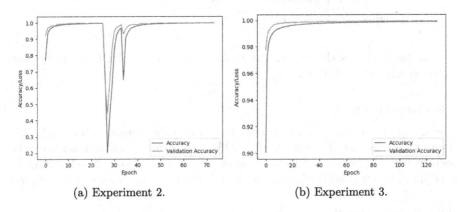

(a) Experiment 2.   (b) Experiment 3.

Fig. 7. Experiment 2 and 3: Training and Validation Accuracy.

6.5   Discussion

The best performing approach towards signer-independent SLR was Experiment 3 with 81.22% accuracy, closely followed by Experiment 2 with an accuracy of 80.992%. Experiments 2 and 3 implemented MediaPipe Holistic pose estimation to extract skeletal points, which were subsequently fed to an LSTM architecture for training. Experiment 1 was the worst performing of the three experiments yielding an accuracy of 74.22%. Performance comparison of the training and test accuracies and losses can be found in Table 2.

Table 2. Performance comparison of the Experiments.

Dataset	Training		Testing	
	Loss	*Accuracy*	*Loss*	*Accuracy*
Experiment 1	0.0016	100.00%	0.9799	74.22%
Experiment 2	0.0069	99.77%	1.6905	80.92%
Experiment 3	0.0033	99.89%	1.9815	81.22%

The performance in Experiment 1 could be improved through video augmentation and pre-training the InceptionV3 with weights generated from the LSA64 dataset or another isolated SLR dataset. This would increase the robustness and generalisation ability of the model.

Figure 8 visualises the successful and failed detections in both the original Experiment 2 and the augmented Experiment 3 datasets. The right hand (RH) and body pose landmarks were evaluated for successful and failed detections, as both the right hand and body should be in all video frames. MediaPipe pose was successful in both experiments, only failing to detect 219 frames in the augmented dataset. MediaPipe Hands struggled when presented with the augmented data failing to detect the right hand in 579,936 of the frames in the augmented data.

The failed detections could result from the augmentation ranges being too excessive. Therefore, looking into using smaller ranges may reduce the number of failed detections while improving the model's robustness. As the failed detections were not manually removed from the dataset, this may have adversely affected the results in Experiment 3 with the high number of failed detections. Therefore, due to the higher proportion of successful detections, Experiment 2 would better reflect the best-performing model for signer-independent SLR on the LSA64 dataset.

Compared to existing results on another signer-independent dataset, namely the AUTSL dataset, Experiment 2 achieved results close to the MediaPipe BiL-STM, which achieved an accuracy of 82.14% on the AUTSL dataset.

Overall the pose estimation combined with RNN seems to be the best approach for signer-independent SLR on the LSA64 dataset. However, looking into other CNN architectures such as Residual Neural Networks (ResNet) [10] and

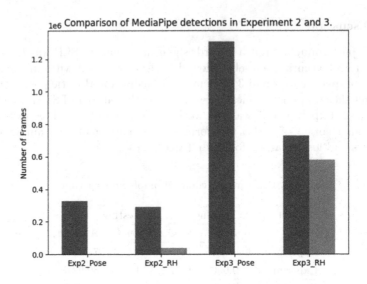

Fig. 8. MediaPipe comparison of detections in Experiment 2 and 3.

applying augmentation to the videos may improve the generalisation ability and performance of the CNN-RNN hybrid architecture. Convolutional Autoencoders have proven successful in dimensionality reduction and image processing tasks in the medical image analysis [6] and therefore may benefit SLR systems as a feature extraction technique through learning and extracting the key features. In contrast to utilising InceptionV3 with ImageNet weights.

7   Conclusion

This study investigates signer-independent SLR on the LSA64 dataset, comparing the different feature extracting techniques. The two techniques compared were pose estimation versus using CNNs to extract features from raw images, specifically MediaPipe Holistic and the InceptionV3 model. Experiment 3 was the best performing, with an accuracy of 81.22% using a MediaPipe-LSTM model combined with transfer learning and augmentation. However, there were many failed MediaPipe right-hand detections in the video frames. Consequently, Experiment 2, yielding an accuracy of 80.92%, is a true reflection of the result of the MediaPipe-LSTM model without augmentation.

This study notably contributes to utilising pose estimation, MediaPipe, towards the signer-independence problem within SLR. The signer-independence problem is a real-world challenge, as the signer would be unknown to the SLR systems in a real-world scenario.

Future expansions on this study would look into more subtle augmentations to improve pose estimation detections. Working with a larger isolated SLR dataset such as AUTSL may improve the models' robustness and generalisation ability. Convolutional Autoencoders may be a better alternative to the InceptionV3 feature extraction architecture through unsupervised learning to extract the key features for SLR.

References

1. Al-qurishi, M., Khalid, T., Souissi, R.: Deep learning for sign language recognition?: current techniques, benchmarks, and open issues. IEEE Access **9**, 126917–126951 (2021). https://doi.org/10.1109/ACCESS.2021.3110912

2. Aloysius, N., Geetha, M.: Understanding vision-based continuous sign language recognition. Multimed. Tools Appl. **79**(31–32), 22177–22209 (2020). https://doi.org/10.1007/s11042-020-08961-z

3. Bazarevsky, V., Grishchenko, I., Raveendran, K., Zhu, T., Zhang, F., Grundmann, M.: BlazePose: on-device real-time body pose tracking. CoRR abs/2006.10204 (2020). https://arxiv.org/abs/2006.10204

4. Camgoz, N.C., Koller, O., Hadfield, S., Bowden, R.: Sign language transformers: joint end-to-end sign language recognition and translation. In: Proceedings of the IEEE/CVF Conference on Computer Vision and Pattern Recognition, pp. 10023–10033 (2020)

5. Cao, Z., Hidalgo, G., Simon, T., Wei, S.E., Sheikh, Y.: OpenPose: realtime multi-person 2D pose estimation using part affinity fields. IEEE Trans. Pattern Anal. Mach. Intell. **43**(1), 172–186 (2021). https://doi.org/10.1109/TPAMI.2019.2929257

6. Chen, M., Shi, X., Zhang, Y., Wu, D., Guizani, M.: Deep feature learning for medical image analysis with convolutional autoencoder neural network. IEEE Trans. Big Data **7**(4), 750–758 (2021). https://doi.org/10.1109/TBDATA.2017.2717439

7. Cho, K., et al.: Learning phrase representations using RNN encoder-decoder for statistical machine translation. In: Proceedings of the 2014 Conference on Empirical Methods in Natural Language Processing (EMNLP), pp. 1724–1734. Association for Computational Linguistics, Doha, Qatar (2014). https://doi.org/10.3115/v1/D14-1179, https://aclanthology.org/D14-1179

8. Cooper, H., Holt, B., Bowden, R.: Sign language recognition. In: Moeslund, T., Hilton, A., Krüger, V., Sigal, L. (eds.) Visual Analysis of Humans, pp. 539–562. Springer, London (2011). https://doi.org/10.1007/978-0-85729-997-0_27

9. Deng, J., Dong, W., Socher, R., Li, L.J., Li, K., Fei-Fei, L.: ImageNet: a large-scale hierarchical image database. In: 2009 IEEE Conference on Computer Vision and Pattern Recognition, pp. 248–255 (2009). https://doi.org/10.1109/CVPR.2009.5206848

10. He, K., Zhang, X., Ren, S., Sun, J.: Deep residual learning for image recognition. In: 2016 IEEE Conference on Computer Vision and Pattern Recognition (CVPR), pp. 770–778 (2016). https://doi.org/10.1109/CVPR.2016.90

11. Hochreiter, S., Schmidhuber, J.: Long short-term memory. Neural Comput. **9**(8), 1735–1780 (1997). https://doi.org/10.1162/neco.1997.9.8.1735

12. Hossin, M., Sulaiman, M.N.: A review on evaluation metrics for data classification evaluations. Int. J. Data Min. Knowl. Manage. Process **5**(2), 1 (2015)

13. Khan, A., Sohail, A., Zahoora, U., Qureshi, A.S.: A survey of the recent architectures of deep convolutional neural networks. Artif. Intell. Rev. **53**(8), 5455–5516 (2020). https://doi.org/10.1007/s10462-020-09825-6

14. Konstantinidis, D., Dimitropoulos, K., Daras, P.: Sign language recognition based on hand and body skeletal data. In: 2018–3DTV-Conference: The True Vision-Capture, Transmission and Display of 3D Video (3DTV-CON), pp. 1–4. IEEE (2018)

15. LeCun, Y., Bengio, Y., Hinton, G.: Deep learning. Nature **521**(7553), 436–444 (2015)

16. Lipton, Z.C.: A critical review of recurrent neural networks for sequence learning. CoRR abs/1506.00019 (2015). http://arxiv.org/abs/1506.00019

17. Lugaresi, C., et al.: MediaPipe: a framework for building perception pipelines. CoRR abs/1906.08172 (2019). http://arxiv.org/abs/1906.08172

18. Marais, M., Brown, D., Connan, J., Boby, A.: An evaluation of hand-based algorithms for sign language recognition. In: 2022 International Conference on Artificial Intelligence, Big Data, Computing and Data Communication Systems (icABCD), pp. 1–6 (2022). https://doi.org/10.1109/icABCD54961.2022.9856310

19. Moryossef, A., et al.: Evaluating the immediate applicability of pose estimation for sign language recognition. In: Proceedings of the IEEE/CVF Conference on Computer Vision and Pattern Recognition, pp. 3434–3440 (2021)

20. Munea, T.L., Jembre, Y.Z., Weldegebriel, H.T., Chen, L., Huang, C., Yang, C.: The progress of human pose estimation: a survey and taxonomy of models applied in 2D human pose estimation. IEEE Access **8**, 133330–133348 (2020). https://doi.org/10.1109/ACCESS.2020.3010248

21. Rastgoo, R., Kiani, K., Escalera, S., Sabokrou, M.: Sign language production: a review. In: 2021 IEEE/CVF Conference on Computer Vision and Pattern Recognition Workshops (CVPRW), pp. 3446–3456 (2021). https://doi.org/10.1109/CVPRW53098.2021.00384

22. Ronchetti, F., Quiroga, F., Estrebou, C., Lanzarini, L., Rosete, A.: LSA64: A dataset of argentinian sign language. In: XXII Congreso Argentino de Ciencias de la Computación (CACIC), pp. 794–803 (2016)

23. Szegedy, C., et al.: Going deeper with convolutions. In: 2015 IEEE Conference on Computer Vision and Pattern Recognition (CVPR), pp. 1–9 (2015). https://doi.org/10.1109/CVPR.2015.7298594

24. Szegedy, C., Vanhoucke, V., Ioffe, S., Shlens, J., Wojna, Z.: Rethinking the inception architecture for computer vision. In: 2016 IEEE Conference on Computer Vision and Pattern Recognition (CVPR), pp. 2818–2826 (2016). https://doi.org/10.1109/CVPR.2016.308

25. Wang, Y.Y., Acero, A., Chelba, C.: Is word error rate a good indicator for spoken language understanding accuracy. In: 2003 IEEE Workshop on Automatic Speech Recognition and Understanding (IEEE Cat. No.03EX721), pp. 577–582 (2003). https://doi.org/10.1109/ASRU.2003.1318504

26. Williams, R.J., Zipser, D.: Experimental analysis of the real-time recurrent learning algorithm. Connection Sci. **1**(1), 87–111 (1989). https://doi.org/10.1080/09540098908915631

27. Williams, R.J., Zipser, D.: Gradient-based learning algorithms for recurrent. Backpropagation: Theory Archit. Appl. **433**, 17 (1995)

28. Zhang, F., et al.: MediaPipe hands: on-device real-time hand tracking. CoRR abs/2006.10214 (2020). https://arxiv.org/abs/2006.10214

Attacks and Defenses of Smart Speakers: Voice Command Fingerprinting on Alexa

Rohan Kathuria[1] and Vinish Kathuria[2](✉) ⓘ

[1] The Shriram, Gurgaon, India
[2] Indian Institute of Management, Lucknow, India
efpm07014@iiml.ac.in

Abstract. Smart speakers, such as Amazon Alexa and Google Home, are a form of voice-based interactive technology that helps consumers solve queries with real-time responses. Smart speaker adoption has increased significantly over the last few years, and this growth is expected to continue. Voice AI, specifically voice commands, have made people's lives more convenient by helping them save time while avoiding physical contact. However, smart speakers also have security risks, including listening to and recording private conversations. In this paper, we review and analyze attacks on Amazon Alexa, their implementation, consequences, and defenses. We also dive into voice command fingerprinting and take inspiration from websites and video streaming fingerprinting to propose new potential defenses. This paper aims to highlight the attacks and protection in the newly emerging field of smart speakers.

Keywords: Smart speakers · Alexa · Voice AI · Cybersecurity · Machine Learning · Voice Command Fingerprinting

1 Introduction

A smart speaker is a voice-activated device that can carry out user commands to control other smart devices, play music, and provide weather information. For instance, after uttering the wake word, which activates a smart speaker, "Alexa," a user can query an Amazon Echo, "What is the traffic like near my house?" and the device will verbally respond with real-time traffic information. Smart speakers with intelligent voice assistants have been the most extensively used IoT (Internet of Things) gadgets in homes [1]. With its Amazon Echo, Amazon currently leads the market for smart speakers. Google Home, which became a serious rival to Amazon after 2020, is second [2].

The ease with which consumers can use smart speakers is one of the main factors driving their rapid growth in popularity. Without lifting a finger, owners of smart speakers may perform things like changing the color of their smart lighting, turning down the fan, or ordering a cab. More consumers have begun to recognize the usefulness of this voice-based product as new businesses add distinctive and specialized functions to smart speakers, such as restaurants allowing customers to book a table using their smart speaker. The promise of speech AI has been demonstrated to smartphone users by phone

© Springer Nature Switzerland AG 2023
D. Garg et al. (Eds.): IACC 2022, CCIS 1782, pp. 429–443, 2023.
https://doi.org/10.1007/978-3-031-35644-5_35

assistants like Siri on Apple iPhones, Google Assistant on Google Phones, and Bixby on Samsung phones, encouraging more people to buy smart speakers [3].

While speed, efficiency, and contactless interactions make smart speakers convenient, privacy problems are a concern [4]. Smart speakers have access to more private data, such as house codes, conversation recordings, customer voice profiles, and the shared data utilized by phones and computers. Due to their extensive access, smart speakers have more attack surfaces than other devices. An attack surface is defined as the total number of locations where an unauthorized user can attempt to enter or extract data from an environment [5]. Additionally, as more smart appliances, including smart air conditioners and televisions, are being used in homes, smart speakers have gained access to more user data than any similar software. With more technological advancements in the smart speaker attack area, prospective attacks like dolphin attacks and voice command fingerprinting attacks have become more prevalent, accurate, and effective. A user profile could be established as a result of these assaults and sold for marketing purposes, for example. There may also be more intimate repercussions, such as identity theft, hacking into one's accounts, or a threat to one's home safety [6]. Furthermore, businesses might be harmed by using smart speakers, not just regular users. As an illustration, Burger King ran a commercial in 2017 that activated Google Homes and Google Assistant on Android phones to narrate the Whopper burger's Wikipedia entry. Attackers changed the title of this Wikipedia article to "worst hamburger," adding cyanide as one of the components. As a result, misleading and harmful information about Burger King was disseminated to thousands of users.

Unfortunately, as data availability has increased, so has the frequency of attacks against smart speakers. Attackers are developing various technical strategies to compromise a smart speaker system, from employing imperceptible orders to nefarious abilities to breaking the system through other smart devices [7, 8]. The purpose of this study is to identify the most common attacks against smart speakers as well as relevant countermeasures. The Amazon Echo (Alexa) will be our primary focus for the remainder of the article as we explore assaults and responses because most research in the field is restricted to Alexa.

The structure of the essay is as follows. The context of the field research is presented in Sect. 2, focusing on the Alexa attack surfaces, voice command fingerprinting, website, and video fingerprinting. Section 3 then delves into six well-known attacks against smart speakers while briefly examining their present and future defenses. The tradeoff between security and field performance is discussed in Sect. 4, along with five alternative voice command fingerprinting defenses. In Sect. 5, we explore the necessity of smart speaker defenses and their effects, and in Sect. 6, we wrap up the paper.

2 Background

Alexa Attack Surfaces. Attacks on Alexa can be better understood by referring to the six different attack surfaces, as shown in Fig. 1 [5].

1. *Voice Capturing.* Attacks on this surface can get beyond Alexa's noise suppression technology and profit from the fact that Alexa doesn't offer voice-based verification. Such assaults use the wake word "Alexa" to introduce background noise and activate

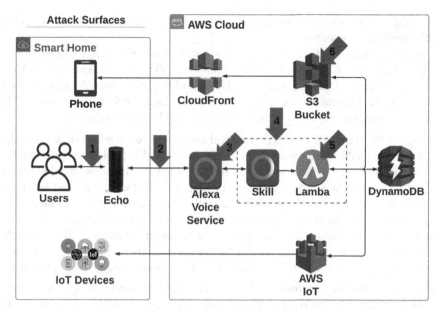

Fig. 1. Alexa Attack Surfaces [3]

the Amazon Echo remotely. This surface has been subjected to man-in-the-middle, dolphin, and remote voice attacks.

2. *Voice transmission.* Attacks against this surface use fingerprinting, a cybersecurity approach that refers to data that can be used to identify software, hardware, operating systems, network protocols, and more. When an attacker uses voice command finger-printing on Alexa, they can listen in on both encrypted outgoing and incoming voice commands, or what the user says to the smart speaker and what the smart device says back.

3. *Alexa Voice Surface.* Alexa uses automatic speech recognition and natural language understanding to enhance the user experience. These technologies do not take context or intent into account, and they are not always accurate at identifying and analyzing human sounds. This has made it possible for assaults like skill squatting, which uses homophones and homonyms, to penetrate an Alexa ecosystem without suffering many repercussions.

4. *Alexa Voice Skills.* Alexa skill is a voice-controlled function that enables users to upgrade and customize an Alexa by adding additional features. Using the Alexa Developer Console, these skills can be produced and made available to the public; however, the procedure through which they are approved for publication is brief and leaves room for the publication of damaging skills. Attacks like harmful attacks and ruse attacks have grown in popularity.

5. *Lambda Functions.* Attacks on Lambda functions are based on serverless architecture, like Alexa's, which might result in the creation of apps with shoddy programming. Due to these vulnerabilities, attackers can pretend to be Amazon employees and

enter queries to obtain customer data using standard application-level techniques like Command/SQL injection.

6. *Amazon S3 Bucket.* Alexa uses Amazon S3, also known as Amazon Simple Storage Service, as a cloud storage platform to keep the media assets associated with Alexa skills. As a result, there is a chance for S3 Bucket Misconfiguration Attacks, in which hackers could access private data or modify data on open S3-based websites. The latter is what was employed in the earlier discussed Burger King attack.

Four of the six attack surfaces mentioned above will be examined in detail in this paper: Attacks on the voice-capturing surface include "dolphin" and "man in the middle" attacks; attacks on the voice transmission surface include "voice command fingerprinting"; attacks on the Alexa voice service surface include "skill squatting"; and attacks on the Alexa voice skill surface have "malicious skills" and "masquerading." These assaults were selected due to their rising popularity, accuracy, efficacy, and simplicity of use. In addition to these assaults, Alexa can potentially be compromised using Bluetooth, the Alexa mobile app, or programs downloaded onto Alexa. These assaults have not been further discussed since they are less potent or damaging than those covered in this study.

Voice Command Fingerprinting. Using voice command fingerprinting, a hacker can access data. An intrusive party can access the Wi-Fi AP or Wi-Fi access point, the Internet Service Provider, the Cloud Server, and both outgoing (the packets of a voice command) and incoming (the packets of the smart speaker answer) traffic. This makes voice command fingerprinting one of the most damaging attacks on Alexa, which is why this article focuses extensively on these attacks and possible countermeasures (Fig. 2).

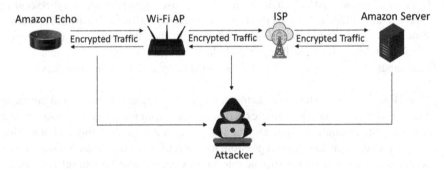

Fig. 2. Attacker Access with Voice Command Fingerprinting [9]

Attacks using voice command fingerprinting make it possible for an attacker to listen in on a speaker's encrypted speech communication. This is accomplished using side channel data, such as packet size, direction, and order, to infer encrypted voice commands without decrypting them. The usage and data of millions of Alexa users may be unintentionally disclosed if these commands are made public. Additionally, this information may benefit additional Alexa attacks like skill squatting or ma-licious skills. For instance, an attacker may utilize voice command fingerprinting to track the frequently used commands of a user and subsequently build a malicious skill based on these instructions to access the user's data.

Most research on voice command fingerprinting focuses on the precision and effectiveness of improvised attacks. This is because fingerprinting, a supervised learning challenge, is fundamentally an encrypted traffic analysis attack. As demonstrated by Kennedy et al. [10] and Wang et al. [6], machine-learning approaches can significantly improve voice command fingerprinting attacks.

Voice fingerprinting attacks were not common before smart speakers since they offered little benefit to attackers. Additionally, voice fingerprinting was not widely employed in general; nonetheless, music recognition algorithms were one application. Initial algorithms for identifying songs, like those used by Shazam, were partly based on voice fingerprinting. The algorithm would capture small segments of the songs and record them; voice fingerprinting would then be used to infer these segments and match them with a database of songs to provide the song's title to the user. Even now, some music detection systems use voice fingerprinting [11].

Website and Video Streaming Fingerprinting. Website fingerprinting, often known as browser, device, or online fingerprinting, is a method certain websites employ to gather user data. Identifying the websites the user is connected to involves looking at the encrypted data between the user and anonymous network portals. Similarly, video streaming fingerprinting is used to gather data on a user by identifying and extracting specific parts of a movie that the user is watching to keep track of it [12, 13]. Because they can provide an attacker access to a wealth of data about a user, website and video streaming fingerprinting attacks are among the most hazardous types of browser-based assaults. For instance, some malicious Google Chrome extensions gather information and create user profiles for use in advertising by using website fingerprinting. Because Alexa can access far more information than websites and movies, thanks to the proliferation of smart homes with connected smart gadgets, voice command fingerprinting might be far more dangerous. Additionally, because website and video streaming fingerprinting are far more mature domains in terms of study and practical application, attackers have drawn inspiration from several websites and video fingerprinting attack approaches to enhance the precision of voice command fingerprinting [14].

On the other hand, website fingerprinting and video fingerprinting have several safeguards against these assaults because they are more mature fields. It is possible to adapt these countermeasures with voice command fingerprinting. For instance, Wang et al. adapted differential privacy to voice command fingerprinting by drawing inspiration from differential privacy as a video fingerprinting defense. Differential privacy was employed in video fingerprinting to add random video and image data, making it more difficult for an attacker to deduce the actual contents of the video. To make it more difficult for attackers to figure out speech commands, Wang et al. changed this to include noise in both incoming and outgoing voice packets [6].

Additionally, differential privacy made it more difficult to deduce one-way traffic in video streams. To conceal bidirectional communication for voice command fingerprinting in Alexa, Wang et al. [6] adapted methods for reducing latency (delays during data transfer) learned in website fingerprinting to the defenses against voice command fingerprinting. The adversarial machine learning defensive system utilized in website fingerprinting is another security mechanism from which this article suggests drawing inspiration. In Sect. 4, these defenses will be covered in more detail [15].

3 Attacks on Alexa

The typical attacks on Alexa are shown in Fig. 3.

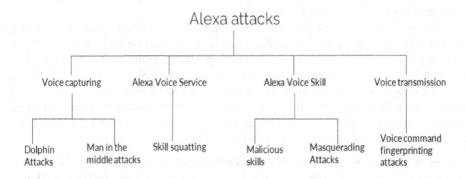

Fig. 3. Attacks on Alexa

Voice Capturing

Dolphin Attacks. An example of a remote attack called a dolphin attack is when Alexa is activated using whispered commands. Ultrasound transducers, ordinarily 2 m from the smart speaker, are used to carry out the procedure. The transducer's sound is outside the 20–20,000 Hz range of human hearing. Since the Alexa microphones can pick up sounds outside of this range, Alexa will receive the inaudible commands rather than the user. This might result in an attacker issuing a command that causes Alexa to reveal personal information, such as "Alexa, what is the balance of my savings account?"

While a physical object must be close to the smart speaker for these attacks to succeed, this distance may someday grow, making dolphin attacks more common and dangerous. Most potential countermeasures against dolphin attacks are hardware-based. For instance, the issue of inaudible orders being used to trigger Alexa might be resolved by restricting the hearing range of a smart speaker microphone to that of humans or by adding a module to smart speaker microphones that only detects modified speech commands within a specific frequency range. Eliminating the basic presumption that an ultrasonic transducer is within Alexa's field of vision may significantly decrease or even completely stop dolphin assaults. However, these hardware alterations can only be made if Alexa manufacturers are willing to incur higher costs and customers are willing to pay a higher price for Alexa [16].

Man in the Middle Attacks. When an IoT device hijacks communication between Alexa and a user, it is known as a man-in-the-middle assault. This second IoT device secretly records talks without Alexa's or the user's knowledge using inaudible command jamming techniques. The next step is to gather user data using data retrieval techniques. A user profile that can be used for advertising can be created using this data.

Furthermore, imagine if these recorded chats include sensitive data, such as a user's CVV or card verification value. Attackers could then use this information to hack into the user's other accounts. These attacks could become more prevalent as more IoT gadgets are put in homes.

Man-in-the-middle attacks presuppose that a hacker can gain access to a different IoT device in the home, like a smart TV. Increasing the security features of other IoT devices is one potential answer, but this may be prohibitively expensive, take time to create, and be outside the control of manufacturers of smart speakers. Additional software-based Alexa-specific solutions can also be used. The key to defending against not just man-in-the-middle attacks but also attacks that fall under the voice-capturing attack surface is to investigate how software that can distinguish between live and recorded voices (both a lightweight voice liveness detection system and a sonar-based detection system) can be used. A simple voice liveness detection system can stop such attacks by identifying distinctions between the vocal patterns of real people and recorded people. Sonar-based liveness detection systems provide a non-user intrusive method of determining the origin of a voice and the location of a user, which can be used to recognize man-in-the-middle attacks. Unfortunately, these defense systems may take years to develop and are inaccurate [17].

Alexa Voice Services

Skill Squatting. This hack takes advantage of Alexa's shoddy skill verification mechanism and unreliable speech recognition technologies. It requires developing malevolent talents that mimic trustworthy skills so that consumers think they are using a reliable skill. For instance, a malicious skill called "Goldman Sacks" is being constructed so that there is a possibility that it would open when consumers ask Alexa to open the actual skill, "Goldman Sachs," because it sounds so similar to the actual skill. As a result, users might divulge their Goldman Sachs account details to the bogus skill, allowing an outside opponent to get personal information. Additionally, skill squatting can be altered based on various user demographics. A malicious talent, such as "US Banc," could be made specifically to target users who typically open the "US Bank" skill by an attacker utilizing voice command fingerprinting, for example.

The lax Alexa skill publishing procedure, which is covered in more detail later in this paper, is the primary cause of skill squatting. By strengthening this procedure, it will be possible to stop the development and distribution of malicious talents and defend thousands of users against this more prevalent and intrusive attack. A context-sensitive detector can be developed from the perspective of cybersecurity software to take user intent and previous conversations into account before launching a skill. Unfortunately, we are still far from developing this technology effectively, leaving thousands of Alexa users open to skill squatting attempts [18].

Alexa Voice Skill

Malicious Skills. Any talent that has been purposefully created to act against a user's interests is considered malicious. Unlike skill squatting, these talents are not constrained to homonyms or homophones, which makes malevolent skills. It may be anything from a talent that gathers data from a cloud server to a skill that tracks other IoT devices in a home. Due to Alexa's lax certification process, these skills are accessible to users. According to a study, researchers could publish multiple skills on the Alexa Skill Store that were against Alexa's rules [5]. It is due to the publication process's minimal intervention design. One employee must examine a talent and decide whether it is hazardous. It introduces ambiguity and a personal viewpoint, which renders the system unreliable. Additionally, the procedure depends on the honesty and integrity of qualified professionals. The skill will probably be confirmed and published if a developer has checked the box to verify that their talent does not have malicious intent.

Making certification far more stringent and possibly adding an automated component that checks the skill's code and warns an employee when it discovers anything suspect are two apparent ways to decrease the publishing of dangerous skills. Additionally, the more thorough screening procedure can cause Alexa lag, which might discourage producers from using it. In Sect. 4, the security versus latency issue will be thoroughly covered.

Masquerading Attacks. This type of Alexa attack entails the development of a malicious skill by an advertiser that users mistake for being dependable and trustworthy or that completely duplicates another skill. Users can manage all their bank accounts in one location, for instance, using the "Overall Banking" talent, while an enemy keeps track of all this private financial data. Alternatively, a "Weather" skill imitates Alexa's standard weather skill while keeping track of the places where users ask about the weather. Masquerading attacks are hazardous because they allow an attacker to gather a lot of data about a user while posing as a reliable source. It may create a highly customized user profile that can be sold for marketing purposes. Masquerading attacks similarly rely on the shoddy certification procedure for Alexa skills. Therefore they share the same defenses as malicious skills.

Voice Transmission

Voice Command Fingerprinting Attacks. Since it allows an adversary access to such a large amount of data, this attack, as was already noted, is one of the key foci of this article due to its tremendous potential to harm users. This section will concentrate on how voice command fingerprinting attacks are being improved since Sect. 2 explains voice command fingerprinting attacks. Machine learning has been used in research on voice command fingerprinting attacks to improve attack accuracy significantly. Wang et al. [6] have suggested a stacked autoencoder, a convolutional neural network, and an extended short-term memory network. The output from all three systems is combined using ensemble learning to create a weighted ensemble used in the voice command fingerprinting attack. The attack on Alexa had an accuracy of 86.09% in the numeric format using this weighted ensemble in a closed-world environment and on only incoming traffic. In an open-world environment with only incoming traffic, the attack accuracy on Alexa achieved a numeric accuracy of 100% using the weighted ensemble. These attacks consider both trained and untrained data to obtain trustworthy figures for attack accuracy. Voice command fingerprinting will become an even bigger concern with further work on increasing attack accuracy.

These attacks can result in the creation of vulnerable and personal user profiles, the hacking of other user accounts, or the use of data for other Alexa attacks, such as the demo-graphic-based skill squatting that was covered earlier in this section, based on the extensive information gathered from voice command fingerprinting. Wang et al.

and Kennedy et al. have proposed five potential defenses, which will be explored in the following section of the study, even though there is little research on voice command fingerprinting protection mechanisms (Sect. 4).

4 Voice Command Fingerprinting Defenses

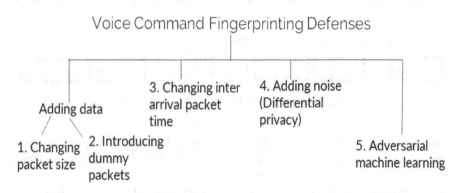

Fig. 4. Voice Command Fingerprinting Defenses

Figures 4 and 5 illustrate the five alternative defense strategies Wang et al. [6] and Kennedy et al. [10] suggest being employed to fend off voice command fingerprinting attacks. These include altering the packet size, adding fake packets, altering the inter-arrival packet time, adding noise using differential privacy, and utilizing adversarial machine learning. In a closed-world context, combining these strategies can reduce the accuracy of voice command fingerprinting assaults from 89.41% to 1.07% when trained with original traffic and from 28.42% when introduced with obfuscated traffic.

Changing Packet Size. This defense strategy adds data to various voice packets to fix packet sizes. It augments the initial command packets with voice data (shown in red) (shown in blue). A constant packet size makes it more difficult for an attacker to deduce the contents of a packet because they can't look for patterns or distinguish between voice instructions. Unfortunately, factors like timestamps and traffic duration that suggest spoken commands are not obscured by modifying packet size. If this security system is employed alone, deep learning-based attacks like those above will succeed. Additionally, it was discovered that the additional communication cost increases linearly as packet size is raised to a specific point (a maximum value of 1500). Accordingly, depending on the maximum packet size, the expense for this defense and the delay it causes may be significant.

Introducing Dummy Packets. To reduce traffic gaps or traffic bursts that may occur in a flow of voice commands, adding new packets is a type of adaptive padding, which refers to adding packet data without introducing latency. Transaction bursts are described as a series of subsequent packets traveling in the same direction, whereas traffic gaps

Changing packet size

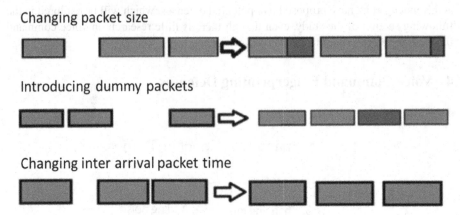

Introducing dummy packets

Changing inter arrival packet time

Fig. 5. A visual of different defense mechanisms

occur when there aren't any of these following packets. Adaptive padding makes it more difficult for attackers to deduce information about the flow of voice packets by inserting new packets. The new packet (in red) will prevent patterns from forming where they would otherwise, like the gap on the diagram's left-hand side. Additionally, adding fresh packets reduces latency by sending buffered data sooner. However, this protection mechanism, like increasing packet size, cannot fend against machine learning-based attacks if employed alone.

Changing Inter-arrival Packet Time. Changing inter-arrival packet time is another type of adaptive padding that relies on fixed timestamps between packets to function. As depicted in the diagram, a defense system can stop a time-based pattern from being produced by altering the inter-arrival packet time. The size of the incoming and outgoing voice instructions is typically considered while creating these patterns. It provides an attacker with a greater understanding of the type of question posed to Alexa and the answer provided, which might assist an attacker in deducing various voice commands. An attacker won't be able to determine the size and contents of a voice packet by removing this time pattern, as indicated on the right side of the diagram. Implementing adaptive padding techniques in every Amazon Echo can be expensive; therefore, changing inter-arrival packet timings can also result in extra communication delays and raise prices for producers. Changing inter-arrival packet time is useless against neural network-based attacks, much like the other two protection strategies mentioned.

Differential Privacy-Adding Noise. This type of differential privacy is applied to real-time, random packet size obfuscation. Wang et al. use d* privacy to further alter packet sizes, a version of differential privacy applied to time-series data. This defense method makes it more difficult for attackers to decipher the contents of speech packets by introducing noise into them, forcing them to infer random noise. For Alexa users, on the other hand, this random noise will be eliminated to deliver the necessary voice command. The differential privacy in video streaming fingerprinting, which uses differential privacy over data bins, served as the model for this protection mechanism (classified groups).

Because voice command fingerprinting has two-way or bidirectional traffic, Alexa adds noise directly to voice packets, unlike video streaming fingerprinting.

Additionally, since different packets do not need to be sorted into bins, adding noise directly to packets saves latency. In addition to the inherent advantages of adaptive padding, this application of differential privacy still adds another degree of protection against voice command fingerprinting. Combining adaptive padding and differential privacy may thwart neural network-based assaults, significantly reducing attack accuracy. The figures mentioned at the beginning of this section, particularly the 88.34% decrease in attack accuracy in a closed-world environment, are based on applying this double layer of adaptive padding and differential privacy. It is anticipated that the server will disguise incoming traffic, and the Amazon Echo will obfuscate outgoing traffic for all four defenses mentioned above.

Adversarial Machine Learning. In this study, a novel method of resistance against voice command fingerprinting is put forth. Zhang et al. [11] advocated adversarial machine learning as a defense against video streaming fingerprinting since it focuses on combating the usage of other machine learning techniques. Advanced voice command fingerprinting attacks rely on machine learning methods like convolutional neural networks and layered autoencoders. Such machine learning-based attacks can be less effective by adversarial machine learning. Adversarial machine learning, which employs the Fast Gradient Sign Method (FGSM) to produce adversarial samples, might diminish the efficacy of assaults using convolutional neural networks by generating random noise samples to deter machine learning attacks. Zhang et al. research show that.'s adversarial machine learning can significantly lower attack accuracy. Voice command fingerprinting defensive systems can be compelling, even against neural network-based attacks, by including adversarial ML as a third layer over adaptive padding and differential privacy.

However, additional research on adversarial machine learning in voice command fingerprinting is required to draw more significant conclusions about its advantages and disadvantages. Additionally, using adversarial machine learning can be expensive, which causes customers to experience lengthy delays. Finally, adversarial machine learning-based defenses can only be effective if the attacker also employs machine learning. Utilizing adversarial machine learning might be pointless if this supposition cannot be made for most voice command fingerprinting attacks [19–21].

Tradeoff. While these voice command fingerprinting measures can offer users of Alexa high levels of security, they can also result in less effective user interactions. In the realm of Alexa, the traditional tradeoff between security and performance in the cybersecurity industry is very common.

On the one hand, the above-discussed protections can lessen attack precision, especially in high-level deep learning-based attacks, and boost Alexa user security. In-depth user profiles are less likely to be built because the user's private and sensitive data will be safer. Additionally, it means that, based on the data a smart speaker has access, there is less likelihood that a user's account will be compromised. Additionally, as voice command fingerprinting attacks are used to support other attacks on Alexa, including skill squatting, the decrease in accuracy of these attacks may result in fewer attacks overall.

Finally, and from a broader perspective, improved smart speaker security may increase their widespread adoption globally. This could result in the global adoption of voice AI-driven contactless engagements, bringing ease to millions of consumers without losing appreciable security issues. For populations like the disabled and the visually impaired, for whom voice is a much more practical method of interfacing with technology, it can be advantageous.

However, as was said before when discussing different protection strategies, their implementation entails higher latency levels, implying that consumers would experience longer delays. It is severe when it comes to smart speakers because their popularity is based mainly on the convenience they offer. Customers will use smart speakers less and less because of this latency's decreased convenience. Therefore, companies like Amazon might be reluctant to deploy these defense strategies because they will reduce demand due to less convenience. Cost is another issue that should be raised about voice command fingerprinting defense strategies. Most defense systems will need more bandwidth, which manufacturers of smart speakers will have to pay for. As a result, producers' expenses will increase, which can cause them to increase the price of smart speakers. It can not only cause a decline in the market for smart speakers but also limit their accessibility to lower-income groups, making it challenging to advance speech AI and smart speakers [22, 23].

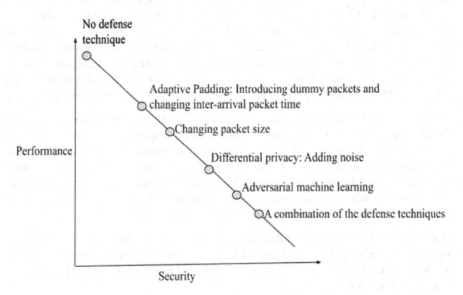

Fig. 6. Tradeoff Between Security and Performance for Voice Command Fingerprinting Defenses

Figure 6 represents the tradeoff between security and performance for the defense techniques discussed in this paper. The figure is subjective and has been used to give an overview of the intricacies of the system and the challenges that we face in the field. It is not based on concrete calculations and does not consider other external factors.

5   Discussion and Future Work

This essay attempts to emphasize the necessity of these defenses in the modern world and the present protection techniques used in the world of smart speakers. Our research and analysis have revealed that (a) security threats from smart speakers are real, (b) there are numerous attack surfaces, (c) there is no one-size-fits-all solution, and (d) multiple defense mechanisms may need to be implemented; (e) consumer education, understanding, and adoption of appropriate defense mechanisms is likely to be the solution. Defense mechanisms must be strengthened to ensure user security as voice AI and smart speakers spread globally. However, the convenience of smart speakers must not be sacrificed to achieve this security. There is much room for research in this area, including implementing various fingerprinting defense techniques to voice command fingerprinting, assessing the efficacy of the current defenses on smart speakers besides Alexa, or comprehending the effect of voice commands that have been encrypted being decrypted [24].

Future research can concentrate on how producer-independent methods, like differential privacy, can be applied in more practical contexts. Other smart speakers like the Google Home and Apple Home Pod, as well as other speech AI technologies like personal assistants like Siri on Apple smartphones, the Google Assistant, Bixby on Samsung devices, and Cor-tana on Windows devices, can be included in a future study. It is a sizable domain that needs to be looked into because there is a chance that attackers may have access to more extensive and perhaps more private amounts of data. Understanding how new or old updated defenses can be used to help in these broader areas will help advance the use of speech AI and smart speakers. With this attack scope, there is also a defense scope [25–27].

6   Conclusion

Because of the ease they offer users, smart speakers have changed how people interact with technology and contribute to the rise of speech AI. This ease, meanwhile, also comes with several security threats, such as the creation of user profiles for advertising purposes and the exposure of private account information. This article explores a variety of assaults on Alexa, including their implementation, potential effects, and countermeasures. During the research process, we learned about the severe consequences of voice command fingerprinting assaults, and we dug deeper into five possible responses, which decreased attack accuracy by 88.34%. We also looked into how defense techniques could be adjusted for voice command fingerprinting in the more established sectors of website fingerprinting and video stream fingerprinting. We concluded by discussing the tradeoff in the field of Alexa attacks and the necessity for vendor-dependent and vendor-independent action.

References

1. Kang, H., Oh, J.: Communication privacy management for smart speaker use: integrating the role of privacy self-efficacy and the multidimensional view. New Media Soc. (2021)

2. Laricchia, F.: Topic: smart speakers. Statista (2022)
3. Apthorpe, N., Huang, D.Y., Reisman, D., Narayanan, A., Feamster, N.: Keeping the smart home private with smart(er) IoT traffic shaping. In: Proceedings of the PETS (2019)
4. Kathuria, R., Kathuria, V.: Role of privacy management and human-centered artificial intelligence in driving customer engagement with smart speakers. In: Stephanidis, C., Antona, M., Ntoa, S., (eds.) HCI International 2022 Posters. HCII 2022. Communications in Computer and Information Science, vol. 1580, pp. 412–418. Springer, Cham (2022). https://doi.org/10. 1007/978-3-031-06417-3_55
5. Lit, Y., Kim, S., Sy, E.: A survey on amazon alexa attack surfaces. In: IEEE 18th Annual Consumer Communications & Networking Conference (CCNC). IEEE (2021)
6. Wang, C., et al.: Fingerprinting encrypted voice traffic on smart speakers with deep learning. In: Proceedings of the 13th ACM Conference on Security and Privacy in Wireless and Mobile Networks (2020)
7. Mao, J., et al.: A novel model for voice command fingerprinting using deep learning. J. Inf. Secur. Appl. **65**, 103085 (2022)
8. Zhang, N., Mi, X., Feng, X., Wang, X., Tian, Y., Qian, F.: Dangerous skills: understanding and mitigating security risks of voice-controlled third-party functions on virtual personal assistant systems. In: Proceedings of the IEEE S&P (2019)
9. Sciuto, A., Saini, A., Forlizzi, J., Hong, J.I.: Hey alexa, what's up?": studies of in home conversational agent usage. In: Proceedings of the 2018 Designing Interactive Systems Conference (2018)
10. Kennedy, S., et al.: I can hear your Alexa: Voice commands fingerprinting on smart home speakers. In: IEEE Conference on Communications and Network Security (CNS). IEEE (2019)
11. Jovanovic, J.: How does shazam work? music recognition algorithms, fingerprinting, and processing. Toptal (2015)
12. Juarez, M., Imani, M., Perry, M., Diaz, C., Wright, M.: Toward an efficient website fingerprinting defense. In: Askoxylakis, I., Ioannidis, S., Katsikas, S., Meadows, C. (eds.) ESORICS 2016. LNCS, vol. 9878, pp. 27–46. Springer, Cham (2016). https://doi.org/10.1007/978-3-319-45744-4_2
13. Zhang, X., et al.: Statistical privacy for streaming traffic. In: Proceedings of the 26th ISOC Symposium on Network and Distributed System Security (2019)
14. Dyer, K.P., Coull, S.E., Ristenpart, T., Shrimpton, T.: Peek-a-Boo, i still see you: why efficient traffic analysis countermeasures fail. In: Proceedings of the IEEE S&P 2012 (2012)
15. Goodfellow, I.J., Shlens, J., Szegedy, C.: Explaining and harnessing adversarial examples. arXiv preprint arXiv:1412.6572 (2014)
16. Zhang, G., Yan, C., Ji, X., Zhang, T., Zhang, T., Xu, W.: DolphinAttack: inaudible voice commands. In: Proceedings of the ACM CCS (2017)
17. Roy, N., Shen, S., Hassanieh, H., Choudhury, R.R.: Inaudible voice commands: the long-range attack and defense. In: Proceedings of the 15th USENIX Symposium on Networked Systems Design and Implementation, NSDI (2018)
18. Kumar, D., et al.: Skill squatting attacks on amazon alexa. In: Proceedings of the USENIX Security (2018)
19. Yuan, X., et al.: Command song: a systematic approach for practical adversarial voice recognition. In: Proceedings of the USENIX Security (2018)
20. Sirinam, P., Imani, M., Juarez, M., Wright, M.: Deep fingerprinting: understanding website fingerprinting defenses with deep learning. In: Proceedings of the ACM CCS (2018)
21. Li, S., Guo, H., Hopper, N.: Measuring information leakage in website fingerprinting attacks and defences. In: Proceedings of the ACM CCS (2018)

22. Shmatikov, V., Wang, M.-H.: Timing analysis in low-latency mix networks: attacks and defenses. In: Gollmann, D., Meier, J., Sabelfeld, A. (eds.) ESORICS 2006. LNCS, vol. 4189, pp. 18–33. Springer, Heidelberg (2006). https://doi.org/10.1007/11863908_2
23. Rahman, M.S., Sirinam, P., Mathews, N., Gangadhara, K.G., Wright, M.: Tik Tok: the utility of packet time in website fingerprinting attacks. In: Proceedings of the PETS (2020)
24. Xiao, Q., Reiter, M.K., Zhang, Y.: Mitigating storage side channels using statistical privacy mechanisms. In: Proceedings of ACM CCS (2015)
25. Sirinam, P., Imani, M., Juarez, M., Wright, M.: Deep fingerprinting: undermining website fingerprinting defenses with deep learning. In: ACM SIGSAC (2018)
26. Wang, T., Cai, X., Nithyanand, R., Johnson, R., Goldberg, I.: Effective attacks and provable defenses for website fingerprinting. In: USENIX Security Symposium (2014)
27. Cai, X., et al.: A systematic approach to developing and evaluating website fingerprinting defenses. In: Proceedings of the 2014 ACM SIGSAC Conference on Computer and Communications Security (2014)

Video Tampering Detection Using Machine Learning and Deep Learning

Siddhi Deo⊙, Simran Mehta⊙, Digha Jain⊙, Charu Tiwari⊙, Aniket Thorat⊙,
Sudhanshu Mahara⊙, Sudhanshu Gonge⁽⊠⁾⊙, Rahul Joshi⁽⊠⁾⊙, Shilpa Gite⁽⊠⁾⊙,
and Ketan Kotecha⊙

Department of Computer Science and Engineering, Symbiosis Institute of Technology, Pune,
India
{siddhi.deo.btech2019,simran.mehta.btech2019,
digha.jain.btech2019,charu.tiwari.btech2019,
aniket.thorat.btech2019,sudhanshu.mahara.btech2019,
sudhanshu.gonge,rahulj,shilpa.gite}@sitpune.edu.in,
head@scaai.siu.edu.in

Abstract. Digital recordings are now affordable, quick to make, and straight-forward to upload on web platforms because of the widespread availability of video recording technology in smartphones and other digital devices. The truth of films published on social media cannot be trusted. With the latest tools used for video editing tools, movies may now be readily changed (faked) for political ends or unlawful profit. Over the years, a lot of effort has gone into creating novel methods for identifying various forms of video manipulation. The objectives of video tampering detection include identifying signs of change and assessing the validity and integrity of the video file. These methods are divided into two groups: active & passive (blind) techniques. Based on the forgeries that passive video tampering detection systems can see, they may be divided into three groups: region tampering detection, double or multiple compressed video detection, and video inter-frame forgery detection. The previous studies under consideration are provided in a condensed tabular format, together with the criteria they employed and any limitations they had. The research work concluded by outlining a number of problems that might be used to inspire new research topics for the identification of passive video manipulation. In this paper, few AI/ML algorithms were tested for video tampering detection to find out which one gives out the most accurate results.

Keywords: Video Tampering · Forgery detection · Machine learning · Deep learning

1 Introduction

Digital video tampering has become easier in this day and age, thanks to readily available sophisticated and ready-to-use editing tools like Adobe Photoshop. As a consequence, it's impossible to tell the difference between modified and genuine videos. Video tampering

© Springer Nature Switzerland AG 2023
D. Garg et al. (Eds.): IACC 2022, CCIS 1782, pp. 444–459, 2023.
https://doi.org/10.1007/978-3-031-35644-5_36

or video forging refers to the unauthorized or objectionable altering of a video. Videos and photos on various social networking sites, such as YouTube and Facebook, have an important role in scientific growth and socioeconomic perspective. Videos are also employed in a range of applications such as legal evidence, video lessons, marketing, and video surveillance. Even if this reflects their important position in today's world, there are also negative aspects to it. It involves the misuse of videos or the dissemination of false information. This implies that footage on social networking sites like YouTube or shown on television may have been tampered with [1, 2].

To discover the best algorithm for detecting video tampering utilising a variety of deep learning and ML approaches. One of the fundamental issues that harms the economy, the environment, and puts human lives in danger is security. Therefore, it is crucial to identify video counterfeit as soon as possible. The goal of this research is to employ image processing and computer approaches to identify regions that are vulnerable to falsification and to extract meaningful information from photographs inside manipulated recordings [3].

Audio can also be included along with video. Better algorithms can be used like GANS so that we can collect data easily and better results can be obtained. In place of ResNet50, we can use ResNet34 or other algorithms like VGG16 or VGG19 can be used as these have less layers and so it will take less time [4, 5].

1.1 Literature Survey

Using semi-fragile watermarks embedded in DCT coefficients, Xiaoling et al. [1] suggested a technique that authenticates and identifies altered algorithms using Compressing Sensing Theory. They conducted content verification of inner I-frames and tamper detection of P-frames on MPEG-2 compression video as his study object. The Semi-fragile Watermarking algorithm performed very well in terms of ability and accuracy, according to the results.

Even when the placement of frame duplication is off for small forged components, Wang et al. [2] developed a method for diagnosing frame duplication using temporal and geographic correlation. Similar to this, a technique based on two types of assaults was created: the MPEG0-2 GOP format was used to identify a temporal copy-move attack, and the Histogram of Oriented Gradients(HOG) was used to identify a spatial (pixel) copy-move assault.

A technique for identifying video tampering based on the recognition of duplicate frames was also proposed by Wang & Farid et al. [3]. In this approach, frames are modified and then stored again as a double compressed MPEG video, providing unique static and temporal statistical disarrangement that may be used in place of the initially encoded MPEG compression method.

In the meanwhile, one of the most common techniques of frame forging was used by Thou-Ho Chen et al. [4] to remove multiple moving frames of objects from a video clip. To extract the changes in features throughout a video of frames, compressed sensing, The attributes were transmitted into the lower-dimensional subspace clustered by k-means using K-SVD (k-Singular Value Decomposition) and random projection. The results of the detection are finally combined for each frame.

Through the use of noise residue correlation, Hsu et al. [5] devised a technical approach for identifying counterfeit frame segments in a movie. The approach is based on the idea that changed frames change how the correlation of noise remnants on each frame correlates, allowing altered sections to be distinguished from unaffected ones [14–16]. The trials' results demonstrate that noise correlation, albeit subject to noise quantization, is a rather dependable characteristic when applied to high-quality video [14–18]. Furthermore, noise residue extraction is a challenging process that requires construction of both space (intra-frame) and time (inter-frame). In the first, tamper-free variant, the video's inter-frame frames are utilised for tampering, and the exact same movies are used for clipping.

In a related work [6], a technique based on the properties and methodology of the Tamura texture was proposed, using the movie's vector matrix, which was acquired by video frame extraction. This method determines the difference between the Tamura texture feature vector and the neighbouring vector matrix. To detect the copy-move sequences, the distance between the differences and the serial number is compared to the threshold if the differences are less than it. Pairs of serial numbers with distances above the threshold are noted.

Davarzani et al. [7, 8] suggested a useful technique to identify copy-move fraud using Multire solution Local Binary Patterns in a related study (MLBP) [9, 10]. Even after rotation, scaling, JPEG compression, blurring, and the addition of noise, the technique is excellent in revealing variation and abnormalities in repetitive sections [11, 12]. Each block in the split image is extracted using the LBP and RANSAC algorithms.

2 Proposed Work

To improve Video Tampering Detection through the use of variety of AI-ML/DL approaches. It can be used to find out the ideal algorithm for the task.

2.1 Scope

- To get tampered video dataset
- To Grab image from the video
- To Detect forgery

2.2 Objectives

- Various algorithms are used to detect tampered video at no additional expense to the current system.
- System may be deployed in all the cases where there is a requirement to identify tampering in videos.
- Print the accuracy of the used algorithms.

3 System Design

3.1 System Design

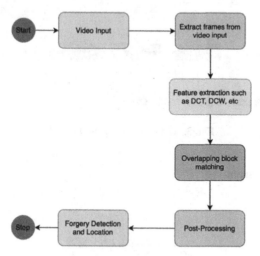

Fig. 1. System Design

Video will be taken as input which will be then extracted intro frames. The feature extraction is carried out using DCT and DWT (Fig. 1).

3.2 Data Flow Diagrams

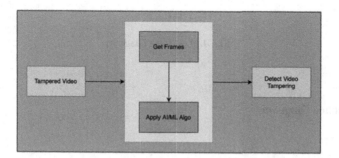

Fig. 2. Data Flow Diagram Level 0

These diagrams map out the flow of information in this project. Figure 2 shows DFD at level 0 and Fig. 3 shows DFD at level 1.

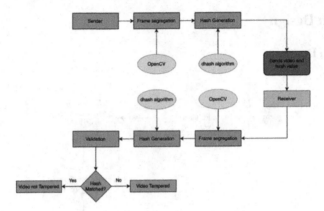

Fig. 3. Data Flow Diagram Level 1

3.3 Use Case Diagram

See Fig. 4.

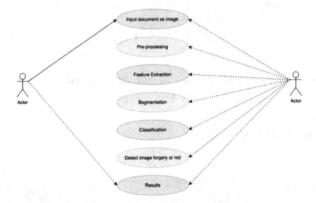

Fig. 4. Use Case Diagram

3.4 Sequence Diagram

See Fig. 5.

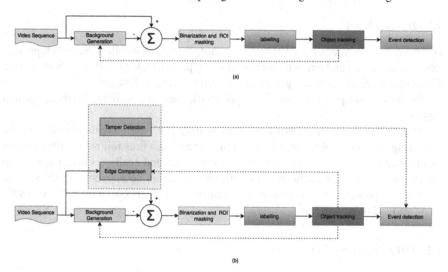

Fig. 5. Sequence Diagram

4 Implementation

Proposed Methodology can be depicted with the below mentioned Figure (Fig. 6).

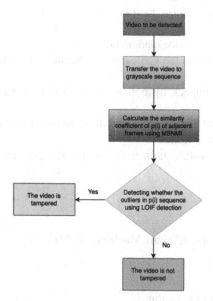

Fig. 6. Flowchart of Implementation

4.1 Dataset Used

For this research project, the CVIP group's manipulated video collection was employed. One original video and one with eight tampering patterns added to it were both used in this verification. The following were the eight tampering techniques:

Rotation, multiple, no transformation, RGB, shearing, scaling, brightening, and flipping.

The modified video's dataset was obtained from [19], therefore the specifics of the tampering processes are unclear, however the general idea is as follows. Multiple refers to simultaneous execution of operations like rotation and scaling. Furthermore, "No transformation" describes the act of duplicating a certain component exactly as it is, without any processing. The algorithm "rotation" and other techniques are frequently employed in image processing.

4.2 Data Preprocessing

Step 1: Traverse the drive folder by folder until you reach the folder with the required file

Step 2: Use os.listdir(root) to get a list of files in the folder and traverse the folder according to the list

Step 3: Create an object cap which stores information returned by VideoCapture()

Step 4: Read frame using read() and store value in retn and frame

Step 5: If retn is true then break else for every 20th frame enter the if block

Step 6: In the if block first resize the frame to 64 × 32 size.

Step 7: Convert it to grayscale.

Step 8: Blur the image to reduce random noise.

Step 9: Using sobel, retrieve the vertical and horizontal edge information and sum the information.

Step 10: Using hog() unpack histogram information in 2 variables namely fd and hog_image

Step 11: Append the information to a list after running it through itertools.chain() to convert it to an acceptable format

Step 12: Append the feature information to training_set and label information to training_labels list

5 Algorithms

5.1 Algorithm 1: Support Vector Machine (SVM)

// Input: Video Frame F

// Output: Accuracy

Step 1: Import the project's libraries

Step 2: Extract the X variables and Y variables of the video frames independently after importing the dataset.

Step 3: Break the dataset into training and validation models.

Step 4: Creating the SVM classifier model from scratch

Step 5: SVM classifier model fitting
Step 6: Obtaining forecasts
Step 7: Performance evaluation of the model

See Figs. 7 and 8.

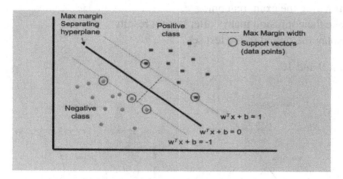

Fig. 7. Representation of algorithm in graphical format [20]

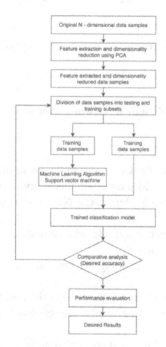

Fig. 8. Flowchart for the SVM Algorithm

5.2 Algorithm 2: Logistic Regression

// Input: Video Frame
// Output: Accuracy
Step 1: Data preparation step
Step 2: Logistic regression is fitted to the training set.
Step 3: Estimating the exam outcome.
Step 4: Make the confusion matrix after testing results
Step 5: Display the output of the test set.

See Figs. 9 and 10.

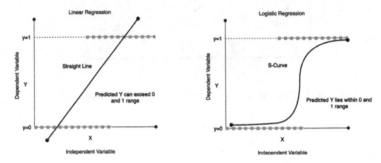

Fig. 9. Difference between Linear and Logistic Regression

5.3 Algorithm 3: Artificial Neural Network (ANN)

// Input: Video Frame
// Output: Accuracy
Step 1: Select a dataset. Read the Dataset from the Drive in our example.
Step 2: Passing weight to the hidden layer will then prepare the dataset for training. There might be anything from 1 to n hidden layers. Neurons in each layer are interconnected with one another.
Step 3: Using the obtained activation rate, hidden nodes, and links to output, ascertain the output nodes' activation rates.
Step 4: Recalibrate it after determining the error rate for each connectivity between hidden and output nodes.
Step 5: Utilizing weights and errors discovered at the result node, reduce hidden layer error. Back propagation is used for both of these reasons as well as to decrease the error if it is significant.
Step 6: Weights between the input and concealed nodes may be adjusted.
Step 7: Repeat the process up until the threshold value is reached.
Step 8: Print the model's accuracy and score.

See Figs. 11 and 12.

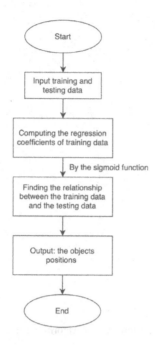

Fig. 10. Flowchart for Logistic Regression

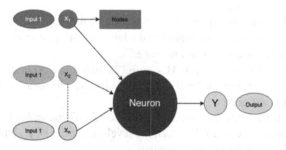

Fig. 11. Representation of Artificial Neural Network (ANN)

5.4 Algorithm 4: ResonNet–Recurrent Neural Network

The model is built using the "Adam" optimizer, which combines gradient descent with momentum and rmsprop and quickly and easily reaches the global minima (learning rate taken into account is 0.001, beta1 is 0.9, beta2 is 0.99, and decay is 1e-09); loss is categorical cross entropy since our motive is multiclass classification; and metric is accuracy. The model was tested on a testing and validation set of photos after being trained on the training images for 30 epochs with a batch size of 64.

// Input: Video Frame
// Output: Accuracy

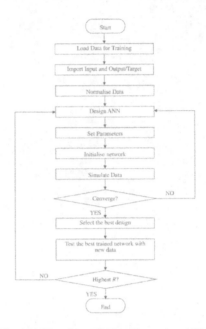

Fig. 12. Flowchart of Algorithm using ANN

Step 1: 64 filters in a 7x7 convolutional layer (CL)

Step 2: An upper pool layer

Step 3: A 3x3 CL with 64 filters, a 1x1 CL with 256 filters, and a 1x1 CL with 64 filters that is repeated three times. Between the levels, there are skip connections as well. Consequently, there are nine levels altogether.

Step 4: A 1x1 CL with 128 filters, a 3x3 CL with 128 filters, and an iteratively repeated 1x1 CL with 512 filters. Between the levels, there are skip connections as well. Consequently, there are 12 layers altogether.

Step 5: A 1x1 CL with 256 filters, a 3x3 CL with 256 filters, and a 1x1 CL with 1024 filters that is repeated six times. Between the levels, there are skip connections as well. Consequently, there are 18 layers altogether.

Step 6: 512-filter 1x1 CL, 512-filter 3x3 CL, and a 2048-filter 1x1 CL that is repeated three times. Between the levels, there are skip connections as well. Consequently, there are nine levels altogether.

Step 7: A fully linked layer with 1000 nodes and a softmax activation function that is the final average pool layer. Consequently, there are 50 layers altogether.

Step 8: The model training is generalised by the skip connections, which help lessen overfitting that could develop when employing the optimizers.

Step 9: In our version, the last fully connected layers were eliminated and replaced with a flatten layer, a dense layer with 128 nodes and ReLU activation, a dropout layer with probability 0.5, and a final dense layer with 28 nodes and softmax activation.

Step 10: The input is sent to the RNN in unit time step.

Step 11: Utilizing the present input set and the previous state, ascertain the system's current state.

Step 12: For the upcoming time step, the current time becomes time-1 (ht).

Step 13: Based on above step, blend the data from all the prior stages and go back as many time steps as necessary.

Step 14: The output is achieved at every state using the final current state.

Step 15: The mistake is created after comparing the result with the desired output, which is the actual output.

Step 16: After the mistake is back-propagated to the network (RNN), it is trained to update the weights.

Step 17: Output the obtained accuracy.

See Fig. 13.

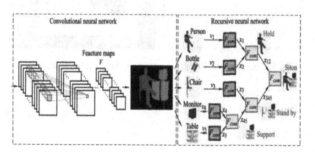

Fig. 13. Representation of Convolutional NN and Recursive NN [13]

6   Results and Discussion

6.1   For SVM

ACCURACY: 82.6%
PRECISION: 81.3%

See Fig. 14.

6.2   For Logistic Regression

ACCURACY: 92.5%
PRECISION: 93.9%

See Fig. 15.

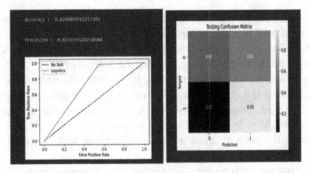

Fig. 14. Graphical Representation of Accuracy and Precision

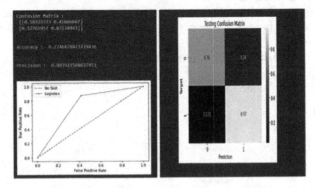

Fig. 15. Graphical Representation of Accuracy and Precision

6.3 For Artificial Neural Network

ACCURACY: 89%
PRECISION: 90%

See Fig. 16.

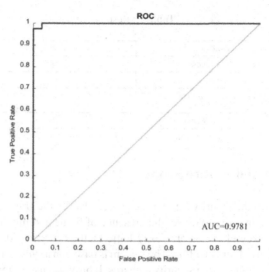

Fig. 16. Graphical Representation

6.4 For ResoNet–RNN

ACCURACY: 92%
PRECISION: 94.8%

See Fig. 17.

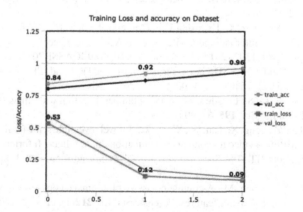

Fig. 17. Graphical Representation of loss and accuracy on dataset

Through the observations it can be inferred that **ResoNet-Recurrent Neural Network** combination provides the best accuracy for video tampering detection using frame tampering detection (Table 1).

Table 1. Results

ALGORITHM	ACCURACY
LOGISTIC REGRESSION	*77%*
SVM	*82%*
ARTIFICIAL NEURAL NETWORK	*89%*
ResoNet - RECURRENT NEURAL NETWORK	*92%*

7 Conclusion and Future Scope

The system monitors the security camera and gathers data on the grayscale, colour, shape, and mobility of fire in order to detect the presence of flame and fire. The suggested fire detection system's key elements are fuzzy logic method, motion identification, shape verification, and fire colour detection. The system is based on a synthesis of numerous fire detection techniques employing security cameras. It provides us the ability to modify the system by combining various video image processing-based fire detection techniques and putting the system in place in accordance with various area needs. In terms of a reduced false fire detection rate, which raises the system's accuracy, it also gives us the best approach for precisely identifying the flame and fire.

References

1. Wang, W.: Digital video forensics (Doctoral dissertation, Dartmouth College Hanover, New Hampshire) (2009)
2. Sun, T., Wang, W., Jiang, X.: Exposing video forgeries by detecting MPEG double compression. In: 2012 IEEE International Conference on Acoustics, Speech and Signal Processing (ICASSP), pp. 1389–1392 (2012). https://doi.org/10.1109/ICASSP.2012.6288150
3. Suhail, M.A., Obaidat, M.S.: Digital watermarking-based DCT and JPEG model. IEEE Trans. Instrum. Meas. **52**(5), 1640–1647 (2003)
4. Di Martino, F., Sessa, S.: Fragile watermarking tamper detection with images compressed by fuzzy transform. Inf. Sci. **195**, 62–90 (2012)
5. Chen, H., Chen, Z., Zeng, X., Fan, W., Xiong, Z.: A novel reversible semi-fragile watermarking algorithm of MPEG-4 video for content authentication. In: Intelligent Information Technology Application, 2008. IITA'08. Second International Symposium on, vol. 3, pp. 37–41. IEEE (2008)
6. Peng, F., Nie, Y.Y., Long, M.: A complete passive blind image copy-move forensics scheme based on compound statistics features. Forensic Sci. Int. **212**(1), e21–e25 (2011)
7. Shivakumar, B.L., Santhosh Baboo, L.D.S.: Detecting copy-move forgery in digital images: a survey and analysis of current methods. Global J. Comput. Sci. Technol. **10**(7), 61–55 (2010)
8. Esmaeilani, R.: Source identification of captured video using photo response non-uniformity noise pattern and SVM classifiers (2014)
9. Lin, C.S., Tsay, J.J.: A passive approach for effective detection and localization of region-level video forgery with spatio-temporal coherence analysis. Digit. Invest. **11**, 120–140 (2014)
10. Davarzani, R., Yaghmaie, K., Mozaffari, S., Tapak, M.: Copy-move forgery detection using multiresolution local binary patterns. Forensic Sci. Int. **231**(1), 61–72 (2013)

11. Amerini, I., Ballan, L., Caldelli, R., Del Bimbo, A., Del Tongo, L., Serra, G.: Copy-move forgery detection and localization by means of robust clustering with J-Linkage. Sig. Process. Image Commun. **28**(6), 659–669 (2013)

12. Shanableh, T.: Detection of frame deletion for digital video forensics. Digit. Invest. **10**(4), 350–360 (2013). https://doi.org/10.1016/j.diin.2013.10.004. ISSN 1742–2876

13. Huang, L., Peng, J., Zhang, R., Li, G., Lin, L.: Learning deep representations for semantic image parsing: a comprehensive overview. Front. Comp. Sci. **12**(5), 840–857 (2018). https://doi.org/10.1007/s11704-018-7195-8

14. Hiroki Ueda, Hyunho Kang, and Keiichi Iwamura. 2021. Video tampering detection based on high-frequency features using machine learning. In: 2020 3rd Artificial Intelligence and Cloud Computing Conference (AICCC 2020). Association for Computing Machinery, New York, USA, pp. 19–24. https://doi.org/10.1145/3442536.3442540

15. Andujar, R., et al.: Video tampering detection for decentralized video transcoding networks. In: Campilho, A., Karray, F., Wang, Z. (eds.) ICIAR 2020. LNCS, vol. 12131, pp. 316–327. Springer, Cham (2020). https://doi.org/10.1007/978-3-030-50347-5_28

16. Anbu, T., Milton Joe, M., Murugeswari, G.: A comprehensive survey of detection of tampered video and localization of tampered frame. Wirel. Pers. Commun. **123**(3), 2027–2060 (2021). https://doi.org/10.1007/s11277-021-09227-z

17. Akhtar, N., Saddique, M., Asghar, K., Bajwa, U.I., Hussain, M., Habib, Z.: Digital video tampering detection and localization: review, representations, challenges and algorithm. Mathematics. **10**(2), 168 (2022). https://doi.org/10.3390/math10020168

18. Kumar, V., Singh, A., Kansal, V., Gaur, M.: A comprehensive survey on passive video forgery detection techniques. In: Khanna, A., Singh, A.K., Swaroop, A. (eds.) Recent Studies on Computational Intelligence. SCI, vol. 921, pp. 39–57. Springer, Singapore (2021). https://doi.org/10.1007/978-981-15-8469-5_4

19. Ardizzone, E., Mazzola, G.: A tool to support the creation of datasets of tampered videos. In: Murino, V., Puppo, E. (eds.) ICIAP 2015. LNCS, vol. 9280, pp. 665–675. Springer, Cham (2015). https://doi.org/10.1007/978-3-319-23234-8_61

20. Jekyll & Minimal Mistakes, Data Science Blog (2022). https://www.reneshbedre.com/blog/support-vector-machine.html. Accessed 17 Apr 2021

Artificial Intelligence Enabled IOT System for Football Identification in a Football Match

Mahesh Kumar Singh[1]([✉]) [iD], Akhilesh Kumar Singh[2,3] [iD], Pushpendra Singh[4] [iD], Kalpana[1] [iD], and Om Prkash Rishi[5] [iD]

[1] Department of Computer Science, ABES Engineering College, Ghaziabad 201009, India
maheshkrsg@gmail.com
[2] Department of Computer Science and Engineering, Jaypee Institute of Information Technology, Noida, India
[3] Department of Information Technology, GL Bajaj Institute of Technology and Management, Gr Noida, Uttar Pradesh 201306, India
[4] Department of Information Technology, Raj Kumar Goel Institute of Technology, Ghaziabad, Uttar Pradesh 201003, India
[5] Department of Computer Science, Informatics University of Kota, Kota, Rajasthan 324010, India

Abstract. Due to growth of AI enabled IOT devices, their use in sports feature identification can be beneficial in terms of recognition quality. Computer Vision is a powerful tool for moving object recognition and tracking. Football identification and recognition problem can be implemented using OpenCV libraries with the help of a programming language like Java, Python etc. OpenCV has special modules that contain specific algorithms and features for moving object recognition and tracking. Internet of things provides a way to connect hardware components through software implementation. In the proposed model the automatic camera module has been implemented through IoT with the help of a servo motor and raspberry pi. The main aim of this paper is to automate the work of a cameraman in a football match by automatically tracking and recognizing the football and broadcasting it with the help of an automatic camera. The initial loss was about 1749, and after 1600+ epochs iterations, the loss reduced to 0.09 in the final model.

Keywords: Automatic Camera · Y.O.L.O. · IoT · Digital Image Processing · Convolutional Network · Deep Learning

1 Introduction

Image processing is a process of conversion of image into digital form for manipulation, extraction of useful information and transformation of it to improve the quality of appearance. The input of the process is image and outputs are the features and properties associated to that image. In today's scenario digital image processing [1, 2] is one of the best emerging technologies for the researchers. Image processing typically has three basic steps: Image analysis, transformation and processing. Output or result is a report based on modified images or image analysis.

© Springer Nature Switzerland AG 2023
D. Garg et al. (Eds.): IACC 2022, CCIS 1782, pp. 460–472, 2023.
https://doi.org/10.1007/978-3-031-35644-5_37

Image analysts can use different interpretation methods to visualized the image, on the other hand digital image processing techniques [3, 4] manipulate digital images [5] using computers. Image processing is used to process image of football and extract useful information from it. It works by processing a signal whose output is an image or information or function related to football [6, 7]. Football has to go through several stages: preprocessing, enrichment, display, and information extraction. We need solid cameras and a powerful computer to detect a football in real-time (See Fig. 1). In our problem statement, we need to install the camera at a suitable distance from the football ground to have a clear vision of the football. We need large data sets to create training data for this work. The data set loaded images of the football used to play the football match from every angle possible, which helped us to identify and recognize the football from every angle of the camera. The process is similar to a football identification in a single image. The primary function camera is to take the live feed and send it frame by frame to our image processing model. The implemented model required to detect [8, 9] the concerned football that is the football in the input frame provided by the camera. The process used for the detection of football involved- an algorithm named the Y.O.L.O. Algorithm.

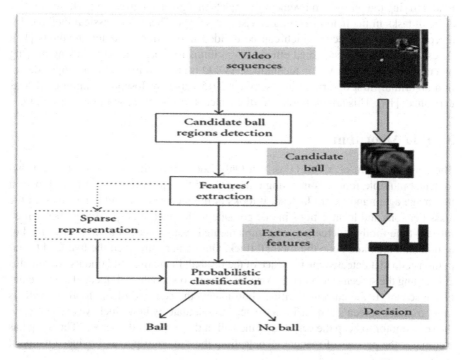

Fig. 1. Architecture of football detection process in real-time

2 Related Work

Although there is no common origin for the concept of image processing, it is concluded that image processing was invented in the 1960s. It was first conceived by Aaron Cragg, a British molecular biologist at the University of Cambridge. The concept has since been worked on by the Jet Propulsion Laboratory, Massachusetts Institute of Technology, Bell Labs, and the University of Maryland. It was an expensive process as there was no sophisticated hardware at the time and no computers that could easily perform the necessary calculations. However, as time went on, technology began to flourish, and since 2000 computers have been used efficiently to process digital images. Since then, image processing has become an important area of research and development in all areas of computer science and its applications. In digital image processing, the feature of image is transform into two dimensional matrix form for manipulation by the computer since computer understand only numeric terms for manipulation and mathematical computation.

Any digital image can be represented by a sequence of real numbers into finite number of bits.The main advantages of digital image processing methods are versatility, reproducibility, and preservation of original data accuracy. Motion detection [10] refers to identifying the physical movement of objects in a given environment. These are very difficult tasks in the field of computer vision research. There are classical methods for detecting moving objects, which can be divided into various classical methods [11]. A research paper [12] specified efficient algorithms for detecting and tracking moving objects using computer vision techniques. YOLO is an effective real-time object detection algorithm, first described in a seminal 2015 paper by Joseph Redmon et al. was explained. [13]. This article introduces the concept of object recognition in Y.O.L.O.

3 Yolo Algorithm

The complete form of Y.O.L.O. is You Only Look Once. It is based on the fact that to detect multiple footballs in a single image, and this algorithm doesn't need to scan the image again and again. Instead, it looks at the picture once and determines all the classifications and localizations in one go. Due to this fact, it is speedy and best suited for real-time football detection. The implemented system needed to take a live feed of a football match and keep the football track. Our camera streamed the live feed to our python code that detected the presence of the football in the field and find its coordinates concerning the screen size. Our primary focus been to keep the ball located at the center of the screen. If the current position coordinates, the centroid of the football (ball) is away from the screen's center. Then we need to calculate by how much we need to rotate the servo motor to keep the centroid of the ball in the center of the screen. The setup has automated the process of manually controlling the camera tripod and reduced the need for a cameraman.

3.1 Convolutional Network in Y.O.L.O

With the help of the Convolutional Network [14, 15] (See Fig. 2), we process only those sections of the football that are most likely to give us a significant result. It is determined using a filter matrix. There is a filter matrix [16, 17] for each important feature of the football to be detected. This process generates a vector of properties. The vector has a size of at least 5. The size can be much more if the number of classes to be detected is more or if the number of football in a grid cell is more than one.

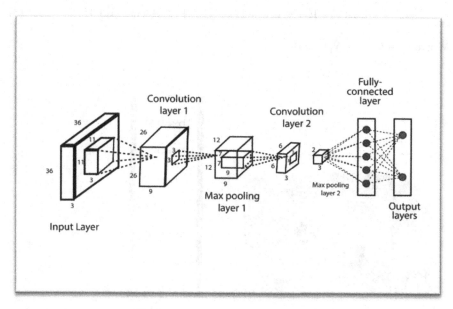

Fig. 2. Convolutional Process Workflow

The general form of the output vector is-

$$Y = \left[P_c, bx, by, b_h, b_w, c_1, c_2, c_3 \ldots \ldots \right] \tag{1}$$

where,

P_c = Probability of Football being detected in this particular cell. ($0 \geq P_c \geq 1$)
b_x = x-coordinate of the center of the border-box surrounding the football ($0 \geq b_x \geq 1$)
b_y = y-coordinate of the center of the border-box surrounding the football ($0 \geq b_y \geq 1$)
b_h = height of the border-box surrounding the football ($b_h \geq 0$)
w = width of the border-box surrounding the football ($b_w \geq 0$)
$c_1, c_2, c_3 \ldots c_n$ = probability of the football belonging to each class C_1 to C_n.

The output vector for football is shown in Fig. 3. If the value of $P_c = 0$ is below, then all the other values do not matter and should be ignored.

3.2 Loss Function

The loss function of is Y.O.L.O. algorithm is of the form

$$\sum_{i=0}^{S^2} 1_i^{obj} \sum_{c \in classes} (P_i(c) - \hat{P}_i(c))^2 \tag{2}$$

Where, $1_i^{obj} = 1$ if an object appears in cell i, otherwise 0.

$\hat{P}_i(c)$ denotes the conditional class probability for class c in cell I, which becomes a complex function upon expanding. In simpler words, if we have an output vector as Y = $[y_1, y_2, y_3, \ldots, y_n]$, then the loss can be computed as

$$loss(Y) = [(y_1 - \hat{y}_1)^2 + (y_2 - \hat{y}_2)^2 + \cdots + (y_n - \hat{y}_n)^2]$$ (3)

Where $y_1 > 0, (y_1 - \hat{y}_1)^2 = 0$

Fig. 3. Output Vector for Football

The loss is minimized using the backward feed convolutional neural network [18]. In this process, first, the receptor neurons create a hypothesis and sense the input. If the information is enough to fire their activation function, they send it to the next layer (hidden layer). There can be as many hidden layers as per the convenience of the user. But with the increase in the number of hidden layers, the speed of execution becomes less, while at the same time, the accuracy becomes high. The neural network's output is fed to a supervisor (training data), and it tells whether the judgment is correct or not. As we know, that error can never be minimized to zero; hence this is an endless cycle, and so the user has to set a fixed number of iterations he wants the neural network to go through. The unit is epochs with each iteration, the loss changes [19]. The loss need not decrease in all iterations as is a hill climb type of algorithm. But eventually, it can be seen that the error tends to move towards its minima and will surely reach a very close value to zero. It can be seen in the form of the graph (see Fig. 4), which shows the minimization of error in gradient descent algorithm-

The process of minimization depends on the nature of the loss function and the learning rate. If there are multiple minima in the curve, the minimization will be achieved

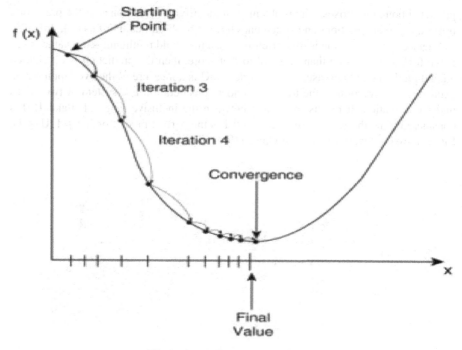

Fig.4. Graph Showing convergence

at the nearest local minima.The formula for minimizing loss function is-

$$repeat\ until\ convergence = \left\{ \theta_0 = \theta_0 - \alpha\frac{1}{m}\sum_{i=1}^{m}(h_\theta(x^{(i)}) - y^{(i)}) \right.$$

$$\left. \theta_1 = \theta_1 - \alpha\frac{1}{m}\sum_{i=1}^{m}(h_\theta(x^{(i)}) - y^{(i)}) \cdot x^{(i)} \right\} \quad (4)$$

where, h_θ is the hypothesis function value at a point and **y** is the actual value obtained at an end.

Convergence is that point of time when,

$$\theta_0 = \theta_0 - \alpha\frac{\partial(loss)}{\partial y}\ AND\ \theta_1 = \theta_1 - \alpha\frac{\partial(loss)}{\partial y} \quad (5)$$

At this point, there is approximately zero change in the hypothesis parameters, and then we consider that we have reached the minima of the error function curve, and the error has been minimized.

3.3 Intersection over Union (IoU)

This technique is used to counter the case when a football is being surrounded by more than one bounding box. One of those boxes is the actual bounding box, and the others are predicted bounding boxes. The problem is in identifying which ones of the prediction boxes are good predictions and which ones have to be discarded. For this task, IoU [20] or Intersection over Union is used. Before this, a threshold minimum score value is set. If the IoU score is more than or equal to that score, then the prediction is considered a good prediction. Otherwise, it is discarded. IoU is a measure of the overlapping area expressed as a fraction of the total area under consideration is a system of two boxes under observation. It results in a value between the inclusive range of 0 and 1. 0 is considered to be the wrong prediction, and 1 is the perfect prediction. ($0 \leq IoU \leq 1$), IoU = (Area of Overlap)/(Area of Union) (Fig. 5).

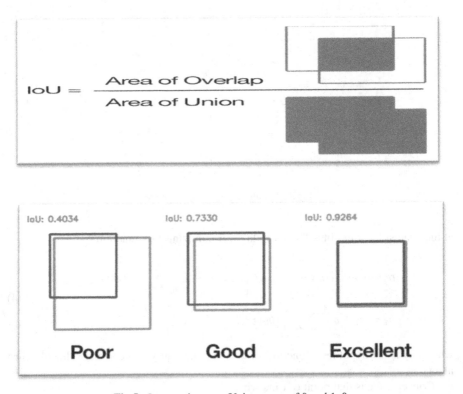

Fig.5. Intersection over Union range of 0 and 1. 0

3.4 Non-Max Suppression

For each thing in the image of football, the Y.O.L.O. algorithm makes a binding box. The objects in the football can have different shapes and sizes, and to detect each of these objects ideally for the Y.O.L.O. algorithm, create multiple bounding boxes. As there are numerous bounding boxes, therefore Y.O.L.O. algorithm needs to select the best bounding box [21]. For the selection of the best bounding box Y.O.L.O. algorithm uses non-Max suppression [22]. This technique discards all other bounding boxes and selects the best bounding box. Initially boundary box of the required image has been selected for highest score and remove all the other boxes because these are highly overlapped. The exact process (see fig 6) continues for the other boxes and until no more reduction possible of boxes. In the end, we will be left with the only box that has the highest objective score and which best localizes the concerned object.

Fig. 6. Working of non-Max suppression

3.5 Anchor Boxes

In this case center of more than one bounding box lie in a single frame or box. The Y.O.L.O. algorithm provides the solution to this with the concept of anchor boxes [23]. Anchor boxes detect different objects of multiple sizes for which center is in the same frame or box (see Fig. 7). The number of anchor boxes in a cell defines the dimensions of the output vector from that particular cell of the grid. If there are two anchor boxes, both the boxes must have their exclusive features. They should have a separate group of values for P_c, b_x, b_y, b_h, b_w, c_1, c_2.

3.6 Working of Y.O.L.O. Algorithm

The image is segmented into a 19 × 19 grid by default (see Fig. 8). For each of the cells in the grid, a convolution is fired, and a vector is made. It results in 19 × 19 vectors. If there is at most one football in each cell of the image, then the size of the resulting 3D vector of vectors will be-

Size of 3D feature vector = 19*19*(size of one vector), Size of one vector = (5 + number of classes).

An example of this 3D vector can be seen in the figure given below. Note that for the sake of convenience, we divided the image in a 3x3 grid and initialized three classes. So, the minimum size of the 3D vector will be, Size = 3 × 3 × 8 = 72. The general formula of the dimensions of this 3D vector can be written as-

$$Size = S * S * \{(5 + C) * B\} \tag{6}$$

Were, S = Number of rows or columns in which the grid is divided, hence (S*S) = number of grid cells. C = number of classes defined, B = number of boxes inside one

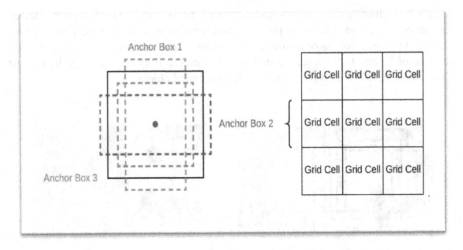

Fig. 7. Anchor box detection different objects of multiple sizes

grid cell. The 5 in the formula is the count of mandatory parameters for each box/cell. It includes - P_c, B_x, B_y, B_h and B_w.

4 Experimental Setup

IoT will be used to control the motion of the camera. When the football is detected, the IoT will help the camera move in the same direction as the football to keep track of the football.

4.1 Dataset and Training

For training our model, we used pictures from the FIFA world cup 2018, Russia. We collected around 200 pictures of the match ball from various angles through the footage of multiple matches in the tournament. Most of the images contained a part or whole image of a football. For labeling the images, we used an open-source software named labeling. It extracted the coordinates of the image of the ball and save them into a text file with the same name as the image file. We need to open the picture and draw a box outside the image [24]. For example, if the image is named football.jpg, after labeling the picture, a text file will be generated, named football.txt.

For training the model, we have used google collab, an interactive cloud platform that provided powerful processors and GPUs. We have used a cloud platform as we required a computer with high specifications, and google collab does this for us in a hassle-free and cost-effective way. It has generated a weights file which is the trained Y.O.L.O. model. The initial loss was about 1749, and after 1600+ epochs iterations, the loss reduced to 0.09 in the final model.

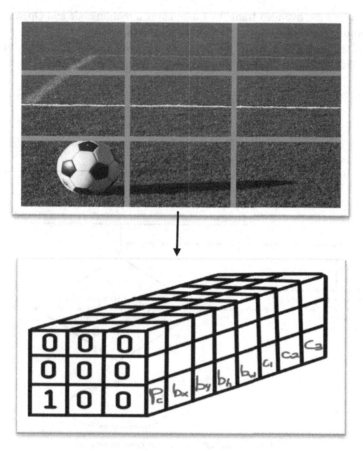

Fig. 8. Working of Y.O.L.O. Algorithm

4.2 Moving Camera Module

Step 1: Fix the camera over servo motors
Step 2: Receive the coordinates of the football from the recognition module
Step 3: Determine the position of football concerning the center.
Step 4: Send a signal to turn the camera in the required direction
Step 5: The camera will move accordingly and track the football

4.3 Working of Proposed Model

The worhing of the proposed model is explained in the Fig. 9. There are following steps

Step 1. Connect the positive and negative terminal of the battery to the breadboard.
Step 2. Connect the VCC and GND inputs of the servo motor to the equipotent cells of the battery's positive and negative terminal, respectively.
Step 3. Fix the camera over the servo motorhead.

Step 4. Process the live feed frame by frame using a python code and Open CV-library and determine the coordinates of the center of the ball.

Step 5. If the position is not in the center of the screen, move the servo motor in a direction that will bring the centroid back to the center of the screen.

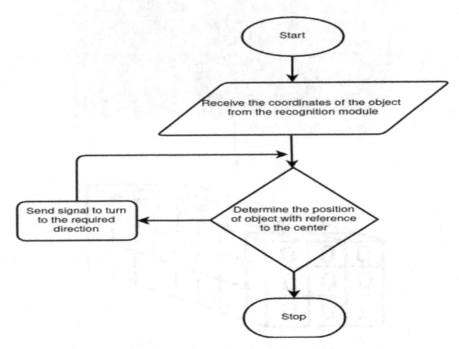

Fig. 9. Flowchart for moving camera module

4.4 Result and Discussion

With the help of image matrix numbers, face features, and other libraries present in OpenCV, we have recognized the football on the screen and get its coordinates. The image of the football is converted into a matrix of numbers. Now positional details of the football are sent to a module that fired a signal to the controller [25] to shift the camera's focus towards the football. The Arduino has moved the camera till the image is near the center and keep it steady till it receives the next signal. At last, we have focused the camera on the moving football for the whole transition.

5 Conclusion and Future Work

This research is based upon the concepts of image processing and IoT. Football recognition and tracking are the main tasks of computer vision. Computer vision applications aim to bring the capabilities of human beings to machines and computers. OpenCV provided us with the feature of computer vision, which helped in the project build-up. Y.O.L.O. Algorithm helped for the football recognition part for which we have pre-defined libraries in OpenCV, which we used. For the automatic camera part, we used the IoT (Internet of things) concept. With the help of Arduino and Servo motor, the camera has detected the required football and change its view. In future player detection and goal identification system can be potential problems for research with good accuracy of results.

References

1. Amat, S., Donat, R., Liandrat, J., Trillo, J.: A fully adaptive PPH multiresolution scheme for image processing 1 (2019). https://doi.org/10.1201/9780429081385-8
2. Hegadi, R.: Image processing: research opportunities and challenges (2010)
3. Wang, X., Chen, T., Li, D., Yu, S.: Processing methods for digital image data based on the geographic information system. Complexity, **2021**, Article ID 2319314, 12 pages (2021). https://doi.org/10.1155/2021/2319314
4. Pratt, W.K.: Digital Image Processing. Wiley, New York (1978)
5. Gonzales, R.C., Wintz, P.: Digital Image Processing. Mass., Reading: Addison-Wesley Publishing Company, Inc., Boston (1977)
6. Girshick, R., Donahue, J., Darrell, T., Malik, J.: Rich feature hierarchies for accurate object detection and semantic segmentation. In: Proceedings of the IEEE Conference on Computer Vision and Pattern Recognition, pp. 580–587 (2014)
7. Singh, M.K., Rishi, O.P.: Event-driven recommendation for e-commerce using knowledge-based collaborative filtering technique. Scalable Comput. Pract. Exp. **21**(3), 369–378 (2020). https://doi.org/10.12694/scpe.v21i3.1709. ISSN 1895-1767
8. Szegedy, C., Toshev, A., Erhan, D.: Deep neural networks for object detection. In: Advances in Neural Information Processing Systems, pp. 2553–2561 (2013)
9. Khan, A.I., Wani, M.A.: Patch-based segmentation of latent fingerprint images using convolutional neural network. Appl. Artif. Intell. **33**(1), 87–100 (2019). https://doi.org/10.1080/08839514.2018.1526704
10. Ngoc, L.Q., Tin, N.T., Tuan, L.B.: A new framework of moving object tracking based on object detection-tracking with removal of moving features. Int. J. Adv. Comput. Sci. Appl. (IJACSA), **11**(4) (2020). https://doi.org/10.14569/IJACSA.2020.0110406
11. Kulchandani, J.S., Dangarwala, K.J.: Moving object detection: Review of recent research trends. Int. Conf. Pervasive Comput. (ICPC) **2015**, 1–5 (2015). https://doi.org/10.1109/PERVASIVE.2015.7087138
12. Chen, C., Li, D.: Research on the detection and tracking algorithm of moving object in image based on computer vision technology. Wirel. Commun. Mob. Comput. 2021, Article ID 1127017, 7 pages (2021). https://doi.org/10.1155/2021/1127017
13. Redmon, J., Farhadi, A.: YOLO9000: better, faster, stronger (2016)
14. Siddique, F., Sakib, S., Siddique, M.A.B.: Recognition of handwritten digits using convolutional neural network in python with tensorflow and comparison of performance for various hidden layers. In: 2019 5th International Conference on Advances in Electrical Engineering (I.C.A.E.E.), Dhaka, Bangladesh, pp. 541–546 (2019). https://doi.org/10.1109/ICAEE48663.2019.8975496
15. Singh, M.K., Rishi, O.P., Sharma, A., Akthatar, Z.: Knowledge extraction through page rank using web mining techniques for e-business: a review. In: Maximizing Business Performance and Efficiency through Intelligent Systems, pp 1–30 (2017). http://www.igi-global.com/book/maximizing-business-performance-efficiency-through/173010.

16. Akgul, O., Penekli, H.I., Genc, Y.: Applying deep learning in augmented reality tracking. In: 12th International Conference on Signal-Image Technology & Internet-Based Systems (S.I.T.I.S.) 2016, pp. 47–54 (2016)
17. Schmidhuber, J.: Deep learning in neural networks: an overview. Neural Netw. **61**, 85–117 (2015)
18. Pushpendra, S., Hrisheekesha, P.N., Singh, V.K.: Ensemble visual content based search and retrieval for natural scene images. Recent Adv. Comput. Sci. Commun. **14**(2), 580–592 (2021). https://doi.org/10.2174/2213275912666190327175712
19. LeCun, Y., Bengio, Y., Hinton, G.: Deep learning. Nature **521**(7553), 436 (2015)
20. He, K., Zhang, X., Ren, S., Sun, J.: Deep residual learning for image recognition. In: Proceedings of the IEEE Conference on Computer Vision and Pattern Recognition, pp. 770–778 (2016)
21. Mahesh Kumar, S., Om Prakash, R.: Knowledge-based recommendation system for online business using web usage mining. In: Rathore, V.S., Dey, N., Piuri, V., Babo, R., Polkowski, Z., Tavares, J.M.R.S. (eds.) Rising Threats in Expert Applications and Solutions. Advances in Intelligent Systems and Computing, vol. 1187, pp. 293–300. Springer, Singapore (2021). https://doi.org/10.1007/978-981-15-6014-934
22. Szegedy, C., Vanhoucke, V., Ioffe, S., Shlens, J., Wojna, Z.: Rethinking the inception architecture for computer vision. In: Proceedings of the IEEE Conference on Computer Vision and Pattern Recognition, pp. 2818–2826 (2016)
23. Liu, Y., Zhou, G.: Key technologies and applications of internet of things. In: 2012 Fifth International Conference on Intelligent Computation Technology and Automation (I.C.I.C.T.A.), pp. 197–200 (2012)
24. Singh, P., Hrisheekesha, P.N., Singh, V.K.: CBIR-CNN: content-based image retrieval on celebrity data using deep convolution neural network. Recent Adv. Comput. Sci. Commun. **14**(1), 257–272 (2021). https://doi.org/10.2174/2666255813666200129111928
25. Van Kranenburg, R.: The internet of things: a critique of ambient technology and the all-seeing network of RFID, Institute of Network Cultures (2008)
26. Van Kranenburg, R., Anzelmo, E., Bassi, A., Caprio, D., Dodson, S., Ratto, M.: The internet of things. In: Proceedings of the First Berlin Symposium on Internet and Society (2011)
27. Evans, D.: The internet of things: how the next evolution of the internet is changing everything. CISCO White Paper **1**(2011), 1–11 (2011)
28. Singh, P., Gupta, V.K., Hrisheekesha, P.N.: A review on shape based descriptors for image retrieval. Int. J. Comput. Appl. **125**(10), 27–32 (2015)

Author Index

D. Garg et al. (Eds.): IACC 2022, CCIS 1782, pp. 473–476, 2023.
https://doi.org/10.1007/978-3-031-35644-5

Printed in the United States
by Baker & Taylor Publisher Services